MYTH AND POETICS

A series edited by

GREGORY NAGY

Greek Mythology and Poetics
by GREGORY NAGY

Also in the series

The Ravenous Hyenas and the Wounded Sun: Myth and Ritual in Ancient India
by STEPHANIE W. JAMISON

Poetry and Prophecy: The Beginnings of a Literary Tradition
edited by JAMES KUGEL

The Traffic in Praise: Pindar and the Poetics of Social Economy
by LESLIE KURKE

Epic Singers and Oral Tradition
by ALBERT BATES LORD

The Language of Heroes: Speech and Performance in the Iliad
by RICHARD P. MARTIN

Myth and the Polis
edited by DORA C. POZZI and JOHN M. WICKERSHAM

Homer and the Sacred City
by STEPHEN SCULLY

GREEK MYTHOLOGY AND POETICS

GREGORY NAGY

CORNELL UNIVERSITY PRESS

ITHACA AND LONDON

First published 1990 by Cornell University Press.
Second printing 1992.
First printing, Cornell Paperbacks, 1992.

International Standard Book Number 0-8014-1985-9 (cloth)
International Standard Book Number 0-8014-8048-5 (paper)
Library of Congress Catalog Card Number 89-17447
Printed in the United States of America
Librarians: Library of Congress cataloging information appears on the last page of the book.

♾ The paper in this book meets the minimum requirements of the American National Standard for Information Sciences—Permanence of Paper for Printed Library Materials, ANSI Z39.48-1984.

Contents

Foreword vii
Acknowledgments x
Introduction 1

PART I. The Hellenization of Indo-European Poetics

1 Homer and Comparative Mythology 7
2 Formula and Meter: The Oral Poetics of Homer 18
3 Hesiod and the Poetics of Pan-Hellenism 36

PART II. The Hellenization of Indo-European Myth and Ritual

4 Patroklos, Concepts of Afterlife, and the Indic Triple Fire 85
5 The Death of Sarpedon and the Question of Homeric Uniqueness 122
6 The King and the Hearth: Six Studies of Sacral Vocabulary Relating to the Fireplace 143
7 Thunder and the Birth of Humankind 181
8 Sêma and Nóēsis: The Hero's Tomb and the "Reading" of Symbols in Homer and Hesiod 202
9 Phaethon, Sappho's Phaon, and the White Rock of Leukas: "Reading" the Symbols of Greek Lyric 223
10 On the Death of Actaeon 263

PART III. The Hellenization of Indo-European Social Ideology

11 Poetry and the Ideology of the Polis: The Symbolism of Apportioning Meat 269

12 Mythical Foundations of Greek Society and the Concept of the City-State 276
13 Unattainable Wishes: The Restricted Range of an Idiom in Epic Diction 294

Bibliography 303
General Index 329
Index of Scholars 360

Foreword

Greek Mythology and Poetics is the second book in the Myth and Poetics series. My goal, as series editor, is to encourage work that will help integrate literary criticism with the approaches of anthropology and that will pay special attention to problems concerning the nexus of ritual and myth.

For such an undertaking, we may look to the comparative testimony of relatively complex societies, such as the Ndembu of Zambia, and also of the very smallest, such as the Yukuna of the Colombian Amazon.[1] Just as important, we must pursue the varied testimonies of the most stratified societies, including those which go under the general heading "Western civilization." It is precisely here that the meaning of myth is the most misleading—and challenging. In a small-scale society myth tends to be viewed as the encoding of that society's concept of truth; at the same time, from the viewpoint of Western civilization, myth has become the opposite of fact, the antithesis of truth.[2]

Since the ancient Greek concept of *politeíā* serves as the foundation for the very word "civilization" and for our concept of Western civilization, more than one of the books in this series will deal primarily with ancient Greece and the ancient Greek city-state, or *pólis.* The testimony of the Greeks is particularly instructive with regard to our central concern, the relationship between ritual and myth. The very word "myth,"

[1] V. Turner, *The Forest of Symbols: Aspects of Ndembu Ritual* (Ithaca, N.Y., 1967), and P.-Y. Jacopin, *La parole générative: De la mythologie des Indiens Yukuna* (diss., University of Neuchâtel, 1981).

[2] See especially M. Detienne, *L'invention de la mythologie* (Paris, 1981), and my review in *Annales: Economies Sociétés Civilisations* 37 (1982) 778–780.

as derived from Greek *mûthos*, is a case in point: the meaning of this word brings to life, in microcosm, the relationship between myth and ritual in ancient Greek society.

In order to grasp the special meaning of Greek *mûthos*, let us consider the distinction between *marked* and *unmarked* speech (in the terminology of Prague School linguistics). We find that marked speech occurs as a rule in ritual contexts, as we can observe most clearly in the least complex or smallest-scale societies. It is in such societies also that we can observe most clearly the symbiosis of ritual and myth, and the ways in which the language of ritual and myth is marked, whereas "everyday" language is unmarked. The Greek language gives us an example of these semantics: *múō* means "I have my eyes closed" or "I have my mouth closed" in everyday situations, but "I see in a special way" or "I say in a special way" in ritual. Hence *mústēs* is "one who is initiated" and *mustḗrion* is "that into which one is initiated, mystery (Latin *mysterium*)." Hence also *mûthos*, "myth": this word, it has been argued, is a derivative of *múō* and had at an earlier stage meant "special" as opposed to "everyday" speech.

A later Classical example of such early patterns of thought occurs in Sophocles, *Oedipus at Colonus* 1641–1644: the visualization and the verbalization of what happened to Oedipus in the precinct of the Eumenides at Colonus are restricted, in that the precise location of his corpse is a sacred secret (1545–1546, 1761–1763). Only Theseus, by virtue of being the proto-priest for the Athenians of the here-and-now, is to witness what happened, which is called the *drṓmena* (1644). This word is what Jane Harrison used to designate "ritual" in her formulation: "myth is the plot of the *drṓmenon*." Thus the visualization and the verbalization of the myth, what happened to Oedipus, are restricted to the sacred context of ritual, controlled by the heritage of priestly authority from Theseus, culture-hero of the Athenian democracy.

From an anthropological point of view, "myth" is indeed "special speech" in that it is a means by which society affirms its own reality. Such a thought pattern is pertinent to the theories of J. L. Austin and J. R. Searle concerning the performative aspects of language. A speech-act, according to Austin and Searle, entails a situation in which the word *is* the action; the antithesis of word and action is neutralized. Here we may invoke Barbara Johnson's application of Austin's notion of speech-act to *poetry*—an application that Austin himself resisted. We may go also one step further, with the help of Richard Martin's *Language of Heroes*, the first book in Myth and Poetics.[3] Martin applies the notion of speech-act

[3] R. P. Martin, *The Language of Heroes: Speech and Performance in the* Iliad (Ithaca, N.Y., 1989).

to the oral performance of oral poetry, the dynamics of which have been made well known through the pathfinding works of Milman Parry and Albert Lord. As Martin argues, the *mûthos* is not just any speech-act reported by poetry: it is also the speech-act of poetry itself.

Viewed in this light, myth implies ritual in the very performance of myth. And that performance is the essence of poetics.

GREGORY NAGY

Cambridge, Massachusetts

Acknowledgments

I thank the Classics Department of Harvard University for the allocation of a subsidy that has helped make this book more affordable. At an early stage of the project, Lenore Savage, with her expertise at the keyboard, navigated through vast stretches of unwieldy text. The final printed version was achieved by Gary Bisbee, master compositor and scholar.

I wish to record my deep gratitude to all those who gave me advice at various stages in the evolution of this book. Special thanks go to Victor Bers, Deborah Boedeker, Martha Cowan, Gregory Crane, Olga Davidson, Marian Demos, Scott Ettinger, Thomas J. Figueira, Douglas Frame, John Hamilton, Leonard Muellner, Blaise Nagy, Joseph Nagy, Jogesh Panda, Dan Petegorsky, Dale Sinos, Laura Slatkin, Roger Travis, Brent Vine, Calvert Watkins, Michael Witzel.

I offer special thanks to John Peradotto, editor of *Arethusa.* It was he who provided the original occasions for the essays rewritten as Chapters 4 and 8 in this book.

Finally, I dedicate this book to my genial daughter, Antónia, whose radiant company has been for me a priceless treasure.

G. N.

GREEK MYTHOLOGY AND POETICS

Introduction

This book concentrates on what ancient Greek society inherited through its language, described by linguists as belonging to the Indo-European language family. The span of time covered is roughly between the eighth and the fifth centuries B.C. My emphasis on the language of the Greeks, calling for comparison with the testimony of related Indo-European languages including Latin, Indic, and Hittite, reflects my long-standing interest in Indo-European linguistics, a discipline that has in the past been successfully applied to the systematic study of society in such pioneering works as Emile Benveniste's *Le vocabulaire des institutions indo-européennes.*[1] This discipline of Indo-European linguistics aims to reconstruct, from various related Indo-European languages, a proto-language once described as "a glorious artifact, one which is far more precious than anything an archaeologist can ever hope to unearth."[2] To put it in more modest terms: the attempt to reconstruct a proto-language translates into an attempt to recover various patterns in society as articulated by language. Throughout the pages that follow, the primary aim is to examine the Greek language, by way of comparison with cognate languages, as a reflection of Greek society, with special attention to the function of language as a vehicle of mythology and poetics.

The emphasis of this book, however, is not on the Indo-European heritage of the Greek language. Rather, it is on the forces that transformed this Indo-European heritage into a distinctly Greek heritage; let us call it Hellenism. As for the process of transformation, let us call it

[1] Benveniste 1969.
[2] Haas 1969.34; cf. Watkins 1969.xx, 1973b.

Hellenization. Hence the titles of the three parts into which the book is divided:

I: The Hellenization of Indo-European Poetics
II: The Hellenization of Indo-European Myth and Ritual
III: The Hellenization of Indo-European Social Ideology

The use of such terms as "poetics," "myth," "ritual," and "social ideology" will be brought into sharper focus as the discussion proceeds, but another question of meaning must be addressed at the very start. The term "Indo-European" will never be used here as any sort of racial or ethnic classification: to say that something is Indo-European is merely to reconstruct an aspect of that thing by way of *comparing cognate languages*, inasmuch as language is a reflection of society and its institutions.[3]

In the case of ancient Greek society—and the same goes for the Romans and the Hittites and so on—it is misleading to speak of it as "Indo-European" just because comparative linguistics has established that the Greek language is predominantly Indo-European in nature. Still, the story of Hellenization can be at least partly retold in the history of an Indo-European language that has settled into a Mediterranean setting.

In the historical context of the ancient Greeks, the Indo-European heritage of their language can be expected to elucidate some, though hardly all, the inherited institutions of their society. Other institutions will have been inherited from layers of language speakers that preceded the Indo-European layer. Still others will have been borrowed at different times from different societies. One thing is sure: all Greek social institutions, whatever their provenience, will have continued to interact and change in the course of history. That process of interaction and change I am describing as Hellenization. In this book, the distinctive Hellenism or "Greekness" of Hellenization is the decisive empirical given.[4]

It follows that there can be no such thing as a controlling Indo-European model for the Greek heritage of mythology and poetics. In particular, the influence of the Near East is pervasive in the ongoing process of Hellenization. In the poetics of Sappho, for example, as we shall see in Chapter 9, the Indo-European myths about the Morning Star and Evening Star have merged with the Near Eastern myths about the Planet

[3] Here again I look to the *démarche* of Benveniste 1969.

[4] I stress the distinctness or "otherness" of Hellenism, not its perceived affinities with "Western Civilization." Such perceptions lead to the impulse of "Orientalism," as dissected by Saïd 1978.

Ištar, known to the Greeks as the Planet Aphrodite, and to us as the Planet Venus.

A particularly valuable contribution to the issue of cultural interaction in ancient Greece is the work of Walter Burkert, who has consistently mined the vast testimony of the Near East for valuable parallelisms with various Greek institutions that have long defied our understanding.[5] For example, he can show that the various myths and rituals of the Greeks connected with the goddess Demeter are closely matched by the patterns inherent in the Hittite Telepinu- and the Mesopotamian Inanna/Ištar figures.[6] Call it *Urerlebnis* or archetype, the fact is that in this particular case Burkert finds no other closely corresponding figures as he surveys other cultures of the world in search of further matches. It is difficult, then, to resist the conclusion that we are dealing here with some sort of contact or borrowing; further analysis of such parallelisms may benefit from techniques of investigation that have been employed by linguists in studying the phenomenon known as *Sprachbund*.[7]

Mention of the myths and rituals connected with the goddess Demeter brings us to a major problem in the history of classical scholarship, where studies of myth and ritual have tended to be segregated. For example, the longtime standard work on Greek religion, Martin Nilsson's reliable *Handbuch*,[8] studiously avoids any consideration of myth as it relates to ritual, with the one notable exception being the myths of Demeter, which even Nilsson cannot divorce from the corresponding rituals.[9] In Chapter 1, I offer working definitions of myth and ritual. For now, however, I stress only the methodological need to treat them as interrelated phenomena in society, along the lines of Burkert's handbook, *Greek Religion*.[10]

[5] Cf. Burkert 1984 on the era stretching between roughly 900 and 600 B.C.

[6] Cf. e.g. Burkert 1979a.139.

[7] Jakobson 1931. In the work of Burkert 1984, I note in particular the emphasis on the role of itinerant artisans, who are described as *dēmiourgoí* 'artisans in the community [*dêmos*]' at *Odyssey* xvii 381–385. (On *dêmos* 'administrative district, population' in archaic Greek poetic diction in the sense of 'local community', with reference to a given locale's own traditions, customs, laws, and the like, see N 1979a.149 §11n6; also Donlan 1970.) The professions listed in that passage are the *aoidós* 'singer, poet', the *mántis* 'seer', the *iētḗr* 'physician', and the *téktōn* 'carpenter'; elsewhere, the term *dēmiourgós* applies to the *kêrux* 'herald' (*Odyssey* xix 135), and we may compare other passages where the *aoidós* is juxtaposed with the *téktōn* and the *kerameús* 'potter' (Hesiod *Works and Days* 25–26). Such a class of artisans was socially mobile not only within the Greek-speaking area (on which see further at N pp. 233–234) but also far beyond, and we must also take into account the possibilities of interchangeability between Greek and non-Greek artisans.

[8] Nilsson 1967 / 1974.

[9] Discussion in Burkert 1979a.138.

[10] Burkert 1985.

To grasp the essence of Greek religion, I suggest, is to understand the relationship between myth and ritual in the historical context of ancient Greece.[11] Moreover, it is at times impossible to achieve an understanding of a given myth without taking into account a corresponding ritual, or the other way around: in the myths and rituals of Adonis, for example, we can see clearly that the factor of sacrifice in ritual corresponds to the factor of catastrophe in myth, and that "play acting" the catastrophe of Adonis in sacrifice is supposed to avert catastrophe for the sacrificers.[12]

The relationship of myth to ritual can have a direct bearing on poetics. In the myth of the Divine Twins, for example, the rituals connected with these figures are a key to understanding not only the historical setting of the dual kingship at Sparta but also the poetics of Alcman PMG 7, concerning the alternating *kôma* of the Twins, their death-sleep. In the case of the Adonis myth, for another example, the connections of this figure with rituals of mourning are pertinent to a general anthropological assessment of mourning as demonstrative self-humiliation and self-aggression.[13] Further, these connections are pertinent to the poetics of Sappho, where the explicit theme of mourning for Adonis may be connected with the implicit theme of Sappho's self-identification with Aphrodite.[14] In this context, we may note Burkert's observation that the standard mythmaking sequence, as formulated by Vladimir Propp, of a successful quest ending in marriage finds its inverse in Sappho's poetry as the disquieting and Adonic sequence of love's abruptly ending in failure.[15]

Some of the essays collected in this book took shape some years ago, the one on Sappho as early as 1973 (recast as Chapter 9). Another of the essays appeared recently, in 1987 (recast as Chapter 12). For this reason and for the purposes of the ensemble in general, there has had to be a great deal of reorganization and rewriting. New references to additional secondary sources, however, have been kept to a minimum. Such new references as there are tend to concentrate on those works that had a role in reshaping various specific lines of argumentation. There are undoubtedly many other works that should have played a role, but some of these have been saved for future reference in altogether new projects to be undertaken.[16]

[11] A crucial work in this regard: Burkert 1970.

[12] Cf. Burkert 1979a.121.

[13] Burkert 1979a.99–122, esp. p. 121. A definitive work on the Greek institutions of mourning: Alexiou 1974.

[14] See pp. 259ff.

[15] Burkert 1979a.121–122.

[16] Notable examples: Gamkrelidze and Ivanov 1984, Witzel 1984.

The frequent cross-references to the author's other publications, most of which represent later work, are intended as a continuation and reinforcement of the arguments here presented, not as empty self-advertisement. With the publication of *Greek Mythology and Poetics,* in combination with the books published in 1974, 1979, 1985 (with T. J. Figueira), and 1990 (*Pindar's Homer: The Lyric Possession of an Epic Past*), as listed in the Bibliography, all of the author's major works from 1973 to date have become easily available.

PART I

THE HELLENIZATION OF INDO-EUROPEAN POETICS

CHAPTER 1

Homer and Comparative Mythology

Still under the spell of Heinrich Schliemann's rediscovery of Troy, students of ancient Greece have been accustomed to regard the Greek epic tradition of Homer as a reporting of events that really happened in the second millennium B.C., the Mycenaean Bronze Age.[1] This view must be modified by the perspective of comparative mythology, as most clearly articulated in a three-volume series, *Mythe et épopée,* by Georges Dumézil.[2] This perspective takes the methodology of Indo-European linguistics beyond the level of pure language and applies it on the level of myth as expressed by language. In this sense, it is appropriate to think of comparative mythology, more broadly, as *comparative philology*:

> One of the services that "comparative philology" can render the "separate philologies" [as, for example, Classical philology] is to protect them against their own unchecked attitudes concerning "origins," to orient them toward the kind of empirical process, positive or negative, that goes beyond the uncertainty and consequent arbitrariness that can result from evaluating facts purely from a Greek or Roman or Indic or Scandinavian point of view.[3]

Just as the Greek *language* is cognate with other Indo-European languages, including Latin, Indic, and Old Norse, so also various Greek *institutions* are cognate with the corresponding institutions of other peoples speaking other Indo-European languages. In other words, such

[1] A notable example is Page 1959.
[2] Dumézil 1968, 1971, 1973.
[3] Dumézil 1985.15 (my translation).

diverse groups as the ancient Greek and Indic peoples have a common Indo-European heritage not only on the level of *language* but also on the level of *society*. To appreciate the breadth and the depth of this Indo-European heritage in Greek institutions, one has only to read through the prodigious collection of detailed evidence assembled by Emile Benveniste in *Le vocabulaire des institutions indo-européennes*.[4] For now, however, we shall concentrate on Dumézil's argument that one such Indo-European institution is the tradition of epic as reflected, for example, in the Indic *Mahābhārata*. The comparative approach, as we shall see, gives a vision of epic that is significantly different from the picture emerging from a "separatist" approach that restricts the field of vision to Homeric standards.

What comparative philology teaches us is that epic is a reflection not so much of historical events as of myth. According to this scheme, epic allows myth to take precedence over reality as we know it. Even where epic utilizes the raw material of real events, the argument goes, it will reshape these events to accommodate the requirements of myth.

This insight from comparative mythology concerning myth is a far cry from our own contemporary usage of the word "myth," which conveys the opposite of reality. Myth, in societies where it exists as a living tradition, must not be confused with fiction, which is a matter of individual and personal creativity. Rather, myth represents a collective expression of society, an expression that society itself deems to be true and valid. From the standpoint of the given society that it articulates, myth *is* the primary reality.[5] For the purposes of the present argument, then, "myth" can be defined as "a traditional narrative that is used as a designation of reality. Myth is applied narrative. Myth describes a meaningful and important reality that applies to the aggregate, going beyond the individual."[6]

The links between myth and epic are explored from another angle in the researches of Milman Parry and Albert Lord on the nature of traditional oral epic poetry.[7] From their fieldwork in the living South Slavic oral poetic traditions, we can witness directly how the composition and performance of epic are aspects of the same process, how myth is literally re-created in each new performance, and how there can be

[4] Benveniste 1969.

[5] Cf. N 1982b, reviewing Detienne 1981, and Martin 1989. On the truth-value of myth: Leach 1982.2–7.

[6] My translation, with slight modifications, of Burkert 1979b.29. Although I recognize the need for the additional term "legend," besides "myth," in the work of others, I find it unnecessary for the purposes of this book.

[7] The basics: Parry 1971 (collected works) and Lord 1960.

countless variations in tradition without any deviation from tradition itself. Parry and Lord have successfully applied to the Homeric *Iliad* and *Odyssey* the criteria that they developed from their experience in fieldwork, and their demonstration that these marvels of Western literature are composed in the traditions of oral poetry may further justify applying the criteria that Dumézil has developed from his experience in the systematic comparison of surviving epic texts.[8] As we can ascertain independently with Parry and Lord, Homer is a master of *mythe et épopée.*

There are serious problems, however, in connecting the epic traditions of ancient Greece with those of other societies belonging to the Indo-European language family. Dumézil himself gives the clearest account of these problems, which can be summarized as follows:[9]

> (1) generally, it is difficult to connect the narrative of the Homeric poems with the basic patterns of Indo-European society as reconstructed from comparable narratives in languages related to Greek;
> (2) specifically, the themes associated with the major Homeric heroes seem not to match the themes associated with gods—at least, they do not match as they do, for example, in the clearly Indo-European epic traditions of the Indic *Mahābhārata.*[10]

A solution to these problems may be found in archaeology—not in the evidence of the second millennium B.C., the represented era of the Homeric heroes, but in the evidence of the eighth century B.C., the era of the incipient Homeric audience. Whereas the archaeology of the second millennium has encouraged students of Hellas to concentrate on the historical realities found in Greek epic, the archaeology of the eighth century may lead them to perceive the mythmaking framework that integrates these realities.

A 1971 book by Anthony Snodgrass, *The Dark Age of Greece*, has made it plain that the eighth century B.C., the era in which the *Iliad* and *Odyssey* were reaching their ultimate form, is as important for our understanding of Homeric poetry as is the late second millennium B.C., the era that provides the overt subject matter for both of these epics.[11] Granted, Homeric poetry draws on details that archaeologists can indeed assign to the late second millennium.[12] But the point is that it also reflects the

[8] Cf. also Martin 1989.1–42.

[9] Dumézil 1968.580–581; cf. also 1982.8, 52, 112–113

[10] Throughout this book, I use the word "theme" (and "thematic") as a shorthand reference to *a basic unit in the traditional subject patterns of myth.* My model for a sensible deployment of this word is Lord 1960.68–98.

[11] Snodgrass 1971 (see esp. pp. 421, 435; also pp. 352, 376, 416–417, 421, 431).

[12] Again, Page 1959.

overall orientation of the eighth century, which is a watershed for the evolution of Hellenic civilization as we know it: in this era, alongside the phenomenon of the *pólis* 'city-state', the heir to localized traditions in cult, law, and so on, there emerged a complementary phenomenon of pan-Hellenism, formalized in such institutions as the Olympic Games, the Delphic Oracle, and the Homeric poems themselves.[13]

In fact, Homeric poetry is a formalization of both these phenomena: it synthesizes the diverse local traditions of each major city-state into a unified pan-Hellenic model that suits the ideology of the polis in general, but without being restricted to the ideology of any one polis in particular.[14] Perhaps the clearest example is the Homeric concept of the Olympian gods, which incorporates yet goes beyond the localized religious traditions of each polis; the pan-Hellenic perspective of Homeric poetry has transcended local phenomena such as the cult of gods, which is functional only on the local level of the polis.[15] By "cult" I mean a set of practices combining elements of ritual as well as myth. For a working definition of "ritual," I choose the following formulation: "Ritual, in its outward aspect, is a programme of demonstrative acts to be performed in set sequence and often at a set place and time—sacred insofar as every omission or deviation arouses deep anxiety and calls forth sanctions. As communication and social imprinting, ritual establishes and secures the solidarity of the closed group."[16] The insistence of ritual on a set order of things should not be misunderstood to mean that all rituals are static and that all aspects of rituals are rigid. Even in cases where a given society deems a given ritual to be static and never changing, it may in fact be dynamic and ever changing, responding to the ever-changing structure of the society that it articulates.

Besides the cult of gods, another example of interplay between polis and pan-Hellenism in Homeric poetry is its attitude toward the cult of heroes. Erwin Rohde's monumental book *Psyche* remains one of the most eloquent sources for our understanding the *hḗrōs* 'hero' as a very old and distinct concept of traditional Greek religion, requiring ritual practices that were distinct from those associated with the gods.[17] What archaeology now tells us is that this Hellenic institution of hero cults, without much difference from what we see attested in the Classical period of the fifth century, is shaped in the eighth century B.C., the same

[13] Snodgrass 1971.421, 435. Hereafter, the word *pólis* will appear in plain roman print: polis.

[14] Cf. N 1979a.115–117.

[15] Rohde 1898.1:125–127.

[16] Burkert 1985.8.

[17] Rohde 1898; for a survey of Rohde's treatment of hero cults, see N 1979a.115–117.

era that shaped the *Iliad* and *Odyssey*.[18] It is of course tempting to explain the upsurge of hero cults throughout the city-states as a phenomenon motivated by the contemporaneous diffusion of Homeric poetry,[19] but it would be better to follow Snodgrass in looking for a more comprehensive explanation.[20] Again, the key is the twin eighth-century phenomena of the polis on one hand and pan-Hellenism on the other. I cite Rohde's thesis that the *cult of heroes* was a highly evolved transformation of the *worship of ancestors*—a transformation that took place within the social context of the polis.[21] This thesis, perhaps most appealing from the viewpoint of cultural anthropology,[22] allows room for considering the constituent elements of hero cults to go back far beyond the eighth century.[23] In other words, we can posit a lengthy prehistory for not only the epics of heroes but also the cults of heroes, with this qualification: the ultimate forms of the epics and of the cults were definitively shaped in the eighth century. The strong eighth-century upsurge in the local cults of heroes can thus be viewed as a phenomenon parallel to—rather than derivative from—the pan-Hellenic epics of heroes, namely, the *Iliad* and *Odyssey*.

Thus the ideological heritage of Greek heroes may still in principle be reconstructed as Indo-European in character. But there are problems in extracting comparative evidence about the hero from Greek epic, especially about the religious dimension of the hero. It is worth stressing that the hero as a figure of cult must be local because it is a fundamental principle in Greek religion that his supernatural power is local.[24] On the other hand, the hero as a figure of epic is pan-Hellenic and consequently cannot have an overtly religious dimension in the narrative. Still, we may expect to find at least latent traces of this religious dimension within the Homeric poems. I have in fact produced a book with this expectation in mind.[25] Even further, it can be argued that these latent traces have cognates in the comparative evidence of other Indo-European epic traditions.

Both the *Iliad* and the *Odyssey* reveal a pervasive theme that implicitly tells of a hero's parallelism, not only in character but also in action, with a corresponding god. This theme is particularly manifest in the case of

[18] Snodgrass 1970.190–193. Cf. Snodgrass 1987, esp. pp. 160, 165.

[19] Cf. Coldstream 1976.

[20] Snodgrass 1971.398–399; also Snodgrass 1987, esp. pp. 160, 165, and Morris 1988.754–755. For a reappraisal, stressing regional variations, see Whitley 1988.

[21] Rohde 1898.1:108–110.

[22] Cf. Brelich 1958.144n202 and Alexiou 1974.19.

[23] Cf. again Snodgrass 1971.398–399.

[24] Rohde 1:184–189.

[25] N 1979a. Cf. also Vernant 1985.101, 104, 106.

Achilles and Apollo in the *Iliad.* For example, both the hero and the god have *mênis* 'anger' (I 1/I 75) that inflicts *álgea* 'pains' (I 2/I 96) so as to be a *loigós* 'devastation' for the Achaeans (I 341/I 97).[26] Moreover, the hero and the god are traditionally represented as look-alikes, for example both appearing unshorn in the manner of a *koûros* 'uninitiated male'. Their physical parallelism has led Walter Burkert to describe Achilles as a *Doppelgänger* of Apollo.[27] We see here a remarkable analogue to the five epic heroes known as the *Pāṇḍava*-s in the Indic *Mahābhārata,* heroes whose parallelism with corresponding gods (Dharma, Vāyu, Indra, and the two Aśvin-s) has been traced in detail by Dumézil.[28]

In Greek epic there is a consistent pattern of mutual antagonism between a god and the hero who is parallel to him. Moreover, this pattern of antagonism on the level of myth is matched by a pattern of symbiosis on the level of cult.[29] As a case in point, I cite the relationship of Apollo with Pyrrhos/Neoptolemos, son of Achilles: this hero is killed by the god himself within his own divine precinct (e.g. Pindar *Paean* 6.117–120), the very place where Pyrrhos/Neoptolemos is believed to be buried and where he is worshiped as the chief cult hero of Delphi (e.g. Pindar *Nemean* 7.44–47).[30] This and many other similar themes of god-hero antagonism suit an Indo-European pattern documented by Dumézil, who links the story patterns of the Old Norse hero Starkaðr, the Indic hero Śiśupāla, and the Greek hero Herakles. With the myth of Herakles, Dumézil himself has admirably demonstrated that the Indo-European pattern of god-hero antagonism is indeed attested in the realm of Greek myth. What I would add here is that this same pattern is central to the narrative traditions of Greek epic in particular, as exemplified in the *Iliad* and *Odyssey.*[31] In fact, the compressed retelling of the Herakles story in *Iliad* XIX 95–133 is a clear attestation of the same Indo-European pattern that Dumézil has reconstructed from such nonpoetic retellings as in Diodorus Siculus (4.8–39).[32]

The claim can be made, then, that the themes associated with the major Homeric heroes do indeed match the themes associated with

[26] Further discussion in N 1979a ch.5.

[27] Burkert 1975.19; cf. N 1979a.142–143.

[28] Dumézil 1968.33–257.

[29] Cf. Burkert 1975.19; cf. N 1979a ch.7.

[30] Cf. N 1979a ch.7.

[31] On the antagonism of Achilles and Apollo, I refer again to N 1979a ch.7; on the antagonism between Odysseus and Poseidon, see Hansen 1977. It is fitting that a complex figure like Odysseus should have more than one divine antagonist. On the implicit antagonism between Odysseus and Athena, see Clay 1984.

[32] See Davidson 1980.

gods, and that Dumézil's doubts about the applicability of his reconstructions to Greek epics can in the end be dispelled. Moreover, since the Greek evidence shows parallelisms of god and hero attested *even on the level of cult,* Dumézil's vision of epic as structured by myth may even be extended one level further: from epic to myth to *ritual.*

There is a striking attestation of all three levels in the *Homeric Hymn to Herakles* (*Hymn* 15), which can be described as a brief and stylized *prayer* in worship of the hero Herakles, invoked as the son of Zeus (verses 1 and 9) and implored to grant success and wealth (9). Within this prayer Herakles is described as *áristos* 'best' among the *epikhthónioi* 'earth-bound men' of Thebes (1–2), and each of these words conjures up a specific heroic theme. Considering *epikhthónioi* first, we note that this word can mean more than 'earth-bound men' pure and simple: it is also attested in the context of designating heroes as worshiped in cult (e.g. Hesiod *Works and Days* 123).[33] As for *áristos* 'best', it serves as a formal measure of a given hero's supremacy in his own epic tradition, as we see from the deployment of the expression *áristos Akhaiôn* 'best of the Achaeans' in the Homeric poems: the *Iliad* and the *Odyssey* each appropriate this epithet to fit the central figures Achilles and Odysseus, respectively.[34]

There are other epic touches as well in *Homeric Hymn* 15, as for example in these verses describing the Labors of the hero Herakles:

πλαζόμενος πομπῆσιν ὑπ' Εὐρυσθῆος ἄνακτος
πολλὰ μὲν αὐτὸς ἔρεξεν ἀτάσθαλα, πολλὰ δ' ἀνέτλη

Homeric Hymn to Herakles 15.5–6

Set off-course on missions at the direction of Eurystheus the king,
many are the reckless [*atásthala*] things that he did, many the things that he endured.

Let us compare the verses beginning the *Odyssey:*

ἄνδρα μοι ἔννεπε Μοῦσα πολύτροπον ὃς μάλα πολλὰ
πλάγχθη, ἐπεὶ Τροίης ἱερὸν πτολίεθρον ἔπερσε.
πολλῶν δ' ἀνθρώπων ἴδεν ἄστεα καὶ νόον ἔγνω,
πολλὰ δ' ὅ γ' ἐν πόντῳ πάθεν ἄλγεα . . .

Odyssey i 1–4

About the man sing to me, Muse, the one of many turns [*polú-tropos*], the

[33] N 1979a.153–154. Cf. also Vernant 1985.101, 104, 106.
[34] N 1979a ch.2.

one who many times
was set off-course after he destroyed the holy citadel of Troy.
Many are the men whose cities he saw, and he came to know their way of thinking,
and many are the pains that he suffered at sea.

In the *Hymn to Herakles*, the anaphora of πολλὰ ... πολλὰ 'many things ... many things' at verse 6 in the context of πλαζόμενος 'set off-course' at verse 5 is parallel to the anaphora of πολύτροπον ... πολλὰ/πολλῶν .../πολλὰ 'the one of many turns' ... 'many'/'many' .../'many' at *Odyssey* i 1/3/4 in the context of πλάγχθη 'was set off course' at i 2. Further, the expression πολλὰ ... ἀνέτλη 'he endured many things' at *Hymn* 15.6 describing Herakles is parallel to πολλὰ ... πάθεν ἄλγεα 'he suffered many pains' at *Odyssey* i 4 describing Odysseus, while the ἀτάσθαλα 'reckless' deeds of Herakles at *Hymn* 15.6 correspond to the characterization of Achilles in his own dark moments of savagery as ἀτάσθαλος (e.g. XXII 418).[35]

The study of the diction in *Hymn* 15 could be taken much further, but the point has already been made: this composition is not only a functional prayer to a hero in his capacity as a cult figure but also a glorification of his epic attributes—the very same epic attributes that seem to be divided up between Achilles and Odysseus in the overall epic diction of the *Iliad* and *Odyssey*.[36]

It is as if the epic figures of Achilles and Odysseus resulted from a split of characterizations that we can find in one heroic figure, Herakles. In light of Dumézil's work on Herakles in *Mythe et épopée* II,[37] we see that Herakles is in fact far closer to an Indo-European model of the hero than is either Achilles or Odysseus. We may even add another factor, this time in light of Dumézil's work in *Mythe et épopée* I.[38] Such heroes as the five *Pāṇḍava*-s in the Indic *Mahābhārata* are not only each parallel to specific gods in traits and actions: they are also sired by these very same gods.[39] So also with Herakles: the best of heroes, as he is described in the *Homeric Hymn to Herakles* (15.1–2), is sired by the best of gods. By

[35] For more on the thematic connection of Achilles with the epithet *atásthalos* (ἀτάσθαλος) 'reckless', see N pp. 163ff.

[36] The nonspecialization of the Herakles figure in comparison with the main heroes of attested Greek epic suggests that the Herakles theme may be appropriate to poetic forms other than epic: cf. Burkert 1979a.94.

[37] Dumézil 1971.

[38] Dumézil 1968.117–132.

[39] The father/son combinations (to repeat: in each case the fathers are gods and the sons are mortals): Dharma/Yudhiṣṭhira, Vāyu/Bhīma, Indra/Arjuna, the two Aśvin-s/Nakula and Sahadeva.

contrast, most Homeric heroes are several generations removed from divine parentage, just as they are several stages removed from the Indo-European model of the hero.

There is a striking reflex of this state of affairs on the formal level of poetic diction. The word in question is *hēmí-theoi* (ἡμίθεοι) 'demigods', which as we see from Hesiod F 204.100 MW and elsewhere clearly denotes *direct divine parentage on one side* (ἡμίθεοι at verse 100 = τέκνα θεῶν at verse 101), not simply *semidivine status.*[40] In Hesiod *Works and Days* 160, this same word *hēmí-theoi* designates the heroes of the generations that fought at Thebes and Troy.[41] Yet Homeric diction consistently refers to this same generation of heroes as *hḗrōes* (ἥρωες) 'heroes', not *hēmí-theoi* (ἡμίθεοι) 'demigods'. The only exception is at *Iliad* XII 23, where *hēmí-theoi* does indeed refer to the Achaean heroes who fought at Troy—*but the reference here is made from the standpoint of the Homeric audience,* as it looks back, centuries later, at the remains of the Trojan War (see especially *Iliad* XII 26–32).[42] The point remains, then, that Homeric poetry—unlike other traditional forms of poetry—cannot as a rule designate its own heroes as *hēmítheoi* 'demigods', being restricted instead to the word *hḗrōes.* It is as if the Indo-European model of hero were no longer appropriate for the Homeric tradition of epic narrative, whereas it remained so for other poetic traditions such as the Hesiodic.[43]

I return to Hesiod F 204 MW for a remarkable illustration of this principle. At verses 95 and following, we find a tightly compressed narrative about the beginnings of the Trojan War: how the Olympian gods were split into pro-Achaean and pro-Trojan factions ever since the *éris* 'strife' at the Judgment of Paris (verses 95–96),[44] how the Will of Zeus ordained the deaths of heroes in the Trojan War (96–123). By good fortune, a corresponding passage is attested in a fragment from the epic *Cycle,* specifically from the beginning of the epic *Cypria* (F 1 Allen). Here, too, we find a reference to *éris* 'strife', this time designating the Trojan War itself (*Cypria* F 1. 5), and how it was the Will of Zeus that heroes should die at Troy (F 1.6–7).[45] So much for the convergences. One major divergence, however, is that the heroes of the Trojan War are called *hḗrōes* in the Cyclic version (F 1.7 Allen) but *hēmítheoi* 'demigods' in the Hesiodic (F 204.100 MW). It appears that the epic format is more specialized,

[40] Cf. West 1978.191.

[41] More on these heroes at p. 126.

[42] More on this passage in N 1979a.159–161. Cf. also Vernant 1985.101, 104, 106.

[43] More at p. 126 on the Hesiodic visualization of heroes.

[44] More in N pp. 219–221.

[45] On the Will of Zeus theme as represented in the *Iliad* (I 5), see N p. 82 § 25n2, with further references.

more restricted, than other forms of poetry, and that it cannot easily tolerate the semantics of an Indo-European model that contradicts the genealogies of its own more specialized, more restricted heroes.

And yet the general themes shared by these Cyclic and Hesiodic passages are distinctly Indo-European in character. Even if the Cyclic *Cypria* avoids calling its heroes *hēmítheoi* 'demigods', these epic figures nonetheless share a vitally important theme with their distant Indic cousins, the divinely sired *Pāṇḍava*-s of the *Mahābhārata*: Zeus brings the *éris* 'strife' of the Trojan War *because he intends to depopulate the Earth of the myriad heroes that weigh upon her* (*Cypria* F 1.1–6 Allen). Similarly in the *Mahābhārata*, the war of the *Pāṇḍava*-s is a divine solution to the overpopulation of heroes weighing upon the earth.[46] In this way the major epic narratives of the Greek and the Indic peoples are inaugurated with a cognate theme, and it is hard to imagine more compelling evidence for the Indo-European heritage of the epic traditions about the Trojan War.[47]

A related theme, equally important as evidence for an Indo-European heritage in Greek epic, is apparent in the *Iliad*'s own compressed reference to the beginnings of the Trojan War—a theme elaborated in detail by the *Cypria*. We have already seen that the war itself is an *éris* 'conflict' (*Cypria* F 1.5 Allen), just as the Judgment of Paris is an *éris* (Hesiod F 204.96 MW). The *éris* that marks the beautiful shepherd's judgment took the form of *neîkos* (νεῖκος) 'quarreling' (*Cypria*/Proclus summary p. 102.15 Allen), and the *Iliad* itself refers to the whole affair as *éris* (III 100) or *neîkos* (XXII 116). I emphasize the words *éris* 'strife' and *neîkos* 'quarreling' not only because of their thematic importance as a plot motivation of epic but also because of their programmatic significance beyond epic. It so happens that the language of Greek praise poetry designates its own converse, blame poetry, with these very words, *éris* and *neîkos*.[48] Moreover, epic itself uses the word *neikéō* as 'blame' in opposition to *ainéō* 'praise' (e.g. *Iliad* X 249–250).[49]

This opposition fits the larger pattern of a complementary interplay between praise and blame, particularly on the level of poetry, in such Indo-European societies as the Italic, Celtic, and Indic.[50] Marcel Detienne has extended the comparison to the Greek evidence,[51] and I in turn have described in detail the diction of praise and blame specifically

[46] See Dumézil 1968.168–169.
[47] Cf. Vian 1970, esp. p. 55.
[48] N 1979a ch.11–ch.15.
[49] N pp. 34–35, 240.
[50] Dumézil 1943; updated in Dumézil 1969.
[51] Detienne 1973.

in Greek poetry.[52] The point to be made now, however, is more fundamental: as we can see from the Iliadic references to the Judgment of Paris, *Greek epic presents its own genesis in terms of the opposition between praise and blame.* As the *Iliad* puts it, the Judgment of Paris entailed the *blaming* of the goddesses Hera and Athena along with the *praising* of Aphrodite:

> ὃς νείκεσσε θεάς, ὅτε οἱ μέσσαυλον ἵκοντο,
> τὴν δ' ᾔνησ' ἥ οἱ πόρε μαχλοσύνην ἀλεγεινήν
>
> *Iliad* XXIV 29–30

> [Paris] who blamed [verb *neikéō*] the goddesses [Hera and Athena], when they came to his courtyard,
> but he praised [verb *ainéō*] her who gave him baneful sensuality.

Thus the primary narrative of Greek epic, which is the Trojan War, is self-motivated by the Indo-European social principle of counterbalancing praise and blame.

It is precisely in this theme, the Judgment of Paris, that Dumézil has found the most overt Greek example of a general Indo-European social ideology that he describes as trifunctionalism. In Dumézil's formulation, society as reflected by the Indo-European languages tends to divide along the following three lines of ideological organization: (1) sovereignty and the sacred, (2) warfare, (3) agriculture, herding, and fertility in general.[53] The theme of the Judgment of Paris reflects this pattern of trifunctionalism. Paris the herdsman is being offered a gift from each of the three functions: (1) sovereignty, from Hera; (2) military supremacy, from Athena; and (3) sexual relations with Helen, the most beautiful woman on earth, from Aphrodite.[54]

Thus the Judgment of Paris, the ultimate point of departure for the narrative traditions that we know as Homer's epics, can itself be judged as an epic theme with an Indo-European foundation. More broadly, Homer can be judged an authoritative source for the myths inherited by and through the Greek language.

[52]N 1979a ch.11–ch.15.

[53]See Dumézil 1958.

[54]Dumézil 1968.580–586. For further important observations on the Judgment of Paris theme, see Dumézil 1985.15–30.

CHAPTER 2

Formula and Meter: The Oral Poetics of Homer

Since the discoveries of Milman Parry[1] and Albert Lord[2] about the nature of "oral poetry," some problems have developed over how to define the formula. Parry's own definition will serve as a useful point of departure: the formula is "a group of words which is regularly employed under the same metrical conditions to express a given essential idea."[3]

It is pointless here to launch into a bibliographical survey of scholars' reactions; I propose instead to consider some of the general problems to be found in the definition itself. The most important of these, one that requires extensive discussion, has to do with Parry's original frame of reference. To put it simply, Parry was basing his definition on one body of evidence alone, the Homeric corpus (that is, the *Iliad* and *Odyssey*). If we look again at Parry's words, we see that he actually prefaced his definition with "The formula in the Homeric poems may be defined as . . . ."[4]

In fact, it is fair to say that the study of oral poetry down to our time has been destined to develop in a certain direction and almost in a certain order not so much because Homeric poetry had been a preeminent topic of academic interest for centuries but rather because Milman Parry in particular based his initial findings exclusively on Homeric poetry. As late as six years after publication of his two fundamental French theses

[1] Parry 1928a, b. The writings of Parry were collected by his son, Parry 1971. I will follow the pagination of this edition, placing in square brackets the original dates of publication (notably 1928a, b; 1930).

[2] Esp. Lord 1960.

[3] Parry 1971 [1930].272.

[4] Parry p. 272.

(Parry 1928a, b), at a time when he was already starting fieldwork on South Slavic oral poetry, Parry was still relying on criteria based squarely on Homeric poetry. Albert Lord gives us a fascinating glimpse of this stage in his teacher's thinking when he quotes statements like the following from Parry's own field notes (dictated at Dubrovnik, from December 1, 1934, to February 2, 1935): "for some reason, that does not exist for the South Slavic poetry, there existed for the Greek heroic songs a fixity of phrasing which is utterly unknown in the South Slavic."[5] Much more fieldwork was yet to follow, and the subsequent research of both Parry and Lord has led to an entirely different conclusion, that the fixity of phrasing in South Slavic oral poetry is in fact all-pervasive.[6]

The experience of fieldwork, then, has here ultimately corrected an initial impression induced under the Homeric influence. It should be emphasized, however, that Homeric poetry did not mislead the fieldworker about Homeric poetry; rather, it misled him about South Slavic poetry. And yet, why should one archaic text, the Homeric corpus, have had more to say about the nature of oral poetry than the myriad songs sung by singers in the living South Slavic tradition? The answer is simple: one knew a great deal more about the Homeric tradition. Centuries of philology had already passed in pursuit of every imaginable aspect in the evolution of the *Iliad* and *Odyssey*. Prodigious efforts at discovering the genesis of Greek epic had a way of inspiring confidence that one was on the track of its essence as well. No matter what we call this quest—the "Homeric Question" or whatever—the assumption is there: *essence through origins.*

Here the evolution of another field of study, that of linguistics, teaches the student of oral poetry an important lesson: searching for origins does not necessarily lead to our grasping the essence. In the nineteenth century the study of language was preoccupied mainly with its genealogy rather than its structure. Historical linguistics took precedence over other approaches, as we can see from Pedersen's eloquent account in *The Discovery of Language* (1931). But historical linguistics is by no means adequate as the sole approach to language. For example, we will not really know the Latin language simply by tracing it back to an Indo-European protolanguage—even though the technique of reconstructing Latin and all the other Indo-European languages to a common prototype has been justifiably called, by a prominent linguist who was not even an Indo-Europeanist himself, "more nearly perfect than that of any other science dealing with man's institutions."[7] Granted, a

[5] Lord 1968.33.
[6] See esp. Lord 1960.47.
[7] Sapir 1929.207.

reconstructed protolanguage may perhaps justifiably be called "a glorious artifact, one which is far more precious than anything an archaeologist can ever hope to unearth."[8] Nevertheless, the point remains that reconstruction cannot yield all the answers. What is also needed is a thorough description of the structure of a given language as it exists at a given time and place. Since the influential work of the linguist Ferdinand de Saussure, such a perspective on language has been called "synchronic," in contrast to the "diachronic" perspective, where we see the structure of a language as it evolves through time.[9] For solving most problems of language, it is now generally recognized that both perspectives are needed.[10]

These concepts of synchronic and diachronic are readily applicable to the study of oral poetry. What I propose to do throughout this presentation is to stress their abiding usefulness. But first, let us quickly compare the history of oral studies with the history of linguistic studies. Fieldwork on South Slavic epic, which is an example of synchronic analysis, came about much later than philological research into the genesis of the Homeric corpus, which is clearly diachronic analysis. In general, then, the evolution of linguistics and oral studies is parallel. In particulars, too, it was the historical perspective, I submit, that had led Parry at the outset of his fieldwork to believe that South Slavic oral poetry lacked the degree of fixity in phrasing that could be found in the *Iliad* and *Odyssey*. Let it not go unsaid, though, that Parry's own approach to the Homeric corpus was strictly synchronic: he was studying its formulas as blocks of a real *system* of traditional diction. My point is simply that Parry's initial impressions of South Slavic oral poetry were influenced by the diachronic standpoint of his Homerist predecessors. Once his own synchronic perspective took hold, the essence of South Slavic oral poetry presented him with an altogether different picture.

The synchronic approach, however useful it has been for Parry when he was analyzing Homeric poetry, was even more effective as a tool for analyzing South Slavic oral poetry. In the case of the *Iliad* and *Odyssey*, Parry had to confront the philological problem of a fixed text containing a finite length of discourse—vestiges of an oral tradition long dead even by the time of Plato. Moreover, we know precious little even about the setting of ancient Greek oral poetry—beyond what we learn from the texts themselves. By contrast, Parry's fieldwork in Yugoslavia was an open-ended situation: here he had access to as many performances as

[8] Haas 1969.34.

[9] Saussure 1916; new ed. 1972.117. For a particularly accessible discussion of these concepts, with essential bibliography, see Ducrot and Todorov 1979.137–144.

[10] Cf. Watkins 1973b, 1978b.

he could record from as many singers as he could find who practiced the living tradition of oral poetry. It is in fact from the synchronic fieldwork of Parry and Lord that we gain the most important new fact about oral poetry—one that we could perhaps never have learned from philological work on the Homeric texts alone. Each and every performance that Parry recorded from the singers of the living tradition turned out to be, as he discovered, a distinct composition. Lord sums it up this way: "Singer, performer, composer, and poet are one under different aspects *but at the same time.* Singing, performing, composing are facets of the same act."[11]

This aspect of oral poetry, which Parry learned from his fieldwork in Yugoslavia, had vital significance for Parry's concept of the formula. The Homeric evidence had taught him that the formula is a traditional group of words regularly recurring in a given rhythmical framework, that is, in given metrical slots. Now he learns from the South Slavic evidence that oral poetry may require you to compose while you perform, perform while you compose. Such a medium, it follows, puts pressure on the poet/singer to have a ready-made phrase available to fill every position in the verse, which is the overall frame for his phraseology. Then too, the singer has to make verse follow verse rapidly. As Lord puts it, "The need for the 'next' line is upon him even before he utters the final syllable of a line. There is urgency. To meet it the singer builds patterns of sequences of lines, which we know as the 'parallelisms' of oral style."[12]

We may all follow intuitively such observations offered by Parry and Lord about the demands made by performance on composition. But the Hellenist who has been reared on the classical approaches to the *Iliad* and *Odyssey* begins to wonder how an oral system so seemingly automatic could still result in compositions that seem so integral—so premeditated esthetically, even psychologically. He wonders even more when he reads some other Hellenists who have championed the findings of Parry. For example, defining what he calls Parry's "law of economy," Denys Page says the following about the Homeric formula: "Generally speaking, for a given idea within a given place in the line, there will be found in the vast treasury of phrases one formula and one only."[13] Page then goes on to give a particularly elegant illustration of this principle of thrift by examining all the Homeric attestations for "the sea." I quote his conclusions in full:[14]

[11] Lord 1960.13.
[12] Lord p. 54.
[13] Page 1959.224.
[14] Page pp. 225–226.

> For this one idea, "the sea," and for its expression in noun + epithet phrases only, he [the poet] relied upon his memory to provide him with a ready-made formula for almost every requirement; and the traditional vocabulary was now so highly developed, so refined and reduced, that for each requirement he found never, or hardly ever, more than one single formula. He has no freedom to select his adjectives: he must adopt whatever combination of words is supplied by tradition for a given part of the verse; and that traditional combination brings with it an adjective which may or may not be suitable to the context.

Such assertions about "metrical utility as a primary determinant in the choice of words"[15] have vexed legions of Homerists devoted to the artistry of the *Iliad* and *Odyssey*.

Most of the outraged reactions, however, are based on overinterpretation of the Parry-Lord theories. To infer that "Homer" cannot do this or that—even against his own artistic wishes—is to misunderstand Parry and Lord altogether; a careful rereading of Albert Lord's *Singer of Tales* chapter 3 ("The Formula") is then in order.[16] What Parry was saying is that the Homeric language is "free of phrases which, having the same metrical value *and expressing the same idea*, could replace one another."[17] Moreover, the context of Parry's statement is a discussion of fixed epithets that are *distinctive* rather than *generic*, like πολύτλας δῖος 'much-suffering brilliant', which is applied to Odysseus only, ποδάρκης δῖος 'swift-footed brilliant', applied to Achilles only, μέγας κορυθαίολος 'great flashing-helmeted', to Hektor only, and so on.[18] Let us pursue the distinction between generic and distinctive epithets. The former class of adjectives is appropriate to any hero, *under the right metrical conditions.* Where the generic and the distinctive epithets have the same metrical shape, *either can be applied to the hero,* depending on the requirements of the theme at hand.[19] When we add this regular Homeric phenomenon of interchange between generic and distinctive epithets to the sporadic phenomenon, as also noted by Parry himself, of interchange among distinctive epithets,[20] we begin to see more clearly that the Homeric "thrift

[15] To borrow the apt phrasing of Holoka 1973.258.

[16] Lord 1960.30–67.

[17] Parry 1971 [1930].276 (italics mine).

[18] Cf. Parry [1930].276–278. On the distinction between generic and distinctive types of epithets, see Parry [1928a].64. Both *generic* and *distinctive* epithets belong to the larger category of *fixed* epithets, as distinct from *particularized* epithets, on which see Parry [1928a].153–165. For a useful bibliographical survey of recent work on the subject: [M. W.] Edwards 1986.188–201.

[19] Cf. Parry [1928a].149.

[20] Parry [1928a].177–180.

of expression," to use Parry's own words,[21] is not really a conditioning principle.

In fact, it can be argued that the principle of economy is not a cause but an effect of traditional diction. From the diachronic standpoint, we can imagine a scenario for the development of a distinctive into a generic epithet. Suppose that a traditional theme about one given hero with a given epithet becomes applied and reapplied to a succession of other heroes. Within parallel epic actions, then, his epithet would follow these other heroes. If the theme is broad enough, and influential enough, it may in time accommodate a whole class of heroes, such as the figures assigned by tradition to the times of the Trojan War. By then, one original hero's epithet may have become appropriate to a whole set of other heroes cast in the same epic mold, so to speak.

As for epithets that still function in a distinctive phase, one sees them from the diachronic standpoint as capsules of traditional themes associated with the noun described. A distinctive epithet is like a small theme song that conjures up a thought-association with the traditional essence of an epic figure, thing, or concept. To cite an example that has deservedly become a commonplace: Odysseus is πολύτλας 'much-suffering' throughout the *Iliad* because he is already a figure in an epic tradition about adventures that he will have after Troy. My saying "after" here applies only to the narrative sequence: the *Iliad* is recording the fact that Odysseus already has an *Odyssey* tradition about him—which is certainly not the final *Odyssey*, the fixed text that has come down to us. In sum, the diachronic viewpoint suggests that the prime regulator of Homeric epithet in particular and formula in general is traditional *theme* rather than current *meter*.[22]

Of course, a great deal remains to be said about *meter* and its synchronic/diachronic relation to *formula*. For now, however, the point is simply that the gaps in the Homeric principle of thrift prove nothing more than the fact that meter does not automatically trigger ready-made words. The ready-made words are determined by the themes of the composition, and the degree of thrift that we do find is due to a long-term streamlining of these themes in the context of the metrical frame. In this connection, the evidence of the Hesiodic corpus helps supplement what we know about the Homeric corpus. From the important work of G. P. Edwards, we learn that Hesiodic poetry is just as formulaic as the Homeric, and that here, too, we can find regular instances where the

[21] Parry [1930].279.

[22] For a particularly elegant illustration in detail, I cite the work of Shannon 1975 on the Homeric epithets describing ash spears (for an important earlier work using similar methodology, see also Whallon 1961).

principle of economy is observed and sporadic instances where it is not.[23] Significantly, the areas of nonobservance in Homeric and Hesiodic poetry often differ.[24] From the diachronic point of view, we may wish to posit here the factor of chronological variation, where the principle of economy is waived in order to leave room for an older or newer expression that is more apt for an older or newer theme. There may also be regional variation: the inherited themes of Homeric and Hesiodic poetry must have been filtered through different traditions from different places. As the boasting Aeneas says to the boasting Achilles in a mutually menacing encounter:

ἐπέων δὲ πολὺς νομὸς ἔνθα καὶ ἔνθα

Iliad XX 249

There is a great range of epics from place to place.

I will defer the reasons for my translating as I did until later. For now, the argument is simply that both the regular observance and the sporadic nonobservance of the thrift principle may reflect the force of traditional themes. Finally, considering all the instances of nonobservance and following Roman Jakobson's useful concept of distinguishing poetic *trends* from *constants*,[25] I will henceforth refer to the "trend toward thrift" instead of "law of thrift / economy."

On the subject of thrift, we may develop a better synchronic insight from the fieldwork of Parry and Lord in South Slavic poetry. Their findings suggest that there is a trend toward thrift that is parallel to what is found in the Homeric corpus—*but primarily on the level of the individual singer's composition.* Lord puts it this way: "Indeed, it seems to me that the thriftiness which we find in individual singers and not in districts or traditions is an important argument for the unity of the Homeric poems. Homer's thriftiness finds its parallel in the individual Yugoslav singer, but not in the collected songs of a number of different singers."[26] An important amplification seems in order: from the synchronic evidence of South Slavic oral poetry, where we see that composition and performance are one, we may also infer that the composition of the *Iliad* and that of the *Odyssey* are also a matter of performance. Homeric poetry is a performance medium, no matter how difficult it is for us to imagine any

[23] Edwards 1971.
[24] Edwards pp. 55–73, ch. 5: "The Principle of Economy."
[25] Jakobson 1952.
[26] Lord 1960.53.

possible context for actual recitation of epics that size.[27] Otherwise such Homeric phenomena as the strong trend toward thrift would be absent. Having discounted meter as the primary cause of fixity in formulaic behavior, we may now attempt to take a diachronic look at the evolution of formula systems. Lord's fundamental observations about the formula in *Singer of Tales*,[28] though they are based on the synchronic perspective of his experiences in the field, are also replete with valuable diachronic insights. In what amounts to a manifesto, he declares: "For the singing we hear today, like the everyday speech around us, goes back in a direct and long series of singings to a beginning which, no matter how difficult it may be to conceive, we must attempt to grasp, because otherwise we shall miss an integral part of the meaning of the traditional formula."[29]

He considers the genesis of formulas not only within the tradition at large but also within the individual singer:[30] "Even in pre-singing years rhythm and thought are one, and the singer's concept of the formula is shaped though not explicit. He is aware of the successive beats and the varying lengths of repeated thoughts, and these might be said to be his formulas. Basic patterns of meter, word boundary, melody have become his possession, and in him the tradition begins to reproduce itself." Surely the dictum applies: *ontogeny recapitulates phylogeny*.[31] How, then, does tradition generate formulas in the singer? The key, it seems, is to be found in the traditional *themes* inherited by the singer:[32] "The fact of narrative song is around him from birth; the technique of it is in the possession of his elders, and he falls heir to it. Yet in a real sense he does recapitulate the experiences of the generations before him stretching back to the distant past." Accordingly, although I agree with Lord's statement that, in making his lines, "the singer is not bound by the formula,"[33] I would also add that the singer is indeed bound by the traditional theme. The theme, I submit, is the key to all the other levels of fixity in oral poetry—including both the formulaic and the metrical levels.

The degree of the singer's adherence to the traditional theme can best be shown by examining the content as well as the form of epic. It is particularly instructive to consider the evidence from Homeric poetry and beyond, as we see from Marcel Detienne's careful investigation of

[27] For a discussion of such contexts, see p. 38.

[28] Lord 1960.30–67.

[29] Lord p. 31.

[30] Lord p. 32.

[31] It is also from the present vantage point that I find it pertinent to adduce the "generative" theory of Nagler 1967 and 1974.

[32] Lord 1960.32.

[33] Lord p. 54.

the attitude of Hellenic society toward the *aoidós* 'singer' and the attitude of the singer toward his craft.[34] The traditional boast of the Hellenic singer, as an individual performer, is that he preserves the truth about heroic actions without having to be an eyewitness. Instead, the truth is his simply by virtue of his hearing from the Muses what they saw. As the singer declares at the beginning of the *Catalogue*,

ὑμεῖς γὰρ θεαί ἐστε, πάρεστέ τε, ἴστέ τε πάντα
ἡμεῖς δὲ κλέος οἶον ἀκούομεν οὐδέ τι ἴδμεν

Iliad II 485–496

You [Muses] are gods: you are there [when things happen] and you know everything.
But we [singers] know nothing: we just *hear* the *kléos*.

The claim of knowing nothing masks a highly sophisticated boast. From its etymology, we know that the Greek word κλέος (*kléos*) was originally an abstract noun meaning simply "the act of hearing." The word came to mean "fame" because it had been appropriated by the singer *in his traditional role as an individual performer* to designate what he sang about the actions of gods and heroes. The meaning "fame" betrays merely the consequences. It shows the social prestige of the poet's art form. The actions of gods and heroes gain fame through the medium of the singer, and the singer calls his medium *kléos,* from "the act of hearing."[35] Since the singer starts his performance by asking his Muse to "tell him" the subject, his composition is in fact being presented to his audience as something that he *hears* from the very custodians of all stages of reality. The Muses are speaking to him, and they have the *ipsissima verba* of the Heroic Age.

The poet's inherited conceit, then, is that he has access not only to the content but also to the actual form of what his eyewitnesses, the Muses, speak as they describe the realities of remote generations. I should emphasize that this conceit is linked with the poet's inherited role as an individual *performer,* and that "only in performance can the formula exist and have clear definition."[36] The formulas are the selfsame words spoken by the Muses themselves: they are recordings of the Muses who were there when everything happened. In fact, the frame in which these formulas are contained, the dactylic hexameter, was actually called

[34] Detienne 1973.
[35] For an extended discussion, see N 1974a.244–252; on the cognate Slavic words *slava* 'glory' and *slovo* 'word, epic tale', see N 1979a.16 § 2n3.
[36] Lord 1960.33.

ἔπος (*épos*) by the composer/performer himself, as Hermann Koller has argued in detail.[37] Since the dactylic hexameter, as well as all verses, has an inherited tendency to be syntactically self-contained,[38] the *épos* is truly an epic utterance—an epic sentence—from the standpoint of the Muses or of any character quoted by the Muses. The word introducing Homeric quotations is in fact regularly *épos.* There are even some subtle grammatical distinctions, in traditions of formulaic behavior, between the *épos* that the Muses quote and the *épos* that they simply narrate.[39] In a medium that carries with it such inherited conceits about accuracy and even reality, we can easily imagine generations after generations of audiences conditioned to expect from the performer the most extreme degree of fixity in content, fixity in form.

Of course, different audiences in different places may be raised on traditions that are variants. When the heroic figures of Aeneas and Achilles meet on the battlefield (*Iliad* XX), they try to intimidate each other by boasting of the variant epics serving as background for their heroic exploits. Aeneas tells Achilles not to try to frighten him with the *épea* (XX 200–201)—let us call them his "epics." There is further allusion to the power of *épea* as Aeneas continues:

> ἴδμεν δ' ἀλλήλων γενεήν, ἴδμεν δὲ τοκῆας
> πρόκλυτ' ἀκούοντες ἔπεα θνητῶν ἀνθρώπων
> ὄψει δ' οὔτ' ἄρ πω σὺ ἐμοὺς ἴδες οὔτ' ἄρ' ἐγὼ σούς
>
> *Iliad* XX 203–205

> We know each other's birth, we know each other's parents,
> hearing the famed *épea* from mortal men.
> And yet you have never seen my parents, nor I yours.

There are, as Aeneas warns Achilles, variant *épea* about the same heroes:

> στρεπτὴ δὲ γλῶσσ' ἐστὶ βροτῶν, πολέες δ' ἔνι μῦθοι
> παντοῖοι, ἐπέων δὲ πολὺς νομὸς ἔνθα καὶ ἔνθα
> ὁπποῖόν κ' εἴπῃσθα ἔπος, τοῖόν κ' ἐπακούσαις
>
> *Iliad* XX 248–250

> The tongue of men is twisted, and there are many words there
> of every kind; there is a great range of *épea* from place to place.

[37] Koller 1972.
[38] Cf. N 1974a.143–145.
[39] Cf. Kelly 1974.

The kind of *épos* that you say is the kind of *épos* that you will hear in turn
about yourself.

The most striking feature of this Aeneas/Achilles episode is that the *Iliad* in Book XX actually allows part of the Aeneas tradition to assert itself at the expense of Achilles, who had taunted Aeneas by predicting that he will never replace Priam as king of Troy (XX 178–183). The god Poseidon himself then predicts the opposite (XX 302–308); the dynasty of Aeneas will prevail in the Troad, and there will be a vindication of his *mênis* 'anger' against King Priam (XIII 460–461)—a theme that finds a parallel in the *mênis* 'anger' of Achilles against King Agamemnon in *Iliad* Book I, verses 1 and following.

One of the most obvious traces of a variant epic tradition in *Iliad* XX is the surprising rescue of Trojan Aeneas by one of the most pro-Achaean Olympians, the god Poseidon. From the researches of Felix Jacoby[40] and others,[41] we can reconstruct a motivation for the use of such a tradition. During the times that our *Iliad* was evolving into its ultimate form, there may well have existed a special cult affinity between the god Poseidon and a dynasty of Aeneadae claiming descent from Aeneas. In *Iliad* XX (302–308) as well as in the *Homeric Hymn to Aphrodite* (196–197), the contemporary importance of such a dynasty is being retrojected into the Heroic Age by such epic devices as the prophecy to Aeneas that his descendants, not Priam's, will be the ones who are to hold sway in the Troad.[42] What has not been sufficiently stressed in previous studies, however, is that the traditions about the Aeneadae must themselves have been transmitted through the medium of epic.[43] In other words, the wording of the Aeneas/Achilles episode shows that there had been a regional epic tradition about Aeneas that was destined to glorify the Aeneadae—to give them *kléos*.[44]

I have gone to such lengths in discussing this particular Homeric scene in order to illustrate how regional variations may result in oral traditions with different themes appropriate to different places; and the different themes can in turn lead to corresponding differences in formulaic behavior. In other words, fixity of form in oral poetry should not be confused with uniformity.

[40] Jacoby 1961 [1933] 1:39–48, 51–53.

[41] Most notably Donini 1967.

[42] This is not to say that the *Hymn to Aphrodite*, let alone the *Iliad*, was expressly composed for an audience of Aeneadae: for further discussion, with bibliography, see N 1979a. 268–269.

[43] Further discussion N pp. 268–269.

[44] N pp. 268–269.

Lack of uniformity is caused by the dimension of time as well as that of space. Although the medium of oral poetry may look upon itself as containing the original, actual words of the Heroic Age, "irreplaceable and immortal,"[45] its *Dichtersprache* will nevertheless undergo change in time, much as everyday language does. Since, however, epic deliberately resists change in order to preserve the *ipsissima verba*, the linguistic innovations that do occur in its *Dichtersprache* will not keep apace with the linguistic innovations of the everyday language from which it evolves. Consequently, the language of a body of oral poetry like the *Iliad* and *Odyssey* does not and cannot belong to any one time, any one place: in a word, it *defies synchronic analysis.*[46] Such chronological stratification in form can surely be expected to affect content. Meanwhile, content, too, can be expected to shift with the passage of time—even if the actual shifts in the presentation of a given traditional theme to audiences from one generation to the next might be too subtle for detection at any one occasion of performance/composition. Change is possible even if both performer and audience expect strict adherence to the traditional theme.

Once having made due allowances for some degree of evolution and variation in traditional theme, I must now return to emphasizing its remarkable stability and archaism. The fixity of phrasing in oral poetry, as I have argued, is actually due primarily to the factor of traditional theme rather than meter. Accordingly, I now offer a working definition of the formula that leaves out the factor of meter as the prime conditioning force: *the formula is a fixed phrase conditioned by the traditional themes of oral poetry.* Furthermore, I am ready to propose that *meter is diachronically generated by formula rather than vice versa.*

By applying the linguistic techniques of comparative reconstruction[47] to the fixed phraseology of native Greek and Indic poetry, I have argued elsewhere[48] that it is possible to find cognate phrases containing identically shaped rhythms. The existence of such comparanda would corroborate the theory that the speakers of these two Indo-European languages have preserved two cognate poetic systems.[49] In the oldest attested phases of Indic poetry, moreover, it can be shown that phraseology is regular even where meter is irregular.[50] This set of facts can be

[45] In the words of Page 1959.225.

[46] Cf. Householder and Nagy 1972.738–745.

[47] Cf. Meillet 1925 for the most elegant model.

[48] N 1974a.

[49] Cf. Meillet 1923, Jakobson 1952, Watkins 1963 and 1982a, West 1973a and 1973b, N 1974a and 1979b, Vine 1977 and 1978.

[50] N 1974a.191–228.

supplemented with the discovery, made by Antoine Meillet,[51] that in early Indic poetry *metrical trends do not create new phrases.* Rather, there are traceable tendencies of preferring phrases with one kind of rhythm over phrases with other kinds of rhythm. Predictable patterns of rhythm emerge from favorite traditional phrases with favorite rhythms; the eventual regulation of these patterns, combined with regulation of the syllable count in the traditional phrases, constitutes the essentials of what we know as *meter.* Granted, meter can develop a synchronic system of its own, regulating any new incoming phraseology; nevertheless, its origins are from traditional phraseology. In short, the comparative evidence of Indic poetry leads to a parallel formulation about meter and traditional phraseology in early Greek poetry.[52] In this case, however, we may specify "formula" instead of the more general "traditional phraseology."

The comparative approach, to be sure, allows us to extend our notions about phraseology and meter only to a degree. The metrical perspective in this case is restricted to those features of meter in general that the cognate Greek and Indic poetic material *in particular* happen to preserve as cognate phenomena, namely isosyllabism, regular patterning of long and short syllables, and so on.[53] The additional perspective on phraseology[54] is likewise restricted, at least for the moment, to what the evidence from the cognate Greek and Indic material reveals. Ideally, the comparative method requires at least three cognate systems.[55] With these allowances duly recorded, an important point can still be made simply by combining the diachronic with the synchronic view of Greek and Indic poetic phraseology. From a synchronic study of cognate Greek and Indic phrases as they are found functioning independently in each of the two poetic traditions, we discover that the regularities governing the behavior of the given phrases are also cognate; furthermore, in the case of the Greek evidence, the regularities are formulaic.[56] Accordingly, the comparative method suggests that the cognate regularities in Indic poetry, most notably in the *Rig-Veda,* are also formulaic.[57]

If indeed Rig-Vedic poetry is formulaic, may we therefore call it oral poetry? In order to answer such a question, we shall have to reckon at a later point with a problem peculiar to the *Rig-Veda,* to wit, that we see

[51] Meillet 1920.
[52] N 1974a.140–149.
[53] For bibliography, see n49.
[54] N 1974a.
[55] Meillet 1925.38.
[56] Cf. N 1974a.103–117.
[57] For another example of the comparative approach to formulaic analysis, see Sacks 1974 on the subject of cognate Old Norse and Old English formulas in cognate metrical contexts.

here a *fixed text* with a *nonwritten transmission* extending over what appears to have been immense stretches of time.[58] As we shall see, there is an analogous problem with Homeric and Hesiodic poetry.[59]

Throughout this presentation I have allowed myself to make reference to meter as something that *contains* or *frames* formulas. Such a point of view, however, is strictly synchronic. From the diachronic point of view, I have now also maintained that formula generates meter. A demonstration is far easier on the basis of the Indic material than on that of the Greek, mainly because Indic meters tend to be so much simpler in structure and because their origins are consequently so much easier to trace. For example, the short verse lengths in Rig-Vedic poetry regularly coincide with syntactical phrase or clause lengths,[60] whereas Greek hexameter is such a comparatively long verse that it regularly accommodates two phrases and over, or even two clauses and over. In this connection, it is pertinent to cite Hermann Fränkel's theory that the Greek hexameter is innately divisible into four "cola," and that the divisions are determined by (1) the places where the verse begins and ends with word-breaks, (2) the places within the verse where word-breaks predictably recur (that is, caesuras and diaereses).[61]

Word-breaking, however, is only a surface phenomenon. What is really going on is that the colon lengths regularly coincide with syntactical phrase or clause lengths.[62] Of course, even before the colon theory had ever been propounded, Parry himself had shown the way when he observed that the canonical word breaks of Greek hexameter mark the places where formulas begin and end.[63]

We come back, then, to the question posed at the outset: how are we to imagine the strict correlation between formula and meter as part of a here-and-now poetic process, where the performer is actually composing? The imagination boggles at the degrees of formal strictness that we discover from reading a book like J. B. Hainsworth's *The Flexibility of the Homeric Formula*, concerning the interaction of Homeric formula and meter.[64] The key word in this book's title, *flexibility*, is a counterweight to Parry's original definition of the formula, with its overemphasis on

[58] See p. 41.

[59] See p. 41.

[60] Cf. Renou 1952.334.

[61] Fränkel 1960.

[62] Cf. Russo 1966. A similar point is made by Ingalls 1972 in his discussion of how to define the formula. He implicitly takes up Russo's suggestion that there is an intimate relation between metrical blocks (cola) and syntactical blocks (formulas). Cf. the bibliographical discussion in [M. W.] Edwards 1986.188–201.

[63] Parry 1928b.

[64] Hainsworth 1968.

identical metrical positioning and identical phrasing.[65] And yet, flexibility should not be confused with irregularity. Hainsworth's study of flexibility in Homeric phraseology shows really just the opposite of irregularity, in that the processes whereby one formula is transformed into another, with different metrical position, inflection, qualifier, and so on, are themselves highly regulated. The flexibility is also regular. In other words, the variations on the regularities are also regular. The strictness is still there, and the synchronic perspective is simply not adequate to account for all its aspects.

Here is where the diachronic approach is needed. It is from this perspective, as we see implicitly from the work of Russo and others,[66] that the interaction between formula and meter can be best understood. The colon system of Greek hexameter, Russo argues, is correlated with a formula system *that in turn is correlated with a syntax system.* Russo here is intuiting something about the evolution of traditional Greek poetry that can be seen readily from the comparative evidence of Indic poetry. (As in linguistics, the comparative method is invaluable for the diachronic perspective.) In the *Rig-Veda* we find that the correlations between metrical units (verse) and syntactical units (phrase or clause) are much more simple and basic than those in Greek epic. Furthermore, as a synchronic examination will show, the regularities of meter are clearly subordinate to the regularities of phrasing; the inference, then, is that metrical units were diachronically generated from phraseological units.[67] Meter may then become a viable structure in its own right, and it may even develop independently of traditional phraseology. The Greek hexameter, as I have argued elsewhere, is an example of such a development; it is built from smaller inherited meters, and thus it can regularly accommodate two formulas and over.[68]

Even if formula lengths do not correspond to the overall verse lengths of the Greek hexameter, they do correspond to the metrical components of the verse length, namely, the cola. Such correspondences are verifiable from a synchronic description,[69] but it is important not to overemphasize the factor of cola and underemphasize the factor of formulas. Again, the diachronic perspective suggests that formula shapes generated colon shapes, not vice versa.[70] Accordingly, from the syn-

[65] Cf. Ingalls 1972.111–114.

[66] Russo 1966. For earlier works leading in the same direction, I cite O'Neill 1942 and Porter 1951.

[67] N 1974a.140–149.

[68] N pp. 49–102, modified in N 1979b.

[69] Cf. Ingalls 1972.

[70] N 1974a.49–82.

chronic perspective, we can expect formula structure to be regular *even where colon structure is irregular.*[71] Where a structure B evolves diachronically from structure A, the patterns of A are not automatically predictable from those of B. Certain patterns in A will seem irregular in terms of B, which has evolved beyond A in the continuing process of regularization.

For an illustration, I cite the following two verses from the *Odyssey*, using Fränkel's notation for the relevant colon junctures:[72]

ἄνδρα μοι ἔννεπε Μοῦσα (B2) πολύτροπον (C2) ὃς μάλα πολλὰ

Odyssey i 1

Tell me, Muse, of the man of many turns, who in very many ways

ἦ σύ γ' Ὀδυσσεύς ἐσσι (B2) πολύτροπος (C2) ὅν τε μοι αἰεί

Odyssey x 330

You must be Odysseus of many turns, whom to me always

From the standpoint of pure phraseology, the combinations

πολύτροπον (accusative) + ὅς (nominative)
πολύτροπος (nominative) + ὅν (accusative)

seem to be part of a formulaic unit that bridges the colon juncture labeled C2 above. From the standpoint of meter, on the other hand, the same combinations have a break at the same colon juncture C2, and this metrical break is even accompanied by a syntactical break. Because meter in this instance seems at odds with phraseology, there is some concern whether we have here "a chance combination or a formula."[73] On the basis of this and other examples, it has been suggested that the Homeric corpus may contain some repetitions that are simply "due to chance."[74] Instead, I would suggest that any phraseological "spilling" over caesuras, diaereses, or even verse junctures may be traditional rather than innovative. In Homeric diction, the traditional phraseology can reflect rhythmical patterns older than the current norms of the hexameter.[75] Then, too, in the case at hand, the adjective πολύτροπος

[71] N pp. 82–102.
[72] Fränkel 1960.
[73] Ingalls 1972.120.
[74] Ingalls p. 121.
[75] Cf. N 1974a.82–98.

(*polútropos*) 'of many turns' is functioning in place of the generic epithet διίφιλος (*diiphilos*) 'dear to Zeus', ready-made for the slot ⏑ – ⏑⏑ between B2 and C2.[76]

The formulaic nature of this adjective πολύτροπος (*polútropos*) 'of many turns' is made apparent in the *Homeric Hymn to Hermes*, where we see its placement in exactly the same slot ⏑ – ⏑⏑ between B2 and C2 of verses 13 and 439. In both these verses, it serves as the epithet of Hermes, god of mediation between all the opposites of the universe. As mediator between light and dark, life and death, wakefulness and sleep, heaven and earth, and so on, Hermes is πολύτροπος (*polútropos*) 'of many turns'. The application of this traditional Hermetic characterization to Odysseus in line 1 of Book i in the *Odyssey*, by virtue of its very prominence, sets an overall tone for the multiple (self-)characterizations of Odysseus that will follow in this epic. The second and only other application, in x 330 of the *Odyssey*, reveals just as much in particular as the first application had in general. The immediate context becomes clear when we reexamine the verse in combination with the verse that follows:

ἦ σύ γ' Ὀδυσσεύς ἐσσι (B2) πολύτροπος (C2) ὅν τε μοι αἰεὶ
φάσκεν ἐλεύσεσθαι χρυσόρραπις ἀργειφόντης

Odyssey x 330–331

You must be Odysseus *polútropos* [= of many turns], about whose
future coming he used to talk to me always—the one with the golden rod,
the Argeiphontes.

The subject is Hermes, and the speaker is the beautiful witch Circe, whose wiles have just been overcome by Odysseus with the help of Hermes. She actually identifies Odysseus on the basis of knowledge from and of Hermes. Here again, then, we see traditional theme motivating formula, which in turn motivates meter or—if we want to become more specific—the presence of a colon juncture at C2 in verses i 1 and x 330 of the *Odyssey*. Such a minute metrical detail is but a trivial consequence in the overall hierarchy of the traditional epic diction. As Gerald Else has said of the Greek bards, "their language and their narrative technique has a structure, is a structure, which gives more than firmness to their work. The qualities which Matthew Arnold attributed to 'Homer' are in the main a function of the technique."[77]

[76] Parry 1971 [1928a].156–157.
[77] Else 1967.348.

I close with a general statement that again links the study of oral poetry with linguistics. In the intellectual history of linguistics as an academic discipline, the diachronic approach preceded the synchronic. For the actual methodology of linguistics, it is now recognized that the synchronic analysis of language must precede the diachronic. For solving the manifold mysteries of language, however, the synchronic approach is not sufficient and must be supplemented with the diachronic approach. I am proposing the same program for solving the problem of formula and meter in the study of oral poetry. The synchronic approach, although it is the essential first step, is not sufficient. As Albert Lord says about traditional poetry,[78]

> It cannot be treated as a flat surface. All the elements in traditional poetry have depth, and our task is to plumb their sometimes hidden recesses; for there will meaning be found. We must be willing to use the new tools for investigation of multiforms of themes and patterns, and we must be willing to learn from the experiences of other oral traditional poetries. Otherwise "oral" is only an empty label and "traditional" is devoid of sense. Together they form merely a façade behind which scholarship can continue to apply the poetics of written literature.

[78]Lord 1968.46.

CHAPTER 3

Hesiod and the Poetics of Pan-Hellenism

The Hesiodic Question

From the vantage point of the ancient Greeks themselves, no accounting of Homer is possible without an accounting of Hesiod as well. In the fifth century B.C., Herodotus was moved to observe (2.53.2) that the Greeks owed the systematization of their gods—we may say, of their universe—to two poets, Homer and Hesiod. The current fashion is to argue, from the internal evidence of their poetry, that both lived sometime in the latter half of the eighth century, roughly three hundred years before Herodotus composed his *Histories*—although there is considerable controversy about which of the two was earlier. For Herodotus, as for all Greeks of the Classical period, however, the importance of Homer and Hesiod was based not on any known historical facts about these poets and their times. Whatever Homer and Hesiod may have meant to the eighth century, the only surviving historical fact about them centers on what their poems did indeed mean to the succeeding centuries extending into the historical period. From Herodotus and others, we know that the poems of Homer and Hesiod were the primary artistic means of encoding a value system common to all Greeks.[1]

In this connection it is worthwhile to correct a common misconception: Homer is not simply an exponent of *narrative* any more than Hesiod is an exponent of purely *didactic* poetry.[2] The explicitly narrative

[1] Cf. also Xenophanes B 10 DK on Homer, Heraclitus B 57 DK on Hesiod.

[2] On Hesiodic poetry as a type of "Mirror of Princes," see Martin 1984a; cf. also Watkins 1979.

structure of epic, as is the case with mythmaking in general, frames a value system that sustains and in fact educates a given society.[3] Conversely, as we shall see, the teachings of Hesiod frame an implicit narrative about the poet and his life.

The question is, why were these two poets universally accepted by the Greeks of Classical times? Such acceptance is especially remarkable in view of the striking diversity that characterizes Greece throughout this period. Each polis or 'city' was a state unto itself, with its own traditions in government, law, religion. Moreover, the diversity that prevailed among the many city-states of Greece had already taken shape by the eighth century, the very era that scholars agree in assigning to Homer and Hesiod. How, then, could the diversification of the Greeks coincide with the consolidation of their poetic heritage? The evidence of archaeology helps provide a partial answer. In the eighth century the emergence of distinct city-states with distinct localized traditions was simultaneous with a countertrend of intercommunication among the elite of these city-states—the trend of pan-Hellenism.[4] The patterns of intercommunication were confined to a few specific social phenomena, all datable starting with the eighth century: the organization of the Olympic Games; the establishment of Apollo's sanctuary and oracle at Delphi; organized colonizations (the Greek word for which is *ktísis*); the proliferation of the alphabet.[5]

Another phenomenon that may be included is Homeric and Hesiodic poetry, featuring overall traditions that synthesize the diverse local traditions of each major city-state into a unified pan-Hellenic model that suits most city-states but corresponds exactly to none.[6] Erwin Rohde cites in particular the Homeric and Hesiodic concept of the Olympian gods, which transcends the individual concepts of these same gods as they are worshiped on the level of cult in the localized traditions of the city-states.[7] We have in this example what amounts to internal evidence corroborating the external evidence summed up in Herodotus' statement: Homeric and Hesiodic poetry systematized the city-states' diverse ideologies about the gods into a set of attributes and functions that all Hellenes could accept. (The earliest unambiguous attestation of the word *panéllēnes* in the sense of "pan-Hellenes" or "all Greeks" is in Hesiod *Works and Days* 528.)

[3] See pp. 8ff.
[4] See pp. 9ff.
[5] Cf. Snodgrass 1971.421, 435.
[6] Cf. N 1979a.7.
[7] Rohde 1898 1:125–127. Cf. pp. 10ff.

The notion that the Homeric and Hesiodic poems were a pan-Hellenic phenomenon going back to the eighth century leads to the tempting scenario of connecting a likewise pan-Hellenic phenomenon, alphabetic writing: the formative stage of the Greek alphabet, after all, is dated to the eighth century. According to this scenario, the Homeric and Hesiodic poems were enshrined for the Greeks because they were written down, thus becoming fixed texts that proliferated throughout the Hellenic world. The problem is, how exactly are we to imagine this proliferation? It is clear that literacy was a tenuous phenomenon at best throughout the archaic period of Greece, and the pan-Hellenic spread of the Homeric and Hesiodic poems during this period stretching from the eighth to the fifth century could hardly be attributed to some hypothetical circulation of manuscripts. To put it bluntly: it seems difficult to imagine an incipient eighth-century reading public—let alone one that could have stimulated such widespread circulation of the Homeric and Hesiodic poems.

The argument for an archaic reading public is actually rendered pointless by the historical fact that the medium of transmitting the Homeric and Hesiodic poems was consistently that of performance, not reading. One important traditional context of poetic performance was the institution of pan-Hellenic festivals, though there may well have been other appropriate public events as well.[8] The competing performers at such public events were called *rhapsōidoí* 'rhapsodes' (as in Herodotus 5.67.1), one of whom has been immortalized in Plato's *Ion.* We learn that the rhapsode Ion has come from his home in Ephesus to compete with other rhapsodes by reciting Homer at the Feast of the Panathenaia at Athens, after having already won at another festival, the Feast of Asclepius in Epidauros (*Ion* 530ab). In the dialogue as dramatized by Plato, Socrates ascertains that Ion is a specialist in Homer, to the exclusion of Hesiod and Archilochus (*Ion* 531a and 532a)—the implication being that there are other rhapsodes who specialize in these other poets.[9] Socrates and Ion then go on to discuss the different repertoires required for the rhapsodes' recitation of Homer and Hesiod (see especially *Ion* 531a-d). In fact, Plato elsewhere presents Homer and Hesiod themselves as itinerant rhapsodes (*Republic* 600d). The examples could be multiplied, but the point is already clear: the proliferation of the Homeric and Hesiodic poems throughout Greece in the archaic period (and beyond) did not depend on the factor of writing.

[8] Cf. N 1979a.8 § 15n1.

[9] For more on the rhapsodic recitation of the poetry of Archilochus, see e.g. Clearchus F 92 Wehrli.

Even if Homer and Hesiod were meant to be heard in performance, not read, there are those who insist that writing was an essential factor at least in the composition and transmission of their poetry. Here we must turn to the study of oral poetry, as perfected by Milman Parry and Albert Lord.[10] The fieldwork of these scholars was based on the living poetic traditions of the South Slavic peoples, and the theories that were developed from their fieldwork were then tested on Homeric—and later on Hesiodic—poetry.[11] The findings of Parry and Lord have on occasion been viewed with suspicion by prominent Hellenists, who fear that the analogy between the typical South Slavic *guslar* and a Homer demeans the latter and overly exalts the former. This is to misunderstand the intellectual basis of fieldwork—and of anthropological research in general. The mechanics of living traditions, however lowly they may seem to Hellenists, can provide indispensable information for extensive typological comparison with those of other traditions, living or dead.

We learn from the experience of fieldwork that composition in oral poetry becomes reality only in performance, and that the poet's interaction with his audience can directly affect the form and content of composition as well as of performance. Moreover, the actual workings of formulaic diction are to be ascertained directly in the dimension of performance—a dimension that is of course now extinct in the case of the Homeric and Hesiodic texts. In studying this factor of performance as reflected by the living South Slavic traditions, Parry and Lord worked out criteria of formulaic behavior that, when applied to the Homeric text, establish it, too, as oral poetry. For example, one reliable indication of oral poetry is the principle of economy as it operates on the level of each individual performance; each position in the verse tends to allow one way, rather than many ways, of saying any one thing.[12] As it turns out, this principle is at work in Homeric poetry as well, which suggests that the composition of the *Iliad* and the *Odyssey* is also a matter of performance.[13] The principle of economy, as G. P. Edwards has demonstrated,[14] is also at work in Hesiodic poetry; moreover, both Homeric and Hesiodic poetry reveal parallel patterns of general adherence to and occasional deviation from this principle.[15]

If, then, the Homeric and Hesiodic poems are reflexes of oral poetry, we can in theory eliminate writing as a factor in the composition of these

[10] Parry 1971 and Lord 1960.
[11] See pp. 18ff.
[12] See pp. 21ff.
[13] See pp. 21ff.
[14] Edwards 1971.
[15] See pp. 23ff.

poems, much as we have eliminated it as a factor in their performance. The absence of writing would suit, at least superficially, the findings of Parry and Lord: in the South Slavic traditions, oral poetry and literacy are incompatible. But now we have to reckon with a new problem, one raised by the study of oral poetry itself. The findings of Parry and Lord also suggest that composition and performance are aspects of the same process in oral poetry, and that no poet's composition is ever identical even to his previous composition of the "same" poem at a previous performance, in that each performance entails a recomposition of the poet's inherited material.

The problem, then, is this: how could the Homeric and Hesiodic poems survive unchanged into the historical period without the aid of writing? One solution is to posit that the poems were dictated by their illiterate composers. But we have already noted that the hypothetical existence of fixed texts in, say, the eighth century cannot by itself account for the proliferation of Homeric and Hesiodic poetry throughout the city-states. That process, as we have also noted, must be attributed long-range to the recurrent competitive performances of the poems over the years by rhapsodes at such events as pan-Hellenic festivals. Thus we must resort to positing the existence of early fixed texts only if the competing rhapsodes really needed to memorize written versions in order to perform, and for this there is no evidence.

On the contrary, there is evidence that the rhapsodes preserved in their performances certain aspects of poetic diction that would not have been written down in any early phase of the textual transmission. In the postclassical era of the Alexandrian scholars, when accentual notation was for the first time becoming canonical, it was observed that rhapsodes maintained in their recitations certain idiosyncratic accent patterns that did not match current pronunciation.[16] We now know from cognate accentual patterns in Indo-European languages other than Greek that these aspects of rhapsodic pronunciation are deeply archaic—surely the heritage of Homeric and Hesiodic diction.[17] To repeat, there seems no way for these patterns to be preserved textually from the archaic period, and we are left with the conclusion that the rhapsodes were much more than mere memorizers of texts.

True, the rhapsodes were not oral poets in the sense that this concept is defined by Parry and Lord on the basis of their fieldwork on South Slavic traditions: by the time of Plato rhapsodes seem to have been performers only, whereas the oral poet technically performs while he

[16] Wackernagel 1953.1103.
[17] Wackernagel p. 1103.

composes, composes while he performs. Looking beyond Yugoslavia, however, we find oral poetic traditions in other cultures where the factor of performance has become separated from that of composition—as revealed, for example, in the Old Provençal contrast of *trobador* (composer) and *joglar* (performer). There are also oral traditions, like those of the Somali, where composition may precede performance without any aid of writing. These and other examples are discussed in Ruth Finnegan's *Oral Poetry*,[18] which is useful for its adjustments on the Parry-Lord theories, though it sometimes confuses oral poetry with the kind of free-associative improvisations that mark certain types of modern poetry in the West.

"Improvise" is a particularly pernicious word when applied to traditional oral poetry—including that of Homer and Hesiod. An oral poet in a traditional society does not "make things up," since his function is to re-create the inherited values of those for whom he composes/performs. As perhaps the most striking available example, I cite the Vedas of the Indic peoples—a vast body of sacred poems displaying the strictest imaginable regulation in form as well as content—and formalizing the ideology of the priestly class without perceptible change for well over two millennia. It should be added that, despite the availability of writing, the authority of the Vedas to this day abides in the spoken word, not in any written text. Moreover, the Vedas have been transmitted unchanged, as a fixed "text," for all these years *by way of mnemonic techniques that had been part of the oral tradition.*[19] Given the authority of the Homeric and Hesiodic poems by the time they surface in the historical period of Greece, it is not unreasonable to suppose that their rhapsodic transmission entailed comparable mnemonic efforts—which need not have required writing at all. In theory, though, written texts of the Homeric and Hesiodic poems could have been generated at any time—in fact, many times—during the lengthy phase of rhapsodic transmission.

In the case of Homeric and Hesiodic poetry, composition and proliferation need not have been separate factors. It is not as if a composition had to evolve into perfection before it was disseminated throughout the city-states. Rather, in view of the pan-Hellenic status ultimately achieved by the Homeric and Hesiodic poems, it is more likely that their composition and proliferation were combined factors. These poems, it appears, represent the culmination of compositional trends that were reaching their ultimate form, from the eighth century onward, in the context of competitive performances at pan-Hellenic festivals and other

[18] Finnegan 1977.73–87.
[19] Kiparsky 1976.99–102.

such events. By way of countless such performances for over two centuries, each recomposition at each successive performance could become less and less variable. Such gradual crystallization into what became set poems would have been a direct response to the exigencies of a pan-Hellenic audience.[20]

Recalling the testimony of Herodotus and others to the effect that Homer and Hesiod provide a systematization of values common to all Greeks, we may go so far as to say that "Homer" and "Hesiod" are themselves the cumulative embodiment of this systematization—the ultimate poetic response to pan-Hellenic audiences from the eighth century onward. An inevitable consequence of such evolution from compositional trends to set poems is that the original oral poet, who composes while he performs and performs while he composes, evolves with the passage of time into a mere performer. We must not be too quick to dismiss the importance of the rhapsode, however: he must have been a master of mnemonic techniques inherited directly from oral poets. Even in such minute details as accentual patterns, as we have seen, he preserved the heritage of a genuine oral poet. The etymology of *rhapsōidós* 'stitcher of songs' reveals a traditional conceit of the oral poet as overtly expressed by the poet himself in cognate Indo-European poetic traditions.[21] There is, then, no demotion implicit in the formal distinction between *rhapsōidós* and *aoidós* 'singer'—which is the word used by the Homeric and Hesiodic poems to designate the genuinely oral poet.[22] It is simplistic and even misleading to contrast, as many have done, the "creative" *aoidós* with the "reduplicating" *rhapsōidós*. We must keep in mind that even the traditional oral poet does not really "create" in the modern sense of authorship; rather, he re-creates for his listeners the inherited values that serve as foundations for their society. Even the narrative of epic, as we have noted, is a vehicle for re-creating traditional values, with a set program that will not deviate in the direction of personal invention, away from the traditional plots known and expected by the audience.[23] If, then, the *aoidós* is an upholder of such set poetic ways, he is not so far removed from the *rhapsōidós* as from the modern concept of "poet."

The more significant difference between *aoidós* and *rhapsōidós* lies in the nature of their respective audiences. The *rhapsōidós*, as we have seen, recites the Homeric or Hesiodic poems to Hellenes at large—to listeners from various city-states who congregate at events like pan-Hellenic

[20] Further discussion in N 1979a.5–9.
[21] Durante 1976.177–179.
[22] For internal evidence, see e.g. N 1979a.15–20.
[23] Cf. N pp. 265–267.

festivals—and what he recites remains unchanged as he travels from city to city. On the other hand, the typical *aoidós* as portrayed in, say, the *Odyssey* (ix 3–11) sings to a strictly local community. As the studies of Wilhelm Radloff concerning the oral poetry of the Kirghiz peoples have made clear, the oral poet in a local situation will of course adjust his composition/performance to the nature of his audience. For example, the presence of rich and distinguished members of society will prompt the Kirghiz *akyn* 'poet' to introduce episodes reflecting traditions that glorify their families.[24] Now, the local audiences of Greece in the eighth century must have challenged the poet with a veritable kaleidoscope of repertoires; each city would have had its own poetic traditions, often radically different from those of other cities. We have a reference to the regional variety of poetic repertoires in the *Iliad* (XX 249).[25] Moreover, even the traditions of any given city could change radically with successive changes in population or government; the genre of *ktísis* 'foundation' poetry seems particularly vulnerable.[26]

The obvious dilemma of the oral poet is that each of the various local traditions in his repertoire will have validity only when it is performed in the appropriate locale. With the surge of intercommunication among the cities from the eighth century onward, the horizons for the poet's travels would continually expand, and thus the regional differences between one audience and the next would become increasingly pronounced. The greater the regional differences, the greater the gap between what one community and another would hold to be true. What was held to be true by the inhabitants of one place may well have been false to those of another. What is true and false will keep shifting as the poet travels from place to place, and he may even resort to using alternative traditions as a foil for the one that he is re-creating for his audience. This device is still reflected in *Homeric Hymn* 1, where the poet declares in his prayer to Dionysus that the god was not born in Drakanos or in Ikaria or in Naxos or by the banks of the Alpheios or even in Thebes (verses 1–5), and that those who claim any of these proveniences are *pseudómenoi* 'lying' (6); he goes on to say that the god was really born at the mountain Nyse (6–9; compare *Hymn* 26.5). The localization of this Nyse is a separate problem, and the point now is simply that various legitimate local traditions are here being discounted as false in order to legitimize the one tradition that is acceptable to the poet's audience.

[24] Radloff 1885.xviii-xix. See also Martin 1989.6–7.
[25] See pp. 27–28.
[26] N 1979a.140–141, 273.

There is a parallel poetic device that inaugurates the *Theogony* of Hesiod, at verses 22–34, which we will understand only by first examining the testimony of Homeric poetry about poetry itself. In the *Odyssey* Odysseus himself tells stories like an oral poet who has to keep adjusting his composition/performance to the exigencies of his diverse audiences,[27] and in such contexts the resourceful hero is explicitly likened to a poet (xi 368, xviii 518). It is in the manner of a poet that he tells his "Cretan lies" (compare xvii 514, 518–521). As he finishes telling one such Cretan tale to Penelope, Odysseus is described in these words:

> ἴσκε ψεύδεα πολλὰ λέγων ἐτύμοισιν ὁμοῖα
>
> *Odyssey* xix 203

> He assimilated many falsehoods [*pseúdea*] to make them look like genuine things.

Earlier, Eumaios had described other wanderers who, just as the disguised wanderer Odysseus is doing now, would come to Penelope with stories about Odysseus that are calculated to raise her hopes:

> ἀλλ' ἄλλως κομιδῆς κεχρημένοι ἄνδρες ἀλῆται
> ψεύδοντ', οὐδ' ἐθέλουσιν ἀληθέα μυθήσασθαι
>
> *Odyssey* xiv 124–125

> It's no use! Wanderers in need of food
> are liars [*pseúdontai*], and they are unwilling to tell true things [*alēthéa mūthḗsasthai*].

Odysseus himself fits this description: before telling his major tale of the *Odyssey* in the court of Alkinoos, he asks the king to let him eat first, since his *gastḗr* 'belly' is making him forget his tales of woe until it is filled with food (vii 215–221). Such a gambit would be typical of an oral poet who is making sure that he gets an appropriate preliminary reward for entertaining his audience.[28]

The root for 'forget' in this last passage is *lēth-* (*lēthánei* vii 221), the functional opposite of *mnē-* 'remember, have in mind', a root that can also mean 'have the mnemonic powers of a poet' in the diction of archaic poetry. *Mnēmosúnē* 'Memory', mother of the Muses (*Theogony* 54, 135, 915), is the very incarnation of such powers. The conventional

[27] N 1979a.233–237.
[28] Cf. Svenbro 1976.50–59. See also pp. 274–275 below.

designation of poetic powers by *mnē-* has been documented by Marcel Detienne, who also shows that the word *a-lēth-ḗs* 'true' is thus originally a double-negative expression of *truth by way of poetry.*[29] The wanderers who are described in the passage above as being unwilling to tell the truth, *alēthéa mūthḗsasthai*, are cast in the mold of an oral poet who compromises poetic truth for the sake of his own survival. Similarly in the court of Alkinoos, Odysseus as poet is implicitly threatening to withhold the truth of poetry by explicitly blaming his *gastḗr* 'belly'.[30]

With these passages in mind, we come finally to *Theogony* 22–34, retelling Hesiod's encounter with the Muses. These goddesses, as daughters of *Mnēmosúnē* 'Memory', not only confer the mnemonic powers of poetry on the poet of the *Theogony* but also offer to endow his poetry with truth, as they themselves announce to him:

ποιμένες ἄγραυλοι, κάκ' ἐλέγχεα, γαστέρες οἶον,
ἴδμεν ψεύδεα πολλὰ λέγειν ἐτύμοισιν ὁμοῖα,
ἴδμεν δ', εὖτ' ἐθέλωμεν, ἀληθέα γηρύσασθαι

Theogony 26–28

Shepherds living in the fields, base objects of reproach, mere bellies [*gastéres*]!
We know how to say many falsehoods [*pseúdea*] that look like genuine things,
but we can also, whenever we are willing, proclaim true things [*alēthéa gērū́sasthai*].

"Truth," which itinerant would-be oral poets are "unwilling" to tell because of their need for survival (*oud' ethélousin* at *Odyssey* xiv 124–125), may be "willingly" conferred by the Muses (*ethélōmen*). We see here what can be taken as a manifesto of pan-Hellenic poetry, in that the poet Hesiod is to be freed from being a mere "belly"—one who owes his survival to his local audience with its local traditions: all such local traditions are *pseúdea* 'falsehoods' in face of the *alēthéa* 'true things' that the Muses impart specially to Hesiod. The conceit inherent in the pan-Hellenic poetry of Hesiod is that this overarching tradition is capable of achieving something that is beyond the reach of individual local traditions. As in the *Homeric Hymn* 1 to Dionysus, the mutually incompatible traditions of various locales are rejected as falsehoods, in favor of one single tradition that can be acceptable to all. In the case of *Hymn* 1 this

[29] Detienne 1973.

[30] Svenbro 1976.54; for other passages concerning the poetic *gastḗr* 'belly', see N 1979a.229–233, 261 § 11n4.

goal seems to be achieved by assigning the remotest imaginable traditional place of birth to the god (Nyse is pictured as "near the streams of Aigyptos," verse 9). In the case of the *Theogony* we see this sort of process in a global dimension: the many local theogonies of the various city-states are to be superseded by one grand Olympian scheme.

As we have noted already, the Olympus of Hesiodic and Homeric poetry is a pan-Hellenic construct that elevates the gods beyond their localized attributes. It is a historical fact about Greece in the archaic period that whatever can be classified as religious practice or ideology was confined to the local level, and a survey of the attested evidence, as gleaned from sources like Pausanias or epichoric inscriptions, reveals clearly that each city had a very distinct pattern of cults. A given god as worshiped in one city could be radically different from a god bearing the same name as he was worshiped in another city.

Under these circumstances, the evolution of most major gods from most major cities into the integrated family at Olympus amounts to a synthesis that is not just artistic but also political, comparable with the evolution of the pan-Hellenic games known as the Olympics, another crucial phenomenon originating in the eighth century. As in any political process, the evolution of the pan-Hellenic poems would afford some victories and many concessions on the part of each region: some one salient local feature of a god may become accepted by all audiences, while countless other features that happen to contradict the traditions of other cities will remain unspoken. For example, Cythera and Cyprus may well be recognized as places that the newborn Aphrodite first visited (the narrative specifies that she did so *in that order*, see *Theogony* 192–193), but very little else about their local lore will ever come to the surface in Hesiodic and Homeric poetry.

The oral poet as represented by the poetry itself is one who can sing both epics and theogonies, as we learn in this description of the poetic repertory of Phemios:

ἔργ' ἀνδρῶν τε θεῶν τε, τά τε κλείουσιν ἀοιδοί

Odyssey i 338

the deeds of men and gods, upon which the singers confer glory [*kléos*]

So also in this description of a generic poet:

αὐτὰρ ἀοιδὸς
Μουσάων θεράπων κλεῖα προτέρων ἀνθρώπων

ὑμνήσει μάκαράς τε θεοὺς οἳ Ὄλυμπον ἔχουσιν

Theogony 99–101

But when a poet,
attendant [*therápōn*] of the Muses, sings the glories [*kléos* plural] of earlier men
and the blessed gods who hold Olympus.

In view of the diversity that existed among the cities, an oral poet would have needed for his repertoire a staggering variety of traditions for composing epics and theogonies, which could in the end be rejected as *pseúdea* 'falsehoods' by the poets of the ultimate epic and ultimate theogony, Homer and Hesiod. Pan-Hellenic poetry can still tell us how an actual epic was being composed by Phemios in the *Odyssey* (i 326–327), or how Hermes composed a theogony for Apollo in the *Hymn to Hermes* (425–433). Yet such pan-Hellenic poetry, ascribed to the ultimate poets, is itself no longer oral poetry in the strict sense: it is being performed by rhapsodes. In the case of the Homeric poems, the compositions have even become too long for any single performance.[31] Moreover, oral poetry, at least in the form represented by the medium itself, has not survived. The emergence of a monumental marvel like the uniquely "truthful" and pan-Hellenic *Theogony* of Hesiod from among countless "deceitful" and local theogonies of oral poets entails not only the crystallization of the one but also the extinction of the many.

Hesiod, Poet of the Theogony

It would be simplistic to assume that the "truth" of the Muses about the genesis of all the gods the Greeks have in common would ever be conferred upon just any poet. Hesiod's *Theogony* in fact presents its composer as the ultimate poet. The very name *Hēsíodos* at *Theogony* 22 means something like 'he who emits the Voice'. The root *i̯eh$_1$– of *Hēsi-* recurs in the expression *óssan hieîsai* 'emitting a [beautiful/immortal/lovely] voice', describing the Muses themselves at *Theogony* 10/43/65/67, while the root *h$_2$uod- of *-odos* recurs as *h$_2$ud- in *audḗ* 'voice', designating the power of poetry conferred by the Muses upon the poet at *Theogony* 31.[32]

[31] N 1979a.18–20.

[32] N 1979a.296–297, following DELG 137–138, 417. On possible explanations for the fact that there is no trace of laryngeal *h$_2$ in such forms as *Hēsíodos*, see Peters 1980.14 and Vine 1982.144–145. Another possible factor: laryngeals (*h$_1$, *h$_2$, *h$_3$) are frequently lost without trace in the second half of compounds (see Beekes 1969.242–243 for a list of examples; also Mayrhofer 1986.125, 129, 140).

In this way *Hēsíodos* embodies the poetic function of the very Muses who give him his powers.[33]

Also, the generic poet's epithet, "*therápōn* [attendant] of the Muses" (*Theogony* 100), literally identifies Hesiod with these divinities and implicitly entails not only his ritual death but also his subsequent worship as cult hero.[34] The poetic word *therápōn*, conventionally translated as 'attendant', is apparently borrowed from an Anatolian word, attested as Hittite *tarpan-alli-* 'ritual substitute'.[35] We may compare the generic warrior's epithet, "*therápōn* [attendant] of Ares" (*Iliad* II 110, VI 67, for instance), which identifies the hero with the god of war at the moment of his death.[36] Although the Homeric poems offer little direct testimony about the cults of dead warriors, they reveal extensive indirect references to the ideology of hero cults. The actual evidence for the existence of hero cults in the eighth century and thereafter comes from archaeology,[37] and there is reason to believe that the historically attested cults of the Homeric heroes are no mere reflex of Homeric poetry; rather, both the cults and the poetry represent interacting aspects of a broader phenomenon.[38] By the same token, it appears that an ideology reflecting the cult of the poet Hesiod is built into the poetry of Hesiod.[39]

This statement would of course be an absurdity were it not for the fact that the very identity of Hesiod within his poetry is consistently determined by the traditions that are the foundation of this poetry. As we are about to see time and again, the persona of Hesiod as reflected by his poetry is purely generic, not historical. This is not to say that Hesiod is a fiction: his personality, as it functions within his poetry, is just as traditional as the poetry itself, and he is no more a fiction than any other aspect of Hesiodic poetry.[40] A word more suitable than "fiction" is "myth"—provided we understand genuine mythmaking to be a traditional expression of a given social group's concept of truth.[41]

[33] For similar implications as built into the name *Hómēros*, see N pp. 297–300.

[34] N p. 297.

[35] Van Brock 1959. Further details at pp. 129–130 below.

[36] N pp. 292–295. Cf. p. 135n58 below.

[37] Snodgrass 1971.191–193, 398–399.

[38] See pp. 9–11 above; see also N 1979a.115 § 28n4.

[39] N pp. 296–297.

[40] I do not deny the notion of "poets within a tradition," as advocated by Griffith 1983.58n82. I am not arguing generally, as Griffith claims, that tradition creates the poet, but I am arguing specifically that the pan-Hellenic tradition of oral poetry appropriates the poet, potentially transforming even historical figures into generic ones who merely represent the traditional functions of their poetry. To put it another way: the poet, by virtue of being a transmitter of tradition, can become absorbed by the tradition (detailed examples in N 1985a).

[41] See pp. 8ff.

Of course, Hesiodic poetry refers to itself not as the gradual evolution of poetic traditions into compositions on a pan-Hellenic scale but, rather, as the one-time creation of one ultimate poet whose self-identification with the Muses, for him both a bane and a blessing, makes him a cult hero. Besides the poet's name and the epithet "*therápōn* of the Muses," the most striking sign of Hesiod's stance as hero is dramatized in the scene describing his first encounter with the Muses. The goddesses are antagonistic to the poet's local origins but aid him anyway by transforming his repertoire from localized "falsehoods" into the "truth" that all Hellenes can accept; they give Hesiod a *skêptron* 'staff, scepter' as an emblem of his transformation from shepherd to poet (*Theogony* 30).

This narrative is typical of traditional Greek myths that motivate the cult of a poet as hero. In the *Life of Archilochus* tradition, for example, the diffusion of which can be historically connected with the actual cult of Archilochus as hero on his native island of Paros from the archaic period onward,[42] we find another story about the poet and the Muses. The paraphrase that follows is from the Mnesiepes Inscription (Archilochus T 4 Tarditi). On a moonlit night young Archilochus is driving a cow toward the city from a countryside region of Paros known as the *Leimônes* 'Meadows' when he comes upon some seemingly rustic women, whom he proceeds to antagonize with mockery.[43] The disguised Muses respond playfully to his taunts and ask him to trade away his cow. Agreeing to do so if the price is right, Archilochus straightaway falls into a swoon. When he awakens, the rustic women are gone, and so, too, is the cow; but in its place Archilochus finds a lyre that he takes home as an emblem of his transformation from cowherd to poet.

The similarities between Archilochus and Hesiod extend further. As a clue, we note that the epithet "*therápōn* of the Muses" is applied to Archilochus precisely in the context of the story retelling the poet's death (Delphic Oracle 4 PW). Then again, just as Archilochus was worshiped as cult hero in his native Paros, so was Hesiod in Askra—until his homeland was obliterated by the neighboring city of Thespiai, and the reputed remains of the poet were transferred by the refugees from Askra to a new cult precinct at Orkhomenos, a rival of Thespiai (Aristotle *Constitution of the Orkhomenians* F 565 Rose; Plutarch by way of Proclus commentary). According to another tradition, contradicting the one emanating from Orkhomenos (Plutarch *Banquet of the Seven Sages* 162c), Hesiod was

[42] N 1979a.303–308.

[43] Cf. Herodotus 5.83 for a reference to the ritual insulting of local women by choral groups.

buried and venerated as hero in the cult precinct of Zeus Nemeios at Oineon in Ozolian Lokris (*Contest of Homer and Hesiod* p. 234 Allen; cf. Thucydides 3.96).[44] In the myth that serves to validate this tradition, the murdered poet's corpse is said to have been originally cast into the sea, only to be carried ashore on the third day by dolphins (*Contest of Homer and Hesiod* p. 234.229–236 Allen)—a narrative scheme that is particularly appropriate to a cult hero in whose honor a festival is founded, as in the case of Melikertes and the Isthmian Games.[45]

In short, the lore about Hesiod fits a general pattern that is characteristic of a local cult hero.[46] The parallelism of Hesiod and Archilochus in this regard becomes even more noteworthy. The local cult of Archilochus at Paros, as we have seen, is the actual source of the myth about the poet's transformation from cowherd into poet. In the case of Hesiod's transformation from shepherd into poet, however, the myth is built into the *Theogony* itself. Since the hero cult of Hesiod is just as much a historical fact as the cult of Archilochus, and since both these cults are deeply archaic in nature, it is possible that the Hesiodic cult is ultimately a locus of diffusion for the Hesiodic poems, just as the Archilochean cult seems to be for the Archilochean vita.

Moreover, the Archilochean vita tradition may well have been the actual context for the preservation of Archilochean poetry itself, with a narrative superstructure about the poet's life serving as a frame for "quoting" the poet's poems; there is a comparable pattern of "quoting" Aesop's fables in the *Life of Aesop* tradition.[47] This arrangement is in fact suggested by the format of the Mnesiepes Inscription (Archilochus T 4 Tarditi), the Parian document that proclaims the hero cult of Archilochus and then proceeds to tell the story of his life (starting with the incident of the cow and the lyre). Granted, this document is late (third century B.C.) and may reflect literary mannerisms characteristic of the Hellenistic era. It is also true that the genre of any archaic poet's vita in general tends to degenerate—from traditional narratives that are parallel to the poems into what can only be called fictions that are arbitrarily derived from the poems.[48] Still, the program of the Mnesiepes Inscription is to document and motivate cult practices in a sacred precinct that

[44] Commentary in Pfister 1909 1:231n861.

[45] On which see Pfister pp. 214–215n788. For more on the myths concerning the death and revival of Hesiod: Scodel 1980, especially with reference to the epigram in *Life of Hesiod* p. 51.9–10 Wilamowitz (1916), comparable with Plato Comicus F 68 Kock, a passage concerning the death and revival of Aesop. More on the *Life of Aesop* tradition in N 1979a.279–316.

[46] Brelich 1958.322.

[47] N 1979a.279–288.

[48] N p. 306.

is actually named after Archilochus (the *Arkhilókheion*), and in such an ancestral religious context invention seems out of the question.

The relevance of this information about Archilochus to Hesiod becomes clear when we consider the name of the man to whom Apollo is said to have given the command to institute the hero cult of Archilochus: *Mnēsi-épēs*, meaning 'he who remembers the word(s) [*épos*]'. It seems as if the foundation of the poet's cult goes hand in hand with remembering the poet's words.[49] Given the historical fact that the poems of Archilochus, like those of Homer and Hesiod, were recited at public competitions by rhapsodes (Athenaeus 620c, Clearchus F 92 Wehrli, Plato *Ion* 531a and 532a), we may envision a pattern of evolution parallel to that of the Homeric and Hesiodic poems. In other words, the oral poetic traditions of Paros could eventually have become crystallized into a fixed collection of poems retrojected as creations of the ultimate poet Archilochus and disseminated by way of rhapsodic transmission in the context of the poet's hero cult. We may directly compare the *Homērídai* 'sons of Homer' (Strabo 14.1.33–35 C 645; Pindar *Nemean* 2.1, with scholia; Plato *Phaedrus* 252b; *Contest of Homer and Hesiod* p. 226.13–15 Allen)[50] and the *Kreōphuleîoi* 'sons of Kreophulos' (Strabo 14.1.18 C638; cf. Callimachus *Epigram* 6 Pfeiffer),[51] organizations of reciters whose very names imply that their "founding fathers" were cult heroes.[52]

In this connection a brief word is in order about a pan-Hellenic tendency inherent in all archaic Greek poetry—not just the Homeric and Hesiodic. It is a historical fact that each major poetic genre in the archaic period tends to appropriate the surface structure of a single dialect to the exclusion of all others. For example, the elegiac poetry of even the Doric areas is characterized by Ionic diction, as we see in the poems of Theognis of Megara and Tyrtaeus of Sparta; conversely, the diction of choral lyric will be a synthetic form of Doric even for Ionic poets like Simonides and Bacchylides.

Before we consider any further the evolution of the local Boeotian poetic traditions of Hesiod into the Ionic hexameters of the pan-Hellenic *Theogony*, it is instructive to ask this related question: why should the local Doric traditions of a city like Megara evolve into the Ionic elegiacs of a Theognis? The answer is given by the poetry itself:

[49] N p. 304 § 4n3.

[50] For other references to the Homeridai of Chios, see Acusilaus FGH 2 F 2, Hellanicus FGH 4 F 20 (both by way of Harpocration s.v.); Isocrates *Helen* 65; Plato *Republic* 599d, *Ion* 530c.

[51] The basic testimonia are conveniently available in Allen 1924.228–229 and Burkert 1972.76n10. Cf. N 1979a.165–166.

[52] Brelich 1958.320–321; cf. N pp. 8–9.

the goal of this poetry, the poet says, is to be heard by all Hellenes everywhere (Theognis 22–23, 237–254). It seems as if such a goal can be reached only with the evolution of the local poetry into a form that is performable at pan-Hellenic events. In the case of the elegiac, that form would be Ionic. And such evolution entails, again, the eventual crystallization of oral poetic traditions into the kind of fixed poems that are the repertoire of rhapsodes. Who, then, is the poet? As we shall observe in the next section, Theognis too—like Archilochus and other masters of lyric—may be considered an idealized creation of the poetry in which he has an integral function—and which he is credited with creating.

There is an important difference, however, between the poems of a Hesiod, on the one hand, and of a Theognis or an Archilochus, on the other. The difference is one of degree: these three figures, among others, seemingly have in common an intent to address all Hellenes, but Hesiod has far more authority than all the other poets. A Theognis or an Archilochus speaks from the perspective of his own city, though the localized aspects of the city are shaded over and the pan-Hellenic aspects are highlighted. In the case of Hesiod, however, the perspective is meant to be that of all cities. This transcendence is of course facilitated by the historical fact that the figure of Hesiod has no native city to claim him, since Askra was destroyed by Thespiai. Because Askra is no more, its traditions need not infringe on those of other cities. By allowing Hesiod to speak as a native of Askra, the pan-Hellenic tradition is in effect making him a native of all Greek cities, as we shall see in our survey of the *Works and Days.* The *Theogony,* too, expresses this transcendence, in two interrelated ways: the form in which the Muses are invoked and the nature of the gift that they confer on Hesiod.

We begin with the second. Whereas the mark of Archilochus' transformation from cowherd to poet in his nighttime encounter with the Muses is a lyre, Hesiod's transformation from shepherd to poet in his likewise nighttime encounter (*Theogony* 10) is marked by their gift of a *skêptron* 'staff, scepter' (verse 30). There has been much fruitless debate over such questions as whether this gift implies that Hesiod had not learned how to play the lyre, and not enough attention has been paid to the implications of the word *skêptron* as it is actually used in archaic poetry. The *skêptron* is a staff held by kings (*Iliad* I 279, II 86), by Chryses as priest of Apollo (I 15, 28), by Teiresias as prophet (*Odyssey* xi 90), by *kḗrūkes* 'heralds' (*Iliad* VII 277), or generally by one who stands up to speak in the *agorā́* 'assembly' (*Iliad* III 218, XXIII 568).[53]

[53] For an Indic parallel to the *skêptron* 'staff, scepter': Minkowski 1986.49–78.

Perhaps the most revealing example of such an *agorā́* is in the *Iliad* (XVIII 497), where it is presented as the context of an archetypal *neîkos* 'quarrel' (497) visualized on that timeless microcosm of a frozen motion picture, the Shield of Achilles.[54] While the two nameless litigants are seen formally quarreling with one another, partisans of each side shout their preferences (*Iliad* XVIII 502), and each of the seated *gérontes* 'elders' at the assembly waits for his turn to stand up with *skêptron* in hand and speak in favor of one side or the other (XVIII 505–506). As each elder speaks, taking the staff from the attending heralds, he is described as rendering *díkē* 'judgment/justice' (XVIII 506); moreover, a prize awaits the one who 'speaks *díkē* in the most straight manner' (XVIII 508).

Such an elder is the equivalent of the generic *basileús* 'king' as described in the *Theogony* (80–93). Moreover, the king's function of speaking *díkē* at the *agorā́* 'assembly' is in fact a gift of the Muses, as the *Theogony* itself tells us. The just king is imbued, from childhood on, by the Muses (*Theogony* 81–84), and he decides what is *thémis* 'divine law' (85) by way of 'straight *díkē* (plural)' (86)—in the context of the *agorā́* 'assembly' (ἀγορεύων 86, ἀγορῆφι 89, ἀγρομένοισιν 92).

In sum, the *skêptron* given to Hesiod by the Muses indicates that the poet will speak with the authority of a king—an authority that emanates from Zeus himself (*Theogony* 96; *Iliad* I 238–239, IX 97–99). The point is, just as Zeus has authority over all other gods, so also the poet who formalizes this authority by telling how it all happened thereby implicitly has authority over all other poets.

Next we turn to the invocation of the Muses in the *Theogony*. Our first impression may be that Hesiod might not fit the image of a poet whose authority transcends that of all other poets. He is situated in Askra (*Works and Days* 640), a remote Boeotian settlement at the foot of Mount Helikon, which in turn is described as the local cult place of the Muses (*Theogony* 1–7). Such a localization, as well as the poet's self-identification as Hesiod, has conventionally been interpreted as a primitive assertion of individualism in contrast with Homer's elevated anonymity.

This is to misunderstand the inherited conventions of the *Theogony*. As we can see from the theogony performed by Hermes himself to the accompaniment of his lyre in the *Homeric Hymn to Hermes* 425–433, the traditional format of such a composition is that of a prelude (the Classical Greek word for which is *prooímion*). There is considerable internal

[54] On the connection of this *neîkos* 'quarrel' with the one between Achilles and Agamemnon in *Iliad* I: N 1979a.109, following Muellner 1976.105–106.

evidence for this format in the actual words used by poetry in referring to it.[55] A prominent example is the expression *amboládēn* 'playing a prelude' in the *Homeric Hymn to Hermes* 426. It is crucial to note that the Homeric *Hymns*, including the *Hymn to Hermes*, are also preludes (thus Thucydides at 3.104.4 refers to the *Homeric Hymn to Apollo* as a *prooímion*). The conventional closure of the *Hymns*, *metabḗsomai állon es húmnon* (as at *Hymn to Aphrodite* 293), literally means 'I will move on to the rest of my song' (not 'to another hymn', as most translators render it).[56] The rest of a performance introduced by a prelude may be technically any poetic/musical form, but the one form that is specified by the Homeric *Hymns* themselves is the *érga/érgmata* 'deeds' of heroes (*Hymn* 31.19, 32.19)—which would be some form of epic (cf. *kléa phōtôn* . . . | *hēmithéōn* 'glories [*kléos* plural] of men who were demigods' at *Hymn* 32.18–19) or catalogue poetry (cf. *génos andrôn* | *hēmithéōn* 'genesis of men who were demigods' at *Hymn* 31.18–19).

Still, the fact is that the *Iliad* and the *Odyssey* have survived without any fixed preludes, although the availability of such preludes is documented by Crates of Pergamon (*Vita Homeri Romana* p. 32 Wilamowitz). The prelude is the prime context—practically the only context—for the archaic poet to identify himself, speak in his own persona, and describe the circumstances of his performance (cf. Theognis 22; Alcman PMG 39); even in choral lyric it is the prelude in which the first person is more appropriate to the poet than to the chorus. Thus the notorious distinction, claimed by generations of scholars, between Hesiodic self-identification and Homeric anonymity is invalid—if indeed the self-identification of Hesiod is happening within a prelude. Moreover, the self-identification of Homer is attested in another genuine prelude, the *Homeric Hymn to Apollo* (166–176).[57]

The proposition that the *Theogony* can be classified, from a purely formal point of view, as a complex prelude that invokes all the gods can be tested by adducing the larger Homeric *Hymns* as simplex preludes, each of which invokes one god. Admittedly these *Hymns* are unwieldy as functional preludes precisely because of their sheer size, and there may well be an element of *ars gratia artis* in their evolution. Since preludes traditionally appear in a variety of metrical forms,[58] the fact that the Homeric

[55] Cf. Koller 1956.

[56] Detailed discussion in Koller pp. 174–182. Koller p. 177 stresses that *húmnos* is the totality of performance; cf. ἀοιδῆς ὕμνον '*húmnos* of the song' at *Odyssey* viii 429. Of course, the "rest of the song" that supposedly follows each of the Homeric *Hymns* may be a stylized formal convention rather than an actual sequel.

[57] N 1979a.5–6, 8–9.

[58] Koller 1956.170–171.

Hymns were composed in hexameter suggests that they were closely affected by the specific form of the epic poetry that they preceded; moreover, if the epic compositions were to evolve into monumental size, then so could the preludes that introduced the epic performances. Despite the monumental size of the larger *Hymns*, however, the point remains that they maintain the traditional program of a functional prelude, one that is worthy of pan-Hellenic performance. This program can be divided into five stages:

1. The invocation proper; naming of the god.
2. Application of the god's epithets, conveying either explicitly or implicitly his/her efficacy on the local level of cult.
3. A description of the god's ascent to Olympus, whereby he/she achieved pan-Hellenic recognition.
4. A prayer to the god that he/she be pleased with the recognition that has been accorded him/her so far in the performance.
5. Transition to the rest of the performance.

These fives stages may or may not be explicit in any given *Hymn*. For instance, in the shorter *Hymn to Hermes* (18.5–9) the admission of Hermes as an Olympian god (stage 3) is suggested by way of mentioning the delay of his admission during the confinement of Maia in her cave; in the longer *Hymn to Hermes* (4.5–9), by contrast, the closely corresponding mention of this delay is followed by a lengthy narrative that elaborates on the god's subsequent admission. This narrative in the longer *Hymn* takes us all the way to verse 578, where we finally reach stage 4; by contrast, stage 4 in the shorter *Hymn to Hermes* is reached by verse 10.

Such an example of extreme length and brevity in two Homeric *Hymns* to the same god, achieved by expansion and compression, respectively (the mechanics of both phenomena are a clear indication of oral poetics),[59] can be compared with the length of the *Theogony* and the brevity of *Homeric Hymn* 25. Technically, both *Hymn* 25 and the *Theogony* are hymns to the Muses, and the first six hexameters of the seven-hexameter prelude have direct formal analogues in the longer:

Hymn 25.1	*Theogony* 1
Hymn 25.2–5	*Theogony* 94–97
Hymn 25.6	*Theogony* 963

[59] On the potential for expansion and compression in oral poetics, see Lord 1960.99–123.

Whereas the short hymn is a simplex prelude that motivates the genesis of the Muses, the long hymn is a complex prelude that first motivates the genesis of the Muses, who are then invoked to motivate the genesis of all the gods, which is the theogony proper. But from verse 964 onward, the *Theogony* is no longer formally a theogony, in that the subject matter shifts from the *theôn génos* 'genesis of gods' (as at *Theogony* 44, 105; cf. 115) to the genesis of demigods born of gods who mated with mortals (cf. *Theogony* 965–968); the latter theme, which amounts to catalogue poetry about heroes and heroines, is actually expressed as *génos andrôn* | *hēmithéōn* 'genesis of men who were demigods' at *Homeric Hymn* 31.18–19—a theme to which *Hymn* 31 announces itself as a formal prelude.

To repeat, verses 1–963 of the *Theogony* are from the standpoint of form a hymn to the Muses, serving as a prelude to the catalogue of heroes and heroines that survives at verses 965–1020 of the *Theogony*—and that interconnects with Hesiod fragment 1 MW.[60] The significant modification in this hymn to the Muses is that it becomes primarily a monumental hymn to Zeus and all the Olympian gods; thus at stage 4, where the poet may be expected to pray that the Muses be pleased with what has been composed so far, he in fact prays to win the pleasure of all the Olympians generated in his *Theogony*.

Thus verses 1–963 of the *Theogony* are not a single, but rather a composite, hymn in comparison with most Homeric *Hymns*. The hymn proper is at verses 36–103, culminating at 104 in a separate stage 4 in which the poet prays exclusively to the Muses; then, starting at verse 105, the expected stage 5 of transition (to whatever composition might follow the prelude) is implicitly postponed and replaced by a reapplied hymn to the Muses running all the way to verse 962, followed at last by a reapplied but cumulative stage 4 at verse 963. We may compare *Hymn to Apollo* 165–166, a stage 4 appropriate to Apollo as he is worshiped in the pan-Ionian context of his birthplace Delos: the poet first prays to Apollo and then greets the Deliades, a chorus of female singers/dancers[61] who seem to be a local manifestation of the Muses, with a formula that elsewhere conveys a stage 4 prayer. Then, at verses 177–178, the expected stage 5 of transition is explicitly postponed and followed at verses 179–544 by a reapplied hymn to Apollo as he is worshiped in the pan-Hellenic context of his abode at Delphi; there is a reapplied stage 4 at verse 545, where the poet again prays to Apollo, followed at last by the stage 5 of transition at verse 546.

[60] On the interconnection: N 1979a.213–214 § 3n1, n3.
[61] Cf. Thucydides 3.104.5.

In the case of the *Theogony*, verses 105–962 amount to an expanded variant of the compressed hymn at verses 36–103, just as verses 179–544 in the *Hymn to Apollo* amount to an expanded variant of the compressed hymn at verses 1–165. There is an important formal difference, however, between the compressed version at verses 36–103 of the *Theogony* and the expanded version of verses 105–962: whereas both are simultaneously a prelude and a theogony—just like the composition performed by Hermes in *Hymn to Hermes* 425–433—the compressed version is more of a prelude and the expanded version is more of a theogony.

The expanded version is the *Theogony* proper, told by Hesiod in his own persona and "retelling" what the Muses had told him. The compressed version, on the other hand, is told only indirectly: in this case the theogony related by the Muses to Hesiod is merely paraphrased, as it were, in the context of describing what the goddesses sang as they went up to Mount Olympus.

Verses 1–21 of the *Theogony* present yet another indirect version (thus there are altogether three versions of theogony in the *Theogony*). Here, too, the theogony related by the Muses is paraphrased, this first time in the context of describing what the goddesses sang as they came down from Mount Helikon. In this version the Muses are invoked as Helikonian (*Theogony* 1–2), not Olympian as everywhere else in the *Theogony*. Moreover, the thematic order of the Muses' theogony, which they sing and dance (*Theogony* 3–4) as they come *down* from the summit of Mount Helikon, is the inverse of what they sing and dance (*Theogony* 70) as they go *up* to the summit of Mount Olympus (which is stage 3 in the program of a pan-Hellenic hymn).

In the first theogony, at *Theogony* 11–20, the Muses are described as starting their narrative with Olympian Zeus (11) and moving their way "down" from the other Olympian gods—Hera, Athena, Apollo, Artemis, Poseidon (11–15)—all the way to the previous divine generations (16–19) and then to the primordial forces, Earth, Okeanos, Night (20). These same Muses, after they encounter Hesiod at the foot of Mount Helikon, are described in the second theogony (*Theogony* 36–52) as starting their narrative with Earth / Sky (45) and moving their way "up" to the Olympian gods, culminating with Zeus himself (47; the word *deúteron* 'next' here denotes merely the order of this theogony and therefore does not slight the importance of Zeus). It is important that this narrative direction of the Muses' second theogony, which determines the direction of Hesiod's third and definitive theogony at verses 105–962, corresponds to stage 3 in the program of a pan-Hellenic hymn, the ascent to Olympus of the divinity who is being praised.

We see here a transformation of the Muses from local goddesses on Mount Helikon into pan-Hellenic goddesses on Mount Olympus. As they start their way down the slopes of Helikon, they are described as *énthen apornúmenai* 'starting from there' at *Theogony* 9—corresponding to *énthen apornúmenos* (same meaning) at *Hymn to Apollo* 29, where the verse goes on to proclaim the transformation of Apollo from lord of his native Delos into lord of all mankind. In their local setting the singing *and dancing* Helikonian Muses resemble the Deliades of the *Hymn to Apollo*. Like the Muses (for example, *Hymn to Apollo* 189–190), the Deliades are Apollo's attendants (157), and the poet seems to be praying to them and Apollo together at stage 4 of his hymn (177–178). Further, the Deliades, too, seem to sing *and dance* (cf. *khorós* at Thucydides 3.104.5; cf. also Euripides *Herakles* 687–690); it is as if the performances of the Helikonian Muses and the Deliades were envisioned as lyric rather than hexameter poetry.

Moreover, the relationship of Hesiod to the Helikonian Muses parallels the relationship of Homer to the Deliades (the *Hymn to Apollo* unmistakably claims Homer as its composer).[62] The self-dramatized encounter of Homer with the Deliades leads to the poet's promise that he will spread their *kléos* 'glory' by mentioning them in his poetry *as he travels throughout the cities of mankind* (*Hymn to Apollo* 174–175; compare verse 156, where this *kléos* is already presented as a fait accompli); in other words, the Deliades will have a place in pan-Hellenic poetry.[63] Similarly, the encounter of Hesiod with the Helikonian Muses leads to the poet's glorifying them with the *Theogony*, which is technically a pan-Hellenic hymn to the Muses; in this way the local goddesses of Helikon are assimilated into the pan-Hellenic goddesses of Olympus.

We may also compare Hermes' miniature theogony as paraphrased in the *Hymn to Hermes* 425–433; this theogony is technically a hymn to the mother of the Muses, *Mnēmosúnē* (429), who is described as the deity presiding over and defined by the characteristics of Hermes (for the diction, cf. Callimachus *Hymn to Apollo* 43). In the same way the Helikonian Muses preside over and are defined by the characteristics of Hesiod—characteristics that they themselves had conferred upon him.

And here we finally see why it is essential for the *Theogony* that Hesiod should have his local origins at the foot of Mount Helikon. As an expression of the Helikonian Muses, he possesses characteristics that are beyond the immediate sphere of the Olympian Muses. As we have noticed, the goddesses confer upon him a staff (*Theogony* 30), an emblem of authority that is the province of kings and that emanates from Zeus himself. Also, as his very name *Hēsíodos* proclaims, the Muses

[62] N 1979a.5–6, 8–9.
[63] N pp. 8–9.

of Helikon endow the poet with *audḗ* (*Theogony* 31), a special voice that enables him not only to sing a theogony (33–34) but also to tell the future as well as the past (32). Whereas the generic protégé of the Olympian Muses and Apollo is an *aoidós* 'poet' who composes the equivalent of Homeric epos and hymns (cf. *Homeric Hymn* 25.2–3 and *Theogony* 94–103), Hesiod as protégé of the Helikonian Muses has the powers not only of a poet but also of what the Greeks would call a *kêrux* 'herald' and a *mántis* 'seer'.

The Indo-European heritage of Greek poetry goes back to a phase where the functions of poet/herald/seer are as yet undifferentiated. Traces of such a phase survive not only in the characterization of Hesiod as protégé of the Helikonian Muses but also in the paradigm of Hermes as protégé of *Mnēmosúnē*. By virtue of singing a theogony, Hermes is said to be *kraínōn* 'authorizing' the gods (*Hymn to Hermes* 427). The verb *kraínō* denotes sovereign authority as exercised by kings and as emanating from Zeus himself.[64] It conveys the notion that kings authorize the accomplishment of something and confirm that it will be accomplished (as at *Odyssey* viii 390). A cross-cultural survey of ritual theogonic traditions throughout the world reveals that a basic function of a theogony is to confirm the authority that regulates any given social group.[65] By singing a theogony and thus "authorizing" the gods, Hermes is in effect confirming their authority.

Hermes later enters into an agreement with Apollo whereby the two gods divide their functions between themselves, and in the process Hermes gives Apollo his lyre along with the powers that go with it (*Hymn to Hermes* 434–512), while Apollo gives Hermes a *rhábdos* 'staff' described as *epi-kraínousa* 'authorizing' the *themoí* 'ordinances'[66] that Apollo has learned from Zeus himself (531–532). While granting this much authorization to Hermes, Apollo specifically excludes the sphere of divination that is appropriate to the oracle at Delphi (533–549); but Apollo does include the sphere of divination that is appropriate to the Bee Maidens of Mount Parnassos (550–566). These Bee Maidens also *kraínousin* 'authorize' (559): when they are fed honey, they are in ecstasy and tell *alētheíē* 'truth' (560–561), but they *pseúdontai* 'lie' when deprived of this food (562–563). Such ecstatic divination is achieved with fermented honey—a pattern typical of an earlier phase when *aoidós* 'poet' and *mántis* 'seer' were as yet undifferentiated.[67] When the Bee Maidens are in

[64] Benveniste 1969 2:35–42.
[65] Cf. West 1966.1–16.
[66] Cf. Hesychius s.v. θεμούς· διαθέσεις, παραινέσεις.
[67] Scheinberg 1979.16–28.

ecstasy, they *kraínousin* 'authorize' by telling of future things that will really come to pass.

The division of attributes between Apollo and Hermes dramatizes the evolutionary separation of poetic functions that are pictured as still integral at the time when Hermes sang the theogony. But then Hermes cedes the lyre to Apollo and confines himself to the primitive shepherd's pipe (*Hymn to Hermes* 511–512) so that Apollo can take over the sphere of the *aoidós* 'poet'. Apollo also takes over the sphere of the *mántis* 'seer' on a highly evolved pan-Hellenic level (his oracle at Delphi), leaving to Hermes the more primitive sphere of the *mántis* 'seer' as a local exponent of the sort of *alētheíē* 'truth' that is induced by fermented honey. But the "newer" god's dramatized affinity with the more primitive aspects of poetry and his actual inauguration of Apollo's poetic art by way of singing a theogony indicate that Hermes—not Apollo—is in fact the older god, and that his "authorizing" staff and his "authorizing" Bee Maidens are vestiges of an older and broader poetic realm. From a historical point of view, Apollo and his Olympian Muses are the newer gods: they represent a streamlining of this older realm into the newer and narrower one of pan-Hellenic poetry.

Similarly, Hesiod's relationship with the Helikonian Muses represents an older and broader poetic realm that the poet then streamlines into the newer and narrower one of a pan-Hellenic theogony by way of synthesizing the Helikonian with the Olympian Muses. The *skêptron* 'staff' and the prophetic voice that Hesiod receives from the Helikonian Muses, speakers of both falsehoods and truth, are analogous to the Hermetic *rhábdos* 'staff' and Bee Maidens, likewise speakers of both falsehoods and truth. It seems as if the Muses of Olympus inherit the genre of theogony from the Muses of Helikon, just as Apollo gets the lyre from Hermes, composer of the first theogony. For a pan-Hellenic theogony to happen, the Muses have to come down from Helikon and go up to Olympus, through the intermediacy of Hesiod.

Just as Hermes is the archetypal *kêrux* 'herald' and *mántis* 'seer', so Hesiod embodies these two functions along with that of the *aoidós* 'poet' by way of the Helikonian Muses. (These local Muses, as Pausanias 9.29.2–3 reports, are *Melétē* 'practice', *Mnḗmē* 'memory', and *Aoidḗ* 'song'; these names correspond to the processes involved in the composition and performance of oral poetry.)[68] The figure of Hesiod requires these local Muses in order to compose a theogony, but he also requires the Olympian Muses in order to compose pan-Hellenic poetry. His own implicit reward for assimilating the Helikonian Muses into the Olympian

[68] Cf. Detienne 1973.12.

is that his local gifts, a staff and a voice that are both appropriate to a local theogony, become in a pan-Hellenic context the emblems that establish his ultimate authority as poet, emanating from the ultimate authority of Zeus as king.

The Language of Hesiod

The figure of Hesiod can proudly announce his local origins and still speak in a language that has evolved to match the language of pan-Hellenic hymns, which in turn have evolved to match the language of the epics that they inaugurate. The poet of the *Theogony* can even equate the artistry of composing a pan-Hellenic theogony with that of composing an epic (100–101)—and the ritual context that a local theogony would surely entail is for us all but forgotten.

In fact, the diction of Hesiodic poetry is so akin to the Homeric that its self-proclaimed Boeotian provenience would be nearly impossible to detect on the basis of language alone. What is more, the Ionic phase of evolution and eventual crystallization is actually even stronger in the Hesiodic tradition than in the Homeric.[69]

Granted, there have been attempts to establish linguistic differences between Homer and Hesiod, the most interesting of which is the finding that the first- and second-declension accusative plural endings *-ās* and *-ous* occur in preconsonantal position far more often in Hesiodic than in Homeric diction; also, that in prevocalic position they occur less often.[70] This phenomenon has been interpreted to mean that we are somehow dealing with the native speaker(s) of a dialect in which these accusative plurals have been shortened to *-ăs* and *-ŏs*; this way the beginning of the next word with a consonant would not matter because the resulting *-ăs* C- and *-ŏs* C-[71] do not produce overlength, whereas *-ās C- and -ous* C- do. Now, it is true that Homeric diction tends to avoid overlength (-V̄C C- as distinct from -V̆C C- or -V̄ C-), but it does not follow that Hesiodic diction should neatly match this tendency; rather, in line with the fact that the formulaic behavior of Hesiod generally reveals fewer constraints, and hence less archaism, than that of Homer, it could be that the higher proportion of preconsonantal *-ās* and *-ous* in Hesiod reveals simply a greater tolerance for this type of overlength than in Homer.

[69] Janko 1982.85, 197.
[70] Edwards 1971.141–165.
[71] In what follows, C = "consonant," V = "vowel."

As it happens, accusative plurals ending in *-ăs* and *-ŏs* are decidedly not a feature of the Boeotian dialect. As for the sporadic occurrences of first-declension *-ăs* before vowels, it is not true that this phenomenon is limited to Hesiodic diction, as is generally claimed. There are sporadic occurrences in Homeric diction as well, including the *Hymns* (for instance, at *Iliad* V 269, VIII 378; *Odyssey* xvii 232; *Hymn to Hermes* 106). It is difficult, granted, simply to rule out the possibility that this phenomenon is a reflex of Doric dialects, where first- and second-declension *-ăs* V- and *-ŏs* V- are indeed attested. Still, it seems preferable to account for the entire problem in terms of the Ionic dialects, which represent the final and definitive phase in the evolution of both Homeric and Hesiodic poetry. The formulaic evidence could go back to a pre-Ionic stage common to all Greek dialects, with accusative plurals ending in

-ăns V-	*-ăns* C-
-ŏns V-	*-ŏns* C-

Then we may posit an intermediate stage common to all dialects (and still attested in some) with

-ăns V-	*-ăs* C-
-ŏns V-	*-ŏs* C-

In the final Ionic stage, prevocalic *-ăns/-ŏns* became *-ās/-ous,* which were extended to preconsonantal position as well:

-ās V-	*-ās* C-
-ous V-	*-ous* C-

But the intermediate stage, by way of formulaic repositionings of words from prevocalic to preconsonantal contexts and vice versa, could have left sporadic traces of "contaminations":

-ăs V-	*-ās* C-
-ŏs V-	*-ous* C-

There would be more such traces in Hesiodic than in Homeric poetry simply because the Hesiodic reflects a longer span of evolution in the Ionic hexameter tradition. The point remains: not only does Hesiodic poetry implicitly claim to be like Homeric poetry (as at *Theogony* 100–101) but it also shares extensively in its formal heritage.

Even within Homeric poetry, the *Odyssey* is perceptibly different from the *Iliad* in featuring more instances of preconsonantal *-ās/-ous* and fewer instances of prevocalic *-ās/-ous*, although this gap between the *Odyssey* and the *Iliad* is not nearly as great as the one between the Hesiodic poems, on the one hand, and the Homeric, on the other.[72] Still, these data correspond to an overall pattern, as established on the basis of several other linguistic criteria: the *Odyssey* had a longer span of evolution in the Ionic hexameter tradition than the *Iliad*, while the Hesiodic poems combined had an even longer span than the *Odyssey*.[73]

The pervasive Ionic heritage of Hesiodic poetry extends from form to content. The one month name overtly mentioned in the *Works and Days*, *Lēnaiṓn* (504), happens to occur in many Ionian calendars (though not in the Athenian), and even the morphology (ending in *-ṓn*) is distinctly Ionic. Now, each city-state had its own idiosyncratic calendar, and there were significant variations in the naming of months even among states that were closely related; it comes as no surprise, then, that the overt mentioning of month names was generally shunned in archaic Greek poetry, with its pan-Hellenic orientation. Thus it is all the more striking that an exclusively Ionic name should surface in the poetry of Boeotian Hesiod. At best, we can justify the name *Lēnaiṓn* as tending toward a pan-Hellenic audience in that it is native to most Ionian cities at least; moreover, the meaning of the name is transparent, in that it is derived from *lênai* 'devotees of Dionysus'. Even so, the name and its form are more pan-Ionian than pan-Hellenic. Moreover, the description of the wind Boreas as it blows over the sea from Thrace in the verses immediately following the mention of *Lēnaiṓn* reflects a geographically Ionian orientation parallel to what we find in the *Iliad*.[74]

In sum, not only does Hesiodic poetry implicitly claim to be like Homeric poetry, but it also shares its predominantly Ionic formal heritage.

Hesiod, Poet of the Works and Days

Hesiod's ultimate authority as poet, emanating from the ultimate authority of Zeus as king, is put to the test in the *Works and Days*. In the prelude to the poem (1–10), which is formally the equivalent of a hymn to Zeus, the supreme god is implored to "straighten the divine laws [*thémis* plural] with your judgment [*díkē*]" (9) while the poet proceeds to

[72] Data in Janko 1982.
[73] *Ibid.*
[74] West 1978.27.

say *etḗtuma* 'genuine things' to his brother Perses (10). Thus the actions of Zeus and the words of Hesiod are drawn into an explicitly parallel relationship.

The actions of Zeus are a model for the ideal king as visualized in the *Theogony:* imbued by the Muses (80–84), he "sorts out the divine laws [*thémis* plural] with straight judgments [*díkē* {plural}]" (85–86). Thanks to his straight judgments, the king is also able to bring to an end even a great *neîkos* 'quarrel' (87). We are reminded of the *neîkos* pictured on the Shield of Achilles (*Iliad* XVIII 497), adjudicated by elders who pronounce *díkē* 'judgment' with *skêptron* in hand (505–508).[75] Curiously, the idealized king in the *Theogony* is not represented as holding a *skêptron*; instead, this symbol of the authority that emanates from Zeus is conferred by the Muses upon Hesiod (*Theogony* 30). It is as if the Muse-imbued king were cast in a mold that could fit the poet.

This is not to say that Hesiod is a king; rather, as we shall see, the *Works and Days* elaborates an authority that replaces and transcends that of kings. The impetus for the entire poem is in fact a *neîkos* 'quarrel' between Hesiod and Perses (35), but this quarrel will not be stopped by any ideal king; the poet wishes that he and his brother would settle it themselves (35), "with straight judgments [*díkē* plural], which are the best, being from Zeus" (36). The original cause of the quarrel between the two brothers is this: after they had divided up their inheritance from their father (37), Perses forcibly took some of Hesiod's fair share (38), thereby enhancing the prestige of greedy kings "who wish to pronounce this judgment [*díkē*]" (38–39). These kings, characterized by Hesiod as *dōrophágoi* 'gift-devouring' (39, 221, 264), are anything but ideal, and the poet threatens that they will be punished for their "crooked judgments [*díkē* plural]" (250, 264).

As we shall see, what ultimately settles the quarrel of Hesiod and Perses is not any king, but the *Works and Days* itself, elaborating on the concept of *díkē* in the sense of 'justice'. So far, the translation offered for *díkē* has been 'judgment', which is how we must interpret the word in the immediate contexts of *Works and Days* 39, 249, and 269. In each of these instances, an accompanying demonstrative (*tḗnde*; see also *táde* 'these things' at 268) forces a translation such as 'this judgment', referring short-range to the unjust pronouncement that the greedy kings wish to make. Such contexts even help us understand the etymology of *díkē*: the ideal king 'sorts out' (verb *diakrī́nō*, at *Theogony* 85) what is *thémis* 'divine law' and what is not (85) by way of *díkē* (86), which is an *indication* (as in Latin *indic-āre*, where *-dic-* is cognate with Greek *díkē*), hence

[75] See p. 53.

'judgment'. Long-range, however, any ad hoc 'judgment' can be turned into 'justice' by Zeus, who is the authority behind all human judgments. Thus, when Hesiod implores Zeus to "straighten the divine laws [*thémis* plural] with *díkē*" (*Works and Days* 9), the supreme god's 'judgment' is the same as 'justice'. This action of Zeus, to repeat, is coefficient with the words of Hesiod to Perses (10), in the context of a *neîkos* 'quarrel' that the two of them must 'sort out' for themselves (verb *diakrī́nō* again, this time in the middle voice; verse 35).

The figure of Hesiod resorts to words in reacting to the violent seizure of his property by Perses. First he tells Perses the story of Prometheus and Pandora (*Works and Days* 42–105), motivating the prime theme of man's inherent need to work the land for a living. Then he tells Perses the myth of the five generations of mankind (106–201), which shows in detail how mankind becomes elevated by *díkē* 'justice' and debased by its opposite, *húbris* 'outrage'.[76] The fifth and present generation, which is the Age of Iron, is a time when *díkē* and *húbris* are engaged in an ongoing struggle. As happens elsewhere in myths about the ages of mankind, the present encompassed by the final age merges with the future and becomes a prophecy:[77] in a deeply pessimistic tone Hesiod predicts that *díkē* will finally lose to *húbris* (*Works and Days* 190–194). Next, Hesiod tells the fable of the hawk and the nightingale (202–212), addressing it to kings whom he diplomatically presupposes to be *phronéontes* 'aware' (202). Again the tone is pessimistic, at least in the immediate context: the hawk seizes the nightingale, described as an *aoidós* 'singer', that is, 'poet' (208), simply because he is more powerful (206, 207, 210), and he boasts of having the ultimate power of either releasing or devouring his victim (209).

At this point Hesiod turns to Perses and, applying all that he has just told him, concludes by urging his brother to espouse *díkē* and reject *húbris* (*Works and Days* 213). He warns that the fulfillment of *díkē* is an eventual process, and that *díkē* will in the end triumph over *húbris* (217–218). Personified as a goddess, *Díkē* will punish greedy men who "sort out divine laws [verb *krī́nō*; noun *thémis*] with crooked judgments [*díkē* plural]" (220–223), and "who drive her out, making her not straight" (224; cf. *Iliad* XVI 387–388). Then follows the paradigm of the two cities: the polis of *díkē* becomes fertile and rich (225–237; cf. *Odyssey* xix 109–114), while the polis of *húbris* becomes sterile and poor (238–247).

[76] N 1979a.151–165, following Vernant 1960, 1966. See also the updated observations of Vernant 1985.101, 104, 106.

[77] West 1978.176.

Having defined justice as an eventual process (*Works and Days* 217–218), Hesiod invites the greedy kings to reconsider "this judgment [*díkē*]" (269) that they had wanted to pronounce in response to the forcible taking of Hesiod's property by Perses (39). We now see that kings who make "this judgment [*díkē*]" (269) are thereby making the goddess *Díkē* "not straight" (224), and that the goddess will eventually punish such men through the power of her father, Zeus (220–224, 256–269). The eventuality of *Díkē* is also clearly defined in the poetry of Solon: men who forcibly take the property of others (F 4.13 W) are thereby guilty of *húbris* (4.8) in violating the foundations of *Díkē* (4.14), who will come to exact just punishment "with the passage of time" (4.16).

The *Works and Days* dramatizes the actual passage of time required for the workings of *Díkē*. At the beginning of the poem we find the goddess implicitly violated through the forcible taking of Hesiod's property by Perses and through the crooked judgment pronounced in the unjust brother's favor by the greedy kings. At verse 39 "this judgment [*díkē*]" is still implicitly crooked as the poet begins to teach about *Díkē*, and the initial teachings are still pessimistic about the outcome of the struggle between *húbris* and *díkē*, as also about the power of the hawk/king over the nightingale/poet. By the time we reach verses 249 and 269, however, "this judgment [*díkē*]" is seen in the light of the vengeance that *Díkē* herself will take on those who violated her. Perses is now urged to espouse *díkē* in the sense of 'justice' (275), since those without it will devour each other like wild beasts (275–278).

The "moral" of the fable about the hawk and the nightingale hereby becomes explicit: the hawk/king who threatens to devour the nightingale/poet as proof of his power is utterly disqualified as an exponent of *díkē* 'justice'. Moreover, since only those kings who are *phronéontes* 'aware' will understand the fable (202; cf. the idealized kings at *Theogony* 88, who are *ekhéphrones* 'aware'), the greedy kings are implicitly disqualified even from understanding the "moral," in view of their general ignorance (see *Works and Days* 40–41).[78] And if the kings cannot be exponents of *díkē*, they are utterly without authority and their raison d'être is annihilated. In fact, after verse 263, the kings are never heard of again in the *Works and Days*.

As for Perses, he is being taught that, in the end, it is the man of *díkē* who gets rich (*Works and Days* 280–281), while the man who forcibly takes the property of others (320–324) will have wealth "only for a short while" (325–326). By the time we reach verse 396 of the *Works and Days*,

[78] On the importance of *ornithomanteíā* 'divination by birds' in the whole poem, cf. *Works and Days* 828 in the context of the comments by West 1978.364–365.

Perses has been reduced to utter penury and "now" comes to beg from Hesiod. But the poet refuses to give him anything, teaching him instead to work the land for a living (396–397). While the authority of *díkē* as emanating from Zeus and as represented by Hesiod is eventually taking hold, even the sense of indignation originally felt by the poet against his brother begins to recede; already by verse 286 he is expressing his good intentions toward Perses. Toward the latter half of the poem, the figure of Perses recedes in favor of a generalized second-person singular: it is as if Perses were now tacitly ready to accept the teachings of his righteous brother.

In the end, then, *díkē* 'justice' is totally vindicated in the *Works and Days*, and its eventual triumph is dramatized in the time that elapses in the course of the poem. Moreover, the function of the *basileús* 'king' as the authority who tells what is and what is not *thémis* 'divine law' by way of his *díkē* 'judgment' is taken over by the poem itself. The vantage point is pan-Hellenic, in that all the cities of the Hellenes are reduced to two extreme types, the polis of *díkē* (225–237) and the polis of *húbris* (238–247). Even the consistently plural use of *basileîs* 'kings' in the *Works and Days* suggests a pan-Hellenic perspective: from the Homeric tradition we see that each city is ruled by a single king.

With the elimination of kings, the *Works and Days* can address itself to any polis of, say, the eighth century or thereafter—whether its government is an oligarchy, a democracy, or even a tyranny. And what the poem in effect communicates is the universal foundation of the law codes native to each Greek city-state.

Even in a democracy like Athens, the laws of Solon, as his own poetry proclaims, are founded on the authority of Zeus as king (F 31 W). Just as Zeus is the one who "straightens what is crooked and withers the overweening" (*Works and Days* 7), as he is implored by Hesiod to "straighten the divine laws [*thémis* plural] with *díkē*" (9), so also Solon's *Eunomíā* 'good government by way of good laws' is a goddess who "shackles those without *díkē*" (F 4.33 W), "blackens *húbris*" (4.34), "withers the sprouting outgrowths of derangement" (4.35), and "straightens crooked judgments [*díkē* plural]" (4.36). In the *Theogony* we find that Zeus himself fathered *Eunomíā*, as well as *Díkē* (902); moreover, their mother is *Thémis*, the incarnation of divine law and order (901), and it is significant that Zeus married her after defeating Typhoeus and swallowing Metis, the last two remaining threats to cosmic order.

Assuming the stance of a lawgiver, Solon says in his poetry that he "wrote down" his *thesmoí* 'laws' after having adjusted "a *díkē* that is straight" for the noble and the base alike (F 36.18–20 W). But besides this written law code, we must also keep in mind the poetic traditions attributed to Solon; and in these traditions the figure of Solon functions not only as a lawgiver, as we see here, but also as a personal exponent of *díkē* by virtue of his life as dramatized through his poetry. In one poem, for example, Solon prays to the Muses that they give him wealth and fame (F 13.1–4 W), and that they should allow him to help his friends and hurt his enemies (13.5–6). He yearns to own *khrḗmata* 'possessions' but renounces any thought of forcibly taking any from others, which would be "without *díkē*" (13.7–8); sooner or later *díkē* would have revenge (13.8). More specifically, deeds of *húbris* will surely be punished by Zeus, who appears like a violent wind (13.16–25; cf. again *Iliad* XVI 384–392).

In the poetic traditions of the city-state of Megara, as represented by the figure of Theognis, we find a remarkable parallel: here, too, the poet prays to Zeus that he may help his friends and hurt his enemies (Theognis 337–338). If Theognis could only exact retribution, by the time he dies, from those who had wronged him, then he would have the fame of a god among men (339–340).[79] We may note the similarity between this aspiration and what happens to Lycurgus of Sparta: this lawgiver is declared to be like a god by Apollo's oracle at Delphi (Herodotus 1.65.3) and is made a cult hero after death (1.66.1).[80] Theognis goes on to say how he has been personally wronged: his possessions were forcibly taken from him (Theognis 346–347). So, too, with Hesiod: Perses had forcibly taken some of his possessions (*Works and Days* 37, in conjunction with 320).

Like Hesiod, moreover, Theognis initially admits pessimism about any success at retribution (Theognis 345), and in his apparent helplessness he expresses the ghastly urge to drink the blood of those who had wronged him (349). The cryptic mention here of a *daímōn* 'spirit' who would supervise such a vengeance (349–350) reminds us of the countless invisible *phúlakes* 'guardians' of *Díkē* who stand ready to punish wrongdoers in *Works and Days* 249–255 and who are identical to the *daímones* or stylized cult heroes at verses 122–126.[81] The guardians of *díkē* 'justice' are described as coefficients of the personified goddess *Díkē*, who is likewise pictured as standing ready to punish wrongdoers (*Works and Days* 256–262); similarly in the poetry of Solon, it is *Díkē* who in due time punishes wrongdoers (F 4.14–16 W). Theognis, however, has conjured up the starker alternative of a bloodthirsty revenant, who may even turn out to be the poet's own self after death.[82]

[79] Commentary in N 1985a.68–74.
[80] N p. 69.
[81] N pp. 72–73. Cf. also Vernant 1985.101, 104, 106.
[82] N p. 73.

Although the particulars may vary, Theognis, like Hesiod and Solon, is presented through his poetry as a personal exponent of *díkē* by virtue of his life as dramatized through his poetry. But, unlike Solon's poetry, which can refer to the *díkē* of a written law code as well (F 36.18–20), the poetry of Theognis can refer only to the *díkē* that emerges from his teachings, addressed to his young *hetaîros* 'comrade' Kyrnos and to various minor characters. Still, this *díkē* has the force of a law code handed down by a lawgiver, as Theognis himself proclaims:[83]

χρή με παρὰ στάθμην καὶ γνώμονα τήνδε δικάσσαι
Κύρνε δίκην, ἶσόν τ' ἀμφοτέροισι δόμεν,
μάντεσί τ' οἰωνοῖς τε καὶ αἰθομένοις ἱεροῖσιν,
ὄφρα μὴ ἀμπλακίης αἰσχρὸν ὄνειδος ἔχω

Theognis 543–546

I must pronounce this *díkē,* Kyrnos, along [the straight line of] a carpenter's rule and square,
and I must give to both sides their equitable share,
with the help of seers [*mántis* plural], portents, and burning sacrifice,
so that I may not incur shameful reproach for veering.

Like Solon, who protects "both sides" and allows "neither side" to win (ἀμφοτέροισι/οὐδετέρους at F 5.5/6), Theognis presents himself as giving an equal share to "both sides" (ἀμφοτέροισι at 544 above), elsewhere advising Kyrnos to walk "the middle road" (219–220, 331–332) and to give to "neither side" that which belongs to the other (μηδετέροισι 332).

The fact that Theognis pronounces "this *díkē*" (verse 544) in a setting of sacrifice and ritual correctness (545) is significant in view of Hesiod's instructions in the latter part of the *Works and Days,* where moral and ritual correctness are consistently made parallel. At verses 333–335 Hesiod's concluding moral injunction to shun "deeds without *díkē*" is followed up by further advice, this time a ritual injunction:

κὰδ δύναμιν δ' ἔρδειν ἱέρ' ἀθανάτοισι θεοῖσιν
ἁγνῶς καὶ καθαρῶς, ἐπὶ δ' ἀγλαὰ μηρία καίειν·
ἄλλοτε δὲ σπονδῇσι θύεσσί τε ἱλάσκεσθαι,
ἠμὲν ὅτ' εὐνάζῃ καὶ ὅτ' ἂν φάος ἱερὸν ἔλθῃ,
ὥς κέ τοι ἵλαον κραδίην καὶ θυμὸν ἔχωσιν,

[83] Commentary in N pp. 37–38.

ὄφρ' ἄλλων ὠνῇ κλῆρον, μὴ τὸν τεὸν ἄλλος

Hesiod *Works and Days* 336–341

To the best of your ability, sacrifice to the immortal gods
in a holy and pure manner, burning sumptuous thigh-portions;
and at other times propitiate them with libations and burnt offerings,
both when you go to bed and when the holy light comes back,
so that they may have a gracious heart and disposition,
and so you may buy another man's holding, rather than have him buy yours.

As the *Works and Days* proceeds, the advice becomes more and more meticulous: for example, one must not cut one's nails at a "feast of the gods" (742–743). Or again, a man must not urinate while standing up and facing the sun (727), or in a road (729), or into rivers or springs (757–758). We may compare the parallel advice in the Indic *Law Code of Manu* 4.45–48: "Let him not void urine on a road . . . nor while he walks or stands, nor on reaching the bank of a river. . . . Let him never void faeces or urine, facing the wind, or a fire, or looking towards a Brahman, the sun, water, or cows."[84]

The legal traditions of the Indic peoples are clearly cognate with those of the Greeks, and in this connection it is especially interesting to observe the uses of *memnēménos* 'being mindful' at *Works and Days* 728, in the specific context of the injunctions now being considered, as well as elsewhere (*Works and Days* 298, 422, 616, 623, 641, 711). The root *men-/*mneh$_2$– of *memnēménos* recurs in the Indic name *Mánu-*, meaning 'the mindful one': this ancestor of the human race gets his name (which is cognate with English *man*) by virtue of being 'mindful' at a sacrifice. Manu is the prototypical sacrificer, whose sheer virtuosity in what Sylvain Lévi has called "the delicate art of sacrifice" confers upon him an incontestable authority in matters of ritual.[85] Since ritual correctness is the foundation of Indic law, the entire Indic corpus of juridical/moral aphorisms is named after him.

There is a parallel thematic pattern in the *Precepts of Cheiron*, a poem attributed to Hesiod (scholia to Pindar *Pythian* 6.22) in which Cheiron the Centaur instructs the boy Achilles. The one fragment that we have (Hesiod F 283 MW) contains the initial words spoken by the centaur, in which he tells Achilles that the very first thing the young hero must do when he arrives home is to sacrifice to the gods. In a fragment from the

[84] Cf. West 1978.334–335; cf. Watkins 1979.

[85] Lévi 1966 [1898].121. Cf. N 1985a.38–41. See also pp. 110–111 below.

Epic Cycle (*Titanomachy* F 6 p. 111 Allen), Cheiron is described as the one who "led the race of mortals to justice [*dikaiosúnē*] by showing them oaths, festive sacrifices, and the configurations [*skhḗmata*] of Olympus." There are also parallel formal patterns shared by the *Precepts* and by the *Works and Days* (336–337, 687–688), as well as by Theognis (99–100, 1145 in conjunction with 1147–1148).

The interaction between Cheiron and Achilles in the *Precepts of Cheiron* is so strikingly similar to the one between Hesiod and Perses and the one between Theognis and Kyrnos that F. G. Welcker was led to propose, in the preface to his 1826 edition of Theognis, that Perses and Kyrnos are generic figures whose dramatized familiarity with Hesiod and Theognis makes it possible for these poets to offer well-intended advice to their audiences, who really consist of strangers.[86] Such Near Eastern typological parallels as *Ahiqar and Nadan* and the *Proverbs of Solomon* add to the probability that these figures are indeed generic.[87] Nevertheless, at least in the case of Perses, scholars resist accepting this probability, primarily because the historicity of even Hesiod is thereby endangered, "and no one supposes Hesiod himself to be an assumed character."[88]

Throughout this presentation it has been generally argued that the persona of the poet in any given archaic Greek poem is but a function of the traditions inherited by that poem; accordingly, the assumption of Hesiod's historicity, as in the statement just quoted, requires no ad hoc rebuttal here. Suffice it for now to observe that there are analogues to the complementary characterizations of Hesiod and Perses even in Homeric poetry. One example is the challenge issued by Odysseus to the suitor Eurymakhos at *Odyssey* xviii 366–375:[89] the resourceful king, disguised as beggar-poet,[90] is challenging the idle usurper of his possessions to a hypothetical contest (the word for which is *éris* 'strife' at xviii 366; cf. *Works and Days* 11–26, especially 26) in the activity of 'working the land' (the word for which is *érgon*, again at xviii 366, and also at xviii 369; cf. *Works and Days* 20).

Or again, there are analogues to the complementary characterizations of Theognis and Kyrnos in the *Works and Days*. For example, Hesiod pointedly teaches that one should not make one's *hetaîros* 'comrade' equal to one's own brother (707). This negative injunction then becomes an excuse for displaying the poetic traditions available for teaching a *hetaîros* instead of a brother, since Hesiod goes on to say in

86 West 1978.33–34.
87 West p. 34.
88 West p. 34.
89 On which see Svenbro 1976.57–58.
90 Cf. N 1979a.228–242.

the next verse: "but if you *should* do so [make your *hetaîros* equal to your own brother], then . . ." (708). What follows in the next several verses is a veritable string of aphorisms that deal precisely with the topic of behavior toward one's *hetaîros* (708–722), and there are numerous striking analogues to the aphorisms explicitly or implicitly offered by Theognis to his *hetaîros* Kyrnos (for instance, *Works and Days* 710–711, 717–718, 720 and Theognis 155–158, 945, 1089–1090, respectively). Conversely, Theognis pointedly defines a true *phílos* 'friend' as a man who puts up with a difficult *hetaîros* as if he were his brother (97–100 = 1164a-d). By implication, one simply has to put up with a difficult brother. Theognis is uncertain whether his being a *phílos* 'friend' to Kyrnos is actually reciprocated: he challenges the fickle youth either to be a genuine *phílos* (89 = 1082e) or to declare that he is an *ekhthrós* 'enemy', overtly starting a *neîkos* 'quarrel' between the two of them (89–90). We may compare the *neîkos* between Hesiod and Perses, which is indeed overt (*Works and Days* 35) but at least is settled in the course of the poem. By contrast, no overt *neîkos* ever develops between Theognis and Kyrnos, and neither is Theognis ever assured that Kyrnos is a genuine *phílos.*

In reckoning with different samples of archaic Greek poetry, we must of course avoid the assumption that parallel passages are a matter of text referring to text; rather, it is simply that any given composition may refer to traditions other than the ones that primarily shaped it, and such different traditions may be attested elsewhere. Still, it is almost as if Theognis here were alluding to Perses, or as if Hesiod were actually giving advice on how to treat a fickle Kyrnos.

Hesiod and Perses are not the only key characters in the *Works and Days.* Their father's very essence retells some of the key themes that shape the composition. He came from Kyme in Asia Minor (636), sailing the seas in an effort to maintain his meager subsistence (633–634), until he settled on the mainland at Askra, a place that is harsh in the winter, unpleasant in the summer—in short, never agreeable (639–640).

This description of Hesiod's Askra, generally accepted as empirical truth by scholars from Strabo onward, seems exaggerated at best: the region is in fact fertile, relatively protected from winds, replete with beautiful scenery, and actually mild in the winter as well as the summer.[91] Why, then, does Hesiod present a deliberately negative picture of his native Askra? The answer emerges when we reconsider the city of Kyme, which, in sharp contrast with Askra, is the place that Hesiod's father left, "fleeing from poverty [*peníā*], not from wealth" (*Works and*

[91] Wallace 1974.8.

Days 637–638). We see here a pointed contrast with a theme characteristic of *ktísis* ('foundation') poetry, a genre that concerned itself with the great colonizations launched toward distant lands from cities of the mainland and its periphery.[92]

One of the thematic conventions of foundation poetry is that the great new cities that sprang up in Asia Minor and elsewhere in the era of colonizations were founded by intrepid adventurers fleeing from the poverty that overwhelmed them in the old cities. A worthy example is Kolophon, one of whose founders was 'the man in rags', *Rhákios,* who got his name "because of his poverty and shabby clothes" (scholia to Apollonius of Rhodes 1.308).[93] So also in the poetic traditions of Megara, which celebrated the city's role as starting point for the foundation of many great cities, including Byzantium, in the era of colonizations.[94] Theognis of Megara urges that one must travel over land and sea in search of relief from baneful *peníā* 'poverty' (Theognis 179–180). In sum, when Hesiod's father traveled all the way to Askra from Kyme, thereby fleeing *peníā* 'poverty' (*Works and Days* 638), he was in effect reversing the conventional pattern of colonization as narrated in *ktísis* poetry.

To repeat, we have here a pointed negative reference as well: Hesiod's father fled from *peníā* 'poverty' (*Works and Days* 638) and did not flee from wealth (637). The theme of wealth conjures up a distinctive feature of foundation poetry, where the colonizers advance from rags to riches, eventually making their new cities fabulously wealthy.[95] Again a worthy example is the city of Kolophon, which in time grew excessively rich (Athenaeus 526a, quoting Xenophanes of Kolophon F 3 W). From Theognis 1103–1104 we learn that the mark of this excess was *húbris* 'outrage', which led to Kolophon's utter destruction. This fate, as the poet warns, is now looming over Megara as well. Further, we see that the *húbris* afflicting Megara is manifested specifically as greed for the possessions of others, and that it brings about the ultimate debasement of the city's nobility (Theognis 833–836).

Such warnings about debasement and even destruction by *húbris* recall the Hesiodic scheme of the two cities: while the city of *díkē* becomes fertile and rich (*Works and Days* 225–235), so that no one needs to sail the seas for a living (236–237), the city of *húbris* becomes sterile and poor (238–247), and its people are afflicted either by wars (246) or by the storms that Zeus sends against them as they sail the seas

92 For a collection of fragments and commentary, see Schmid 1947.
93 Schmid pp. 28–29.
94 See Hanell 1934.95–97.
95 N 1985a.51–60.

(247). From the standpoint of *ktísis* poetry, as we have seen in the instance of Kolophon, the same city can begin at one extreme and end at the other. As he leaves Kyme, Hesiod's father flees the poverty of a city implicitly ruined by *húbris* (*Works and Days* 637–638), and he is in effect fleeing from the debris of what had been the golden age of colonization (for a Homeric reference to foundation poetry, specifically to narrative conventions that picture colonization in a golden age setting, see *Odyssey* ix 116–141).[96]

Settling down in Askra, Hesiod's father has found a setting marked by a stylized harshness that conjures up the iron age.[97] Whereas *díkē* and *húbris* characterize the golden and the silver ages, respectively (*Works and Days* 124, 134), both characterize the iron age simultaneously. So, too, with Askra: it is neither a city of *díkē* nor a city of *húbris*. Still, the place is full of characteristics that pull in one direction or the other. For example, the name *Askrā* itself means 'sterile oak' (Hesychius, s.v. Ἄσκρη· δρῦς ἄκαρπος). While barrenness marks the city of *húbris* (*Works and Days* 242–244), a fertile acorn-bearing oak is a prime image in the city of *díkē* (232–233: note here the phonetic similarity of *drûs ákrē* 'top of the oak' with *Askrē*). The local lore as reported by Pausanias (9.29.1) has it that Askra was founded by *Oioklos* ('he who is famous for his sheep': cf. *Works and Days* 234 and *Theogony* 26), son of a personified Askra who mated with Poseidon; and that it was also founded by Otos and Ephialtes, who were the "first" to sacrifice on Helikon to the Muses. These two brothers, however, are elsewhere clearly exponents of *húbris* (*Odyssey* xi 305–320, especially 317 in conjunction with *Works and Days* 132, preliminary to the destruction of the Silver Generation because of their *húbris*, verse 134).

As we have seen earlier, the struggle of *díkē* against *húbris* in the iron age of mankind appears at first to be a lost cause, but the corresponding struggle, in Askra, of Hesiod as exponent of *díkē* against Perses as exponent of *húbris* turns into a universalized triumph for justice and for the authority of Zeus. In this light we may consider the meaning of the name *Pérsēs*. Since this character, unlike Hesiod, is confined to the *Works and Days*, the meaning may have something to do with the central themes inherited by this composition. Now, the form *Pérsēs* is a residual variant, through a split in declensional patterns, of *Perseús*, and we may compare such other formal pairs as *Kíssēs* (*Iliad* XI 223) and Classical *Kisseús*.[98] Moreover, the form *Perseús* is related to the compound formant

[96] Cf. N 1979a.180–181.
[97] Cf. West 1978.197.
[98] For these and other examples, see Perpillou 1973.239–240.

persi- of the verb *pérthō* 'destroy',[99] and it is not without interest that the direct objects of *pérthō* are confined in Homeric tradition to *pólis* 'city', its synonyms *ptolíethron* and *ástu*, or the name of a polis. Since Perses is primarily an exponent of *húbris* in the *Works and Days*, we may recall the traditional theme expressed in the poetry of Theognis: *húbris* destroys the city (1103–1104, for example).

Of course *húbris* destroys cities only figuratively: more precisely, it is Zeus who destroys cities because of their *húbris*—which is actually what he does to the archetypical city of *húbris* at *Works and Days* 238–247 (especially 239, 242). In this sense the name *Pérsēs* formalizes the negative side of what Zeus does to those mortals who are marked by *húbris*. Thus it may be significant that Perses is addressed as *dîon génos* 'descendant of Zeus' by his brother Hesiod at *Works and Days* 299—and that this title is elsewhere applied only to the children of Zeus (for instance, Artemis at *Iliad* IX 538). Moreover, from the fifth century onward, the name of the father of Hesiod and Perses is attested as *Dîos* (see, for example, Ephorus of Kyme FGH 70 F 1). Thus the split between Hesiod and Perses as exponents of *díkē* and *húbris*, corresponding to the split between the city of *díkē* and the city of *húbris*, is genetically reconciled in a figure whose name carries the essence of Zeus, much as Hesiod and Perses become reconciled in the course of the *Works and Days* through the utter defeat of *húbris* by the *díkē* of Zeus.

Hesiod's pervasive affinities with Zeus, as with Apollo and his Olympian Muses, are paralleled by his affinities with the goddess Hekate as she is celebrated in *Theogony* 404–452. Like Zeus, this goddess is an ideal paradigm for the pan-Hellenic nature of Hesiodic poetry. Thanks to the sanctions of the supreme god (*Theogony* 411–415, 423–425), Hekate has title to a share in the divine functions of all the gods (421–422). Accordingly, the invocation of Hekate at a sacrifice is tantamount to a blanket invocation of all the other gods as well (416–420). Because of her relatively recent, maybe even foreign, origins,[100] this synthetic goddess Hekate is an ideal pan-Hellenic figure (we may compare the choice of "foreign" Nyse as the genuine birthplace of Dionysus in the *Homeric Hymn to Dionysus* 1.8–9): she can manifest even her ritual dimensions in Hesiodic poetry, unlike the historically older gods who are each worshiped in different ways by each city-state—and whose ritual dimensions are therefore consistently screened out by the pan-Hellenic poems of Hesiod as well as Homer.

[99] Perpillou p. 231.
[100] West 1966.278.

The parallelism of Hekate with Apollo and his Muses also has a bearing on the pan-Hellenic authority of Hesiod. We start with the fact that Apollo and Hekate are actually cousins: their mothers, Leto and *Asteríā*, are sisters (*Theogony* 405–410), and the latter name is identical to the "god-given" name of Delos, Apollo's birthplace (Pindar *Paean* 5.42 in conjunction with Callimachus *Hymn* 4.36; also Pindar F 33c.6 SM). The shared grandparents of Apollo and Hekate are *Phoíbē* and *Koîos*; the first name is the feminine equivalent of Apollo's primary epithet *Phoîbos* (as at *Theogony* 14), while the second is cognate with the Indic *kaví-* 'poet/seer'[101] (we may compare the discussion, above, of Apollo's relationship to the generic *aoidós* 'singer/poet' and *mántis* 'seer'). The name *Hekátē* is the feminine equivalent of Apollo's epithet *Hékatos* (as at *Hymn to Apollo* 1). Most important, the name of Hekate's father, *Pérsēs* (*Theogony* 409), is identical to that of Hesiod's brother.

Hekate is the only legitimate child of Perses the god, and as such she is *mounogenḗs* 'only-born' (*Theogony* 426, 448). By contrast, Perses the man is distinctly not the only child of *Dîos*, being the brother of Hesiod, who in turn implicitly wishes he were an only child: he advises that the ideal household should indeed have a *mounogenḗs* 'only-born' to inherit the possessions of the father (*Works and Days* 376–377). What would happen if Hekate were not *mounogenḗs* is suggested by the story about the birth of *Eris* 'Strife' in *Works and Days* 11–26, presented as a traditional alternative to the story reflected in *Theogony* 225. The *Works and Days* affirms that there is not just a *moûnon . . . génos* 'single birth' of Eris (11), the version that we see in the *Theogony* (225), but that there are in fact two Erides (*Works and Days* 11–12). The younger and secondary one of these Erides is negative in her stance toward mankind, but the older and primary one is positive: she instills the spirit of competition that motivates even the idler to work the land for a living (*Works and Days* 12–24). In that *Eris* is parent of *Neîkos* 'quarreling' (*Theogony* 229), the *neîkos* between Hesiod and Perses (*Works and Days* 35) is motivated by Eris. At first it seems as if it had been the maleficent and secondary Eris that had done so, but, as the *neîkos* eventually reaches a resolution with the triumph of Hesiod's *díkē* over Perses' *húbris* in the *Works and Days*, we realize that it must have been the beneficent and primary Eris all along.[102] The point is, just as an undivided negative Eris can split into a primary positive and secondary negative pair, so also an undivided positive Hekate could by implication split into a primary negative and a

[101] DELG 553 (cf. also Greek *koéō* 'perceive', Latin *caueō* 'beware, take precautions, provide guarantees').
[102] N 1979a.313–314.

secondary positive pair. Thus it is beneficial for mankind that Hekate should remain an only child: the primary child in a hypothetical split of the *mounogenḗs* Hekate figure would presumably take after the father *Pérsēs*, whose name conveys the negative response of gods to the *húbris* of mankind.[103] Similarly, Hesiod and Perses themselves are a primary positive and secondary negative pair, while the secondary child *Pérsēs* has a name that conveys, again, the negative response of Zeus to the *húbris* of mankind. As for the father of Hesiod and Perses, his name, *Dîos*—to repeat—carries the essence of Zeus.

The special thematic relationship of Hesiod with the figure of Hekate raises questions about a revealing detail in the *Works and Days.* Despite all the advice given by Hesiod to Perses about sailing, the poet pointedly says that he himself has never sailed on a ship except for the one time when he traveled from Aulis to the island of Euboea (650–651). There follows a pointed reference to the tradition claiming that the Achaean expedition to Troy was launched from Aulis (651–653). The *Iliad* acknowledges Aulis as the starting point of the Trojan expedition (II 303–304), and according to most versions it was there that Agamemnon sacrificed his daughter Iphigeneia to Artemis (for instance, *Cypria* Proclus summary p. 104.12–20 Allen). In the Hesiodic *Catalogue of Women* (F 23a.15–26 MW), we read that the sacrificed Iphigeneia (here called Iphimede, verses 15, 17) was thereupon made immortal by Artemis, and that, as a goddess, Iphigeneia became Artemis-of-the-Crossroads, otherwise known as Hekate (Hesiod F 23b = Pausanias 1.43.1).

Hekate, as the *Theogony* (435–438) tells us, aids those who compete in contests, and the poet cites athletic contests in particular. When Hesiod crosses over from Aulis to Euboea, he is traveling to an occasion of contests, the Funeral Games of Amphidamas at Chalkis (*Works and Days* 654–656). Moreover, Hesiod competes in a poetic contest at the games—and wins (656–657). He goes home with a tripod as prize and dedicates it to his native Helikonian Muses (657–658). Finishing his narrative about the prize that he won in the poetic contest, Hesiod pointedly says again that this episode marks the only time that he ever made a sea voyage (660).

Hesiod's only sea voyage is ostentatiously brief, with the distance between Aulis and Euboea amounting to some 65 meters of water.[104] There is a built-in antithesis here with the long sea voyage undertaken by

[103] On the maleficent aspects of Hekate, as represented in archaic Greek iconography: Vermeule 1979.109.
[104] West 1978.320.

the Achaeans when they sailed to Troy. Perhaps the antithesis was meant to extend further: Aulis is an original setting for the *Catalogue of Ships* tradition, transferred to a Trojan setting in the *Iliad* only because this particular epic starts the action in the final year of the war. But even the *Iliad* acknowledges Aulis as the starting point of the Achaean flotilla. Moreover, the strong Homeric emphasis on navigation as a key to the Achaeans' survival (for example, *Iliad* XVI 80–82)[105] is in sharp contrast with the strong Hesiodic emphasis on the poet's personal inexperience in navigation—especially in view of Hesiod's additional emphasis on Aulis as the starting point for not only his short sea voyage but also for the long one undertaken by the Achaeans. Perhaps, then, this passage reveals an intended differentiation of Hesiodic from Homeric poetry.

In this light it is not out of place to consider a variant verse reported by the scholia at *Works and Days* 657. In this variant we find Hesiod declaring that his adversary in the poetic contest that he won was none other than Homer himself:

> ὕμνῳ νικήσαντ' ἐν Χαλκίδι θεῖον Ὅμηρον
>
> variant at *Works and Days* 657
>
> defeating god-like Homer in song, at Chalkis

instead of

> ὕμνῳ νικήσαντα φέρειν τρίποδ' ὠτώεντα
>
> Hesiod *Works and Days* 657
>
> winning in song, [I say that I] carried away [as a prize] a tripod with handles on it

There is no proof for the conventional explanation that this variant verse is a mere interpolation (with the supposedly interpolated verse matching a verse found in an epigram ascribed to Hesiod in *Contest of Homer and Hesiod* p. 233.213–214 Allen). Also, to argue that this verse may be part of a genuine variant passage is not to say that the surviving version about the tripod is therefore not genuine. In archaic Greek poetry, reported variants may at any time reflect not some false textual alteration but, rather, a genuine traditional alternative that has been gradually ousted in the course of the poem's crystallization into a fixed text.[106]

Furthermore, there is an attested traditional story that tells of the contest of Homer and Hesiod (*Contest* pp. 225–238 Allen), juxtaposing the

[105] Commentary in N 1979a.333–347.
[106] Cf. Lamberton 1988.45–48.

Life of Homer and the *Life of Hesiod* traditions. In its present form it is a late and accretive reworking that has generated much controversy about its authorship, a problem that cannot be addressed here.[107] One thing is sure, however: the basic premise of the story—that Homer and Hesiod competed in a poetic contest—exhibits the characteristics of a traditional theme. This theme, moreover, corresponds to a basic truth about archaic Greek society: the performance of poetry, from the days of the oral poets all the way to the era of the rhapsodes, was by its nature a matter of competition.[108]

Prospects

To treat Hesiod simply as an author will only accentuate our inability to appreciate fully his poems, in that he represents a culmination of what must have been countless successive generations of singers interacting with their audiences throughout the Greek-speaking world. Whatever poetic devices we admire in the poems have been tested many thousands of times, we may be sure, on the most discerning audiences. Even the unmistakable signs of a Hesiodic poem's structural unity are surely the result of streamlining by the tradition itself, achieved in the continuous process of a poem's being recomposed in each new performance. Instead of referring to *a poem* in such a context, moreover, it would be better to speak in terms of *a tradition of performing a certain kind of poem.*

With the important added factor of pan-Hellenic diffusion, the successive recompositions of Hesiodic poetry could in time become ever less varied, more and more crystallized, as the requirements of composition became increasingly universalized. Of course the rate of such crystallization, and even the date, could have been different in each poem or even in different parts of the same poem. From this point of view, we can in principle include as Hesiodic even a composition like the *Shield of Herakles,* though it may contain references to the visual arts datable to the early sixth century. Scholars are too quick to dismiss this poem as not a genuine work on the basis of the dating alone, and it then becomes all the easier for them to underrate its artistic qualities on the grounds that it is merely an imitation of Hesiod.

[107] See Janko 1982.259–260n80; cf. also Dunkel 1979.252–253. For a useful perspective on the problem: Lamberton pp. 5–10.

[108] Detailed discussion in Durante 1976.197–198. Cf. also Dunkel 1979 and N 1979a.311 §2n6. For an example of a myth about such a competition, I cite the story of a contest between Arctinus of Miletus and Lesches of Mytilene, two of the poets of the Epic Cycle (Phaenias F 33 Wehrli, in Clement *Stromateis* 1.131.6).

Critics also have noticed that the conclusion of the *Theogony* at verses 901–1020 is formally and even stylistically distinct from the previous parts of the poem.[109] But this part is also functionally distinct from the rest, and we may note in general that different themes in oral poetry tend to exhibit different trends in formal—even linguistic—development. To put it another way: different contexts are characterized by different language. An explanation along these lines is surely preferable to a favorite scenario of many experts, in which the *Theogony* was somehow composed by a combination of one Hesiod and a plethora of pseudo-Hesiods. Worse still, some will even attribute the constitution of the poem to a dreary succession of redactors. Whatever the arguments for multiple authorship may be, there is predictably little agreement about how much or how little can be attributed to the real Hesiod. In sum, it seems preferable to treat all Hesiodic poems, including the fragments, as variable manifestations of a far more extensive phenomenon, which is Hesiodic poetry.

Another obstacle to our understanding of Hesiodic poetry, perhaps even harder to overcome, is the commonplace visualization of Hesiod as a primitive landlubber of a peasant who is struggling to express himself in a cumbersome and idiosyncratic poetic medium clumsily forged out of an epic medium that he has not fully mastered. Hesiod's self-dramatization as one who works the land for a living is thus assumed to be simply a historical fact, which can then serve as a basis for condescending speculations about an eighth-century Boeotian peasant's lowly level of thinking. It is as if the poetry of Hesiod, and of Homer, for that matter, were primitive raw material that somehow became arbitrarily universalized by the Greeks as a point of reference for their poetry and rhetoric in particular, and as the foundation of their civilization in general. Of course, if critics go on to treat such poetry as a producer rather than a product of the Greek poetic heritage, it is easy to find fault whenever we fail to understand. Over the years Hesiod especially has been condemned for many offenses against the sensibilities of modern literary critics. Perhaps the most shortsighted of the many charges leveled against him is that he is, on occasion, capable of forgetting his starting point.

There are, to be sure, those who have articulately conveyed the cohesiveness and precision of Hesiodic poetry. I single out the work of Jean-Pierre Vernant, whose findings about such key Hesiodic themes as Prometheus and the ascendancy of Zeus are so definitive that no attempt need be made here to offer a summary.[110] There is also the work of

[109] West 1966.398.
[110] Vernant 1974.103–120, 177–194.

Peter Walcot, whose repertoire of Near Eastern parallels to aspects of the *Theogony* and the *Works and Days* serves to illuminate the inner workings of Hesiodic composition.[111] The value of these analogues is not to be underrated, and the absence of any mention of them up to this point can be remedied by citing Martin West's commentaries, which contain an illustrative collection of references.[112] It is worth noting, however, that such Near Eastern parallelisms may in any given instance be a matter of typology rather than of direct borrowing. Given the pervasiveness of cross-cultural parallelisms in patterns of mythmaking, even the most striking convergences in detail may turn out to be nothing more than a typological analogue: I cite for example the Inca parallels to the Pandora myth,[113] which seem closer to the Hesiodic version than do some of the Near Eastern parallels generally cited as Hesiod's "sources."

One of the most neglected areas in the general study of Hesiod, as also in this specific presentation, is the artistry of the poems. With our fragmentary understanding of the Hesiodic tradition, some special effects that would have delighted the intended audience will be forever lost to us, while others will emerge only in their barest outlines. It seems appropriate to bring this survey to a close with one such dimly perceived set of special effects, illustrating simultaneously the richness of the poetry and our own poverty of understanding.

In *Works and Days* 504–563, a portrait of winter and its harshness, the North Wind is described as it descends upon trees along the side of a mountain, penetrating the skin of all living things in its path with its cold blast (507–518). The imagery here is pointedly sexual, as a study of parallel imagery in other Indo-European tradition clearly shows.[114] Then follows (519–525) the contrasting image of a sensuous young girl taking a bath in her warm and comfortable boudoir, safely sheltered from the piercing wind and "not yet knowing the ways of golden Aphrodite" (521); meanwhile, the *anósteos* 'boneless one' is gnawing at his own foot in his cold and wretched haunts (524–525). Now, the Greek word *anósteos* has an Indic cognate *anasthá-* 'boneless one', a kenning for "penis,"[115] while the Greek word for 'gnaw', *téndō* (525), is related to the Irish *teinm* (*laído*), 'gnawing [of marrow]', a magical process leading to *knowledge* by divination.[116] Thus the 'boneless one', by gnawing his foot,

[111] Walcot 1966.
[112] West 1966, 1978.
[113] Sinclair 1932.13.
[114] Watkins 1978a.231.
[115] References in Watkins p. 233.
[116] Watkins p. 232.

is one who "knows," in contrast with the inexperienced young girl, who does not "know" (εἰδυῖα 521).

But the allusiveness extends even further. The 'boneless one' is also to be understood as an octopus (compare the syntax of *Works and Days* 524, containing *anósteos*, with that of Hesiod F 204.129 MW, containing *átrikhos* 'hairless one' = snake), an animal that is conventionally pictured in Greek lore as eating its own feet when it is hungry.[117] The hungry octopus gnawing at its foot is described as living in cold and wretched haunts (*Works and Days* 525), and this image of poverty takes us back to an earlier image of a poor man in winter, holding his swollen foot in his emaciated hand (496–497); the Proclus commentary here cites an Ephesian law to the effect that a child could not be exposed until his father's feet were swollen with famine.[118] Our thoughts turn to *Oidípous* 'he whose feet are swollen', and the story of his exposure.

In this connection we come to yet another occurrence of the word *poús* 'foot' in this passage about winter: at *Works and Days* 533–535, the winter storm is described as making everyone hunch over like a *trípous* 'three-footed' man (533; compare 518). This kenning, which designates a man leaning on a walking stick, corresponds to the *aínigma* 'riddle' of the Sphinx as solved by *Oidípous* (Sophocles *Oedipus Tyrannus* 393, 1525).[119] Like the 'boneless one' who 'gnaws' his foot (*Works and Days* 524) and thereby *knows* by way of divination, Oedipus *knows* by virtue of solving the riddle of the Sphinx. The oracular tone of this passage is sustained later (at *Works and Days* 571) with another kenning, *pheréoikos* 'he who carries his house' (= snail), which is introduced by the expression *all' hopót' an* 'but whenever . . .' (571), a frequent introductory phrase in oracles.[120]

This much said, we are still typically far from understanding all the implications of this passage, just as we are far from understanding all that can be understood about Hesiod and his world.

A definitive assessment of Hesiod's poems is elusive, since we still know so little about their background. The best hope is that there will be further progress in rigorous internal analysis and in systematic comparison with other attested Greek poetic traditions, so that tomorrow's reader may better appreciate the mechanics and esthetics of Hesiodic poetry. Even so, we shall always fall far short, unable ever to recover all that this poetry presupposes of its own audience at large.

[117] References in West 1978.290.
[118] West p. 284.
[119] Cf. Asclepiades FGH 12 F 71 and the comments of West 1978.293.
[120] West p. 302.

PART II

THE HELLENIZATION OF INDO-EUROPEAN MYTH AND RITUAL

CHAPTER 4

Patroklos, Concepts of Afterlife, and the Indic Triple Fire

The rituals occasioned by the Funeral of Patroklos, as narrated in *Iliad* XXIII, have been compared with the royal funerary rituals of the Hittites.[1] The parallelisms in details and in ideology suggest a common Indo-European heritage, in view of additional comparative evidence available from the Indic traditions.[2] If indeed the Funeral of Patroklos reflects an ideology so early as to be of Indo-European heritage, then a basic criterion for the dating of narrative traditions in the Homeric poems has to be revised. Archaeologists tend to interpret the cremation of Patroklos in particular and of Homeric heroes in general as inspired by practices that went into effect only in the first millennium B.C., when cremation and inhumation are found to exist side by side; in this respect, then, Homeric poetry is supposed to reflect a near-contemporary state of affairs, as opposed to a more archaic heritage dating back to the Mycenaean era of the second millennium B.C., a period when cremation is sporadic and inhumation is the norm.[3] The comparative evidence, on the other hand, now suggests that the procedures and ideologies of cremation as attested in Homeric poetry are in fact so archaic as to predate the second millennium B.C., thus reflecting—albeit distantly— customs that go back to a time even before the entry into Greece, in the beginning of the second millennium, of the Indo-European language that

[1] Christmann-Franck 1971, esp. pp. 61–64; cf. Vieyra 1965. The edition of the Hittite royal funerary texts: Otten 1958.

[2] Cf. Lowenstam 1981.152 on *Rig-Veda* 10.16.4 and 10.16.7 as compared with *Iliad* XXIII 167–169; in both the Indic and the Greek passages, the corpse is covered with layers of the fat of sacrificial animals.

[3] Cf. Andronikos 1968, esp. p. 76.

ultimately became the Greek language. Even more important for my purposes, the comparative evidence also suggests that the cremation of Patroklos is a traditional theme founded upon concepts of afterlife beyond Hades.

For the moment, I choose the word "afterlife" instead of "rebirth" or "eschatology." These other words too are pertinent to my inquiry: as we shall see in what follows, the Indo-European languages, Greek included, abound with earlier patterns of thought concerning life after death.[4] Still, it is useful to start with the most general term possible.

The concept of afterlife, as I argue, is implicit in the Homeric narrative of the cremation of Patroklos. Comparable concepts, as we shall see, are explicitly attested in Indic institutions, especially as represented in prayers to the god Savitr̥ and in rituals involving the so-called Triple Fire. After a detailed exposition of the Indic evidence, soon to follow, we shall also see that closely analogous concepts are represented—albeit indirectly— in the Greek evidence, specifically in the diction of Homeric poetry.[5]

In correlating various concepts of afterlife with the practice of cremation, I am not about to claim that cremation was the definitive Indo-European funerary ritual. I argue only that cremation was clearly one of perhaps several different types of Indo-European funerary ritual. In any discussion of differences in funerary practices, as in the case of cremation and inhumation, I wish to stress from the start that no universals can be assumed for the thought-patterns—let us continue to call them ideologies—traditionally associated with such practices. The ritual dimensions of cremation and inhumation may "mean" different things in different societies or in different phases of the same society.[6] Where the two practices coexist in one society, they may conceivably convey two distinct meanings.[7] In other situations, coexistence may reflect a blurring of distinctions.[8] In some contexts, a practice like inhumation may not even imply anything about a given society's concepts of afterlife.[9] In other contexts, however, there is good reason to think that the same

[4] For an introduction to the topic of "Indo-European eschatology," cf. Lincoln 1986.119–140.

[5] My comparative approach leads to conclusions that differ, at least in part, from those of some more recent studies on the Greek concept of the "soul," such as Claus 1981 and Bremmer 1983. For an accounting of these works, as well as those of Ireland and Steel 1975, Darcus 1979ab, and Garland 1981, I cite the dissertation of Caswell 1986, to be published as a monograph.

[6] Cf. Bremmer 1983.94–95.

[7] Cf. Bérard 1970.48–53, with reference to archaic Eretria.

[8] Cf. Bremmer 1983.95.

[9] Bremmer p. 95.

practice of inhumation does indeed imply the concept of rebirth.[10] To take the stance of doubting in general the presence of such an ideology, on the grounds that "a simple inhumation without the accompanying idea of rebirth is often found,"[11] seems to me unjustified.[12]

Let us begin with the briefest possible summary of the evidence from the Indic Vedas, representing the oldest attested Indic concepts of after-life.[13] Before death the realm of consciousness, of both rational and emotional functions, is the *mánas-*. When death occurs, this *mánas-* is separated from the body, and in the process of this separation *mánas-* can be either equated or paired with the word *ásu-*. After death, *mánas-* and *ásu-* designate the disembodied conveyor of the dead person's identity, sometimes represented as a frail and vulnerable homunculus who is a miniature vision of the deceased as he seemed in life.[14] Eventually, *mánas-* and/or *ásu-* arrive at the "third sky," where the *pitṛ́-s* 'ancestors' abide.[15] The *mánas-* and/or *ásu-* are destined to be reintegrated with the body, and cremation of the body is the key to this eventual reintegration.[16]

From a preliminary comparison with the archaic Greek evidence, we see some striking convergences and divergences. Before death the realm of consciousness, of rational and emotional functions, is the *thūmós*,[17] which can be paired in this context with the word *ménos*.[18]

[10] Cf. Bérard p. 52 on the inhumation of children in archaic Eretria.

[11] Bremmer 1983.97.

[12] More on distinct ideologies associated with cremation, inhumation, and exposition in chapters 5 and 6 below.

[13] For a most useful synthesis, see Arbman 1926/1927. These articles also offer important typological observations on the Greek evidence. For bibliography surveying the influence of Arbman's work on further scholarship: Bremmer p. 10.

[14] In the story of Sāvitrī, for example (*Mahābhārata* 3.281, critical ed.), Yama the king of the ancestors and god of the dead extracts from the body of Sāvitrī's husband a thumb-sized person, whereupon the body's breathing stops and symptoms of death appear. See the commentary by Arbman 1927.79, 105–106, 110.

[15] For a collection of passages, see Oldenberg 1917.533–534. See also his pp. 527–528 for a survey of passages in the *Atharva-Veda* where incantations are offered for the dying: it is a persistent theme that *mánas-* and *ásu-* must stay in the body for the dying to stay alive.

[16] See Arbman 1927.90–100, esp. p. 93. This reintegration of body and *mánas-/ásu-* is envisioned as an eschatological process. In *Jaiminīya-Brāhmaṇa* 1.49.1 and following, for example, the identity of the deceased leaves the body and "goes from the smoke into the night" (*dhūmād vai rātrim apy eti*) by way of cremation, then moving from the night into the day and then into the dark half of the month and then into the light half of the month and then into the month itself, whereupon the body and *ásu-* are finally reunited. Note that the original separation of identity and body is here simultaneous with cremation, whereas in other versions it is simultaneous with the moment of death. For more on the theme of *dhūmá-* 'smoke' in the fire of cremation, see pp. 115–116.

[17] See Arbman 1926.185–191 and Böhme 1929.69–74.

[18] Instances of *thūmós* and *ménos* paired: *Iliad* V 470, VI 72, XI 291, etc. See also N

When death occurs, the *thūmós* is separated from the body, and in the process of this separation *thūmós* can be paired with the words *ménos* or *psūkhḗ*.[19] After death, *psūkhḗ* designates the disembodied conveyor of the dead person's identity, sometimes represented as a homunculus who is a miniature vision of the deceased as he seemed in life.[20] I should stress that the *psūkhḗ* is merely a *conveyor* of identity, not the identity itself: in Homeric diction, the word *autós* 'self' actually designates the body, which the *psūkhḗ* leaves behind when the hero dies (e.g. *Iliad* I 3–4).[21]

Before death, the word *psūkhḗ* is as a rule excluded from designating the realm of consciousness, of rational and emotional functions;[22] after death, the words *thūmós* and *ménos* are as a rule excluded from designating the disembodied conveyor of the dead person's identity.[23] Only in the process of death can all three words *thūmós*/*ménos*/*psūkhḗ* be fully synonymous.[24] As they are separated from the body, they head for Hades.

1979a.136–137 on *Iliad* XX 174 as contrasted with 171. Both words embrace physical as well as mental aspects: on *thūmós* see Redfield 1975.173 and on *ménos* see N 1974a.266–269. Further work on *thūmós*: Caswell 1986.

[19] See Warden 1971 for a list of Homeric attestations. It has been argued that *ménos* does not technically leave the body at death, in that the verb λύθη 'was set loose', for which *ménos* serves as subject in passages like *Iliad* V 296, conveys "a metaphor comparing the collapsing of the dead with the collapsing of horses when they are unharnessed after a tiring ride" (Bremmer p. 76). But we should note the pairing of *ménos* with *psūkhḗ* as a correlative subject in this and other passages such as *Iliad* VIII 123, 315; the fact is, the *psūkhḗ* is indeed regularly conceived as leaving the body at the moment of death (e.g. XVI 856). So, too, with the other potential correlate of *ménos*, that is, *thūmós*: it, too, leaves the body at the moment of death (e.g. XXIII 880). Moreover, the act of releasing a horse, as conveyed by the verb *lúō* 'set loose', can be a matter of *starting to drive it away* (as e.g. at *Iliad* X 498), not just *stopping it* after having driven it (as e.g. at V 369). In other words, the combination of λύθη 'was set loose' with *ménos* as subject may imply that the horse races off while the chariot from which it has just been unharnessed is left behind. Similarly in metaphorical descriptions of fatigue, *ménos* can be visualized as becoming separated from the body (cf. the collocation of *dia-krī́nō* 'separate' with *ménos* at II 387).

[20] For representations of the *psūkhḗ* of Patroklos and even of Achilles as such homunculi in Black Figure iconography, see Stähler 1967, esp. pp. 32–33, 44. On the Münster Hydria (inv. no. 565), the miniature figure of Patroklos is actually labeled ΦΣΥΧΕ '*psūkhḗ*': Stähler p. 14. On pp. 28–29, Stähler argues cogently that such iconographical representations of *psūkhḗ* have a "pre-Homeric" heritage. See further at p. 220 below.

[21] Cf. N 1979a.208. The concept of *psūkhḗ* has a built-in tension between identity and nonidentity, as Jean-Pierre Vernant (1985 [1962].330) observes in connection with the *psūkhḗ* of Patroklos when it appears to Achilles: "c'est la présence de l'ami, mais c'est aussi son absence irrémédiable; c'est Patrocle en personne, mais aussi bien un souffle, une fumée, une ombre ou l'envol d'un oiseau."

[22] See Arbman 1926.191–198. I disagree, however, with the argument against any connection between *psūkhḗ* and the semantic sphere of breathing: see pp. 90–91.

[23] See Arbman 1926.185–191 and 1927.165. Consider also the Homeric expression νεκύων ἀμενηνὰ κάρηνα 'persons of the dead, without *ménos*' (*Odyssey* x 521, 536; xi 29, 49). On the Greek visualizations of "head" as "person," see Warden 1971.97.

[24] Cf. Böhme 1929.103; also Schnaufer 1970.180.

In some Homeric variations, however, arrival at Hades may be delayed. For example, after the *psūkhḗ* of Patroklos has been separated from his body by death (*Iliad* XVI 856), it leaves for Hades (XVI 856), but is thwarted from entering (XXIII 72–74); in a vision (XXIII 65ff.) the *psūkhḗ* of Patroklos asks Achilles to give his body a funeral in general (XXIII 71) and a cremation in particular (XXIII 76), so that his *psūkhḗ* may finally enter Hades (XXIII 71, 75–76). Achilles is astounded that the *psūkhḗ* of Patroklos has *phrénes* (XXIII 103–104).[25] We must note that this word *phrénes* designates the physical localization of *thūmós*[26] and *ménos*[27] in the living. Indeed, what the *psūkhḗ* of Patroklos says to Achilles in *Iliad* XXIII 65–92 are the words of one who appears to be conscious of himself, in possession of his rational and emotional faculties.[28] By implication, the *psūkhḗ* of Patroklos can become detached or distinct from his *thūmós*/*ménos* and become free to enter Hades only after his body is cremated.[29]

On the surface, then, it seems as if the Homeric poems point to Hades as the ultimate destination of the *psūkhḗ*. Moreover, once the process of cremation enables the *psūkhḗ* to arrive at Hades, it is liable to lose consciousness as well as rational and emotional faculties, and we are left with the initial impression that the dead person stays dead forever. Here we see a major divergence from the Indic formulation, where the *mánas-* and/or *ásu-* not only preserve consciousness and the faculties but also become eventually reintegrated with the body *by way of cremation.* Yet the divergence lies not in what the Greek formulation says about the afterlife but rather in what it leaves unsaid. Let us keep in mind that, conscious or unconscious, the *psūkhḗ* is a conveyor of identity. Thus the door is still left open for the possibility that the *psūkhḗ* may yet be reintegrated with the body. A word like *thūmós* or like *ménos* may at first seem from our point of view more appropriate for designating the aspect that is separated and then hypothetically reintegrated with the body, since both *thūmós* and *ménos* designate consciousness and the faculties. In fact, as we have just noted, *thūmós* and *ménos* are synonymous with *psūkhḗ* at the moment of death. Yet these very words *thūmós* and *ménos* cease to apply to the identity once it passes through the gates of Hades: from here on,

[25] See Schnaufer pp. 77–79 for an interpretation of these two verses; the ἀτάρ of verse 104, as he shows, indicates the unexpected and contradictory factor (that is, the presence of *phrénes*). Achilles is in effect saying: "So there really *is* a *psūkhḗ*, even outside of Hades, a mere image—and yet it is conscious (= has *phrénes*)!"

[26] E.g. *Iliad* X 232, IX 462, XIII 487, etc.

[27] E.g. *Iliad* I 103, XXI 145; *Odyssey* i 89, etc.

[28] Moreover, the *psūkhḗ* of Patroklos is at this time *not* miniature (*Iliad* XXIII 66).

[29] At p. 87n16, we have seen a corresponding Indic theme, that the identity of the dead person is separated from his body by way of the *dhūmá-* 'smoke' of cremation.

the identity is conveyed by *psūkhḗ* only. This suspension of synonymity is itself telling us something: that the *psūkhḗ* once had an affinity with consciousness and the faculties—an affinity which is then suspended in Hades.

My interpretation here differs from the view that any absence of synonymity between "Ichseele" (e.g. *thūmós/ ménos*) and "Psycheseele" (e.g. *psūkhḗ*) in the mythopoeic thinking of any "primitive" culture invariably implies an original distinctness between the two concepts.[30] What I propose is that the distinctness, as in the case of *thūmós/ ménos* on one side and *psūkhḗ* on the other, may be a secondary development—a matter of secondary specialization. In other words, the convergence in meaning between *thūmós/ ménos* and *psūkhḗ* may be primary and the divergence, secondary. Then we can account for such rare "exceptions" as *Iliad* VII 131 (where the *thūmós* goes to Hades) and XXI 569 (where the *psūkhḗ* abides in a living hero) as residual traces of an earlier ideology where *thūmós/ ménos* and *psūkhḗ* were as yet undifferentiated in realms where they are later differentiated.

My interpretation is also at odds with the view that the Homeric *psūkhḗ* is not a "Psycheseele" but a mere "Totengeist."[31] The reasoning behind this disputed view is based on the conventional diction describing the swooning of a hero: the *psūkhḗ* is regularly envisaged as leaving the body, *but it is never mentioned as returning when the hero revives.*[32] Only the *thūmós* or *ménos* are mentioned as returning to the hero when he is revived.[33] For some, this restriction in diction means that "Homer" did not know of any function that could be attributed to *psūkhḗ* in the living hero—that the word *psūkhḗ* simply did not denote consciousness.[34]

And yet, as even those who prefer this explanation have to concede,[35] the concept of *psūkhḗ* is indeed derived from the concept of *breathing* (cf. Homeric *psū́khō* 'blow', with "winds" as subject, at XX 40), the loss of which is the primary manifestation of death in the conventional Homeric descriptions. The words *thūmós* and *ménos* are also associated with breathing.[36] Accordingly, the descriptions of both swooning and

[30] E.g. Arbman 1927.159–160.

[31] Böhme 1929.124.

[32] See Schnaufer 1970.194–195 for a useful chart of passages.

[33] For *thūmós* see *Iliad* XXII 475; *Odyssey* v 458, xxiv 349; for *ménos* see *Iliad* XV 60 and 262 as discussed by Schnaufer pp. 192–193.

[34] Böhme 1929.111, 124.

[35] Böhme pp. 22 and 124, *pace* Arbman 1926.194–195; for a fuller discussion, see Schnaufer 1970.198–201.

[36] Consider the collocation of ἄμπνυτο 'he breathed again' with the revival of the *thūmós* at *Iliad* XXII 475, *Odyssey* v 458, xxiv 349; also the collocation of ἐμπνεύσῃσι/ἐνέπνευσε 'he [Apollo] breathes/breathed' with object *ménos* [into Hektor] at *Iliad* XV 60 and 262 (cf. n33).

dying as a loss of *thūmós/ ménos/ psūkhḗ* are physiologically appropriate and proper, and yet the regaining of the hero's breath after swooning is restricted in Homeric diction to *thūmós/ ménos*, with *psūkhḗ* excluded. The reason for this exclusion is surely not physical but ideological. To repeat, it has been argued that *psūkhḗ* is excluded because it does not denote consciousness, whereas *thūmós/ ménos* regularly do. But this argument is predicated on the assumption that *psūkhḗ* is distinct from *thūmós/ ménos* at the moment when they become separated from the body. This is to confuse words with concepts, and I must insist here on returning to the facts of Homeric diction. What leaves the body at the moment of dying or swooning is functionally expressed as *thūmós* and/or *ménos* and/or *psūkhḗ*. At the moment of dying or swooning, all three words are formulaically interchangeable synonyms, expressing the same concept.[37]

If, then, the word *psūkhḗ* is excluded in descriptions of revival from swooning, it is because this synonym of *thūmós/ ménos* at the moment of dying and swooning has at other moments a meaning that goes beyond the concept of breath or even the concept of consciousness. Some would argue that this meaning is simply that of 'ghost': once the *psūkhḗ* is in Hades, the reasoning goes, it cannot return to the body of someone who has swooned because the *psūkhḗ* would already be a ghost—and its owner would already be dead.[38] Yet, this reasoning again fails to account for the fact—as established by observation of Homeric diction—that *psūkhḗ* is synonymous with *thūmós/ ménos* at the moment of dying or swooning. It cannot simply be assumed that *psūkhḗ* should mean one thing when a hero swoons and another thing when he is revived.

There may be a more sublime reason for the avoidance of the word *psūkhḗ* in Homeric descriptions of a hero's revival. As we have noted, the synonymity of *thūmós/ ménos/ psūkhḗ* at the moment of death implies an affinity of *psūkhḗ* with consciousness—an affinity that is then suspended in Hades. If it is simply a matter of suspension, however, then the door is left open for imagining an eventual restoration of synonymity, with all three words *thūmós/ ménos/ psūkhḗ* once again capable of designating the identity of the deceased. The setting for such a restoration is, I submit, the eventual reintegration of the *psūkhḗ* and body, when the deceased comes back to life. In that case, the avoidance of the word *psūkhḗ* in descriptions of a hero's revival from a swoon would be motivated by a need to keep this theme distinct from the theme of a hero's revival from death. Elsewhere, I have attempted to document this theme, the hero's

37 For an instant demonstration, see tables 1, 2, and 3 in Warden 1971.102.
38 Cf. Schnaufer 1970.201.

revival from death, on the basis of the internal evidence available in the diction in Greek poetic traditions.[39] In that effort, however, I did not confront what the *Iliad* has to say, albeit indirectly, about the afterlife of Patroklos. Which is the problem at hand—a problem that may be solved, I submit, by now pursuing even further the semantics of *thūmós/ ménos/ psūkhḗ*.

Exceptionally, the restoration of synonymity for *thūmós/ ménos/ psūkhḗ* can happen in Hades itself. The *psūkhḗ* of the seer Teiresias (*Odyssey* x 492) is described as the only one in Hades to be endowed with *phrénes* (x 493), which as we have seen is the physical localization of *thūmós* and *ménos*.[40] Accordingly, the *psūkhḗ* of Teiresias is the only one in Hades to recognize Odysseus without having to drink blood (xi 91). To be contrasted are the other *psūkhaí* who are as a rule "without faculties" (*aphradées* xi 476) except whenever they get to drink a libation of blood (xi 147–149).[41] The reason for my drawing attention at this point to the exceptional *psūkhḗ* of Teiresias has to do with yet another crucial word, one that serves to explain why Teiresias has *phrénes* even in Hades: Persephone had given him *nóos* (x 494). This word, which here epitomizes the synonymity of *thūmós/ ménos/ psūkhḗ*,[42] is as a rule used in Homeric diction to designate the realm of rational functions only,[43] whereas *thūmós* is used to designate the realm of both rational and emotional functions.[44] As such, *nóos* represents a mere subcategory of *thūmós* in the living Homeric hero. Why, then, should this word be a key, in *Odyssey* x 494, to the synonymity of *thūmós/ ménos/ psūkhḗ* and, by implication, to the reintegration of consciousness and body?

The etymology of *nóos* provides an answer. As the researches of Douglas Frame have established,[45] the root of *nóos* is *nes-, which means not just 'return home', as attested in Greek *néomai* (verb) and *nóstos* (noun), but also 'return to light and life', as apparently attested in Indic

[39] See e.g. N 1979a.165–168 (also p. 208) on *Odyssey* iv 561–569, xi 601–604, and Hesiod F 25.25–28 MW. In the case of *anapsūkhein* 'reanimate' at *Odyssey* iv 568, the themes of revival from death and revival from a swoon actually converge: N 1979a.167–168 §28n2. Cf. also p. 142 on *Iliad* V 677 (Sarpedon is revived from a swoon by a blast from Boreas the North Wind).

[40] See p. 89.

[41] Cf. Schnaufer 1970.67.

[42] See also *Iliad* XVIII 419, where *nóos* is explicitly said to be localized in the *phrénes*. As Böhme 1929.65 puts it, *nóos* can designate the ego while *phrénes* designates "the organ of the ego."

[43] See Böhme p. 75. The description "rational" may be too broad here: cf. Fritz 1943. Such words as "intuitive" or "perceptive" may be more appropriate.

[44] For a list of attestations where rational functions are attributed to *thūmós* in Homeric diction, see Böhme p. 72n1; as for the emotional functions, see his pp. 69–71.

[45] Frame 1978.

Nā́satyau, an epithet of the Indic Divine Twins, the Aśvin-s who bring mortals back to life and who bring about sunrise after the night brought on by each sunset.[46] As Frame also shows, there is in fact a pervasive interplay between the themes of *nóos* and *nóstos* in the *Odyssey*, so that the fundamental meaning of the root *nes-, 'return to light and life', is reenacted within the overall structure of this epic; in other words, the *Odyssey* itself is built on the symbolism of rebirth from death, as visualized in the dynamics of sunrise after sunset and as verbalized in the *nóos/nóstos* of Odysseus himself.[47] Within the space of the present discussion, I cannot do full justice to the evidence and arguments that Frame adduces. Rather, I am simply confining myself to the problem of connecting the death of Patroklos with the semantics of *thūmós/ménos/psūkhḗ*. Still, the etymology of *nóos*, which functions in Homeric diction as a subcategory of *thūmós* and as a principle that reunites *thūmós/ménos/psūkhḗ* in synonymity, can serve as an ideal point of transition to the main part of this presentation—a survey of assorted evidence available in Indic traditions that may throw light on the afterlife of Patroklos. If this evidence will help strengthen Frame's own arguments, then I hope that he will accept my efforts here as a tribute to his own.

Indic traditions formalize the theme of returning to light and life in more ways than one. Besides the *Nā́satyau*, I cite a Vedic sun-god called *Savitŕ̥-*, appropriately meaning 'the vivifier' (root *sū-* 'vivify'). As we shall see, Savitr̥'s solar journey enables the aspects of man that leave the body at death to be reintegrated in the realm of the *pitŕ̥-s* 'ancestors'. Since the comparative evidence of the Savitr̥ tradition is both ample and complex, it may be best to anticipate here the conclusions that I plan to draw from this evidence at a later point. What will emerge is that the Indic words designating the aspects of man that leave the body at death, *mánas-* and *ásu-*, are actually cognate with the Homeric noun + epithet combination *ménos ēú* (μένος ἠύ), designating in general the energetic faculties of heroes (e.g. *Iliad* XX 80) and, in particular, the aspect of Patroklos that has been lost as a result of death (XXIV 6).

The correspondence between the Indic noun *mánas-* and the Greek noun *ménos* is overt. As for the Indic noun *ásu-* and the Greek adjective

[46] For a collection of these themes in Indic lore, see Frame pp. 134–152; cf. also Güntert 1923.253–276 and N 1979a.198–200. On the morphology of Indic *Nā́satyau*, see Frame pp. 135–137; cf. Greek *Lampetíē*, as discussed at p. 249n80. (The attestation of disyllabic scansion for the first vowel of *Nā́satyau* [*naasatyau*] remains a problem.) For a survey of the Indo-European myth of the Divine Twins, see Ward 1968; cf. also Joseph 1983 and Davidson 1987. Further discussion of the Divine Twins, including the Greek Dioskouroi, at pp. 255–256.

[47] Frame pp. 34–80. For other aspects of the theme of rebirth in the *Odyssey*, see Newton 1984.

ēú (ἠύ), the correspondence on the levels of both form and meaning is complicated, and further discussion is useless until we can review the comparative evidence preserved in Iranian traditions.[48]

Suffice it now to add another overt comparandum besides Indic *mánas-* on one side and Greek *ménos* on the other: the Indic word *pitṛ́-* 'ancestor' is directly cognate with the Greek element *patro-* of *Patro-klées*, a name that literally means 'he who has the glory [*kléos*] of the ancestors [*patéres*]'.[49] In view of Erwin Rohde's observation that the Funeral of Patroklos in the *Iliad* bears the distinct features of hero cult[50] and that the cult of heroes is itself an institution that evolved from the worship of ancestors,[51] we may recover an Indo-European theme in comparing the association of *ménos ēú* (= μένος ἠύ) and *Patroklées* in the context of that hero's death with the association of *mánas-/ ásu-* and the *pitṛ́-s* 'ancestors' in the context of their coming back to life after death.

Having anticipated my conclusions from the comparative Indic evidence about Savitṛ and his role in bringing the dead back to life, I will now present this evidence to the extent that I am able to sketch it without oversimplifying its rich complexities.[52]

As we begin to examine the traditions about this specialized sun-god Savitṛ, we note that there are contexts of darkness as well as brightness. Savitṛ protects the righteous *at night* (*Rig-Veda* 4.53.1) and wards off the demonic Rakṣas-es *all night* (1.35.10).[53] The time of these Rakṣas-es is the

[48] See pp. 118ff.

[49] For *patéres* as 'ancestors', see e.g. *Iliad* VI 209; for more on the semantics of *Patroklées*, see N 1979a.102ff.

[50] Rohde 1898 1:14–22, esp. p. 16n1. See also Stähler 1967.32, who argues that the picture on the Münster Hydria (p. 88n20 above) represents the beginning of the hero cult of Patroklos.

[51] Rohde 1:108–110; see also N 1979a.114–115. Cf. p. 116n119 for thematic connections between the concept of 'ancestor' and the actual word *hḗrōs* (ἥρως) 'hero'. In view of the inherited relationship of this word with *hṓrā* (ὥρα) 'season, seasonality, timeliness' (on which see Pötscher 1961), we may compare the Indic representation of seasonal eschatology as outlined at p. 87n16.

[52] The patterns that I have found are clearly not the only ones attested in Indic traditions. I am persuaded by the account, in Witzel 1984, of alternative traditions, featuring alternative visualizations, especially with regard to the "backward" or "reversed" course of celestial bodies, the "oceans" of the sky, and the abode of Yama.

[53] In both these passages, Savitṛ is invoked as Asura (*ásura-*). In a future project, I hope to show in detail that this epithet was primarily appropriate to Dyaus (*dyáus*) 'sky' personified, cognate of Greek *Zeús* (Ζεύς), in contexts where the god Dyaus is ambivalently beneficent or maleficent (cf. the applications of *ásura-* to *dyáus* at *Rig-Veda* 1.122.1, 1.131.1, 8.20.17, etc.). As Dyaus becomes obsolescent, specialized sky-gods like Savitṛ inherit the epithet Asura in contexts of ambivalence. In the plural, however, Asura becomes one-sidedly bad, designating demons only, while Deva (*devá-*), derivative of Dyaus (*dyáus*), becomes one-sidedly good, designating gods only. In the Iranian traditions of the *Avesta*, on the other hand, the original sky-god remains head of the universe, but only under the name of *Ahura-*, cognate of Indic *ásura-*; meanwhile, the Iranian cognate of Indic Dyaus (*dyáus*) survives only in a derivative form, *daēuua-*, cognate of Indic *devá-*. Moreover, all

night (7.104.18); in the east they have no power, because they are wiped out by the rising sun (*Taittirīya-Saṃhitā* 2.6.6.3). As the *Rig-Veda* makes clear, the daily breakthrough to light in the east is caused by Savitr̥ (10.139.1). How, then, can the sun-god Savitr̥ be present at night? As we see from *Rig-Veda* 1.35, the *Savitr̥ Hymn,* the god reverses the course of his chariot with each sunrise and sunset: he travels through the brightness at day and then through the darkness at night. During the night trip, he is the good aspect of darkness, just as he is the good aspect of brightness during the day trip. The night trip of Savitr̥ is especially precarious for mortals not only because of the darkness but also because the daylight course of the sun is reversed. After the forward course of the chariot at daytime comes the backward course at nighttime. This forward/backward movement of Savitr̥ is expressed in terms of downstream/upstream, the words for which are *pravát-/udvát-*:[54]

yā́ti deváḥ pravátā yā́ty udvátā

Rig-Veda 1.35.3

The Deva [god] goes downstream, goes upstream.[55]

It remains to ask where it is that Savitr̥ travels "upstream," from west

---

*daēuua-*s are bad, demons only. I follow Schlerath 1968.144–145 in interpreting the morphological segmentation of Indo-Iranian *ásura- to be *as-ura-, the root of which I am inclined to reconstruct as Indo-European *es- 'to be'. I agree with Schlerath that *ásura- is not derived directly from Indo-Iranian *ásu-; going beyond Schlerath's own arguments, I venture to propose that both forms *ásu- and *ásura- are derived from the root *as- (Indo-European *es-, that is, $*h_1es$-). For more on Indo-Iranian *asu- (Indic *ásu-*, Iranian *ahu-*), see pp. 118ff.

[54]Cf. *Rig-Veda* 5.31, where Indra is represented as driving the chariot of the sun (stanza 11) as he repels the darkness (stanza 3, etc.), and where he specifically makes his chariot go *pravát-* 'downstream' = 'forward':

índro ráthāya pravátaṃ kr̥ṇoti

Rig-Veda 5.31.1

Indra drives the chariot forward

At *Rig-Veda* 1.181.3, Indra's chariot is described as *pravátvant-* 'moving downstream'. Elsewhere in the *Rig-Veda,* as at 7.50.3, *pravát-* means not the downstream specifically but simply the stream: here 'downstream' is further specified as *nivát-*, as opposed to *udvát-* 'upstream'. Just as the unmarked path of the sun is simply *the* path of the sun, so also the unmarked downstream is simply *the* stream. One need specify 'downstream' only in opposition to 'upstream': otherwise it is just 'stream'.

[55]On the word *devá-* 'god', see p. 94n53. It is in the precarious nighttime context of the sun's direction reversed that Savitr̥ is euphemistically called *sunīthá-* 'heading in the good direction' (*Rig-Veda* 1.35.7, 10). It is precisely in this ambivalent context (1.35.10) that Savitr̥ is called Asura (on which see again n53).

to east, during the night.[56] The *Rig-Veda* is ostentatiously cryptic about the sun's whereabouts at nighttime, offering only such indications as in the following verses of the *Savitṛ Hymn*:

kvèdā́nīm sū́ryaḥ káś ciketa
katamā́m dyā́m raśmír asyā́ tatāna

Rig-Veda 1.35.7

Where is the sun now? Who knows?
Which sky has its ray reached?

A further indication about this unmentionable sky occurs in stanza 6 of the same *Savitṛ Hymn*, where Savitṛ is described as having two skies. From such indirect mystical hints we may surmise that the sky of this our world is matched by another sky, of the underworld. Furthermore, there is a third sky mentioned in the same stanza (*Rig-Veda* 1.35.6), this one belonging to Yama rather than Savitṛ; it is in this third sky that immortal things abide (*amṛ́tā́dhi taṣṭhur*), and

ihá bravītu yá u tác cíketat

Rig-Veda 1.35.6

whoever knows it should say it here.

The name Yama refers to the king of the *pitṛ́*-s 'ancestors' (*Rig-Veda* 10.14 passim), particularly the Aṅgiras-es (10.14.3, 5), and his path is death (1.38.5). He is the first person ever to experience death (*Atharva-Veda* 18.3.13), and he is specifically addressed as "our *pitṛ́*" (*Rig-Veda* 10.135.1). Yet the abode of Yama and the *pitṛ́*-s is in the midst of the sky (10.15.14), in the highest sky (10.14.8), in the third sky which has eternal light and where the sun was placed (9.113.7–9). The abode of the *pitṛ́*-s is the highest point of the sun (9.113.9), and they are in communion with it (1.125.6, 10.107.2, 10.154.5). Thus, the third sky of Yama could be visualized as above the first sky of Savitṛ, who goes *pravát-* 'downstream' during the day; come sunset, Savitṛ reaches the dreaded second sky of the lower world, where he travels *udvát-* 'upstream' during the night.

How, then, did Yama the primordial mortal reach the third sky?

[56] The patterns that I have found in answer to this question, as I outline them in what follows, are clearly not the only ones attested in Indic traditions. Again I refer to Witzel 1984.

Come sunrise, he ascends along with the sun, traveling *pravát-* 'downstream':

pareyivā́ṃsam praváto mahī́r ánu
bahúbhyaḥ pánthām anupaspaśā́nām

Rig-Veda 10.14.1

having gone along the great *pravát-* streams,
having discovered a path for many.

In the *Atharva-Veda* (6.28.3, 18.4.7), Yama is described as the first ever to have gone along the *pravát-*. Before reaching the third sky with the coming of sunrise, it may be that Yama, the first person ever to experience death, is imagined as having to traverse the unmentionable second sky with the coming of sunset. A model and guide for this kind of trip could be Savitr̥ himself.

The role of Savitr̥ as psychopomp is illustrated by such passages as *Rig-Veda* 10.17.3–6: according to the Kalpa to *Taittirīya-Āraṇyaka* 6.1.1, this text is a prayer for the dead at the ritual of cremation; Savitr̥ is implored to place the dead man into the abode of the *pitŕ̥-*s:

yátrā́sate sukŕ̥to yátra té yayús
tátra tvā deváḥ savitā́ dadhātu

Rig-Veda 10.17.4

where the doers of good abide, where they have gone,
there may the Deva [god] Savitr̥ put you [the dead man].[57]

In the function of psychopomp, Savitr̥ has a thematic correlate called Pūṣan; in the same Savitr̥ passage (10.17.5) this Pūṣan is implored to guide the dead man "along the least dangerous path" (*ábhayatamena*), being a "bestower of well-being" (*svastidā́*).[58] Like Savitr̥, Pūṣan is associated with the path of the sun (*Rig-Veda* 2.40.4–5, 6.56.3, 6.58.2); in fact, it is the theme of the sun's path that makes Savitr̥ and Pūṣan overlap in identity:

[57] On the word *devá-* 'god', see again p. 94n53.

[58] Cf. the semantics of *sunīthá-* 'heading in the good direction' (*Rig-Veda* 1.35.7, 10), as discussed at p. 95n55.

utá pūṣā́ bhavasi deva yā́mabhiḥ

Rig-Veda 5.81.5

and you, Deva [the god Savitṛ] become Pūṣan by your movements.

Previously, the movements of Savitṛ had just been described:

utá rā́trīm ubhayátaḥ párīyasa

Rig-Veda 5.81.4

and you [Savitṛ] go around the night on both sides.

From the other contexts,[59] we may assume here that Savitṛ goes east to west when night is below us and west to east when night is above us. Savitṛ and Pūṣan are correlates elsewhere, too, in the *Rig-Veda* (3.62.9–10, 10.139.1), but it will suffice here to consider only their correlation in solar movement.[60]

In the same hymn where Savitṛ and Pūṣan function as correlate psychopomps, the solar movements of Pūṣan are described in the following mystical language:

prápathe pathā́m ajaniṣṭa pūṣā́
prápathe diváḥ prápathe pṛthivyā́ḥ
ubhé abhí priyátame sadhásthe
ā́ ca párā ca carati prajānán

Rig-Veda 10.17.6

at the extremity of paths was Pūṣan born,
at the extremity of the sky, at the extremity of the earth;
over both most dear *sadhástha*-s
he goes to and fro, knowing [the way].

Two basic questions are: (1) what is the extremity of sky/earth and (2) what are the two *sadhástha*-s 'abodes' of the sun?

A bivalent answer can be derived from the Indic concept of Sky and Earth as surrounded by Ocean, on all sides. This concept is implicit in a Rig-Vedic theme that has it that all streams and rivers flow into the Samudra 'Ocean' (1.32.2, 1.130.5, 2.19.3), as also in another theme,

[59] See pp. 94ff.

[60] Since Savitṛ is called Asura specifically in the context of his movements (*Rig-Veda* 1.35.10), it is important to stress that Pūṣan, too, is called Asura (5.51.11). See again p. 94n53.

which has it that there is an East Ocean and a West Ocean (10.136.5), or that there are four Oceans (9.33.6). These concepts seem to be based on mythopoeic patterns of cosmic order rather than geographical experience, so that there is room for believing also in an upper Ocean matching the Sky as well as a lower Ocean matching the Earth (cf. 10.98.5, 12). But this distinction is just a sophisticated elaboration: the basic idea remains that the Ocean comes between where the Earth stops and the Sky begins. It follows, then, that the sun submerges in the Ocean at sunset and emerges from it at sunrise; in fact, this concept is explicit in the testimony of the *Taittirīya-Āraṇyaka* (4.42.33) and the *Aitareya-Brāhmaṇa* (4.20.13; cf. also *Atharva-Veda* 13.2.14). Thus the birth of Pūṣan from the extremity of Sky/Earth (again, *Rig-Veda* 10.17.6) must mean that the sun was born of the Ocean.[61] It must be for this reason that Pūṣan's solar correlate Savitr̥ is specifically called *apā́ṃ nápāt* 'progeny of the waters' (1.22.6); furthermore, Savitr̥ as Apām Napāt even knows such secrets as where the fountainhead of the Ocean gushes forth (10.149.2). As for the two *sadhástha*-s 'abodes' of Pūṣan (10.17.6), they must be the Sky and the Ocean: as he travels to and fro (*ā́ ca párā ca carati*), he goes east to west in the Sky at day and, somehow, west to east at night after having plunged into the Ocean.

To be contrasted with the two *sadhástha*-s of Pūṣan are the three *sadhástha*-s of the fire-god Agni (*Rig-Veda* 3.20.2, etc.); in fact, one of Agni's epithets is *tri-sadhasthá-* 'having three *sadhástha*-s' (5.4.8, etc.). Unlike the fire of the sun, which has abodes only in the sky and in the water, Agni as sacrificial fire abides also on earth. The word *agní-* itself means 'fire', cognate with Latin *ignis.* Agni as god links the microcosm of sacrificial fire with the macrocosm of celestial fire. As sacrificial fire, Agni is kindled on earth at dawn so that the sun may rise (4.3.11, 5.6.4). If there were no sacrificial fire at dawn, there would be no sunrise (*Śatapatha-Brāhmaṇa* 2.3.1.5). From a cosmic point of view, Agni himself caused the sun to rise (*Rig-Veda* 10.156.4).[62]

The three *sadhástha*-s 'abodes' of Agni correspond to three different proveniences of Agni, and the *Rig-Veda* reveals them in the following order (10.45.1):[63]

[61] There is a cognate theme in Greek traditions: the sun rises from and sets into the *Ōkeanós* 'Ocean' (e.g. *Iliad* VII 421–423 and VIII 485 respectively), visualized as a cosmic river that surrounds an Earth that is round and flat; for further discussion, see N 1979a.195ff. In the death wish of Penelope, *Odyssey* xx 61–65, the *thūmós* 'spirit' after death is visualized as traveling to the far west, where it is plunged into the Okeanos: see p. 237. This plunge implicitly parallels the plunge of the sun itself: p. 246.

[62] For further discussion of this theme: pp. 147ff.

[63] Cf. also *Rig-Veda* 8.44.16, 10.2.7, 10.46.9.

First, Agni is born in the Sky, as lightning;[64]
Second, Agni is born on Earth, as sacrificial fire;
Third, Agni is born in the Ocean, as the risen sun.

Let us examine in more detail the third provenience of Agni. Like the sun-god Savitr̥, the water-born third Agni is also called *apā́ṃ nápāt* 'progeny of the waters' (*Rig-Veda* 3.1.12–13, 3.9.1, etc.). Elsewhere, Apām Napāt seems to exist as a separate entity (10.30.3–4, etc.); he is celebrated in one whole hymn (2.35), but even here he is identified with Agni in the last stanza. Just as Savitr̥ as specialized sky-god has features derivable from Dyaus 'Sky'[65] so also Apām Napāt: whereas Savitr̥ is called the *prajā́pati-*, the creator of the universe (4.53.2),[66] Apām Napāt is described as the one who "created all things" (*víśvāni . . . bhúvanā jajāna* 2.35.2).[67]

The Vedic figure Apām Napāt is so ancient that there is a formal analogue in the Iranian evidence: the Avestan figure Apąm Napå.[68] While other thematic evidence about Apąm Napå is elusive, he is known to have the epithet *auruuat̰.aspa-* 'having swift horses' (*Yašt* 19.51);[69] otherwise, this word serves only to describe the *huuar-* 'sun' (*Yašt* 10.90, etc.). There is a thematic parallel in the Rig-Vedic word *āśuhéman-* 'driving swift horses', which serves as epithet for Apām Napāt (2.31.6, 2.35.1, 7.47.2); he is transported by horses as swift as thought itself (1.186.5).[70]

In *Rig-Veda* 1.162, a hymn celebrating the sacrificial horse, it is specifically Pūṣan's goat that leads the horse to its immolation (stanzas 2–3). In fact, Pūṣan's chariot is regularly drawn by goats (1.138.4; 6.55.3–4, 6; 6.57.3; 6.58.2); by contrast, Savitr̥'s chariot is drawn by

[64] Cf. *Rig-Veda* 1.143.2, 3.2.13, 6.6.2, etc.; cf. also Agni's common epithet Vaidyuta 'he of the *vidyút-* [lightning]' in the *Brāhmaṇa-*s.

[65] See p. 94n53.

[66] According to the *Taittirīya-Brāhmaṇa* (1.6.4.1), Prajāpati became Savitr̥ and created the universe.

[67] This creation of all things by Apām Napāt is done *asuryàsya mahnā́* 'with the greatness of Asura-power' (*Rig-Veda* 2.35.2). Like the sun-god Savitr̥, Agni too is called Asura (4.2.5, 5.15.1, 7.2.3, etc.). On the title Asura, see again p. 94n53.

[68] Just as the Indic Apām Napāt uses the greatness of Asura-power (see n67), so too the Iranian Apąm Napå is called *bərəzantəm ahurəm* 'the high Ahura' (*Yasna* 2.5, etc.). On the Indic/Iranian correspondences of Asura/Ahura, see p. 94n53.

[69] The context of the epithet 'having swift horses' is this: the fire-god Ātar and the demon Dahāka have been fighting to a standstill over *x^varənah-* 'brilliance of glory'; then Apąm Napå, the *auruuat̰.aspa-* 'having swift horses', seizes the *x^varənah-* and takes it to the bottom of the Ocean. For parallel themes in Persian epic traditions, most notably in the *Shāhnāma* of Ferdowsi, see Davidson 1985.88–103. For Celtic parallels, see Dumézil 1973.21 and following.

[70] Cf. the Laconian custom of sacrificing horses to Helios the sun-god on a peak of Mount Taygetos (Pausanias 3.20.4). On the solar symbolism of horses in Greek mythology: N 1979a.198–200, 209–210 § 50n2.

horses (7.45.1; cf. 1.35.3, 5). Therefore, the ritual symbolism of having the sacrificial goat of Pūṣan precede the sacrificial horse can be related with mythological symbolism: just as the goat is the horse's guide in ritual, so also Pūṣan is Savitr̥'s guide in myth. From the conventional association of Indic Apām Napāt and of Iranian Apąm Napå with horses, it follows that the designation of Savitr̥ the sun-god as Apām Napāt (1.22.6) is old enough to be a part of the shared Indo-Iranian heritage and is due to his own solar association with horses (7.45.1); by contrast, Pūṣan is called Apām Napāt nowhere in the *Rig-Veda*, presumably because he is associated with goats, not horses. In their function as solar psychopomps, Savitr̥ and Pūṣan may be correlates,[71] but not so in terms of the epithet Apām Napāt: the inherited phraseology of this expression requires association with horses, not goats.

When it comes to the death and rebirth of man, Apām Napāt serves as a solar *model* rather than solar *guide*. The celestial fire plunges into the waters at sunset, only to be reborn from them at sunrise. As a parallel, the sacrificial horse is immolated so that it may draw the chariot of the sun come sunrise, but its *guide* is the goat. In the Rig-Vedic hymn to Apām Napāt, sun and horse are parallel as they rise at dawn:

áśvasyā́tra jánimāsyá ca svàr

Rig-Veda 2.35.6

There [in the waters] is the birthplace of the horse and this sun.[72]

For the function of enacting man's rebirth after death, there is an element missing in the figure of Apām Napāt; as the hymn composed specially for him makes clear, Apām Napāt is Apām Napāt only in the waters and in the sky, but on earth he becomes someone else:

só apā́ṃ nápād ánabhimlātavarṇo'
'nyásyevehá tanvā̀ viveṣa

Rig-Veda 2.35.13

Apām Napāt, with imperishable radiance,
is at work here [on earth] with the body of another.

This "other" is then identified in the last stanza of the hymn as Agni himself, in his function as sacrificial fire (2.35.15). Thus whereas Agni is

71 See p. 97.
72 On a cognate theme in the *Iliad*: N 1979a.209–210 § 50n2.

Apām Napāt, Apām Napāt is not Agni in all respects. Specifically, Apām Napāt lacks one of Agni's three aspects: he is not at work on earth.

To round out this complex picture of the tripartite Agni, let us briefly consider his first provenience. Besides the earth-born Second Agni of the sacrificial fire and the water-born Third Agni of the sun, there is also the sky-born First Agni of lightning (*Rig-Veda* 10.45.1–3; also 1.143.2, 3.2.13, 6.6.2). While the water-born Agni has two *sadhástha*-s 'abodes', Sky and Ocean, the sky-born Agni in the form of lightning can go directly from Sky to Earth through the *antárikṣa-* 'intermediate space' (6.8.2, 10.65.2).

The tripartite distribution of Agni is subject to a number of confusions. As lightning, sky-born Agni qualifies as being in the *third* sky (*Rig-Veda* 1.143.2, etc.); yet the sky-born Agni is the *first* Agni. Also, with the concept of celestial waters matching terrestrial waters (1.32.2, 12, etc.), it may seem tempting to imagine the water-born Agni as not only the sun but also lightning; and yet, Indic ritual shows that water-born Agni was basically incompatible with the fire of lightning: according to the *Śatapatha-Brāhmaṇa* (12.4.4.4; cf. *Aitareya-Brāhmaṇa* 7.7), "the Agni in the waters" must be expiated if fire from lightning has been mixed with sacrificial fire.[73]

Lightning, however, is not the only form in which Agni comes from Sky to Earth. We are now about to see the purpose of Agni's tripartition, which links the mystery of afterlife with the mystery of terrestrial fire's origin from celestial fire. We begin with the Vedic concept of human reproduction, where the male plants the *gárbha-* 'embryo' in the uterus of the female: thus when Sky impregnates Earth with rainwater, the embryo is none other than "the Agni in the waters," and this embryo is then lodged within the plants that grow out of the impregnated Earth (*Rig-Veda* 7.9.3, 8.43.9, 1.141.4, etc.).[74] One of the designations of Agni within plants is actually *apā́m gárbha-* 'embryo of the waters' (7.9.3); one of the designations of "plant" is *óṣadhī-*:

apsv àgne sádhiṣ ṭava
saúṣadhīr ánu rudhyase

Rig-Veda 8.43.9

Your station is in waters, Agni;
you grow into *óṣadhī*-s.

[73] Also in the *Atharva-Veda*, there is an explicit distinction between the Agni-s of the waters and the Agni-s of lightning (3.21.1, 7; 8.1.11; 12.1.37).

[74] Cf. Bergaigne 1878 1:17, Oldenberg 1917.113–114.

Etymologically, *óṣadhī-* may be interpreted as being composed of roots *uṣ-* and *dhā-*, meaning 'light-emplacement.'[75]

The one who brought fire from the Sky to the Earth is called Mātariśvan, messenger of Vivasvat (*Rig-Veda* 6.8.2; also 1.93.6, 3.2.13, 1.143.2). Elsewhere, the messenger of Vivasvat is specified as Agni himself (1.58.1, 8.39.3, 10.21.5), and the word *mātaríśvan-* actually serves as Agni's epithet (1.96.4, 3.5.9, 3.26.2). "Though the myth of Mātariśvan is based on the distinction between fire and a personification which produces it, the analysis of the myth shows these two to be identical."[76] It remains to ask how Mātariśvan brought celestial fire to Earth: he produced fire by friction, expressed with verb forms of the root *manth-* (as in 1.71.4, 1.141.3, 1.148.1, 3.9.5). In the language of the *Rig-Veda*, fire is produced by the *manth-* 'friction' of fire-sticks called the *aráṇi-*s:[77]

ástīdám adhimánthanam
ásti prajánanaṃ kr̥tám
etā́ṃ viśpátnīm ā́ bhara
agním manthāma pūrváthā

aráṇyor níhito jātávedā
gárbha iva súdhito garbhíṇīṣu

Rig-Veda 3.29.1–2

This is the friction-place,
birth-giving, it has been prepared;
bring the *viśpátnī* [mistress of the household];
as before, let us rub fire.

Agni the Jātavedas has been emplaced in the two *aráṇi-*s,
well-placed like the embryo in pregnant females.

The fire latent in the wood of the *aráṇi-*s is born as terrestrial fire, and we note that the Agni-epithet Mātariśvan is etymologically appropriate to the theme of latent fire: *mātarí-* 'in the mother' and *-śvan-* 'swelling' (from root *śū-* 'swell'). Here, then, is the key to the mystery of how the terrestrial fire of sacrifice was produced from celestial fire. Agni descends from the Sky as an embryo in rainwater. Then he is lodged in the plants that grow from the impregnation of Earth with rain. Finally, he is

[75] For a survey of the etymological possibilities of *óṣa-dhī* 'plant', including the one chosen here, see Minard 1956.268. For more on this etymology, see p. 150n25.

[76] Macdonell 1897.71.

[77] On the etymology of *aráṇi-* as the 'nurturing, nourishment' of the fire, see p. 156.

rubbed out of wood, thus becoming terrestrial fire. The link between celestial and terrestrial fire is Agni Mātariśvan, messenger of Vivasvat (6.8.2, etc.).

As for Vivasvat, he is the first to receive fire on earth by virtue of being the first to sacrifice on earth, and he is the ancestor of humans (*Maitrāyaṇī-Saṃhitā* 1.6.12, *Taittirīya-Saṃhitā* 6.5.6.1–2, *Śatapatha-Brāhmaṇa* 3.3.1.3–4).[78] To say *sádane vivásvataḥ* 'at the place of Vivasvat' (*Rig-Veda* 1.53.1) is the same as saying 'at the sacrifice'.[79] Vivasvat, father of Yama (10.14.5, 10.17.1) is formally and thematically cognate with the Avestan figure Vīvahvant, father of Yima, who was the first person ever to prepare Haoma (*Yasna* 9.3–4). The association of Vīvahvant with Haoma is important because Soma/Haoma constitutes the Indic/Iranian sacrifice par excellence,[80] and the Vedic Vivasvat also has special associations with Soma (*Rig-Veda* 9.26.4, 9.10.5, etc.). In the context of the breaking dawn, *uṣás-*, the word *vivásvat-* also occurs as an epithet of Agni, meaning 'shining':

> *ámūraḥ kavír áditir vivásvān*
> *susaṃsán mitró átithiḥ śivó naḥ*
> *citrábhānur uṣásām bhāty ágre*
> *apā́m gárbhaḥ prasvà ā́ viveśa*
>
> *Rig-Veda* 7.9.3

> The unerring seer, the Aditi, the Vivasvat,
> the Mitra of good company, our kind guest,
> with majestic brightness he shines in front of the dawns,
> the embryo of the waters has lodged in pregnant plants.

Such thematic connections (cf. also 1.44.1, 1.96.2, 3.30.13) serve as confirmation of the etymology: the *vas-* of *vivásvat-* is derived from the verb *vas-/uṣ-* 'shine', and so, too, is the *uṣ-* of *uṣás-* 'dawn'. Furthermore, the *vas-* of *vivásvat-* is cognate with the Latin *ues-* of Vesta, Roman goddess of the domestic fireplace.[81] As for the domestic aspect of Vivasvat, it is best understood in relation to the Indic Triple Fire. Matching the tripartite nature of Agni, there evolved certain Indic cult practices that involve a triple sacrificial fire, as documented in minute detail by the Brāhmaṇas. Whereas the single sacrificial fire is suitable for domestic purposes, the triple sacrificial fire is a priestly institution associated with

[78] See Dumézil 1954.34–35.
[79] Cf. Dumézil p. 42n43.
[80] Cf. Oldenberg 1917.281–283.
[81] Dumézil 1954.33–34. Cf. pp. 146ff. below.

the cult centers of the Indic peoples (cf. *Śatapatha-Brāhmaṇa* 2.1.4.4). Some sacrifices, such as the offerings at sunrise and sunset, can be enacted with either a single or a triple fire, but others are restricted to one or the other: for example, rites related to family life belong to the single fire, whereas Soma-rites are restricted to a triple fire.[82]

Among the three fires of the Triple Fire, one is still specifically associated with the domestic aspects: it is the Gārhapatya, meaning 'fire of the *gr̥hápati-*'. The word *gr̥hápati-*, like *viśpáti-*, means 'lord of the household'; both are common Rig-Vedic epithets of Agni. Significantly, if the fire of the Gārhapatya is extinguished, it must be rekindled with *aráṇi-*s (*Śatapatha-Brāhmaṇa* 12.4.3.2). By contrast, if another of the three fires, the Āhavanīya (from preverb *ā-* plus root *hav-* 'pour libation'), is extinguished, it is to be relit from the fire of the Gārhapatya (*Śatapatha-Brāhmaṇa* 12.4.3.3). The specific association of the Gārhapatya with the *aráṇi-*s (see also *Śatapatha-Brāhmaṇa* 2.1.4.5–9) is parallel to the association of Vivasvat with the *aráṇi-*s:

> In the Mātariśvan myth, Agni is produced with *manth-* 'friction'.[83]
>
> Mātariśvan is the messenger of Vivasvat.[84]
>
> Vivasvat is the first to receive fire by virtue of being the first sacrificer on earth.[85]
>
> Agni is produced with the *manth-* 'friction' of fire-sticks called *aráṇi-*s in *Rig-Veda* 3.29.1–2.[86]

We note that the fire apparatus in the latter passage, *Rig-Veda* 3.29.1–2,[87] is called *viśpátnī* 'mistress of the household': here, too, the domestic implication is pertinent to the function of the Gārhapatya. Finally, besides the *aráṇi-*s, still another feature of the Gārhapatya links it to the Mātariśvan myth: it is the designation of its enclosure as the *yóni-* 'uterus' (*Śatapatha-Brāhmaṇa* 7.1.1.12).[88]

The connection between Indic Vivasvat / Mātariśvan / Gārhapatya and Italic Vesta extends beyond the general feature of the domestic fireplace. Even in such specific details as the relighting of the Gārhapatya with the

[82] Cf. Oldenberg 1917.347–348.
[83] See p. 103.
[84] See p. 103.
[85] See p. 104.
[86] Quoted at p. 103.
[87] See again p. 103.
[88] On the etymology of *aráṇi-*, which reveals a semantic parallelism with *yóni-*, see pp. 156ff.

friction of wood, the cult of Vesta affords specific parallels. The fire in the Roman sanctuary of Vesta was supposed to be kept going at all times (cf. Cicero *Philippics* 11.10), and it was a grave matter if it ever went out:

> *ignis Vestae si quando interstinctus esset, uirgines uerberibus adficiebantur a pontifice, quibus mos erat tabulam felicis materiae tamdiu terebrare, quousque exceptum ignem cribro aeneo uirgo in aedem ferret.*
>
> Paulus ex Festo 94 ed. Lindsay
>
> Whenever the fire of Vesta was interrupted, the Virgins were beaten by the *pontifex*; their custom was to bore a *tabula* of *fēlix māteria* until a fire could be taken and brought in a brazen *cribrum* to the sanctuary by a Virgin.[89]

We note that the wood used here is called *māteria*, a noun apparently derived from *māter* 'mother', and that *māteria* is qualified as *fēlix*, an adjective appropriate to the theme of fertility. Immediately comparable in theme are the name *mātariśvan-* 'swelling in the mother'[90] and the name for the enclosure of the Gārhapatya, *yóni-* 'uterus'.[91]

If the fire of the Gārhapatya went out, it was likewise a grave matter: the fire must not be relit by borrowing from the fire of the Āhavanīya, nor by substituting the Āhavanīya for the Gārhapatya; rather, fire must be rubbed from the *aráṇi*-s (*Śatapatha-Brāhmaṇa* 12.4.3.3).[92] This ritual hierarchy reflects symbolically the Indo-European custom of borrowing fire from the domestic fireplace of a fellow member of a community: we may compare such expressions as Greek πῦρ αὔειν/λαβεῖν, Lithuanian *ùgnį im̃ti*, Latin *ignem accipere*, Italian *fuoco prendere*, all meaning 'take fire'; as Wilhelm Schulze has noticed, the contexts of these expressions point back to the same ancestral custom.[93] *The point remains that the Gārhapatya, by virtue of being the domestic fire, is the central point from which all other fires emanate.*[94]

Having observed the primacy of the Gārhapatya, let us examine how the distinction between the Gārhapatya and the Āhavanīya symbolizes the distinction between terrestrial and celestial fire. To repeat, whereas terrestrial fire is obviously incompatible with its opposite element, water, the nature of water-born celestial fire is different in Indic myth:

89 The details of the *tabula* and the brazen *cribrum* will be taken up at pp. 168–169, where this same passage will be reexamined at greater length.

90 See p. 103.

91 See p. 105.

92 See Dumézil 1954.30.

93 Schulze 1966 [1918].189–210.

94 For further details: Dumézil 1961.252–257.

—the sun plunges into the waters of the west only to be reborn the next day from the waters of the east;

—celestial fire is hidden in raindrops that impregnate the earth; it remains hidden in plants that grow out of the earth; then it is rubbed out of wood as terrestrial fire.

The distinction in myth, as we shall now see, is ritually conveyed by the interplay of the Gārhapatya and the Āhavanīya.

The fireplace of the Gārhapatya is set up in a circular enclosure, with the space on the inside representing the earth and the space on the outside representing the ocean around it (these ritual symbols are definitively and explicitly recounted in *Śatapatha-Brāhmaṇa* 7.1.1.8, 13); the enclosure, set off with bricks, is circular because the shape of the earth is circular (7.1.1.37). We note that the waters are symbolized as being outside the enclosure that is to receive the terrestrial fire, the Gārhapatya.

By contrast, the fireplace of the Āhavanīya is set up in a quadrilateral enclosure representing the *dyáus* 'sky', with a lotus leaf placed inside the enclosure for the specific purpose of representing the waters (again, these symbols are definitively and explicitly recounted in *Śatapatha-Brāhmaṇa* 7.3.1.9). The enclosure of the Āhavanīya is quadrilateral because the four directions—north, south, east, west—can be ascertained from the dynamics of the sky (the sun's path, the stars' positions); orientation comes from the sky, not from earth—which is therefore symbolized as circular, that is, without directional coordinates of its own. We note that the waters are symbolized as being inside the enclosure that is to receive the celestial fire, the Āhavanīya. Unlike terrestrial fire, celestial fire is compatible with its opposite element, water: in macrocosm, the sun dips into the waters of the west only to be reborn the next day in the waters of the east.

While duly taking into account the distinctions between the cults of the Indic peoples, attested at a nomadic stage, and the cults of the Italic peoples, attested at a sedentary stage of development, Georges Dumézil[95] has noticed a remarkable parallelism between the Indic Āhavanīya and the ordinary Roman *templum*, a quadrilateral precinct drawn along the lines of the four cardinal points of the sky (cf. Vitruvius 4.5); also between the Indic Gārhapatya and the *aedēs* of Vesta, with its foundations built in the shape of a circle (hence the designation *aedēs* instead of *templum*). Just as the Gārhapatya represents the domestic

[95] Dumézil 1954.27–43.

aspects of fire, so also the Roman Vesta is the goddess of the domestic fireplace. Dumézil has also noticed further parallelisms. Just as the Gārhapatya is incompatible with water, so also the *aedēs* of Vesta: in the course of the rituals that take place within the *aedēs*, no water may touch the ground, not even if it is put down in a container. In line with this prohibition is the essence of a water jar called the *futtile*, derived from the adjective *futtilis* ('which is poured'); besides the radical variant *fu-t-*, Latin also preserves *fu-d-* as in *fundō* 'pour'). The use of this jar is explicitly described as follows:

futtile uas quoddam est lato ore, fundo angusto, quo utebantur in sacris Vestae, quia aqua ad sacra Vestae hausta in terra non ponitur, quod si fiat, piaculum est. unde excogitatum uas est, quod non stare posset sed positum statim effunderetur.

Servius on *Aeneid* 11.339

The *futtile* is a container with a wide mouth and a narrow base which they used in the rites of Vesta, since water drawn for the rites of Vesta is not put down. And if it does happen, it is a matter for expiation. Hence the invention of a vase which could not stand up and which, once it is put down, would immediately spill.

The third aspect of the Indic Triple Fire has yet to be mentioned: besides the Gārhapatya situated toward the west and the Āhavanīya toward the east, there is also the Dakṣiṇa toward the south. Meaning 'the right-hand one', the Dakṣiṇa serves primarily to ward off the evil spirits from the sacrifice (*Śatapatha-Brāhmaṇa* 4.6.6.1, 5.2.4.15–16). Given the associations of the earth-born Agni with the Gārhapatya and of the water-born Agni with the Āhavanīya, it follows that the sky-born Agni of lightning should be associated with the Dakṣiṇa.

While the Gārhapatya symbolizes earth and the Āhavanīya symbolizes the sky plus ocean, the Dakṣiṇa symbolizes the *antárikṣa-* 'intermediate space' (as explicitly affirmed in the *Śatapatha-Brāhmaṇa* 12.4.1.3). The sky-born Agni is specifically described as protecting the sacrificial ordinances and spanning the *antárikṣa-*:

sá jā́yamānaḥ paramé vyòmani
vratā́ny agnír vratapā́ arakṣata
vy àntárikṣam amimīta sukrátur
vaiśvānaró mahinā́ nā́kam aspṛśat

Rig-Veda 6.8.2

Born in the highest sky,
Agni the ordinance-guardian watches over the ordinances;

the Sukratu, he spans the intermediate space;
the Vaiśvānara, he touches the sky-vault with his greatness.

The *antárikṣa-* is the context for a fusion of Agni with Indra in the act of smiting the demon Vṛtra in a stylized thunderstorm:

antárikṣam máhy ā́ paprur ójasā

Rig-Veda 10.65.2

they [the gods] filled the intermediate space with their *ójas-*.

The root of *ójas-* 'power' (*$h_2$eu̯g-) is cognate with that of *vájra-* (*h_2u̯eg-), the name of Indra's thunderbolt,[96] which is conferred upon him by Agni:

ā́ bāhvór vájram índrasya dheyām

Rig-Veda 10.52.5

I [Agni] will put the *vájra-* in the arms of Indra.

In fact, the epithet *vájra-bāhu-* 'he who holds the *vájra-* in his arms' is applied to the fused figure of Indra-Agni (*Rig-Veda* 1.109.7) as well as to Indra alone (1.32.15, etc.).[97] To conclude: since the Dakṣiṇa symbolizes the *antárikṣa-* 'intermediate space', it follows that it is proper to the sky-born Agni of lightning.

We are now in a position to summarize the symbolism of the Indic Triple Fire:

1. Dakṣiṇa: sky-born Agni, lightning
2. Gārhapatya: earth-born Agni, fire
3. Āhavanīya: water-born Agni, sun

The three fires have been listed here to match the order of Agni's three births, as revealed by *Rig-Veda* 10.45.1.[98] This Rig-Vedic order of Agni's three births is significant because it helps account for the interpretation of the name Trita Āptya as 'the watery Third one'.[99] It is also significant

[96] On the *vájra-*: pp. 192, 197.
[97] On the Indo-Iranian pedigree of the theme conveyed by *vájra-bāhu-*: Benveniste 1968.74.
[98] See pp. 99–100.
[99] See Rõnnow 1927, esp. p. 178.

because it corresponds to the order in which the Deva-s,[100] had set up the Triple Fire:

1. Dakṣiṇa
2. Gārhapatya
3. Āhavanīya

By contrast, the antagonists of the Deva-s, the Asura-s,[101] had set up the Triple Fire in the following order:

3. Āhavanīya
2. Gārhapatya
1. Dakṣiṇa

The myth of these rival orders is recorded in the *Taittirīya-Brāhmaṇa* (1.1.4.4–7), where it is added that the fortunes of the Asura-s or 'demons' consequently went *backward* and they lost all, while the fortunes of the Deva-s or 'gods' went *forward* and they prospered. But the Deva-s were not to have any progeny; in this respect, the Deva-s are then contrasted with Manu, whose sacrifice brought him both prosperity and progeny. Throughout the Brāhmaṇa-s, this Manu is the ideal sacrificer and the ancestor of the human race. In Sylvain Lévi's description, Manu is the hero of the *śraddhā*,[102] given that this Vedic word designates the sacrificer's attitude toward his sacrifice. As ancestor of the human race, Manu would naturally have the same order of fire placement as that practiced by the Indic peoples; throughout the *Rig-Veda*, whenever a sacrificer kindles fire, he does so *manuṣvát-* 'like Manu' (1.44.11, etc.). Here is the order in which the Indic sacrificer sets up the Triple Fire:

2. Gārhapatya
3. Āhavanīya
1. Dakṣiṇa

The key to Manu's success in progeny—where even the gods have failed—is that he started the order of fire placement with the Gārhapatya, where Agni is born like a human: as the *mātaríśvan-*, the one 'swelling in the mother', Agni is born of the Gārhapatya's *yóni-* 'uterus'.[103] From the *Rig-Veda*, we know that it was Mātariśvan who gave

[100] On whom see p. 94n53.
[101] On whom see again p. 94n53.
[102] Lévi 1966 [1898].120. See also p. 70 above.
[103] Cf. p. 105.

Agni to Manu (1.128.2, 10.46.9), and that Agni abides among the offspring of Manu (1.68.4).

Manu can be described as a specialized multiform of Vivasvat: both figures are primordial sacrificers, both are ancestors of the human race, both have special affinities with Mātariśvan and the Gārhapatya. In fact, Manu is in some versions the "son" of Vivasvat and thus bears the epithet Vaivasvata (*Śatapatha-Brāhmaṇa* 13.4.3.3, etc.). Also "son" of Vivasvat is Yama (*Rig-Veda* 10.14.5, etc.), who likewise bears the epithet Vaivasvata (10.14.1, etc.). As the first person ever to experience death, Yama Vaivasvata is ruler of the dead, while Manu Vaivasvata is ruler of the living sacrificers (*Śatapatha-Brāhmaṇa* 13.4.3.3–5).

The etymology of *mánu-* is transparent: it is derived from the verb *man-* 'to have in mind'. The meaning of Manu as 'the mindful one' is appropriate to the theme of Manu: as Sylvain Lévi points out, his sheer virtuosity in "the delicate art of sacrifice" confers upon him an incontestable authority on matters of ritual.[104] There is no sacrificial error for which he does not know a remedy (*Taittirīya-Saṃhitā* 2.2.10.2, etc.). To the degree that ritual was the informing principle of law in the social history of the Indic peoples, Manu's authority was further extended: he was also regarded as a sort of lawgiver, and it is for this reason that the Indic corpus of juridical and moral aphorisms is named after him.[105]

The semantics of *Mánu-* go beyond the theme of being 'mindful' at a sacrifice. The broader implications are visible in another derivative from the root *man-*, the noun *mánas-*. As we shall see, *mánas-* conveys both the mental power of prayer at sacrifice and the cosmic power triggered by such prayer. It also conveys, along with the noun *ásu-*, the aspect of man that survives death.[106] Just as *Mánu-* assures the perpetuity of the human race by way of sacrificial fire, so also *mánas-* assures the regeneration of the individual human—again by way of Agni as sacrificial fire.[107]

[104] Lévi 1966 [1898].121. Also p. 70 above. See Christensen 1916 for further documentation of the ubiquitous mythological type that equates the first man with the first sacrificer. In this connection we may note that *Mánu-*, the name of the primordial Indic man, is cognate with English *man*. In Germanic lore, as we hear from Tacitus (*Germania* 2), the first man was *Mannus*, son of *Tuisto*; the etymology of the latter name reveals the meaning 'twin', and we may compare the meaning of *Yamá-*, Manu's "brother": it is likewise 'twin'. For documentation, see Güntert 1923.315–343; also Puhvel 1975. On the variation between brother-brother and father-son dyads, see further Davidson 1987.

[105] Cf. Lévi p. 121.

[106] See p. 87.

[107] Keeping in mind not only the connection between Indic *mánas-* and *Mánu-* as 'man' (see n104) but also the cognate relationship of *mánas-* with Greek *ménos* (μένος), we note that the *ménos ēú* (μένος ἠΰ) of Patroklos at *Iliad* XXIV 6 is in collocation with his *androtḗs* 'manhood' (ἀνδροτῆτά τε καὶ μένος ἠΰ).

How, then, is this regeneration concretely visualized with an abstract noun like *mánas-*? As we shall see, the concrete imagery associated with *mánas-* (and with *ásu-*) is vision and breath in microcosm, sun and wind in macrocosm. The focus of this imagery is Agni's aspect as terrestrial fire, which provides the dead with a direct link to Agni's aspect as celestial fire, namely, the sun. The sun-gods Savitr̥ and Pūṣan can be psychopomps only because Agni himself is a psychopomp, by virtue of cremating the dead. Agni is the supreme *model* and *guide* of rebirth.

The cremating fire of Agni ultimately confers upon the dead a communion with the sun:

sū́ryaṃ cákṣur gacchatu vā́tam ātmā́

Rig-Veda 10.16.3

may the eye go to the sun and the breath to the wind[108]

Here we see the elements of vision and breath absorbed into the macrocosm of sun and wind. Elsewhere too, the theme of wind is correlated with that of the sun:

sū́rya ātmā́ jágatas tasthúṣaś ca

Rig-Veda 1.115.1

sun, the breath of everything moving and unmoving

Such correlations of wind with sun can be derived from the microcosm of sacrificial fire: its air-suction and exhaust are simply transferred to the macrocosm of the sun.[109]

Turning now to the associations of these concrete images with the abstract noun *mánas-*, let us examine the deployment of this word in Vedic diction. As "thought" or "power of thought," *mánas-* has speed comparable with that of the Aśvin-s' horse team (*Rig-Veda* 1.181.2, 6.62.3, 4). These Aśvin-s are the *Nā́satyau*,[110] sons of Dyaus 'Sky' (1.183.1, etc.),

[108] The following verses of this stanza present a variant theme that is beyond the scope of this presentation—one that I hope to examine in a projected study of the *óṣadhī-* (on which see p. 102).

[109] In the *Brāhmaṇa*-s, the sacrificial South Fire of the *pitŕ̥*-s 'ancestors' is designated as Vāyu, name of the wind-god (*Taittirīya-Brāhmaṇa* 1.1.8.1–2, etc.), and Vāyu frequently forms a triad with Agni and Sūrya the sun-god (*Taittirīya-Saṃhitā* 3.1.6b, 3.2.4h, etc.). The association of the South Fire with the *pitŕ̥*-s is "natural" because their abode is the highest point in the sky (cf. p. 96), and this position in the Northern Hemisphere can be represented as south in terms of east and west. Further details in Hillebrandt 1927 1:103nn2, 3.

[110] See pp. 92ff.

consorts of the sun-goddess Sūryā (4.43.6) and fathers of Pūṣan (10.85.14); their sunlike chariot (8.8.2) is set in motion by Savitṛ before the dawn (1.34.10). They appear as the sacrificial fire is kindled and as the sun rises (1.157.1, 7.72.4, etc.). The frequent Rig-Vedic theme that their chariot is faster than *mánas-* 'thought' (1.117.2, etc.) implies a comparison of *mánas-* with wind. In the hymn to the Sacrificial Horse, the victim's thought is specifically likened with *vā́ta-*, the wind (1.163.11); the epithet for *vā́ta-* here is *dhrájīmat-* 'rushing', which occurs elsewhere only once:

áhir dhúnir vā́ta iva dhrájīmān

Rig-Veda 1.79.1

the raging serpent, like the rushing wind

The raging serpent here is none other than the fire-god Agni himself.

The Greek cognate of *mánas-*, *ménos* (μένος), generally means not 'thought' or 'power of thought' but 'power', by way of a basic meaning 'having in mind, reminding' common to both Indic *mánas-* and Greek *ménos.* For instance, the goddess Athena *reminded* (*hup-é-mnē-sen*) Telemachus of his father, thereby giving him *ménos*:

τῷ δ' ἐνὶ θυμῷ
θῆκε μένος καὶ θάρσος, ὑπέμνησέν τέ ἑ πατρὸς
μᾶλλον ἔτ' ἢ τὸ πάροιθεν

Odyssey i 320–322

In his *thūmós*
she had put *ménos* and daring; and she had reminded him of his father,
more than before.[111]

Besides the contextual guarantee from the verb root *men-/*mn-eh$_2$- in *hup-é-mnē-sen* (ὑπέμνησεν) here, there is also a thematic guarantee for the interpretation of *ménos* as 'reminding": in order to put *ménos* into Telemachus, Athena has assumed the form of a hero called *Méntēs* (Μέντης i 105ff.), a name that literally means 'the reminder'.[112]

[111] We note that Telemachus gets the *ménos* placed in his *thūmós* (*Odyssey* i 320); elsewhere in Homeric diction, *thūmós* can function not only as the localization of *ménos* but also as its synonym (see pp. 87ff.).

[112] N 1974a.266–269. See also p. 210n22 below. On Greek and Hittite thematic parallels from the same root, cf. Watkins 1985b.

The precise transmission of divine *ménos* is by *breathing*, as the gods *blow* it (ἐμπνεῖν) into the hero (*Iliad* X 482; XV 59–60, 262; XX 110; *Odyssey* xxiv 520). Consequently, warriors eager for battle are literally "snorting with *ménos*," that is, μένεα πνείοντες (*Iliad* II 536, III 8, XI 508, XXIV 364; *Odyssey* xxii 203). The gods also breathe *ménos* into horses:

ὣς εἰπὼν ἵπποισιν ἐνέπνευσεν μένος ἠΰ

Iliad XVII 456

So saying he [Zeus] breathed good *ménos* into the horses.

Parallel to this μένος ἠΰ 'good *ménos*' blown by Zeus is the "good *mánas-*" that Agni is implored to blow into the sacrificers:[113]

bhadráṃ no ápi vātaya mánaḥ

Rig-Veda 10.20.1

blow us a good *mánas-*!

Besides heroes and horses, other entities, too, can have *ménos*, such as the sun (*Iliad* XXIII 190), fire (VI 182, XVII 565), moist winds (*Odyssey* xix 440), and streams (*Iliad* XII 18). Like heroes, cosmic forces have to be *reminded* of their power, and this is precisely what sacrificers have to do. One Vedic word for this reminder is *mánas-*, as when the priests (*vípra-*s) hitch up *mánas-* and thoughts at the coming of the sun-god Savitr̥:

yuñjáte mána utá yuñjate dhíyo

Rig-Veda 5.81.1

they hitch up *mánas-* and they hitch up thoughts

The time of Savitr̥'s coming is sunrise (*Rig-Veda* 5.81.2), and his function as daily "vivifier" (the actual meaning of *savitŕ̥-*)[114] is duly recounted (5.81.2–5). By hitching up *mánas-*, the priests indirectly hitch up the *dhī́yas* 'thoughts, consciousness' of mankind, *insomuch as they have reminded Savitr̥*, whose daily function it is to rouse men by awakening them at sunrise (4.53.3, 6.71.2, 7.45.1). Specifically, it is the consciousness of men that Savitr̥ rouses:

[113] Cf. Schmitt 1967.115.
[114] See p. 93.

tát savitúr váreṇyam
bhárgo devásya dhīmahi
dhíyo yó naḥ pracodáyāt

Rig-Veda 3.62.10

May we receive this choice light
of the Deva Savitr̥,
who will rouse our thoughts.

This stanza is the celebrated Sāvitrī,[115] with which Savitr̥ is invoked at the inception of one's Vedic study. Again, the word for "thoughts" is *dhī́yas*, which was the correlate of *mánas-* in *Rig-Veda* 5.81.1, quoted above.[116] From such contextual evidence, it is possible to infer that not only Savitr̥ but also *mánas-* is connected with *awakening from sleep* as well as *resurrection from death.* In Greek usage, too, *ménos* is an element that is lost during sleep:

οὐ γὰρ παυσωλή γε μετέσσεται, οὐδ' ἠβαιόν,
εἰ μὴ νὺξ ἐλθοῦσα διακρινέει μένος ἀνδρῶν

Iliad II 386–387

There will not be a pause for rest [from battle] in between, not a bit,
unless the night comes and separates the *ménos* from the men.

We come back, then, to our original starting point: that the Greek word *ménos* is synonymous with *thūmós* and *psūkhḗ* at the moment of death in particular and of losing consciousness in general. Now we see from the comparative evidence of the Indic cognate *mánas-* that this Greek word has a heritage of leaving open the possibility of reawakening from death on the model of reawakening from sleep or a swoon. In Indic traditions the context of this reawakening is the realm of the *pitŕ̥-*s 'ancestors'. We also come back, then, to the collocation of the expression *ménos ēú* with the name *Patro-kléēs* 'whose glory is that of the ancestors' in a context where the expression designates the aspect of Patroklos that is separated from his body by death (*Iliad* XXIV 6).

The comparative evidence of the Indic cognate *mánas-* can tell us still more about Greek *ménos*: we now see that there is an inherited affinity between the *ménos* of the sun (*Iliad* XXIII 190) or wind (*Odyssey* xix 440) and the *ménos* of a hero whose name conveys the glory of the ancestors.

[115] Cf. also the name of the epic character discussed at p. 87n14.
[116] See p. 114.

Through the intermediacy of the fire that cremates the body, vision and breath can become one with sun and wind.[117] It is therefore a vital fact that the fire of cremation is itself called "the *ménos* of fire" in *Iliad* XXIII 238 and XXIV 792; moreover, in the first passage, the body that is being cremated is that of Patroklos himself.[118] By way of this intermediacy, we can now see how a verb like *psū́khō*, which designates the blowing of winds at *Iliad* XX 440, has a noun-derivative *psūkhḗ* that can function as the synonym of *ménos* at the moment of dying. Or again, we now see how the Indo-European verb root *an- (*h_2enh_1–), as attested in Indic *ániti* 'blows', leads to noun-derivatives like both *ánemos* 'wind' in Greek and *animus* 'spirit' in Latin. Significantly, the word *ánemoi* (plural) in Greek can also designate 'spirits of the ancestors' (e.g. *Suda* s.v. *tritopátores*, etc.).[119] Further, Latin *fūmus* and Indic *dhūmá-*, both meaning 'smoke', are cognate with Greek *thūmós*: again, we can better understand such semantic specializations when we envision the exhaust of sacrificial fire as it transforms the breath of life into wind (and we have already witnessed this theme in an earlier passage).[120]

We are still left, however, with the problem of the epithet *ēú* in the Homeric expression *ménos ēú* (μένος ἠύ). Semantically, *ēú* corresponds to *bhadrám* 'good' in the Vedic expression *bhadrám . . . mánas*.[121] Formally, as we shall now see, *ēú* corresponds to the noun *ásu-*, which is used in combination with *mánas-* to designate the conveyors of identity after death. Before we can examine this formal connection, however, we shall have to survey the concrete visualizations of *ásu-* at the moment of cremation and thereafter.

[117] See p. 112.

[118] In this connection, let us recall that *ménos* in Homeric diction applies not only to heroes like Patroklos but also to horses (see p. 114). At *Iliad* XVII 456, moreover, Zeus blows *ménos* into horses that are immortal and that belong to Achilles himself. Further discussion in N 1979a.209–210 §50n2, where I argue that Xanthos the immortal horse of Achilles is presented by the *Iliad* as a model of solar rebirth. Xanthos and the other horses of Achilles are represented on the Münster Hydria (see p. 88n20), and it is argued by Stähler (1967.44ff.) that these horses function there as symbols for the death of Patroklos. In view of the semantic range inherited by the word *ménos*, which extends to the sun itself (*Iliad* XXIII 190), I would add that these same horses also function as symbols for the afterlife of Patroklos and of Achilles. Cf. *Rig-Veda* 2.35.6, as quoted at p. 101.

[119] For documentation, see Rohde 1898 1:247–249, esp. pp. 248–249n1. In view of Rohde's analysis of hero cult as a transformation of ancestor worship in the context of the polis or city-state (see p. 93 above), we may compare the word *tritopátores* (τριτοπάτορες e.g. Photius s.v., *Suda* s.v.), as discussed by Rohde, with the Linear B word *ti-ri-se-ro-e* = *tris hērōei (dative; Pylos tablets Fr 1204, Tn 316.5); cf. Homeric *trìs mákar* (τρὶς μάκαρ), as discussed by Sacconi 1960.171ff.

[120] See p. 87.

[121] See p. 114.

As we have already seen, the setting sun can be envisioned as taking along the breath and vision cosmically absorbed from the cremated dead.[122] Significantly, a goat has been cremated together with the corpse (*Rig-Veda* 10.16.4). With the goat as warrant of divine guidance, the righteous dead must travel along the way of the ancestors, the *pitṝ́*-s, who have reached the *ásu-* and who have been *avr̥kā́s* 'unharmed by the wolf':

ásuṃ yá īyúr avr̥kā́ r̥tajñā́s

Rig-Veda 10.15.1

who have reached the *ásu-*, unharmed by the wolf, knowing righteousness

Not only the cremation of the goat but also the threat of the wolf point to the psychopomp Pūṣan: it is he who fends off the wolf from the traveler's path (*Rig-Veda* 1.42.2). Another threat are Yama's hounds, who are *asutŕ̥pā* '*ásu*-robbers' (10.14.11). It is because of these hounds that the following prayer must be recited:

tā́v asmábhyaṃ dr̥śáye sū́ryāya
púnar dātām ásum adyéhá bhadrám

Rig-Veda 10.14.12

may these two [hounds], so that we may see the sun,
give us back, here today, our good *ásu-*

Thus "good *ásu-*," with the same epithet *bhadrá-* 'good' that we have already seen applied elsewhere to *mánas-*,[123] is a key to the vision of sunlight.

With Agni / Savitr̥ / Pūṣan as psychopomp, the dead must travel along the *ásunīti-* 'path leading to *ásu-*' (*Rig-Veda* 10.12.4, 10.15.14, 10.16.2); elsewhere, *ásunīti-* is personified as a goddess, *implored to give back to the dead their vision of sunlight* (10.59.5–6). As the dead near the end of their trip from west to east, sleepers are ready to waken and Uṣas 'Dawn' is awaited:

úd īrdhvaṃ jīvó ásur na ā́gād
ápa prā́gāt táma ā́ jyótir eti
ā́raik pánthāṃ yā́tave sū́ryāya

[122] See p. 112.
[123] See p. 114.

áganma yátra pratiránta ā́yuḥ

Rig-Veda 1.113.16

Arise! The living *ásu-* has come to us;
darkness has gone away, light draws near;
she [Uṣas] has made free the path for the sun to go;
we have arrived where they continue life.

At the same moment that sleepers awake, the dead are resurrected. After the righteous dead have successfully traveled along the underworld path, they rise with the sun on the *pravát-* stream, following the example of Yama, to the abode of the *pitṛ́-*s 'ancestors', the highest point of the sun (*Rig-Veda* 9.113.9), where they may stay in communion with it (1.125.6, 10.107.2, 10.154.5).

A suitable psychopomp for the ascent (with Yama: 10.14.8) into the abode of the *pitṛ́-*s is the sun-god Savitṛ himself (10.17.4).[124] Or Agni can serve as a cosmic model, in the function of Apām Napāt.[125] There is even a variant of *apā́ṃ nápāt* that is specially applicable to Agni, namely, *praváto nápāt* 'progeny of the *pravát-* stream' (*Atharva-Veda* 1.13.2). We may also compare this declaration in the Vedas:

pravát te agne jánimā

Rig-Veda 10.142.2

The *pravát-* stream is your birthplace, Agni!

Since *ásu-* in the highest heaven is the ultimate goal of the righteous dead, it is significant that every time Agni is lit again on the sacrificial altar, he himself returns to his own *ásu-*:

devó yán mártān yajáthāya kṛṇván
sī́dad dhótā pratyáṅ svám ásuṃ yán

Rig-Veda 10.12.1

When the Deva [Agni] helps mortals sacrifice,
abiding as Hotṛ, returning to his *ásu-*. . .

When flames die down, it is Agni who quickens them with *ásu-*:

[124] Quoted at p. 97.
[125] See pp. 100ff.

tā́sāṃ jarā́m pramuñcánn eti nā́nadad
ásuṃ páraṃ janáyañ jīvám ástr̥tam

Rig-Veda 1.140.8

taking away from them their oldness, he comes roaring,
producing a higher, living, unsurpassable *ásu-*

There is an Iranian cognate for the expression *ásuṃ páram* 'higher *ásu-*' here: it is Avestan *parāhu-* 'higher existence' (*Yasna* 46.19), describing the place where the righteous dead abide. The translation of *parāhu-* as 'higher existence' is warranted by the synonym *parō.asti-* 'higher existence' (*Yašt* 1.25).[126] These Iranian formations *para-ahu- and *para-asti- both seem to be noun-derivatives of the verb *(h_1)es-, namely, *es-u- and *es-ti-, in terms of Indo-European morphology.[127] If indeed Iranian *ahu-* and Indic *ásu-* are cognates derived from *es-u-, then it is possible to translate *ásu-* in a passage like *Rig-Veda* 1.140.8, quoted immediately above, as 'existence'.

That Indic *ásu-* and Iranian *ahu-* are truly cognates is suggested by other evidence as well.[128] For example, in the same passage that contained the collocation of *pára-* and *ásu-* (*Rig-Veda* 1.140.8),[129] corresponding to Avestan *parāhu-* (*Yasna* 46.19), there is also the collocation of *jīvá-* 'alive, living' and *ásu-*,[130] corresponding to the Avestan expression *juiiō aŋhuš* 'living *ahu-*' (*Hadōxt Nask* 2.2). Moreover, there is the collocation of verb *jan-* 'produce, beget' and *ásu-* (again, *Rig-Veda* 1.140.8),[131] corresponding to the Avestan expression *aŋhə̄uš zą̄θōi* 'in the begetting of *ahu-*' (*Yasna* 43.5). I draw attention to the context of the last expression, where the supreme god Ahura[132] is being described as the primal being 'in the begetting of essence [*ahu-*]'. The identical expression *aŋhə̄uš zą̄θōi* 'in the begetting of *ahu-*' occurs elsewhere (*Yasna* 48.6) in a description of Ahura as he causes the plants to grow at the begetting of primaeval essence (*ahu-*), and we may compare a stanza immediately preceding the one where the collocation of *pára-* and *ásu-* occurs (*Rig-Veda* 1.140.8):[133] here we find a description of Agni as he causes the plants to grow (1.140.7).

126 Schlerath 1968.149.
127 Schlerath p. 149. Cf. EWA 147.
128 Schlerath pp. 147–148, 152.
129 Quoted immediately above.
130 Quoted immediately above.
131 Quoted immediately above.
132 On whom see p. 94n53.
133 Quoted immediately above.

The Avestan *ahu-* 'essence' of afterlife is ambivalent: for the good, it is *vahišta- ahu-* 'best essence' (*Yasna* 9.19, etc.), while for the bad it is *acišta-ahu-* 'worst essence' (*Yasna* 30.4, etc.). There is a semantic parallel in the Vedic combination of *ásu-* and the epithet *bhadrá-* 'good' (*Rig-Veda* 10.14.12).[134] In the Indic evidence, the contexts of *ásu-* are one-sidedly good. It happens, however, that the Avestan analogue to the Rig-Vedic combination of *ásu-* plus root *nī-* 'lead' (as in *ásu-nīti-* 'path leading to *ásu-*')[135] is in an evil context: *tə̄m . . . ahūm . . . naēšat̰* 'may it lead to such an [evil] *ahu-*' (*Yasna* 31.20). As for the good essence, another term for it is *ahu- manahiia-* 'essence of *manah-*, spiritual essence' (*Yasna* 57.25, etc., as opposed to the negative *ahu- astuuant-* 'essence of bones', *Yasna* 28.2, etc.). Not only is Avestan *ahu-* cognate with Vedic *ásu-* but Avestan *manah-* is cognate with Vedic *mánas-*, and it is these two Vedic words, *ásu-* and *mánas-*, that designate the elements of afterlife in the Indic traditions.[136] Furthermore, just as Vedic *ásu-* and *mánas-* can function as correlates (*Atharva-Veda* 18.2.24, etc.), so also Avestan *ahu-* and *manah-*:[137]

yaθācā aŋhat̰ apə̄məm aŋhuš
acištō drəguuatąm *at̰ ašāunē vahištəm manō*

Yasna 30.4

as the *ahu-* will be finally.
It [the *ahu-*] of the unrighteous will be the worst [*acišta-*],
but the righteous will have the best [*vahišta-*] *manah-*

The Iranian comparative evidence, where we see not only noun *manah-* coordinated with noun *ahu-* but also the adjective of noun *manah-* subordinated to noun *ahu-* (*ahu- manahiia-*), helps account for the Greek evidence, where the adjective *ēú* (ἠύ) is subordinated to the noun *ménos* (μένος) in the expression *ménos ēú* (μένος ἠύ, as in *Iliad* XX 80, XXIV 6).[138] In brief, then, we find coordination and subordination in Iranian (*manah-* plus *ahu-*, *manahiia-* plus *ahu-*), but only coordination in Indic (*mánas-* plus *ásu-*) and only subordination in Greek (*ménos ēú*). The directions of subordination, moreover, are reversed in Greek and Iranian.

[134] See p. 117.
[135] On which see p. 114.
[136] See p. 87.
[137] Schlerath 1968.153.
[138] See pp. 93ff.

Even if we may not be certain about the precise phonological prehistory of Greek *ēú-* (ἠύ-) in comparison with Indic *ásu-* and Iranian *ahu-*, one thing seems certain: that all are derived from root *es- 'to be'. The semantic specialization of 'good' in adjectival derivatives of *es- is commonplace: we have only to cite the Greek adjective *es-thlós* (ἐσθλός) 'good' as perhaps the most immediate example.[139]

In the case of *ménos ēú* (μένος ἠύ) in *Iliad* XXIV 6, where the expression applies to the aspect of Patroklos that has been lost as a result of death, I propose that we are witnessing an archaic context where the meaning 'good' for *ēú* is only on the surface. Beneath the surface, we find the echo of a Homeric hero's afterlife.

[139]For more on *esthlós* (ἐσθλός): Watkins 1972, 1982b.

CHAPTER 5

The Death of Sarpedon and the Question of Homeric Uniqueness

It has been argued often, and in many ways, that the poetry of Homer is unique, transcending his poetic heritage. The point of departure for this presentation is a confrontation with one such argument, concerning the meaning of the Homeric expression *kléos áphthiton* 'fame ... imperishable' at *Iliad* IX 413, cognate with the Indic expression *śrávas ... ákṣitam* 'fame ... imperishable' at *Rig-Veda* 1.9.7. I stress, at the very beginning, my own conclusion about these two expressions, following a long series of previous works leading to the same conclusion:[1] that Greek *kléos áphthiton* and Indic *śrávas ... ákṣitam* are reflexes of a common Indo-European poetic expression.[2] An article concerning these two cognate expressions, however, stresses the differences between the Greek and the Indic contexts, concluding that the Homeric vision of imperishable fame is distinct and therefore unique to Homer.[3] In

[1]For a thorough bibliographical dossier, see Schmitt 1967.61–71.

[2]N 1974a, esp. pp. 140–149, 244ff. On the metrical factors that may be involved in the tmesis of *śrávas* and *ákṣitam*, see N 1979b.630n6.

[3]Floyd 1980. The germ of the present chapter is derived from the article N 1981a, which was written in response to Floyd's arguments. There is another article that goes further than Floyd, Finkelberg 1986 (who cites Floyd 1980 but not N 1981a), claiming that the Homeric expression *kléos áphthiton* at *Iliad* IX 413 is not even an inherited formula. For a critique of Finkelberg, see [A. T.] Edwards 1988; also Watkins 1989. In response to Finkelberg's argument that *kléos áphthiton* as used at *Iliad* IX 413 is not a "a self-contained unit," I point to the discussion in N 1974a.104–109, where the relationships that link the phrase-types κλέος ἄφθιτον ἔσται (as at IX 413), κλέος ἔσται (as at VII 458), and κλέος ἄφθιτον (as at Sappho F 44.4 V) are explored from the perspective of a less narrow understanding of "formula." I agree with Finkelberg that κλέος ἄφθιτον ἔσται at IX 413 is coefficient with κλέος οὔποτ' ὀλεῖται as at II 325. I can also accept the possibility that κλέος οὔποτ' ὀλεῖται does not occur at IX 413 because ὤλετο is already present at the beginning of the line. But I disagree with her inference that the presence of κλέος ἄφθιτον ἔσται

reacting to this conclusion, I shall argue that, even if the Homeric expression *kléos áphthiton* 'fame . . . imperishable' has a distinctive meaning in comparison with the corresponding Indic expression, such distinctiveness can be explained nonetheless in terms of the actual traditions inherited by Homeric poetry. In other words, the themes underlying the Homeric expression *kléos áphthiton*, even if they have become semantically specialized in the overall context of the *Iliad*, may still reflect an Indo-European heritage. I shall also argue that these themes center on the concept of immortalization, transcending concerns about material wealth and security. Finally, I shall examine in detail, as further illustration of these themes, the Homeric story about the death and funeral of the Anatolian hero Sarpedon, as narrated in *Iliad* XVI.

Let us begin with the *kléos* 'fame' that Achilles predicts will be *áphthiton* 'imperishable' for him, in the sense that the reputation of this hero as conferred by epic poetry will survive him and last forever:[4]

εἰ μέν κ' αὖθι μένων Τρώων πόλιν ἀμφιμάχωμαι,
ὤλετο μέν μοι νόστος, ἀτὰρ κλέος ἄφθιτον ἔσται·
εἰ δέ κεν οἴκαδ' ἵκωμαι φίλην ἐς πατρίδα γαῖαν,
ὤλετό μοι κλέος ἐσθλόν, ἐπὶ δηρὸν δέ μοι αἰὼν
ἔσσεται, οὐδέ κέ μ' ὦκα τέλος θανάτοιο κιχείη

Iliad IX 412–416

If I stay here and fight in the siege of the city of the Trojans,
my homecoming [*nóstos*] is destroyed, but my fame [*kléos*] will be
imperishable [*áphthiton*].
But if I return home to the beloved land of my ancestors,
then my genuine fame [*kléos*] is destroyed, but I will have a lengthy
lifetime [*aiṓn*],
and my end in death will not overtake me quickly.

By contrast, it seems at first glance that the *srávas* 'fame' for which the priests are praying in stanza 7 of *Hymn* 1.9 of the *Rig-Veda* is to be *ákṣitam* 'imperishable' only in the sense that it should last for a lifetime. In this instance, it has been claimed, the fame is contemporary, manifested in

instead of κλέος οὔποτ' ὀλεῖται at IX 413 is an innovation; it could be an archaism that survives precisely for the stylistic purpose of avoiding word duplication. As a general approach to poetics, I suggest that allowance should always be made for the possibility that more archaic forms can be activated in situations where the more innovative device is inappropriate. For an illuminating discussion of the usage of relatively older and newer forms in poetics, see Meillet 1920.

[4] See N 1974a.244–255.

"secure material possessions, festive celebrations, long life."[5] The same claim is made for the related Indic expression *ákṣiti śrávas* at *Rig-Veda* 1.40.4, 8.103.5, 9.66.7.[6]

If, then, we are to defend the basic idea that Greek *kléos áphthiton* and Indic *śrávas . . . ákṣitam* are reflexes of a common Indo-European poetic expression, we must confront such claims of semantic differences between them. Let us for the moment concede that these differences do in fact exist. On the basis of such posited differences, it has been argued that "the Vedic pattern may actually be closer to the original meaning of the formula."[7] According to this argument, the emphasis on material security in the context of Indic *śrávas . . . ákṣitam* follows an Indo-European model, whereas the context of Greek *kléos áphthiton* in the *Iliad* supposedly represents something of a Homeric innovation, as we witness Achilles deliberately rejecting the material security of a *nóstos* 'homecoming' (the word is used at IX 413) in favor of a transcendent "fame," a poetic tradition that will survive him and will sing his glory forever.

This view concerning the distinctness of *kléos áphthiton* in *Iliad* IX 413 is at odds with the one that is advanced in my monograph on Greek and Indic meter, where I take the position that not only the Greek *kléos áphthiton* but also the Indic *śrávas . . . ákṣitam* convey the transcendent notion of a poetic tradition that will last forever, beyond today's material wealth and security, and that this notion is in fact an inherited Indo-European poetic theme.[8] The disagreement can best be summed up by observing two different interpretations of *viśvā́yur*, one of the three epithets—besides *ákṣitam*—that qualify *śrávas* 'fame' at lines b and c of *Rig-Veda* 1.9.7.[9] Whereas I translate *viśvā́yur* as 'everlasting',[10] it has been suggested that the more appropriate rendering would be 'lasting our lifetime.'[11] Two other epithets are cited in support of the second interpretation: at line a of the same stanza, *Rig-Veda* 1.9.7 *śrávas* is also

[5] Floyd 1980.135.

[6] Floyd p. 135.

[7] Floyd p. 139.

[8] N 1974a.244–255. For an effective answer to those who question the antiquity of this theme, see Risch 1987, esp. p. 4, where he points out a crucial oversight on the part of most experts who have expressed their views on the Greek epithet *áphthito-* 'imperishable' and its Indic cognate *ákṣita-*. Cf. also Watkins 1989.

[9] I follow Schmitt 1967.19n114 and 73n446 in interpreting the form *viśvā́yur* at *Rig-Veda* 1.9.7 as the neuter of *viśvā́yus-*, agreeing with *śrávas* 'fame', rather than *viśvā́yu-*, supposedly agreeing with *índra*. Granted, there are passages where *viśvā́yu-* is indeed attested as agreeing with *índra-* (e.g. *Rig-Veda* 6.34.5), but there are also clear attestations of neuter *viśvā́yus-* (Wackernagel and Debrunner 1930.291; concerning the tendency for *-ā́yu* to be displaced by *-ā́yus-* in the second part of compounds, see Wackernagel and Debrunner 1954.479). For a reading of *viśvā́yur* at *Rig-Veda* 1.9.7 as agreeing with *índra*, see Watkins 1989.

[10] N 1974a.110.

[11] Floyd 1980.136n6.

qualified as *vā́javat* 'rich in booty' and *gómad* 'rich in cattle'. It seems pertinent that Achilles himself, speaking of booty in general and mentioning cattle in particular at IX 406–407, goes on to say that all the booty that could be seized from Troy or Delphi is not worth as much as his own life (IX 401–405, 406–409), but that he will nevertheless lose his life in order to get something else that is indeed worth it, namely, *kléos áphthiton* (IX 413). By contrast, the *śrávas . . . ákṣitam* of *Rig-Veda* 1.9.7 is manifested precisely in the material security of booty in general and cattle in particular.

This disagreement over interpreting the Indic word *viśvā́yur* as epithet of *śrávas* 'fame' could be resolved by considering the etymology of the element *-ā́yur*, derived from *ā́yu-/ā́yus-*, a noun meaning 'lifetime' on two levels, the human and the cosmic. In an important article, Emile Benveniste establishes the formal relationship of this Indic noun, along with its Greek cognate *aiṓn*, also meaning 'lifetime', with such other words as Greek *aieí* 'forever, always', Latin *aeternus* 'eternal', Avestan *yauuaētāt-* 'eternity', and so on.[12] It is not without interest that Greek *aiṓn* 'lifetime' occurs at *Iliad* IX 415, in the context of contrasting, on the one hand, the *kléos* that will outlast Achilles (*Iliad* IX 413) and, on the other, the material security that would be his if he went home (IX 414; the theme of material security here is made explicit at IX 400). The *nóstos* 'homecoming' of Achilles (IX 413) is associated with material security as expressed by *aiṓn* (IX 415), and yet, to repeat, this same word *aiṓn* is related to another word *aieí* which actually means 'forever'! Moreover, the formulaic combination *áphthiton aieí* is attested in Homeric diction (II 46, 186; XIV 238), and there is even an instance of the combination *kléos áphthiton aieí* in an archaic piece of poetry inscribed in the seventh century B.C. (κλεϝος απθιτον αιϝει: DGE no. 316).

It seems safe to conclude, then, that from the standpoint of the Indo-European language family the notion of material wealth and security is not incompatible with the notion of eternity. To put it another way: the transcendent notion of eternity is actually visualized in terms of the material. Thus, for example, the word *aiṓn*, which is to be realized for Achilles in his possession of material wealth after a safe homecoming, has a built-in temporal sense by virtue of designating the vital force that keeps one alive and without which one would not be alive.[13] The notion of 'duration' extends to 'age', 'generation', with an open-ended perspective on the future: the cosmic vital force maintains an unending succession of generations, as we see clearly from the semantics of the Latin

[12] Benveniste 1937. Not cited by Floyd 1980.
[13] Benveniste p. 109.

cognate *aetas/aeternus.*[14] The Greek adverb *aieí* corresponding to the noun *aiṓn* is 'forever' in the original sense of a perpetual starting over (e.g. *Iliad* I 52).[15] Such a perpetual starting over can be described as an "eternal return."[16]

Moreover, the theme of personal immortalization is conventionally expressed in archaic Greek poetry by images of material wealth and security: witness the epithet *ólbioi* 'blessed' (from *ólbos* 'wealth') as applied to the immortalized heroes of the fourth generation of mankind (Hesiod *Works and Days* 172).[17] To cite another example: when the mortal Ino becomes immortalized as the White Goddess after death, she gets a *bíotos* 'life' that is *áphthitos* 'imperishable' (Pindar *Olympian* 2.29).[18] Similarly, whenever one's *aiṓn* is threatened by destruction, this threat can be expressed by verbs with root *phthi-* 'perish' (*Odyssey* v 160, xviii 204). Further, just as *á-phthi-to-* 'imperishable' can express personal immortalization, it can combine with *kléos* 'fame' to express the perpetuity of the poetic tradition that glorifies the one who is immortalized. Thus, for example, Ino not only gets a *bíotos* 'life' that is *áphthitos* 'imperishable': she also gets a *kléos* 'fame' that is, again, *áphthiton* (Hesiod F 70.7 MW).

By contrast, Achilles must give up his *aiṓn* 'lifetime' (IX 415), dependent on his *nóstos* 'return, homecoming' (IX 413), if he is to achieve a *kléos* that is *áphthiton* (IX 413). And yet, the word *aiṓn*, to repeat the conclusions of Benveniste, conveys the theme of an "eternal return."[19] This theme of returning into an afterlife is also pertinent to the word *nóstos* 'return, homecoming', as the work of Douglas Frame has shown.[20] Here, then, is the basic difference between the *kléos áphthiton* of *Iliad* IX 413 and the *śrávas ... ákṣitam* of *Rig-Veda* 1.9.7: Homeric poetry has separated not so much the theme of material wealth from the theme of perpetuity but rather the theme of personal immortalization from the theme of immortalization by way of poetry. Achilles is in effect saying

[14] Benveniste pp. 105, 109.

[15] Benveniste pp. 105, 109.

[16] Benveniste p. 100.

[17] See N 1979a.169–170 §30n2. On heroes as portrayed in the *Works and Days*, cf. also Vernant 1985.101, 104, 106. I interpret the μὲν at line 166 of the *Works and Days* as parallel to μὲν at lines 122, 137, 141, 161, not to μὲν at line 162 (*pace* West 1978.192). The discussion of cyclical regeneration at N pp. 168–172 is in line with Benveniste's notion (p. 112) that *aiṓn* is visualized as the synthesis of the finite and the infinite in the form of a circle.

[18] See N pp. 175 §1n4, 203 §41n2.

[19] Benveniste 1937.110.

[20] Frame 1978. See also pp. 92ff.; the discussion here of the relationship between *nóos/nóstos* and *psūkhḗ* is pertinent to the expression ψυχὴ πάλιν ἐλθεῖν 'that the *psūkhḗ* come back' at *Iliad* IX 408. The observations of Frame pp. 145–152 about the links between the themes of immortality and cattle in Indo-European poetic traditions are pertinent to the discussion above of the epithet *gómad* 'rich in cattle' at *Rig-Veda* 1.9.7.

that he chooses immortality as conferred by the *Iliad* over immortality as conveyed by the material visualizations of *aiṓn* and *nóstos*.[21]

The point remains, however, that the themes of material wealth and security, as conveyed by the epithet *áphthito-* 'imperishable', are in fact compatible with the themes of transcendent personal immortalization.[22] If the *kléos áphthiton* 'fame . . . imperishable' of Achilles is to be considered distinct, it is so only to the extent that this hero of the *Iliad* places the importance of his being immortalized by epic even higher than the importance of his own personal immortalization.

This is not to say, however, that the theme of personal immortalization is minimized by Homeric poetry. Given the specialized value system of Achilles, we may note that the *Iliad* itself provides the backdrop of a more generalized outlook where the theme of personal immortalization is clearly not incompatible with the theme of immortalization by epic in general and by the *Iliad* in particular. The case in point is the death and funeral of the Lycian hero Sarpedon, as narrated in the *Iliad*.

In considering this narrative about Sarpedon, I shall adduce three general principles established in three distinct fields, each of which has a direct bearing on the question of Homeric uniqueness. The fields are: (1) archaeology, (2) comparative linguistics, and (3) the study of "oral poetry." I propose to outline the three principles field by field, and then to correlate them with the passage describing the death and funeral of the hero Sarpedon, *Iliad* XVI 419–683.

First, we consider archaeology. We have already seen that the eighth century B.C., the era in which the *Iliad* and *Odyssey* were reaching their ultimate form, is as important for our understanding of Homeric poetry as is the late second millennium B.C., the era that provides the overt

[21] For more on the Iliadic theme of Achilles' immortalization by way of epic, see N 1979a.174–210. Note, too, that the hero Odysseus, unlike Achilles, achieves both a *kléos* and a *nóstos* (N pp. 36–41). From this point of view at least, the epic about Odysseus may indeed be considered to be closer to the Indo-European pattern. Moreover, in light of the connotations of the epithet *ólbioi* 'blessed' as discussed above, we may note in passing the expression *lāoì* . . . | *ólbioi* at *Odyssey* xi 136–137, mentioned in the context of Odysseus' ultimate 'homecoming': the setting of Odysseus' future death implies rebirth into an Elysian status, parallel to the status of the immortalized heroes on the Islands of the Blessed (as at Hesiod *Works and Days* 172, cited above). For other aspects of the theme of rebirth in the *Odyssey*, see Newton 1984.

[22] In the course of arguing that *kléos áphthiton* is a Homeric innovation, Finkelberg 1986.5 asserts that the application of *áphthito-* to an "incorporeal entity" like *kléos* 'fame' is a "semantic innovation"; at p. 4 she argues that, on the grounds that *áphthito-* applies mostly to "material objects," the "concrete associations of the term must have been the original ones." I question such a weighing of statistical predominance in determining what is "original." And I point out a salient feature, not noted by Finkelberg, in the contexts where *áphthito-* applies to "material objects": the concrete associations are otherworldly ones (cf. N 1974a.244–255).

subject matter for both of these epics.[23] What archaeology tells us is that the Hellenic institution of hero cults is shaped in the eighth century B.C., the same era that shaped the *Iliad* and *Odyssey*.[24] As Erwin Rohde emphasizes, the hero as a figure of cult must be local because it is a fundamental principle in Greek religion that his supernatural power is local.[25] On the other hand, the hero as a figure of epic is pan-Hellenic and consequently cannot have an overtly religious dimension in the narrative.[26] Such a restriction on the self-expression of Homeric poetry led Rohde to misunderstand the elusive evidence of the *Iliad* and *Odyssey* on heroes as cult figures. His belief was that the general Homeric silence on the subject of hero cults implies an absence of even the ideological background.[27] And yet, even Rohde had to admit that a central scene like the Funeral of Patroklos in *Iliad* XXIII preserves pervasive and unmistakable signs of cult.[28]

In fact, a general argument can be made that Homeric poetry is permeated with references—direct as well as oblique—to heroes in their religious dimension as figures of cult.[29] For the moment, however, I confine myself to citing the one central scene that Rohde himself acknowledged as just such a reference. This scene, the Funeral of Patroklos in *Iliad* XXIII, happens to be an ideal point of transition to the second of the three principles to be considered in evaluating the narrative about the death and funeral of Sarpedon in *Iliad* XVI. This time the field is comparative linguistics. As for the principle in question, the briefest of summaries will suffice: as we have already seen, not only is the Greek *language* cognate with other Indo-European languages such as Hittite and Indic, but also various Greek *institutions* are cognate with the corresponding institutions of other peoples speaking other Indo-European languages.[30] The case in point is one particular set of details where the evidence about a Greek institution can be matched with corresponding evidence attested in other societies with an Indo-European linguistic heritage. I refer to the Funeral of Patroklos in *Iliad* XXIII, as compared with the royal funerary rituals that are recorded in official Hittite documents.[31] The convergences in detail between the Iliadic scene and the standard Hittite ritual are so strikingly close as to

[23] See pp. 9–10.
[24] See pp. 10–11.
[25] Rohde 1898 1:184–189.
[26] Cf. N 1979a, esp. p. 342.
[27] For a sensible critique, see Hack 1929.
[28] Rohde 1898 1:14–22.
[29] N 1979a.69–117.
[30] See p. 2.
[31] As edited by Otten 1958.

suggest a common Indo-European heritage.[32] When we add the comparative evidence of funerary rituals and ancestor worship in the Indic traditions, the thesis of a common Indo-European heritage is further reinforced.[33]

The relevance of the Hittite and the Indic comparative evidence to the archaeologist's perspective cannot be emphasized enough: for instance, the evidence of cognate Hittite and Indic procedures in cremation makes obsolete the archaeological controversy over the cremation of Patroklos. Since inhumation seems to have been the standard procedure for the Hellenic people in the second millennium B.C., with cremation becoming common only in the first millennium, the cremation of Patroklos and other heroes in Homeric poetry has been interpreted as a phenomenon characteristic of the first millennium from the archaeological point of view.[34] The evidence of comparative linguistics, however, suggests that the procedures of cremation as attested in Homeric poetry are in fact so archaic as to reflect customs going back to a time even before the entry into Greece, in the beginning of the second millennium, of the Indo-European language that ultimately became the Greek language.[35] To put it another way: the literary testimony of Homeric poetry is in this case far more archaic than the archaeological testimony of Mycenaean civilization.

This is not to say, however, that the evidence of comparative linguistics on matters of ritual simply bypasses the second millennium B.C. I cite the Greek word *therápōn*, which is a borrowing, sometime in the second millennium, from one of the Indo-European languages spoken at that time in the area of Anatolia.[36] The given language may have been Hittite, Luvian, or some unattested near-relative, but in any case the evidence that we have for the word that was borrowed as *therápōn* comes primarily from Hittite: there the word appears as *tarpan(alli)-* or *tarpašša-*, corresponding to Greek *therápōn* and its by-form *théraps* respectively. In Hittite the word means 'ritual substitute'. The entity requiring substitution is as a rule the king himself, and *tarpan(alli)-/ tarpašša-* designates his alter ego ("un autre soi-même"), a projection upon whom the impurities of the king and of the community that he represents may be ritually transferred.[37] Here again the evidence is applicable to the death and

[32] See p. 85.
[33] See p. 85.
[34] E.g. Andronikos 1968.76.
[35] As I stressed in ch.4, I do not claim that cremation was the definitive Indo-European funerary ritual. I argue only that cremation was clearly one of perhaps several different types of Indo-European funerary ritual.
[36] Van Brock 1959; cf. N 1979a.33, 292–293; also p. 48 above.
[37] Van Brock p. 119.

funeral of Patroklos: there is a Greek reflex of the Hittite semantics in the Iliadic application of the title *therápōn* to Patroklos (*Iliad* XVI 244, etc.), the hero who was killed while wearing the armor of Achilles and who functions in the *Iliad* as the actual surrogate of Achilles.[38]

Mention of the Greek word *therápōn* is pertinent to the focus of this presentation in what follows, namely, the death and funeral of Sarpedon in *Iliad* XVI. We shall have occasion to see the deployment of another key word that is, again, of Anatolian origin, and again this word conveys the ritual dimension of the hero in epic. Before we can examine the word in question, however, the actual tradition of the Sarpedon story in the *Iliad* has to be defended. Some influential Homerists have cast doubt upon the authenticity of this tradition, arguing that the death of Sarpedon in *Iliad* XVI is a derivative story modeled on the death of Memnon as reflected in the *Aithiopis*.[39] This point of view has been seconded on an iconographical as well as literary basis by those who argue that the theme of the dead Memnon's removal by Eos is a basic and pervasive tradition among the Hellenes, and that the parallel theme of the dead Sarpedon's removal by Apollo seems by comparison marginal and flawed by artistic inadequacies.[40]

Such a line of argumentation, however, misses one of the most basic principles to be learned from the fieldwork of Milman Parry and Albert Lord in the realm of "oral poetry." This principle is also the third and last of the three principles to be considered and then applied to the Iliadic passage describing the death and funeral of Sarpedon. To put it briefly: in oral poetry, a given theme may have more than one version or variant, but such multiplicity of thematic variants does not mean that any one of them is somehow basic while the others are derivative. In terms of any operating system of oral poetics, each thematic variant is but a multiform, and not one of any variants in a given isolated grouping may be treated as a sort of *Ur*-form.[41] The same principle applies also to the study of myths in general. In the case of the Sarpedon story, to prove that it has artistic inadequacies that do not exist in the Memnon story is not the same thing as proving that one was modeled on the other. Each multiform can be expected to have its own inadequacies, and all we can say is that some may have more inadequacies than others. But even this value judgment may be a matter of cultural bias: it is possible that the very criteria of adequacy and inadequacy are in this and other instances

[38] Householder and Nagy 1972.774–776; cf. also Sinos 1980 and Lowenstam 1981.
[39] E.g. Schadewaldt 1965.155–202.
[40] Clark and Coulsen 1978.
[41] Cf. Lord 1960.100.

too narrowly based on the vantage point of one particular multiform that has for whatever reason become canonical.

The kind of reasoning that leads to the discounting of one variant as an invention based on another variant is but a symptom of a more general oversight that commonly afflicts the study of Homer: in our struggle to come to terms with the concept of "oral poetry," we tend to forget something more fundamental, that oral poetry is traditional poetry. An oral poet does not make up stories: rather, he retells stories that his audience has heard before and expects to hear again. As Albert Lord observes, "The picture that emerges is not really one of conflict between preserver of tradition and creative artist; it is rather one of the preservation of tradition by the constant re-creation of it. The ideal is a true story well and truly retold."[42]

With these thoughts in mind, we are ready to consider the Greek word of Anatolian origin that occurs in the Iliadic passage telling of the death and funeral of Sarpedon, son of Zeus himself. After this prominent Lycian prince dies at the hands of Patroklos, the plan of Zeus is that Apollo should remove his body by having the twins *Húpnos* 'Sleep' and *Thánatos* 'Death' convey it to his homeland of Lycia (*Iliad* XVI 454–455, 671– 673). At this point, the following sequence of events is to happen:

> ἔνθα ἑ ταρχύσουσι κασίγνητοί τε ἔται τε
> τύμβῳ τε στήλῃ τε· τὸ γὰρ γέρας ἐστὶ θανόντων
>
> *Iliad* XVI 456–457 = 674–675

> and there his relatives and comrades will give him a funeral [verb *tarkhúō*]
> with a tomb and a stele, for that is the privilege of the dead.

The conventional translation, 'give a funeral to', for the verb *tarkhúō* is inadequate, as we shall presently see. If indeed this story of Sarpedon—as also other Homeric stories—is a faithful retelling of a genuine tradition, then its Lycian setting assumes added significance. As it happens, the Lycian language is Indo-European in origin and closely related to Hittite and Luvian. In Lycian, there is a word *trqqas*, which designates a god described as one who smashes the wicked;[43] this form is directly related to Luvian *Tarḫunt-*, which is the name of the storm-god who is head of the Luvian pantheon.[44] There is also a Hittite version, attested as

[42] Lord p. 29.
[43] Laroche 1958.98–99; Heubeck 1959.32–35.
[44] Laroche pp. 98–99; cf. Watkins 1974.107.

Tarḫu- in theophoric names; it is also attested as the adjective *tarḫu-*, meaning 'conquering, victorious'.[45] This whole family of noun-formations stems from the verb *tarḫ-* 'conquer, overcome', which can be reconstructed as the Indo-European root *terh$_2$-.[46]

To sum up the point of this brief etymological survey: all indications are that the Greek verb *tarkhúō* is a second-millennium borrowing from an Anatolian language, and that the form borrowed was something like *tarḫu-* 'conquering, victorious'. This explanation of *tarkhúō* has been tentatively accepted in Pierre Chantraine's authoritative *Dictionnaire étymologique de la langue grecque*.[47]

We are still left, however, with the problem of translating Greek *tarkhúō*. Since the form *tarḫu-*, as we have seen, can designate a divinity in the Anatolian languages, Chantraine follows Paul Kretschmer's example in interpreting the Greek expression ἔνθα ἑ ταρχύσουσι at *Iliad* XVI 456 = 674 as 'and there they will treat him like a god'.[48] We may compare the Hittite expression designating the death of a king or queen in the royal funerary ritual: DINGIR^{LIM}-*iš kišat* '[he or she] becomes a god'.[49] The adverb ἔνθα 'there' in the Greek expression ἔνθα ἑ ταρχύσουσι refers to the *dêmos* 'district' of Lycia (*Iliad* XVI 455, 673; cf. 683).[50] I draw attention to this word *dêmos* in the context of the aforementioned fact that cult is a localized phenomenon in archaic Greek religion. I also draw attention to the following Homeric expression involving this same word *dêmos*:

> . . . θεὸς δ' ὣς <u>τίετο</u> <u>δήμῳ</u>
>
> *Iliad* V 78, X 33, XI 58, XIII 218, XVI 605
>
> . . . and <u>he got *tīmḗ* [honor]</u> in the <u>*dêmos*</u>, like a god

The verbs *tī́ō*/ *tīmáō* 'honor', and the corresponding noun *tīmḗ* 'honor', are crucial, since one of their uses in Greek is to designate the 'honor' that a god or hero gets *in the form of cult*; this usage is not recognized as a distinct category in the dictionary of Liddell and Scott, although it is richly attested in the language of archaic poetry and prose.[51] If indeed

[45] Laroche pp. 90–96.

[46] Laroche p. 96. Also Watkins 1990.

[47] DELG 1095.

[48] DELG 1095; Kretschmer 1940.103–104.

[49] Otten 1958.119–120.

[50] For the semantics of *dêmos* as 'district', see DELG 273–274; by extension, the word comes to mean 'people of the district' (e.g. *Odyssey* vii 11).

[51] *Prose:* cf. the use of *tīmḗ* at Herodotus 1.118.2 (cult of god) and 1.168 (cult of hero); cf. also the use of *tīmáō* at 1.90.2, 2.50.3, 2.75.4, 5.67.4–5. *Poetry:* cf. the use of *tīmḗ* in the *Homeric Hymn to Demeter* 311–312, where the theme of the gods' getting "honors" is correlated explicitly with the observance of their cults by mortals (also lines 353, 366–369); for

cult is also implied in the Homeric formula presently under consideration, then we could immediately justify Chantraine's interpretation of ἔνθα ἑ ταρχύσουσι at *Iliad* XVI 456 = 674 as 'and there they will treat him like a god': in the *dêmos* of Lycia, Sarpedon will get *tīmḗ* 'honor' just as a god would.[52]

What still stands in the way, however, is that the Homeric formula θεὸς δ' ὣς τίετο δήμῳ 'and he got *tīmḗ* [honor] in the *dêmos*, like a god' applies in each attestation to a hero who is still alive, whereas Sarpedon has already died. In fact, the procedure designated by the verb *tarkhúō* at *Iliad* XVI 456–674 is equated at *Iliad* XVI 457 = 675 with the procedure of providing the dead Sarpedon 'with a tomb and a stele, for that is the privilege of the dead'. We should keep in mind the archaeological evidence of the second millennium B.C. and thereafter, which suggests that a tomb and a stele are indeed standard features that mark the burial of the dead.[53] The problem is, how to reconcile this perspective of the hero as an apparent figure of cult with that of the hero as a figure of epic?

The solution to this problem, I suggest, lies in the actual contexts of the formula announcing that a given hero 'got *tīmḗ* [honor] in the *dêmos*, like a god' (*Iliad* V 78, X 33, XI 58, XIII 218, XVI 605). In each of these contexts, the hero appears in the function of either priest or king:

V 77–78	Dolopion as priest of Skamandros
X 32–33	Agamemnon as king of all the Argives
XI 58–60	Aeneas as grouped with the Antenoridai; at II 819–823, he and the Antenoridai are described as joint leaders of the Dardanians
XIII 216–218	Thoas as king of the Aetolians
XVI 604–605	Onetor as priest of Zeus Idaios

The sacral aspect of priests is in these cases overt, but not that of kings. As we turn from Homeric to Hesiodic poetry, however, we find an overt attestation showing that kingship is not only sacral but also intrinsic to the hero as a cult figure who gets his due *tīmḗ*.

The passage in question is the Hesiodic description of the Gold and Silver Generations of mankind, *Works and Days* 109–142. As Erwin Rohde has shown, the essence of the Gold and Silver Generations is that

commentary, see Richardson 1974.260–261. For more evidence from poetry, see Rudhardt 1970.6–7. See also in general Rohde 1898 1:99n1.

[52] See Kretschmer 1940.104 on the later literary and epigraphical evidence for the local cult of Sarpedon and Glaukos as heroes in Lycia. In Lycian Xanthos, there is also epigraphical evidence for a *dêmos* 'deme, district' named *Sarpēdónios* (Kretschmer p. 104).

[53] Andronikos 1968.114–121.

together they form a complete picture of the generic cult hero.[54] A review of the manifold details would go far beyond the scope of this presentation,[55] and I confine myself here to the themes of kingship and *tīmḗ*.

After the death of the Gold Generation is narrated (*Works and Days* 116, 121), they are described as possessing what is called the *géras basilḗion* 'honorific portion of kings' (γέρας βασιλήιον 126). We have already seen the word *géras* 'honorific portion, privilege' in a context where it designates the funerary honors accorded to the corpse of Sarpedon—honors that included the procedure designated by the verb *tarkhúō*:

ἔνθα ἑ ταρχύσουσι κασίγνητοί τε ἔται τε
τύμβῳ τε στήλῃ τε· τὸ γὰρ γέρας ἐστὶ θανόντων

Iliad XVI 456–457 = 674–675

and there his relatives and comrades will give him a funeral [verb *tarkhúō*] with a tomb and a stele, for that is the privilege of the dead.

It is worth noting in this connection that the Gold Generation 'died as if overcome by sleep' (θνῆσκον ... ὥσθ' ὕπνῳ δεδμημένοι *Works and Days* 116), whereas the corpse of Sarpedon was flown to Lycia by *Húpnos* 'Sleep' and *Thánatos* 'Death', who are described as "twins" (*Iliad* XVI 672). Since the word *géras* 'honorific portion, privilege' in Hesiodic diction and elsewhere represents a specific manifestation of *tīmḗ* (as in *Theogony* 392–396),[56] we can correlate what is said at *Works and Days* 126 about the Gold Generation's royal *géras* with what is said later about the Silver Generation: after the death of this next generation is narrated, they are described as

δεύτεροι, ἀλλ' ἔμπης τιμὴ καὶ τοῖσιν ὀπηδεῖ

Hesiod *Works and Days* 142

second in rank—but nevertheless they too get *tīmḗ*.

The irony here is that the Silver Generation, which represents the nega-

[54] Rohde 1898 1:91–110.
[55] I have attempted such a review in N 1979a.151–173.
[56] Benveniste 1969 2:43–50.

tive and latent side of the cult hero, earned an untimely death from Zeus for the following reason:

οὕνεκα τιμὰς
οὐκ ἔδιδον μακάρεσσι θεοῖς οἳ Ὄλυμπον ἔχουσιν

Works and Days 138–139

because they did not give *tīmḗ* [plural] to
the blessed gods who control Olympus.

This theme, that a hero gets *tīmḗ* even though he failed to give *tīmḗ* to the gods, is a key to understanding the religious ideology of god-hero antagonism, but a proper treatment of this subject would again go far beyond the scope of this presentation.[57] It will suffice for now to observe that the Silver Generation's failure to give *tīmḗ* to the gods is in part equated with their failure to make sacrifice to them:

ὕβριν γὰρ ἀτάσθαλον οὐκ ἐδύναντο
ἀλλήλων ἀπέχειν, οὐδ' ἀθανάτους θεραπεύειν
ἤθελον οὐδ' ἔρδειν μακάρων ἱεροῖς ἐπὶ βωμοῖς,
ἣ θέμις ἀνθρώποισι κατ' ἤθεα

Hesiod *Works and Days* 134–137

for they could not keep wanton outrage [*húbris*]
from each other, and they were unwilling either to be ministers to [verb *therapeúō*] the immortals[58]
or to sacrifice on the altars of the blessed ones,
which is the socially right thing for men, in accordance with their local customs.

In other words, the factor of *tīmḗ* is here expressed directly in terms of ritual sacrifice.

Our survey of formulas involving the concepts of *tīmḗ* and *dêmos* leads to the following conclusion: the hero who gets *tīmḗ* from the *dêmos* is said to be "like a god" *because he is thereby being treated as a cult figure.* In Homeric poetry, of course, the generic hero is predominantly a figure of

[57] See N 1979a.118–150.

[58] The use of *therapeúō* 'be a *therápōn* [minister]' may have deeper significance. As Sinos 1980 has shown, the *therápōn* in Homeric narrative is an inferior look-alike who can function as the equal of his superior look-alike and thus be invulnerable—*so long as he serves him.* Once he leaves his superior look-alike and acts on his own, however, the *therápōn* loses his invulnerability and dies, thus fulfilling his function as ritual substitute; see p. 48 above.

epic, and his dimension as figure of cult has to be latent—basically because he is still alive. Once he is dead, however, the perspective may change, as in the case of Sarpedon: the verb *tarkhúō*, designating what his relatives and comrades do to the dead hero, conveys the notion that he is being treated like a god—which is the epic way of saying that he is being treated like a cult figure.

It does not follow, however, that we may dismiss as poetic fancy the traditional notion that a hero is being treated like a god by virtue of getting *tīmḗ* from the *dêmos*. The institution of hero cult is visualized, from the religious standpoint of the institution itself, as a form of *immortalization after death*. In the *Homeric Hymn to Demeter*, for instance, the young hero who is protégé of the goddess loses his chance to be exempt from death (verses 260–264) but is offered as compensation a *tīmḗ* that is *áphthitos* 'imperishable' (verse 263).[59] In the following three verses, the ritual form of this *tīmḗ* is then actually made explicit: the youths of Eleusis will hold a festival of mock battles at a given season every year for all time to come (265–267). In other word, the cult hero is being awarded the permanent institution of a yearly ritual in his honor.[60] It is not without interest that the name of this young protégé of Demeter who becomes a cult hero is *Dēmophóōn* (e.g. 234), which apparently means 'he who shines for the *dêmos*'.[61]

If we now contrast Demophon as hero of cult with Achilles himself as a hero of epic, we can see more clearly the Homeric perspective on the very nature of being a hero. Whereas Demophon gets as compensation for his mortality a *tīmḗ* that is *áphthitos* 'imperishable', Achilles says that he will get as compensation for his own untimely death a *kléos* 'fame' that is *áphthiton* 'imperishable' (*Iliad* IX 413). As we have already seen, this word *kléos* designates the 'fame' that a hero gets *specifically by way of poetry*.[62] The ultimate hero of the *Iliad* is in effect saying that he will be immortalized by his own epic tradition. We have here the essence of the Homeric perspective: the theme of a hero's immortalization has been shifted from the realm of cult to the realm of epic itself. Accordingly, Homeric poetry tends not to speak in a direct fashion about immortalization because Homeric poetry presents itself as the very process of immortalization.

This is not to say, however, that Homeric poetry ignores the dimension of cult: rather, it places itself above cult. The *kléos* that the hero

[59] On the semantics of *áphthito-*, see pp. 124ff.

[60] Richardson 1974.245–248.

[61] Fuller discussion in N 1979a.181–182. In Greek vase inscriptions, the form ΔΕΜΟΦΑΟΝ is actually attested: see Richardson pp. 236–237.

[62] See p. 26.

earns in Homeric poetry by way of valor in battle serves to validate and even justify the *tīmḗ* 'honor' that he gets at home from his *dêmos* 'district'. While he is still alive in the *Iliad*, Sarpedon himself says so:

Γλαῦκε, τίη δὴ νῶι τετιμήμεσθα μάλιστα
ἕδρῃ τε κρέασίν τε ἰδὲ πλείοις δεπάεσσιν
ἐν Λυκίῃ, πάντες δὲ θεοὺς ὣς εἰσορόωσι,
καὶ τέμενος νεμόμεσθα μέγα Ξάνθοιο παρ' ὄχθας,
καλὸν φυταλιῆς καὶ ἀρούρης πυροφόροιο;
τῶ νῦν χρὴ Λυκίοισι μέτα πρώτοισιν ἐόντας
ἑστάμεν ἠδὲ μάχης καυστείρης ἀντιβολῆσαι,
ὄφρα τις ὧδ' εἴπῃ Λυκίων πύκα θωρηκτάων·
"οὐ μὰν ἀκλεέες Λυκίην κάτα κοιρανέουσιν
ἡμέτεροι βασιλῆες, ἔδουσί τε πίονα μῆλα
οἶνόν τ' ἔξαιτον μελιηδέα· ἀλλ' ἄρα καὶ ἶς
ἐσθλή, ἐπεὶ Λυκίοισι μέτα πρώτοισι μάχονται."

Iliad XII 310–321

Glaukos, why is it that you and I get the most honor [verb *tīmáō*, from *tīmḗ*] of all,
with a special place to sit, with choice meats, and with full wine-cups,
in Lycia, and everyone looks at us as gods,
and we are allotted a great *témenos* [sector of land] at the banks of the Xanthos,
fine land, orchard and wheat-bearing ploughland?
And so it is our duty to take our stand in the front ranks of the Lycians, and to meet blazing battle head-on,
so that one of the heavily armored Lycians may say of us: "Indeed it is not without *kléos* that our kings
are lords of Lycia, who feed upon fat sheep
and drink choice sweet wine, since they have genuine strength
and since they fight in the front ranks of the Lycians."

On one level, the examples of *tīmḗ* recounted by Sarpedon to Glaukos can function as attributes of a living epic hero who happens to be a king; on another level, however, each example can be matched with a corresponding sacral honor accorded to a cult figure. As we know from Greek religious practices attested in the historical era, cult heroes receive libations,[63] choice cuts of meat placed on a special table,[64] and

[63] Burkert 1985.194, 205.

[64] On the practice of *trapezṓmata*, see Gill 1974. Sarpedon's royal diet of mutton (*Iliad* XII 319) may be correlated with archaeological discoveries at Eretria showing that sheep are the usual victims sacrificed to heroes (see Hadzisteliou Price 1973.136).

the allotment of a *témenos* in the sense of 'sacred precinct'.[65]

From the standpoint of the *Iliad*, then, Sarpedon's goal is to get a *kléos* that matches the *tīmḗ* that he already has at home in Lycia. From the standpoint of cult, however, this *tīmḗ* would be possible only after he dies, so that the epic perspective has the logical sequence reversed: by placing epic above cult, Homeric poetry allows the hero, *even before he dies*, to have the kind of *tīmḗ* that befits a cult hero. What he still has to earn by dying is *kléos* itself.

Sarpedon then goes on to say that he and Glaukos should be prepared to die in battle at Troy (*Iliad* XII 326–328), and that he would choose to escape from battle only if escaping entailed immortality (322–325). The implication seems to be that the welcoming of death may succeed in bringing immortality where the avoidance of death has failed: after all, both *tīmḗ* and *kléos*, which are in store respectively for the hero of cult and the hero of epic after death, are *áphthito-* 'imperishable' (τιμὴ ... ἄφθιτος *Homeric Hymn to Demeter* 263; κλέος ἄφθιτον *Iliad* IX 413).

The same sort of implication can be found in the words of Hera at *Iliad* XVI 440–457, where she tells Zeus that he must not permit Sarpedon to escape death in battle and thus send him back home to Lycia alive (see especially line 445). Implicitly, Sarpedon would then have *tīmḗ* without having had to experience death. The exemption of Sarpedon from death in battle, Hera says to Zeus, would be without precedent: in her words, "beware lest some other divinity may wish to send his or her son back home, away from the battle" (*Iliad* XVI 446–447). Instead, Hera suggests, Zeus should let his own dear son die at the hands of Patroklos, after which *Thánatos* 'Death' and *Húpnos* 'Sleep' will take Sarpedon's body back home to the *dêmos* 'district' of Lycia (XVI 450–455). Immediately after these verses, we come upon the verse that describes the ritual performed on Sarpedon's corpse, as designated by the verb *tarkhúō* (XVI 456, repeated at 674). From the context of Hera's words, we now see that the action conveyed by this verb is presented as a compensation for the death that Sarpedon must experience. From the other contexts that concern the theme of compensation for mortality, we also see that the verb *tarkhúō* entails the theme of immortalization after death—in a way that is yet to be defined. That is to say, the verb *tarkhúō* indicates not only that the relatives and comrades of Sarpedon will treat him like a cult figure but also that he will thereby attain some form of immortalization after death.[66]

[65] On the *témenos* as a sacred precinct, see Burkert 1985.84–87; on the precincts of Pelops and Pyrrhos, see Burkert 1983.93–103 and 119–120, respectively.

[66] This interpretation can be extended to the only other Homeric attestation of *tarkhúō*

The explanation of *tarkhúō* that I have just offered is corroborated by the evidence of comparative linguistics. The Indo-European root *terh$_2$-, which survives as Hittite *tarḫ-* 'conquer, overpower, overcome', also survives as Indic *tar(i)-* 'overcome, cross over', which takes the shape *-tur-* in compounds (e.g. *ap-túr-* 'crossing over the water'). The latter formation corresponds to the *-tar-* of Greek *nék-tar*, the substance that sustains the immortality of the Olympian gods; furthermore, the root *nek-* in *nék-tar* is the same as in Latin *nex* 'death' and Greek *nék-ūs*/ *nek-rós* 'corpse'.[67] Thus the word *nék-tar* must once have meant something like 'overcoming death'; in fact, there is a kindred combination of concepts, even words, in archaic sacral Indic poetry, where the verb *tar(i)-* 'overcome' is actually attested in a context where *mr̥tyú-* 'death' is its direct object (*Atharva-Veda* 4.35.1d-6d).[68]

This evidence not only provides yet another argument for the heritage of an Indo-European poetic language.[69] More immediately, it also gives us a broader perspective on the semantics of Greek *tarkhúō*. To put it another way: the meaning of Greek *-tar-* in *nék-tar*, where the root is directly inherited from Indo-European, may help us comprehend the meaning of Greek *tarkhúō*, where the stem *tarkhu-* is indirectly inherited from Indo-European by way of a Greek borrowing from the Anatolian language family.[70] I draw special attention to the corresponding Anatolian form *tarḫu-* as it appears in Hittite *tarḫu-* 'victorious' and in Luvian *Tarḫunt-*, the name of the storm-god who is head of the Luvian pantheon—and who wields the thunderbolt as his attribute.[71] Perhaps these formations convey the theme of overcoming not just evildoers or other such immediate obstacles, but also the ultimate obstacle of death itself.[72]

Let us look for a parallel in the figure of Zeus himself, head of the Greek pantheon and wielder of the thunderbolt in his own right. With

besides *Iliad* XVI 456 = 674, namely, *Iliad* VII 85. The dead body in this case is that of the hypothetical hero who is to answer Hektor's challenge to fight whoever is the "best of the Achaeans" (see VII 50) in one-to-one combat (VII 67–91). Elsewhere, I argue that the words of Hektor ironically apply to Achilles himself (N 1979a.26–41), and that Achilles himself is destined for personal immortalization in alternative epic traditions that are implicitly recognized by the *Iliad* (N pp. 174–210 and 317–347).

[67] Thieme 1952. See also Schmitt 1967.186–192. The objections raised against this etymology have been convincingly refuted by Schmitt 1974.

[68] Schmitt 1967.190.

[69] Schmitt pp. 190–191; cf. Householder and Nagy 1972.771–772.

[70] DELG 1094 at least allows for the possibility that the Greek word *tárīkhos* 'smoked fish, mummy' is a related borrowing. In Herodotus 9.120 the word is applied to the corpse of the hero Protesilaos, who in this context is believed to be endowed with supernatural powers. See N 1987c.

[71] On *Tarḫunt-* and the thunderbolt, see Laroche 1958.95.

[72] Cf. the contexts assembled by Laroche pp. 90–91.

his thunderbolt, Zeus can cause both the death and the immortalization of heroes. We may take for example the poetic tradition that tells how Semele became immortalized as a direct result of dying from the god's thunderbolt (Pindar *Olympian* 2.25, in conjunction with Hesiod *Theogony* 942).[73] Then there is the case of Herakles, son of Zeus, who is struck by the thunderbolt of his divine father and thereby elevated to Olympus as an immortal (Diodorus Siculus 4.38.4–4.39.1).[74] Finally, we may consider yet another son of Zeus, none other than the Lycian king Sarpedon, whose dead body undergoes a process designated by the verb *tarkhúō*. I submit that this process entails immortalization of the hero after death.

The fundamental difference, however, between the explicit immortalization of Herakles and the implicit immortalization of Sarpedon is that the first is narrated as an event on the level of myth whereas the second is narrated as an event on the level of ritual. Still, the myth and the ritual are complementary aspects of one ideology. The rituals of cult are a code that can convey the same message as that conveyed by the code of the myth. On a formal level, we can see most clearly the complementary function of myth and ritual in expressing the theme of immortality by considering the name *Ēlúsion* 'Elysium'. We may turn to the renowned passage in *Odyssey* iv 561–569 where this name designates a special place of immortalization for heroes, and indeed the concept of Elysium has become a permanent fixture of Western civilization. But we seldom hear of what ancient commentators on Greek religion have to say about *ēlúsion* as a plain noun. In the Alexandrian lexicographical tradition (Hesychius s.v. Ἠλύσιον), the word is glossed as κεκεραυνωμένον χωρίον ἢ πεδίον 'a place or field that has been struck by the thunderbolt', with this added remark: καλεῖται δὲ καὶ ἐνηλύσια 'and it is also called *enēlúsia*'. This definition is confirmed by the testimony of Polemon (F 5 Tresp), who explains that *enēlúsion* is a place made sacred by virtue of having been struck by a thunderbolt; also, the adjective *enēlúsios* is attested in Aeschylus TGF 17 as an epithet of the hero Kapaneus, who was struck dead by the thunderbolt of Zeus.[75] We may compare the semantic relationship of *enēlúsios/enēlúsion* with that of *hierós/hierón* 'sacred'/'sacred place'. Moreover, the body of the thunderstruck Kapaneus is described as *hieró-* 'sacred' in Euripides *Suppliants* 935.[76]

[73] In the Pindaric narrative, Semele's abode of immortality is Olympus itself. See also Diodorus Siculus 5.52, Charax FGH 103 F 14, and so on.

[74] Cf. Rohde 1898 1:320–322.

[75] Burkert 1961.

[76] Cf. also the testimony of the Thurian gold leaves at A1.4, A2.5, A3.5 (Zuntz 1971.301–305), where the persona of the dead man is represented as declaring in each instance that his immortalization was preceded by death from the thunderbolt.

Besides *Ēlúsion*, there is also another example of a form that serves to designate both a place of immortalization on the level of myth and a cult site on the level of ritual. In Hesiod *Works and Days* 171 we hear of a place called *Makárōn nêsoi* 'Islands of the Blessed', where heroes who fought in the Theban and Trojan wars are immortalized after death (167 and following).[77] But there is also a tradition according to which the name *Makárōn nêsos* 'Island of the Blessed' was actually applied to the old acropolis of Thebes, the Kadmeion; specifically, the name designated the sacred precinct where Semele, the mother of Dionysus, had been struck by the thunderbolt of Zeus (Parmenides in *Suda* and in Photius s.v. Μακάρων νῆσος; Tzetzes on Lycophron 1194, 1204).[78]

Let us return for one last viewing of the corpse of Sarpedon. It is appropriate to notice that the *Iliad* contains other indications of his impending immortalization besides the verb *tarkhúō* at XVI 456 = 674. Each of these indications requires a discussion that would go beyond the scope of this presentation, and I will content myself with merely listing them as signposts for future elaboration:

Apollo bathes the body of the dead hero Sarpedon in a river (*Iliad* XVI 669 and 679).[79]

Apollo anoints the body of Sarpedon with *ambrosíē* 'ambrosia' (XVI 670 and 680)[80] and clothes it in vestments that are *ámbrota* 'immortalizing' (same lines).[81]

The name *Sarpēdṓn* applies not only to the hero but also to various places associated with the mythological theme of abduction by winds or by birdlike Harpies.[82] This theme is expressed by way of various forms containing the verb-root *harp-* 'snatch' (as in *hárpuia* 'Harpy' and *harpázō* 'snatch'), which may be formally connected with the element *sarp-* of *Sarpēdṓn*.[83] In this connection, I cite the following observation: "It is not too surprising that Homer makes Sarpedon the subject of the only big

[77] On the association, at Hesiod *Works and Days* 172, of the word *ólbioi* with the heroes who inhabit the Islands of the Blessed, see N 1979a.170 § 30n2. Cf. also p. 126 above.

[78] Burkert 1961.212n2.

[79] Cf. the theme of the "baths of Okeanos" at *Iliad* XVIII 489 = *Odyssey* v 275, as discussed in N 1979a.201–204. In the case of *Iliad* XVI 669 and 679 it is possible that these verses referred originally to the local waters of the Lycian river Xanthos (cf. *Iliad* II 877, V 479, VI 172).

[80] Note that *ambrosíē* is used in Homeric diction as a synonym of *néktar*; in other words, ambrosia and nectar do not seem to be specialized always as food and drink respectively (see Schmitt 1974.158).

[81] On the use of *ámbroto-* and its derivatives to designate the notion of 'immortalizing' as well as 'immortal', see Thieme 1952.

[82] See Vermeule 1979.242n36 and 248n36 on the "Harpy Tomb" of Xanthos. On the theme of death / immortalization in the form of abduction by winds, see N 1979a.190–203.

[83] On the morphology of *-ēdṓn*, see Risch 1974.61. More on Harpies at pp. 243ff. below.

snatch in the *Iliad*, though he transformed the carriers from lady birds to Sleep and Death, to match more familiar configurations of epic mortality."[84]

The snatching of Sarpedon's body by *Húpnos* 'Sleep' and *Thánatos* 'Death' (XVI 454, 672, 682) can be correlated with the manner in which the hero faints and dies. As in the case of other Homeric heroes, Sarpedon loses his *psūkhḗ* when he dies (XVI 453) as also earlier when he falls into a swoon from a terrible wound (V 696). Nowhere in Homeric poetry, however, is a hero ever described as regaining his *psūkhḗ* when he is revived from a swoon.[85] This rigorous stricture in Homeric diction implies that the reintegration of the *psūkhḗ* with the body is understood as immortalization, the overt expression of which is programmatically avoided in the *Iliad* and *Odyssey*.[86] Still, the manner in which Sarpedon recovers from his swoon seems to be a latent expression of this hero's destiny of immortalization: Sarpedon is revived by a blast from Boreas the North Wind (V 697). We note that it was to a rock named *Sarpēdṓn* that Boreas snatched Oreithuia away (scholia to Apollonius of Rhodes 1.211 = Pherecydes FGH 3 F 145).[87]

Coming now to the end of this inquiry into the death of Sarpedon, we are left perhaps even more mystified than ever by this uncanny Anatolian analogue of a Herakles. There are so many ramifications waiting to be explored that this presentation amounts to a set of questions more than answers. But this much at least is certain: Homeric epos is a repository of secrets about life and death—secrets that it will never fully reveal. In the case of Sarpedon, his Anatolian heritage allows a glimpse behind the veil of Homeric restraint—and the secrets are almost given away.

[84] Vermeule 1979.169.
[85] See p. 90.
[86] See pp. 90ff.
[87] Cf. Vermeule 1979.242n36.

CHAPTER 6

The King and the Hearth: Six Studies of Sacral Vocabulary Relating to the Fireplace

In the *Electra* of Sophocles, Clytemnestra dreams that Agamemnon has come back from the dead to the realm of light (417–419; ἐς φῶς 419). The king seizes the *skêptron* 'scepter' (σκῆπτρον 420) that had once been wielded by him, but which is now held by the usurper Aegisthus (420–421), and he places it firmly into the royal hearth, the *hestíā* (ἐφέστιον | πῆξαι 419–420). From the hearth, there then grows out of the scepter a shoot so vigorous that it covers with its shade all the kingdom of Mycenae (421–423).[1] The focus in the inquiry that follows is this very symbol of the *hestíā* 'hearth' as the generatrix of the authority that is kingship.

The general symbolism of the Greek noun *hestíā* and of the goddess Hestia, who is the personification of the hearth, has been studied by Jean-Pierre Vernant as a model of Greek society in general and of the family in particular.[2] Vernant draws our attention to the traditional themes of Hestia's virginity (*Homeric Hymn* [5] *to Aphrodite* 21–32) and immobility (e.g. *Homeric Hymn* [29] *to Hestia* 3).[3] He explains these themes in terms of the exogamous and patrilocal ideology of Greek society at large. Whereas in real life women are as a rule mobile, being

[1]In *Iliad* I 233–237, this same *skêptron* 'scepter' is viewed as a thing of nature that has been transformed into a thing of culture; commentary in N 1979a.179–180, 188–189. Here in Sophocles *Electra* 421–423, the transformation is in the other direction. On the cult of Agamemnon's *skêptron* at Khaironeia, where its local name is the *dóru* 'wood, shaft', see Pausanias 9.40.11–12. Discussion by N 1974a.242–243n16, with emphasis on the epithet *áphthiton* 'imperishable' as applied to the *skêptron* at *Iliad* II 46, 186.

[2]Vernant 1985, esp. pp. 165–169; cf. also Gernet 1968.387.

[3]Vernant pp. 156–157.

shifted from hearth to hearth in the exogamous pattern of Greek marriages, myth presents an opposite image, that of the virginal and immobile goddess Hestia, who conveys the ideal, the myth, of an unbroken male line, an ever-renewed cloning of the father, by way of the paternal hearth.[4] On the level of family, the very legitimacy of generation, of reproduction, is warranted by the paternal hearth of the family.[5]

On the level of archaic Greek society in general, legitimacy is seen as a prolongation of the paternal line. Legitimacy is a global symbol for society, inasmuch as the body politic is embodied in kingship. The symbolism is at work in the vision taken from Clytemnestra's dream, where the legitimate king is seen as sprouting from the hearth. And we must keep in mind that the Mycenaean Royal Hearth, as pictured in this dream, is destined to become the Public Hearth of the polis.[6] It is in fact a distinguishing feature of the Classical city-state that the Public Hearth is housed in the *prutaneîon* 'presidential building':[7] in Athens, for example, the arkhon's authority is said to be derived from the Common Hearth (Aristotle *Politics* 1322b), and he actually resides in the *prutaneîon* (Aristotle *Constitution of the Athenians* 3.5).[8]

This symbolism of the Greek *hestíā* 'hearth' as the generatrix of authority is a matter of Indo-European heritage. Turning to the evidence of other Indo-European languages, specifically the hieratic diction of such disparate organizations as the Atiedian Brethren of Umbrian Iguvium and the Brahmans of the Indic Vedas, we shall find some striking convergences with the Greek model. Since we are dealing with societies that spoke cognate languages, I am encouraged to see in such convergences the actual traces of cognate religious attitudes, or even of cognate institutions.

The form that is central to my six studies of sacral vocabulary relating to the fireplace is the Indo-European root $*h_2es$-. As a verb, $*h_2es$- must have meant something like 'set on fire'—or so we might infer from the comparative evidence of various Indo-European languages that we are

[4] Vernant pp. 163–165.

[5] Concerning the ritual of the Amphidromia, where the naming of the newborn child literally revolves around the *hestíā*, see Vernant pp. 189–195: for the naming to be formalized, the father runs around the hearth carrying his new baby on the fifth day after birth and then sets down the child in the sacred area thus circumscribed (scholia to Plato *Theaetetus* 160e; Hesychius s.v. Δρομιάμφιον ἦμαρ; scholia to Aristophanes *Lysistrata* 758). On the Eleusinian ritual concept of the παῖς ἀφ' ἑστίας 'boy from the hearth [*hestíā*]' (Harpocration s.v. ἀφ' ἑστίας, *Anecdota Graeca* 204.19 ed. Bekker), see the discussion in Vernant pp. 164–168 and the updating of sources in Burkert 1983.280n31.

[6] Vernant p. 187.

[7] Vernant pp. 181, 186.

[8] Vernant p. 186.

about to examine. Let us begin with the Hittites. Purely on phonological grounds, we may expect the root *$h_2$es- to survive in the Hittite language as *ḫaš-*, and there is indeed an attested Hittite noun *ḫašša-* meaning 'sacrificial fireplace'.[9] This noun, it is generally agreed, is related in form to Latin *āra* 'sacrificial fireplace, altar'.[10]

The problem is, there is also a Hittite verb *ḫaš-* meaning not 'set on fire' but 'beget'.[11] Despite this semantic anomaly, I propose to relate this Hittite verb *ḫaš-* 'beget' to the noun *ḫašša-* 'sacrificial fireplace'. As I hope to show in due course, the actual context for a semantic relationship between the concepts of "beget" and "fireplace" may be latent in the heritage of myth and ritual.

There is a related problem, I suggest, in the semantics of the Hittite noun *ḫaššu-*, meaning 'king', which has been connected in some studies with the verb *ḫaš-* 'beget'.[12] In what follows, I shall be arguing that both this noun and *ḫašša-* 'sacrificial fireplace' are derived from the same Hittite verb *ḫaš-* 'beget'.[13] Already at this point, we may note an analogous semantic relationship, even if we fail to understand as of now the precise application of the notion "beget." The English noun *king* and the German cognate *König* stem from a Germanic formation *kuningaz. This noun is a derivative of *kun- (as in Gothic *kuni* 'race, family'), a root with cognates in Latin *gēns, genus, gignō*, etc.[14] We may note especially the meaning of *gignō* as 'beget' (e.g. Ennius *Annals* 24S). As I also hope to show in due course, the actual context for a semantic relationship between the concepts of "beget" and "king" may be latent in the heritage of myth and ritual.

[9] Cf. Benveniste 1962.14.

[10] Benveniste p. 14.

[11] For a survey of various etymologies that have been proposed for this Hittite verb, see Tischler 1983.191–194.

[12] See the survey in Tischler pp. 207–209, who lists other suggested etymologies as well.

[13] The Hittite verb *ḫaš-* 'beget' is spelled with a single *s* in the third person singular (*ḫa-a-ši*) and with a double *s* in the third plural (*ḫa-aš-ša-an-zi*). Such derivatives as *ḫaššatar* 'begetting, *gēns*' show double *s* (*ḫa-aš-ša-tar*), and so too the proposed derivative *ḫaššu-* (*ḫa-aš-šu-*). By contrast, consider the Luvian and Palaic adjective *wašu-* 'good', with single *s*, which seems to be derived from the verb *wašš-* 'be agreeable', attested in Hittite with double *s*. Instead of *wašu-*, however, the Hittite word for 'good' is *aššu-*, with double *s*. Even if we are not prepared to explain them, it is important to note the existence of such *s/ss* variations. I find a similar *s/ss* problem in the contrast of Latin *āra* and Umbrian *asa*, both meaning 'sacrificial fireplace, altar'. Like Latin, Umbrian rhotacizes single intervocalic *-s-, so that we have to reconstruct an inherited Italic contrast of **āsā* vs. **ăssā* in order to account for the respective Latin and Umbrian forms. Again, I merely note the existence of this *s/ss* variation, rather than attempt an explanation.

[14] Benveniste 1969 2:85.

Greek *Hestia*, Latin *Vesta*, Indic *Vivasvat*

According to Georges Dumézil, the root *u̯es- of Greek *hestíā* 'hearth' (ἑστία) and Latin *Vesta*, Roman goddess of the hearth, has a cognate in the Indic form *vi-vás-vat-*.[15] The mythical figure Vivasvat (*vi-vás-vat-*), as we have already seen, is the first person ever to receive fire on earth, by virtue of being the first sacrificer on earth; he is ipso facto the ancestor of the human race.[16] In Vedic diction, to say *sádane vivásvataḥ* 'at the place of the Vivasvat' (*Rig-Veda* 1.53.1, etc.) is the same as saying 'at the sacrifice'. Vivasvat, father of Yama (10.14.5, 10.17.1), is formally and thematically cognate with a figure in the Zoroastrian *Avesta*, Vīvahvant-, father of Yima. Vīvahvant was the first person ever to prepare Haoma (*Yasna* 9.3–4). The association of Iranian Vīvahvant with Haoma is crucial because the Indic Vivasvat likewise has special associations with Soma (*Rig-Veda* 9.26.4, 9.10.5, etc.), and, further, because Soma/Haoma (from Indo-Iranian *sauma) constitutes the Indo-Iranian sacrifice par excellence.[17]

The Indic form *vivásvat-* is an adjective derived from the verb *vas-*, with the attested meaning 'shine'.[18] The Vedic god of sacrificial fire, Agni himself, is called the Vivasvat at the morning sacrifice, as Uṣas the goddess of dawn appears (*Rig-Veda* 1.44.1, 7.9.3).[19] Uṣas the Dawn is in turn called the feminine equivalent, Vivasvatī:

dídr̥kṣanta uṣáso yā́mann aktór
vivásvatyā máhi citrám ánīkam

Rig-Veda 3.30.13

at the coming of Uṣas from the darkness,
they yearn to see the great shining visage of the Vivasvatī

When the fire-god Agni begot the human race, his "eye" was *vivásvat-*:

imā́ḥ prajā́ ajanayan mánūnām
vivásvatā cákṣasā dyā́m ca apáś ca

Rig-Veda 1.96.2

[15] Dumézil 1954.34–35.
[16] See p. 104.
[17] See pp. 104ff.
[18] Dumézil 1954.34.
[19] Cf. p. 104, where *Rig-Veda* 7.9.3 is quoted.

he [Agni] begot this progeny of men [and]
with his shining [*vivásvat-*] eye, the sky and the waters

In Vedic diction, the causative stem *janáya-* is used indifferently to denote either 'beget' or 'create'. For another example of *janáya-* in the sense of 'create', I cite the following verses, again concerning the fire-god Agni:

tvám bhúvanā janáyann abhí krann
ápatyāya jātavedo daśasyán

Rig-Veda 7.5.7

your sound is heard, as you create the world,
O Jātavedas [Agni], helpful for progeny

The macrocosmic principle inherent in Agni, god of sacrificial fire, is anchored in a belief that the rising of the sun is dependent on the kindling of the sacrificial fire. The sacrificers pray as follows:

ā́ te agna idhīmahi
dyumántaṃ devā̆járam
yád dha syā́ te pánīyasī
samíd dīdáyati dyávi

Rig-Veda 5.6.4

may we, Agni, kindle
your bright, ageless fire,
so that your wondrous brand
may shine in the sky

In fact, it is Agni whom the sacrificers implore to make the sun ascend the sky (*Rig-Veda* 10.156.4). The *Śatapatha-Brāhmaṇa* puts it even more bluntly (2.3.1.5): without the morning sacrificial fire, there would be no sunrise. The macrocosmic *cákṣas-* 'eye' of Agni in the passage cited above, *Rig-Veda* 1.96.2, is clearly the sun (cf. also 6.7.6). With the sun, Agni *ajanayat* 'created' or 'begot' the world and mankind. To repeat, the epithet of this solar symbol *cákṣas-* is *vivásvat-*, derived from the verb *vas-* 'shine'.

By now we have seen three important contexts for the adjective *vivásvat-* in Vedic poetry:

1. epithet of Agni, god of sacrificial fire
2. epithet of Agni's eye, the sun, when he begot mankind

3. name of the first sacrificer on earth, ancestor of mankind

From these Vedic contexts of *vivásvat-*, then, it appears that the usage of the Indic verb *vas-* was appropriate to three parallel themes: the shining of the sun, the kindling of the sacrificial fire, and the begetting of progeny. Furthermore, as we have also seen, *vas-* implied creation as well as procreation.

To repeat, Dumézil argues that the root of this Indic verb *vas-* is cognate with the root *u̯es- of Greek *hestíā* 'hearth' (ἑστία) and of Latin *Vesta*, Roman goddess of the hearth.[20] Going beyond Dumézil's position, we may consider the possibility that this root *u̯es- could be reconstructed further as *h_2u̯es-, despite the absence of any phonological trace of word-initial *h_2 before *u̯ in Greek *u̯estiā, whence *hestíā* 'hearth' (ἑστία).[21] This reconstruction is not essential to the main points still to be raised. Still, if it turns out to be valid, then the root *h_2u̯es- of the Greek noun *hestíā* 'hearth' may possibly be interpreted as a variant of the root *$h_2$es- as in the Hittite noun *ḫašša-* 'hearth'—and, I would add, in the Hittite verb *ḫaš-* 'beget'. Such a root-variation *$h_2$es- vs. *h_2u̯es- would be in line with an Indo-European pattern attested in a series of possible examples

[20] Dumézil 1954.34–35. In Ionic and other Greek dialects as well, there is a variant of Attic *hestíā* (ἑστία), namely *histíā* (Ionic ἱστίη): see DELG 379. I draw attention to the raising of *e to *i after the labial *u̯ in *histíā*, to be reconstructed as *u̯istíā. Such replacement of *e by *i in the vicinity of labials is a feature of the "standard" Mycenaean dialect: see Householder and Nagy 1972.784–785. In other words, there is a possibility that the variant form *histíā* is a reflex of the "standard Mycenaean" dialect of the second millennium B.C. For a working definition of "standard Mycenaean," see Risch 1966 (updating in Risch 1979). For an alternative explanation of the *i in *histíā*, see Vernant 1985.199–200.

[21] The absence of *h_2 before *u̯ in a hypothetical Greek formation *u̯estiā may conceivably be explained on the basis of a combination of morphological and phonological factors. First, the morphology: the suffix-formation of *u̯estiā, as DELG 379 points out, suggests that this noun is derived from an adjective *u̯esto-, or possibly from *u̯estā-. Formations like *u̯esto- are typical of what we find in the second half of compounds. Which brings us to the second consideration, that of phonology. It appears that laryngeals (*h_1, *h_2, *h_3) can disappear without trace in the second half of compounds (see Beekes 1969.242–243 for a list of examples; cf. Mayrhofer 1986.125, 129, 140). If, then, we accept the argument in DELG that the Greek noun *u̯estiā may be a derivative of compound-formations, then we may expect phonological instability in the retention of laryngeal reflexes. Even more important, there is another factor leading to a pattern of phonological instability in Greek *u̯estiā: in many inscriptions featuring dialects that normally retain initial *u̯, the expected digamma (= *u̯) of *u̯estiā is not spelled out (DELG 379). What seems to be at work here is the force of analogy: we may posit a pairing, in Greek usage, of *hestíā* (ἑστία) with another word designating 'fireplace', *eskhárā* (ἐσχάρα); it is clear that *eskhárā* never had an initial *u̯, as DELG 379 makes clear. Besides the semantic convergences between these two words for 'fireplace', *hestíā* and *eskhárā*, we should note, already at this point, an important divergence that is pertinent to the semantics of other words for 'fireplace' to be studied later on in this presentation: unlike the *hestíā*, the *eskhárā* is potentially movable: see Risch 1981 [1976].537 (also DELG 379–380).

shaped CeC(C)- vs. Cu̯eC(C)-.[22] To repeat: given that Indic *vas-* 'shine' conveys simultaneously the themes of the shining sun, the kindling of sacrificial fire, and the begetting of progeny, the reconstruction *h_2u̯es- of this root, entertained here simply as a remote possibility, would make it a formal variant of *$h_2$es-, as in Hittite *ḫaš-* 'beget' and *ḫašša-* 'sacrificial fireplace'.[23]

The Indic verb *vas-* 'shine', which I have tentatively reconstructed as *h_2u̯es-, has a noun-derivative *uṣás-* 'dawn', which in turn can be reconstructed as *$h_2$us-os-. There is an e-grade variant, $h_2$eus-os-, attested in Latin *aurōra* 'dawn' and in Greek *aúōs/ ḗōs* (Aeolic αὔως/ Ionic ἠώς) 'dawn'.[24] According to this scheme, there is a possibility that both Latin and Greek have words for the macrocosm of 'dawn' built from the root *$h_2$eu̯s- and for the microcosm of 'sacrificial fireplace' built from the same root, but with a different configuration: *h_2u̯es- as in Greek *hestíā* (ἑστία) and Latin *Vesta.*[25]

[22] Where C = consonant. For the formulation of this Indo-European pattern of root-variation, see Kuryłowicz 1927 (*pace* Benveniste 1969 1:22–25). Some suggested examples of CeC(C)- vs. Cu̯eC(C)-: *$h_1$esu- vs. *h_1u̯esu-, as in Greek ἐυ- 'good', Hittite *aššu-* 'good', vs. Indic *vásu-* 'good', Iranian (Avestan) *vohu-* 'good', Luvian and Palaic *wašu-* 'good'; *teks- vs. *tu̯eks-, as in Indic *takṣ-* 'fashion' vs. Indic *tvakṣ-* 'fashion', Iranian (Avestan) θ*uuaxš-* 'fashion'; *$h_1$ers- vs. *h_1u̯ers, as in Indic *arṣ-* 'flow', Hittite *arš-* 'flow' vs. Indic *varṣ-* 'rain', Greek ἕρση / ἐέρση 'dew', Hittite *warša-* 'dew'.

[23] Moreover, the reconstruction *h_2u̯es- may possibly fit the Hittite verb *ḫuiš-* 'live' (if, however, Luvian *ḫuit-* is a cognate, on which see Tischler 1983.264–266, then this connection is to be rejected). If Hittite *ḫuiš-* is conceivably cognate with Indic *vas-* 'shine', the meaning 'live' rather than 'shine' would be in line with the semantics of Hittite *ḫaš-*, meaning 'beget' rather than 'set on fire', despite the meaning of *ḫašša-* 'sacrificial fireplace'. We may note that the suffix of the Hittite adjective *ḫuišwant-* 'alive' is cognate with that of the Indic adjective *vivásvat-*. The root *h_2u̯es-, this hypothetical reconstruction from Greek *hestíā* 'hearth' (and conceivably from Hittite *ḫuiš-* 'live'), is not to be confused with the *h_2u̯es- of the Greek aorist *áesa* (ἄεσα) 'spend the night', which is a variant of *$h_2$eu̯s- as in the Greek present *iaúō* (ἰαύω) 'sleep'. The distinctness of the roots is reflected in Indic, where *vas-* 'spend the night' (present third singular *vásati*) is conjugated differently from *vas-* 'shine' (present third singular *uccháti*).

[24] Alternatively, we may conceivably reconstruct Greek *aúōs/ ḗōs* as *$h_2$us-os- instead of *$h_2$eu̯s-os- (cf. Peters 1980.31–32). In any case, the spelling of Aeolic αὔως reflects an underlying *au̯u̯ōs; the gemination of *u̯ reflects the Aeolic device for poetic lengthening of initial syllables with shape *Vu̯- (where V = vowel), on which subject one of the most informative works remains Solmsen 1901. By contrast, the Attic-Ionic device for poetic lengthening of initial syllables with shape *Vu̯- is not gemination of the *u̯ but lengthening of the *V-: *hau̯ōs to *hāu̯ōs to ἠώς in Ionic (Homeric), ἕως in Attic. For a summary of the diachronic motivations for poetic lengthening of the initial syllable, see Kuryłowicz 1956.264–269; also Householder and Nagy 1972.754. Alternatively, *au̯u̯ōs and *āu̯ōs may perhaps be direct phonological reflexes of *ausōs.

[25] Just as the posited root-variant *h_2u̯es- may have survived in Greek as *hestíā* 'hearth' (ἑστία), without a phonological trace of *h_2 (see n21), so also the root-variant *$h_2$eu̯s- apparently survives as *heúō* (εὕω) 'singe', again without a trace of *h_2. Cognates of Greek *heúō* are Latin *ūrō* 'burn' and Indic *óṣati* 'burn'. In this case, the loss of *h_2 in the Greek reflex of the posited root *$h_2$eu̯s- may be attributed to the secondary nature of e-grade

The semantic connection between the macrocosm of dawn and the microcosm of the sacrificial fireplace is explicit in the *Rig-Veda,* where the coming of dawn is treated as an event parallel to the simultaneous kindling of the sacrificial fire (1.124.1, 11; 5.75.9; 5.76.1; 5.79.8; 7.41.6; etc.). The link or *dūtá-* 'messenger' between dawn and the sacrificial fireplace is the fire-god Agni:

tvā́m íd asyā́ uṣáso vyùṣṭiṣu
dūtám kr̥ṇvānā́ ayajanta mā́nuṣāḥ

Rig-Veda 10.122.7

at the lighting-up of this dawn [*uṣás-*],
men [= "descendants of Manu"][26] have sacrificed, making you [Agni] the messenger [*dūtá-*]

In the stanza immediately following (*Rig-Veda* 10.122.8), the Vasiṣṭha-s ('the Best') are described as archetypal sacrificers who summoned Agni to the sacrifice. These same priestly Vasiṣṭha-s are also the first to waken Uṣas 'Dawn' with their songs of praise (7.80.1). Elsewhere in the *Rig-Veda,* it is Uṣas who awakens men for the morning sacrifice (e.g. 1.113.8–12), as opposed to the converse theme where the sacrificers awaken Uṣas:

yāvayád dveṣasaṃ trā
cikitvít sūnr̥tāvari
práti stómair abhutsmahi

Rig-Veda 4.52.4

by songs of praise, with awareness,
we awakened you [Uṣas]
who ward off the foe, O Sūnr̥tāvarī![27]

formations of the type *heúō/ ūrō/ óṣati,* apparently built on the zero-grade of the root (on such a pattern of derivation, see Kuryłowicz 1968.221). Parallel to secondary verb-formations of the type *óṣati* 'burn', Indic preserves secondary adjective- and noun-formations of the type *-óṣa-,* as in *dur-óṣa-* 'hard to kindle' and *óṣa-dhī* 'plant'. I interpret the latter form as a compound consisting of the roots *uṣ-* (from *$h_2$us-) 'light' and *dhā-* (from *dheh$_1$-) 'put, place', meaning something like 'light-emplacement'; see p. 103. For thematic evidence in support of this etymology, see pp. 102ff. For a survey of the etymological possibilities of *óṣa-dhī* 'plant', including the one suggested here, see again Minard 1956.268. We may compare the semantics of the English idiom "*set* on fire."

[26] More on Manu at pp. 110ff.

[27] The root *nr̥t-* 'dance' in the epithet of Uṣas, *sūnr̥tāvari* may be compared with the collocation of *khoroí* 'dances' and *Ēṓs* 'Dawn', as at *Odyssey* xii 4. For more on the goddess Eos 'Dawn' and her relation to the dance, see Boedeker 1974.58–63, 87–88.

Radical *$h_2$es- and Latin *āra*

Hittite *ḫašša-* is comparable in both form and meaning to Italic *āsā / *ā̆ssā 'sacrificial fireplace, altar', as in Latin *āra*, Umbrian *asa*, Oscan *aasaí* (locative).[28] The length of the radical vowel, guaranteed by Latin *āra* and Oscan *aasaí*, may be a secondary Italic development.[29] If the original Italic root is *ăs-, we may then reconstruct *ăs(s)-ā- from *$h_2$es(s)-oh_2-, vs. *$h_2$os(s)-o-, as in Hittite *ḫašša-*.

Also apparently related to Latin *āra* and Hittite *ḫašša-* is a series of Germanic derivatives nouns with root *as-/*az- (from *$h_2$es-). The following list shows some of the most plausible examples:

Old Norse *arinn* 'sacrificial fireplace', from *az-ina- (cf. also the Finnish borrowing *arina* 'hearthstone');

German *Esse* 'smith's fireplace' = 'forge', from *as-jōn; likewise Old High German *essa*, Old Norse *esja* (cf. also the Finnish borrowing *ahjo* 'fireplace');

English *ash(es)*, from *as-kōn; likewise Old English *aesce*, Old Norse *aska*, Old High German *asca*.

For the meaning of English *ashes*, we may compare the Indic cognate, *ā́sa-* 'ashes'.[30] This masculine noun can be reconstructed as *$h_2$os-o-,

[28] Cf. p. 145n13 above.

[29] As we may possibly infer from such contrasts as in Latin *ăcuō* vs. *ācer*.

[30] For an especially interesting attestation, let us consider the context of *ā́sa-* 'ashes' at *Śatapatha-Brāhmaṇa* 4.5.1.9, where *ā́sa-* is being described as a creative substance. The *ā́sa-* is what becomes of the *aṅgā́ra-s* 'coals' mentioned in *Śatapatha-Brāhmaṇa* 4.5.1.8, where the *aṅgā́ra-s* are in turn described as the creative substance from which the priests known as the *Áṅgiras-*es originate (cf. EWA 48). Cf. also *Aitareya-Brāhmaṇa* 3.34, and *Śatapatha-Brāhmaṇa* 1.7.4.4, 2.3.2.1.3, 12.4.1.4. We may compare the forms and meanings of Indic *aṅgā́ra-* 'coal' and *Áṅgiras-*, the name for the fire-priests, with the forms and meanings of Greek *ánthrax* 'coal' and *ánthrōpos* 'human', which I interpret etymologically as 'he who has the looks of embers'. In a future study I hope to connect this proposed etymology with the context of *thūmálōps* 'piece of burning wood, charcoal' in Aristophanes *Acharnians* 321, which may be a veiled reference to a local anthropogonic tradition; see especially *ánthrakes* 'charcoal', as associated with the Acharnians, at lines 34, 332. On the anthropogonic theme of First Man as First Sacrificer, see pp. 70, 110–111. (On the possibility of a related theme, that of First Man as First *Mántis* 'Seer', see p. 198n120.) I draw attention to two of the mock-names of members of the chorus of Acharnians: *Marīládēs* 'son of embers' (*Acharnians* line 609), derived from *marī́lē* 'embers of charcoal' (as at line 350: see p. 198n120), and *Prīnídēs* 'son of holm oak' (line 612), parallel to the general description of the Acharnians as *prī́ninoi* 'made of holm oak' (line 180; on the connections of anthropogony with the material of wood, see p. 198n120). The latter description of the Acharnians is coupled with *stiptoí* 'tough' (line 180), in the sense of "compressed by treading down," like the charcoal used by smiths (Theophrastus *On fire* 37; cf. Sommerstein 1980.176); moreover, the *ánthrakes*

which also fits Hittite *ḫašša-* 'sacrificial fireplace'.[31] For a parallel to the semantic contrast of *ḫašša-* 'sacrificial fireplace' vs. *ā́sa-* 'ashes', we may compare Lithuanian/Latvian *pẽlenas/pęlns* 'domestic fireplace, hearth' (singular) vs. *pelenaĩ/pęlni* 'ashes' (plural).

Another possible reflex of the root *as- (from *$h_2$es-) occurs in Greek *ás-bolos/ as-bólē*, traditionally translated as 'soot'.[32] A clear example is the following passage, where a woman is being blamed for laziness about her household tasks:

οὔτε πρὸς ἰπνὸν ἀσβόλην ἀλευμένη
ἵζοιτ'

Semonides F 7.61–62 W

Nor would she sit by the oven, [thus] avoiding the *asbólē*.

The preceding survey of noun-derivatives of root *$h_2$es- points to the basic form of a verb. The intransitive sense of this verb, I suggest, is 'be on fire', as we may infer from the following correspondences in the Indic evidence:

kā́ma- 'desire'	from	*kam-* 'be desirous'
śā́ka- 'power'	from	*śak-* 'be powerful'
etc.		
ā́sa- 'ashes'	from	*as- 'be on fire' (?)

We may consider the following semantic parallel in Lithuanian and Latvian:

pelenaĩ 'ashes'	from	*pel- 'be on fire'[33]
pęlni 'ashes'		

There is another possible attestation of root *$h_2$es- as verb in Latin

'charcoals' are described as *prī́ninoi* 'made of holm oak' (ἀνθράκων πρινίνων 668). Thus the "tough stuff" that men are made of is also the stuff of charcoals (on the wood used for charcoal by the Acharnians, see also Sommerstein p. 171). A pervasive theme of the *Acharnians* of Aristophanes is the ridiculing of the Acharnians' feelings of solidarity and even affection toward the *ánthrakes* 'charcoals' (325–341), which they treat as animate beings, as their *dēmótai* 'fellow district-members' (349; cf. 333).

[31] The lengthening of the radical vowel in *ā́sa-* is secondary: see Kuryłowicz 1968.282–283 on the phenomenon known as Brugmann's Law.

[32] I accept the etymological interpretation "Aschen-wurf": Schwyzer 1939 1:440; for the absence of -o- between ἄσ- and -βολος, cf. ἐπεσ-βόλος, κερασ-βόλος.

[33] As in Old Church Slavonic *polěti* 'be on fire'.

ardeō, ardēre 'be on fire', which can be reconstructed as *ā̆s-edh-[34] plus stative suffix *-ē-.[35] Similarly, I reconstruct Latin *āreō, ārēre* 'be dry' as *ās- plus stative suffix -ē-, without the segment *-edh-. We may compare the reconstructed doublet *ā̆s-edh- (*ardeō, ardēre* 'be on fire') vs. *ās- (*āreō, ārēre*) with Greek *phleg-éth-ō* (φλεγ-έθ-ω) vs. *phlég-ō* (φλέγ-ω), both meaning 'be on fire'; also the solar names *Pha-éth-ōn* (Φαέθ-ων) vs. *Phá-ōn* (Φά-ων), both meaning 'bright, shining'.[36] Within the semantic framework of cause, that is, fire, and effect, that is, no water, it is easy to imagine a development in the meaning of *ās-ē- from 'be on fire' to 'be dry'. In Tocharian there is a verb *as-* (presumably from *$h_2$es-) meaning 'become dry'.[37] For another aspect of the semantic factor "no water" in *ā̆s-, we may consider the usage of the original participle of Latin *ardēre*, that is, *assus*, which means 'roasted, broiled', that is, 'cooked without water' as opposed to *ēlixus* 'boiled'.[38]

An alternative reconstruction of *ardēre*, *ā̆si-dhē-, is disadvantageous because there is no convincing morphological justification for an *-i-.[39] Nor will it do simply to assume that *ardēre* is derived from *āridus* 'dry', by way of a syncope of *-i-*. In attested Latin, the formal and functional correlates of stative adjectives in *-idus* are stative verbs in *-ēre*, not *-(i)dēre*:

calidus 'hot'	*calēre* 'be hot'	(*calor* 'heat')
tepidus 'warm'	*tepēre* 'be warm'	(*tepor* 'warmth')
āridus 'dry'	*ardēre* 'be on fire'	(*ardor* 'burning')

I fail to see how an adjective *āridus* meaning 'dry' could motivate a derivative *ardēre* meaning 'be on fire', especially when there already exists a stative verb *ārēre* meaning 'be dry'.[40]

The semantic distinction between

[34] For an example of a Latin form in which rhotacism precedes syncope, cf. *ornus* 'mountain-ash tree', from *ŏrenos from *ŏsenos (cf. Old Slavonic *jasenĭ* 'ash tree'), on which see DELL 469. Also Leumann 1977.96, 99, who contrasts the type *ornus* with the type *pōnō* (from *po-sinō). Consider also *Faler-nus* (from *Falis-inos; cf. *Falis-cī*).

[35] The Indo-European stative *-ē- is familiar even from the internal evidence of Latin: *calēre* 'be hot', *tepēre* 'be warm', *albēre* 'be white', etc.

[36] Cf. p. 235. For other such doublets, see Schwyzer 1939.703.

[37] We may compare the secondary length in the perfect and causative *ās-* (vs. present *as-*) with the long radical vowel of Latin *ārēre*.

[38] Cf. DELL 51–52.

[39] This rejected etymology figures among those entertained by Sommer 1914.66–67; note Sommer's argument that *arfet*, putative formal equivalent of *ardet*, is a textual corruption.

[40] Granted, a verb like *gaudēre* presupposes an original formant *gāu̯id-, latent in the participle *gauīsus*; note, however, that there is no trace of any *ārid- in the original participle of *ardēre*, which is, to repeat, *assus* (again, DELL 51–52).

ardēre 'be on fire'	from	*ă̄s-edh-ē-
and		
ārēre 'be dry'	from	*ă̄s-ē-

would be an illustration of Kuryłowicz's so-called Fourth Law of Analogy,[41] in that the more evolved form has the basic meaning and the basic form has the more evolved meaning. The basic form in this case, however, that is, *ă̄s-, may still retain the basic meaning of 'burn' in the noun-derivative *ārea,* which means 'ground, space free of buildings or trees'. The association of this word with trees seems to be the earlier situation, as in the following context:

liber ab arboribus locus est, apta area pugnae

Ovid *Fasti* 5.707

the place is free of trees, an area suited for battle

Presumably, the *ārea* was originally a place where trees and bushes had been burned clear for the purpose of farming. We may compare Lithuanian *ìš-dagas* 'arable land', derived from the verb *dèg-ti* 'burn'.[42]

Besides retaining the basic notion of 'burn' in the Latin nominal derivative *ārea,* the root *ă̄s- also retains this notion in the Latin noun-derivative *āra* 'sacrificial fireplace, altar'; attested with the same meaning are the Oscan cognate *aasaí* (locative singular) and the Umbrian cognate *asa.* The Italic form *ă̄ssā-, which I reconstruct further as $*h_2es(s)oh_2$-,[43] is directly comparable with the Hittite form *ḫašša-* 'sacrificial fireplace', from $*h_2os(s)o$-.[44]

Like Hittite *ḫašša-*, Latin *āra* is consistently associated with fire, as in this example:

adolescunt ignibus arae

Virgil *Georgics* 4.379

the altars light up with the fires

[41] J. Kuryłowicz's "Fourth Law": "Quand à la suite d'une transformation morphologique une forme subit la différentiation, la forme nouvelle correspond à sa fonction primaire (de fondation), la forme ancienne est réservée pour la fonction secondaire (fondée)." Quoted from Kuryłowicz 1966 [1945–1949].169.

[42] For further semantic analogues, cf. Reichelt 1914.313–316; Reichelt's interpretation of *āra* differs from the one presented here.

[43] For the secondary character of the lengthened radical vowel overt in Latin and Oscan, cf. the lengthening in *ārēre*; also, cf. again such *ă/ā* variations as in *ăcuō* vs. *ācer,* etc.

[44] Cf. pp. 144–145.

The Oscan cognate of Latin *āra,* namely *āsā-*, is actually combined with an explicit adjectival derivative of *pūr-* 'fire' (cognate of Greek *pûr* = πῦρ 'fire') in the locative phrase *aasaí purasiaí* 'on a fiery *āsā-*' (147 A 16, B 19 Vetter). We may compare, too, the Umbrian sacral formula *pir ase antentu* 'let him put fire on the *ā̆sā-*' in the *Iguvine Tables* (IIa 19–20, III 22–23).

Latin *altāria* and *adolēre*

There is a latent trace of the connection between fire and Latin *āra* in the formation *altāria* 'sacrificial fireplace, altar'. This neuter plural noun arose from an adjectival *alt-āri-*; the first part is traditionally connected with the root of *adoleō,* while the second is explained as the adjectival suffix *-āli-*, with dissimilation of the *-l-*.[45] Instead, I propose that *altāria* is a Bahuvrīhi compound meaning 'whose *ā̆s- is nurtured'. I note the incidental explanation in Paulus ex Festo 5 ed. Lindsay: *altare, eo quod in illo ignis excrescit* 'called *altāre* because fire develops there'; to be contrasted is the folk etymology recorded in Paulus ex Festo 27: *altaria ab altitudine dicta sunt* 'called *altāria* on account of the *alt*itude'.

As justification for my interpretation of the *alt-* in *altāria* as the verbal adjective of *alō* 'nurture', I cite the common Latin expression *ignem alere* 'nurture fire', that is, 'keep the fire going'.[46] The posited Bahuvrīhi compound *al-to- + *ā̆s-i- 'whose *ā̆s- is nurtured' has numerous morphological parallels in Indic, of the type *hatá-mātr̥-* 'whose mother is killed';[47] among the examples from the *Rig-Veda,* I single out the semantically crucial *iddhā́gni-* (1.83.4, 8.27.7), analyzed etymologically as **idh-ta-* + **agni-*[48] and meaning 'whose fire is kindled'. Some morphological parallels in Latin itself are such compounds as *uersipellis* 'whose skin is changed [literally 'turned']'. In Plautus *Amphitruo* 123, Jupiter is so described for having assumed human form; elsewhere, *uersipellis* designates 'werewolf' (Pliny *Natural History* 8.34; Petronius 62). We may compare too the epithet *altilāneus* 'whose wool is nurtured', a specialized word used in the *Acts of the Arval Brethren* to describe sacrificial sheep

45 DELL 24.

46 Cf. Cicero *De natura deorum* 3.37; Livy 21.1.4; Pliny *Natural History* 2.236; Ovid *Metamorphoses* 10.173, *Remedia Amoris* 808; Tacitus *Germania* 45, *Annals* 15.38, *Histories* 3.71; etc.

47 Cf. Whitney 1896.446. For the phonological development from *alto-ā̆si- to *altāri-*, with deleted *-o-, cf. the types *magn-animus, rēm-ex,* etc.

48 Whether Indic *agní-* 'fire' originates from *egni- or *n̥gni- is irrelevant to the reconstruction of *iddhā́gni-*.

(*a.* 183 I 24 ed. Henzen). In Virgil *Aeneid* 12.169–170, a *sacerdōs* 'priest' is sacrificing an *intonsam bidentem* 'unshorn sheep', and the setting is *flagrantibus aris*, 'flaming altars' (*ārae*). The Servian commentary adds (*ad locum*) the following explanation: *quam pontifices altilaneam uocant* 'and the priests [*pontifices*] call it [the unshorn sheep] *altilānea*'. For the reconstructed notion of *lānam alere* 'grow wool' underlying the compound *altilāneus*, we may compare the attested notions of *capillum alere* 'grow hair' (Pliny *Natural History* 24.140) and *pilos alere* 'grow hair' (35.47).

As for the attested Latin notion of *ignem alere* 'nurture fire' = 'keep the fire going', I have found at least three parallels in the Indic traditions. The first of these is an abstract noun derived from *al- 'nurture', which has survived passim in the *Rig-Veda* with the specialized sense of designating the wood with which the fire is kindled. The word for such wood is *áraṇi-*. From the etymological point of view, I am proposing that the *áraṇi-* is the 'nurturing, nourishment' of the fire.[49] Since Latin *alō* can be used in the sense of 'nurture [the embryo] within the uterus' (e.g. Varro *De re rustica* 2.4.13, Gellius 12.1.6, Paulus ex Festo 8, etc.), it may be viewed as a comparable theme that the fire-god Agni of the *Rig-Veda* is born daily from firesticks called *áraṇi*-s (3.29.2, 7.1.1, 10.7.9, etc.).[50] Produced from the *áraṇi*-s, Agni is a newborn infant, hard to catch (5.9.3–4).[51] An epithet of Agni is *mātaríśvan-* (1.96.4, 3.5.9, 3.26.2), which means 'swelling inside the mother' (*śvan-* from *śū-* 'swell'); as the Mātariśvan, Agni "was fashioned in his mother" (*ámimīta mātári* 3.29.11).[52] In short, I conclude that the *áraṇi-* is the *alma māter*, as it were, of fire.

[49] The derivation of *áraṇi-* from *al- 'nurture' is communicated as a possibility by R. Hauschild to M. Mayrhofer; cf. KEWA s.v. (this possibility is more recently rejected in EWA s.v.). There are numerous morphological parallels to the proposed derivation of *áraṇi-*, in the reconstructed sense of 'nurturing, nourishment', from *al- 'nurture': I cite for example Rig-Vedic *dhumáni-* 'blowing', from *dham-* 'blow' (for a list of other such examples, cf. Wackernagel and Debrunner 1954.207); cf. also p. 186n37 below. For an interesting analogue to the proposed semantic specialization of an abstract noun like *áraṇi-* into the concrete designation of the wood with which the fire is "nurtured," I cite the post-Vedic meaning of *taráṇi-*: it is no longer abstract 'crossing'—from root *tar-* 'cross'—but rather concrete 'ship' *or* concrete 'sun'. In other words, the abstract notion of the *act* of crossing becomes specialized as the concrete notion of the *means* of crossing. (For a discussion of the process whereby abstract nouns become concrete, see N 1970.63–65, 68–70; cf. also Ernout 1954.179–183 ch. 6, "Passage de l'abstrait au concret.") On the mythical themes of the sun's crossing from the realm of light to the realm of darkness and back, see N 1979a.192–210.

[50] *Rig-Veda* 3.29.2 is quoted at p. 103.

[51] I note in passing that there are comparable themes concerning the infant Hermes in the *Homeric Hymn to Hermes*.

[52] More on Mātariśvan at pp. 103ff.

This theme brings us to the second of the three Indic parallels to the Latin notion of *ignem alere* 'nurture fire' = 'keep the fire going'. There is a neuter noun *alāta-* 'firebrand, coal', attested for example in the *Mahābhārata,* which can be interpreted etymologically as 'the nurturing one', derivable from an earlier form *ala-.[53] As the third and final example, I note that the Indic root *al- survives in the post-Vedic word for 'fire', *an-ala-*, which has been interpreted as an original adjective meaning 'insatiable';[54] we may compare Greek *án-altos* (ἄν-αλτος) 'insatiable', as in *Odyssey* xvii 228. There is ample thematic evidence that Indic poetic traditions represent fire as the prime insatiable element.[55] As long as a fire is kept going, it must be fed, and it always needs more: hence *an-ala-*, 'the insatiable one'.

I reconstruct the *-al-* of Greek *án-altos* 'insatiable' as *$h_2$el- (the *án-* would reflect *n̥- added at a stage when initial *h_2- was already lost). This root is also to be found in the causative formation *ol-éi̯-e/o- attested in Latin *adoleō* and Umbrian *uřetu.*[56] In the case of Latin *adoleō,* the sequence *ol* presents a phonological problem: word-medial *ol* should survive as *ul,* as we see from the borrowings *crāpula* from κραιπάλη and *anculus* from ἀμφίπολος. In archaic Latin, granted, we do see sporadic traces of *ol* for *ul* (*popolom, Hercolei,* etc.), but the consistency of the form *adoleō* and the total absence of *aduleō is puzzling. There is a similar crux with *subolēs* and *indolēs.* Faced with these phonological problems, one expert finds himself forced to assume morphological interference with phonological change, in that *sub-olēs* 'offshoot' and *ind-olēs* 'inherent nature' must be derivatives of *olēscō* 'increase, be nurtured'.[57] In Festus 402 (ed. Lindsay), we read *suboles ab olescendo, id est crescendo, ut adolescentes quoque, et adultae, et indoles dicitur* '*subolēs*: from *olēscō*; as also *adolēscentēs, adultae, indolēs*', an explanation followed by illustrative citations from Lucretius (4.1232) and Virgil (*Eclogues* 4.49).

We now turn to the actual meaning of *adoleō,* as also of Umbrian *uřetu.* Although this verb is usually translated as 'burn', Latin *adoleō* can be interpreted etymologically as 'nurture' in terms of a causative formation. As contextual affirmation of this etymology, let us test this transla-

[53] For morphological parallels, cf. the Rig-Vedic derivative *śáryāta-* from *śárya-* 'reed, arrow'; the derivational expansion of the base from *-a-* to *-āta-* is especially marked in names of plants or trees, as in *āmrāta-* 'Spondias mangifera', derived from *āmrá-* 'mango' (cf. Wackernagel and Debrunner 1954.269).

[54] Schulze 1966 [1927].215–216. Cf. EWA 70.

[55] Schulze pp. 215–216.

[56] The *h_2 disappears before *o. The etymology of Umbrian *uřetu* as *olētōd, equivalent of Latin *(ad-)olētōd* 'let him burn', is suggested *en passant* by Thurneysen 1907.800.

[57] Leumann 1977.86.

tion in the following passages, where we should note as well the consistent collocation of *adoleō* with derivatives of the root *ā̆s-:

cruore captiuo adolere aras

Tacitus *Annals* 14.30

nurture the *āra*-s with the blood of captives

igne puro altaria adolentur

Tacitus *Histories* 2.3

the *altāria* are nurtured with pure fire

sanguine conspergunt aras adolentque altaria donis

Lucretius 4.1237

they sprinkle the *āra*-s with blood and they nurture the *altāria* with offerings

castis adolet dum altaria taedis

Virgil *Aeneid* 7.71

while . . . nurtures the *altāria* with pure pitch-pine[58]

I propose that the idea behind these expressions involving *adoleō* is that the sacrificial fireplace is being "nurtured" by being kept lit with flames and, indirectly, with the material consumed by the flames. Where *ad-ol-eō* is actually combined with *alt-āria*, the collocation of *-ol-* vs. *alt-* can be said to reflect an inherited *figura etymologica.* We may compare the definition in Paulus ex Festo 5 (ed. Lindsay): *altaria sunt in quibus igne adoletur* '*altāria* are places in which there is *adolēre* with fire'. For the sense of "nurture," we may compare the use of *adoleō* with *penātēs*, a name for the gods of one's native sacrificial fireplace:

flammis adolere penates

Virgil *Aeneid* 1.704

To nurture the *penātēs* with flames

Servius explains (*ad locum*) that the verb *adolēre* is equivalent in usage to

[58] A sacrifice is being described, at which Lavinia's hair seems to catch on fire.

augēre 'increase': *adolere est proprie augere.* We may compare, too, the formal opposite of *adoleō, aboleō,* meaning 'cause to atrophy, check the growth of, abolish'.

In Umbrian, the causative formation *ol-éi̯-e/o- is attested in the sacral formula

pir persklu uřetu

Iguvine Tables III 12; cf. IV 30

with a prayer, let him nurture the fire

The imperative *uřetu* corresponds formally to Latin *(ad-)olētō*; for the change from *-l-* to *-ř-*, we may compare Umbrian *kařetu* 'let him call', from *kal- as in Latin *calāre* 'call'. Semantically, Umbrian *pir . . . uřetu* is comparable with the Latin combination *ignem alere.*[59]

In the case of Latin *adoleō,* its formal and functional connection with *alō* became eroded, so that the contextual association of *adoleō* with the notion of burning promoted a less restricted and etymologically inaccurate usage. Consequently, *adoleō* in the simple sense of 'burn' became capable of taking direct objects designating material meant to be burned, as in the following:

uerbenasque adole pinguis et mascula tura

Virgil *Eclogues* 8.65

burn fertile boughs and male frankincense

Besides the formation *ol-éi̯-e/o- of *adoleō,* which we are translating as 'nurture', Latin has also preserved a stative-intransitive type *ol-ē-, plus iterative suffix *-sk-e/o-, in the verb *adolēscō* 'become nurtured, grow'; the stative-intransitive *ol-ē- is also attested in *adolē-faciō* 'cause to be nurtured', which occurs specifically in the context of thunderstruck trees in the *Acts of the Arval Brethren* (*arborum adolefactarum, a.* 224.16). Even the verb *adolēscō* is attested in the context of burning:

adolescunt ignibus arae

Virgil *Georgics* 4.379

the altars are nurtured [= light up] with the fires

59 Note, however, the absence of Latin "*ignem adolēre.*"

We may compare also the Swedish verb *ala* 'be on fire'.

The participle of *adolēscō* 'become nurtured, grow' had evolved in meaning to become *adolēscēns* 'adolescent', and in this function a clearly attested formal variant *adulēscēns* has been preserved.[60] Thus the function of the word as a noun tolerates the expected phonological development from *ol* to *ul* that is suppressed in the function of the word as an adjective, a participle.

Latin *focus*

Besides the designation of "sacrificial fireplace" by way of *āra*, a less specialized designation for "fireplace" is *focus*, which is attested in not only sacral but also domestic contexts:

> *inde panem facito, folia subdito, in foco caldo sub testu coquito leniter*
>
> Cato *De re rustica* 75
>
> make a loaf, place leaves, and bake slowly on a warm hearth under a crock

In this case Cato is giving a recipe for making the cake called *libum* (cf. also *De re rustica* 76.2). Another clear example of *focus* meaning 'domestic fireplace, hearth' is the following:

> *munda siet. uillam conuersam mundeque habeat. focum purum circumuersum cotidie priusquam cubitum eat habeat*
>
> Cato *De re rustica* 143.2
>
> She [the *uilica* 'housekeeper'] must be neat, and keep the farmstead neat and clean. She must clean and tidy the hearth every night before she goes to bed.

As for the sacral uses of the *focus*, we may consider the testimony of Varro:

> *sane Varro rerum diuinarum refert inter sacratas aras focos quoque sacrari solere, ut in Capitolia Ioui Iunoni Mineruae, nec minus in plurimis urbibus oppidisque , et id tam publice quam priuatim solere fieri . . . nec licere uel priuata uel publica sacra sine foco fieri. quod hic ostendit poeta*
>
> Servius Auctus on Virgil *Aeneid* 3.134

[60] Cf. DELL 23.

Indeed, Varro (*Rerum diuinarum*) reports that amidst the *ārae* that are consecrated, *focī* too are regularly consecrated, as in the Capitolium to Jupiter, Juno, Minerva; likewise in most cities and towns; and that this is regularly done both publicly and privately; . . . and that it is not allowed to perform public or private sacrifices without a *focus*. Which is what the Poet [Virgil] shows here.

Varro's report on the use of the *focus* in the Capitolium can be directly linked with the mention of the derivative word *foculus* in the *Acts of the Arval Brethren*, year A.D. 87: the setting is *in Capitolio* (*a.* 87 I 2), and the *promagister* of the brethren is presiding (I 2 and following); after the preliminary sacral proceedings (I 2– 7), "on the same day *and in the same place*" (*eodem die ibidem in area* I 18), the same *promagister* does the following:

ture et uino in igne in foculo fecit

Acts of the Arval Brethren a. 87 I 19 ed. Henzen

he made a sacrifice with incense and wine on the fire on the *foculus*

In the *Acts of the Arval Brethren* the uses of the *āra* and the *foculus*, both located *in luco* 'in the grove', are in complementary distribution when it comes to the sacrifice of pigs and cows: the *porcae piāculāres* are regularly immolated at the *āra* and the *uacca honorāria*, at the *foculus*.[61] We may compare the following statement:

quae prima hostia ante foculum cecidit

Valerius Maximus 1.6.9

the first sacrificial animal that fell before the *foculus*

Unlike the *āra*, the *focus/foculus* is optionally movable,[62] as the following passages attest:

adde preces positis et sua uerba focis

Ovid *Fasti* 2.542

add prayers and the appropriate words at the *focī* that are set down

61 *Acts of the Arval Brethren aa.* 90.49–50; Domitian-era C I 2–5; 105 II 7–9; 118 I 59–62; 120.36–37; 155.32–34; M. Aurelius-era E 1–2; 183 II 21–22; 218 a 17–19; 240 (= Dessau 9522) II 4.

62 For a standard accounting from an abidingly useful manual: Wissowa 1912.475.

posito tura dedere foco

Ovid *Fasti* 4.334

a *focus* was set down and they offered incense[63]

crateras focosque ferunt

Virgil *Aeneid* 12.285

they take away the craters and *focī*

praetextatum immolasse ad tibicinem foculo posito

Pliny *Natural History* 22.11

to make an immolation while wearing the *praetexta*, to the accompaniment of a reed-player, with a *foculus* set down

bona . . . consecrauit foculo posito in rostris adhibitoque tibicine

Cicero *De domo sua* 123

he consecrated the possessions . . . , with a *foculus* set down at the *rostra* and with a reed-player summoned for the occasion

tu . . . capite uelato . . . foculo posito bona . . . consecrasti

Cicero *De domo sua* 124

you consecrated the possessions . . . with head veiled and with a *foculus* set down

Liberalia dicta, quod per totum oppidum eo die sedent sacerdotes Liberi anus edera coronatae cum libis et foculo pro emptore sacrificantes

Varro *De lingua latina* 6.14

Festival of Liber: throughout the town on that day, the priestesses of Liber, old women wearing ivy on their heads, sit with cakes and a *foculus*, and they sacrifice [the cakes] for any purchaser.

The nature of the *focus/foculus* is strictly ad hoc. In Cato's *De re rustica*, for example, the *foculus* is catalogued simply as a rustic utensil (11.4, 16.3). Any place or thing on which a fire is started qualifies as a *focus*, as we see from the following summary:

[63] Context: before sailing on, the retinue of Claudia Quinta pauses to sacrifice a heifer.

> *quidquid ignem fouet, focus uocatur, siue ara sit siue quid aliud in quo ignis fouetur*
>
> Servius on Virgil *Aeneid* 12.118
>
> Whatever fosters [*fouet*] a fire is called a *focus*, whether it be an *āra* or anything else in which fire is fostered [*fouetur*].[64]

Such a wide range of applications is also illustrated by the semantic development of Latin *focus* into the Romance word for "fire" itself, as in French *feu*, Italian *fuoco*, Spanish *fuego*, and so on.

In light of what we have already seen of this Latin noun *focus*, with its strikingly expansive semantic range of contextual settings, I bring this section to a close by taking note of a striking gap in the history of the Latin language. That is, there is no known etymology for *focus*.[65] Without making the results of the preceding observations on *focus* depend in any way on what now follows, I suggest that there may be an etymological connection between the noun *focus*, this premier word for 'fireplace', and the verb *faciō*, which not only means 'do' or 'make' in a secular dimension but also serves as a premier word for 'sacrifice' in the dimension of the sacred. This is not to say that *focus* can be explained as a direct reflex of a primary Indo-European noun-formation. Rather, the point is that *focus* may perhaps represent a secondary Italic noun-formation, just as the present tense of the verb *faciō* represents a secondary verb-formation. The *-c-* of the present-tense *faciō* is a secondary extension from the *-c-* of the primary perfect formation, *fēcī*, direct cognate of Greek *thêka* (θῆκα) 'placed'. The inherited meaning of 'set, put, place', as explicitly preserved in the Greek cognate, helps explain the meaning of 'sacrifice' in *faciō* (e.g. Virgil *Aeneid* 8.189), and in the compound *sacri-ficō* (e.g. Plautus *Poenulus* 320). More important for now, it also helps explain the traditional collocations of *focus* with verbs meaning 'set, put, place', as we have seen immediately above in the list of contexts illustrating the movable nature of the *focus*. If we are to explain *focus* as a

64 The words *fouet* and *fouetur* here imply an etymological connection between verb *foueō* 'foster' and noun *focus*; but note the lengthened *o* in *fōculum*, the derivation of which from *foueō* seems assured by the collocation of the two words in Plautus *Captivi* 847. Thus we must distinguish between *fōculum*, derivative of *foueō*, and *fŏculus*, derivative of *focus* (as in Cato *De re rustica* 11.4). For attestations showing the distinct vowel lengths, see DELL s.v. *foueō*. The meaning of *fōculum*, conveying the notion of "fostering" or "nurturing" fire, is analogous to that of *altāria* as discussed above. Perhaps the phonological closeness of *fōculo-* and *fŏculo-* is influenced by their semantic parallelism, in that both words designate a movable fireplace. It is conceivable that this parallelism masks an earlier form **faculus*, derived from **facus*, and that **facus* was reshaped as *focus* on the model of an analogized *foculus*. In which case, *focus* could perhaps be explained as a secondary derivative of *faciō*, meaning something like 'setting'. More on this possibility in the discussion that follows.

65 DELL 243.

noun somehow derived from the verb *faciō*, we have to posit the generalization of the secondary *-c-* as part of the verb-stem *fac-* at an early enough stage that it could generate noun-derivatives of the type *focus*.[66] Moreover, we would have to posit that the *-o-* of *focus* is secondary as well, since there seems to be no way to derive a sequence like *foc-* directly from the Indo-European root *dheh$_1$(-k-) / *dhh$_1$(-k-). Still, there is room for positing an Italic or even Latin stage of derivation, with the secondary *-o-* of *focus* being perhaps shaped by analogy.[67]

Umbrian *ahti-* and *aso-*

Corresponding to Latin *focus*, the Umbrian word for "movable fireplace" is *ahti-*,[68] which is etymologically an abstract noun *ag-ti- meaning 'carrying' (from a verb cognate with Latin *agō, agere*); for the form and the semantics, we may compare Latin *uectis* 'bolt, lever', which is likewise an original abstract noun *u̯egh-ti- 'carrying' (from the verb attested as *uehō, uehere*). The usage of the word *ahti-* as 'movable fireplace' is not necessarily a feature of the Umbrian language in general: rather, it is a specialized feature of the repertoire of sacral texts managed by the Atiedian Brethren of the Umbrian city of Iguvium, as recorded in the set of inscriptions known as the *Iguvine Tables*. The *ahti-* is central to the religious life of Iguvium, as is evident from the rites

[66] Cf. Umbrian *façia, faç(i)u, fakust, facurent*, which are functional equivalents of Latin *faciat, facere, fēcerit, fēcerint* respectively. Moreover, there may be a trace of e-grade in the Umbrian imperative *fetu*, also spelled *feitu*. This form cannot correspond to Oscan *factud*, the Umbrian cognate of which would be **faitu*: we may compare the Umbrian imperative *aitu* with the corresponding Oscan *actud*. Thus it is possible to reconstruct Umbrian *fe(i)tu* as **fekitōd*. An argument against the alternative possibility, **fēkitōd*, is that the inherited *ē* of Umbrian is regularly spelled *i* in the Latin alphabet as opposed to *e* in the native Umbrian alphabet (e.g. *filiu* in the Latin alphabet vs. *feliuf* in the Umbrian). Yet, what corresponds to the native Umbrian spelling *fetu / feitu* is the Latin spelling *fetu / feitu / feetu*, never **fitu*.

[67] See n64. Furthermore, the possible derivation of *focus* from the root of *fac-iō* may have a formal parallel: the noun *iocus* 'jesting word(s)' can be derived from the verb *iaciō* 'throw, hurl', with root *i̯eh$_1$(-k-) as in the perfect *iēcī*. For the semantics, we may compare Greek *epes-bólos*, literally 'thrower of words', as in *Iliad* II 275: here the epithet is applied to Thersites as an exponent of blame poetry, which is characterized by words of damaging ridicule (on which subject see N 1979a.253–264, esp. p. 264). The *-k- of zero-grade *i̯h$_1$-k- in present-tense *iaciō* is again a secondary extension from the perfect *iēcī*, just as in *faciō* and *fēcī*. Even in Classical Latin, *iaciō* is frequently used with direct objects denoting things said (e.g. *contumeliam* 'insult' in Cicero *Pro Sulla* 23). On the semantics of Umbrian *iuka* 'sacred words, formula': Poultney 1959.199 and Borgeaud 1982.190. Lithuanian *juõkas* may be a borrowing from German *jōk*, in turn a borrowing from Latin by way of Studentensprache: LEW 197.

[68] For my interpretation of *ahti-*, I have been guided by the critical discussion of textual evidence in Devoto 1937.267–268, 385–386; also Poultney 1959.165.

described in *Iguvine Tables* III 1 and following. After *pir* 'fire' is kindled on the way leading *arven* 'to the field' (III 11–12), and after this fire is later placed *ase* 'on the altar' which is *vuke* 'in the grove' (III 21–22), then a sacrifice is made *iuvepatre* 'to Jupiter' at the right side of the altar (III 22–23) on behalf of the following:

fratrusper atiieřies	'for the Atiedian Brethren'
ahtisper eikvasatis	'for the *ahti-s eikvasatis*
tutaper iiuvina	'for the people of Iguvium'
trefiper iiuvina	'for the *tribus* of Iguvium'[69]

Iguvine Tables III 23–24

Such a hierarchy of values is a most dramatic illustration of the importance of the *ahti-* to the community. This Umbrian collocation of *vuke* 'in the grove' / *ase* 'on the altar' with *ahtisper* 'for the portable fireplaces' is comparable to the Latin collocation of *in luco* 'in the grove' / *in ara* 'on the altar' with *in foculo* 'on the portable fireplace' in the *Acts of the Arval Brethren.*[70]

In what we have just seen quoted from the *Iguvine Tables*, the ablative plural *ahtis* is combined with the postposition *-per*, which is parallel to the Latin preposition *prō* 'for, on behalf of'. This combination of *ahti-* and *-per* is semantically parallel to the Latin phrase *prō ārīs focīsque*, as in the following examples:

sibi pro aris focisque et deum templis ac solo in quo nati essent dimicandum fore

Livy 5.30.1

that they were going to have to fight it out on behalf of the *ārae&focī*, the sacred precincts of the gods, and the soil on which they were born

pro patria pro liberis pro aris atque focis suis cernere

Sallust *Catiline* 59.5

to fight it out on behalf of the *patria*, the household-members, and their *ārae&focī*

69 On the Umbrian word *trifu-* 'tribe' (cognate of Latin *tribus*), see p. 278.

70 See p. 161. For other parallelisms between the *Iguvine Tables* and the *Acts of the Arval Brethren*, see Vine 1986.

We may also compare the highly emotional and affective tone of Cicero's references to *ārae&focī*, as in *Against Catiline* 4.24; *De domo sua* 106, 143; *In Pisonem* 91; *Pro Sestio* 90; and so on.

The sacral importance of the movable fireplace in Umbrian society is apparent not only from the euphemistically abstract etymology of *ahti-* and from the importance of the *ahti-* in the hierarchy just quoted from *Iguvine Tables* 23–24; it is apparent also from the usage of the word in the Atiedian fire ritual. The *Iguvine Tables* contain two versions of this ritual, one written in the native Umbrian alphabet (Ib 10–16) and the other, in the Latin alphabet (VIb 48–53). A careful study of the parallel texts reveals several new details about the sacrificial fireplace in Italic ritual. For the sake of convenience, the texts are divided here into sections A′ to H′ (native alphabet) and A to H (Latin alphabet), on the basis of inherent divisions in subject-matter. In what follows, I print the Latin alphabet in italics, and the native alphabet in roman, marked off by brackets.

	VIb 48–53		Ib 10–16
A	*pone poplo afero heries* when he wishes to perform a lustration of the people	A′	{pune puplum aferum heries} when you wish to perform a lustration of the people
B	*avif aseriato etu* he shall go and observe the birds	B′	{avef anzeriatu etu} go and observe the birds
Ca	*ape angla combifianšiust* when he has announced the *angla*	C′	{pune kuvurtus} when you have returned
Cb	*perca arsmatiam anouihimu* he shall put on the *perca arsmatia*		
Da	*cringatro hatu* he shall hold the *cringatro*	D′	{krenkatrum hatu} hold the {krenkatrum}
Db	*destrame scapla anouihimu* he shall put it on the right shoulder		
E	*pir endendu* he shall place fire	E′	{enumek pir ahtimem ententu} then place fire in the {ahti-}
Fa	*pone esonome ferar pufe pir entelust* when that in which he has placed the fire is brought to the sacrifice	F′	{pune pir entelus ahtimem} when you have placed the fire in the {ahti-}
Fb	*ere fertu poe perca arsmatiam habiest* the one who has the *perca arsmatia* shall carry it		
Fc	*erihont aso destre onse fertu* the same shall carry the *aso* on his right shoulder		
G	*ennom stiplatu parfa desua* then he shall pronounce a *parfa*-bird on the right	G′	{enumek steplatu parfam tesvam} then pronounce a {parfa}-bird on the right

H	*seso tote iiouine* for himself and for the people of Iguvium	H′	{tete tute ikuvine} for yourself and for the people of Iguvium.

Here ends the fire ritual. Then follows the banishment ritual at Acedonia, starting with *ape acesoniame . . . benust* 'when he has come to Acedonia' in the Latin alphabet (VIb 52–53), matched by {pune menes akeřuniamem} 'when you come to Acedonia' in the native alphabet (Ib 15–16).

There are several details to be noted about the fire ritual. To begin, the expression *poe perca arsmatiam habiest* 'the one who has the *perca arsmatia*' (Fb = VIb 50) is a tabu periphrasis occurring elsewhere, too (VIb 53, 63; VIIa 46, 51), to designate the *arsfertur*/{ařfertur}, who is the chief sacrificer in the cult of the Atiedian Brethren (VIa 2, etc.). Henceforth, he will be designated as "Adfertor," the latinized equivalent of the Umbrian title.[71] The *perca* of the Adfertor is something that he wears, as is evident from the use of *perca* with *anouihimu* 'put on, wear' (Cb and Db, = VIb 49) and from its association with *ponisiater*/{puniçate} (VIb 51/Ib 15), a word apparently related to Latin *pūniceus* 'dyed with purple'.[72] In the fire ritual described at Ib 10 and following, two officials called {prinuvatu} are to accompany the Adfertor, and they are to have {perkaf . . . puniçate} (Ib 15). Likewise, in the fire ritual described at VIb 48 and following, two *prinuatur* are to accompany the Adfertor, and they are to have *perca . . . ponisiater* (VIb 51); meanwhile, the Adfertor himself has *perca arsmatiam* (VIb 49, 50). The periphrasis designating the Adfertor as 'the one who has the *perca arsmatia*' is restricted to those parts of the *Iguvine Tables* that are written in the Latin alphabet. From those parts written in the native alphabet, the identity of the {ařfertur} with this man 'who has the *perca arsmatia*' (*poe perca arsmatiam habiest*) becomes obvious: in Ib 41–42 (native alphabet), it is the {ařfertur} who chases a sacrificial heifer while the two {prinuvatu} chase two; in VIIa 51–52 (Latin alphabet), the sacrificial heifers are chased by *poe perca arsmatiam habiest* 'the one who has the *perca arsmatia*' and the *prinuatur*.

In the parallel texts for the fire ritual presently under consideration, the tabu periphrasis *poe perca arsmatiam habiest* in the Latin alphabet version (A-H) cannot be contrasted directly with a counterpart in the native alphabet version (A′-H′), since in one case the Adfertor is instructed in the grammatical third person (A-H) whereas in the other he is instructed in the second person (A′-H′). There is, however, a direct contrast in the

[71] For Celtic parallels to the Italic concept of "Adfertor": Borgeaud 1982.31, with bibliography.
[72] See Ernout 1961.126.

devices used by the two texts in referring to the movable fireplace: version A-H, which shows a reluctance to name the chief sacrificer of the Atiedian Brethren by title, also shows a reluctance to use the brethren's word *ahti-* 'movable fireplace', the equivalent of Latin *focus.* As we have seen, section E has *pir endendu* 'he shall place fire' while section E′ has {enumek pir ahtimem ententu} 'then place fire in the {ahti-}'. We should note, too, the tabu periphrasis in section Fa, *pufe pir entelust,* in place of the word *ahti-*: instead of some direct statement, such as "when the *ahti-* is brought to the sacrifice," we see in section Fa this periphrasis: *pone esonome ferar pufe pir entelust* 'when that in which he has placed the fire is brought to the sacrifice'. In the version with the Latin letters, then, specific words dealing with the cult officers and cult objects of the Atiedian Brethren are treated with special caution; perhaps the same factor of caution explains the regular use of the third person in instructing the Atiedian sacrificers, as opposed to the second person in the version with native letters.

Besides being more circumspect, the instructions in version A-H are also more precise and detailed than in version A′-H′. Greater detail may imply less familiarity with the prescribed way of doing things; consider section Db, where it is specified that the sacrificer must place the garment *cringatro* on his right shoulder; in section D′, by contrast, it had sufficed to prescribe that the sacrificer must hold the {krenkatrum}. (This garment *cringatro*/{krenkatrum} is comparable to Latin *cinctus* or *cingulum.*) Presumably, the stark prescription of section D′ was enough of a reminder about what to do next; section Da, by contrast, also prescribes that the sacrificer must hold the *cringatro,* but further specification has to follow in Db about what to do with it, namely, to put it on. The reason for putting the *cringatro* specifically on the right shoulder becomes apparent later: the sacrificer who puts on the *cringatro*/{krenkatrum} is none other than the *arsfertur*/{ařfertur} 'Adfertor' (cf. Cb: the same sacrificer is putting on the *perca arsmatiam*). The Adfertor then proceeds to place fire in the *ahti-* 'movable fireplace' (cf. E/E′, Fa/F′), which at that point "is brought to the sacrifice" (*esonome ferar*: Fa). The one who brings the *ahti-* to the sacrifice is the Adfertor himself (cf. Fb), and he carries it on his right shoulder (cf. Fc). It appears, therefore, that the garment called *cringatro*/{krenkatrum} may have served to shield the Adfertor's right shoulder from the heat of the *ahti-* which he was to carry. Presumably, this *ahti-* was some kind of brazier: we may compare the brazen *cribrum* used by the Vestal Virgins as a movable fireplace, described as follows:

> *ignis Vestae si quando interstinctus esset, uirgines uerberibus adficiebantur a pontifice, quibus mos erat tabulam felicis materiae tamdiu terebrare, quousque*

exceptum ignem cribro aeneo uirgo in aedem ferret

Paulus ex Festo 94 ed. Lindsay

Whenever the fire of Vesta was interrupted, the Virgins were beaten by the *pontifex*; their custom was to bore a *tabula* of *fēlix māteria* until a fire could be taken and brought in a brazen *cribrum* to the sanctuary by a Virgin.

We may compare the usage of *tabula* 'board' here with the following instruction in *Iguvine Tables* IIb 12: {tafle e pir fertu} 'carry the fire there on a *tafla*', where Umbrian *tafla* is the equivalent of Latin *tabula*. We may note too that the wood used to kindle the fire is called *māteria*. The form of this noun suggests that it is derived from *māter* 'mother'.[73] In addition, the *māteria* is described with the word *fēlix*, an adjective designating fertility and the power of nurturing. Immediately comparable in theme is the expression *ignem alere* 'nurture fire'[74] and the cognate Indic theme of the fire-god as Mātariśvan, that is, the one who is nurtured inside the mother.[75] We may note too that the enclosure of the Indic Gārhapatya, the domestic fireplace, is actually called *yóni-* 'female genitalia' (*Śatapatha-Brāhmaṇa* 7.1.1.12).[76]

In the same set of instructions where the text of the *Iguvine Tables*, quoted above, studiously avoids use of the Atiedian word *ahti-* to designate 'movable fireplace' (E-F), there does occur a synonym, spelled *aso*:

Fc *erihont aso destre onse fertu*

Iguvine Tables VIb 50

the same [= the Adfertor] shall carry the *aso* on his right shoulder

Because of the specification of the right shoulder in section Fc, what is not directly mentioned by name in Fa (*pufe pir entelust* 'that in which he has placed the fire') has to be mentioned again, and this time it is done not by periphrasis but by use of an equivalent word for 'movable fireplace'. This Umbrian word *aso* is apparently not part of the Atiedian sacral vocabulary, and it is probably for this reason that it could be written out in the tabu-conscious ritual instructions of VIb 48–53, whereas *ahti-* was not mentioned directly but by periphrasis.[77] Just as Umbrian *asa*

[73] See p. 106.
[74] See p. 155.
[75] See p. 156; also, p. 106.
[76] See pp. 105–106.
[77] This interpretation of Umbrian *aso* is offered as an alternative to the one found in the handbooks, where *aso* is understood as 'roast meat' or the like (cf. Latin *assum*). The contextual disadvantages of the latter interpretation are apparent from the discussion by Devoto 1937.268–269 and Ernout 1961.111.

(*Iguvine Tables* IIa 38, etc.) can be reconstructed as *ă̄ssā-, so also *aso* (VIb 50) from *ă̄sso-. Removing the factor of geminated *s, we may reconstruct *aso- as $*h_2$es-o-; in other words, I propose that Umbrian *aso* is the cognate of Hittite *ḫašša-* 'sacrificial fireplace'.

The Meaning of Hittite *ḫaš-/ḫašša-/ḫaššu-* from the Standpoint of Myth and Ritual

Among the noun-reflexes of the Indo-European root $*h_2$es-, our survey has suggested that the semantic basis is the notion of 'fireplace':

Hittite *ḫašša-*	sacrificial fireplace
Indic *ā́sa-*	ashes
Old Norse *arinn*, etc.	sacrificial fireplace
German *Esse*, etc.	smith's fireplace
English *ashes*, etc.	ashes
Greek ἀσβόλη, ἄσβολος	soot
Latin *āra, altāria*	sacrificial fireplace, altar
Oscan *aasa-*	sacrificial fireplace, altar
Umbrian *asa*	sacrificial fireplace, altar
Umbrian *aso*	sacrificial fireplace (movable)

The semantically anomalous reflexes of $*h_2$es- remain the Hittite verb *ḫaš-* 'beget' and noun *ḫaššu-* 'king'. In light of the myths and rituals that we have surveyed, however, these meanings fit the broader context of the sacrificial fireplace as the generatrix of kingship and the authority of kingship, which has been all along the focus of this inquiry.

In this connection, we may add that the formula which the Hittite *ḫaššu-* uses in referring to himself is ^{d}UTU*ši* 'my sun', as in the Autobiography of King Ḫattušiliš III (passim). This usage seems distinctly Hittite, in that there is no corresponding mechanism for designating "ego" + first person singular in Akkadian texts (where the expected form would have been *ŠAMŠI* 'my sun' + third person singular). In the Royal Funerary Ritual of the Hittites,[78] which features the cremation of the *ḫaššu-* 'king' and offerings at the *ḫašša-* 'sacrificial fireplace' (passim), one of the prime recipients of these offerings is the great state god ^{d}UTU 'sun'; after the *ḫaššu-* has died, he joins this very god ^{d}UTU.[79] In fact, after the *ḫaššu-* has died, he himself becomes a god.[80] This belief also seems

[78] The texts of the Royal Funerary Ritual have been collected by Otten 1958. For a survey of the specific passages dealing with the afterlife of the king, see Otten pp. 113, 119–120.

[79] Otten pp. 113, 119–120.

[80] Otten pp. 113, 119–120.

distinctly Hittite, as we may see from the attenuated Akkadian translation of the following Hittite statement spoken by King Muršiliš II:

> *ABUYA* DINGIR^{LIM}-*iš kišat*
>
> Otten 1958.120
>
> [when] my father became a god

We may contrast the parallel Akkadian version:

> *ABUYA ARKI ŠIMTIŠU KI ILLIKU*
>
> Otten 1958.120
>
> when my father went to his destiny

We may compare also the following prayer:

> *n[u-?] ka-ru-ú ma-aḫ-ḫa-an an-na-za* ŠÀ-*za ḫa-aš-ša-[a] n-za e-šu-un*
> *n[u-m] u-kán* DINGIR-*YA a-ap-pa a-pu-u-un* ZI-*an an-da ta-a-i*
> *[nu-m] u tu-el ŠA* DINGIR-*YA* ZI-*KA am-mu-uk* [ ] IGI-*an-da*
> *[a] t-ta-aš-ma-aš an-na-aš ḫa-aš-ša-an-na-aš x x x*
> [Z]I$^{\text{HI.A}}$ *ki-ša-an-ta-ru*
>
> Otten 1958.123–124
>
> Already when I was begotten [*ḫaš-*] from the inside of my mother, then you, my god, put this "*animus*" [ZI = *ištanza-*] in for me; and may your divine "*animus*" become for me the "*animī*" of my father, mother, and "*gēns.*"

This theme brings us back to our starting point, that is, the Indo-European pattern of thought that links the rising of the sun at dawn as parallel to the kindling of the sacrificial fire. This parallelism, as we have seen, is explicit in the ritual language of the Vedas and it is implicit in the possible affinity between Indo-European roots in words for 'dawn', notably Greek *ēṓs* and Latin *aurōra,* and in words for 'hearth', notably Greek *hestíā* and Latin *Vesta.* In other words, the possibility remains that the macrocosm of dawn and the microcosm of sacrificial fire are designated with variants of the same root, with *heu̯s- for 'dawn' and *hu̯es- for 'fireplace'.

If indeed the Hittite *ḫaššu-* 'king', as we have just seen, considers his identity to be that of the sun, it follows that the begetting of the king is parallel to the kindling of the sun; in that case, the Hittite verb *ḫaš-* 'beget' is thematically connected to the Hittite noun *ḫaššu-* 'king'. From the etymological point of view, *ḫaš-* may then be translated as 'kindle, light up'. For an example of the reverse in semantic development, we may consider English *kindle*, which had meant 'beget' (Middle English), then 'set on fire'; another example is Old Norse *kveikja* 'beget, kindle' (the noun *kveika* means 'fuel'). Finally, we may compare the Latin noun *adulēscēns / adolēscēns* 'young man', the participial origin of which reveals the built-in metaphor that we have already examined in detail: 'becoming nurtured as fire becomes nurtured'.

Such an etymological interpretation of Hittite *ḫaššu-* as the 'one who is lit up, kindled' is reinforced by a well-known theme in Italic myth, concerning ritual fire. The protagonist of this myth is the Roman king Servius Tullius, whom Georges Dumézil has singled out as representing the features of the ideal king from the standpoint of patterns in Indo-European mythmaking.[81] If indeed it is valid to claim that Latin *āra* is related to Hittite *ḫašša-* 'sacrificial fireplace' and that Latin *focus* is the functional correlate of the *āra*, then the following myth of Servius and the *focus* is decisive:

> *non praeteribo et unum foci exemplum Romanis litteris clarum: Tarquinio Prisco regnante tradunt repente in foco eius comparuisse genitale e cinere masculi sexus eamque, quae insederat ibi, Tanaquilis reginae ancillam Ocresiam captiuam consurrexisse grauidam; ita Seruium Tullium natum, qui regno successit; inde et in regia cubanti ei puero caput arsisse, creditumque Laris familiaris filium; ob id Compitalia ludos Laribus primum instituisse.*
>
> Pliny *Natural History* 36.204

> I will not pass over a famous example of the *focus* in Roman literature. In the reign of Tarquinius Priscus, they say that there suddenly appeared in his *focus* a genital organ of male sex out of the ashes, and that it impregnated Ocresia, who had sat there. She was an enslaved handmaiden of Queen Tanaquil. Thus was Servius Tullius born, and he succeeded to the kingship. When he was a boy sleeping in the palace, his head caught on fire, and he was believed to be the son of the *Lār familiāris*. For this reason he was the first to institute the Compitalia Games for the *Lārēs*.

This version can be supplemented with another:

[81] Dumézil 1943.

namque pater Tulli Volcanus, Ocresia mater
praesignis facie Corniculana fuit.
hanc secum Tanaquil sacris de more peractis
iussit in ornatum fundere uina focum.
hic inter cineres obsceni forma uirilis
aut fuit aut uisa est, sed fuit illa magis.
iussa foco captiua sedet. conceptus ab illa
Seruius a caelo semina gentis habet.
signa dedit genitor tunc cum caput igne corusco
contigit, inque comis flammeus arsit apex.

Ovid *Fasti* 6.625–634

For the father of Tullius was Vulcan, and Ocresia of
Corniculum, distinguished in beauty, was his mother.
When the sacred rites were enacted, according to tradition,
Tanaquil ordered her to pour wine into the ornate *focus.*
At this point, among the ashes, there was, or seemed to be,
the male form of something indecent. More likely there was one.
Ordered to do so, the slave girl sat at the *focus.* Conceived
by her, Servius has the seeds of his *gēns* from the sky.
His father gave a sign, at the time when he touched his head
with flashing fire, and a flame lit up in his hair.

In this remarkable passage the preoccupation of the myth with a ritual context is especially clear. There is also a lengthy account of the same myth in Dionysius of Halicarnassus *Roman Antiquities* 4.2.1–4. Romulus and Remus themselves were begotten likewise, according to a myth recorded by Plutarch (*Romulus* 2.4–8). The same goes for Caeculus, founder of Praeneste and ancestor of the distinguished *gēns* Caecilia (Servius on Virgil *Aeneid* 7.678).[82]

I close by citing once more a striking detail from the myth about the begetting of Servius, the Italic king par excellence, from the sacrificial fireplace. As we have seen in both versions just quoted, there is an outward sign that warrants the truth of the king's being generated from the embers of the hearth. To mark the moment that his kingship is revealed, the head of Servius literally lights up. The radiant visage of the king, the ideal human, is a theme that may be linked with the etymology that I have already suggested for Greek *ánthrōpos* (ἄνθρωπος) 'human', that is,

[82] For a conscientious collection of testimonia about these Italic myths, see Alföldi 1974.182–185; also Bremmer and Horsfall 1987.49–53. Cf. Brelich 1949.70, 96–100; also Dumézil 1966.69n1, 320–321, who adduces Indic parallels; for example, one particular epic figure is begotten by the fire-god Agni in the Gārhapatya 'domestic fireplace' (*Mahābhārata* 3.213.45ff).

'he who has the looks of embers'.[83] In line with a ubiquitous theme of mythmaking, that the first human is the first king,[84] this image of the king with a visage glowing from the fire of the hearth is a symbol for the never-ending search of myth to grasp the celestial affinities of humankind.[85] We come back, full circle, to Clytemnestra's dream in the *Electra* of Sophocles (417–423): in the vision, to repeat, the king of Mycenae places his scepter into the royal hearth (419–420), and from it grows a shoot so vigorous that it covers with its shade all the kingdom of Mycenae (421–423). The hearth, as we have seen, is the focus for reveries about the father's generation of a son without the exogamous intermediacy of a female outsider. The female insider, the ultimate generatrix, is in such reveries the hearth itself, and from it emanates the essence of authority, made manifest in the radiant visage of the ideal king.

Appendix. Conflicting Semiotics of Cremation, Inhumation, Exposition: An Iranian Case in Point

In Avestan usage, the root *ā̆s- (from *$h_2$es-) is attested as the component *ah-(ya-) in the compounding of *sairiia-* plus **ahiia-* = *sairiie.hiia-*. The word *sairiia-* designates the dried manure used as a proper funerary resting place for the corpse, *Vendidad* 8.8; the word *sairiie.hiia-* is attested only once, *Vendidad* 8.83. It has been traditionally interpreted to mean 'apparatus for drying manure',[86] where the semantics of root *ā̆s- correspond to what we find in Latin *ārēre* 'be dry', Tocharian *as-* 'dry', and so on.[87] I propose an alternative explanation of *sairiie.hiia-*, interpreting its etymology as 'apparatus for burning manure'. As we shall see, this interpretation helps explain some crucial details of conflicting Iranian ideologies concerning the funerary practices of cremation, inhumation, and exposition.

[83] See p. 151n30.

[84] A classic on this subject is the two-volume work of Christensen 1918 and 1934.

[85] Such a theme may prove to be the key to understanding the etymological relationship of Greek *anḗr* (ἀνήρ) 'man' with *nṓrops*, a Homeric adjective glossed as λαμπρός 'bright' in Hesychius (e.g. s.v. νῶροψ) and used as a formulaic synonym of *aíthops* 'with looks of fire, fiery-looking' in Homeric diction (e.g. postvocalic νώροπι χαλκῷ vs. postconsonantal αἴθοπι χαλκῷ). On the presence and absence, respectively, of initial *a* as reflex of laryngeal *h_2 in *e*-grade *anḗr* (*$h_2$ner-) and *o*-grade *nōr-* (*$h_2$nor-), see Beekes 1969.75–76.

[86] Bartholomae 1904.1565.

[87] At pp. 153ff., I have argued that the semantics of Latin *ārēre* 'be dry' are secondary, and that the root *ā̆s- of this verb can be reconstructed as meaning 'burn', as reflected in the derivative noun *ārea*.

According to Zoroastrian precepts, exposing a corpse to be eaten by dogs and birds is the proper funerary procedure, rather than cremation or inhumation (*Vendidad* 8 passim). I draw attention here to the contrast with the Indic custom of cremation (e.g. *Rig-Veda* 10.16, etc.),[88] and with the Greek customs of cremation and inhumation, as discussed earlier.[89] More specifically, I also draw attention to the contrast, established in the *Iliad*, between the sacredness of cremating a corpse, which I have argued is considered the key to successful afterlife,[90] and the abomination of exposing a corpse to be eaten by dogs and birds, a custom cited at the very beginning of the *Iliad* (I 4–5) and pervading the rest of the epic as the ultimate image of inhumanity, a symbolic threat to the very afterlife of the deceased.[91]

Zoroastrian ideology, in symmetrical contrast, not only sanctions the exposition of the corpse to dogs and birds: it also singles out the custom of cremation as an abomination, and there are elaborate protective rituals for the true believer to follow in the event that he should come upon *ātrəm nasupākəm* 'a corpse-cooking fire' (*Vendidad* 8.73 and following). Such clear provisions for the eventuality of discovering the practice of cremation suggest that this funerary procedure, though forbidden by the Zoroastrian norm, was widespread in various areas of Iranian society.

In one instance the people of an entire region are singled out for traces of this particular aberration from orthodoxy: in the first book of the *Vendidad*, a tract against *daēuua*-s 'demons', the Zoroastrian religious community is represented by sixteen regions of Iranian society, and from among these, the thirteenth "best" region, called Čaxra 'The Chariot-Wheel', is described as being tainted with the practice of "corpse cooking" (*Vendidad* 1.16). We may compare these other aberrations from Zoroastrian orthodoxy:

> The tenth "best" region, called Harax^{v}aitī (= Old Persian Harahuvatī in the Behistun Inscription, = Arachosia), is tainted with the practice of corpse burying, that is, inhumation (*Vendidad* 1.12).

> The sixth "best" region, called Harōiuua (= Old Persian Haraiva, = latter-day Herāt), is tainted with the practice of keening or funeral dirges (*Vendidad* 1.8: *sraskəmča driuuikāča* 'weeping and howling').

88 Cf. Caland 1896. This is not to say, of course, that cremation is the only type of Indic funerary practice.

89 See pp. 85, 129.

90 See pp. 86ff.

91 Cf. N 1979a.224–227.

In the latter case we may note again a symmetrical contrast with Greek customs, as reflected in the *Iliad*, which not only describes the practice of keening or funeral dirges as the norm but equates the very essence of this institution with the characterization of its main hero, Achilles, that man of constant sorrow.[92] The Zoroastrian ideology shows the converse, where the very building that is designated for the exposition of the corpse is conceived as the Tower of Silence in Parsee usage.[93]

At the end of the first book of the Zoroastrian *Vendidad* (1.20), it is pointed out that there are other regions in the Zoroastrian community-at-large besides the sixteen that are formally listed. As for the choice of the sixteen "best" regions and their arrangement in descending order of value, the desired effect is to symbolize the geographical spread of Zoroastrian orthodoxy.[94]

At the top of the list in *Vendidad* 1 are those regions that were the first to accept Zoroastrian orthodoxy:

1st:	Airiianəm Vaējah = Ariana
2nd:	Suγδa = Sogdiana
3rd:	Mouru = Margiana
4th:	Bāxδī = Bactriana
5th:	Nisāiia
6th:	Harōiuua = Arīa

It has been argued the best Zoroastrian region of all, "the Aryan Vaējah," homeland of Zaraθuštra = Zoroaster, is to be identified as X^{v}ārizm = Chorasmia.[95] The *Avesta* explicitly connects Zaraθuštra with "the Aryan Vaējah" (*Yašt* 5.17–18, 104), and it was at the river Dāitiiā, closely associated with this region, that Zaraθuštra made sacrifice (*Yašt* 5.104, 15.2). The precise localization of "the Aryan Vaējah," which counts as the sacred space of Zoroastrianism itself, seems to have varied in the course of time, following the shifting localizations of power and influence, and it seems clear that Chorasmia, even if it merits the title "the Aryan Vaējah," was not the only region to be described this way.[96] The point remains, in any case, that the six regions heading the list of *Vendidad* 1 are apparently to be located in East Iran, visualized as contiguous with

[92] Full presentation of the argument in N 1979a.94–117.

[93] Cf. Humbach 1961.99.

[94] Cf. Nyberg 1938.313–327. There is considerable disagreement about the precise location of many of the places mentioned in *Vendidad* 1; cf. e.g. Gnoli 1980.23ff.

[95] E.g. Nyberg p. 326.

[96] Cf. Davidson 1985.93–94, 101, with further bibliography (esp. Duchesne-Guillemin 1979.63; also Gnoli 1980.91ff).

each other, and that they are the nucleus of Zoroastrian orthodoxy, from where it spread to regions such as Čaxra.

On the steppes of Central Asia in general, of which East Iran forms a part, the poorly wooded terrain makes cremation impractical, and it is no coincidence that the alternative custom of exposition is a characteristic feature of the peoples living in the Central Asiatic steppes, including the Mongols.[97] Since the nucleus of Zoroastrian orthodoxy is to be located in the East Iranian steppes, it follows that the Zoroastrian custom of exposition was an areal feature acquired by the East Iranians from their Central Asiatic neighbors. As Zoroastrian orthodoxy spread, the custom of exposition came into conflict with that of cremation, such as practiced by the people of Čaxra. The specific mention of "corpse cooking" as the plague of Čaxra (*Vendidad* 1.16) suggests that the inhabitants clung to an older custom that was difficult to uproot.[98] Given the clearly attested Indic custom of cremation (e.g. *Rig-Veda* 10.16, etc.),[99] the Iranian attestations of non-Zoroastrian "corpse cooking" suggest an Indo-Iranian pedigree for the custom of cremation as opposed to exposition.

There is also direct evidence that the Zoroastrian custom of exposition was generally preceded by that of cremation: the actual Zoroastrian word designating the place built for exposing the corpse is *daxma* (*Vendidad* 5.14, 8.2), which from an etymological point of view means "burning" (whence "place for burning, cremation") from verb *dag-* 'burn' (as attested in *Yasna* 71.8, etc.). In other words, I am arguing that the original place of the funeral pyre was converted into the place of exposition, without so much as a change in the word used to designate the place itself.[100] There are instances where the word *daxma* at least implies a

[97] Nyberg p. 310.

[98] Nyberg pp. 321–322.

[99] Cf. Caland 1896. To repeat, this is not to say that cremation is the only type of Indic funerary practice.

[100] The standard etymology of *daxma* as "burning" (whence "place for burning, cremation") from verb *dag-* 'burn', as we find it in e.g. Bartholomae 1904.676, has been challenged by Hoffmann 1975 [1965].338, on the basis of arguments presented by Humbach 1961, who shows that *daxma* in e.g. *Vendidad* 7.49 and following designates something like a "mausoleum," that is, a roofed and sealed building in which the corpse is sheltered from the elements, as distinct from the open-sky format required by the orthodox Zoroastrian place of exposition. And yet, Humbach himself points out (p. 101) that *daxma* in e.g. *Vendidad* 5.14, 8.2 designates an orthodox Zoroastrian place of exposition. In other words, the referent of this word *daxma* in the language of the *Avesta* can vary from the orthodox place of exposition to the anti-orthodox "mausoleum" (for examples of New Persian *daxma* in this sense of "mausoleum" in the epic tradition of the *Shāhnāma* of Ferdowsi, see Humbach p.100). Given this range of variation, we may continue to posit yet another nonorthodox variant among the referents of *daxma*, that is, a place where the corpse is cremated rather than exposed to the elements. And I am arguing that this particular variant represents the earliest meaning of *daxma*.

place of cremation: in *Vendidad* 7.49–58 (cf. also 3.13), we see variations on the theme of an "illegal" *daxma*, described as a place frequented by *daēuua*-s 'demons', fiends who are the primordial enemies of Ahura, head of the pantheon. In line with the opprobrium of "corpse cooking," it seems that the *daēuua*-s are being described as actually devouring the dead who are "cooked" at the *daxma* (*Vendidad* 7.55).

The fact that Zoroastrian teaching holds cremation to be an abomination has a bearing on the context of *sairiie.hiia*- in *Vendidad* 8.83. In *Vendidad* 8.81–96, there is a catalogue of merits to be gained by bringing various kinds of fire to the central fire of purification; the more impure the fire, the greater the merit. The reasoning behind this mentality, as reflected to this day by the ritual practices of the Zoroastrian Parsees, has been described as follows:[101]

> Since the goal of all these procedures is to obtain a fire that is as pure as possible, the question remains why it is necessary to use for these procedures, among other things, the fire that is the most impure that one can imagine, that is, the fire that has burned a cadaver. Clearly, the reason is that the goal is also to deliver the fire from its impurity, to *save* it.

In *Vendidād* 8, the most impure fire of them all is "corpse-cooking" fire:

> *yō ātrəm nasupākəm dāitīm gātum auui auua.baraiti*
>
> *Vendidad* 8.81
>
> who brings corpse-cooking fire to the prescribed place . . .

In this case, the person who brings such impure fire to the central fire of purification merits 10,000 firebrands.

The second in rank among all impure fires is described as follows:

> *yō ātrəm uruzdipākəm dāitīm gātum auui auua.baraiti*
>
> *Vendidad* 8.82
>
> who brings fluid-cooking fire to the prescribed place . . .

In this case, the person who brings such impure fire to the central fire merits 1,000 firebrands. The reference to "fluid" here seems to concern fluids emanating from the body: *Dēnkart* 8.46 offers the explanatory description *hixr pāk* 'excrement cooking'.[102]

[101] Duchesne-Guillemin 1962.82 (my translation).
[102] Bartholomae 1904.1533.

The third in rank among all impure fires is described as follows:

yō ātrəm sairiie.hiiat̰ hača dāitīm gātum auui auua.baraiti

Vendidad 8.83

who brings fire from the *sairiie.hiia-* to the prescribed place . . .

In this case, the one who brings such fire merits 500 firebrands.

From then on, the catalogue lists fires destined for secular uses, such as the fire from a potter's fireplace (*Vendidad* 8.84), from a goldsmith's fireplace (8.87), from a baker's fireplace (8.91), and so on. Last on the list is the fire that is easiest to bring, namely, "from the nearest place":

yō ātrəm nazdištat hača dāitīm gātum auui auua.baraiti

Vendidad 8.96

who brings fire from the nearest place to the prescribed place . . .

In this case, the bringer merits 10 firebrands.

The essential question remains: why does fire from the *sairiie.hiia-* rank so high in degree of abomination that it should be listed directly after fire for burning the body and after fire for burning fluid discharge from the body? The answer may well be concealed in the use of *sairiia-* 'manure' as a resting place for the corpse:

auua.hē gātūm baraiiən ātriiehe vā sairiiehe vā

Vendidad 8.8

they should bring for him [= the corpse] as a place either ashes or manure

The context shows that this practice follows the dictates of Zoroastrian orthodoxy, just like the practice of exposing the corpse in the *daxma*. Yet the *daxma*, if my argument holds, was at an earlier stage the place of cremation, not exposition. Similarly, I propose, *sairiia-* 'manure' was at an earlier stage a fuel, or an ingredient in the fuel, for cremation. In the Zoroastrian orthodoxy, use of the term *daxma* was retained but converted to designate the place of exposition rather than cremation. Similarly, I suggest, any use of manure as fuel for cremating the corpse would have to be converted: the body is to be laid out on manure, but neither the body nor the manure may be burned. We must note that the custom of using manure as an ingredient for cremation has survived in latter-day

India.[103] Moreover, manure is the common domestic fuel in latter-day India. If the custom of using manure for fuel is of Indo-Iranian provenience, then Avestan *sairiie.hiia-* may have at an earlier stage designated simply a place where manure was burned.

To sum up: Zoroastrian orthodoxy prescribes manure as a resting place for the corpse; since corpse burning is forbidden, it follows that manure burning should also be forbidden because of the surviving association of manure with the resting place of the corpse. Because of this association, the use of manure for secular fuel may be forbidden along with its use for cremating the corpse.

In fact, the custom of burning manure may be of Indo-European provenience: we may consider the Latin noun *fimus* 'manure', apparently derived from *-fiō* as in *suffiō* 'fumigate' (Cato *De re rustica* 113.1) or 'burn for the purpose of fumigation' (Pliny *Natural History* 28.42, etc.); we may compare the root-formation *dhu̯ī̆- of *suffiō* with the *dhū- of *fūmus* 'smoke'.[104] We may note also the reports about the *stercus* 'manure' that is ritually swept out of the precinct of Vesta, Roman goddess of the domestic fireplace (Varro *De lingua latina* 6.32, Festus 344 Lindsay).[105]

The subject of fumigation brings this presentation to a close. And aptly so, since the very concept of fumigation is pertinent to the focus of the entire study, the setting of the sacrificial fireplace. I cite the formation of *fūmigō* 'fumigate', which happens to be parallel to *pūrgō* 'purify', from an earlier *pūrigō* (as in Plautus *Miles* 177).[106] Following Rudolf Thurneysen,[107] I interpret *pūrgō/pūrigō* 'purify' as derived from an underlying expression **pūr agere* 'carry fire', formally parallel to *rēmigō* 'row', derived from an underlying expression *rēmum agere* by way of the intermediate formation *rēmex, rēmigis.* Against the conventional rejection of Thurneysen's positing an underlying **pūr agere* 'carry fire',[108] I cite the Umbrian collocation *pir ahtimem ententu* 'place fire in the *ahti-*' in *Iguvine Tables* Ib 12, where *pir* (< **pūr*) is combined with the abstract noun *ahti-* (< **ag-ti-*) derived from a verb surviving in Latin as *agere.*[109] The Umbrian *ahti-*, receptacle of the sacred fire, is the source of purification for the community.

[103] Cf. Dubois 1924.485; also Gonda 1960.130.

[104] Cf. DELL s.v. *suffiō.*

[105] Cf. Dumézil 1959a.97–98.

[106] In this connection, we may compare the obscure gloss *exfir* in Paulus ex Festo 69 Lindsay, where *pūrgāmentum* seems to be equated with *suffitiō:*

> *exfir, purgamentum, unde adhuc manet suffitio*

[107] Thurneysen 1912–1913.276–281; cf. Leumann 1977.550.

[108] E.g. DELL s.v. *pūrgō.*

[109] See pp. 164ff.

CHAPTER 7

Thunder and the Birth of Humankind

In the mythmaking traditions of a wide variety of societies, there is a convergent pattern of thought concerning the origin of fire: that a stroke of thunder can deposit fire into trees or rocks and that this fire of thunder is extracted whenever friction is applied to these materials.[1] Oftentimes the god of the thunderbolt is pictured as being actually incarnated within the material.[2] There are also numerous occurrences of a related line of thought, equating the friction of making fire with the friction of making love. Besides the ample documentation of this equation in the lore of diverse societies,[3] we may consider the formulation of the philosopher Gaston Bachelard, who views the metaphorical syntax of sexual arousal as the inspiration, as it were, for Man's discovery of how to make fire by friction.[4] Theories aside, it can be argued that the infusion of fire into wood and stone is a sexual and anthropogonic theme *in the logic of myth.* What follows is an attempt to present such an argument, with special reference to the anthropogonic traditions of the Greeks. In the course of examining the pertinent myths, we shall see that the stroke of the thunderbolt may be viewed as not only destructive but also procreative. Furthermore, the concept of procreation can presuppose that of creation itself.[5]

[1] Frazer 1930.224–225; also 90, 92, 151, 155 (trees) and 106, 131, 187–188 (rocks/stones).

[2] Frazer p. 90.

[3] Cf. Frazer pp. 220–221.

[4] Bachelard 1949, esp. pp. 45–47.

[5] Cf. Dworak 1938, esp. p. 1.

Two key words in this presentation will be Baltic (Lithuanian) *perkū́nas* and Slavic *perunŭ*, both meaning 'thunderbolt'.[6] In examining the formal and semantic connections between these two words, we shall discover a pervasive association of the concept of "thunderbolt" with traditional lore about two particular kinds of material that attract the thunderbolt, that is, wood and stone. We shall further discover that the very forms of these nouns, *perkū́nas* and *perunŭ*, are related to the forms of other nouns that actually designate wood, especially oak wood, and stone—not to mention still other nouns designating elevated places that attract the thunderbolt, such as mountains, boulders, or wooded hilltops. Even further, we shall see the emergence of a neat pattern of parallelism linking myths about thunderbolts and oaks with myths about thunderbolts and rocks. Finally, we shall consider another dimension of this parallelism, that is, in myths about the creation of humankind. Such myths, as we shall see, are reflected by a Greek proverb that refers to ancient myths of anthropogony with a distancing attitude of indifference, as if humans had originated from *either* oaks *or* rocks. When Penelope challenges the disguised Odysseus to reveal his hidden identity by revealing his lineage (xix 162), she adds the following words:

οὐ γὰρ ἀπὸ δρυός ἐσσι παλαιφάτου οὐδ' ἀπὸ πέτρης

Odyssey xix 163

For surely you are not from an oak, as in the old stories, or from a rock.

To begin at the very beginnings is to begin with the oak and the rock, at least in the logic of the proverb, and it is for this reason, as we shall see, that the persona of Hesiod, reproaching himself for lingering too long at the beginning of beginnings in the *Theogony*, finally declares, with impatience:

ἀλλὰ τίη μοι ταῦτα περὶ δρῦν ἢ περὶ πέτρην;

Hesiod *Theogony* 35

But why do I have these things about the oak or about the rock?

In the interest of making our own beginning, let us without further delay proceed to the Baltic and the Slavic evidence.

[6] For the difficult task of establishing the etymological links between these words, I cite the pathfinding work of Ivanov 1958 and Ivanov and Toporov 1970, following Jakobson 1950, 1955; cf. Watkins 1966.33–34, 1970.350, 1974.107. Book-length treatment in Ivanov and Toporov 1974.

In Slavic, *perunŭ* designates both 'thunderbolt' and 'thunder-god'.[7] By "thunder" I mean both thunder and lightning, in the spirit of the older expression "thunderstruck" as opposed to the newer "struck by lightning." In the case of the Slavic form *perunŭ*, the meaning 'thunderbolt' is basic in the attested Slavic languages (Russian *perun*, Czech *perun*, Polish *piorun*, and so on), while the meaning 'thunder-god' is residual. The second meaning is least obscure in the Russian evidence, where the word *perun* 'thunderbolt' survives also as one of the names constituting the native heathen pantheon. The Old Russian Chronicles[8] tell of wooden idols in the image of the god *Perun*, set up on hills overlooking Kiev and Novgorod. They also tell how the people of Kiev wept as the Christianized Prince Vladimir had the idol of Perun cast down into the Dnepr River. At Novgorod, too, the god was toppled. And yet, as his idol was floating downstream in the Volxov River, Perun took revenge: people believed that he hurled his mace at a bridge, hurting some and frightening the others.[9] The Perun figure has survived also in the folklore of Byelorussia.[10] He is *Piarun*, who lives on mountaintops and smites the Serpent.[11] He even made the first fire ever: it happened accidentally, when he struck a tree in which the Demon was hiding.[12]

In the Baltic languages there is a word that seems formally similar to the Slavic *perunŭ* and that likewise means both 'thunderbolt' and 'thunder-god'. In Baltic languages, unlike Slavic, however, we cannot immediately arrive at a common Baltic form. In Lithuanian the word is *perkū́nas*; in Latvian it is *pērkōns* (standard spelling for *pḕrkuons*). For the Old Prussian forms we have the testimony of the *Elbing Glossary:* the entry *percunis* is glossed as 'thunder'. Formal problems aside, there are striking thematic parallelisms between the Baltic and Slavic figures. Like Slavic Perun, the Latvian *Pērkōns* hurls a mace.[13] Like the Slavic Perun, the Baltic *Perkū́nas* of Lithuanian folklore dwells on lofty mountaintops: such places are called *Perkūnkalnis* 'summit of Perkūnas', and brazen idols of the god are sure to be there.[14] Also, Perkūnas strikes oak trees, which have fire stored up inside.[15]

[7] Cf. REW s.v. *perún.*

[8] The testimonia have been assembled by Gimbutas 1967.741–742.

[9] Cf. Darkevič 1961.91–102.

[10] Cf. Ivanov and Toporov 1968, 1970.

[11] Ivanov and Toporov 1970.1182.

[12] Seržputovski 1930.26 (I no. 268); cf. Ivanov and Toporov p. 1194.

[13] Cf. the expression *Pērkōns mȩt savu milnu* 'Pērkōns throws his mace' (Ivanov and Toporov p. 1195). Note that *milna* 'mace' is related to Old Norse *mjǫllnir*, the word for the hammer of Thor the thunder-god. Note, too, that Thor's mother is *Fjǫrgyn* (from *perkunī). On these forms: Ivanov 1958.104.

[14] Balys 1937.163 nos. 233–236; also p. 149 nos. 4–5. Cf. Ivanov and Toporov p. 1182.

[15] For an attestation of this belief, see the first-person account by the cleric Matthäus Praetorius (late seventeenth century) of his encounter with some Lithuanian woodcutters,

The personification of *perkū́nas*, as we have just seen, is closely associated with the oak tree. Moreover, while the derivative noun *perkū́nija* means 'thunderstorm', as *Perkū́nija* it can also designate the name of a place where a great oak stood; underneath this oak was an idol of Perkūnas.[16] The diction of Lithuanian folklore frequently yields the expression *Perkūno ąžuolas* 'oak of Perkūnas,'[17] which is matched by Latvian *Pērkōna ōzōls* 'oak of Pērkōns'.[18] From story to story, the stroke of Perkūnas either seeks out oak trees or specifically avoids them.[19] Either way, the point remains that there is a thematic link between oaks and the stroke of Perkūnas. There even exist accounts of old Lithuanian rituals involving Perkūnas and oak trees.[20] Finally, Simon Grunau's description of Old Prussian customs (written in the early sixteenth century) tells of a sacred oak with a hollow containing an idol of Perkūnas.[21]

Likewise in Slavic lore, Perun is associated with the oak. Besides the old Russian expression *Perunov dub* 'oak of Perun',[22] there is the additional evidence of a frequently attested Byelorussian folk theme, with Piarun violently striking oak trees.[23]

From both the Baltic and the Slavic evidence, it is clear that the god of the thunderbolt is associated with rocks as well as oaks. In Lithuanian folklore, for example, we find instances where Perkūnas is associated

---

as reprinted in Mannhardt 1936.533–535. For the relative reliability of Praetorius, see Mannhardt pp. 519–520.

[16] Balys 1937.163 no. 246; cf. Ivanov and Toporov p. 1184.

[17] Balys p. 163 no. 241; cf. Ivanov and Toporov p. 1184.

[18] Šmits 1940.1401; cf. Ivanov and Toporov p. 1184.

[19] Balys 1937.158 no. 141 and p. 197 no. 802; cf. Ivanov and Toporov pp. 1193–1194.

[20] For a detailed account by Matthäus Praetorius, see Mannhardt 1936.539–540 (cf. Ivanov and Toporov p. 1189). Perkūnas was venerated with perpetual fires fueled by oak wood (for documentation, see Mannhardt pp. 196, 335, 435, 535, etc.). When Christian zealots extinguished such perpetual fires, the natives believed that Perkūnas would freeze (Mannhardt p. 436).

[21] Mannhardt p. 196; cf. Ivanov and Toporov p. 1187. For a balanced account of Grunau's basic reliability, see Krollmann 1927.14–17. Without reading Krollmann, we would be prone to overinterpret the severe judgment of Jaskiewicz 1952.92–93, who was primarily concerned with the unreliability of a later writer, Jan Łasicki (late sixteenth century). Krollmann argues cogently the unlikelihood of Grunau's having "invented" a Prussian system of gods modeled on a Nordic scheme. It strains credulity to imagine that this wandering beggar-monk (who even spoke Prussian himself) would have created a pastiche based on Adam of Bremen (Krollmann pp. 15–17). Krollmann's inference, however, that the Prussian religious practices described by Grunau were borrowed from Nordic culture (p. 17) is gratuitous. As for Jaskiewicz, I find in his brief discussion of Grunau no facts to support his contention that Grunau's account of Perkūnas and the oak is mere phantasmagoria (pp. 92–93). For a balanced evaluation of Grunau's reliability, see Puhvel 1974.

[22] Ivanov and Toporov pp. 1183–1184.

[23] Seržputovski 1930.9 no. 49; cf. also p. 8 nos. 37–48. Cf. also Ivanov and Toporov pp. 1193–1194.

with striking rocks instead of oaks.[24] Also, in a late seventeenth-century account of a heathen Lithuanian ritual involving Perkūnas, the sacral site features a rock and an oak situated five paces apart.[25] Similarly, the Byelorussian Perun (Piarun) goes about smiting not only oaks but also rocks.[26]

Obviously, all this thematic evidence makes it tempting to trace the Baltic and Slavic words for 'thunder'/'thunder-god' to a common formal source. The task is forbidding, however, as we may see from the skepticism recorded in the standard etymological dictionary of Russian.[27] The received opinion here is that *perunŭ* has the common Slavic agent suffix *-unŭ* and is probably derived from the verb *per- as in Old Church Slavonic *perǫ/pĭrati* 'strike'.[28] While the Slavic *perunŭ* looks like a deverbative meaning 'the striker', the form of Lithuanian *perkū́nas* looks like a denominative. On the basis of such formations as Latin *Portūnus* (from *portūnos), derived from the *u*-stem noun *portus*, Lithuanian *perkū́nas* has been reconstructed as *perkʷūnos, derived from *perkʷus.[29] Such a *u*-stem noun *perkʷus is actually attested in Latin *quercus* 'oak'.[30] Even without the comparative evidence, it seems that *perkū́nas* is a denominative. Other attested Lithuanian nouns with the suffix *-ū́nas* are known to be derived from *u*-stem nouns;[31] only nouns with the suffix *-ũnas* may be derived from verbs.[32]

Despite such internal evidence for the derivation of *perkū́nas* from *perkʷu-, we find skepticism in the standard etymological dictionary of Lithuanian,[33] where *perkū́nas* is linked with the verb *per̃-ti* 'strike', cognate with Old Church Slavonic *perǫ/pĭrati* 'strike'. It is argued that Lithuanian could have preserved a radical variation of *per- (as in *per̃-ti*) and *per-kʷ- (as in *perkū́nas*, with extension of the root by *-kʷ-).[34] We may compare the radical variation of *per- and *per-g- as attested within the conjugation of an Armenian verb meaning 'strike', *hari* (aorist) vs.

[24] Balys 1937.159 nos. 155–164; cf. Ivanov and Toporov p. 1194.

[25] Mannhardt 1936.539–540.

[26] Ivanov and Toporov p. 1193.

[27] REW s.v. *perún.*

[28] Also Russian *peru/prat'*, Czech *peru/prati*, etc.; cf. Lithuanian *per̃-ti* 'strike'. For a typical example of the agent-suffix *-unŭ*, cf. Russian *begún* 'runner' from *begat'* 'run'.

[29] Schulze 1929.287. Cf. also Latin *tribūnus* from *tribus*, *lacūna* from *lacus*, and so on.

[30] DELL s.v. For a survey of Germanic cognates meaning 'oak' or 'fir', see the discussion of Friedrich 1970.136–137. For the semantic shift from 'oak' to 'fir', see Friedrich p. 136n30; also Vendryes 1927.314–315 and Güntert 1914.214.

[31] Specht 1932.215: e.g. *karaliū́nas* 'prince' from *karãlius* 'king'.

[32] Otrębski 1965.206; the suffix *-ũnas* too may be denominative (Otrębski p. 207), but the point remains that *-ū́nas* cannot be deverbative.

[33] LEW s.v.

[34] LEW s.v.; cf. Meillet 1926.171.

harkanem (present).[35] The form *per-g- also survives in Indic *Parjánya-*, which serves as the Rig-Vedic name for the god of the thunderstorm.[36] Also, the internal evidence of Indic suggests that the formation of *Parjánya-* is deverbative.[37]

In short, the comparative evidence is ambivalent about the etymology of Lithuanian *perkū́nas.* Forms like Latin *Portūnus* suggest that *perkū́nas* is derived from a noun *perk^{w}u- as in Latin *quercus* 'oak'. Forms like Slavic *perunŭ* and Indic *parjánya-*, on the other hand, imply that the root *per-k^{w}- of *perkū́nas* is a variant of *per-/*per-g-, meaning 'strike'. The solution, as Roman Jakobson saw, is that *perk^{w}u- had not always meant 'oak'.[38] Rather, the noun *perk^{w}u- is derived from a verb *per-k^{w}- 'strike'. The oak is named *perk^{w}u-, as in Latin *quercus,* because it is the tree consecrated to the god who *strikes* with the thunderbolt.[39] The thematic association of Baltic *Perkū́nas* and Slavic *Perunŭ* with the oak serves as corroboration.[40]

The form *perk^{w}u- is also attested in the Old Norse name *Fjǫrgyn* (feminine), by way of the intermediate form *perk^{w}unī-; the 'son' of Fjǫrgyn is Thor the thunder-god (*Vǫluspá* 56.10, etc.).[41] Considering the thematic associations of the thunder-god Perkūnas with mountaintops, we must also compare the Gothic form *fairguni,* to be reconstructed as *perk^{w}uni̯o- 'mountain, mountain-range'.[42] Its form is matched by a

[35] Meillet p. 171 and LEW s.v. For the derivative *orot* 'thunder', see Lidén 1906.88ff.

[36] Meillet p. 171 and KEWA s.v.

[37] We may note that *-áni-* is a deverbative formant of abstract nouns and adjectives, such as *śar-áṇi-* 'malice' from *śr̥̄-* 'destroy' and *sakṣ-áni-* 'overpowering' from *sah-* 'overpower'. For more examples, see Wackernagel and Debrunner 1954.207, where it is pointed out that abstract nouns in *-eni- are also a productive category in Germanic. (The type *-áni-* becomes infinitival in Indic, and some nouns in *-áni-* seem to be formed by way of infinitives in *-áni-*: see Renou 1937, esp. pp. 73–78.) There are two especially interesting examples: *aś-áni-* 'thunderbolt' and *ar-áṇi-* 'wood for obtaining fire by friction' (on which see p. 156). In neither case has the respective verb of these derivatives even survived in Indic. Sometimes the suffix *-áni-* is found with the accentuation *-aní-*, as in *kṣip-aní-* 'stroke of the whip' from *kṣip-* 'hurl' and *dyot-aní-* 'brightness' from *dyut-* 'shine'. The point is, the suffixes *-anyà-* (= *-anía-*) and *-ánya-* seem to be derivatives of *-aní-* and *-áni-* respectively. (For the derivation of *i̯o*-stems from *i*-stems, cf. Wackernagel and Debrunner pp. 778, 804, 816–817; also Benveniste 1935.73–74.) For examples of the suffix *-anya-*, we may adduce *nabh-anyà-* 'bursting forth' from *nabh-* 'burst' and *abhy-ava-dā-nyà-* 'apportioning' from *abhy-ava-dhā-* 'apportion'; cf. Wackernagel and Debrunner p. 212. In sum, I interpret *parj-ánya-* as 'striking, the striker', from *perg- 'strike'.

[38] Jakobson 1955.

[39] Jakobson 1955. LEW 574 also connects the following words containing the root *per-: Lithuanian *pérgas* 'Einbaum, Fischerkahn', Old English *fercal* 'bolt', Latin *pergula* 'projection from an edifice'. We may perhaps add Czech *prkno* 'board'. For the semantics, cf. Trautmann 1906. On Indic *parkatī*, see KEWA s.v.

[40] Here we have the central point of Ivanov and Toporov 1970.

[41] Meid 1957.126; Ivanov 1958.105; Güntert 1914.213.

[42] Ivanov 1958.104–105, 107; for a discussion of related forms in Germanic, see Feist

Celtic name transliterated as Ἑρκυνιο-.[43] Strabo uses the expression Ἑρκύνιος δρυμός 'Hercynian woodlands' in referring to the central mountain-range of Germany (4.6.9 C207; 7.1.3, 5 C290, 292). There is also a celebrated reference by Caesar to the *Hercynia silva* (*Bellum Gallicum* 6.24.2, 25). The semantic common denominator for the reconstruction *perk^{w}uni̯o- (and feminine *perk^{w}unī / *perk^{w}uni̯ā̆-) seems to be 'wooded mountain'. As in the case of oak trees in particular, we may suspect that wooded mountains were likewise consecrated to the god of the thunderbolt. There is also a suggestive morphological parallel, as V. V. Ivanov saw,[44] between *perk^{w}uni̯o- and *meldhuni̯o-: this second formation survives as Old Norse *mjǫllnir,* the name of Thor's Hammer.[45]

Roman Jakobson has argued convincingly for another parallel to the Celtic and Germanic reflexes of *perk^{w}uni̯o-, in the Slavic word for 'wooded hill', **pergynja* from *perg^{w}ūni̯ā.[46] We see reflexes in Old Church Slavonic *pregynja* 'wooded hill' and Old Russian *peregynja* (and various tabu-deformations) 'wooded hill', as well as in the Polish and Ukrainian toponomastic evidence.[47] Most important of all, we have it on record in East Slavic documents that Christian churchmen took pains to condemn the actual worship of wooded hills.[48] We may compare the Lithuanian toponym *Perkū́nija,* designating a spot where a great oak stood and where an idol of Perkūnas was venerated.[49] Besides the thematic parallelism between the Baltic and Slavic words, there is a formal parallelism as well. Both Baltic *perkū́nija* and Slavic **pergynja* have *-ūn- in the suffix and both feature an extension of the root *per- 'strike'. The important difference is that the radical extension is *-k^w- in Baltic (*per-k^w-ūn-) and *-g^w- in Slavic (*per-g^w-ūn-).

In the Old Russian Chronicles there is an interesting Slavic word closely parallel to the reconstructed **pergynja,* namely, *perynja,* along with two variants, *perynĭ* and *perunĭ*; all three are attested in the locative

1939 s.vv. *fairguni* and *fairhvus*; I draw attention to the delabialization of *k^w to *k: *perk^{w}un- to *perkun-.

[43] Ivanov 1958.104–105, 107; Watkins 1966.33–34; Meid 1956.284–285.

[44] Ivanov 1958.104.

[45] Cf. p. 183n13. The formal type *perk^{w}ŭ-ni̯o- is worth contrasting with the type *perk^{w}ū-no- as in Lithuanian *perkū́nas,* where the derivation from *perk^{w}u- is accompanied by lengthening of the *-u-. The same kind of lengthening, as we have already noted, occurs in Latin: *Port-ūnus* from *portus, trib-ūnus* from *tribus,* and so on. A comparable kind of non-lengthening pattern as in *perk^{w}ŭ-ni̯o- is evident in Indic: *árjuna-* 'bright' (cf. Greek *árgŭ-ros, árgŭ-phos*); cf. also the inner-Indic derivative patterns *śmaśrŭ-ṇá-* 'bearded' from *śmáśru-* 'beard', *dārú-ṇa-* 'sturdy' from *dā́ru-* 'wood', etc. (cf. Wackernagel and Debrunner 1954.485–486, 734; Meid 1956.270, 280).

[46] Jakobson 1955; cf. also Ivanov 1958.107–108, *pace* Vaillant 1948.

[47] Jakobson 1955.

[48] Mansikka 1922.305; Jakobson 1955.616.

[49] See p. 184.

expressions *na peruně, na peryni, na peruni* respectively.[50] The usage of these expressions in the chronicles reveals a highly suggestive context: they refer to a hill overlooking Novgorod, on top of which was a sanctuary that harbored, as the chronicles tell us, the idol of Perun himself.[51] Archaeologists have actually found this sanctuary (1951): it is four kilometers south of Novgorod, situated on top of a hill surrounded by the Volxov River, its tributary, and a swamp.[52]

With this much contextual evidence, we can safely follow Roman Jakobson and V. V. Ivanov in linking the Slavic formations *perunŭ*, *perynja/perynĭ/perunĭ*, and **pergynja.* I should add that we may abandon the notion that *perunŭ* is a deverbative agent noun. A variation like *perynĭ/perunĭ* strongly suggests the prehistoric existence of a **perynŭ* matching *perunŭ.*[53] It also suggests, in my opinion, that we are dealing with denominative rather than deverbative forms, built directly from a *u*-stem noun.[54] We may compare the Latvian variation *pȅrkūns/pȅrkuons/pȅrkauns* 'thunderbolt'.[55] The variation *pȅrkūns/ pȅrkuons* in

[50] Ivanov 1958.107.

[51] Mansikka 1922.65, 380; Ivanov p. 107.

[52] Jakobson 1955.615, Gimbutas 1967.742.

[53] Ivanov 1958.106–107. We may compare the variation in the Slavic word for 'wormwood', **pelynŭ/pelunŭ*, as attested in Old Church Slavonic *pelynŭ*, Polish *piołyn/piołun*, Czech *pelyn/pelun*, and so on. Cf. Būga 1959 [1921].332; cf. also Meid 1956.273–274.

[54] I reconstruct Slavic *-ynŭ/-unŭ* as *-ūnos/*-ōunos, on the basis of comparative evidence from Baltic, especially Latvian. For the clearest example available, I note that the Latvian *u*-stem noun *vìrsus* 'summit' has the variant derivatives *vìrsūne* and *vìrsuone,* both likewise meaning 'summit' (LDW 4:616). We may compare Lithuanian *viršū́nė* 'summit', from *viršùs* 'summit'. Such an alternation *-ūn-/-uon-* clearly suggests an earlier *-ūn-/-ōun- (Endzelin 1923.235, 240; cf. Meid 1956.276 on the type υἱύς/υἱωνός; the negative arguments of Schmeja 1963.40–41 are based mainly on the relative dearth of positive evidence in Greek). Latvian also shows a third variant, *vìrsaune* (LDW 4:610–611), which is significant because inherited *ōu has a bivalent reflex in Baltic, *au* as well as *uo* (Stang 1966.47–48, 75–76). We see the *ū/uo/au* alternation not only in derivatives of *u*-stems such as *vìrsūne/vìrsuone/vìrsaune* but also in the actual declension of both Lithuanian and Latvian *u*-stems (Stang pp. 75–76). And it so happens that we find the same *ū/uo/au* alternation in the attested Latvian variants of the word for 'thunderbolt', *pȅrkūns/ pȅrkuons/ pȅrkauns* (LDW 3:208–209); besides these *o*-stems, we also find the *i̯o*-stems *pę̄rkūnis/ pę̄rkuonis/pę̄rkaunis* (LDW 3:208–209).

[55] See the previous note. Of these three formations, it is *pȅrkuons* that prevails in the standard language (spelled *pērkōns*), largely because agent-nouns in *-uons* are a productive category in Latvian (the suffix *-uonis* is likewise productive in Latvian; cf. Lithuanian *-uonis,* which is productive, whereas *-uonas,* cognate of Latvian *-uons,* is not). Specht 1932 (240–241, 259, 264–265, etc.) has demonstrated that the suffix *-uons* of such agent-nouns is derived ultimately from *-ōn- (as in Greek -ων); the *-ōn- is clearly attested in older Lithuanian *-uõ;* the replacement pattern that prevailed in this language is not the *o*-stem *-uonas* but the *i̯o*-stem *-uonis* (unlike Latvian, where *-uons* and *-uonis* coexist). Specht's demonstration, however, need not lead to the inference that Latvian *pȅrkuons,* as distinct from *pȅrkūns,* is not an inherited form. It is simply a matter of phonological ambiguity in Baltic (both *ōu and *ō yield *uo*), which has led to a morphological reinterpretation. The

Baltic (Latvian) corresponds to the variation *perynĭ/perunĭ* in Slavic, which in turn implies a variant **perynŭ* for *perunŭ*.[56] In sum, we may reconstruct an underlying noun *peru-/*perg^{w}u- in Slavic, and *perk^{w}u- in Baltic.

The chain of derivation that I have posited for Slavic, verb *per- to noun *peru- to noun *perōuno-, has a close parallel in Hittite: verb *tarḫ-* to noun *tarḫu-* to noun *tarḫuna-*.[57] The verb *tarḫ-* 'conquer, overpower, overcome', comparable in meaning to *per- 'strike', has a *u*-stem derivative *tarḫu-*, as attested in the derivative *tarḫuili-* 'heroic'.[58] The *u*-stem noun is also attested as *Tarḫu-*, the name of the Storm-God, who is head of the Luvian pantheon.[59] Moreover, the name *Tarḫu-* has a derivative, with the same meaning, shaped *Tarḫuna-*.[60]

The derivation of *tarḫu-* from verb *tarḫ-* follows a familiar Hittite pattern: we may compare *parku-* 'elevated' from verb *park-* 'lift', *ḫuišu-* 'alive' from verb *ḫuiš-* 'live', and so on.[61] As for the derivation of *Tarḫuna-* from *Tarḫu-*, we may compare the form *peruna-* 'rock', derived from *peru-* 'rock';[62] both forms are used with the prefixed Sumerogram NA$_4$, which also designates 'rock' or 'stone'. The declension of Hittite *peru-* 'rock',

variant *pèrkuons* prevails over *pèrkūns* because its suffix *-uons*, which I reconstruct as *-ōunos, now has the same familiar shape as the productive formant of agent-nouns, *-uons* as derived from *-ōnos. Let us contrast a situation where we find no such inherent parallelism, as in the case of *vìrsūne/vìrsuone/vìrsaune*, discussed in the previous note: here the form that prevails is *vìrsaune*, not *vìrsuone* (for all the forms, see LDW 4:610–611). In considering the displacement of *pèrkūns* by *pèrkuons* in Latvian, we should note, too, that this language does not have a productive category of agent-nouns in *-ūns*. Conversely, Lithuanian *perkū́nas* can prevail over *perkuonas* because the language has no productive category of agent-nouns in *-uonas* (from *-ōnos); rather, the productive suffixes are *-uonis* and *-ūnas*. For vestiges of *perkuonas* (and *viršuonė*) in Old Lithuanian, see Specht p. 265.

56 Just as Latvian *pèrkuons* prevails over *pèrkūns* because of the productive agent-suffix *-uons* (see previous note), so also we may say that Slavic *perunŭ* prevails over **perynŭ* because its suffix *-unŭ*, which I reconstruct as *-ōunos, is shaped like an agent-suffix that is productive in Slavic, *-unŭ*. In this case, I prefer to reconstruct the deverbative agent-suffix also as *-ōunos, the same suffix that is derived from *u*-stem nouns. In other words, deverbative *-unŭ* was once denominative (cf. Specht 1932.268). We may compare Lithuanian *-ūnas* and *-uonis*, which are still denominative as well as deverbative, as distinct from *-ū́nas*, which is formally marked for an exclusively denominative category (cf. Specht pp. 240–241; also Meid 1956.268–270).

57 This is not to say that e.g. *terh$_2$u- cannot be a verb-formation (cf. Hittite *tarḫuzzi*, Indic *tárute, tū́rvati*, etc.).

58 Laroche 1958.90. Also Watkins 1990.

59 Laroche pp. 91–95; on *Tarḫunt-* and the thunderbolt, see Laroche p. 95. Cf. Watkins 1974.107. Cf. also p. 131.

60 Laroche pp. 93, 94.

61 Laroche p. 90. As for the vocalism of *tarḫ-*, etc., Kuryłowicz 1958.228 observes that roots ending in *-erC* tend to generalize the zero-grade in Hittite (*-R̥C* > *-arC*, where *R* = *r, l, m, n*, and *C* = other consonant).

62 Laroche p. 90. Also spelled *piruna-* and *piru-*.

as we see from dative/locative *peruni*, reveals an *r/n*-stem added to the *u*-stem.[63] Hittite *peru-* 'rock' is cognate with Indic *párvan-* 'joint [e.g. of sacrificial animal], knot [in plant]'.[64] The Indic noun can be explained as a derivative of the verb-root *per- 'go to the end point, go over to the other side, arrive at the other side',[65] *with special reference to the successful piercing through or cutting through of the body's joints in the context of sacrifice.*[66] We may compare the Greek verb *peírō*, which can mean either 'pierce' when the object is the body of a victim or 'cross over' when the object is a body of water (as reflected in such derivative nouns as *póros*).[67] These meanings are pertinent to the semantics of the Hittite verb *tarḫ-* 'conquer, overpower, overcome', from which the name of *Tarḫu-* the Storm-God is derived: the Indo-European root *terh$_2$- underlying this Hittite verb also carries the meaning 'cross over' as in the Indic *ap-túr-* 'crossing over the water',[68] and this meaning applies also in specific contexts of immortalization, as in the Greek *nék-tar.*[69] Given the parallelism between the sense of 'cross over' in the verb-root *terh$_2$- and the sense of 'go to the end point, go over to the other side, arrive at the other side' in the verb-root *per-, we arrive at a better understanding of the etymology of Greek *Ēlúsion*, designating both the place where a thunderbolt has struck and the place of immortalization, 'Elysium':[70] this noun-formation is derived from *-ḗlutho-*, from the conjugation ἔρχομαι/ἐλεύσομαι in the sense of 'arrive'.[71] Also, given the parallelism between the Hittite forms *Tarḫu-/Tarḫuna-*, designating the Storm-God, and *peru-/peruna-*, meaning 'rock', we may be ready to connect Hittite *peruna-* 'rock' with Slavic *perunŭ* '(god of) thunderbolt', just as we have connected Latin *quercus* 'oak' with Baltic (Lithuanian) *perkū́nas* '(god of) thunderbolt'. As we have already seen, *rocks as well as oaks were sacred to the god of the thunderbolt.*[72]

The cognate of Hittite *peru-* 'rock', to repeat, is Indic *párvan-* 'joint [e.g. of sacrificial animal], knot [in plant]', derived from the verb-root *per- meaning 'go to the end point, go over to the other side, arrive at

[63] Hoffmann 1975 [1974].332, 336.
[64] Hoffmann pp. 332, 336.
[65] Bergren 1975.62–101, esp. p. 95.
[66] Bergren pp. 67–78, esp. pp. 68–69 on *Rig-Veda* 1.61.12, where Indra hurls his thunderbolt at Vṛtra in order to sever his joints (noun *párvan*), much as the joints of an ox are severed; cf. also Hoffmann 1975 [1974].332.
[67] Cf. DELG 871. Detailed discussion of the semantics in Bergren pp. 95–101.
[68] See p. 139.
[69] See p. 139. Cf. also p. 156n49 on Indic *taráṇi-* in the sense of 'ship'.
[70] See p. 140.
[71] On the level of form, this derivation of *Ēlúsion* is corroborated by DELG 411; my interpretation of the meaning, however, differs from that of DELG.
[72] See pp. 184ff.

the other side', *with special reference to the successful piercing through or cutting through of the body's joints in the context of sacrifice.* Given the implication of sacred violence in this meaning, we may be justified in identifying this verb-root *per- with the verb-root *per- that we have been defining up to now simply as 'strike', attested in the Baltic and the Slavic verbs that yield the words for '(god of) thunderbolt' in these languages. Although I know of no verb shaped *per- in Hittite, we may still cite *parḫ-* 'chase, drive, make (a horse) gallop'. Just as *tarḫ-* 'conquer, overpower, overcome' is traced back to the root *terh$_2$-, so also *parḫ-* might stem from *perh$_2$-, with radical extension *-h$_2$- added to the *per- which hypothetically survives as *peru-* 'rock'. The attested meanings of *parḫ-* might be secondary to a primary meaning 'strike'; we may compare the semantics of Lithuanian *giǹ-ti* 'chase, drive (cattle) to pasture',[73] cognate with Indic *hánti* 'strike, kill', Hittite *kwenzi* (same meaning), and so on.

In further support of the derivation of Hittite *peruna-* from a verb-root *per- 'strike', we may consider the Hittite epithet *kunkunuzzi-* (with prefixed Sumerogram NA$_4$ designating 'rock' or 'stone') as applied to the megalithic monster Ullikummi, who was himself born of a huge *piruna-* (= *peruna-*) 'rock'.[74] The form *kunkunuzzi-* is an instrument-noun derived from the verb *kwenzi* 'strike, kill'.[75] In the Indic *Rig-Veda* the cognate verb *hánti* 'strike, kill' regularly denotes the action of the thunderbolt.[76] For the reduplication in *kun-kun-uzzi-*, we may compare a South Slavic form related to *perunŭ*, *per-per-una*, which is a name for a virgin chosen to dance for rain:[77] "nude and draped with flowers she whirls ecstatically in the middle of a ring, invoking in song the sky or Elijah to moisten and fructify the earth."[78] To repeat: *kun-kun-uzzi-* is an instrument-noun;[79] accordingly, we might have expected the word to designate a weapon—maybe even a projectile at that. Instead, it designates an animated boulder that is destined to be smitten by the Storm-God.[80]

There is a comparable ambiguity in Old Norse: *hamarr* may mean 'rock, boulder, cliff' as well as 'hammer'; the former meaning is attested

[73] Cf. also the derivative *nakti-gonis* 'night-herder of horses': LEW 152.
[74] For the Ullikummi texts, see Güterbock 1952, esp. pp. 37, 146–147.
[75] Ivanov 1958.110, Ivanov and Toporov 1970.1196–1197.
[76] Grassmann 1873 s.v. *han-*, the attestations labeled "1."
[77] Jakobson 1955.616, with a list of tabu-variants.
[78] Jakobson 1950.1026.
[79] For another example of a Hittite instrument-noun in *-uzzi-*: *išḫuzzi-* 'belt', vs. verb *išḫiya-* 'bind'.
[80] See Güterbock 1952.6. The Storm-God is written with the Sumerogram ^{d}U, but the Ullikummi texts (as well as others) reveal the Hittite ending *-unaš*; cf. Güterbock p. 4n14. The full form is probably *Tarḫunaš* (Laroche 1958.94–95).

in toponyms like *Hammerfest.* Conversely, Lithuanian *akmuõ* 'rock, stone' is cognate with Greek *ákmōn,* which means not 'hammer' but 'anvil'. To complicate matters further, there are traces of the meaning 'thunderbolt' in the usage of *ákmōn* in Homeric and Hesiodic diction.[81] We even hear of a god *Akmōn,* father of *Ouranós* 'Sky' (Alcman PMG 61). Also, in a sixteenth-century account of pagan Lithuanian practices, there is a god (mentioned alongside Perkūnas himself) who is named *Akmo* and who is described as *saxum grandius.*[82] Amidst all this complicated evidence, we must keep in mind the basic ambiguity, namely, that the word for the thunder-weapon is being applied to the thunder-target itself; also, that the meaning may become simplified to the extent of designating merely the weapon or the target, without any overt message about the thunder-stroke itself.

As further illustration of the weapon/target ambiguity, we may consider the Indic noun *áśman-,* cognate of Greek *ákmōn* and Lithuanian *akmuõ.* This word is used in the *Rig-Veda* to designate the weapon of Indra (2.30.5, 4.22.1, 7.104.19). The activities of Indra, this national war-god, are as a rule described in a specialized language that is so highly stylized that it tends to blur the naturalistic aspects of his background as thunder-god, more visible in his counterpart *Parjánya-.*[83] Nevertheless, the basic naturalistic attributes of Indra persist in the *Rig-Veda:* he gives rain (4.26.2, etc.), lightning comes from him (2.13.7), he is likened to a thundering cloud-driver (6.44.12), and he is specifically described as equal to Parjanya at raintime (8.6.1). Indra's weapon is predominantly called the *vájra-,* which, in keeping with the stylistic specialization of his descriptions, has become Indra's personal distinguishing feature in the diction of the *Rig-Veda.* Like its owner, however, the *vájra-,* too, has natural attributes that persist: it thunders (1.100.13) and roars (2.11.10). With this *vájra-* of his, Indra conventionally strikes boulders and thereby releases water or light—a theme so common that any listing of the attestations would be superfluous.[84] Suffice it to note here that one of the words for 'boulder' in the *Rig-Veda* is *áśman-* (1.130.3, etc.), the same word that can also designate Indra's weapon (again, 2.30.5, etc.).[85]

[81] Whitman 1970, esp. pp. 39–40.

[82] Rostowski's history of the Jesuit Order in Lithuania (1583): see Mannhardt 1936.435 and Reichelt 1913.26. On the related subject of *Iuppiter Lapis,* see Schwenck 1859.393–394. Cf. also the Laconian cult stone known as *Zeùs Kappṓtās* (Pausanias 3.22.1).

[83] On this figure, see p. 186. For a balanced discussion of the naturalism surrounding the *Parjánya-* figure, see Lommel 1939.38–44. For a contrast of the naturalistic/nonnaturalistic descriptions of Parjanya/Indra, see Oldenberg 1917.137. The relative dearth of naturalism in descriptions of Indra results from intense stylistic elaboration and evolution, not shared by the far less developed Parjanya figure.

[84] For a survey, see Reichelt 1913.34–37.

[85] In *Rig-Veda* 2.12.3, Indra brings forth fire *áśmanor antár* 'between two rocks'. Ivanov

In addition, we should consider a far more common word for 'boulder' in the *Rig-Veda*, a word that is actually derived from *párvan-*, the Indic cognate of Hittite *peru-* 'rock'.[86] The word in question is *párvata-* 'boulder'. The *párvata-* that Indra strikes with his *vájra-* is often a metaphorical substitute for 'cloud'.[87] In the diction of the *Rig-Veda*, the description of streams that burst forth from a smashed boulder is conventionally made parallel to the description of rain flowing from clouds.[88] In the description of rain, the expression *ā́. . .divó br̥hatáḥ* 'from the high Heaven' is parallel to *párvatād. . .ā́* 'from the Boulder' (5.43.11).[89] Indra conventionally smites (verb *hánti*) the Serpent on the *párvata-* (1.32.1, etc.), which in such contexts is traditionally rendered as 'mountain'.[90] In fact, *párvata-* is frequently in apposition to the noun *girí-* 'mountain' (1.37.7, etc.). Alternatively, it is the Demon called Vr̥tra whom Indra smites (verb *hánti*) on the *párvata-*; in the process, Indra is also described as smashing the *párvata-* directly and thus bringing water (1.32.1, 1.57.6).[91]

The mighty Indra not only smashes the *párvata-*: at times he is actually likened to it, as in the expression

sá párvato ná dharúṇeṣu ácyutaḥ

Rig-Veda 1.52.2

like a *párvata-*, unshakable in his fortifications

There is also a personified Parvata, who is Indra's alter ego (*Rig-Veda* 1.32.6, etc.) or his antagonist (8.3.19). Finally, *párvata-* may refer to Indra's weapon itself:

---

and Toporov 1970.1195–1196 compare the Byelorussian theme where Perun (Piarun) rubs two gigantic millstones together, thus producing thunder and lightning.

[86] See pp. 189ff.

[87] See again Lommel 1939.42–43. In a few passages, *áśman-* allows the interpretation 'sky' (e.g. *Rig-Veda* 7.88.2; but see Geldner 1951 2:259 and Kuiper 1964.111n80). Reichelt 1913 has argued that *áśman-* could be used with the meaning 'sky' as well as 'stone' because the sky was thought to have a stone vault once upon a time. We may compare especially Avestan *asan-/asman-* 'rock, stone, sky' (Bartholomae 1904.207–208). For typological parallels from Africa, see Baumann 1936.146–147. Although Reichelt's presentation is persuasive, there is another way to explain the meaning 'sky'. If 'rock' equals 'cloud' by way of metaphor, the notion of 'cloud' could easily evolve into 'sky'. We may compare Hittite *nepiš* 'sky' and Slavic *nebo* 'sky' vs. Indic *nábhas* 'cloud' and Greek *néphos* 'cloud'; cf. also Middle English *sky* 'cloud' or 'sky'.

[88] For Slavic parallels: Ivanov and Toporov 1970.1193. For typological parallels in African myth and ritual: Hocart 1936.56.

[89] Lommel 1939.42–43.

[90] See Geldner 1951 1:36, etc.

[91] See Benveniste and Renou 1934.147n1.

abhí jahi rakṣásaḥ párvatena

Rig-Veda 7.104.19

smite [verb *hán-*] the demons with your *párvata-*[92]

As Louis Renou remarks in his study (with Emile Benveniste) of Vr̥tra and Vr̥trahan in the *Rig-Veda*, there is a curious fact about the attributes proper to Indra the Vr̥trahan or 'Vr̥tra-killer': these same attributes are also proper to his arch-antagonist, Vr̥tra.[93] I would add, from a distinct set of myths, the case of *párvata-*, a word that stands for either Indra's *target* ('rock, boulder, mountain') or his *weapon*,[94] and which is also suitable for comparison with the very likeness of the fulminating Almighty in the myths of the Indic peoples.[95]

No survey of forms related to Baltic (Lithuanian) *perkū́nas* and Slavic *perunŭ* can be definitive without mention of the Greek form *keraunós*, which likewise designates not only the thunderbolt but also the god of the thunderbolt. At Mantineia in ancient Arcadia, for example, *Keraunós* was the epithet of Zeus himself (*IG* V 2.288). From not only the functional but also the formal point of view, it has been observed, *keraunós* seems parallel to Slavic *perunŭ*.[96] One explanation that has been offered is to reconstruct *perunŭ* as *peraunos, to which *keraunós* would correspond as a tabu rhyme-word of the type *Donnerledder* for *Donnerwetter*.[97] According to this scheme, *keraunós* consists of root *ker- as in *keraízō* 'destroy, ravage' plus the suffix *-aunos, which is patterned to rhyme with the *-aunos of *per-aunos;[98] the earlier suffixal pattern, the argument goes, is *ker-u- as in Indic *śáru-* 'missile, arrow'.[99]

I see at least two disadvantages to this explanation. First, the reconstruction *au in *per-aunos is puzzling from the standpoint of Indo-European morphology. Second, we can account for the *au of *keraunós*

[92] In the same stanza, Indra's weapon is called *áśman-*: see Reichelt 1913.44–45. Cf. also *Rig-Veda* 2.30.5, 4.22.1. On the Germanic theme of the whetstone as a symbol of authority, see Mitchell 1985.

[93] Benveniste and Renou 1934.138.

[94] For Slavic parallels, see Ivanov and Toporov 1970.1193–1195.

[95] Ivanov 1958.110 adduces the name of the Anatolian deity *Pirwa-* (on whom see Otten 1951), deriving it from *peru̯-o-. We may note too the Hittite collocation *ḫé-kur pí-ir-wa* (cf. Goetze 1954.356n54), with the *ḫé-kur* preceded by the Sumerogram NA_4, which designates 'rock' or 'stone', and with *pí-ir-wa* once preceded by the Sumerogram ^{d}; the noun *ḫekur* means 'summit, mountain'.

[96] Güntert 1914.215–216.

[97] Güntert pp. 215–216, 221.

[98] Güntert p. 216. Outside of *keraunós*, we find no instance of suffixal *-aunos* in Greek. The word *púraunos* (Pollux 6.88, 10.104) must be a compound formed with the verb *aúō* (on this word see Borthwick 1969).

[99] Güntert p. 216.

more easily in terms of the Greek language itself. The noun *keraunós* may be formed from the base *kerau̯- as attested in the Homeric verb *keraízō* 'destroy, ravage'.[100] The base *kerau̯- (from *kerh$_2$-u̯-) contains the root *kerh$_2$-,[101] clearly visible in the Indic verb *śṛṇā́ti* 'shatter' (from *kṛ-n-eh$_2$-ti).[102] In *Rig-Veda* 3.30.17, this verb actually denotes the action of Indra's bolt against his adversaries, described in metaphorical language that pictures them as trees rather than men. Finally, we may note the apparent formal parallelism between Greek *keraunós* (from *kerh$_2$-u̯-) and Hittite *tarḫuna-* (from *terh$_2$-u̯-).

Even if *keraunós* may not be formally connected with Baltic *perkū́nas* and Slavic *perunŭ*, perhaps *terpikéraunos* can. Like Homeric *argikéraunos* 'he whose thunderbolt shines' (*Iliad* XX 16, XXII 178), *terpikéraunos* too serves exclusively as an epithet of Zeus himself (VIII 2, XII 252, etc.). In fact, the two epithets are formulaic variants. We may note, too, the synchronic morphological parallelism between *terpi-* and *argi-* (from *h$_2$ergi-; cf. Hittite *ḫarki-* 'bright'). If we set up a reconstruction *k^{w}erpi- for *terpi-*, then we may recover an earlier *perk^{w}i- by way of metathesis.[103] If *argikéraunos* means 'he whose bolt shines', perhaps *terpikéraunos* means 'he whose bolt strikes'.[104]

The time has come to ask why oaks and rocks should be singled out for a sacral affinity with the thunderbolt to such an extent that their designations are interchangeable in various Indo-European languages. From our own secular standpoint, it is obvious that rocks, boulders, trees, hills, or mountains are targets of lightning by virtue of their elevation or prominence. But there are other factors as well in attracting the stroke of lightning. I would be out of my field in attempting a strictly scientific discussion about these other factors, but they can be in any case easily intuited even by the unscientific mind. For example, it is an observable fact that different kinds of trees have significantly different degrees of susceptibility to being struck by lightning. In a quaint experiment conducted by the Lippe-Detmold'sche Forstverwaltung over the years 1879 to 1890, the following statistics emerge for the susceptibility,

[100] DELG 519. From the evidence of such pairs as *daíō* (from *dau̯i̯ō) vs. *daízō*, we may expect an earlier form *kerau̯i̯ō: cf. GEW 822.

[101] For reflexes of *h$_2$u̯- as *au* in Greek roots, cf. both GEW and DELG s.v. *kaíō* (cf. also the discussion of Schmeja 1963.29–32).

[102] See KEWA s.v. *śṛṇā́ti*.

[103] Cf. *artokópos* 'baker' from *artok^{w}opos, by metathesis from *artopok^{w}os (on which see DELG 118).

[104] Alternatively, *terpikéraunos* may be explained as the reflex of an expressive reduplication *k^{w}erpi-ker(p)aunos, with dissimilation of *k^w. . .*k^w to *k^w. . .k, from an earlier form *k^{w}er(p)aunos, which in turn would be a tabu-metathesis of *per(k^w)aunos (cf. Watkins 1970.350).

in a given forest, of certain species of tree to lightning strikes:

	% of all trees in forest	number of lightning strikes
oak	11%	56
beech	70%	0
spruce	13%	3 or 4
fir	6%	20 or 21

We may observe especially the dramatic contrast between oaks and beeches—a contrast that was already observed ages earlier through the medium of folklore. In Nordic mythology, for example, Thor the thunder-god smites the giants when they hide under an oak, but he has no power over them when they hide under a beech.[105]

In the logic of myth there is an inference built into the known attraction of oaks to the thunderbolt. There must have been something *intrinsic* in oak trees that is like the thunderbolt and that therefore attracts it. Also, rocks must have some kindred quality. This quality, I suggest, is potential fire. The Lithuanian thunder-god Perkūnas, for instance, was believed to strike oak trees that have fire stored up inside.[106] Or again, the prime material for the heathen German *Notfeuer*, equivalent of English *willfire*, which may be produced only by friction, was oak wood.[107] As for rocks, we may consider again the Byelorussian tradition that pictures Piarun (Perun) rubbing two gigantic millstones together, thus producing thunder and lightning.[108] Indra too brings forth fire *áśmanor antár* 'between two rocks' (*Rig-Veda* 2.12.3).[109] In sum, those earthbound things that we use to kindle fire and that also attract the thunderbolt must tell us something, by dint of their celestial affinity, about how the fire of the thunderbolt comes about. Conversely, the fact that we can rub fire out of wood and rock suggests that these materials were once infused, perhaps even impregnated, with the stroke of some thunderbolt.[110]

As we shall now see, the infusion of thunder-fire into wood and stone is a sexual and anthropogonic theme. Let us begin with instances of overtly creative themes associated with the thunderbolt. In Indic

[105] Grimm 1878 3:64. For a survey of connections between the oak and Thor (as well as other Germanic equivalents), see Wagler 1891 2:43–46.

[106] See p. 183.

[107] Kuhn 1886, with a discussion of the evidence collected by J. Grimm.

[108] See pp. 192–193n85; Ivanov and Toporov 1970.1195–1196.

[109] Ivanov and Toporov pp. 1195–1196.

[110] In the case of wood, we have just noted a pattern of preference for oak wood as the sacral material for rubbing fire, a pattern that can be correlated with the observably stronger attraction of oak trees to lightning.

mythology, for example, Indra's *vájra-*, his stylized thunderbolt, is not only destructive but also procreative.[111] The Iranian cognate, *vazra-*, forms a derivative *vazraka-*, which means 'endowed with generative power' in Old Persian.[112] The radical *u̯eg- of *vájra-/vazra-* recurs in the Rig-Vedic word *vā́ja-* 'generative power residing in vegetation, cattle, etc.'.[113] It also recurs in Latin *uigeō* 'thrive' and *uegeō* 'quicken, arouse'.[114] We may note in this connection the Old Norse lore about Thor's Hammer, which hallows the laps of brides and has the power of bringing his dead goats back to life.[115] Or we may note a Lithuanian belief, reported by the cleric Matthäus Praetorius (late seventeenth century), that lightning could beget human children in the vicinity where it strikes.[116] Or again, if lightning strikes in the daytime as a child is being born, he will thrive; if it strikes at night, the child will die.[117] If a man is struck down in a thunderstorm that is heading west, he dies as a favorite of God; if the thunderstorm was heading east, he has died on account of his sins.[118] Within the framework of this presentation, however, I cannot do justice to the vast subject of the thunderbolt's destructive/creative ambivalence in Indo-European lore.[119] My main purpose instead is to explore specifically the Indo-European traditions concerning the association of the thunderbolt with trees and rocks, and how the action of a thunderstroke on these materials was believed to be sacral and, more than that, creative.

A belief in the creative and even anthropogonic powers of trees or rocks is indirectly attested in a Greek proverb: *surely you or I or anyone else today*, the saying has it, *were not created either from oaks or from rocks* (e.g.

[111] Survey of relevant passages in Gonda 1954.32–55, esp. pp. 36–37.

[112] Liebert 1962.127, who also refutes the reinterpretation as *vazarka-* (e.g. Bartholomae 1904.1389–1390).

[113] Gonda 1954.43ff.; Liebert p. 145. Otherwise Watkins 1986.325 and 327, with the references at n10.

[114] Gonda pp. 43ff. For the vocalisms *uig-/ueg-*, see Watkins 1973a.

[115] Davidson 1965.11–14.

[116] Reprinted in Mannhardt 1936.538.

[117] Mannhardt p. 538.

[118] Mannhardt p. 538.

[119] More on this subject in Gonda 1954.36–37. Also, we may note that the derivation of neuter *śárīra-* 'body' from the root *kerh$_2$- of *śr̥ṇā́ti* 'shatter' is accepted as plausible in KEWA s.v. *śárīra-* (on the associations of the verb *śr̥ṇā́ti* 'shatter' with the thunderbolt at *Rig-Veda* 3.30.17, see p. 195). We may compare the etymological explanation of Latin *corpus* as if derived, albeit indirectly, from the root *per-k^w- (see Vendryes 1927.315). It may be possible to link the verb *śr̥ṇā́ti* not only with *śárīra-* 'body' but also with *śáru-* 'missile, arrow' (on which see p. 194), a word used for comparisons with the thunderbolt in the *Rig-Veda* (1.172.2, etc.). Perhaps also with *śará-* 'reed' and *śáras-* 'ashes' (cf. KEWA s.v.). In view of the latter meaning, 'ashes', it may be pertinent to cite the reflex of the root *perk^w- in Lithuanian *pir̃kšnys* 'glowing ashes' (cf. LEW s.v. *pirkšnis*) and possibly also in Old Irish *richis* 'glowing coals, live ember'.

Plato *Apology* 34d, *Republic* 544d; Plutarch *Consolation to his Wife* 608c; Philostratus *Images* 2.3.1). By implication, as we shall see, earlier humans had just such origins.

Let us return to our starting point, the passage in the *Odyssey* where Penelope challenges the disguised Odysseus to reveal his hidden identity by revealing his lineage (xix 162). She adds the following words:

> οὐ γὰρ ἀπὸ δρυός ἐσσι παλαιφάτου οὐδ' ἀπὸ πέτρης
>
> *Odyssey* xix 163

> For surely you are not from an oak, as in the old stories, or from a rock.

The context of Penelope's utterance reveals a detached attitude, on her own part, toward an old myth. The narrative that frames Penelope's words is itself merely alluding to a theme, without going into details that seem inappropriate to an epic situation. The epithet *palaíphatos* 'spoken of a long time ago', which may be interpreted as referring to both 'oak' and 'rock', is a self-conscious poetic allusion to a genre other than epic. Elsewhere in Homeric diction, the adjective *palaíphato-* is used exclusively to describe *théspbata*, which may be defined as 'words of a *mántis* [seer] or of one who functions as a *mántis*'.[120]

In Hesiodic poetry as well, there is a fastidious attitude toward treating the theme of oaks and rocks with any references that would go beyond mere allusion. There is a passage in the *Theogony* (31–34) where the poet has just told how the Muses infused in him the power to sing about

[120] See *Odyssey* ix 507, xiii 172. For the mantic connotations of *théspbata*, see especially ix 507, xi 151. In connection with the mantic concept, we may note the form of the placename, *Perkṓtē*, as attested at *Iliad* II 835. A *mántis* 'seer' by the name of *Mérops* is identified as *Perkṓsios* 'from *Perkṓtē*' at *Iliad* II 831–832 (Μέροπος Περκωσίου, ὃς περὶ πάντων | ᾔδεε μαντοσύνας). The form *Perkṓtē* may perhaps be reconstructed as *perkō[u]tā (for the phonology, cf. Vine 1982.42–43 on Greek *plōtḗr*), to be derived from an earlier *u*-stem noun *perku- (from *perk^{w}u-) 'oak'. We may note too that *méropes* is a common Homeric epithet for *ánthrōpoi* 'humans' (cf. Koller 1968) and that the sons of *Mérops Perkṓsios* are said to hold sway over a place called *Pitúeia*, at *Iliad* II 829. The latter name is surely derived from the noun *pítus* 'pine'. We may perhaps compare the semantic oscillation between 'oak' and 'fir', on which see p. 185n30. What we see in these associations are perhaps traces of an ancient local myth that equated the First Man with the First *Mántis* 'Seer'. On the anthropogonic theme of First Man as First Sacrificer, cf. pp. 110 and following. Given the anthropogonic themes inherent in the possible etymology of *ánthrōpos* as 'he who has the looks of embers' (p. 151n30), we may consider the possible etymology of *mérops* as 'he who has glowing looks'; cf. *Merópē* as the name of a star at Hesiod F 169.3 MW. I suggest that Μαῖα, the name of another star mentioned in Hesiod F 169.3, be emended to Μαῖρα = *Maîra*, from root *mer- as in *marmaírō* 'glow, flash'; cf. *marī́lē* 'embers of charcoal'. The proposed explanation of *mérops* as 'he who has glowing looks' may be pertinent to the discussion of Indic *márya-* at p. 250.

past and future things, and about the origins of the gods; also, to start and end the song by singing of the Muses themselves. The poet then breaks off with these words:

ἀλλὰ τίη μοι ταῦτα περὶ δρῦν ἢ περὶ πέτρην;

Hesiod *Theogony* 35

But why do I have these things about the oak or about the rock?

With this utterance, the narration is pausing to take a self-conscious look at the point that has been reached so far in the composition of the *Theogony*. In the next verse, the break is followed up with Μουσάων ἀρχώμεθα 'let us start with the Muses', the same expression that had inaugurated the *Theogony* at verse 1. Thus the narration has come full circle from *Theogony* 1 to 36, and Hesiod "has to make a fresh start on the same lines as before."[121] Verse 35 actually anticipates that Hesiod is about to make this fresh start with verses 36 and following. For Hesiod to ask in verse 35 why he has "these things about [= going around][122] the oak or about the rock" is the equivalent of asking why he has lingered at the beginning of beginnings. "Why am I still going around, as it were, the proverbial oak or rock? Let me proceed at last by starting out again!"

Finally, we may consider the passage in *Iliad* XXII where Hektor is deliberating whether he should throw himself at the mercy of Achilles. He then decides against taking this course of action, saying to himself:

ἀλλὰ τίη μοι ταῦτα φίλος διελέξατο θυμός;

Iliad XXII 122

But why do I have these things to talk about with my spirit [*thūmós*]?

Hektor recognizes that Achilles will be merciless and will surely kill him (XXII 123–125). At this point, Hektor expresses his loss of hope in terms of the proverb:

οὐ μέν πως νῦν ἔστιν ἀπὸ δρυὸς οὐδ' ἀπὸ πέτρης

[121] West 1966.170.

[122] West p. 169 argues that περί + accusative regularly conveys a positional ('around') rather than a conceptual ('about') sense in early poetic diction. Perhaps such a formulation is too restrictive: the second sense can be a metaphorical derivative of the first.

τῷ ὀαριζέμεναι

Iliad XXII 126–127

It is by now impossible to converse with him, starting from the oak or from the rock.[123]

In other words, it is no use to begin at the beginning with Achilles. There is no more time to make a fresh start of things.

In these three poetic contexts the proverbial oak or rock connotes not only temporal but also cultural remoteness. In all three instances elaboration on the theme is studiously avoided as if it were inappropriate, perhaps even too primitive. The theme is indeed "primitive," in the sense that we can find it commonly attested in the widest spectrum of societies. In the mythmaking traditions of many peoples of the world, it is a recurrent theme that humankind originated from trees or rocks.[124] A comparable theme can be reconstructed in the traditions of Indo-European languages as well.[125] From the Germanic evidence, we may note in particular the following reflexes of the root *perk^{w}-: Old Norse *fjǫr* 'life'; Old English *feorh* 'life, soul' and *fíras* 'men'; and so on.[126] From the Celtic, there are such examples as the Old Irish name *Macc Daro* 'son of oak', *Macc Cairthin* (also the Ogam genitive *Maqi Cairatini*) 'son of rowan-tree', *Macc Ibair* 'son of yew', and so on.[127] There is also a wealth of further evidence, such as the testimony of Lithuanian folk songs.[128]

Instead of going further with illustrations, however, I simply return to the central point to be made. We have observed an ambivalence in the application of Indo-European *per(k^{w})u- to oaks in some languages

[123] What follows at *Iliad* XXII 127–128 is a description of sweet-talk between unmarried lovers, as if such a pair would take their conversation all the way back to the oak and the rock.

[124] There is a multitude of African examples collected by Baumann 1936.224–235 (trees), 219–220 (rocks). For a survey of European examples, cf. Vadé 1977. For traces in Semitic myth: Dirlmeier 1955.25–26. For a convenient bibliography on the general theme of *Petra Genitrix*, see Eliade 1962.208.

[125] Specht 1944. Cf. also Lincoln 1986.188n29, with emphasis on parallelisms between cosmogonic and sociogonic themes, especially in Germanic traditions.

[126] See also Vendryes 1927.

[127] Cf. Loth 1920.122.

[128] Cf. Meulen 1907.55–72, 121–169. For a useful statement on tree animism, see esp. his p. 127. For a discussion of myths where humankind originates from the ash tree, see Shannon 1975.44–48, 57, 70. Shannon's book shows convincingly that such myths are linked to the theme of Achilles' ash spear in the *Iliad.* He also points out that, in the Hesiodic *Works and Days,* it is the gods in general who create the first and second generations of humankind (109–110, 127–128), but it is Zeus in particular who creates the third generation, and this third creation emerges specifically out of ash trees (143–145). Such an association of Zeus himself with the process of creation out of ash trees is significant in view of his epithets *keraunós, terpikéraunos,* and *argikéraunos,* as discussed at pp. 194–195.

(Latin *quercus*) and to rocks in others (Hittite *peru*). This etymological ambivalence, we now see, is matched by the thematic ambivalence in the obsolescent ancient Greek proverb alluding to the myth that humankind originated *either* from oaks *or* from rocks—whichever of the two. The unifying theme that resolves these two cases of ambivalence, I am suggesting, is the creative action of the Indo-European thunder-god, whose very name is formed from the derivatives of *per(k^w)u- in Baltic (*Perkū́nas*) and Slavic (*Perunŭ*).

CHAPTER 8

Sêma and Nóēsis: The Hero's Tomb and the "Reading" of Symbols in Homer and Hesiod

The word *semiotic*—and *semantic*, for that matter—may be perceived in a new light if we look again at its Greek origins. The basic form in Greek is *sêma* 'sign', a neuter action-noun built on a root-verb that is no longer attested in the language. There is a cognate of Greek *sêma* in the Indic branch of the Indo-European linguistic family. The form is *dhyāma* 'thought', a neuter action-noun, attested only in the late Indic lexicographical tradition.[1] This poorly attested noun is built on a root-verb that is well attested in early Indic. The root is *dhyā-* 'think' (variant of *dhī-* 'think'). Even though the morphological relationship of *dhyā-* and *dhyāma* is transparent in Indic, and even though Indic *dhyāma* and Greek *sêma* would have to be considered cognates on the basis of their parallelism on the level of morphology, students of language are troubled by the apparent lack of parallelism on the level of semantics: how could the meaning 'sign' of Greek *sêma* be connected with the meaning 'thought' of Indic *dhyāma*?[2]

This presentation is an attempt to show that the semantics of *sêma* are indeed connected with the semantics of thinking. The overall approach will emulate that of Emile Benveniste's *Vocabulaire des institutions indo-européennes*,[3] in that the given word will be examined not only in context but also specifically in the contexts of its behavior within the formulaic systems of archaic Greek poetic diction.[4] What will emerge is that the key

[1] KEWA 2:114.
[2] See DELG 998.
[3] Cf. esp. Benveniste 1969 2:58.
[4] For an attempt to outline this methodology: N 1979a.1–11.

to understanding *sêma* as a word connected with the semantics of thinking is to be found in its working relationship with another word connected with mental activity, namely, the noun *nóos* 'mind, sense, perception', along with its derivative verb *noéō* 'perceive, take note, think, think through' (whence the derivative noun *nóēsis*—and the second part of the title for this presentation). In order to grasp the semantic range of this difficult word *nóos* and its derivatives, it will be necessary to consider also its etymology, as explored in a seminal work by Douglas Frame, who traces it back to an Indo-European root *nes- meaning something like 'return to light and life'.[5] Ultimately, then, the etymology of both *sêma* and *nóos* will shed light on the working relationship of these words as reflected in poetic diction. And this working relationship will in turn, it is hoped, shed light on Greek concepts of cognition.[6]

It seems easiest to begin with illustrations of *sêma* as the key to a specific aspect of cognition, namely, recognition. In particular, Homeric diction deploys *sêma* as the conventional word for the signs that lead to the recognition of Odysseus by his *phíloi*, those who are 'near and dear' to him.[7] Thus, for example, the scar of the disguised Odysseus is specified by him as a *sêma* for his old nurse Eurykleia (*Odyssey* xxiii 73), for his loyal herdsmen Eumaios and Philoitios (xxi 217), and for his aged father Laertes (xxiv 329). An appropriate word for the 'recognition' of this *sêma* is the verb *anagignṓskō* (ἀναγνόντος xxiv 329, in the case of Laertes). The same verb recurs in the context of Penelope's 'recognizing' (ἀναγνούσῃ xxiii 206) the *sḗmata* (plural, same line) specified by the disguised Odysseus as the clothes given to the real Odysseus by Penelope herself (that the clothes *are* the *sêma* is confirmed at xix 255–257).

In all these instances the narrative features the recognition of the *sêma* 'sign' as the crucial prerequisite for the recognition of Odysseus himself.[8] Moreover, the recognition of the *sêma* implicitly requires an act of *interpretation*. For example, there is the *sêma* sent by Zeus to the

[5] Frame 1978; cf. pp. 92ff. and 126 above. Also Svenbro 1988a.31n79.

[6] Cf. Svenbro 1988a, esp. p. 53.

[7] On the translation of *phílos* as 'near and dear', cf. Jones 1962.57–58, commenting on Aristotle's definition of *anagnṓrisis* 'recognition' (*Poetics* 1452a30–32) as a shift from ignorance to knowledge, which matches a shift to *philíā* 'nearness and dearness' (or to its opposite). Schwartz 1982 argues that *phílos* is derived from locative *phi*, cognate of English *by* in the sense of 'near'; such a notion of nearness or closeness, if indeed it is built into the word *phílos*, can be connected with the concept of an "ascending scale of affection," which is a mode of self-identification discussed at N 1979a.103–113.

[8] In other instances the narrative may omit the intermediate stage of recognizing the *sêma* before recognizing the person: thus at iv 250 Helen ἀνέγνω (verb *anagignṓskō*) 'recognized' Odysseus (direct object) when he slipped into Troy in disguise. It seems no accident that this particular stretch of narrative is highly compressed.

Achaeans, as reported in *Iliad* II (308): the event of a snake's devouring eight nestlings and their mother (II 308–319) requires the mantic *interpretation* of Kalkhas the *mántis* 'seer', who recognizes it as a portent of Troy's impending destruction (II 320–332). Or again, there are all the Homeric instances of lightning sent by Zeus as a *sêma* (II 353, IX 236, XIII 244, xxi 413, etc.)—one might say as a *code* bearing distinct *messages* that are to be interpreted in context by both the witnesses and the narrative itself.

The word that conveys this basic faculty of recognition and interpretation is *nóos.* As the Trojan hero Polydamas says to Hektor . . .

οὕνεκά τοι περὶ δῶκε θεὸς πολεμήια ἔργα,
τοὔνεκα καὶ βουλῇ ἐθέλεις περιίδμεναι ἄλλων·
ἀλλ' οὔ πως ἅμα πάντα δυνήσεαι αὐτὸς ἑλέσθαι.
ἄλλῳ μέν γὰρ δῶκε θεὸς πολεμήια ἔργα,
ἄλλῳ δ' ὀρχηστύν, ἑτέρῳ κίθαριν καὶ ἀοιδήν,
ἄλλῳ δ' ἐν στήθεσσι τιθεῖ νόον εὐρύοπα Ζεὺς
ἐσθλόν, τοῦ δέ τε πολλοὶ ἐπαυρίσκοντ' ἄνθρωποι,
καί τε πολέας ἐσάωσε, μάλιστα δὲ καὐτὸς ἀνέγνω.
αὐτὰρ ἐγὼν ἐρέω ὥς μοι δοκεῖ εἶναι ἄριστα

Iliad XIII 726–735

Hektor, there is no way you can be helped[9] to heed persuasive words.
Just because the god granted that you excel in deeds of war
you wish also to excel in planning [*boulḗ*] by knowing more than others.[10]
But there is no way you can get everything all to yourself.
The god grants that one man excel in deeds of war
and another in dancing and another in playing the lyre and singing.
And for yet another man, far-seeing Zeus places *nóos* in his breast,
a genuine[11] one; and many men benefit from such a man,
and he saves many of them, and he himself has the greatest powers of

[9] On the semantics of *amḗkhanos* 'irremediable' and the pertinence of this epithet to the present context, see Martin 1983.18.

[10] Hektor not only yearns to excel in *boulḗ* 'planning': he is formally a paragon of *mêtis* 'artifice, stratagem', even earning the epithet 'equal to Zeus in *mêtis*' (VII 47, XI 200). This quality, however, ultimately brings him into conflict with Athena, the goddess of *mêtis* incarnate. Hektor even yearns to have the same *tīmḗ* 'honor' as Athena and Apollo themselves (cf. VIII 538–541, XIII 825–828), and his mortality is thereby underscored as he falls victim to death precisely because his *mêtis* had in the end gone bad (κακὰ μητιόωντι XVIII 312): Athena herself takes away his senses (XVIII 311). See N 1979a.144–147, where it is also argued that the excellence of a hero in a given pursuit is precisely what draws him into a forcefield of antagonism with a corresponding god. The excellence of Polydamas in the realm of planning and stratagem (in this passage as also at XVIII 251–252) is not central: it simply highlights, by way of contrast, Hektor's ultimate failure as he pursues excellence in this very realm.

[11] On the semantics of *esthlós*: Watkins 1972, 1982b.

recognition [verb *anagignṓskō*].
But I will tell you what seems best to me.

It is *nóos*, then, that enables one to 'recognize' (verb *ana-gignṓskō*).[12]

To come back to the clothes of Odysseus as a *sêma* for recognition (xix 250): the narrative suggests that, in order for the clothes to be a *sêma*, Odysseus himself has to *notice* them as such:

τὸν δὲ χιτῶν' ἐνόησα . . .

Odyssey xix 232

. . . and I noticed [verb *noéō*] the tunic . . .

Odysseus here is speaking in a disguised persona as he calls attention to the tunic. In his false identity, he is calling attention to his true identity by way of a *sêma*, and in noticing it first himself within his own narrative, he shows by example what Penelope and the Homeric audience must notice on their own. The verb here for 'notice' is *noéō*, derivative of the noun *nóos*.

In like manner, the appropriately-named *Alkí-noos* is said to 'notice' (verb *noéō*) the weeping of Odysseus, and he thereby discovers a sign that leads to the recognition of the hero. Alkinoos is the only one of the Phaeacians to notice, two times, that the disguised Odysseus weeps whenever the blind bard of the Phaeacians sings tales about the Trojan War:

Ἀλκί-νοος δέ μιν οἶος ἐπεφράσατ' ἠδὲ νόησε

Odyssey viii 94 and 533

Alkí-noos was the only one who observed[13] and noticed [verb *noéō*] him.

The ensuing speech of Alkinoos at viii 536–638 calls on the disguised Odysseus to reveal his identity—which is precisely what then happens at the beginning of Book ix.

There are several passages that show how the verb *noéō* conveys simultaneously the *noticing* of signs and the *recognition* of what they mean. Those in particular who have mantic powers will instantly recognize the facts of a matter simply by noticing a portent. The ultimate *mántis* 'seer'

[12] For a variation on this theme, see xxi 205: Odysseus ἀνέγνω 'recognized' (verb *anagignṓskō*) the *nóos* of Eumaios and Philoitios. *Then* at xxi 217 he specifies for them the *sêma* of the scar. In other words, Odysseus here recognizes the *nóos* that is capable of recognizing the *sêma*.

[13] On *phrázomai* as a verb that denotes the activity of *mêtis* 'artifice, stratagem': Detienne and Vernant 1974.25n32.

is of course Apollo himself, and the following example of Apollo's mode of thinking as he spots a bird flying in the sky can serve as an ideal illustration:

> οἰωνὸν δ' ἐνόει τανυσίπτερον, αὐτίκα δ' ἔγνω
> φηλητὴν γεγαῶτα Διὸς παῖδα Κρονίωνος
>
> *Hymn to Hermes* 213–214
>
> He noticed [verb *noéo*] a long-winged bird, and he recognized [verb *gignṓskō*] instantly
> that the thief was the child of Zeus the son of Kronos.

In such contexts, the verb *noéo* is actually synonymous with *gignṓskō* in the sense of 'recognize'. Similarly, when old Priam *notices* (= verb *noéō*: νοήσας XXIV 294, 312) a bird sent by Zeus, he implicitly recognizes the signal to approach the ships of the Achaeans. Or again, in response to such ominous signals as the uncontrollable laughter of the impious suitors (xx 346) and the ghastly suffusion of the walls with blood (xx 354), the seer Theoklymenos prudently decides to leave the banquet-hall:

> . . . ἐπεὶ νοέω κακὸν ὔμμιν
> ἐρχόμενον
>
> *Odyssey* xx 367–368
>
> since I notice [verb *noéō*] that evil fortune is
> coming upon you.[14]

The translation 'recognize' for *noéō* here would be just as appropriate as 'notice'. By contrast, the suitors themselves fail to recognize the many signs that signal their doom. Even when the disguised Odysseus kills their leader, appropriately named *Antí-noos* (xxii 8–30), they still fail to have *nóēsis* (verb *noéō*: οὐκ ἐνόησαν xxii 32).

All these signs, of course, seem more or less *arbitrary*. A signal like "bird flying in the sky," for example, may correspond to the declarative message "Hermes is the thief" in one context, or to the imperative message "Priam must go to Achilles" in another. But a true recognition of the sign, a true *nóēsis* of the *sêma*, can be achieved only be recognizing the internally coherent system of signals: it is not just a matter of "bird flying in the sky," for example, but rather, of 1 2 3 . . . *n* different kinds

[14] For the diction, cf. Solon F 13.54 W [= F 1 GP]: ἔγνω δ' ἀνδρὶ κακὸν τηλόθεν ἐρχόμενον 'he [= a generic *mántis* 'seer'] recognizes [verb *gignṓskō*] a misfortune, even as it is heading toward a man from afar' (commentary in N 1985a.25).

of birds flying α β γ . . . ω different ways in the sky. The bird that Priam saw was flying in a right-hand direction (XXIV 294, 312); if it had been flying in a left-hand direction, however, the signal would presumably correspond to a message such as "Priam must *not* go to Achilles"! To cite another example: in order to recognize the Dog Star as a *sêma* (XXII 30) bearing a yearly message of the parching in store for mankind (XXII 30–31), one has to know its relation to the other stellar *sḗmata* in the sky, and whatever messages they in turn may bear.[15] Or again, in order to recognize the baleful *sḗmata* that were scratched by Proitos on the tablet that the hero Bellerophon took with him to the king of Lycia (VI 168/176/178), the king has to know their relation to the other *sḗmata* in a *system* of markings and the relation of these markings to a set of meanings. Whether these markings are ideograms or runes or even letters, the point is that the king has to "read" them. And the present argument is that *nóos* would be an appropriate word for designating such "reading," such recognition of the system. The code composed of elements such as A B Γ . . . Ω could be decoded by the *nóos* of the king of Lycia, just as it was encoded by the *nóos* of Proitos.

There is a striking analogy in Latin, which also has a bearing on another important word in the realm of semiotics. The word in question is *signum* 'sign',[16] and the context in question concerns the use of the word by the Roman army in battle. In the parlance of strategy, the Latin phrase for 'obey orders' is *signa sequī*—literally, 'follow the signs' (e.g. Livy 3.28.3, 22.2.6, 23.35.7, 24.48.11, 30.35.6, 42.65.12). Synchronically, the word *signum* in these contexts refers to a military standard carried by the *signifer* 'standard-bearer'. Diachronically, however, *signum* refers to 'that which is followed': if we follow Benveniste in reconstructing this noun as *sek^{w}-nom, then it is actually derived from the verb *sequi* 'follow'.[17] Thus *signa sequi* would be a figura etymologica that encompasses the system of traditional Roman military maneuvers:

signa subsequi	'keep in order of battle'
ab signis discedere	'desert'
signa figere	'encamp'
signa mouere	'decamp, break up the camp'
signa inferre	'attack'
signa constituere	'halt'

[15] Consider also the message of the constellations Arktos and Orion for Odysseus: *Odyssey* v 271–277, in conjunction with v 121–124 (N 1979a.202–203).

[16] For a survey: Benveniste 1969 2:255–263.

[17] Benveniste 1948.122–124.

signa proferre	'advance'
signa conuertere	'wheel, turn, face about'
signa conferre	'engage in close fight'
etc.	

The *signum* in isolation is arbitrary, but each signal in the left column above is part of an internally cohesive system or code. For the Roman soldier, each signal corresponds to a message in the right column above, a particular military action. Thus when the *signum* 'standard' is planted into the ground by the *signifer* 'standard-bearer', the soldier encamps; when it is taken out again, he decamps; and so on. One might say that the Roman soldier recognizes his commands because he recognizes the system of signals. He can effectively obey individual commands because he grasps the overall code.[18]

While such codes as the Roman system of military *signa* leave little room for interpretation on the part of the destined recipients of their messages, there are other codes that require prodigious feats of interpretation. For example, here is the reply given by the disguised Odysseus to a command given him by Eumaios:

γιγνώσκω, φρονέω· τά γε δὴ νοέοντι κελεύεις

Odyssey xvii 281

I understand [verb *gignṓskō*], I am aware. You are commanding these things to one who recognizes [verb *noéō*].

Yet the command of Eumaios is in this case hardly precise: he had told the disguised Odysseus not to dally outside the palace lest 'someone' injure him or chase him away, adding the general command that Odysseus should 'be observant of these things' (xvii 279: pronoun *tá*, verb *phrázomai*).[19] Odysseus is in effect replying that he can obey successfully because he can recognize the essence of 'these things' that Eumaios had told him (xvii 281: pronoun *tá*), and his recognition is expressed by the verb *noéō* (same line).

A given *sêma* will not, of and by itself, explicitly declare or command. To make sense of the message, one must have *recognition* (noun *nóos*, verb *noéō*) of how the *sêma* works within its code. There is an admirable

[18] Note especially the expression at Livy 23.35.7: *signa sequi et in acie agnoscere ordines suos* 'to follow the signals and to recognize their positions in the battle-line'. The system (or *ordines*) of the *acies* 'battle-line' depends on the system of *signa*. To recognize (or *agnoscere*) the system of the *signa* is to recognize the *ordines* of the *acies*.

[19] On *phrázomai* as a verb of *mêtis*: p. 205n13.

illustration in the Homeric narrative of the Chariot Race in the course of the Funeral Games of Patroklos (*Iliad* XXIII). To enable his son Antilokhos to win a prize in the race (XXIII 314), old Nestor gives him a lesson in *mêtis* 'artifice, stratagem' (313, in the context of 315–318).[20] As the key to victory, Nestor gives his son a *sêma* 'sign' (326): when Antilokhos reaches the *térma* 'turning point' in the race, he must risk getting as close to it as possible, making the right side of his chariot's horse-team go faster and the left side, slower—thus effecting the quickest possible turn around the *térma* (327–345):

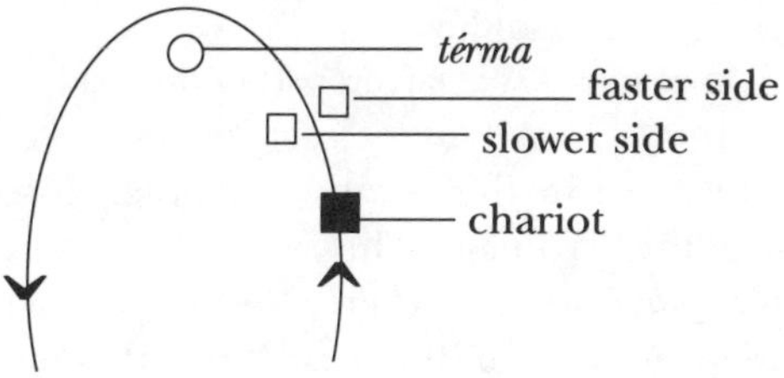

Earlier, Nestor also tells his son that the skilled charioteer keeps his eye on the *térma* as he heads toward it (323), watching for an opportunity to pass a faster chariot (322–325) that is driven without such a sense of goal-directedness (319–321). Antilokhos indeed finds such an opportunity, quickly passing and almost "fishtailing" the faster chariot of Menelaos (417–441). In this context, Antilokhos himself uses the verb *noéō* to express what he is doing (νοήσω 415). What, then, makes Nestor's *sêma* work as a key to victory? It is the ability of his son to *recognize* how the *sêma* works within its code, which is equated with simply *noticing* it. And the word for this noticing / recognition is *noéō*.

Nestor did not have to tell his son explicitly what to do and when to do it. All he did was to give him a *sêma*, and Antilokhos could then *take the initiative* by way of *recognizing* and *interpreting* it correctly (verb *noéō*).[21] The relationship of *sêma* and *nóēsis* is in this passage formally enacted by way of a phrase combining a negative with the verb *lḗthō* 'escape the mind of' (XXIII 326, 414–415):

[20] For more on this passage: N 1979a.47.

[21] On *noéō* in contexts of taking the initiative, see N 1979a.51n. Cf. *sêma* at xxi 231 and the contexts of *nóēsis* at xxi 413–414, 431; xxii 129.

σῆμα δέ τοι ἐρέω μάλ' ἀριφραδές, οὐδέ σε λήσει

Iliad XXIII 326

I [Nestor] will tell you a *sêma*, a very distinct one, and it will not escape your mind.

ταῦτα δ' ἐγὼν αὐτὸς τεχνήσομαι ἠδὲ νοήσω
στεινωπῷ ἐν ὁδῷ παραδύμεναι, οὐδέ με λήσει

Iliad XXIII 414–415

And I myself [Antilokhos] will devise these things and recognize [verb *noéō*] how
to pass him at a narrow part of the road, and it will not escape my mind.

As we see in the second example, this negative phrase is synonymous with the verb *noéō*. This same phrase, which links the noun *sêma* with the verb *noéō*, recurs where Nestor is describing how a skilled charioteer keeps his eyes on the *térma* 'turning point' as he heads toward it:

αἰεὶ τέρμ' ὁρόων στρέφει ἐγγύθεν, οὐδέ ἑ λήθει
ὅππως τὸ πρῶτον τανύσῃ βοέοισιν ἱμᾶσιν,
ἀλλ' ἔχει ἀσφαλέως καὶ τὸν προὔχοντα δοκεύει

Iliad XXIII 323–325

. . . always keeping his eye on the *térma*, he makes a tight turn, and it does not escape his mind,
as soon as he pulls at his ox-hide reins,
but he holds his pace steady, stalking the front-runner.

In view of Nestor's specifically saying that the *sêma* 'sign' of victory (326) centers on the way in which Antilokhos is to make his turn around the turning point (327–345), and in view of the linkage between this *sêma* 'sign' (326) and this *térma* 'turning point' (323) by way of the formula οὐδέ σε/ἑ λήσει/λήθει 'and it will/does not escape your/his mind' (326/323), it is significant that the narrative raises the possibility that the *térma* is itself a *sêma* (σῆμα 331/τέρματ' 333). But here (331) the word *sêma* has the specific meaning of 'tomb', a meaning that cannot be discussed until later. For now it will suffice to stress again the connection of the noun *sêma* with the verb *noéō* by way of this phrase combining a negative with the verb *lḗthō* 'escape the mind of'.[22]

[22] The negative plus the root *lēth-* is a litotes for the root *mnē-* 'have in mind'. (On the

There are two other instances of this phrase that merit special notice:

πάντα ἰδὼν Διὸς ὀφθαλμὸς καὶ πάντα νοήσας
καί νυ τάδ' αἴ κ' ἐθέλησ' ἐπιδέρκεται, οὐδέ ἑ λήθει
οἵην δὴ καὶ τήνδε δίκην πόλις ἐντὸς ἐέργει

Hesiod *Works and Days* 267–269

The Eye of Zeus[23] sees everything and recognizes [verb *noéō*] everything.
If it so pleases him, he casts his glance downward upon these things as well,
and it does not escape his mind
what kind of justice [*díkē*] is this that the city keeps within it.

σῆμα δέ τοι ἐρέω μάλ' ἀριφραδές, οὐδέ σε λήσει

Odyssey xi 126

I will tell you a *sêma*, a very distinct one,
and it will not escape your mind.

From the previous instances of the formula 'and it will not escape my/your/his mind', it is to be expected, in the first passage, that the cognition of Zeus is linked with the *sêma*; and, in the second passage, that getting the sign is linked with its recognition (noun *nóos* or verb *noéō*).

To take the first passage first: there are indeed *sḗmata* linked with the cognition of Zeus, but such *sḗmata* are *encoded* rather than decoded by his *nóos*. Thus, for example, a violent storm can be a sign sent by Zeus to manifest his anger against a city over the violation of *díkē* 'justice' (XVI 384–393; *díkē* at 388); and the most visible manifestation of violent storms is generically the lightning, which is in fact the most ubiquitous *sêma* of Zeus (e.g. XIII 244).[24] What humans must do is to *decode* the various signs *encoded* by Zeus, which is a hard thing to do:

ἄλλοτε δ' ἀλλοῖος Ζηνὸς νόος αἰγιόχοιο,

---

central role of the root *mnē-* in Indo-European poetic diction, see Watkins 1987.270–271.) Note the collocation of *noéō* and *mnē-* at xx 204–205 (. . . ὡς ἐνόησα, δεδάκρυνται δέ μοι ὄσσε | μνησαμένῳ 'Οδυσῆος). Note also the contexts of *lḗthē* as the opposite of *nóos*, surveyed by Frame 1978.36–37, 75–76.

[23] On the Indo-European heritage of the theme "Eye of Zeus," see the discussion of West 1978.223–224. It should be noted, however, that his discussion does not cover the ethical implications of this theme.

[24] In this passage the stylized expression ἀρίζηλοι δέ οἱ αὐγαί 'and his flashes of light are very clear to see' might be connected with the theme "Eye of Zeus" (as at Hesiod *Works and Days* 267; see the previous note).

ἀργαλέως δ' ἄνδρεσσι καταθνητοῖσι νοῆσαι

Hesiod *Works and Days* 483–484

The *nóos* of aegis-bearing Zeus is different at different times,
and it is hard to recognize [verb *noéō*] for mortal men.

In this very context Hesiod gives an example: when the sound of the cuckoo is first heard across the land, that is a sign for rainstorms that allow spring ploughing (*Works and Days* 485–492). These instructions are then summed up as follows:

ἐν θυμῷ δ' εὖ πάντα φυλάσσεο· μηδέ σε λήθοι
μήτ' ἔαρ γινόμενον πολιὸν μήθ' ὥριος ὄμβρος

Hesiod *Works and Days* 491–492

Keep all these things well in mind, and let them not escape your mind
— either the coming of gray[25] spring or the seasonal rainstorm.

The expression 'and let them not escape your mind' implies, again, that the word *sêma* is understood. There is in fact a parallel Hesiodic passage where the word *sêma* is overt: when the sound of the migrating crane is for the first time heard across the land (*Works and Days* 448–449), this is a *sêma* 'sign' (450) for rainstorms that allow autumn ploughing (450–451).

Now to take the second passage: in this instance, the seer Teiresias is giving a *sêma* to Odysseus (xi 126), and, to repeat, the follow-up expression 'and it will not escape your mind' (same line) raises the expectation that getting the sign is linked with its recognition (noun *nóos* or verb *noéō*). The word *nóos* is indeed overtly linked with the concept of *sêma* here, but again the attention is as much on the *encoding* as on the *decoding* of the sign. The narrative stresses that Teiresias, who is giving the *sêma* to Odysseus (xi 126), is exceptional among the *psūkhaí* in Hades in that his cognitive faculties—or *phrénes*—are intact (x 493): it is because Persephone had given him *nóos* (x 494).[26] This *sêma*, then, is implicitly *encoded* by the *nóos* of Teiresias—and presumably must be *decoded* by the *nóos* of Odysseus.

The message of the *sêma* 'sign' given by Teiresias to Odysseus is actually twofold. Before exploring this sign any further, however, it will be

[25] The epithet πολιόν 'gray' seems to suggest 'overcast' (*pace* West 1978.279), reflecting the rainy days, as opposed to an epithet like λευκόν 'bright' (e.g. Theocritus 18.27), reflecting the clear days.

[26] For further discussion: p. 92.

useful to reconsider a *sêma* 'sign' given by Hesiod, namely, the sound of the migrating crane, which signals the season of autumn ploughing (*Works and Days* 450–451). As it turns out, this *sêma* is itself twofold, for the time when one must plough in the autumn is the same time when one must not sail the seas (*Works and Days* 618–623). Besides the contrast of the negative "do not sail" (622) with the positive "do plough" (623), the latter teaching is reinforced with the expression *memnēménos* 'being mindful' (623, picking up from *memnēménos arótou* 'being mindful of ploughing' at 616), which is the positive equivalent of the negative *oudé me/se/he lḗthei* 'and it does not escape my/your/his mind'.[27] One who is *memnēménos* 'mindful', then, is by implication one whose *nóos* reads the *sêma* of the crane and perceives that it is time to plough and time not to sail.[28] Similarly with the *sêma* of Teiresias, the expression *oudé se lḗsei* 'and it will not escape your mind' (xi 126) is by implication challenging the *nóos* of Odysseus with a twofold message: what is an oar for seafarers is a winnowing shovel for inlanders (cf. xi 121–137, xxiii 265–284).

The message of this *sêma,* however, is twofold neither for the seafarers nor for the inlanders, since the former can surely distinguish oars from winnowing shovels while the latter are presented as knowing only about winnowing shovels. Rather, the message is twofold only for Odysseus the traveler, since he sees that the same signal has two distinct messages in two distinct places: what is an oar for the seafarers is a winnowing shovel for the inlanders. In order to recognize that one signal can have two messages, Odysseus has to travel through the cities of many men. In all his travels he will have come to know a wide variety of signs:

πολλῶν δ' ἀνθρώπων ἴδεν ἄστεα καὶ νόον ἔγνω

Odyssey i 3

He saw the cities of many, and he came to know [*gignṓskō*] their *nóos.*

[27] See pp. 210–211n22.

[28] Cf. Theognis 1197–1202: the poet hears the sound of the crane (1197–1198), which signals the season of autumn ploughing for men (1198–1199). But the poet is sad and helpless: he has lost his lands because of a sea voyage, which now weighs on his mind (μνηστῆς . . . ναυτιλίης 1202). In line with the present interpretation of Hesiod *Works and Days* 450–451/618–623, the root *mnē-* expressing 'on my mind' here (Theognis 1202) implies that the sound of the crane is a *sêma* 'sign'. For more on the sound of the migrating crane as a *sêma,* see the commentary at N 1985a.64–68 on Theognis 1197–1202 and related passages.

This verse is suitable for describing what Odysseus would have to do in following the instructions of Teiresias:

ἐπεὶ μάλα πολλὰ βροτῶν ἐπὶ ἄστε' ἄνωγεν ἐλθεῖν

Odyssey xxiii 267–268

... since he [Teiresias] instructed me [Odysseus] to go to very many cities of mortals

Moreover, the gesture of planting the handle of his oar into the ground (xi 129), which is what Odysseus is instructed to do when he reaches a place where the natives mistake his oar for a winnowing shovel, is itself the bearer of a twofold message. To plant the handle of a winnowing shovel in a heap of grain at a harvest festival is a formal act symbolizing that the winnower's work is finished (e.g. Theocritus 7.155–156).[29] And to plant the handle of an oar in the ground is to symbolize that the oarsman's work is likewise finished—as in the case of Odysseus' dead companion Elpenor, whose tomb is to be a mound of earth with the handle of his oar planted on top (xi 75–78, xii 13–15).[30] So also with Odysseus: he too will never again have to sail the seas. Moreover, Odysseus' own oar planted in the ground is a stylized image of his own tomb! And yet, this "tomb" is situated as far away from the sea as possible, whereas Odysseus' death is to come *ex halós* 'out of the sea' (xi 134). There is no need to argue on this basis that the phrase *ex halós* somehow means 'away from the sea'.[31] Rather, the twofold semantic nature of the *sêma* for Odysseus is formalized in the *coincidentia oppositorum* of his finding the sign for his death from the sea precisely when he is farthest away from the sea.[32]

[29] Hansen 1977.38–39.

[30] Hansen pp. 38–39.

[31] *Pace* Hansen pp. 42–48.

[32] For other instances of *coincidentia oppositorum* as a characteristic of Odysseus stories, see N 1979a.206. Compare also the factor of *coincidentia oppositorum* in the latter-day Demotic stories of Saint Elias, whose shrines are in fact on tops of hills and mountains, far away from the sea, but who had lived the life of a seaman; for an acute analysis of these stories about Saint Elias and the oar, strikingly parallel to the story about Odysseus and the oar, see Hansen pp. 27–41. Hansen also calls attention to an ancient shrine on a mountain in landlocked Arcadia, said to have been founded by Odysseus in gratitude to Athena *Sṓteira* 'Savior' and Poseidon (!) after the hero returned safely from Troy (Pausanias 9.44.4). So also with Saint Elias: his chapels are built on tops of hills and mountains, the story goes, because it was on top of a mountain that his oar was mistaken for a "stick" (Hansen p. 29). On the apparently symbiotic relationship of Odysseus here with Poseidon and Athena on the level of cult, as opposed to his antagonistic relationship with them on the level of myth, cf. N 1979a.121, 142–152, 289–295. The antagonism of Odysseus and Athena is of course

The question remains to be asked: why should the *sêma* 'sign' (xi 126) given by Teiresias to Odysseus take the form of a stylized tomb? For an answer, it is necessary to reconsider the word's meaning. The word *sêma* bears not only the general meaning of 'sign' but also the specific meaning of 'tomb', which is conventionally visualized as a mound of earth (e.g. XXIII 45, the *sêma* 'tomb' of Patroklos, and xi 75, the *sêma* 'tomb' of Elpenor). It has in fact already been noted[33] that the meanings 'sign' and 'tomb' can converge. When Nestor gives his son Antilokhos a *sêma* 'sign' (XXIII 326) that will enable him to win a prize in the chariot race, the message of this sign centers on the way in which Antilokhos is to make his turn around the *térma* 'turning point' (XXIII 327–345), and it is significant that the narrative itself ostentatiously raises the possibility that this turning point is a *sêma* 'tomb':

ἤ τευ σῆμα βροτοῖο πάλαι κατατεθνηῶτος,
ἦ τό γε νύσσα τέτυκτο ἐπὶ προτέρων ἀνθρώπων,
καὶ νῦν τέρματ' ἔθηκε ποδάρκης δῖος Ἀχιλλεύς.

Iliad XXIII 331–333

It is either the tomb [*sêma*] of a man who died a long time ago,
or it was a turning post in the times of earlier men.
Now swift-footed brilliant Achilles has set it up as the turning point [*térma* plural].

As Dale Sinos points out,[34] the turning points of chariot racecourses at the pan-Hellenic Games were conventionally identified with the tombs of heroes: Pausanias (6.20.15–19) reports that the spirit of one such hero was called *Taráxippos* 'he who disturbs the horses', and that the Taraxippos often causes the chariots to crash (6.20.15, 19).[35] So also with the chariot race in honor of the dead hero Patroklos: the turning point is the place where Antilokhos must take care not to let his chariot crash (XXIII 341–345).

Sinos also points out that the hero's tomb, from the standpoint of Homeric epos, is a physical manifestation of his *kléos* 'glory' as conferred by poetry (e.g. iv 584).[36] The tomb shared by Achilles and Patroklos, which is to be visible not only for men of their time but also for the generations of the future (xxiv 80–84), along with the Funeral Games for

for the most part latent in the *Odyssey*, but it must have been overt in some *Nostoi* traditions (even as reflected by the *Odyssey*: iii 130ff., xiii 221ff.).

[33] See pp. 209–210.

[34] Sinos 1980.53n6.

[35] Rohde 1898 1:173 and n1.

[36] Sinos 1980.47.

Achilles (xxiv 85–92), are the two explicit reasons for the everlasting *kléos* of Achilles (xxiv 93–94). In this context the etymology of *sêma* 'sign, tomb' can be brought to bear; as a 'sign' of the dead hero, the 'tomb' is a *reminder* of the hero and his *kléos*. Thus the *sêma* 'tomb' of 'a man who died a long time ago' (XXIII 331) is appropriate for Achilles to set as a turning point for the chariot race in honor of the dead *Patroklées* 'he who has the *kléos* of the ancestors'.[37] This meaning of the name of Patroklos converges with the connotations of ἐπὶ προτέρων ἀνθρώπων 'in the times of earlier men' at XXIII 332, describing the heroic era that *may have been* the setting for the use of the turning point, which in turn *may have been* a *sêma* 'tomb' belonging to someone described as βροτοῖο πάλαι κατατεθνηῶτος 'a man who died a long time ago' at XXIII 331. Dale Sinos has written of this passage:[38]

> The *sêma* of the dead man will turn out to be the realization of the hint, the *sêma* of Nestor to his son. The latent function of *sêma* 'tomb' thus becomes overt: the 'hint' becomes the 'tomb'. Likewise, the 'tomb' becomes a 'hint' of a Dead Man's presence, invoked by Achilles. Can one connect this presence of a long-dead hero with the newly dead hero of *Iliad* XXIII? The very name *Patro-klées* helps provide an answer to this question. Patroklos re-enacts the eternal scheme of attaining *kléos*, and his name provides the present epic situation with the past glories of the ancestors. The Patroklos figure validates the *Iliad* by establishing the link with the eternal values of *kléos*. From our point of view, even the name *Patro-klées* is a *sêma*, as it were, for these eternal values. His role enacts his name, and his name is a key to the tradition which gives *kléos* to Achilles and marks the *Iliad* as the heroic present with an eternal past. Tradition is dependent on the continuation of ancestral values by their re-enactment in the present. In *mythos*, the ancestor functions as hero, operating as he does in a timeless scheme. From the standpoint of *mythos*, the Dead Man of XXIII 331 and the Patroklos of Book XXIII *in toto* are parallel figures with parallel functions.

The narrative of the *Iliad* emphatically maintains, to repeat, that the turning point for the chariot race in honor of Patroklos had been in the past *either* just that, a turning point, *or else* a *sêma* 'tomb' (XXIII 331–332). The ostentatiously presented alternative of a *sêma* 'tomb' (331), in view of the *sêma* 'sign' of Nestor to his son only five verses earlier (326), bears its own message: not only the tomb is a sign but *the very mention* of the tomb may be a sign. To put it another way: a *sêma* is a

[37] For more on the meaning of *Patro-klées* as 'he who has the *kléos* of the ancestors': N 1979a.102–103, 111–115, 177, 319. Cf. also p. 94 above.
[38] Sinos 1980.48–49.

reminder, and the very use of the word is a *reminder*. But the attitude of the narrative is one of "take it or leave it." If you reject the alternative that the turning point is a *sêma* 'tomb' of a dead man, then the *sêma* 'sign' of Nestor to Antilokhos has a simplex message about how to take a turn; if you accept it, on the other hand, then the same *sêma* 'sign' has an additional message about the *sêma* 'tomb' as a reminder of *kléos*.

There is reason to think that Antilokhos is to recognize the turning point as *both* a turning point *and* a tomb by virtue of the *sêma* given him by Nestor, just as Odysseus is to recognize the oar as *both* an oar *and* a winnowing shovel by virtue of the *sêma* given him by Teiresias. The key is *nóos*. To begin, the cognition of Nestor and Antilokhos in *encoding* and *decoding* the *sêma*, respectively, is a matter of *nóos*:

μυθεῖτ' εἰς ἀγαθὰ φρονέων νοέοντι καὶ αὐτῷ

Iliad XXIII 305

He [Nestor] spoke to him [Antilokhos], having good intentions toward him, and he [Antilokhos] too was aware [verb *noéō*].

The *kaí* 'too' of 'he too was aware' here stresses that the decoder has *nóos* too, not just the encoder. When the time comes for Antilokhos to take the initiative, in a situation not specifically anticipated by the instructions of Nestor, he says: 'I will have *nóos*' (νοήσω [verb *noéō*] XXIII 415). Then he executes the dangerous maneuver of passing the faster chariot of Menelaos (XXIII 418–441), in an impulsive manner that is condemned by Menelaos as lacking in good sense (XXIII 426; cf. the diction of 320–321). The self-acknowledged impulsiveness of Antilokhos at this point of the action is then counterbalanced by his clever use of verbal restraint after his prize is challenged by an angry Menelaos, who is thus flattered into voluntarily ceding the prize to Antilokhos (XXIII 586–611).[39] The impulsiveness and restraint of Antilokhos in action and in speech, respectively, as Douglas Frame pointed out to me *viva voce* years ago, correspond to the speeding up and the slowing down of his right- and left-hand horses, respectively, as he rounds the *sêma*—which is the feat of *nóos* that Nestor had taught him.[40] Winning his prize,

[39] Ironically, it is the *nóos* of Antilokhos that Menelaos calls into question (XXIII 604, in response to the clever self-deprecation of Antilokhos himself at XXIII 590). I agree with Detienne and Vernant (1974.22–24, 29–31, *pace* Lesher 1981.19 and 24n38) that Antilokhos has succeeded rather than failed in accomplishing a feat of *mêtis*.

[40] See pp. 208ff. I note with interest a parallel theme in the iconography of the Münster Hydria (published in Stähler 1967): the turn of the chariot team is counterclockwise in this Black Figure representation (on the image of the turning point, see further at p. 220), and the right-hand horses have their heads thrust farther ahead than the left-hand horses, as if the impulse and the restraint were greater on the right and the left, respectively.

Antilokhos then hands it over to a companion who is appropriately named *Noḗmōn* (XXIII 612)—a form derived from the verb *noéō*. Another appropriate name is that of Nestor himself, the man whose *nóos* encodes the message decoded by Antilokhos. As Douglas Frame has argued convincingly, the form *Nés-tōr* is an agent-noun derived from the root *nes-, just as *nóos* is an action-noun derived from the same root.[41] Significantly, Nestor, too, gets a prize from Achilles, even though the old man had not competed in the chariot race. And the purpose of this prize, Achilles says, is that it will be a *mnêma* 'reminder' of the funeral of Patroklos (Πατρόκλοιο τάφου <u>μνῆμ</u>' ἔμμεναι XXIII 619)! Thus the narrative comes full circle around the *sêma* of Nestor: the encoder had given a *sêma* 'sign' to Antilokhos about the turning point, which *may have been* used in the chariot races of ancestral times, ἐπὶ προτέρων ἀνθρώπων 'in the times of earlier men' (XXIII 332), or which *may have been* the *sêma* 'tomb' of someone described as βροτοῖο πάλαι κατατεθνηῶτος 'a man who died a long time ago' (XXIII 331), and this hint about *Patro-klées* 'he who has the glory of the ancestors' is then formalized in the prize given by Achilles to Nestor as a *mnêma* 'reminder' of Patroklos' funeral.

The question is: what do these associations of *sêma* have to do with the semantics of *nóos*? As Frame argues in the course of his illuminating book, *nóos* is an action-noun derived from the Indo-European root-verb *nes- meaning 'return to light and life'. This meaning is possibly still attested in Indic *Nā́satyau*, a name of the Divine Twins who bring about sunrise after the night brought on by each sunset.[42] The root-verb *nes- is attested in Greek as *néomai*, but in this case means simply 'return', not 'return to light and life'. One derivative of *néomai* is *nóstos* 'return, homecoming'—and another is *nóos*! As Frame also argues, the theme of 'return to light and life' is recovered by way of the pervasive interplay between the themes of *nóos* and *nóstos* within the overall framework of the *Odyssey*: the key to the *nóstos* 'homecoming' of Odysseus is his *nóos*, and the *nóstos* is endangered whenever the *nóos* is threatened by *lḗthē* 'forgetfulness', as in the story of the Lotus-Eaters.[43] There are in fact two aspects of *nóstos* in the *Odyssey*: one is of course the hero's return from Troy, and the other, just as important, is his return from Hades. Moreover, the theme of Odysseus' descent and subsequent *nóstos* 'return' from Hades converges with the solar dynamics of sunset and subsequent sunrise.[44] The movement is from dark to light, from unconsciousness to consciousness as expressed by *nóos*. In fact, the hero is asleep as he floats

[41] Frame 1978.81–115. See also pp. 225ff. below.
[42] Frame pp. 134–152. Cf. pp. 92ff. above.
[43] Cf. pp. 210–211n22.
[44] See N 1979a.206; cf. N 1985a.74–76.

in darkness to his homeland, and sunrise comes precisely when his boat reaches the shores of Ithaca (xiii 79–95).[45]

But the question still remains: how does the story of Nestor's *sêma* pertain to the semantics of *nóos*? A partial answer is to be found in juxtaposing the semantics of *sêma* and *nóstos*, the overt derivative of root *nes-. Just as *sêma* has the general meaning of 'sign' and the specific meaning of 'tomb', so also *nóstos* has the general meaning of 'return' (from Troy) and the specific meaning of 'return to light and life' (from Hades).[46] This specific meaning of *nóstos* seems to match that of the root *nes- as attested in the verb *néomai* itself in this striking phrase from the poetry of Pindar:

ἀφνεὸς πενιχρός τε θανάτου παρὰ | σᾶμα νέονται

Pindar *Nemean* 7.19–20

Both rich and poor return [verb *néomai*] by going past the *sêma* of Death.

The language is that of chariot racing, it seems, with the verb *néomai* 'return' connoting the "home stretch" after rounding the turning point. Here, too, as with Nestor's *sêma*, the turning point is not just a 'sign': it is

But the *sêma* of the chariot race in honor of the dead Patroklos is not just a 'tomb' that serves as a 'reminder' of 'a man who died a long time ago'. It is also a 'sign' that was encoded by the *nóos* of *Nés-tōr* 'he who brings about a return'[47] (cf. again XXIII 305).[48] And the word *nóos* conveys life after death, not only by virtue of its etymology 'return to light and life' but also by virtue of its usage in Homeric diction: *nóos* is the quality that allows the *psūkhḗ* to be cognitive even after death, as in the case of the seer Teiresias (x 492–494).[49] In other words, *nóos* is the quality that reintegrates the *psūkhḗ* of the dead with *thūmós* and *ménos*, the physical manifestations of consciousness in the body, and in this sense *nóos* is the quality that can reintegrate *psūkhḗ* and body.[50] Thus the *sêma* is not just the 'sign' of death, it is also the potential 'sign' of life after death. In this light, it may be possible to interpret the Pindaric phrase above as follows: 'Both rich and poor return to light and life by going past the *sêma* of Death'. In any case, the *sêma* is a signpost for *nóos*. There is, for

45 Frame 1978.75–76, 78. Cf. Segal 1962.
46 N 1985a.74–81, adducing Theognis 1123–1125 and related passages.
47 For the active diathesis of *Nés-tōr*: Frame 1978:96–115.
48 As quoted at p. 217.
49 For a fuller discussion: pp. 92ff.
50 See pp. 92ff.

example, the *sêma* 'tomb' of Ilos, local hero of Troy, which is where Hektor 'plans his plans' (*boulàs bouleúei*: X 415).[51] Or there is the *sêma* of 'a man who died a long time ago', upon which Antilokhos must fix his eyes as he approaches with his chariot (XXIII 323), waiting for an opportunity to use his *nóos*. Or again, there is the *sêma* of Achilles and Patroklos at the Hellespont, which is *tēlephanḗs* 'shining from afar' as a beacon of salvation for sailors at sea (xxiv 80–84, in conjunction with XIX 374–380).[52] In the Black Figure iconography of the Münster Hydria,[53] this very *sêma* is visualized against a red background as a gleaming white egg-shaped mass rising out of the ground, with the *psūkhḗ* of Patroklos himself hovering over it (the homunculus is actually labeled in the picture, with the lettering ΦΣΥΧΕ); meanwhile, the chariot of Achilles is racing around it, counterclockwise, with horses at full gallop—and with Achilles himself running alongside.[54]

In sum, it seems as if the contextual connections of *sêma* and *nóos* reflect not only the etymology of *nóos* as 'return to light and life' but also the etymology of *sêma* as a cognate of Indic *dhyāma* 'thought'. The related Indic form *dhīyas* 'thoughts' is in fact attested as designating the consciousness of man in awakening and *reminding* the sun, by sacrifice, to rise, as well as the consciousness of man in *being reminded* by the rising sun to awaken and sacrifice.[55] This theme is in turn closely linked with Indic concepts of life after death.[56]

It bears repeating that it was Achilles himself who had chosen the would-be *sêma* 'tomb' as the turning point for the chariot race (XXIII 333). Upon receiving the prize from Achilles, Nestor remarks that he rejoices

ὥς μευ ἀεὶ <u>μέμνησαι</u> ἐνηέος, οὐδέ σε <u>λήθω</u>

[51] For more on the *boulḗ* 'planning' of Hektor, see p. 204n10.

[52] See N 1979a.338–341. In this connection, we may note with the greatest interest the description of cult heroes in Pausanias 2.12.5: their gravestones are visible from afar, located on top of a hill, and before the celebration of the Mysteries of Demeter, the natives are described as specifically looking at these *mnḗmata* 'monuments', ἐς ταῦτα βλέποντες τὰ μνήματα, as they invoke the heroes to attend the libations.

[53] Published in Stähler 1967.

[54] See Stähler pp. 15, 32–33, 44, who argues that the represented activity of racing around the tomb of Patroklos, with the chariot rider jumping off and running alongside, can be conceived simultaneously as an athletic event *and* a ritual act of hero worship; cf. also p. 88n20, above. The athletic event, as featured for example at the Panathenaia, involves the feat of leaping in full armor from a racing chariot and then leaping back on again; the athlete who performs this feat is the *apobátēs* (cf. Dionysius of Halicarnassus 7.73; Harpocration s.v.; also the bibliography assembled in Connor 1987.45).

[55] See pp. 114ff.

[56] See pp. 114ff.

τιμῆς ἧς τέ μ' ἔοικε τετιμῆσθαι μετ' Ἀχαιοῖς

Iliad XXIII 648–649

because you always keep me in mind, benevolent that I am, and I do not escape your mind
when it comes to the honor that is my due among the Achaeans.

By implication, then, Achilles himself had *nóos* both in choosing the turning point and in rewarding Nestor for having the *nóos* to recognize this turning point as a *sêma* 'tomb'. Nestor prays that the gods reward Achilles for having rewarded him (XXIII 650), and the narrative then concludes his speech by calling it an *aînos* (XXIII 652). This is not the place to attempt a thorough definition of this poetic form called *aînos*, and it will suffice here to offer a summary: the *aînos* is a complex poetic discourse that is deemed worthy of a prize or reward, which is meant specifically to praise the noble, and which bears two or more *messages* within its one *code*.[57] In the last respect, the *aînos* of Nestor matches the *sêma* of Nestor.

It could even be said that the *aînos* of Nestor *is* a *sêma*, and that poetry itself can be a *sêma*.[58] Homeric diction makes this clear by occasionally equating an *épos* 'utterance' with a *sêma*. For example, Odysseus prays to Zeus for *both* a portent *and* a *phḗmē* 'prophetic utterance' as indications of his future success against the suitors (xx 98–101). In response, Zeus sends *both* lightning (103–104) *and* a *phḗmē* (105). The *phḗmē* takes the form of words spoken by a slave woman who is grinding grain with her mill, and she prays to Zeus to punish the suitors, who have made her work so hard (105–119). The narrative introduces her words by calling them an *épos* (111), which is specifically identified as a *sêma* for Odysseus (same line). The poetic format of what the woman says is apparent not only from such parallels as *Carmina Popularia* PMG 869 but also from the use of *épos*, which is attested in archaic poetic diction as meaning not just 'utterance' but also specifically 'poetic utterance'.[59] And again, the faculty for encoding the verbal *sêma* is *nóos*:[60] thus after Zeus expresses his Will by way of nodding his head (I 524–527), Hera goads him for not telling what it is, that is, for not making an *épos* out of what he has in his *nóos* (verb *noéō*: I 543). Zeus replies that the *mûthos* 'utterance' that he has in his *nóos* (verb *noéō*: I 549) is for him alone to know. But of course

[57] See N 1979a.235–241.

[58] Similarly in the case of the Indic cognate *dhyā-/dhī-* 'think' and its derivative *dhīyas* 'thoughts': these words can designate the inspiration of poetry (see pp. 114ff.).

[59] See Koller 1972; also N 1979a.236.272.

[60] For other instances of encoding words, as expressed by *noéō*, see VII 358, XII 232.

the Homeric audience knows, since the *Iliad* declares programmatically that its plot *is* the Will of Zeus (I 5).[61] In this sense the entire *Iliad* is a *sêma* reinforcing the Will of Zeus.

The end of this presentation is by necessity also a prelude to other presentations, in that the testimony of Greek poetry about *sêma* and *nóēsis* turns out to be a lesson in how to read this poetry: the Greek poem is a *sêma* that requires the *nóēsis* of those who hear it.[62]

[61] On which see N 1979a.81–82n2 and the references there.

[62] The same applies to the poetic utterances of the Oracle of Apollo at Delphi: cf. Theognis 808 and Heraclitus B 93 DK. There is also an example where the poem seems to be implicitly a *sêma* not only in the sense of 'sign' but also in the sense of 'tomb': in Theognis 1209–1210 (quoted at pp. 273–274 below) the poet seems to be saying that this poetry is his *sêma* 'tomb' (commentary in N 1985a.76–81). Cf. Svenbro 1988a, esp. p. 96.

CHAPTER 9

Phaethon, Sappho's Phaon, and the White Rock of Leukas: "Reading" the Symbols of Greek Lyric

In the arcane Greek myths of Phaethon and Phaon there are latent themes that help resolve three problems of interpretation in Greek poetry. The first of these problems is to be found in the *Partheneion* of Alcman (PMG 1). It concerns a wondrous horse conjured up in a simile describing the beauty of the maiden Hagesikhora, center of attention in the song-and-dance ensemble:

δοκεῖ γὰρ ἤμεν αὔτα
ἐκπρεπὴς τὼς ὥπερ αἴτις
ἐν βοτοῖς στάσειεν ἵππον παγὸν ἀεθλοφόρον καναχάποδα
τῶν ὑποπετριδίων ὀνείρων

Alcman PMG 1.45–49

For she appears
outstanding, as when someone
sets among grazing beasts a horse,
well-built, a prize-winner, with thundering hooves,
from out of those dreams underneath the rock.

So the problem is, what is the meaning of ὑποπετριδίων? I translate 'underneath the rock' following the scholia of the Louvre Papyrus, which connect this adjective with πέτρα = *pétrā* 'rock' and quote the following passage from the *Odyssey*:

πὰρ δ' ἴσαν Ὠκεανοῦ τε ῥοὰς καὶ Λευκάδα πέτρην

ἠδὲ παρ' Ἠελίοιο πύλας καὶ δῆμον ὀνείρων

Odyssey xxiv 11–12

And they passed by the streams of Okeanos and the White Rock [*Leukàs pétrā*]
and past the Gates of the Sun and the District of Dreams.

This interpretation has been rejected by Denys Page, who argues: "The reference to [*Odyssey*] xxiv 11f is irrelevant; nothing is said there about dreams living 'under rocks'."[1] Instead, Page follows the *Etymologicum Magnum* (783.20), where we read ὑποπτεριδίων 'sustained by wings', so that the wondrous horse being described would be something 'out of winged dreams'; in support of this interpretation, Page adduces passages where dreams are represented as winged beings (e.g. Euripides *Hecuba* 70).[2] All the same, Page retains the reading ὑποπετριδίων in his edited text, so that we are left to assume some sort of ad hoc metathesis of ὑποπετριδίων to ὑποπτεριδίων, as if the local Laconian dialectal pronunciation of the word for 'wing' were *petr-* rather than *pter-*. Other experts, though hesitantly, go along with the interpretation 'under rocks', allowing for some vague notion of dreams abiding underneath some mysterious rock in the Laconian poetic imagination.[3] In the most accessible chrestomathy of Greek lyric, the editor chooses to take ὑποπετριδίων at face value: "the dreams are those of siestas taken underneath a shady rock'.[4]

The second problem of interpretation, then, is the significance of the White Rock, *Leukàs pétrā*, in *Odyssey* xxiv 11. This mysterious place has to be viewed in the overall context of *Odyssey* xxiv 1–14, describing the passage of the spirits of the suitors of Penelope, who have just been killed by Odysseus, into the realm of the dead. This description, known as the Introduction to the Second Nekyia, represents a distinct subgenre of Greek epic. It is replete with idiosyncrasies in both theme and diction,[5] and its contents afford a precious glimpse into early Greek concepts of

[1] Page 1951.87.

[2] Page p. 87.

[3] Wilamowitz 1897.252n2.

[4] Campbell 1976.203. I infer that the editor had in mind passages like Hesiod *Works and Days* 588–589.

[5] For a survey, see Page 1955.116–119. For some, including Page, such idiosyncrasies mean that the passage is an insertion and does not intrinsically belong where it is found in the text. I disagree, believing that the epic genre consists of several subgenres, and that each subgenre has its idiosyncrasies in theme and diction. For a survey of the principle that each epic subgenre (such as that of similes) has its own distinctive archaisms as well as innovations, see Householder and Nagy 1972.741–743.

afterlife. Nowhere else in Homeric diction do we find the puzzling expressions Ἠελίοιο πύλας 'Gates [*púlai*] of the Sun', δῆμον ὀνείρων 'District [*dêmos*] of Dreams', and Λευκάδα πέτρην 'White Rock [*Leukàs pétrā*]'. On the level of content, however, there do exist Homeric parallels to the first two of the three expressions.

In the instance of Ἠελίοιο πύλας 'Gates [*púlai*] of the Sun', there is a thematic parallelism between *púlai* 'gates' and Homeric *Púlos* 'Pylos'. As Douglas Frame has demonstrated, the royal name *Néstōr* and the place-name of King Nestor's realm, *Púlos* 'Pylos', are based on mythological models.[6] I should stress that Frame's arguments are used not to negate a historical Nestor and the historical Pylos, but rather to show that the kernel of the epic tradition about Nestor and Pylos was based on local myths linked with local cults. The clearest example is a story, represented as Nestor's own tale within the *Iliad*, that tells of the hero's retrieving the cattle of Pylos from the Epeians (XI 671–761). Frame argues convincingly that the retrieved cattle are a thematic analogue to the Cattle of the Sun.[7] The etymology of *Néstōr*, explained by Frame as 'he who brings back to light and life', is relevant.[8] We have already noted the association of words built out of the root *nes- with the theme of sunrise.[9] In fact, the entire plot of Odysseus' travels is interlaced with diction that otherwise connotes the theme of sunset followed by sunrise. To put it more bluntly, the epic plot of Odysseus' travels operates on an extended solar metaphor, as Frame argues in adducing the internal evidence of Homeric theme and diction.[10] Likewise, when Nestor returns the cattle to Pylos, it is implicit that Pylos is the Gate of the Sun and an entrance to the underworld.[11] There are survivals of this hieratic connotation in the local Pylian lore of classical times (Pausanias 4.36.2–3).[12] In a Homeric allusion to the myth about Herakles' descent into the underworld and his wounding of Hades (*Iliad* V 395–404), the name Pylos actually serves to connote the realm of the otherworld rather than any realm of this world:

[6] Frame 1978.81–115.

[7] Frame pp. 87–90, 92. Just as Nestor brings his cattle back to Pylos, so also another figure, Melampous, on whose solar significance see Frame pp. 91–92.

[8] See p. 218.

[9] See p. 218. Cf. also pp. 92ff., with reference to Frame's (1978) demonstration of the traditional theme that represents sunrise as symbolically parallel with a return to consciousness, the Greek word for which is *nóos*.

[10] Note esp. Frame pp. 75–76, 78 on *Odyssey* xiii 79–95, where the 'return' of Odysseus coincides with sunrise, at which point the hero can finally awaken from the deathlike sleep that had held him for the duration of his nighttime sea voyage homeward. Cf. p. 218. Also Segal 1962.

[11] Frame pp. 92–93.

[12] For details, see Frame pp. 90–91.

ἐν Πύλῳ ἐν νεκύεσσι

Iliad V 397

in Pylos, among the dead

Hades himself is the *pulártēs* 'gate-closer' (*Iliad* VIII 367, etc.). In short, the thematic associations of *Púlos* imply that the Gate of the Sun is also the Gate of the Underworld, and thus we have a parallel to the context of Ἠελίοιο πύλας 'Gates [*púlai*] of the Sun' in xxiv 12. Accordingly, a Homeric expression like πύλας Ἀίδαο περήσειν 'pass by the gates of Hades' (V 646; cf. XXIII 71) implies that the *psūkhaí* 'spirits' of the dead traverse to the underworld through the same passage traveled by the sun when it sets.

In the instance of δῆμον ὀνείρων 'District [*dêmos*] of Dreams' (*Odyssey* xxiv 12), the concept of a community of dreams situated past the Gates of Hades is thematically consistent with other Homeric expressions involving dreams. After a person dies, his *psūkhḗ* 'spirit' flies off ἠύτ' ὄνειρος 'like a dream' (xi 222). Hermes, who is conducting the *psūkhaí* of the dead suitors (xxiv 1), is also the conductor of dreams, ἡγήτορ' ὀνείρων (*Hymn to Hermes* 14). Since it is Hermes who leads the *psūkhaí* of the suitors past the Gates of the Sun (xxiv 11), it is significant that another of his inherited epithets is *pulēdókos* (*Hymn to Hermes* 15), to be interpreted as 'he who receives [the *psūkhaí*] at the Gates'.[13] These are the Gates of Hades, or we may call them the Gates of the Sun. But there is also another name available. Since Hermes conducts dreams as well as the ghosts of the dead, and since dreams move like ghosts, it is not surprising that dreams, too, have gates (*Odyssey* xix 562; cf. iv 809).[14] Since the Ἠελίοιο πύλας 'Gates [*púlai*] of the Sun' are already mentioned in xxiv 12, we may expect δῆμον ὀνείρων 'District [*dêmos*] of Dreams' in the same line to be a periphrastic substitute for a redundant concept 'Gates of Dreams'.

In the instance of Λευκάδα πέτρην 'White Rock [*Leukàs pétrā*]' (*Odyssey* xxiv 11), we find no parallel in Homeric theme and diction. All we can say about the White Rock at this point is that its collocation with δῆμον ὀνείρων 'District [*dêmos*] of Dreams' (xxiv 12) seems parallel to the

[13] This epithet serves as a counterexample to the argument of Page 1955.117 that in Homeric poetry Hermes functions as psychopomp only in *Odyssey* xxiv. Cf. also Whitman1958.217–218 on *Iliad* XXIV.

[14] As for the epithet ἀμενηνῶν 'without vital force [*ménos*]' applied to ὀνείρων 'dreams' here at *Odyssey* xix 562, we may note that it is applied in the *Odyssey* exclusively to the dead throughout its other attestations (νεκύων ἀμενηνὰ κάρηνα at x 521, 536; xi 29, 49).

expression ὑποπετριδίων ὀνείρων 'from dreams underneath a rock' in Alcman's *Partheneion* (PMG 1.49).

As we begin to examine the attestations of *Leukàs pétrā* 'White Rock' beyond Homer, we come upon the third problem of interpretation, concerning the White Rock and a figure called Phaon:

οὗ δὴ λέγεται πρώτη Σαπφὼ
τὸν ὑπέρκομπον θηρῶσα Φάον'
οἰστρῶντι πόθῳ ῥῖψαι πέτρας
ἀπὸ τηλεφανοῦς. ἀλλὰ κατ' εὐχὴν
σήν, δέσποτ' ἄναξ, εὐφημείσθω
τέμενος πέρι Λευκάδος ἀκτῆς

Menander F 258K[15]

where they say that Sappho was the first,
hunting down the proud Phaon,
to throw herself, in her goading desire, from the rock
that shines from afar. But now, in accordance with your sacred utterance,
lord king, let there be silence throughout the sacred precinct of the headland of Leukas.

This fragment, alluding to a story about Sappho's jumping into the sea for love of Phaon, is from a play of Menander's entitled *The Leukadia.* We infer from Menander's lines that Sappho leapt off the White Rock of Leukas in pursuit of Phaon. It is to Strabo that we owe the preservation of these verses (10.2.9 C452). He is in the process of describing Cape Leukas, a prominent white rock jutting out from Leukas into the sea and toward Kephallenia.[16] From this rock Sappho is supposed to have jumped into the sea after Phaon. Strabo goes on to describe a shrine of Apollo Leukatas situated on Cape Leukas and an ancestral cult practice connected with it. Every year, he reports, some criminal was cast down from the white rock into the sea below for the sake of averting evil, ἀποτροπῆς χάριν (*ibid.*). Wings and even birds would be fastened to him, and men in fishing boats would be stationed below the rock in order to retrieve the victim after his plunge (*ibid.*).

As Wilamowitz has convincingly argued,[17] Menander chose for his play a setting that was known for its exotic cult practice involving a white rock and conflated it in the quoted passage with a literary theme likewise

[15] This passage must have belonged to the introductory anapests of the play (scholia A to Hephaestion περὶ ποιημάτων 6.3).

[16] Corinthian settlers called the entire territory Leukas, after Cape Leukas; cf. Strabo 10.2.8 C452.

[17] Wilamowitz 1913.25–40.

involving a white rock. There are two surviving attestations of this theme. The first is from lyric:

> ἀρθεὶς δηῦτ' ἀπὸ Λευκάδος
> πέτρης ἐς πολιὸν κῦμα κολυμβῶ μεθύων ἔρωτι

Anacreon PMG 376

> One more time taking off in the air, down from the White
> Rock into the dark waves do I dive, intoxicated with lust.

The second is from satyr drama:

> ὡς ἐκπιεῖν γ' ἂν κύλικα μαινοίμην μίαν
> πάντων Κυκλώπων ⟨μὴ⟩ ἀντιδοὺς βοσκήματα[18]
> ῥῖψαί τ' ἐς ἅλμην Λευκάδος πέτρας ἄπο
> ἅπαξ μεθυσθεὶς καταβαλών τε τὰς ὄφρυς.
> ὡς ὅς γε πίνων μὴ γέγηθε μαίνεται

Euripides *Cyclops* 163–168

> I would be crazy not to give all the herds of the Cyclopes
> in return for drinking one cup [of that wine]
> and throwing myself from the white rock into the brine,
> once I am intoxicated, with eyebrows relaxed.
> Whoever is not happy when he drinks is crazy.

In both instances, falling from the white rock is parallel to falling into a swoon—be it from intoxication or from making love. As for Menander's allusion to Sappho's plunge from a *Leukás* 'white rock', Wilamowitz reasonably infers that there must have existed a similar theme, which does not survive, in the poetry of Sappho. Within the framework of this theme, the female speaker must have pictured herself as driven by love for a certain Phaon, or at least so it was understood by the time New Comedy flourished.[19] So the third and the last of the three problems is, why should Sappho seem to be in love with a mythical figure?

About Phaon himself we have no reports beyond the meager fragments gathered in Sappho F 211 V. It appears that he was an old *porthmeús* 'ferryman' who was transformed into a beautiful youth by Aphrodite herself; also, the goddess fell in love with this beautiful Phaon

[18] For a discussion of the restoration ⟨μὴ⟩, see Wilamowitz pp. 30–31n2; following Wilamowitz, Dieterich 1913.vii retracts his earlier reading without ⟨μὴ⟩.
[19] Wilamowitz pp. 33–37.

and hid him in a head of lettuce. Besides specifically attesting the latter myth in Cratinus (F 330 Kock), Athenaeus (69d-e) also cites striking parallels in Eubulus (F 14 Kock) and Callimachus (F 478 Pfeiffer), where we see that Adonis, too, was hidden in a head of lettuce by Aphrodite. This thematic parallelism of Aphrodite and Phaon with Aphrodite and Adonis becomes more important as we come to another myth about the second pair.

According to the account in Book VII of the mythographer Ptolemaios Chennos (ca. A.D. 100; by way of Photius *Bibliotheca* 152–153 Bekker),[20] the first to dive off the heights of Cape Leukas was none other than Aphrodite herself, out of love for a dead Adonis. After Adonis died (how it happened is not said), the mourning Aphrodite went off searching for him and finally found him at 'Cypriote Argos', in the shrine of Apollo *Eríthios.* She consults Apollo, who instructs her to seek relief from her love by jumping off the white rock of Leukas, where Zeus sits whenever he wants relief from his passion for Hera. Then Ptolemaios launches into a veritable catalogue of other figures who followed Aphrodite's precedent and took a ritual plunge as a cure for love. For example, Queen Artemisia I is reputed to have leapt off the white rock out of love for one Dardanos, succeeding only in getting herself killed. Several others are mentioned who died from the leap, including a certain iambographer Charinos, who expired only after being fished out of the water with a broken leg, but not before blurting out his four last iambic trimeters, painfully preserved for us with the compliments of Ptolemaios (and Photius as well). Someone called Makēs was more fortunate: having succeeded in escaping from four love affairs after four corresponding leaps from the white rock, he earned the epithet *Leukopetrās.* We may follow the lead of Wilamowitz in questioning the degree of historicity in such accounts.[21] There is, however, a more important concern. In the lengthy and detailed account of Ptolemaios, Sappho is not mentioned at all, let alone Phaon. From this silence I infer that the source of this myth about Aphrodite and Adonis is independent of Sappho's own poetry or of later distortions based on it.[22] Accordingly, the ancient cult practice at Cape Leukas, as described by Strabo (10.2.9 C452), may well contain some intrinsic element that inspired lovers' leaps, a practice also noted by Strabo (*ibid.*). The second practice seems to be derived from the first, as we might expect from a priestly institution that becomes independent of the social context that

[20] Westermann 1843.197–199.
[21] Wilamowitz 1913.28.
[22] *Pace* Wilamowitz 1913.28.

had engendered it. Abstracted from their inherited tribal functions, religious institutions have a way of becoming mystical organizations.[23]

Another reason for doubting that Sappho's poetry had been the inspiration for the lovers' leaps at Cape Leukas is the attitude of Strabo himself. He specifically disclaims Menander's version about Sappho's being the first to take the plunge at Leukas. Instead, he offers a version of the *arkhaiologikṓteroi* 'those more versed in the ancient lore', according to which Kephalos son of Deioneus was the very first to have leapt, impelled by love for Pterelas (Strabo 10.2.9 C452). Again, I see no reason to take it for granted that this myth concerning historical *Leukás* had resulted from some distortion of the cult's features because of Sappho's literary influence.[24] The myth of Kephalos and his dive may be as old as the concept of *Leukás*, the White Rock. I say "concept" because the ritual practice of casting victims from a white rock such as that of Leukas may be an inheritance parallel to the epic tradition about a mythical White Rock on the shores of the Okeanos (as in *Odyssey* xxiv 11) and the related literary theme of diving from an imaginary White Rock (as in the poetry of Anacreon and Euripides). In other words, it is needless to assume that the ritual preceded the myth or the other way around.

Actually, there are other historical places besides Cape Leukas that are associated with myths about diving. For example, Charon of Lampsakos (v B.C., FGH 262 F 7)[25] reports that Phobos, of the lineage Kodridai, founder of Lampsakos, was the first to leap ἀπὸ τῶν Λευκάδων πετρῶν 'from the White Rocks', located apparently on the north shore of the Smyrnaean Gulf, not far from Phokaia.[26] We may compare, too, the myth about the death of Theseus. He was pushed by Lykomedes and fell into the sea from the high rocks of the island *Skûros* (Heraclides by way of Pausanias 1.17.6; scholia to Aristophanes *Ploutos* 627). The island derives its name *Skûros* from its white rocks (LSJ s.vv. *skûros* and *skîros/skírros*).[27] In fact, the entire Theseus myth is replete with themes

[23] For an articulate discussion of this general tendency, see Jeanmaire 1939, esp. p. 310 on the Mysteries.

[24] *Pace* Wilamowitz 1913.27.

[25] By way of Plutarch, *De mulierum uirtutibus* 255a-e.

[26] See the commentary of Jacoby FGH 262 F 7, p. 16.

[27] Gruppe 1906.585. The basic meaning of *skîros* 'hard rock' (whence 'chalk, gypsum') survives in the variant reading for *Iliad* XXIII 332–333, preserved by Aristarchus (Scholia Townley). Nestor is telling about a landmark, an old tree trunk (XXIII 326–328), with this added detail:

λᾶε δὲ τοῦ ἑκάτερθεν ἐρηρέδαται δύο λευκὼ

Iliad XXIII 329

and two white rocks are propped up on either side

involving names derived from *skûros/skîros*. Even the "grandfather" of Theseus is *Skū́rios* (Apollodorus 3.15.5), while Theseus himself casts *Skī́rōn* off the *Skīrōnídes pétrai* (Strabo 9.1.4 C391; Plutarch *Theseus* 10; Pausanias 1.33.8).[28] For the moment, I merely note in passing the ritual nature of the various plunges associated with Theseus and his "father" Aigeus,[29] and the implications of agonistic death and mystical rebirth in both ritual and myth.[30]

A more immediate concern is that the mythological examples I have cited so far do not attest the lovelorn theme as a feature of the plunges from white rocks. There is, however, a more basic sexual theme associated with the *Thoríkios pétros* 'Leap Rock' of Attic Kolonos (Sophocles *Oedipus at Colonus* 1595). Kolonos itself, meaning 'summit', is proverbially white or shining-bright (ἀργὴς κολωνός Sophocles *Oedipus at Colonus* 670). As for the name *Thoríkios*, it is formally derivable from the noun *thorós* 'semen' (e.g. Herodotus 2.93.1) by way of the adjective *thorikós*; the noun *thorós* is in turn built on the aorist *thoreîn* of the verb *thrṓiskō* 'leap'.[31] Even the verb can have the side-meaning 'mount, fecundate' (Aeschylus *Eumenides* 660). From the form *Thoríkios* itself, it is difficult to ascertain whether the name may connote leaping as well as fecundating. And yet, thematic associations of the formally related name *Thórikos* suggest that leaping is indeed involved. The provenience of Kephalos, son

---

In the vulgate, at *Iliad* XXIII 331–333, this image of two white rocks propped up on a tree trunk is described as either a *sêma* 'tomb' or a *nússa* 'turning post' belonging to a past generation (quoted at p. 215). Instead of the two verses 332–333, describing the alternative of a turning post, Aristarchus reads the following single verse:

ἠὲ σκῖρος ἔην, νῦν αὖ θέτο τέρματ' Ἀχιλλεύς

or it was a *skîros*, but now Achilles set it up as a turning point

In the *Tabulae Heracleenses* (DGE no. 62.19, 144), *skîros* designates a rocky area unfit for planting, on which trees grow wild. For a useful discussion of words formed with *skīr-*, see Robert 1885.

[28] Pausanias tells us (1.33.8) that the specific name of Skiron's white rock was Molouris, and that it was sacred to Leukothea, the White Goddess (on whom see N 1985a.79–81). It is from the Molouris that Leukothea flung herself into the sea with her "son" Melikertes (Pausanias 1.44.7). At the top of Molouris was a shrine of Zeus Aphesios, the 'Releaser' (Pausanias 1.44.8).

[29] As for the agency of *Lyko*medes (*Lukomḗdēs*) in the plunge of Theseus (Heraclides by way of Pausanias 1.17.6; scholia to Aristophanes *Ploutos* 627), we may compare the agency of *Lyko*urgos (*Lukoûrgos*) in the plunge of Dionysus (*Iliad* VI 130–141). We may note, too, the words describing what happened to Dionysus after he dove into the sea: Θέτις δ' ὑπεδέξατο κόλπῳ 'and Thetis received him in her bosom' (VI 136). For the ritual significance of the wolf theme, see Jeanmaire 1939.581.

[30] For a detailed discussion, see Jeanmaire pp. 324–337. We may note in general the parallelism between the procedure of initiation (ritual) and the story of death (myth). Cf. N 1986a. For a pathfinding work on the theme of rebirth in the *Odyssey*, see Newton 1984.

[31] DELG 444.

of Deioneus, the figure who leapt from the white rock of Leukas (Strabo 10.2.9 C452), is actually this very Thorikos, a town and deme on the southeast coast of Attica (Apollodorus 2.4.7).[32]

The sexual element inherent in the theme of a white rock recurs in a myth about Kolonos. Poseidon fell asleep in this area and had an emission of semen, from which issued the horse *Skīrōnítēs*:

> ἄλλοι δέ φασιν ὅτι περὶ τοὺς πέτρους τοῦ ἐν Ἀθήναις Κολωνοῦ καθευδήσας ἀπεσπέρμηνε καὶ ἵππος Σκύφιος ἐξῆλθεν, ὁ καὶ Σκιρωνίτης[33] λεγόμενος
>
> Scholia to Lycophron 766
>
> Others say that, in the vicinity of the rocks at Athenian Kolonos, he [Poseidon], falling asleep, had an emission of semen, and a horse *Skúphios* came out, who is also called *Skīrōnítēs*.

The name Skironites again conjures up the theme of Theseus, son of Poseidon, and his plunge from the white rocks of Skyros.[34] This Attic myth is parallel to the Thessalian myth of *Skúphios* 'Skyphios':

> Πετραῖος τιμᾶται Ποσειδῶν παρὰ Θεσσαλοῖς, ... ὅτι ἐπί τινος πέτρας κοιμηθεὶς ἀπεσπερμάτισε, καὶ τὸν θορὸν δεξαμένη ἡ γῆ ἀνέδωκεν ἵππον πρῶτον, ὃν ἐπεκάλεσαν Σκύφιον
>
> Scholia to Pindar *Pythian* 4.246
>
> Poseidon *Petraîos* [= of the rocks] has a cult among the Thessalians ... because he, having fallen asleep at some rock, had an emission of semen; and the earth, receiving the semen, produced the first horse, whom they called *Skúphios*.

There is a further report about this first horse ever:

> φασὶ δὲ καὶ ἀγῶνα διατίθεσθαι τῷ Πετραίῳ Ποσειδῶνι, ὅπου ἀπὸ τῆς πέτρας

[32] The leap of Kephalos into the sea was at first probably localized in Thorikos and only later transposed to Cape Leukas. For a discussion of the political motivations for such a mythographical transposition, see Gruppe 1912.373.

[33] The reading Σκιρωνίτης is preferable to Σκειρωνίτης, as we know from the evidence of vase inscriptions; see Kretschmer 1894.131ff.

[34] Gruppe 1912.372 argues that Kolonos marks one of the places claimed to be the spot where Theseus descended into the underworld.

ἐξεπήδησεν ὁ πρῶτος ἵππος

Scholia to Pindar *Pythian* 4.246

and they say that there was a festival established in worship of Poseidon *Petraîos* at the spot where the first horse leapt forth.[35]

The myth of Skironites/Skyphios, featuring the themes of leaping, sexual relief, and the state of unconsciousness, may help us understand better the puzzling verses of Anacreon, already quoted:

ἀρθεὶς δηὖτ' ἀπὸ Λευκάδος
πέτρης ἐς πολιὸν κῦμα κολυμβῶ μεθύων ἔρωτι

Anacreon PMG 376

One more time[36] taking off in the air, down from the White
Rock into the dark waves do I dive, intoxicated with lust.

The theme of jumping is overt, and the theme of sexual relief is latent in the poetry,[37] while the situation is reversed in the myth. In the poem the unconsciousness comes from what is likened to a drunken stupor; in the myth it comes from sleep.[38] As for the additional theme of a horse in the myth, we consider again the emblem of Hagesikhora's charms, that

[35] The rock associated with Skyphios is the *Pétrē Haimoníē*: Apollonius *Argonautica* 3.1244 and scholia. Note, too, the Argive custom of sacrificing horses by throwing them into the sea (Pausanias 8.7.2); see Nilsson 1906.71–72.

[36] For an appreciation of the contextual nuances in δηὖτε 'one more time', I recommend as an exercise in associative esthetics the consecutive reading of the passages cited by Campbell 1976.266, with reference to the triple deployment of δηὖτε at Sappho F 1.15,16,18 V.

[37] If plunging is symbolic of sexual relief, it follows that the opposite is symbolic of sexual frustration:

ἀναπέτομαι δὴ πρὸς Ὄλυμπον πτερύγεσσι κούφης
διὰ τὸν Ἔρωτ'. οὐ γὰρ ἐμοὶ [. . .]θέλει συνηβᾶν

Anacreon PMG 378

I flutter up toward Olympus on light wings
on account of Eros. For he [. . .] refuses to join me in youthful sport.

[38] Note the association of wine with the shade from a rock in the following words of Hesiod: εἴη πετραίη τε σκιὴ καὶ βίβλινος οἶνος 'let there be a shade under the rock and wine from Biblos' (*Works and Days* 589; see further at 592–596).

wondrous horse of Alcman's Laconian fantasy, who is 'from those dreams under the Rock', τῶν ὑποπετριδίων ὀνείρων (PMG 1.49).

We may note that, just as Poseidon obtains sexual relief through the unconsciousness of sleeping at the white rocks of Kolonos, so also Zeus is cured of his passion for Hera by sitting on the white rock of Apollo's Leukas (Ptolemaios Chennos by way of Photius *Bibliotheca* 152–153 Bekker). At Magnesia, those who were *hieroí* 'sacred' to Apollo would leap from precipitous rocks into the river *Lēthaîos* (Pausanias 10.32.6). This name is clearly derivable from *lḗthē* 'forgetfulness'. In the underworld, Theseus and Peirithoos sat on the θρόνος τῆς Λήθης 'throne of *Lḗthē*' (Apollodorus *Epitome* 1.24; Pausanias 10.29.9). I have already quoted the passage from the *Cyclops* of Euripides (163–168) where getting drunk is equated with leaping from a proverbial white rock. We may note the wording of the verses that immediately follow that equation, describing how it feels to be in the realm of a drunken stupor:

> ἵν' ἔστι τουτί τ' ὀρθὸν ἐξανιστάναι
> μαστοῦ τε δραγμὸς καὶ παρεσκευασμένου
> ψαῦσαι χεροῖν λειμῶνος, ὀρχηστύς θ' ἅμα
> κακῶν τε λῆστις
>
> Euripides *Cyclops* 169–172

> where it is allowed to make this thing stand up erect,
> to grab the breast and touch with both hands
> the meadow[39] that is made all ready. And there is dancing
> and forgetting [*lêstis*] of bad things.

Again, we see the theme of sexual relief and the key concept *lêstis* 'forgetting'.

In short, the White Rock is the boundary delimiting the conscious and the unconscious—be it a trance, stupor, sleep, or even death. Accordingly, when the Suitors are led past the White Rock (*Odyssey* xxiv 11), they reach the *dêmos oneírōn* 'District of Dreams' (xxiv 12) beyond which is the realm of the dead (xxiv 14).

Even with the accumulation of this much evidence about the symbolism of the White Rock, it is still difficult to see how it relates to the mythical figure Phaon and how he relates to Sappho. One approach that might yield more information is to study the mythical figure Phaethon, who shares several characteristics with Adonis and Phaon. For now, I postpone the details and citations, offering only the essentials. Like

[39] Euphemism for female genitalia.

Adonis and Phaon, Phaethon is loved by Aphrodite, and like them, he is hidden by her. Like Adonis, Phaethon dies. Like Phaon, Phaethon means 'bright' (for the morphology of *Pháōn/Phaéthōn*, we may compare Homeric *phlégō/phlegéthō* 'burn').[40] Unlike Phaon, however, about whom we have only meager details, the Phaethon figure confronts us with a wealth of testimony, much of it unwieldy and conflicting; we now turn to this testimony.

In the commentary to his edition of the Hesiodic *Theogony*, Martin West observes that *Phaéthōn* (line 987), like *Huperíōn*, is a hypostasis of the sun-god *Hḗlios*.[41] The thematic equation of *Hḗlios* with *Huperíōn* and *Phaéthōn* is apparent in epic diction, where *huperíōn* 'the one who goes above' (*Odyssey* i 8, etc.) and *phaéthōn* 'the one who shines' (*Iliad* XI 735, etc.) are ornamental epithets of *Hḗlios*. The mythological differentiation of identities is symbolized in genealogical terms: in one case, *Huperíōn* is the father of *Hḗlios* (*Odyssey* xii 176, Hesiod *Theogony* 371–374), while in the other, *Phaéthōn* is the son of *Hḗlios*. The latter relationship is a basic feature of the myth treated by Euripides in the tragedy *Phaethon*.[42] What follows is an outline of the myth as found in the Euripidean version.

Phaethon, the story goes, was raised as the son of Merops and Klymene. His real father, however, is not the mortal Merops but the sun-god Helios. At his mother's behest, Phaethon travels to Aithiopia, the abode of Helios, in a quest to prove that the Sun is truly his father. He borrows the chariot of Helios for a day; driving too near the earth, he sets it afire. Zeus then strikes him dead with his thunderbolt, and Phaethon falls from the sky.[43]

A cross-cultural perspective reveals many myths, indigenous to a wide variety of societies, that are analogous to this Greek myth. There are parallels, for example, in the myths of the Kwakiutl and Bella Coola Indians, British Columbia. From the traditions collected by the anthropologist Franz Boas,[44] the following outline emerges. The Sun impregnates a woman, who bears him a son (called Born-to-be-the-Sun in the Kwakiutl version). When the boy goes to visit his father, he is permitted to take the Sun's place. Exceeding his limits, the boy sets the earth on fire, whereupon he is cast down from the sky.[45]

[40] Cf. p. 153.

[41] West 1966.427.

[42] Fragments edited by Diggle 1970.

[43] For attestations of the same myth beyond Euripides, cf. Diggle pp. 3–32.

[44] Boas 1910.123, 125, 127; also Boas 1898.100–103.

[45] For detailed comparisons with the Greek myth, see Frazer 1921 2:388–394, appendix xi: "Phaethon and the Chariot of the Sun."

There seems to be, a priori, a naturalistic element in these myths. The personalized image of the sun's surrogate descending from the sky is parallel, let us say, to the actual setting of the sun. In the specific instance of the Phaethon myth, his fall has indeed been interpreted as a symbol of sunset.[46] I intend to adjust this interpretation later, but at the moment I am ready to argue that there is at least a thematic connection between the Phaethon story and the actual process of sunset as described in Greek epic diction. An essential link is the parallelism between Okeanos and Eridanos, the river into which Phaethon falls from the sky (Choerilus TGF 4; Ion of Chios TGF 62). By the banks of this river Eridanos, the Daughters of the Sun mourn for the fallen Phaethon:

ἀρθείην δ' ἐπὶ πόντιον
κῦμα τᾶς Ἀδριηνᾶς
ἀκτᾶς Ἠριδανοῦ θ' ὕδωρ,
ἔνθα πορφύρεον σταλάσ-
σουσ' εἰς οἶδμα τάλαιναι
κόραι Φαέθοντος οἴκτῳ δακρύων
τὰς ἠλεκτροφαεῖς αὐγάς

Euripides *Hippolytus* 735–741

Let me lift off, heading for the seawave
of the Adriatic headland and the water of Eridanos,
where the wretched girls, in sorrow for Phaethon,
pour forth into the seething swell
their shining amber rays of tears.

To understand the meaning of the Eridanos, we must review the role of Okeanos in epic diction. Before I even begin such a review, I wish to outline the eventual conclusion. Like the White Rock and the Gate of the Sun, the Okeanos and Eridanos are symbolic boundaries delimiting light and darkness, life and death, wakefulness and sleep, consciousness and unconsciousness. Birth, death, and the concept of *nes-, which Frame explains as 'return to life and light',[47] are the key acts that cross these boundaries.

[46] Robert 1883.440: "Allabendlich stürtzt der Sonnengott im Westen nieder und allabendlich erglänzen das Firmament und die Berge in roter Glut, als sollte die Welt in Flammen aufgehen. Es brauchte nun bloss dieser regelmässig wiederkehrende Vorgang als einmaliges Ereignis aufgefasst und der Sonnengott Helios-Phaethon zu dem Heros, dem Sonnenkind Phaethon, hypostasiert zu werden und der Mythus war fertig." Paraphrased at p. 239.

[47] See pp. 225ff.; also pp. 92ff., 126, 203, 218, 225.

The river Okeanos marks the extremities beyond Earth and seas (cf. *Iliad* XIV 301–302). It is from Okeanos that Helios the Sun rises (VII 421–423; cf. *Odyssey* xix 433–434); likewise, it is into Okeanos that the Sun falls at sunset (VIII 485). Thus Okeanos must surround this our world.[48]

The *thūmós* 'spirit' of one who dies is visualized as traveling to the far west and, like the sun, plunging into Okeanos (xx 63–65).[49] Bordering on the Okeanos is the land of the Aithiopes (*Iliad* I 423–424, XXIII 205–207). Just as the Okeanos flows both in the extreme east and in the extreme west, so also the land of the Aithiopes is located in the two extremities (*Odyssey* i 23–24). This instance of *coincidentia oppositorum*, a mythological theme where identity consists of two opposites,[50] is reinforced thematically in *Odyssey* xii 1 and following. In this passage there are two opposite places that add up to the same place. From the overall plot of the *Odyssey*, we know that Odysseus is wandering in the realms of the extreme west when he comes upon the island of Aiaie (x 135). It is from Aiaie, island of Circe, that Odysseus is sent on his way to the underworld by traveling beyond the sea until he and his men reach the Okeanos (xi 21–22).[51] Later, on the way back from the underworld, the ship of Odysseus leaves the Okeanos and returns to Aiaie, which is now described as situated not in the extreme west but in the extreme east. In fact, Aiaie now turns out to be the abode of Eos and sunrise (xii 1–4).[52] The head-spinning directional placements of mythical Okeanos in the epic tradition lead to confused and divergent localizations in later traditions. I cite for example Pindar *Pythian* 4.251, where the Argonauts reach the Red Sea by way of Okeanos. On rational grounds, Herodotus ridicules the concept of an Okeanos surrounding Earth (4.36.2), and he uses the name to designate the seas in the vicinity of Gades/Cadiz (4.8.2), thus clearly distancing himself from the mythical sense of 'cosmic river' and approaching the still-current geographical sense of 'ocean'.

Similarly with Eridanos, there are several exotic localizations of this mythical river. The poetry of Aeschylus places it in Spain and identifies it with the Rhone (TGF 73; cf. Pliny *Natural History* 37.31–32),[53] while the words of Euripides, in the passage quoted above, picture it emptying

[48] On the circularity of the Okeanos: pp. 238ff.; cf. N 1979a.194, 206.

[49] The passage is quoted at pp. 243–244. Cf. N 1979a.194–195.

[50] See also p. 214 above; cf. Eliade 1963.419–423, 428–429.

[51] Cf. Frame 1978.57–60, who also discusses the thematic intrusion of a northerly direction into the narrative.

[52] See also Frame pp. 68–73.

[53] Diggle 1970.27–32.

into the Gulf of Venice (*Hippolytus* 736–737). Rejecting still another such contrivance, Herodotus specifically volunteers that Eridanos is myth rather than reality (3.115; cf. Strabo 5.1.9 C215). The basic difference in the post-epic treatments of Eridanos and Okeanos is that the former still counts as a river whereas the latter, thanks to expanding geographical information about the Atlantic, came to designate the varied concepts of 'ocean' in the current sense of the word.

From the standpoint of Homeric diction, however, the Okeanos is a *potamós* 'river' (*Iliad* XVIII 607, *Odyssey* xi 639; cf. Hesiod *Theogony* 242); it surrounds the Earth, and for that reason the macro- and microcosmic visual themes on the Shield of Achilles are actually framed by a pictorial Okeanos along the circular rim (*Iliad* XVIII 607–608; cf. Hesiodic *Shield* 314). To repeat, the Sun plunges into the Okeanos (*Iliad* VIII 485) and rises from it (*Iliad* VII 421–423, *Odyssey* xix 433–434); ultimately, all rivers and streams flow from it (*Iliad* XXI 195–197). With such a thematic heritage from the *Iliad* and *Odyssey*, it is not surprising that the name Okeanos came to designate the 'ocean' in post-Homeric times.

From the standpoint of epic in general, the more obscure Eridanos is thematically parallel to Okeanos. In fact, Eridanos is the "son" of Okeanos, according to Hesiod (*Theogony* 337–338); this relationship would be insignificant, since Okeanos sired several major rivers,[54] if it were not for other special features of Eridanos. Besides the distinction of being mentioned straightaway in the first line of the catalogue of rivers (*Theogony* 338 in 338–345), Eridanos gets the epithet *bathudī́nēs* 'deep-swirling', which is otherwise reserved for Okeanos himself in the *Theogony* (133; also *Works and Days* 171).[55] There is another example of Eridanos in a variant verse of the *Iliad*. For the context, I cite the following verses describing the birth of the magic horses of Achilles:

τοὺς ἔτεκε Ζεφύρῳ ἀνέμῳ ἅρπυια Ποδάργη
βοσκομένη λειμῶνι παρὰ ῥόον Ὠκεανοῖο

Iliad XVI 150–151

Their father was the wind Zephyros and the mother who conceived them
was the Harpy Podarge [*Podárgē* = 'bright/swift of foot'],[56]
as she was grazing in a meadow on the banks of the stream Okeanos.

[54] *Theogony* 337–345. Some of the rivers in this catalogue are real while others are only mythical; see West 1966.259–263.

[55] I propose to study elsewhere the application of *bathudī́nēs* to Alpheios (Hesiod F 193.9 MW) and to Skamandros/Xanthos (XX 73, XXI passim).

[56] More on Harpies at pp. 243ff.

There survives a variant reading for Ὠκεανοῖο 'Okeanos' in this passage, namely, Ἠριδανοῖο 'Eridanos'. We may note the thematic parallelism of *Ōkeanós/Ēridanós* here with the *Thoríkios pétros* 'Leap Rock':[57] wondrous horses were born at either place, and the name *Skīrōnī́tēs* conjures up a mythical White Rock.[58]

I turn now to parallelisms between Okeanos and Eridanos that relate directly to the Phaethon figure. We know from Pliny's testimony (*Natural History* 37.31–32) that in Aeschylus' treatment of the Phaethon myth, the daughters of the Sun were turned into poplars on the banks of the Eridanos (TGF 73), into which river Phaethon had fallen (Choerilus TGF 4; Ion of Chios TGF 62).[59] There is a parallel association in the *Odyssey,* where poplars grow on the banks of the Okeanos, at the edge of the underworld (x 508–512). Like Okeanos, Eridanos, too, is associated with the theme of transition into the underworld. Besides the specific instance of Phaethon's death, there are also other attestations linking Eridanos with the underworld. For example, in the *Codex Vaticanus* 909 of Euripides' *Orestes,* there is a scholion to verse 981 that reads εἰς τὸν Ἠριδανὸν ποταμὸν κρέμαται ὁ Τάνταλος 'Tantalos is suspended at the river Eridanos'.[60]

I conclude from such parallelisms between Eridanos and Okeanos that the fall of Phaethon into the Eridanos is an analogue to the fall of the sun into the Okeanos at sunset, as in *Iliad* VIII 485. There is also a genealogical dimension to this mythological analogy: just as Phaethon is the son of Helios, so also Eridanos is the son of Okeanos (as in *Theogony* 337–338). In a pseudo-rationalist story of the mythographer Dionysius Scytobrachion (ii/i B.C.), who seems not concerned with the ties that bind myth to ritual and to the general notion of the sacred, Helios himself is cast in the role of plunging to his death in the Eridanos (Dionysius F 6 Rusten, by way of Diodorus 3.57.5).

It does not necessarily follow, however, that the Phaethon myth merely represents the sunset. I sympathize with those who are reluctant to accept the theory that "Phaethon's fall attempts to explain in mythical terms why the sun sinks blazing in the west as if crashing to earth in flames and yet returns to its task unimpaired the following day."[61] One counterexplanation runs as follows: "Phaethon's crash is an event out of

[57] See p. 231.
[58] See p. 231.
[59] Murr 1890.17.
[60] See Dieterich 1913.27. For a more familiar reference to the underworld Eridanos, see Virgil *Aeneid* 6.659 (also Servius on *Aeneid* 6.603). The name Eridanos also figures in the myths about Herakles in the far west; Pherecydes FGH 3 F 16–17, 74.
[61] Diggle 1970.10n3, paraphrasing and rejecting the formulation of Robert 1883.440, quoted at p. 236n46.

the ordinary, a sudden and unexpected calamity, occurring once and not daily."[62] In such matters, however, I would heed the intuitively appealing approach of Lévi-Strauss. A myth, he concedes, "always refers to events alleged to have taken place long ago."[63] Nevertheless, "what gives the myth an operational value is that the specific pattern described is timeless; it explains the present and the past as well as the future."[64] Accordingly, I find it unnecessary to entertain the proposal, based only on naturalistic intuition, that the Phaethon myth represents the fall of a meteorite.[65] The meteorite explanation, as also the sunset explanation, operates on the assumption that the message of the Phaethon myth is simply a metaphorical expression of some phenomenon that occurs in the sky. I disagree. The Phaethon myth presents a problem, not a solution. Furthermore, this problem addresses the human condition, not just celestial dynamics. We may consider again the analogues of the Phaethon myth from British Columbia. In the Bella Coola version, the boy is angry because other children laugh at him for claiming that his father is the sun. In the Kwakiutl version, Born-to-be-the-Sun, as yet unaware of his true identity, weeps when his playmate laughs at him for not having a father. The parallel *Angst* of Phaethon, ridiculed by his youthful friend, is well known from Ovid's treatment:

erubuit Phaethon iramque pudore repressit

Ovid *Metamorphoses* 1.755

Phaethon blushed and in his shame held back his anger

We must not confuse the code of a myth with its message. Whatever its message, the Phaethon myth operates on a code of solar behavior combined with human behavior. For example, the theme of riding across the sky counts as a solar *function* for Helios but as a human *deed* for Phaethon. Phaethon may re-enact what Helios does because his father is the Sun, but he fails in his solar role because his mother is human. The Phaethon figure projects a crisis of identity. He seeks proof that his father is really the Sun, according to what he suspects, what his own name suggests, and what his mother actively affirms. This dilemma is fundamental to the myth dramatized by Euripides. Phaethon's mother, Klymene, assures him that Helios rather than Merops is his real father, and that Phaethon is entitled to one request

[62] Diggle p. 10n3.
[63] Lévi-Strauss 1967.205.
[64] Lévi-Strauss p. 205.
[65] Diggle 1970.10n3.

from Helios. She promises Phaethon that, if his request is granted, he will have proof that his origin is divine (θεοῦ πέφηκας Euripides *Phaethon* 48). Phaethon wavers (51) but finally decides to go to Helios (61–62). His one request, to drive the chariot of Helios, is of course granted by his father. Ironically, however, this proof of his divine nature, inherited from his father, leads to fiery death. His death in turn is proof of his human nature, inherited from his mother. The self-delusion of Phaethon is that he overrated the relationship with his father. His real identity is composed of two ingredients, part "father" = immortal, part "mother" = mortal, but his imagined identity is all "father," that is, he imagines that he can function as an immortal since his father is immortal. His imagined identity impels him to assume the solar role of his father, but his real identity, part mortal, destines him to fail and die. Viewed from a standpoint outside the myth, Phaethon's real identity is indeed that of the Sun, by way of hypostasis. Inside the myth, however, this identity is simply Phaethon's imagination, and his real identity is only partially solar. The self-delusion of Phaethon is comparable to that of another tragic figure, Oedipus. The delusion of Oedipus is that he underrated the relationship with his wife. His real identity is both "husband" and "son" of the same woman, but his imagined identity is only "husband."[66] A basic distinction between the delusions of Phaethon and Oedipus is that one forgets his real identity whereas the other is unaware of it. Forgetting that his mother is human, Phaethon tries to be the Sun. Not knowing who his mother is, Oedipus marries her. In both cases, the imagined identity is then tragically shattered.

Aside from telling us about the dilemma of being human, the Phaethon myth also tells us something about the mystery of the sun. A priori, we expect Helios the sun-god to be immortal. In the diction of Greek epic, he is counted among the ranks of the immortal gods. Yet the movements of the sun suggest the theme of death and rebirth. With the waning of day, the old sun submerges beyond the horizon into the west Okeanos; then, after night has passed, a new sun emerges from the east Okeanos with the waxing of another day. Given the inescapable fact of human mortality, the fundamental dichotomy of man vs. god extends into the dichotomy of man = mortal vs. god = immortal, as we see throughout Greek epic diction: *athánatoi* 'immortals' is a synonym of *theoí* 'gods'. Accordingly, it becomes inappropriate to associate any inherent death/rebirth of the sun directly with Helios the sun-god, who

[66] I benefit here from the discussion of Lévi-Strauss 1967, who treats the Oedipus problem from several vantage points, including Freud's. I should note that my use of the terms "overrate" and "underrate" differs from that of Lévi-Strauss.

must be immortal. The Phaethon myth fills a gap. At sunset, when the sun undergoes a process naturally suggestive of death, it is personified not as Helios the sun-god but as Phaethon, child of the immortal Helios, also child of a mortal. The father Helios represents the divine permanence of the sun's cycle, while his child Phaethon represents the mortal aspect of the sun's alternating death/rebirth cycle. This dichotomy accommodates the traditional veneration of Helios as sun-god, still reflected in Homeric diction. We may contrast the contrivance of Dionysius Scytobrachion (F 6 Rusten, by way of Diodorus 3.57.5): no longer concerned with any inherent divine element in the sun, he imagines Helios himself in the role of Phaethon, and we are left with a secularistic allegory about sunset.

There is another Phaethon myth, preserved in Hesiodic poetry, which is preoccupied with both aspects of the solar cycle, not only with death but also rebirth. In this myth Phaethon is the son not of Helios but of Eos the dawn-goddess (*Theogony* 986–987). In the same context we hear first that Eos mates with Tithonos, bearing Memnon, king of the Aithiopes, and Emathion (984–985); then she mates with Kephalos, bearing Phaethon (986–987); then Aphrodite mates with Phaethon (988–991), having abducted him (990).[67] The parallelism between the mating of Eos with Kephalos and the mating of Aphrodite with their son, Phaethon, is reinforced in the *Hymn to Aphrodite*: when Aphrodite seduces Anchises, the goddess herself cites the abduction of Tithonos by Eos as precedent (218). There are also other parallels, as when a hero called Kleitos is abducted by Eos (*Odyssey* xv 250–251). Or again, the nymph Kalypso cites the abduction of the hero Orion by Eos as a precedent for her abduction of Odysseus (v 121–124).[68]

Traditional poetic diction preserves traces, albeit indirect, of the manner in which such abductions were envisaged. For a clearer impression, though, let us first examine the following verbs that designate the events:

Aphrodite abducts Phaethon, *Theogony* 990: *anereipsaménē* 'snatching up'
Eos abducts Kephalos, Euripides *Hippolytus* 455: *anḗrpasen* 'snatched up'
Eos abducts Tithonos, *Hymn to Aphrodite* 218: *hḗrpasen* 'snatched'
Eos abducts Kleitos, *Odyssey* xv 250: *hḗrpasen* 'snatched'
Eos abducts Orion, *Odyssey* v 121: *héleto* 'seized'

[67] For a more detailed discussion of Hesiod *Theogony* 986–991, see N 1979a.191.

[68] It is pertinent to note here the argument that Kalypso is a hypostasis of Aphrodite herself, in the aspect *Melainís* 'the black one': see Güntert 1909, esp. p. 189. For a definitive treatment of the Kalypso figure, see Crane 1988.

There is another abduction that is parallel to these, that of Ganymedes. The parallelism is explicit in the *Hymn to Aphrodite*, where Aphrodite herself cites the fates of Ganymedes (202–217) and Tithonos (218–238) as a precedent for the fate of Anchises. We may note that, when the gods abduct Ganymedes for Zeus, it is for the following reason: κάλλεος εἵνεκα οἷο, ἵν' ἀθανάτοισι μετείη 'on account of his beauty, so that he may be with the immortals' (*Iliad* XX 235). Similarly, when Eos abducts Kleitos, it is for the following reason: κάλλεος εἵνεκα οἷο, ἵν' ἀθανάτοισι μετείη 'on account of his beauty, so that he may be with the immortals' (*Odyssey* xv 251). These thematic parallelisms of Ganymedes/Tithonos and Ganymedes/Kleitos are important because the verb used in the *Iliad* to designate the abduction of the Ganymedes figure is *anēreípsanto* 'snatched up' (XX 234), aorist indicative corresponding to the aorist participle *anereipsaménē* 'snatching up', which designates the abduction of the Phaethon figure (*Theogony* 990). Furthermore, in the *Hymn to Aphrodite* the verb used to designate the abduction of Ganymedes is *anḗrpase* 'snatched up' (208). Only, the subject here is more specific than the general *theoí* 'gods', subject of *anēreípsanto* 'snatched up' in *Iliad* XX 234:

ὅππῃ οἱ φίλον υἱὸν ἀνήρπασε θέσπις ἄελλα

Hymn to Aphrodite 208

where the wondrous gust of wind [*áella*] snatched up
[*anḗrpase*] his son

Not only here but also in every other Homeric attestation of *anēreípsanto* 'snatched up' besides *Iliad* XX 234, the notion 'gusts of wind' serves as subject of the verb. When Penelope bewails the unknown fate of the absent Telemachus, she says that it was *thúellai* 'gusts of wind' that *anēreípsanto* 'snatched up' her son (*Odyssey* iv 727). When Telemachus bewails the unknown fate of the absent Odysseus, he says that it was *hárpuiai* 'snatching winds, Harpies' that *anēreípsanto* 'snatched up' his absent father (i 241). The identical line is used when Eumaios bewails the unknown fate of his absent master Odysseus (xiv 371).

The meaning of *thúella* 'gust of wind' is certain (cf. ἀνέμοιο θύελλα VI 346, etc.). As for *hárpuia* 'snatching wind, Harpy', there is further contextual evidence from the only remaining Homeric attestation of the verb *anēreípsanto* 'snatched up'. When Penelope prays that Artemis smite her dead and take her *thūmós* 'spirit' straightaway, she adds:

ἢ ἔπειτά μ' ἀναρπάξασα θύελλα
οἴχοιτο προφέρουσα κατ' ἠερόεντα κέλευθα,

ἐν προχοῇς δὲ βάλοι ἀψορρόου Ὠκεανοῖο

Odyssey xx 61–65

or, after that, may a gust of wind [*thúella*]
carry me off, taking me down the misty paths,
and may it plunge me into the streams of the backwardflowing Okeanos.

As precedent for being snatched up by a gust of wind and cast down into the Okeanos, she invokes the fate of Pandareos' daughters:

ὡς δ' ὅτε Πανδαρέου κούρας ἀνέλοντο θύελλαι

Odyssey xx 66

as when gusts of wind [*thúellai*] seized [*anélonto*] the daughters of Pandareos

We may compare the use of *anélonto* 'seized' here with that of *héleto* 'seized' when Eos abducts Orion (*Odyssey* v 121). After further elaboration in the story of the daughters of Pandareos, the central event is presented with the following words:

τόφρα δὲ τὰς κούρας ἅρπυιαι ἀνηρείψαντο

Odyssey xx 77

then the Harpies [*hárpuiai* 'snatching winds'] snatched up
[*anēreípsanto*] the girls.

So much for all the Homeric attestations of *anēreipsanto* 'snatched up' and the solitary Hesiodic attestation of *anereipsaménē* 'snatching up'. As for *hárpuia* 'snatching wind, Harpy', the only other Homeric attestation besides those already surveyed is in the *Iliad*, where the horses of Achilles are described as follows:

Ξάνθον καὶ Βαλίον, τὼ ἅμα πνοιῇσι πετέσθην,
τοὺς ἔτεκε Ζεφύρῳ ἀνέμῳ ἅρπυια Ποδάργη
βοσκομένη λειμῶνι παρὰ ῥόον Ὠκεανοῖο

Iliad XVI 149–151

Xanthos and Balios, who flew with the gusts of wind.
Their father was the wind Zephyros and the mother who conceived them was the Harpy [*hárpuia* 'snatching wind'] Podarge [*Podárgē* = 'bright/swift of foot'],

as she was grazing in a meadow on the banks of the stream Okeanos.[69]

Finally, we may consider the Hesiodic description of the *hárpuiai* 'snatching winds' or 'Harpies', two in number, in *Theogony* 267–269: one is called *Aellṓ* (267, from *áella* 'gust of wind'), and the other, *Ōkupétē*, the one who is 'swiftly flying' (267). In short, the epic attestations of *hárpuia* betray a regular association with wind. Furthermore, this noun may be formally connected with the verb transmitted as ἀνηρείψαντο 'snatched up' and ἀνερειψαμένη 'snatching up' in Homer and Hesiod, respectively, as we may infer from the variant *arepuîa*, attested in the *Etymologicum Magnum* (138.21) and on a vase inscription from Aegina.[70]

The prime significance of this contextual survey is that it establishes how Phaethon, Kephalos, Tithonos, Kleitos, Orion, and Ganymedes were abducted in the poetic imagination: *they were snatched away by a gust of wind.* The imagery is most explicit in the story of Ganymedes. The *immediate agent* of the abduction is a gust of wind, and Ganymedes' father does not know where the *áella* 'gust of wind' has 'snatched up' his son, *anḗrpase* (*Hymn to Aphrodite* 208). We should observe, however, that the *ultimate agent* is Zeus himself, who is the subject of the verb *hḗrpasen* 'snatched' designating the abduction of Ganymedes (*Hymn to Aphrodite* 202–203). As compensation for the abduction of Ganymedes, Zeus gives to the boy's father a team of wondrous horses (*Hymn to Aphrodite* 210–211), who are described as having *feet of wind* (ἀελλοπόδεσσιν 217). In this instance, both themes, of taking and giving in return, center on the element of wind.

After having ascertained *how* the likes of Phaethon were abducted, we may still ask *where* they were taken. The most explicit Homeric imagery about this aspect of *thúellai*/ *hárpuiai*, the snatching gusts of wind, occurs in the passage already quoted from the *Odyssey*, where Penelope wishes for a gust of wind to snatch her up and drop her into the Okeanos (xx 63–65).[71] The *immediate agent* is the *thúella* 'gust of wind' (xx 63), but the ultimate agents are the gods themselves (xx 79). In this connection, we may note again that it is on the banks of the Okeanos that the *hárpuia* 'Harpy' called Podarge [*Podárgē* = 'bright/swift of foot'] gave birth to the wind-horses of Achilles (*Iliad* XVI 149–151). And we may also note again that the variant reading for Ὠκεανοῖο 'Okeanos' at *Iliad* XVI 151 is Ἠριδανοῖο 'Eridanos'.[72]

[69] Cf. p. 238.
[70] Kretschmer 1894.208–209.
[71] See pp. 243–244.
[72] Cf. 238–239, 244–245.

By dying, Penelope will have the experience of having her *thūmós* 'spirit' plunge into the Okeanos (*Odyssey* xx 65), but later there is a further detail, that *she will have gone underneath the earth* (xx 80–81). These themes of (1) falling into Okeanos and (2) going underneath the earth also apply to the movements of the sun itself (e.g. *Iliad* VIII 485, *Odyssey* x 190–193).[73] For humans, Okeanos has a function that can be described as follows: when you die, a gust of wind carries your spirit to the extreme west, where it drops you into the Okeanos; when you traverse the Okeanos, you reach the underworld, which is underneath the earth. For the sun itself, Okeanos has an analogous function: when the sun reaches the extreme west at sunset, it likewise drops into the Okeanos; before the sun rises in the extreme east, it stays hidden underneath the earth. When the sun does rise, it emerges from the Okeanos in the extreme east (*Iliad* VII 421–423; cf. *Odyssey* xix 433). Thus the movements of the sun into and from the Okeanos serve as a cosmic model for death and rebirth. From the human standpoint, the sun dies in the west in order to be reborn in the east. Since Okeanos is thematically parallel with Eridanos, the sunset theme of a dead Phaethon falling into Eridanos implies an inverse sunrise theme of a reborn Phaethon emerging from Eridanos.

In this respect, a detail about Phaethon's mother *Ḗṓs* 'the Dawn' becomes especially significant. Homeric Eos has a fixed epithet *ēri-géneia* 'early-generated' (or 'early-generating') that is exclusively hers (e.g. *Odyssey* ii 1). This epithet is built on what survives as the old locative adverb *êri* 'early', and Homeric diction actually preserves *êri* in collocation with *ēṓs* 'dawn' (xix 320). This form *ēri-géneia* is comparable to *Ēri-danós*, the first part of which is likewise built on *êri*; the second part *-danos* seems to mean 'dew' or 'fluid' (cf. Indic *dā́nu-* 'fluid, dew').[74]

We come now to the association of Phaethon with Aphrodite in *Theogony* 988–991. It arises, I propose, from a sexual theme implicit in a solar transition from death to rebirth. In the logic of the myth, it appears that the setting sun mates with the goddess of regeneration so that the rising sun may be reborn. If the setting sun is the same as the rising sun, then the goddess of regeneration may be viewed as both mate and mother.

Such an ambivalent relationship actually survives in the hymns of the *Rig-Veda*, where the goddess of solar regeneration, the dawn Uṣas, is the wife or bride of the sun-god Sū́rya (1.115.1, 7.75.5, etc.) as well as his mother (7.63.3, 7.78.3).[75] In the latter instance, the incestuous

[73] Cf. pp. 98–99. For more on *Odyssey* x 190–193, see N 1979a.320–321.

[74] Güntert 1923.36n1. The semantics of the form *Ēri-danós* are pertinent to the work of Boedeker 1984.

[75] For more on Indic sun-gods, see pp. 93ff.

implications are attenuated by putting Uṣas in the plural, representing the succession of dawns; similarly, Uṣas in the plural can designate the wives of Sūrya (4.5.13). Yet even if each succeeding dawn is wife of the preceding dawn's son, the husband and son are always one and the same Sūrya, and the basic theme of incest remains intact.

This comparative evidence from the *Rig-Veda* is important for understanding the Greek evidence, because Indic *Sū́rya-* 'Sun' and *Uṣás-* 'Dawn' are formally cognate with Greek *Hḗlios* 'Sun' and *Ēṓs* 'Dawn';[76] furthermore, the epithets of Uṣas in the *Rig-Veda, divá(s) duhitár-* and *duhitár- divás,* both meaning 'Daughter of the Sky', are exact formal cognates of the Homeric epithets *Diòs thugátēr* and *thugátēr Diós,* meaning 'Daughter of Zeus'.[77] The Homeric hexameter preserves these epithets only in the following patterns:

A. – ⏔ – ⏔ – | θυγάτηρ Διός | – ⏑ ⏑ – ⏓	6 times
B. – ⏑ Διὸς θυγάτηρ | ⏔ – ⏔ – ⏑ ⏑ – ⏓	8 times
C. – ⏔ – ⏔ – ⏑ | Διὸς θυγάτηρ ⏑ ⏑ – ⏓	18 times

We see from this scheme that it is cumbersome for the meter to accommodate the name of Eos, 'Ηώς, in a position contiguous with these epithets. Thus it is not surprising that Eos is not combined with these epithets anywhere in attested Greek epic, despite the comparative evidence that such a combination had once existed, as we see from the survival of the Indic cognates *divá(s) duhitár-* and *duhitár- divás* in the *Rig-Veda.*

Within the framework of the Greek hexameter, we may have expected at least one position, however, where the name of Eos could possibly have been combined with *thugátēr Diós* 'Daughter of Zeus':

D. *– ⏔ – ⏔ – ⏔ – | θυγάτηρ Διὸς 'Ηώς

And yet, when 'Ηώς 'Dawn' occupies the final portion of the hexameter and when it is preceded by an epithet with the metrical shape ⏑ ⏑ – ⏑ ⏑, this epithet is regularly ῥοδοδάκτυλος 'rosy-fingered' (or 'rosy-toed'), not θυγάτηρ Διός = *thugátēr Diós* 'Daughter of Zeus'. I infer that the epithet θυγάτηρ Διός = *thugátēr Diós* 'Daughter of Zeus' in position D must have been ousted by the fixed epithet ῥοδοδάκτυλος 'rosy-fingered', as in the familiar verse

[76] Schmitt 1967 ch. 4.
[77] Schmitt pp. 169–173.

ἦμος δ' ἠριγένεια φάνη ῥοδοδάκτυλος Ἠώς

Iliad I 477, etc.

when early-born rosy-fingered Dawn appeared . . .

In short, for both metrical and formulaic reasons, Greek epic fails to preserve the combination of *Ēṓs* 'Dawn' with *Diòs thugátēr* and *thugátēr Diós,* meaning 'Daughter of Zeus'.[78] By contrast, when the name *Aphrodī́tē* occupies the final position of the hexameter, her fixed epithet is *Diòs thugátēr.*

– ⏖ – ⏖ – ⏑ | Διὸς θυγάτηρ Ἀφροδίτη

Iliad III 374, etc.

. . . Daughter of Zeus, Aphrodite

From the standpoint of comparative analysis, then, Aphrodite is a parallel of Eos in epic diction. Furthermore, from the standpoint of internal analysis, Aphrodite is a parallel of Eos in epic theme. Just as Eos abducts Tithonos (*Hymn to Aphrodite* 218), Kleitos (*Odyssey* xv 250), Orion (v 121), and Kephalos (Euripides *Hippolytus* 455), so also Aphrodite abducts Phaethon (*Theogony* 990). When Aphrodite seduces Anchises, she herself cites the abduction of Tithonos by Eos for an actual precedent (*Hymn to Aphrodite* 218–238), as we have already seen. Throughout the seduction episode, Aphrodite is called *Diòs thugátēr* 'Daughter of Zeus' (*Hymn to Aphrodite* 81, 107, 191).

The archaic parallelism of Eos and Aphrodite suggests that Aphrodite became a rival of Eos in such functions as that of *Diòs thugátēr* 'Daughter of Zeus'. From the comparative evidence of the *Rig-Veda,* we would expect Eos to be not only mother but also consort of the Sun. There is no such evidence in Greek epic for either Helios or any hypostasis such as the Phaethon figure. Instead, the Hesiodic tradition assigns Aphrodite as consort of Phaethon, while Eos is only his mother (*Theogony* 986–991). In other words, the Hesiodic tradition seems to have split the earlier fused roles of mother and consort and divided them between Eos

[78] I disagree with Schmitt's statement that Eos is Daughter of Helios (pp. 172–173). Technically, she does appear as Daughter of the Sun in *Theogony* 371–374, but here the name of her "father" is Hyperion; as for Helios, he is her "brother" (*ibid.*). For the image of Eos as Daughter of the Sun, we may compare the special image of Uṣas as Daughter of the Sun-God Sūrya in the *Rig-Veda* (2.23.2), as distinct from the usual image of Uṣas as Daughter of the Sky-God Dyaus, *divá(s) duhitár-* (*Rig-Veda,* passim); the noun *dyáus* 'sky', personified as the Sky-God Dyaus, is cognate of Greek *Zeús.*

and Aphrodite respectively. This way, the theme of incest could be neatly obviated.

There are, however, instances in Homeric diction where the relationship of *Ēṓs* and *Phaéthōn* is directly parallel to the relationship of Uṣas and Sūrya in the *Rig-Veda*. We have already noted the fact that *phaéthōn* 'the one who shines' is an ornamental epithet of *Hḗlios* (*Iliad* XI 735, etc.). Moreover, the name *Phaéthōn* is assigned to one of the two horses of Eos:

Λάμπον καὶ Φαέθονθ' οἵ τ' Ἠῶ πῶλοι ἄγουσι

Odyssey xxiii 246

Lámpos and *Phaéthōn*, the horses [*pôloi*] that draw *Ēṓs*

We may note that *Lámpos,* the name of her other horse, is also associated with the notion of brightness.[79] There is a striking parallel in the *Rig-Veda*: Sūrya the sun-god is called the 'bright horse', *śvetám* . . . *áśvam,* of the dawn-goddess Uṣas (7.77.3; cf. 7.78.4).

There is also, within Greek epic, an internal analogue to the combination of *Phaéthōn* and *Lámpos* in *Odyssey* xxiii 246. The names for the daughters of Helios the sun-god are *Phaéthousa* and *Lampetíē* (*Odyssey* xii 132), which are feminine equivalents of *Phaéthōn* and *Lámpos.*[80] Again we may note a striking Indic parallel: in the *Rig-Veda* the name for the daughter of *Sū́rya-* the sun-god is *Sūryā́* (1.116.17), which is a feminine equivalent of the masculine name.

The comparative evidence of this contextual nexus suggests that the Horses of the Dawn in *Odyssey* xxiii 246 had once been metaphorical aspects of the Sun. As in the *Rig-Veda,* the Sun could have been called the bright stallion of the Dawn—by such names as *Phaéthōn* or *Lámpos.* Once the metaphor is suspended, then the notion 'Horse of the Dawn' must be taken at face value: if the Dawn has a horse, she will actually require not one but two for a chariot team, and the two kindred solar aspects *Phaéthōn* 'bright' and *Lámpos* 'bright' will do nicely as names for two distinct horses. Yet the surviving role of *Phaéthousa* and *Lampetíē* as daughters of Helios serves as testimony for the eroded personal connotations of the names *Phaéthōn* or *Lámpos.* By contrast, the metaphor is maintained in the *Rig-Veda,* where Sūrya the sun-god is both bridegroom

[79] We may note, too, that *Odyssey* xxiii 246 is the only place in either the *Iliad* or the *Odyssey* where a solar deity has a chariot team.

[80] For the morphology of *Lampetíē,* see N 1970.43–44n121; also Frame 1978.135–137 on Indic *Nā́satyau.*

and horse of the dawn-goddess Uṣas. There is even a special word that incorporates both roles of Sūrya, namely, *márya-* (1.115.2, 7.76.3).[81] In fact, the metaphorical equation of stallion and bridegroom is built into various rituals of Indic society, such as those of initiation, and a key to this equation is the same word *márya-* and its Iranian cognates.[82]

Significantly, there is a corresponding Greek attestation of such a metaphorical equation, in the hymenaeus 'wedding-song' of Euripides *Phaethon* 227–235, where the *pôlos* 'horse' of Aphrodite (234) is the hero Hymen himself.[83] We have seen the same word *pôlos* designating the horses of Eos, Phaethon and Lampos (*Odyssey* xxiii 246).[84] Hymen's epithet νεόζυγι 'newly yoked' in Euripides *Phaethon* 233 marks him as Aphrodite's bridegroom (compare the diction in Aeschylus *Persians* 514–515; Euripides *Medea* 804–805; TGF 821). As for the appositive σῶν γάμων γένναν 'offspring of your wedding' (*Phaethon* 235), it conveys that Hymen is not only the bridegroom but also the son of Aphrodite. We may note in this connection that the hymenaeus 'wedding-song' in *Phaethon* 227–235 is being sung in honor of Phaethon, and that his bride-to-be is in all probability a Daughter of the Sun.[85] Finally, we may note that Aphrodite functions in this context as τὰν Διὸς οὐρανίαν 'the celestial daughter of Zeus' (*Phaethon* 228).

Besides Eos and Aphrodite, other Homeric goddesses, too, qualify as *Diòs thugátēr/ thugátēr Diós* 'Daughter of Zeus': they are Athena (*Iliad* IV 128, etc.), the Muse of the *Odyssey* (i 10), Atē (*Iliad* XIX 91), Persephone (*Odyssey* xi 217), Artemis (xx 61), and Helen (iv 227).[86] It is beyond the scope of this investigation to examine the contexts of *Diòs thugátēr/ thugátēr Diós* 'Daughter of Zeus' and to correlate them with the contexts of the Rig-Vedic cognate *divá(s) duhitár-/ duhitár- divás* 'Daughter of Sky', which applies only to Uṣas the dawn-goddess.[87] Instead, I confine myself here to observations that relate to the theme of abduction.

The Rig-Vedic Uṣas is an overtly beneficent goddess, well known for her function of dispelling the darkness (1.92.5, 2.34.12, etc.). Yet her epithet *divá(s) duhitár-/ duhitár- divás* is ambivalent. In a hymn that is part of the Vedic liturgical canon for animal sacrifice, Uṣas combined

[81] The Indic noun *márya-* may be pertinent to the semantics of Greek *mérops*, as discussed at p. 198n120.

[82] Wikander 1938.22–30, 81–85, esp. p. 84.

[83] Diggle 1970.148–160. The passage is quoted in N 1979a.199–200.

[84] See p. 249.

[85] So Diggle 1970.158–160.

[86] On the divine aspects of Helen in Homeric diction and on the relationship of *Diòs thugátēr/ thugátēr Diós* 'Daughter of Zeus' to *Diòs koûroi* 'sons of Zeus', see Clader 1976.

[87] For a pathfinding survey, see Boedeker 1974.

with the Night are together called *divó duhitárā* (*Rig-Veda* 10.70.6). In other words, both Dawn and Night are Daughters of the Sky, Indic *Dyáus* (cognate of Greek *Zeús*). When Dawn drives away the Night, the latter is actually called her sister (*Rig-Veda* 1.92.11, 4.52.1). There is a parallel ambivalence in the cognate epithet *Diòs thugátēr/ thugátēr Diós*. In one instance, it can describe a beneficent Athena who has just rescued Menelaos and who is compared to a mother fostering her child (*Iliad* IV 128). This function of the *Diòs thugátēr/ thugátēr Diós* as patroness of the Hero is typical.[88] In another instance, however, the epithet describes a maleficent Persephone, goddess of the dead (*Odyssey* xi 217). In still another instance, it describes Artemis when Penelope wants to be shot and killed by her (xx 61).

Although the epithet *Diòs thugátēr/ thugátēr Diós* does not survive in combination with Eos, the goddess herself is in fact likewise ambivalent. Homeric diction features her snatching up youths as if she were some Harpy, and yet she gives them immortality. For review, the example of Kleitos will suffice (xv 250–251).[89] Such an ambivalence inherent in the Eos figure is so uncomfortable that it tends to be attenuated in the diction. For instance, the verb used to describe the abduction of Orion by Eos is not the concretely violent *hḗrpasen* 'snatched' but the more abstract *héleto* 'seized' (*Odyssey* v 121).[90] Once the wording *hḗrpasen* 'snatched' is removed, the connotation of death from Harpies disappears and a new theme is introduced, death from Artemis (*Odyssey* v 121–124). We may note that death is at least not violent at the hands of Artemis (ἀγανοῖς βελέεσσιν 'with her gentle darts' v 124). Similarly, when Penelope wants to be killed by Artemis, the death is implicitly gentle (xx 61–65).

The alternative to a gentle death from Artemis is a violent abduction by a *thúella* 'gust of wind' (*Odyssey* xx 63), the action of which is described as *anarpáxāsa* 'snatching up' (*ibid.*). As precedent for being abducted by a gust of wind and plunged into the Okeanos, Penelope's words evoke the story of the daughters of Pandareos, abducted by *thúellai* 'gusts of wind' (xx 66), the action of which is described as *anélonto* 'seized' (*ibid.*). This mention of abduction is followed by a description of how the daughters of Pandareos had been preserved by the Olympian goddesses (xx 67–72); the preservation of the girls is then interrupted by death, at the very moment that Aphrodite is arranging for them to be married (xx 73–74). Death comes in the form of abduction by *hárpuiai*

[88] Other examples: Athena/Odysseus (*Odyssey* xiii 369), Aphrodite/Alexander (*Iliad* III 374), Aphrodite/Aeneas (V 312).

[89] See p. 242.

[90] See p. 242.

'snatching winds' (xx 77), the action of which is now described as *anēreípsanto* 'snatched up' (*ibid.*).[91]

In this story about the daughters of Pandareos (*Odyssey* xx 66–81), we see a sequence of *preservation followed by abduction/death.*[92] In the story about Orion and Eos (v 121–124), by contrast, the pattern is *abduction/preservation followed by death,* in that Eos abducts and preserves the hero while Artemis arranges for his death.[93] Finally, the story about Aphrodite and Phaethon (Hesiod *Theogony* 986–991) presents yet another pattern, that of *abduction/death followed by preservation.*[94] In each of these narrative patterns, we see various patterns of differentiation in the ambivalent function of Eos as the undifferentiated agent of abduction, death, and preservation.

The abduction of Phaethon by Aphrodite is most directly comparable to the abduction of Kleitos by Eos (*Odyssey* xv 251–252), where again we see the pattern *abduction/death followed by preservation.* The Kleitos figure is represented as son of Mantios (xv 249) and grandson of the seer Melampous (xv 242). As Frame has shown, the Melampous myth centers on the theme of retrieving the Cattle of the Sun.[95] The solar function of the Melampous figure and his genetic affinity with the Kleitos figure imply a solar affinity as well. The wording *hḗrpasen* for the abduction of Kleitos at *Odyssey* xv 251 implies that he was taken by a maleficent Harpy and dropped into the Okeanos. This theme of death is parallel to sunset. On the other hand, the subject of *hḗrpasen* is Eos herself, and the theme of sunrise is parallel to rebirth. Since the abductor of Kleitos is represented as the Dawn, it is at least implicit that Kleitos is to be reborn like the Sun and thus preserved.

So long as the Dawn is present, the day waxes. Once the Sun reaches noon, however, the Dawn ceases and the day wanes. This vital role of Eos is explicit in Homeric diction (e.g. *Iliad* XX 66–69). Implicitly, the Sun is united with the light of Dawn until noon; afterwards, the Sun descends into the Okeanos, only to be reborn the next day. In the story of Eos and Kleitos a parallel death and rebirth are implied. The sequence of events, to repeat, is *abduction/death followed by preservation.*[96] In the

[91] For further details on this difficult passage concerning the daughters of Pandareos, *Odyssey* xx 66–81, see N 1979a.195 § 25n2.

[92] Further discussion at N p. 201 § 37n3.

[93] More detailed discussion at N pp. 201–203.

[94] N pp. 191–192. As for the Tithonos story in the *Hymn to Aphrodite,* the sequence is suspended: *abduction = preservation, with no death ensuing.* Appropriately, Tithonos therefore never rises from the Okeanos, as would a reborn Sun. Whenever Eos rises, she leaves Tithonos behind (*Iliad* XIX 1–2 vs. *Odyssey* v 1–2; *Hymn to Aphrodite* 227, 236).

[95] Frame 1978.91–92. Suffice it here to note the suggestive verses at *Odyssey* xv 235–236.

[96] See immediately above.

Orion story (*Odyssey* v 121–124), on the other hand, the sequence is the inverse: *abduction/preservation followed by death.*[97] We may note that Orion's relation to the Dawn is the inverse of the Sun's. Translated into the symbolism of celestial dynamics, Orion's movements are accordingly astral, not solar, and we see an astral representation of the Orion figure already in Homeric poetry (v 274; *Iliad* XVIII 488).[98] Like the Sun, the constellation Orion rises from the Okeanos and sets in it (v 275, *Iliad* XVIII 489), but, unlike the Sun, it rises and sets at nighttime, not daytime. In the summer, at threshing time, Orion starts rising before Dawn (Hesiod *Works and Days* 598–599). In the winter, at ploughing time, Orion starts setting before Dawn (*Works and Days* 615–616). In summer days the light of Dawn catches up with the rising Orion, and he can be her consort in the daytime.[99] In winter days the light of Dawn arrives too late to keep Orion from setting into the Okeanos. One related star that does not set, however, is Arktos (v 275 = *Iliad* XVIII 489). The Arktos 'Bear' watches Orion, *dokeúei* (v 274 = *Iliad* XVIII 488), and the verb *dokeúei* implies doom. In Homeric diction it is used when marksmen or savage beasts take aim at their victims (*Iliad* XIII 545, XVI 313, XX 340).[100] As for the Arktos 'Bear', the name implies the goddess Artemis.[101] In other words, the astral passages of *Odyssey* v 273–275 and *Iliad* XVIII 487–489 implicitly repeat the theme of Orion's dying at the hands of Artemis, explicit in *Odyssey* v 121–124.[102] The latter passage involves two goddesses, a beneficent Eos and a maleficent Artemis.[103] We may contrast the passage about Kleitos, involving an ambivalent Eos who is both maleficent and beneficent (*Odyssey* xv 251–252).[104] The theme of death is implicit in *hḗrpasen* 'snatched' (251), while the theme of preservation is explicit in ἵν' ἀθανάτοισι μετείη 'so that he may be with the immortals' (252).

Similarly, Aphrodite is ambivalent in the Hesiodic passage about Phaethon (*Theogony* 989–991). Again, the theme of death is implied in *anereipsaménē* 'snatching up' (990). The epithet *daímōn* 'supernatural being' (991), on the other hand, implies divine preservation, as we see from the context of *daímōn* in *Works and Days* 109–126.[105] We may

[97] See p. 252.

[98] More detailed discussion in N 1979a.201–203.

[99] This theme is pertinent to the name *Ōríōn* (*Ōaríōn*), which seems to be connected with *óar* 'wife', *óaros* 'companionship, keeping company', etc.

[100] Survey of contexts in N 1979a.202 § 39n1.

[101] The argument is presented at N p. 202.

[102] On the implications of the Orion myth for the fate of Odysseus in the *Odyssey*, see N pp. 202–203. See also p. 207n15 above.

[103] See p. 251.

[104] See p. 242.

[105] Further details at N 1979a.190–192.

compare, too, the preservation of the hero Erechtheus by Athena in *Iliad* II 547–551, where the goddess is explicitly described as *Diòs thugátēr* 'Daughter of Zeus' (548). The preservation of both Phaethon and Erechtheus is represented in these passages in terms of hero cult.[106] If the hero is situated in a sacred precinct and if he is propitiated at set times, then he is being treated like a god and it follows that he must be like a god; thus he must be in some sense alive.[107] From the standpoint of myth, he is explicitly dead, but from the standpoint of cult, *he is implicitly reborn and thus alive.* Myth has it that, like Phaethon, Erechtheus, too, had once been struck dead by the thunderbolt of Zeus (Hyginus 46). It is clear that Erechtheus has an underworld phase, in that he is described as hidden in a χάσμα . . . χθονός 'chasm of the earth' (Euripides *Ion* 281). Similarly, the adjective *múkhios* 'secreted' describing Phaethon in *Theogony* 991 implies a stay in the underworld, as we see from the usage of *mukhós* 'secret place' in *Theogony* 119. As for Aphrodite, the goddess who abducted Phaethon and made him *múkhios,* she herself is known as *Mukhíā* in the context of one of her cults (as at Gyaros: IG XII v 651; cf. Aelian *De natura animalium* 10.34).[108] Another such cult title of Aphrodite, again implying an underworld phase, is *Melainís* 'the dark one' (Pausanias 2.2.4, 8.6.5, 9.27.5). In the Phaethon myth preserved by Euripides, even the mother's name *Kluménē* connotes the underworld. The masculine equivalent, *Klúmenos,* was a euphemistic epithet of Hades himself, as in the epichoric cults of Hermione (Pausanias 2.35.9). Behind the Hermionian precinct of *Khthoníā* 'the chthonic one' is the 'Place of *Klúmenos*', and in this place is a γῆς χάσμα 'chasm of the earth' through which Herakles brought up the Hound of Hades (Pausanias 2.35.10). Accordingly, I am inclined to view Phaethon's *Kluménē* as a hypostasis of chthonic Aphrodite.

To sum up: like Eos, Aphrodite is both maleficent and beneficent in the role of abductor, since she confers both death and preservation. When Phaethon's parents are Helios and Klymene, the stage is set for his death, implicit in the Klymene figure. When his parents are Kephalos and Eos, the stage is set for both his death and his preservation, implicit in the Eos figure as well as in her alternate, Aphrodite. Thus, I disagree with the spirit of the claim that "on the evidence available to us the son of Helios and the son of Eos and Cephalus must be pronounced entirely different persons."[109] Such an attitude is overly prosopographical. We

[106] N pp. 190–192.

[107] Rohde 1898 1:189–199. The rationalizations about priest-kings in Farnell 1921.17 amount to an exercise in euhemerism.

[108] Cf. also Güntert 1909.185 on the mystical function of the word *mukhós* 'secret place' and its relation to the name *Kalupsṓ* in the *Odyssey.*

[109] Diggle 1970.15n3.

are dealing not with different persons, but with different myths, cognate variants, centering on the inherited personification of a solar child and consort.

Since the epithet *múkhios* 'secreted' as applied to Phaethon in *Theogony* 991 implies that he was hidden by Aphrodite, we see here an important parallelism with Phaon and Adonis, who were also hidden by Aphrodite.[110] Just as Phaethon implicitly attains preservation in the cult of Aphrodite, so also Adonis in the cult of Apollo *Eríthios.*[111] As for Phaon, he explicitly attains preservation in the myth where he is turned into a beautiful young man by Aphrodite (Sappho F 211 V). From the myths of Phaethon, we see that the themes of concealment and preservation are symbolic of solar behavior, and we may begin to suspect that the parallel myths of Phaon and Adonis are based on like symbolism.

The very name *Pháōn,* just like *Phaéthōn,* suggests a solar theme.[112] His occupation too, that of ferryman (Sappho F 211 V), is a solar theme, as we see from the studies of Hermann Güntert on other mythological ferrymen.[113] As an interesting parallel to Phaon, I single out a solar deity in the *Rig-Veda,* Pūṣan,[114] who regularly functions as a psychopomp and who is at least once featured as traveling in golden boats (6.58.3); he is the wooer of his mother (6.55.5) and the lover of his sister (6.55.4, 5). A frequent and exclusive epithet of Pūṣan is *ā́ghr̥ṇi-* 'glowing, bright', comparable in meaning to *Pháōn* and *Phaéthōn.*

In light of these characteristics associated with the specialized Indic sun-god Pūṣan, we may note that the standard Indic sun-god Sūrya in the *Rig-Veda* is both son and consort of the dawn-goddess Uṣas (8.63.3, 7.78.3; 1.115.2, 7.75.5, etc.).[115] The 'fathers' of Pūṣan, the solar Divine Twins known as the Aśvin-s (*Rig-Veda* 10.85.14), share with Pūṣan his affinity with boats; they, too, are described as traveling about in boats (1.116.3).[116] The Aśvin-s are described as 'born differently' (*nā́nā jātáu* 5.73.4) and born 'here and there' (*ihéha jātā́* 1.181.4); one is the son of *Súmakha-* 'Good Warrior' and the other, the son of *Dyáus* 'Sky'.[117] In Yāska (Nirukta 12.1), a passage is quoted about the Aśvin-s where "one is

[110] See pp. 228–229.

[111] See pp. 229–230.

[112] See p. 235.

[113] See esp. Güntert 1909 and 1923.273. For the problem of the Aśvin-s (on whom see also pp. 112–113), see immediately below.

[114] On whom see pp. 97ff.

[115] In the Greek tradition, we have seen that Eos can be represented as the sister of Helios (Hesiod *Theogony* 371–374). See p. 248.

[116] More on the Aśvin-s at pp. 92–93, 112–113.

[117] The adjectives *makhá-* and *súmakha-* in Indic poetry serve as epithets denoting the heroic aspect of both men and gods.

called the son of Night, the other the son of Dawn." I view these images as solar symbols of day/night, bright/dark, immortal/mortal, alive/dead. When the two Aśvin-s are treated as a pair, on the other hand, only one side of their split personalities is revealed.[118] Accordingly, the two of them together are the sons of *Dyáus* 'Sky' (1.182.1, etc.) and the sons of Uṣas (3.39.3, to be supplemented by the comments of Sāyana concerning this passage).

As solar figures, Aśvin-s also represent the morning/evening star.[119] The female solar divinity Sūryā, Daughter of the Sun, relates to the Aśvin-s in their astral function, much as Uṣas the dawn-goddess relates to them in their solar function. The Aśvin-s are Sūryā's two husbands (4.43.6). As Douglas Frame has argued, the Twins' epithet *Nā́satyau* means 'retrievers', because they retrieved the light of the sun.[120] The essence of the *Nā́satyau* theme is that the morning star, as it rises from the horizon, 'recovers' the light of the sun, represented by Sūryā. The night before, the evening star had dipped beyond the horizon, plunging after the sinking sun, in order to effect its recovery, another morning, by the alter ego, the morning star.[121]

The Indic Aśvin-s are parallel to the Greek Dioskouroi, *Diòs koûroi* 'sons of Zeus, Dioscuri'.[122] Just as the Aśvin-s are named after the word for 'horse', *áśva-*, the Dioskouroi are known as *leukópōloi* 'bright horses' (e.g. Pindar *Pythian* 1.66).[123] We may note that the Dioskouroi have a horse called *Hárpagos* 'snatcher', son of *Podárgā* 'bright/swift of foot' (Stesichorus PMG 178.1); the latter name may be compared with that of the Harpy *Podárgē* = 'bright/swift of foot' who bore the horses of Achilles at the banks of Okeanos/Eridanos (*Iliad* XVI 150–151).[124] We may note, too, a Laconian ensemble of priestesses called *Leukippídes* 'bright horses' (Pausanias 3.16.1), who are associated with the cult of Helen (cf. Euripides *Helen* 1465–1466); Helen in this context functions as a dawn-goddess, analogous to or perhaps even identical with the dawn-goddess *Aōtis* in Alcman PMG 1.87.[125]

[118] For more on this characteristic of the Divine Twins, see Davidson 1987.103–104; cf. Wikander 1957.

[119] A central point argued by Güntert 1923.

[120] Frame 1978.134–152; see pp. 92–93, 112–113 above; see also Güntert p. 268.

[121] For a discussion of the Indic equivalent to the Greek Okeanos beyond the horizon, see pp. 98ff.

[122] See Güntert 1923.260–276.

[123] On the Old English traditions about the twin brothers *Hengest*, cognate of German *Hengst* 'stallion', and *Horsa*, as in latter-day English *horse*, who reportedly led the Saxons in their invasion of the British Isles, see Ward 1968.54–55 and Joseph 1983. On the Iranian *Lohrāsp* and *Goshtāsp*, a Dioscuric father-son dyad in the *Shāhnāma* of Ferdowsi, where the element *-āsp* is cognate with Indic *áśva-* 'horse', see Davidson 1987.

[124] See pp. 238–239, 244–245.

[125] For details and discussion, see Calame 1977 1:326–330, 2:124–125, who also argues

To return to our current center of attention, the solar figure Phaon in the poetics of Sappho: another solar theme associated with Phaon is his plunge from a white rock, an act that is parallel to the solar plunge of Phaethon into the Eridanos. We have seen that the Eridanos is an analogue of the Okeanos, the boundary delimiting light and darkness, life and death, wakefulness and sleep, consciousness and unconsciousness. We have also seen that the White Rock is another mythical landmark delimiting the same opposites and that these two landmarks are mystical coefficients in Homeric diction (*Odyssey* xxiv 11). Even the Phaethon figure is connected with the White Rock, in that his "father" Kephalos is supposed to have jumped off Cape Leukas (Strabo 10.2.9 C452)[126] and is connected with the placename *Thórikos* (Apollodorus 2.4.7).[127] The theme of plunging is itself overtly solar, as we see from Homeric diction:

> ἐν δ' ἔπεσ' Ὠκεανῷ λαμπρὸν φάος Ἠελίοιο
>
> *Iliad* VIII 485
>
> and the bright light of Helios plunged into the Okeanos.

In the Epic Cycle the lover of Klymene is not Helios but "Kephalos son of Deion" (Κεφάλῳ τῷ Δηΐονος *Nostoi* F 4 Allen),[128] a figure whose name matches that of Kephalos son of Deioneus, the one who leapt from the white rock of Leukas (Strabo 10.2.9 C452) and who hails from Thorikos (Apollodorus 2.4.7).[129]

If indeed the Phaon and Adonis myths operate on solar themes, it remains to ask about the relevance of Aphrodite. Most important of all, how do we interpret Aphrodite's plunge from the White Rock? We hear of her doing so out of love for Adonis (Ptolemaios Chennos by way of Photius *Bibliotheca* 152–153 Bekker),[130] and the act itself may be connected with her known function as substitute for the Indo-European dawn-goddess of the Greeks, Eos. As we have seen, Aphrodite has even usurped the epithet of Eos, *Diòs thugátēr* 'Daughter of Sky', as well as the roles that go with the epithet. From the Homeric standpoint, Aphrodite is actually the *Diòs thugátēr* par excellence, in that even her "mother's"

---

that the theme of radiant horses is a sacred symbol for the dawn, a cult topic shared by the figure of Helen with the Leukippides, who in myth are consorts of the Dioskouroi, brothers of Helen.

126 See p. 230.

127 See p. 232.

128 The son of Klymene and Kephalos is named as Iphiklos (*Nostoi* F 4 Allen).

129 See p. 232.

130 See p. 229.

name is *Diṓnē* (*Iliad* V 370, 381). It still remains, however, to explain Aphrodite's plunge from the White Rock as a feature characteristic of a surrogate Indo-European dawn-goddess.

Here we may do well to look toward Aphrodite's older, Near Eastern, heritage. As the Greek heiress to the functions of the Semitic fertility goddess Ištar, Aphrodite has as her astral symbol the planet of Ištar, better known to us as Venus.[131] The planet Venus is of course the same as *Hésperos* the Evening Star and *Heṓsphoros* ('dawn-bearer', *Ēṓs*- bearer') the Morning Star. In the evening Hesperos sets after sunset; in the morning Heosphoros rises before sunrise. We have the testimony of Sappho's near contemporary, Ibycus (PMG 331), that Hesperos and Heosphoros were by this time known to be one and the same. From the Indo-European standpoint, on the other hand, Hesperos and Heosphoros must be Divine Twins, as represented by the Dioskouroi, the Greek 'Sons of Zeus' who are cognates of the Indic Aśvin-s.[132] At the battle of Aigospotamoi, there is supposed to have been an epiphany of the Dioskouroi in the form of stars, on either side of Lysander's admiral ship; after their victory the Spartans dedicated two stars of gold at Delphi (Plutarch *Lysander* 12, 18).

In the poetics of Sappho, the Indo-European model of the Morning Star and Evening Star merges with the Near Eastern model of the Planet Aphrodite. On the one hand, Sappho's Hesperos is a nuptial star, as we know directly from the fragment 104 V and indirectly from the celebrated hymenaeus 'wedding-song' of Catullus 62, *Vesper adest.* Since Hesperos is the evening aspect of the astral Aphrodite, its setting into the horizon, beyond which is Okeanos, could have inspired the image of a plunging Aphrodite. If we imagine Aphrodite diving into the Okeanos after the sun, it follows that she will rise in the morning, bringing after her the sun of a new day. This image is precisely what the Hesiodic scholia preserve to explain the myth of Aphrodite and Phaethon:

> ὁ ἠῷος ἀστήρ, ὁ <u>ἀνάγων</u> τὴν ἡμέραν καὶ τὸν Φαέθοντα
>
> Scholia to Hesiod *Theogony* 990
>
> the star of Eos, the one that <u>brings back to light and life [verb *an-ágō*]</u> the day and Phaethon, Aphrodite[133]

For the mystical meaning of *an-ágō* as 'bring back the light and life [from

[131] Scherer 1953.78–84, 90, 92, 94.

[132] Güntert 1924.266–267. See pp. 255ff.

[133] Both Wilamowitz 1913.37n3 and Diggle 1970.15n1 find this statement incomprehensible.

the dead]', I cite the contexts of this verb in Hesiod *Theogony* 626 (εἰς φάος 'into the light'), Plato *Republic* 521c (εἰς φῶς 'to light'), Aeschylus *Agamemnon* 1023 (τῶν φθιμένων 'from the realm of the dead'), and so on.[134]

From Menander F 258K, we infer that Sappho spoke of herself as diving from the White Rock, crazed with love for Phaon. The implications of this image are cosmic. The "I" of Sappho's poetry is vicariously projecting her identity into the goddess Aphrodite, who loves the native Lesbian hypostasis of the Sun-God himself. By diving from the White Rock, the "I" of Sappho does what Aphrodite does in the form of Evening Star, diving after the sunken Sun in order to retrieve him, another morning, in the form of Morning Star. If we imagine her pursuing the Sun the night before, she will be pursued in turn the morning after. There is a potential here for *amor uersus*, a theme that haunts the poetry of Sappho elsewhere:

καὶ γὰρ αἰ φεύγει, ταχέως διώξει

Sappho F 1.21 V

for even if she now flees, soon she will pursue

Sappho's special association with Aphrodite is apparent throughout her poetry. The very first poem of the Sapphic corpus is, after all, an intense prayer to Aphrodite, where the goddess is implored to be the *súmmakhos* 'battle-ally' of the poetess (F 1.28 V). The "I" of Sappho pictures herself and Aphrodite as parallel rather than reciprocal agents:

ὄσσα δέ μοι τέλεσσαι θῦμος ἰμέρρει, τέλεσον

Sappho F 1.26–27 V

and however many things my spirit [*thūmós*] yearns to
accomplish [verb *teléō*, active], I pray that you [Aphrodite]
accomplish [verb *teléō*, active]

I draw attention to the wording τέλεσσαι 'to accomplish', an active infinitive instead of the expected passive τελέσθην 'to be accomplished'.[135] If someone else needs something done by Aphrodite,

[134] See again Frame 1978.150–162 on the epithet of the Aśvin-s, *Nā́satyau*, which he interprets as 'they who bring back to life and light'; for the Aśvin-s as Evening/Morning Star, see pp. 255–256.

[135] For a similar effect, we may compare the opposition of active *faciam* 'that I do' and passive *fieri* 'to be done', both referring to the verbs *odi et amo* in Catullus 85.

Sappho's poetry opts for the passive infinitive τελέσθην 'to be accomplished', not active τέλεσσαι 'to accomplish':

> Κύπρι καὶ] Νηρήιδες ἀβλάβη[ν μοι
> τὸν κασί]γνητον δ[ό]τε τυίδ' ἴκεσθα[ι
> κὤσσα F]οι θύμῳ κε θέλῃ γένεσθαι
> πάντα τε]λέσθην
>
> Sappho F 5.1–4 V

> Aphrodite and Nereids, grant that my brother
> come back here unharmed,
> and that however many things he wishes in his spirit [*thūmós*] to happen
> may all be accomplished [verb *teléō*, passive]

The figure of Sappho projects mortal identity onto the divine explicitly as well as implicitly. I cite the following examples from one poem:

> πόλ]λακι τυίδε [ν]ῶν ἔχοισα
> . . . . . .
> σε θέᾳ σ' ἰκέλαν ἀρι-
> γνώτᾳ, σᾷ δὲ μάλιστ' ἔχαιρε μόλπᾳ
> . . . . . .
> ε]ὔμαρ[ες μ]ὲν οὐ[κ] ἄ[μ]μι θέαισι μόρ-
> φαν ἐπή[ρατ]ον ἐξίσω-
> σθαι
>
> Sappho F 96.2–5, 21–23 V

> Many times turning your attention [*nóos*] in this direction
> . . . . . .
> you, a likeness of the well-known goddess.
> And it is in your song and dance that she delighted especially.
> . . . . . .
> It is not easy for us
> to become equal in lovely shape
> to the goddesses

An even more significant example is Sappho F 58.25–26 V, two verses quoted by Athenaeus 687b. Sappho is cited as a woman who professes not to separate *tò kalón* 'what is beautiful' from *habrótēs* 'luxuriance':

> ἐγὼ δὲ φίλημμ' ἀβροσύναν, [. . .] τοῦτο, καί μοι

τὸ λά⌞μπρον ἔρως[136] ἀελίω καὶ τὸ κά⌟λον λέ⌞λ⌟ογχε

Sappho F 58.25–26 V

But I love luxuriance [*(h)abrosunā*]. . . . this,
and lust for the sun has won me brightness and beauty.[137]

From *Oxyrhynchus Papyri* 1787 we can see that these two verses come at the end of a poem alluding to mythical topics. According to Lobel and Page, verses 19 and following refer to Tithonos (F 58 LP). Be that as it may, we do see images about growing old, with hair turning white and the knees losing their strength (Sappho F 58.13–15 V). The fragmentary nature of the papyrus prevents certainty about the speaker and the speaker's predicament, but somebody is feeling helpless, asking rhetorically what can be done, and bemoaning some impossibility (58.17–18). Also, the Lesbian Eos is mentioned: βροδόπαχυν Αὔων 'rosy-armed Dawn' (58.19).

As a coda to this poem, the last two verses, which I interpret as proclaiming Sappho's 'lust for the sun', amount to a personal and artistic manifesto. The *(h)abrosúnā* 'luxuriance' of Sappho transcends the banal discussion of Athenaeus, who quotes these two verses. For Sappho, *(h)ábros* 'luxuriant' is the epithet of Adonis (F 140 V), as also of the Kharites 'Graces' (128 V), on whose chariot Aphrodite rides (194 V). At Sappho F 2.13–16 V, *(h)ábrōs* (14) is the adverb describing the scene as Aphrodite is asked to pour nectar. The use of *(h)ábros* 'luxuriant' / *(h)abrosúnā* 'luxuriance' in Sappho reminds us of the Roman neoterics and their allusive use of *lepidus/lepos* in expressing their artistic identity. As for Sappho's 'lust for the sun' and 'love of *(h)abrosúnā* [luxuriance]', these themes combine profound personal and artistic ideals. In verses preceding the coda, the words of Sappho perhaps alluded to Phaon as an old man, compared with Tithonos. Or perhaps Phaon was son of Tithonos. We do hear of a myth where Phaethon is son of Tithonos (Apollodorus 3.14.3); just as Phaethon was son of *Ēṓs* 'Dawn', perhaps Phaon was son of the Lesbian cognate, *Aúōs* 'Dawn' mentioned in the same poem, Sappho F 58.19. The expression ἔσχατα γᾶς φέροισα['[she], taking to the ends of the earth' in the following

[136] Cf. Hamm 1957 § 241.

[137] This interpretation differs from that of e.g. Campbell 1982.101, who reads τὠελίω (τὸ ἀελίω), agreeing with τὸ λάμπρον. Even if we were to accept the reading τὠελίω, we could theoretically interpret the crasis along the lines of τῶ ἀελίω = τὠελίω (cf. e.g. πω ἔσλον = πὦσλον at Alcaeus 69.5 V; cf. Hamm p. § 91e).

verse 20 of this poem, along with ἔμαρψε 'snatched' in the following verse 21, remind us of Okeanos / Eridanos and Harpies.

In any case, the fact remains that there is a Lesbian myth about Phaon as an old man (Sappho F 211 V); significantly, in this same myth Aphrodite herself assumes the form of an old woman, whom the old Phaon generously ferries across a strait (*ibid.*). I suspect that the figure of Sappho identifies herself with this figure of an old woman. Similarly, we may compare the myth of the mourning Aphrodite's plunge from the White Rock out of love for the dead Adonis (Ptolemaios Chennos by way of Photius *Bibliotheca* 152–153 Bekker)[138] as pertinent to the poetics of Sappho, where the explicit theme of mourning for Adonis (F 168 V) may be connected with the latent theme of Sappho's self-identification with Aphrodite.

In short, there is a mythical precedent for an aging lady to love Phaon. The implicit hope is retrieved youth. After Aphrodite crossed the strait, she became a beautiful goddess again, conferring youth and beauty on Phaon, too (again, Sappho F 211 V). For all these reasons, perhaps, Sappho loves Phaon.

[138] See pp. 229ff.

CHAPTER 10

On the Death of Actaeon

The myth of Actaeon the hunter is famous from the version in Ovid *Metamorphoses* 3.13 and following, where Artemis literally turns Actaeon into a stag. The hapless victim is then torn to shreds by his own hounds. One critic has claimed that the same theme recurs in Stesichorus PMG 236.[1] This fragment has been derived from the following passage:

> Στησίχορος δὲ ὁ Ἱμεραῖος ἔγραψεν ἐλάφου περιβαλεῖν δέρμα Ἀκταίωνι τὴν θεόν, παρασκευάζουσάν οἱ τὸν ἐκ κυνῶν θάνατον ἵνα δὴ μὴ γυναῖκα Σεμέλην λάβοι
>
> Pausanias 9.2.3

> Stesichorus of Himera wrote that the goddess [Artemis] flung the hide of a stag around Actaeon, arranging for him a death that came from his own hounds so that he might not take Semele as wife.

If we follow this interpretation, the expression ἐλάφου περιβαλεῖν δέρμα Ἀκταίωνι 'flung the hide of a stag around Actaeon' reflects the actual words of Stesichorus, and it means figuratively that the goddess, by flinging the *dérma* 'hide' of a stag around Actaeon, thereby transformed the *dérma* 'hide' of Actaeon into that of a stag. For this purportedly traditional usage of *peribállō* 'fling around [someone]' in the sense of 'transform', a striking parallel passage has been adduced, where we find the gods in the act of transforming Philomele into a nightingale:[2]

[1] Rose 1931.
[2] *Ibid.*

περέβαλον γάρ οἱ πτεροφόρον δέμας

Aeschylus *Agamemnon* 1147

for they [the gods] have flung [verb *peribállō*] around her [Philomele] a feather-wearing body [*démas*]

While conceding that the verb *peribállō* implies 'transform' in this passage, another critic rejects the argument that this usage applies also to the context of Stesichorus PMG 236.[3] Rather, he reads *peribállō* in the Stesichorus fragment to mean that Artemis merely flung a deerskin around Actaeon. For support, he cites the evidence from Greek iconography, where the motif of a dying Actaeon clad in deerskin is clearly attested.[4] As a prime example, he singles out a metope from Temple E in Selinus (middle fifth century B.C.),[5] which features Actaeon wearing the decrskin and his hounds lunging more at it than at him.[6]

Such evidence, however, is inconclusive: the theme of Actaeon's wearing rather than having the hide of a stag may be a *visual* as well as *verbal* metaphor. On the verbal level *peribállō* implies clothing, as in the Philomele passage of Aeschylus quoted above. The gods transform Philomele into a nightingale, but the words of Aeschylus represent the action as if the gods *clothed* her with the *démas* 'body' of a nightingale. The meaning of *peribállō* as 'clothe' is commonplace in Greek (*Odyssey* v 231, xxii 148; Herodotus 1.152.1, 9.109.1; Euripides *Iphigeneia in Tauris* 1150, and so on), and the derivative *períblēma* actually means 'garment' (Aristotle *Problemata* 870a27, etc.). I propose, then, that the wording *peribállō* in Stesichorus PMG 236 is also metaphorical: ἐλάφου περιβαλεῖν δέρμα Ἀκταίωνι '[that the goddess] flung the hide of a stag around Actaeon', meaning that the goddess transformed him into a stag.

In favor of the nonmetaphorical interpretation, the objection still remains that "δέρμα [*dérma* 'skin'] is not the same as δέμας [*démas* 'body']."[7] This objection does not reckon, however, with the traditional theme of equating one's identity with one's "hide." The lexical evidence of the Indo-European languages reveals traces of this equation. We may consider, for example, a cognate of Indic *tvác-* 'hide' and Greek *sákos* 'cowhide-shield', namely, Hittite *tweka-*: besides meaning 'body', this word is also regularly used to designate 'person, self, one's own self'. We

[3] Bowra 1961.99–100.

[4] Bowra pp. 99–100, 125–126, with the alternative representation of Actaeon as sprouting antlers also taken into account.

[5] Richter 1950 fig. 411.

[6] Bowra 1961.125.

[7] Bowra p. 100.

may consider also Latin *uersipellis*, meaning literally 'he whose hide is turned' (from verb *uertō* 'turn' and noun *pellis* 'hide, skin'). In Plautus *Amphitruo* 123, *uersipellis* designates Jupiter when he transformed himself into the human Amphitruo; in Pliny *Natural History* 8.34 and Petronius 62, *uersipellis* means 'werewolf'.

Thus we have comparative evidence in favor of the argument that the text of Stesichorus PMG 236 reflects a traditional usage, which we can interpret metaphorically to mean that Actaeon was indeed transformed into a stag. The iconographical evidence may be explained as an equally symbolic means of representing the same conception as we find in the poetic evidence.

One last problem remains. It has been argued that such expressions as *peribállō* in Stesichorus PMG 236 "are ultimately not metaphorical" on the grounds that the Actaeon *myth* seems to be connected with *rituals* of hunting.[8] If I understand this argument, its underlying assumption is that metaphor must be incompatible with ritual. Such an assumption seems to me unjustified: for a ritual participant to wear the skin of a stag in a ritual context is potentially just as much a matter of metaphor as it is for an audience of myth to hear that Artemis flung the deerskin on Actaeon's body.

[8]Renner 1978.286n16, citing e.g. Burkert 1983.111–114.

PART III

THE HELLENIZATION OF INDO-EUROPEAN SOCIAL IDEOLOGY

CHAPTER 11

Poetry and the Ideology of the Polis: The Symbolism of Apportioning Meat

Φιλόχορος δέ φησιν κρατήσαντας Λακεδαιμονίους Μεσσηνίων διὰ τὴν Τυρταίου στρατηγίαν ἐν ταῖς στρατείαις ἔθος ποιήσασθαι, ἂν δειπνοποιήσονται καὶ παιωνίσωσιν, ᾄδειν καθ' ἕνα ⟨τὰ⟩ Τυρταίου· κρίνειν δὲ τὸν πολέμαρχον καὶ ἆθλον διδόναι τῷ νικῶντι κρέας

Philochorus FGH 328 F 216 from Athenaeus 630 f

Philochorus says that the Spartans, after having defeated the Messenians on account of the leadership of Tyrtaeus, instituted a custom in their military organization: whenever they would prepare dinner and perform paeans, they would each take turns singing the poems of Tyrtaeus. The polemarch would serve as judge and award a cut of meat to the winner.

This passage, if its testimony is to be believed, illustrates an ideology basic to the polis, namely, the notion of community through the participation of social equals. The ritual that is being described, the awarding of a cut of meat to the winner of a contest, dramatizes such an ideology. As the studies of Jean-Pierre Vernant and Marcel Detienne have shown, the archaic Greek custom of competing for prizes in contests presupposes the communalization of property that is to be apportioned and distributed in a manner that is egalitarian in ideology—but without excluding the option of awarding special privileges.[1] Where the prize is a cut of meat, the communalization takes place through the central act that integrates the community, namely, the sacrifice of a victim and the apportioning of its meat.[2]

[1]Vernant 1985.202–260, esp. pp. 210–215; Detienne 1973.82–99.

[2]Detienne and Vernant 1969, in particular the article by Detienne, "Pratiques

In the passage under consideration the prize is being awarded for the best performance of the poetry of Tyrtaeus. It is my contention that the very contents of this poetry are pertinent to the ritual of awarding the cut of meat. The poetics of Tyrtaeus in particular and elegiac poetics in general amount to a formal expression of the ideology of the polis, in that the notion of social order is envisaged as the equitable distribution of communal property among equals. Giovanni Cerri adduces a striking illustration from the elegiac poetry of Theognis, in a passage where the poet condemns the breakdown of the social order:[3]

χρήματα δ' ἁρπάζουσι βίῃ, κόσμος δ' ἀπόλωλεν,
δασμὸς δ' οὐκέτ' ἴσος γίνεται ἐς τὸ μέσον

Theognis 677–678

They seize possessions by force, and order [*kósmos*] has been destroyed.
There is no longer an equitable distribution [*ísos dasmós*],[4]
directed at the center [*es tò méson*].[5]

In the language of elegiac poetry, the *dasmós* 'distribution' is envisaged specifically as the distribution of food at a feast, as we see from Solon's condemnation of the elite for their destroying the social order:

δήμου θ' ἡγεμόνων ἄδικος νόος, οἷσιν ἑτοῖμον
ὕβριος ἐκ μεγάλης ἄλγεα πολλὰ παθεῖν.
οὐ γὰρ ἐπίστανται κατέχειν κόρον οὐδὲ παρούσας
εὐφροσύνας κοσμεῖν δαιτὸς ἐν ἡσυχίῃ

Solon F 4.7–10 W [= F 3 GP]

The intent of the leaders of the community[6] is without justice [*díkē*]. What

culinaires et esprit de sacrifice," pp. 10, 23–24; also the article by Detienne and Svenbro (1979), "Les loups au festin ou la Cité impossible," esp. pp. 219–222. To repeat, the apportioning and distribution of meat, though conducted in an egalitarian manner, does not exclude the option of awarding special privileges. See also Svenbro 1982, esp. pp. 954–955. Cf. Loraux 1981.616–617.

[3] Cerri 1969. For an analysis of Theognis 667–682, the poem in which this passage occurs: N 1985a.22–24.

[4] The *ísos* 'equal, equitable' of *ísos dasmós* refers to the *virtual* equality of the participants; cf. Detienne 1973.96.

[5] Cf. the paraphrase of *es tò méson* 'directed at the center' by Cerri 1969.103: 'under the control of the community'. This expression *es tò méson* 'directed at the center' evidently refers to an agonistic communalization of possessions that are marked for orderly distribution by the community. I cite Cerri's survey of parallel passages.

[6] I disagree with West 1974.68 that the expression 'leaders of the community [*dêmos*]' (as here and at Solon F 6.1 W = F 8 GP) means 'popular leaders' i.e. champions of democracy: see N 1985a.43–44. On *dêmos* in the sense of 'community', see p. 3n7 above.

is in store for them
is the experiencing of many pains as a result of their great
outrage [*húbris*].
For they do not know how to check insatiability or
to make order [*kósmos*] for the merriment [*euphrosúnē* plural][7] that goes on
in the serenity of the feast [*daís*].

The word *daís* 'feast' is derived from the verb *daíomai*, meaning 'divide, distribute, apportion'.[8] The very poem of Solon from which this passage is taken centers on the concept of *Eunomíā*, personified as a goddess (Solon F 4.32 W). Like the word *īsonomíā*,[9] *Eunomíā* is derived from the verb *némō*, meaning 'distribute, apportion'.[10] The same word *Eunomíā* is reported by Aristotle (*Politics* 1306b40) and Strabo (8.4.10 C362) as the name of a poem by Tyrtaeus concerning the constitution of Sparta (F 1–4 W).

The *daís* 'feast' that is described by Solon as being disrupted because of *húbris* 'outrage' is to be envisaged specifically as an occasion for the distribution of meat, as we see from the following condemnation of *húbris* in the elegiac poetry of Theognis:

δειμαίνω μὴ τήνδε πόλιν Πολυπαίδη ὕβρις
ἥ περ Κενταύρους ὠμοφάγους ὀλέσῃ

Theognis 541–542

I fear, son of Polypaos, that *húbris* will destroy this polis
[the same *húbris*] that destroyed the Centaurs, eaters of raw meat.[11]

In the *Odyssey* (xxi 295–304), the leader of the suitors, Antinoos himself, retells a myth about the disruption of a feast by the Centaur Eurytion—a disruption that precipitated the battle of the Centaurs and Lapiths. This retelling entails an irony unintended by Antinoos, since the suitors themselves violate all the norms of a *daís* 'feast', an activity

[7] On the programmatic connotations of *euphrosúnē* 'merriment' as the occasion for poetry at a feast: N 1979a.19, 92 (with § 39n7), 236 (with § 15n5).

[8] Cf. N 1979a.127–128 et passim, with bibliography.

[9] For documentation and bibliography: Cerri 1969.103–104.

[10] For an illuminating note on the meaning of *eunomíā* in Solon (F 4.32 W) and in Aristotle (*Politics* 1294a4–7), see Svenbro 1982.962n27, who also discusses the differences in political nuance between *eunomíā* and *īsonomíā*.

[11] Cf. Apollodorus 2.5.4: the Centaur Pholos offers roast meat to his guest Herakles, while he himself eats his own portions of meat raw (αὐτὸς δὲ ὠμοῖς ἐχρῆτο). Cf. also Theognis 54, with an implied description of debased aristocrats in language that suits the Cyclopes (cf. *Odyssey* ix 215); discussion in N 1985a.44 § 29n4 (also p. 51 § 39n2).

that conventionally centers on the ritual core of the sacrifice of a victim and the distribution of its meat.[12]

Thus the evidence of elegiac poetry, as supplemented by that of epic poetry, implies a coherent picture of *dī́kē* 'justice' in terms of an orderly apportioning of meat at a feast that centers on a correctly executed sacrifice; conversely, *húbris* 'outrage' is represented as the disruption and perversion of this process.[13] Given that the poems of Tyrtaeus, one of which is even called *Eunomíā* (as we have seen), are representative of the function of elegiac poetry as an expression of the polis, the performance of this poet is ideologically suited to the ritual reported by Philochorus, namely, the awarding of a cut of meat to the one who gives the best performance.

I therefore call into question the opinions expressed on this matter by Felix Jacoby, who thought that the practice reported by Philochorus cannot be dated further back than the early fourth century B.C.[14] Jacoby argued *ex silentio* that, in the fifth century B.C. and in the first decade of the fourth, there was nothing known about Tyrtaeus in Sparta.[15] According to Jacoby, the references to Tyrtaeus by the likes of Philochorus (FGH 328 F 215, 216; second half of the fourth century B.C., first half of the third), the orator Lycurgus (*Against Leocrates* 106–107), and Plato

[12] On the suitors' violation of social norms through violation of the *daís* 'feast': Saïd 1979.

[13] Aesop *Fable* 348 Perry, about the Wolf as Lawgiver and the Ass, is comparable to the story in Herodotus 3.142–143, where Maiandrios, successor to the tyrant Polycrates of Samos, declares to the assembly of citizens that he will place his political power *es méson* 'under the control of the community', proclaiming *īsonomíā* (3.142.3). On *es tò méson* 'directed at the center' in the sense of 'under the control of the community', see p. 270n5. As Detienne and Svenbro point out (1979.220–221, 230), both the wolf as lawgiver and the tyrant commit the same perversion of the principles of community: just as the wolf as lawgiver reserves portions of meat for himself *before* the procedure of placing all seized meat *es tò méson* (Aesop *Fable* 348.4), so also Maiandrios reserves special privileges for himself *before* placing his political power *es méson* (Herodotus 3.142.3). On the wolf as the symbolic antithesis of the Law, see the bibliography assembled by Detienne and Svenbro 1979; also Davidson 1979 and Grottanelli 1981, esp. p. 56. On the possible etymology of *Lukoûrgos* (= Lycurgus), lawgiver of the Spartans, as 'he who wards off the wolf': Burkert 1979a.165–166n24.

[14] Jacoby FGH IIIb vol. 1 pp. 583–584 and IIIb vol. 2 pp. 479–480. See also Jacoby 1918, esp. pp. 1–12.

[15] Jacoby thought that Herodotus did not know of the poetry of Tyrtaeus, on the grounds that there is no mention of him in the discussion of how Sparta achieved *eunomíā* in Herodotus 1.65–66. And yet, what Herodotus says does leave room for the possibility that he did indeed know of Tyrtaeus. Herodotus rejects a version of the Lycurgus story according to which the lawgiver got his laws from the Delphic Oracle, preferring a version that he attributes to the contemporary Spartans themselves, to the effect that Lycurgus got his laws from Crete. In my opinion, this version leaves room for the notion that both Lycurgus and Tyrtaeus made contributions to the constitution of Sparta—Lycurgus with laws from Crete and Tyrtaeus with laws from the Delphic Oracle (see Tyrtaeus F 4.1–2 W).

himself (*Laws* 629b) are based on an Athenian transmission of Tyrtaeus, as supposedly evidenced by the tradition that the poet himself was a native Athenian.[16]

But this is to misunderstand the accretive nature of myths about poets and their poetry: even if we concede that the detail about the Athenian provenience of Tyrtaeus reflects an anachronistic elaboration, it does not follow that the other details of the Tyrtaeus story as reported by Athenian sources are likewise anachronistic.[17] Moreover, there is reason to doubt the notion that the story of an Athenian Tyrtaeus is necessarily an Athenian tradition. There is evidence to suggest that the stories about the foreign proveniences of Sparta's poets are not foreign but native Spartan traditions, suited to the overall ideology of the polis.[18] Besides, it is a common traditional theme that the culture hero of a given polis is really a foreigner or at least one who introduces his cultural boon from a foreign source.[19]

In the case of stories about cultural boons introduced from foreign sources, there is an interesting example in the elegiac poetry of Theognis: here the poet's model of social cohesion is the foundation not of his native Megara but of Thebes (Theognis 15–18), which is the city where the poet represents his own tomb, in the mode of an epigram:

Αἴθων μὲν γένος εἰμί, πόλιν δ' εὐτείχεα Θήβην

[16] References to the Athenian provenience of Tyrtaeus: Philochorus FGH 328 F 215 and Callisthenes FGH 124 F 24 from Strabo 8.4.10 C362.

[17] From the standpoint of literary history as well, one can argue against Jacoby's notion that there was a lacuna in the transmission of Tyrtaeus in the fifth century. There is reason to believe that the poetry of Tyrtaeus—and all archaic elegiac poetry, for that matter—was being continually recomposed in the process of transmission through performance (see N 1985a.46–51). The factor of continual recomposition would account for the anachronistic accretions of given passages and testimonia.

[18] Note the parallelisms of themes in the testimonia about the foreign proveniences of archaic Sparta's poets, as collected by Fontenrose1978: Q 18 (Tyrtaeus), Q 53 (Terpander), and Q 54 (Thaletas); cf. also Q 118. For the testimonia on these and other poets of Sparta, including Alcman, see Calame 1977 2:34–36. As Calame emphasizes (p. 35), the poetry of all these poets is integral to the ritual complex of Spartan festivals (cf. Brelich 1969.186ff.). I would argue, therefore, that such traditions as the report about the Lydian provenience of Alcman (PMG 13a; also PMG 1 Schol. B., Velleius Paterculus 1.18.2, Aelian *Varia Historia* 12.50) must be correlated with the fact that there were Spartan rituals that centered on Lydian themes, such as τῶν Λυδῶν πομπή, the 'Procession of the Lydians' mentioned in Plutarch *Aristeides* 17.10 in connection with the cult of Artemis Orthia. We may compare an event known as the "Dance of the Lydian Maidens," at a festival of Artemis at Ephesus (Autocrates F 1 Kock, from Aelian *De natura animalium* 12.9 and Aristophanes *Clouds* 599–600; see the discussion of Calame 1977 1:178–185). In this case, it seems clear to me that the term "Lydian Maidens" in fact designates a ritual role played by the local girls of Ephesus.

[19] For a brief survey of examples, see Pfister 1909 1:130–133: "Verehrung des fremden Heros wegen seiner Verdienste."

οἰκῶ, πατρῴας γῆς ἀπερυκόμενος

Theognis 1209–1210

I am *Aíthōn* by birth, and I have an abode in well-walled Thebes,
since I have been exiled from my native land.[20]

That the poet here pictures himself as already dead becomes clear from the verses that immediately follow: after some further cryptic words that are beyond the scope of this inquiry (Theognis 1211–1213), the poet reiterates that he is an exile (1213–1214), and then he indicates overtly that his abode is next to the Plain of Lethe (1215–1216).[21]

These themes are strikingly analogous to what we find in the story of Lycurgus: the Spartan lawgiver is said to have introduced his laws from a foreign source, in this case, Crete (Herodotus 1.65.4; Plutarch *Lycurgus* 4.1), which is where he returns in self-imposed exile and starves himself to death in order to make these laws permanent (Plutarch *Lycurgus* 29.8, 31; Ephorus FGH 70 F 175, from Aelian *Varia Historia* 13.23).[22] The theme of Lycurgus' death by hunger brings us back to the name *Aíthōn* assumed by Theognis as an exile speaking from his tomb (1209–1210). The adjective *aíthōn* can mean 'burning [with hunger]' and is used as an epithet for characters known for their ravenous hunger, such as Erysikhthon (Hesiod F 43 MW).[23] Odysseus himself assumes the name *Aíthōn* (*Odyssey* xix 183), and he does so in a context of assuming the stance of a would-be poet (xix 203, in conjunction with xiv 124–125 and vii 215–221). This poet-like stance of Odysseus is symbolized by the concept of the *gastḗr* 'belly' (as at *Odyssey* vii 216): hunger can impel a man to use ambiguous discourse in order to ingratiate himself with his audience—and thus feed his *gastḗr*.[24] But this ambiguous discourse of the poet, the technical word for which is *aînos* (as at *Odyssey* xiv 508), is not

[20] For an analysis of this passage, see N 1985a.76–81. Note especially the parallel usages of *oikéō* 'I have an abode' in this passage of Theognis (1210) and in Sophocles *Oedipus at Colonus* 27, 28, 92, 627, 637. In N pp. 76–77, I argue that *oikéō* in such contexts refers to the establishing of a corpse in a sacred precinct for the purposes of hero cult. On historical evidence for the cultural debt of pre-Dorian Megara to Thebes, see Hanell 1934.95–97.

[21] On the poetic convention that pictures the poet who speaks as one who is already dead, with further discussion of Theognis 1209–1210 and related passages, see N pp. 68–81. On the convention of representing the poet's poetry as his own *sêma* 'tomb', see p. 222n62. In this connection, we may note that elegiac poetry, as represented by the likes of Theognis and Tyrtaeus, is a reflex of the poetic traditions of lamentation as removed from the tribal context and as appropriated and reshaped by the polis. On this subject, see Edmunds 1985.

[22] N pp. 31–32; cf. Szegedy-Maszak 1978.199–209, esp. p. 208.

[23] For further elaboration: N pp. 76–91.

[24] See p. 44. Cf. Svenbro 1976.50–59.

just a negative concept. It can also be a positive social force: when the disguised king Odysseus is begging for food at the feasts of the impious suitors, he is actually speaking not only in the mode of an *aînos*[25] but also in the role of an exponent of *díkē* 'justice'.[26] The role of Aesop, master of the *aînos* in both the general sense and in the specific sense of 'fable',[27] is analogous: he uses this discourse to indicate cryptically what is right and wrong,[28] and we must keep in mind the *aítion* 'cause' of his death, which was that he ridiculed the ritualized greed of a Delphic rite where meat is being apportioned in a disorderly and frenzied manner (*Oxyrhynchus Papyri* 1800).[29] In the praise poetry of Pindar, the technical word for which is likewise *aînos* (in the testimony of the poetry itself),[30] the concept of the *gastḗr* can again be seen as a positive social force (*Isthmian* 1.49).

In elegiac poetry as well, we have seen that the poet as exponent of *díkē* 'justice' associates the social order of the polis with the orderly apportioning of meat at a feast. At the beginning of this presentation we observed this association in the negative context of the poet's condemning the behavior of the elite, as when Solon compares their acts to the disruption of a feast or when Theognis compares the perpetrators of disruption to unruly Centaurs. There is also an important positive context in the description by Theognis of the foundation of Thebes by Kadmos, which is celebrated by the poet as the inauguration of his own poetry (15–18):[31] myth has it that the actual occasion for the foundation was a feast, featuring an egalitarian distribution of food (Nonnus *Dionysiaka* 5.30–32). And the bride of Kadmos the Founder is none other than *Harmoníā* incarnate (cf. Hesiod *Theogony* 937, 975).[32]

In sum, the Spartan ritual practice involving the award of a cut of meat as reported by Philochorus is perfectly in accord with the ideology of the archaic polis as expressed in the elegiac poetry of Tyrtaeus. To perform the poetry of an exponent of *díkē* 'justice' is perfectly in accord with the prize of meat that is awarded to the winning performer.

[25] For documentation, see N 1979a.231–242.

[26] N pp. 231–242. On Odysseus as the quintessentially just king, see esp. *Odyssey* xix 109–114.

[27] N p. 239 § 18n2.

[28] N pp. 281–284.

[29] N pp. 284–288.

[30] N pp. 222–223, following Detienne 1973.21.

[31] Quoted, with commentary, in N 1985a.27–29.

[32] Elaboration in N p. 28.

CHAPTER 12

Mythical Foundations of Greek Society and the Concept of the City-State

The kinship terminology of the various Indo-European languages, as outlined in Emile Benveniste's *Le vocabulaire des institutions indo-européennes* (1969), shows clearly that the basis of Indo-European social organization was the tribe.[1] For the word "tribe," I find the working definition of Montgomery Watt, in his study of pre-Islamic Arab society, particularly useful: "a body of people linked together by kinship, whether in the male or in the female line."[2] The kinship, of course, may be a matter of confederation, not just genetic affiliation, and the common ancestry of the given body of people may be a matter of mythopoeic thinking, not just reality.[3]

The problem is, efforts to study the Indo-European heritage of tribal organization have been impeded by the fact that most Indo-European languages are attested in the historical context of societies that happen to reflect what we recognize as institutions of a state, not of a tribe. At the present time there is much uncertainty, particularly in the case of the ancient Greek evidence, where the current consensus among specialists in archaic and Classical Greek history is that the institutions of the Greek *pólis* 'city-state' cannot be derived from the institutions of any tribal form of society. The object of my presentation is to argue against this consensus and to show that the ancient Greek evidence affords a

[1]For a detailed study of Indo-European kinship terminology, with a rich bibliography, see Szemerényi 1978.

[2]Watt 1962.153.

[3]Watt p. 153. For an instructive essay on descent and symbolic filiation, see Moore 1964; also Calame 1987.

particularly valuable comparative insight into the nature of Indo-European society.

To illustrate the current consensus against the notion of a tribal heritage in the Greek polis, I cite the detailed book of Denis Roussel (1976). He deplores the equation, made by Classicists in general, between the notion of "tribe" and the Greek word *phūlḗ*,[4] which is glossed in the dictionary of Liddell and Scott as 'race, tribe'. As Roussel recognizes, the *phūlḗ* is in fact a subdivision of society in the polis, as we see from the traditional four-*phūlaí* system of Ionian cities and the traditional three- or four-*phūlaí* systems of Dorian cities. For Aristotle, it is hard even to imagine the existence of a polis without subdivisions into *phūlaí*, not to mention sub-subdivisions into *ph(r)ātríai* (*Politics* 1264a8). The fact that the *phūlḗ* was a distinctive feature of the polis but not of the *éthnos*[5] had led Max Weber to postulate that the *phūlḗ* was the invention, as it were, of the polis.[6] Even in myth, the *phūlaí* were treated as inventions made for and in the city (e.g. Ion institutes the four old *phūlaí* of Athens: Herodotus 5.66.2, Euripides *Ion* 1579–1588; Aletes institutes the eight *phūlaí* of Corinth: *Suda* π 225 Adler s.v. *pánta oktṓ*). Accordingly, the reasoning goes, the *phūlaí* were never tribes. For Roussel, if indeed the *phūlḗ* was a functional subdivision of the polis, there is then no reason to think that this institution was a reflex of tribal society.[7]

What is misleading here, I suggest, is the assumption that the reflex of the tribe—if there is to be a reflex at all—should be the *phūlḗ* of the polis. Rather, it should be the polis itself. We must keep in mind that, from an anthropological point of view, the concept of politics—as derived from the word *pólis*—is not incompatible with the concepts of tribe in general and kinship in particular.[8] Just like the polis, the tribe is a social totality—from the standpoint of the tribe. For example, Benveniste notes the semantics of Indic *viś-* 'tribe, people' and of the derivative *viśva-* 'all'.[9] And the totality of the polis, as Roussel's findings suggest, is

[4] Roussel 1976.163.

[5] For more on the *éthnos*, see Snodgrass 1980.42–47.

[6] Weber [1956].776–780; cf. Latte 1941.994–995.

[7] See esp. Roussel 1976.257–260.

[8] On tribal politics, see e.g. Gluckman 1965.

[9] Benveniste 1969 1:366. Note that the concept of *viś-* stands for a whole community *as ruled by a king:* see the discussion by Drekmeier 1962.20, 49. Cf. Old Persian *viθ* 'royal house, court'. There is a parallel concept in Old Irish, where the *tuath* 'tribe, people' is ruled by the *rí* 'king'. For the Irish evidence, see Byrne 1971, esp. p. 132; cf. also Dillon 1975.98–105. I should add that the reference to the choosing of a king by the *viśaḥ* [plural of *viś-*] in *Rig-Veda* 10.124.8 seems comparable to the choosing of an over-king by a grouping of *tuatha* in Old Irish traditions (on which see Byrne p. 133 and Dillon p. 105). In the diction of the *Rig-Veda* the theme of universal kingship as applicable to gods leads to an emphasis on the concept of over-kingship, so that a given god as *rājan-* 'king' is predominantly described as lord over *viśaḥ* (plural), not over any single *viś-*. The compound

the sum of its *phūlaí.* I would suggest, therefore, that if the polis developed from the tribe, then the *phūlḗ* developed from a subdivision of the tribe.

In this connection, we may consider the etymology of the Umbrian word *trifu-* 'tribe' (cognate of Latin *tribus*),[10] used correlatively with the word *tuta* 'city' or 'people' (cognate of Old Irish *tuath* 'tribe, people' and German *Deutsch*) in referring to the city of Iguvium (*Iguvine Tables* III 24–25, 29–30: *tutape(r) Iiuvina trefiper Iiuvina*).[11] As Benveniste argues,[12] Umbrian *trifu-* is apparently derived from a combination of *tri- and *bhu-, where the second element is cognate with the *phū-* of *phūlḗ.* As cognate concepts of a social totality subdivided into three parts, Benveniste connects the Greek place-name *Triphūlíā*[13] and the distinctly Dorian patterns of subdividing the citizens of the polis into three *phūlaí.*[14]

As for the Latin word *tribus,* it seems to have undergone a semantic shift of subcategorization:[15] instead of designating the totality of society, as is the case with the Umbrian cognate *trifu,* Latin *tribus* applies to each of the three primordial constituencies of Rome (Cicero *De republica* 2.14: [*Romulus*] *populum. . .in tribus tris curiasque triginta discripserat;* also Livy 10.6.7). I would attribute this particular shift to a process of *sunoikismós* 'urban consolidation'[16] that could have operated on the ideological principle of trifunctionalism: three parts make a whole that in turn becomes part of a new totality of three.[17] In short, I understand the Roman model

---

viśpati- 'lord of the *viś-*' seems to be synonymous with *rājan-:* cf. *Atharva-Veda* 4.22.3 and the comments of Gonda 1976.139n66. But note the attestation of the periphrases *viśaḥ pati-* 'lord of the *viś-* [singular]' at *Rig-Veda* 10.152.2 and *viśām pati-* 'lord of the *viśaḥ* [plural]' at e.g. *Atharva-Veda* 1.21.1. I would compare Old Irish *rí tuaithe* 'king of the *tuath* [singular]' and *rí tuath* 'king of the *tuatha* [plural]' = over-king, respectively (see Byrne pp. 132–134). As for the cognate of Indic *viśpati-,* Lithuanian *viešpats* '[sovereign] lord', I find no evidence to justify the translation 'chief of clan' (as in Benveniste 1:295). For arguments against translating Indic *viś-* as 'clan', see Gonda pp. 138–139, who adduces passages like *Rig-Veda* 4.4.3, where the poet refers to his community as 'this *viś-* [singular]'. Note, too, that the semantics of Lithuanian *viẽškelis* 'Landstrasse, öffentlicher Weg' (LEW 1244) suggest that *viẽš-* stands for the concept of a whole community.

[10] The semantics of Latin *tribus* are discussed immediately below.

[11] The correlation seems to be in terms of political vs. territorial distinctions: whereas *tuta* is political, *trifu* is territorial. Cf. the usage of *"tribus"* in Umbrian place-names as reported by Livy 31.2.6 and 33.37.1 (Poultney 1959.274). For more on the semantics of Umbrian *tuta,* Old Irish *tuath,* and German *Deutsch,* see Benveniste 1969 1:364.

[12] Benveniste 1:258–259. Otherwise Watkins 1966.45–49.

[13] Benveniste 1:258–259; there is no need to posit, as Benveniste does, that the name "Triphylia" reflects a specifically Dorian pedigree.

[14] Benveniste 1:258–259.

[15] On this topic, see further at p. 284n51.

[16] For a parallel, cf. the discussion of the *sunoikismós* at Rhodes at p. 285n53.

[17] On the trifunctional association of the three primordial *tribūs* with the three distinct ethnic groups of Latins/Etruscans/Sabines, I cite the updated views of Dumézil 1969.214. Also Alföldi 1974.59–60, who points to patterns of Etruscan linguistic borrowings from

of *tribus*, a "third" of the whole, to be a secondary development, as distinct from an earlier semantic pattern represented by the Umbrian model, where the equivalent of Latin *tribus* is a "triad" that *is* the whole.[18] This Roman model leads to the Latin usage of translating Greek *phūlḗ*, which is clearly *part* of the whole, by way of *tribus*. Even in the earlier model, the principle of division is built in, as we see from the verb *tribuō*.

Benveniste's basic explanation of Latin *tribus* and Umbrian *trifu-* as a combination of *tri- and *bhu-, where the second element is cognate with the *phū-* of *phūlḗ*, is dismissed as "de la pure acrobatie linguistique" by Roussel,[19] for whom the three-*phūlaí* subdivisions of citizens in Dorian cities are a matter of relatively recent cultural diffusion, not of common inheritance.[20] But this is to underestimate the weight of not only comparative but also internal evidence, as we shall now see.

In a recent study of the epigraphical testimonia of official city documents, it has been argued that, in Dorian cities where the three-*phūlaí* subdivision prevails, there is a traditional hierarchy in the ranking of the *phūlaí*.[21] Citizens of Dorian cities like Megara and Cos are consistently listed in the following order of three *phūlaí*: (1) *Dumânes* (2) *Hulleîs* (3) *Pámphūloi*.[22] Alongside this principle of hierarchy there is a complementary principle of egalitarianism, in that all three *phūlaí* get to share in certain aspects of civic life on an equal basis. Thus, for example, the terms of certain magistracies seem to be divided equally among the *phūlaí* within the space of one year. Also, the principle of rotation applies: the sequence 1/2/3 of *Dumânes/Hulleîs/Pámphūloi* will be followed by 2/3/1, then by 3/1/2, back to 1/2/3, and so forth. To quote directly the formulation of Jones: "the Dorian *phūlaí*, wherever found, followed a common, traditional order that might, on occasion, be rotated in such a way that in any given document any of the three *phūlaí* might hold first, second, or third position."[23]

Still, the hierarchy of the *phūlaí* is maintained, as we see from the fact that the third *phūlḗ*, the *Pámphūloi*, is specifically excluded from certain

---

Italic in arguing against the notion that the Roman concept of *tribus* was borrowed from the Etruscans.

[18] *Pace* Täubler 1930, who considers the Roman model primary, and the Umbrian, secondary. I should add that the pattern of three cities in the territory of the Vestini (Täubler pp. 6–10), as also the tripartition of the territory of the Paeligni (pp. 12–14), resembles the Roman model to the extent that the equivalent of *tribus* in these instances figures as a "third" of a larger whole (whence the description by Ovid *Amores* 2.16.1 of his home town Sulmo as a "third" of Paelignian territory: *pars me Sulmo tenet Paeligni tertia ruris*).

[19] Roussel 1976.166.

[20] Roussel pp. 221–263.

[21] Jones 1980a.

[22] As for the hierarchy in Dorian cities with four *phūlaí*, see below.

[23] Jones 1980a.204.

civic roles, such as certain aspects of public sacrifice.[24] Thus the *basis* for rotation has to be the order *Dumânes/Hulleîs/Pámphūloi.* Moreover, in Dorian cities where a fourth *phūlḗ* had been instituted to accommodate the supposedly pre-Dorian elements,[25] this *phūlḗ* could still rank above that of the *Pámphūloi.* Thus at Argos, for example, the order of *phūlaí* in an inscription dated ca. 460–450 (DGE no. 96 [1]) is as follows: (1) *Dumânes* (2) *Hulleîs* (3) *Hurnáthioi* (4) *Pámphūloi.*[26] Later inscriptions, however, reflecting a change from an oligarchical to a democratic form of government,[27] show a changed order of *phūlaí*: (1) *Dumânes* (2) *Hulleîs* (3) *Pámphūloi* (4) *Hurnáthioi.*[28] Such a promotion of the *Pámphūloi* in the specific context of a democratic ideology is additional evidence that the *Pámphūloi* had been the lowest of the three *phūlaí.*

In sum, we have internal evidence for the traditional convention of a fixed order in the three-*phūlaí* and modified four-*phūlaí* systems of Dorian cities. As Jones concludes, "the observance of the convention throughout the Dorian region shows that the fixed order must, like the *phūlaí* themselves, have antedated the dispersal of the Dorians to their historical centers."[29] He adds the opinion that "the practice of rotating the order—a sophisticated and . . . egalitarian device—did not evolve until well into the historical period."[30]

[24] In an inscription from Cos (DGE no. 253), for example, we read of a resolution by "those *phūlaí* who share in the rites of Apollo and Herakles" (lines 1–6). Further evidence from this and other related inscriptions from Cos leads to the conclusion that the *phūlḗ* associated with the rites of Apollo was in this case the *Dumânes*; that the *phūlḗ* associated with the rites of Herakles was the *Hulleîs*; and that the *phūlḗ* excluded from these rites was the *Pámphūloi.* See e.g. Jones 1980a.210.

[25] For testimonia on the incorporation of non-Dorian elements at Sikyon, Phleious, Epidauros, Trozen, Hermione, see Pausanias 2.6.7, 2.13.1–2, 2.26.1–2, 2.30.10, 2.34.5, respectively. Cf. Wörrle 1964.13, who adduces the interesting remarks of Isocrates 12.177f.

[26] Jones 1980a.205. In Argive inscriptions of this period, the naming of citizens follows the pattern: name plus adjective naming the *phūlḗ* (no patronymic necessary). See Wörrle pp. 16–19.

[27] This change is dated to some time in the 460s, but no later than 462 B.C.; see Wörrle p. 20, 122–126; also Jones p. 206.

[28] Jones p. 206.

[29] Jones p. 212.

[30] Jones p. 212. He finds just two exceptions to the sequence *Dumânes/Hulleîs/-Pámphūloi* (pp. 209, 211). Both occur in one set of inscriptions, DGE no. 251 (Cos, iv/iii B.C.) A 10–13 and C 1–5. The first passage concerns the selection of an ox to be sacrificed to Zeus Polieus. A priest and a panel of *hieropoioí* 'sacrificers' must select one ox out of three triads of oxen, each triad being presented by each of the three *phūlaí.* If no ox is selected from the triad presented by the *Pámphūloi*, then the *Hulleîs* are to present their triad; if no ox is selected from the triad presented by them, then the *Dumânes* are to present their triad. In the second passage, which will be discussed again in another context below, three sheep are to be selected for sacrifice, one on behalf of each of the three *phūlaí* in three different sacred precincts. The sequence of enumeration is *Hulleîs/Dumânes/Pámphūloi.* I should note that, exceptionally, both these passages are concerned with the

All this internal evidence can lead to valuable comparative insights. For example, the semantic relationship between the name of the lowest in the order of three *phūlaí*, the *Pámphūloi*, and the word *phūlḗ* itself, corresponds to the semantic relationship between the name of the lowest in the order of the three leading social classes or *varṇa*-s in Indic traditions,[31] the *vaiśya-*, and the word from which it is derived, *viś-* 'tribe': just as the word *Pámphūloi* implies the whole community while designating the lowest of three parts, so also the word *vaiśya-*, by virtue of its derivation, implies the whole community, the *viś-*, while specifically designating, again, the lowest of three parts. We have in fact already noted that the word *viś-* stands for the concept of a whole community, as we could see from the semantic relationship between *viś-* and the derivative *viśva-* 'all'.[32] Moreover, in *Rig-Veda* 8.35.13, the expression *devāsaḥ sarvayā viśā,* literally 'gods, with the *viś-* complete', denotes the completion of the speech-act of listing the gods of all three social functions corresponding to the three leading *varṇa*-s: Mitra-Varuṇa as the first (sovereignty/priesthood), the Maruts as the second (warrior class), and the Aśvins as the third (agriculture/herding).[33] The symbolic inclusiveness of the third part is evident in other ways as well: for example, the word *viś-* is sufficient for designating, all by itself, the lowest of the three

---

rituals of sacrifice. In the first passage the sequence may reflect an ascending order of importance in a climactic ideology of sacrifice. In the second passage the sequence may have been affected by the special importance of the cult of Herakles at Cos (to repeat, the precinct of Herakles was associated with the *phūlḗ* of the *Hulleîs*: p. 280n24). In any case, the expression *parà tà Anaxílea,* to be discussed below, suggests that the *Dumânes* outranked the *Hulleîs.*

[31] The stratification of the *varṇa*-s is attested already in e.g. *Rig-Veda* 10.90.11–12: cf. Dumézil 1958.7–8 and Benveniste 1:279–288. The people of the fourth *varṇa-*, namely the *śūdra-*, are ideologically the servants of the leading three *varṇa*-s.

[32] Cognate with Indic *viśva-* is Avestan *vispa-* 'all', just as Indic *viś-* is cognate with Avestan *vīs*. In Iranian society the *vīs* seems to have been a subdivision of the *zantu* (< *gen-tu-): see Benveniste 1969 1:294–295. Whereas the Vedic *viś-* and the Avestan *vīs* may not necessarily represent any longer the same type of social organization, the convergence of meanings in Vedic *viśva-* and Avestan *vispa-*, both meaning 'all', suggests that the Indo-Iranian **viš-* is analogous to, say, the Old Irish *tuath.* Both the Indic *viś-* and the Old Irish *tuath,* as we have seen (p. 277n9), apparently designate a community *as ruled by a king.* In this light, we may note the findings of Dubuisson (1978a and 1978b), on the basis of Indo-Iranian and Celtic rituals of royal inauguration, to the effect that the Indo-European king embodies a totality of the triad of three social functions. If, then, we maintain that the third social function is the completing function that allows the totality to happen, it follows that the image of the king as a totality should be articulated expressly in terms of the third function. I cite as an example the generative connotations of Germanic *kuningaz 'king' (root akin to Latin *gen-* as in *genitor;* cf. also Hittite *ḫaššuš* 'king'—in light of the argument that this word is derived from *ḫaš-* 'beget': see pp. 145ff.). Then the Avestan expression *vīsō puθra,* as discussed by Benveniste 1:305, may represent a variation on this theme.

[33] For more on *Rig-Veda* 8.35.13, see Dumézil 1977.226.

leading *varṇa-*s, the *vaiśya-* (e.g. *Rig-Veda* 8.35.18).[34] The semantic bivalence of the Indic word *viś-*, in designating both the third part of totality and totality itself, has been compared by Georges Dumézil with the situation in Latin, where the word *Quirītes,* related to *Quirīnus,* the god representing the third function in the pre-Capitoline triad, designates not only 'civilians' as opposed to *milites* but also the totality of the Roman people (note the proposed etymology: **co-uiro-*).[35] I might add that, just as Indic *viś-* may alternatively include the two upper functions or exclude them,[36] so also Greek *dêmos* may designate either the whole community[37] or else the community minus its *hēgemónes* 'leaders'.[38]

The parallelisms between the third in the triad of Dorian *phūlaí,* the *Pámphūloi,* and the third in the triad of Indic *varṇa-*s, the *vaiśya-*, extend beyond the realm of pure semantics. Just as the *Pámphūloi* are ranked the third and lowest of the three *phūlaí,* so also the *vaiśya-* are ranked third and lowest of the three leading *varṇa-*s.[39] Moreover, just as the *Pámphūloi* have the lowest priority in certain aspects of sacrifice,[40] so too the *vaiśya-*.[41]

The institutions of sacrifice also reveal other aspects of trifunctionality in the Dorian triad of *phūlaí.* In an inscription from Cos (DGE no.

[34] For a commentary on *Rig-Veda* 3.35.16–18, see Dumézil 1977.213–215. Note, too, *Śatapatha-Brāhmaṇa* 4.2.2.13 (also 2.1.4.12): universal totality is equated with the triad *brahma/kṣatram/viś-*, the three characteristics of the three functions. Cf. Gonda 1976.132n30.

[35] Dumézil 1977.218n2, 226n3, 255.

[36] For an informative collection of contexts where the *viś-* is in conflict with upper strata of society, see Rau 1957.59–61.

[37] N 1979a.149. Cf. p. 3n7 and pp. 132–133 above.

[38] N 1985a.43–44. Cf. also Donlan 1970. On the implications of third function in the word *dêmos*, I cite the semantics of *dēmiourgoí*, the word for 'artisans'. According to Strabo 8.7.1 C383, Ion divided the population of the Athenians into four classes: the *geōrgoí* 'cultivators', *dēmiourgoí* 'artisans', *hieropoioí* 'priests', and *phúlakes* 'guardians'; on the affinities of this grouping system with the four-*phūlaí* structure of certain Ionian city-states and with the trifunctional Indo-European ideology of (1) sovereignty/priesthood, (2) warrior class, (3) cultivators/herders and artisans, see Benveniste 1969 1:289–291 (*pace* Nilsson 1951). On the differentiation of the third function between cultivators/herdsmen and artisans, see Dumézil 1977.256, with reference to his valuable outline of four different historically attested ways of integrating the emerging classes of a given society into the inherited scheme of trifunctionalism.

[39] Note the corporeal imagery in *Rig-Veda* 10.90.11–12.

[40] See p. 280n24.

[41] See the ample documentation in Gonda 1976.131–133, with instances of either third-ranking or complete omission of the *vaiśya-*. On the imagery of the first two *varṇa-*s as resting on top of the third for support, see the citations compiled by Gonda p. 135. It goes without saying that I disagree with Gonda's view that such hierarchization of the *varṇa-*s amounts to an argument against Dumézil's construct of trifunctionalism. In this connection, I quote the following useful formulation: "La coupure initiale qui sépare les représentants des deux premières classes et ceux de la troisième est une donnée indo-européenne commune": Dumézil 1958.56. Cf. also Dumézil 1959b.26.

251C),[42] it is specified that three sheep are to be selected for sacrifice, each on behalf of each of the three *phūlaí* (lines 1–5):

sheep of the *Hulleîs: parà tò Hērakleîon* 'at the precinct of Herakles'

sheep of the *Dumânes: parà tà Anaxílea* 'at the precinct [called] *Anaxílea*'

sheep of the *Pámphūloi: parà tò Dā̃matrion* 'at the precinct of Demeter'.

The name *Anaxílea* is evidently composed of the elements *anak(t)-* 'king' and *lāós* 'people, host'; the latter word for 'people', as Benveniste points out, expresses the personal relation of a group of men with a leader.[43] As for the kind of leadership implicit in the word, we may consider the derivative *lā́iton* = *lḗiton,* which Herodotus (7.197.2) glosses as the Achaean word for *prutaneîon* or 'presidential building'.[44] Clearly, then, the association of the *Dumânes* with a precinct named *Anaxílea* reflects an aspect of the first social function of trifunctionality, that is, sovereignty or legitimation. And, just as clearly, the association of the *Pámphūloi* with the precinct of Demeter reflects an aspect of the third social function, that is, agriculture.

As for the association of the *Hulleîs* with the precinct of Herakles, we may note the tradition according to which *Húllos,* evidently the eponymous ancestor of the *Hulleîs,* was the son of Herakles. In myth, *Húllos* the Heraclid was the leader of the initial attempt of the Dorians to conquer the Peloponnesus (cf. e.g. Herodotus 9.26.2–5). *Húllos* was the adopted son of Aigimios, son of *Dôros,* the eponymous ancestor of the Dorians, while Aigimios had two sons of his own, *Dumā̃n* and *Pámphūlos,* eponymous ancestors of the *Dumânes* and the *Pámphūloi* (Ephorus FGH 70 F 15; cf. Strabo 9.4.10 C427 and Apollodorus 2.8.3). Of the three eponymous ancestors, the second or warrior function of the non-Dorian *Húllos* is evident from the theme of his military leadership: in referring to the Dorian Conquest, which according to myth was successfully executed under the leadership of three great-grandsons of *Húllos,* the words of Pindar describe the Dorian invaders as Ὕλλου τε καὶ Αἰγιμιοῦ Δωριεὺς . . . στρατός 'the Dorian Host of Hullos and Aigimios' (*Isthmian* 9.2–3). As for the three great-grandsons of *Húllos,* they became ancestors of the three great royal houses of the Peloponnesus, the Dorian dynasties of

[42] Already discussed at pp. 280–281n30.
[43] Benveniste 1969 2:90.
[44] See further Benveniste 2:92–93.

Argos, Sparta, and Messenia (Apollodorus 2.8.4–5).[45] Thus, for example, King Leonidas of Sparta traced himself back to Herakles, twenty generations removed (Herodotus 7.204).[46]

The genealogical association of Dorian royalty with the second *phūlḗ*, the *Hulleîs*, is comparable to the historically verifiable fact that the kings of India generally came from the second *varṇa-*, the warrior class of the *kṣatriya-*.[47] The appropriation of kingship by the *kṣatriya-s* is reflected even in the Indic usage of the very word *kṣatriya* to designate the second or warrior function: of and by itself, the base-form *kṣatram* 'dominion, power' seems to designate kingliness in general, not necessarily the second function in particular.[48] Moreover, the higher stratum within the category of *kṣatriya-* in Vedic diction is *rājanya-* (e.g. *Rig-Veda* 10.90.12 = *Atharva-Veda* 19.6.6), where the derivation from *rājan-* 'king' reveals most clearly the appropriation of kingliness by the second function.

In light of such comparisons, it seems reasonable to infer that the three-*phūlaí* organization of Dorian cities is a reflex of Indo-European trifunctionalism.[49] It seems also reasonable to explain the epithet *trikhā́ïkes*, applied to *Dōriees* 'Dorians' at *Odyssey* xix 177, as a combination of an adverbial element meaning 'in three parts', **trikhā* (?),[50] and a radical element *u̯eik-/*u̯oik-, cognate with Indic *viś-*.[51] In a fragment of

[45] On which see Sergent 1977/1978.

[46] So also King Leotychides of Sparta, at Herodotus 8.131.2. In light of the tradition according to which *Húllos* was a Dorian only by adoption (as the adopted son of Aigimios son of *Dôros*), we may note the anecdote at Herodotus 5.70.3 about King Kleomenes of Sparta: when he was barred from Athena's inner sanctum at the Athenian acropolis on the grounds that he was a Dorian, he protested that he was not a *Dōrieús* but rather an *Akhaiós*. On the semantics of self-identification by Greeks as Dorians and Ionians, see Alty 1982; on Herodotus 5.70.3, see Alty p. 13.

[47] See Drekmeier 1962.81–85. Note, too, the evidence of Vedic diction: at *Atharva-Veda* 4.22.1, for example, the king is overtly described as a *kṣatriya-*.

[48] See the survey of passages by Gonda 1976.141. It does not follow, however, as Gonda seems to think, that these passages disprove Benveniste's (1969 1:280) definition of the *kṣatriya-* as the man "qui a le pouvoir guerrier (qui a le pouvoir de *rāj-*)." The point remains that the derivative of *kṣatram, kṣatriya-*, clearly designates the second function in particular, and that this designation in turn particularizes the meaning of the base-form *kṣatram*. Thus the attestations of an earlier, more general, meaning cannot vindicate Gonda's counterargument. Cf. Dumézil 1977.255.

[49] So Dumézil 1941.254–257. The idea is retracted, however, in Dumézil 1953.25.

[50] Cf. τριχῇ (= τριχῆ ?) at Herodotus 3.39.2; the context of this passage is pertinent.

[51] See Benveniste 1969 1:310. In connection with this proposed etymology, I note the claim by Roussel 1976.230 that Benveniste confuses the semantic subdivisions of family/clan/tribe. This is to miss one of Benveniste's main points, which is that the diachronic perspective reveals shifts in meaning from category to subcategory or from subcategory to category. As for the morphology of *trikhā́ïkes*, it is admittedly opaque, partly because the phonology is opaque: Homeric and Hesiodic traditional diction guarantees only the vowel quantities here, not the precise vowel qualities (in this case, *u̯eik- ? *u̯oik- ? *u̯īk-?).

Hesiod (233 MW), this same epithet of the Dorians is actually glossed by the poetry as meaning *having land divided into three parts.* The territorial implications of the Indic root *viś-* 'to settle' are compatible with such a description of the Dorians. That their traditional tripartition into three *phūlaí* reflects territorial as well as political subdivision is also suggested by the description of the settlement of the Dorian island of Rhodes in the Homeric *Catalogue of Ships:* the settlers *trikhthà . . . oíkēthen kataphūladón* 'were settled [root *u̯oik-] in three parts, *phūlḗ* by *phūlḗ*' (*Iliad* II 668).[52] The adverb *trikhthá* 'in three parts' tells us that each *phūlḗ* is part of a whole (cf. *Iliad* XV 189, on the three-way division of the universe among the sons of Kronos).[53]

Such indications of the territorial aspect of subdivision into *phūlaí* need not be taken to mean that a typical polis and its surrounding territory were simply divided into a given number of sectors inhabited by a corresponding number of *phūlaí.*[54] The example of Athens is instructive

[52] Whether *kataphūladón* reflects an underlying noun *phūlḗ* or *phûlon* is irrelevant to the argument, since Homeric *phûlon* can be used in the sense of Classical *phūlḗ* (*Iliad* II 362, on which see further below).

[53] I interpret *Iliad* II 655 (in conjunction with 668) as saying that the whole island was subdivided into three cities, Lindos, Ialysos, and Kameiros, and that this tripartition *of the whole island* was like a subdivision into three *phūlaí within one city.* The three cities are mentioned explicitly as cities in Herodotus 1.144.3. The Homeric testimony should not be misinterpreted to mean that each of these cities did not have its own *phūlaí.* On the available epigraphical evidence for the existence of *phūlaí* in each of the three Rhodian cities and for the political principle of rotation-by-*phūlḗ*, see Fraser 1953, esp. pp. 40–41n1; one *phūlḗ* at Lindos is known as *Argeíā*, which leads to his inference that the traditional Dorian names of *Dumânes/Hulleîs/Pámphūloi* became obsolete in Rhodes, possibly at an early stage (cf. also the discussion in Roussel 1976.261). In the *sunoikismós* 'urban consolidation' of 408/7, the three cities were united as the one city of Rhodes, apparently consisting of three *phūlaí* known as Lindia, Ialysia, and Kameiris (Latte 1941.996). Note that *Kamirís* is attested as the name of a *phūlḗ* in Hierapytna (DGE no. 200.1). For further discussion of the subdivisions of Rhodes, see Momigliano 1936, esp. pp. 60–63. Momigliano points out (p. 51) that the *Iliad* (II 653–657) assigns the three cities of Rhodes to a single leader, Tlepolemos. (In this connection, note the report of Pherecydes FGH 3 F 80 that the maternal grandfather of Tlepolemos was one *Phū́lās*; cf. Robertson 1980.8.) Even before the *sunoikismós* of 408/7, certain sacral institutions of one of the three cities, Lindos, are known to have been shared by the other two (Momigliano p. 51); note, too, the report that the text of Pindar's *Olympian* 7, in honor of Diagoras of Ialysos, was inscribed in gold and deposited at the temple of Athena at Lindos (scholia to Pindar *Olympian* 7.1 p. 195 Drachmann; cf. Momigliano p. 51). Finally, I should note that it may be productive to study further the Rhodian institution of the *ktoínā*, which is obviously a territorial subdivision (see Momigliano p. 59) and at the same time an aristocratic kinship subdivision (cf. Hesychius s.v. κτύναι ἢ κτοῖναι · χωρήσεις προγονικῶν ἱερειῶν ἢ δῆμος μεμερισμένος '*ktoînai*: categories of inherited priesthoods or a subdivision of a district [*dêmos*]'). Note, too, the morphological parallelism of Rhodian *ktoinétai* (DGE no. 281, note to line 14) and Linear B *ko-to-ne-ta* (Pylos Eb901.1).

[54] Thus the Rhodian model of three cities seems in fact exceptional in its outward simplicity—hence perhaps the emphasis on the theme of the tripartition of Rhodes in the *Iliad.* See again p. 285n53. As for the testimony of Socrates of Argos FGH 310 F 6 about a locale within the city of Argos called the *Pamphūliakón*, it is hard to determine whether this

here: after the reform of Kleisthenes (Herodotus 5.69.1–2; Aristotle *Constitution of the Athenians* 21.2–6), the polis was subdivided into ten *phūlaí*, each further subdivided into three *trittúes*, each of which was further subdivided into a number of *dêmoi* 'demes'. The mechanism for the territorial distribution of the *phūlaí* was not the number 10 of the *phūlaí* but the number 3 of the subdivisions of the *phūlaí*, the *trittúes*: the territory of Athens was subdivided into three categories, (A) urban, (B) coastal, and (C) interior, and each of these categories of *trittúes* was further subdivided into subterritories assigned to the ten *phūlaí*.[55] In other words, the ten *phūlaí* were separately distributed in each of the three areas A B C.[56] Thus the ten *phūlaí* were in effect territorial subdivisions of the A B C categories of the *trittúes*, not of the one polis, while the A B C *trittúes* were political subdivisions of the ten *phūlaí*.

As for the political system of Athens before the reform of Kleisthenes, there is a report that the polis had been politically subdivided into four *phūlaí*, which were each subdivided into three *trittúes* or *phrātríai*, which were each subdivided into thirty *génē* 'lineages' (Aristotle *Constitution of the Athenians*, F 385 Rose).[57] The earlier four *phūlaí* of Athens, the *Geléontes*, the *Aigikoreîs*, the *Argadeîs*, and the *Hóplētes*, were recognized as cognate with the basic traditional four *phūlaí* of the Ionians (see Herodotus 5.66.2, 5.69.1).[58] From the epigraphical evidence, we know that most Ionian cities preserved these four *phūlaí*, usually along with added *phūlaí*.[59] Moreover, as Benveniste has argued, the four basic Ionian *phūlaí* can be explained as a reflex of the three Indo-European social functions, with the third function differentiated into the two separate functions of cultivators/herdsmen, on the one hand, and artisans, on the other.[60]

Having just surveyed the basics of what little we are told about the political system of Athens before the reform of Kleisthenes, I raise the

---

locale is a city sector or just a place of assembly: see Wörrle 1964.13. For possible evidence adduced in favor of territorial subdivisions implied by *phūlaí*-divisions, see Szanto 1906 [1901].226. In this connection, I cite the interesting usage of the concept *Zeùs homóphūlos* in Plato *Laws* 843a.

[55] It is instructive to study a map that shows only the *phūlaí* and the *trittúes* of Attica, not the *dêmoi*: see Lévêque and Vidal-Naquet 1964.15.

[56] On the politics of this distribution, see Lévêque and Vidal-Naquet pp. 13–18.

[57] For an extensive commentary on this fragment, see Bourriot 1976.460–491. In discussing the concept of *phrātríā*, I shall use this form throughout, though there exist other by-forms: *phrā́trā*, *phā́trā*, etc.

[58] The form *Argádai* in Herodotus corresponds to *Argadeîs* elsewhere (e.g. Plutarch *Solon* 23.4).

[59] For a survey of the situation in Miletus, Ephesus, Teos, and Samos, see Roussel 1976.209–220.

[60] Benveniste 1969 1:289–291.

possibility, however tenuous, of an inherited territorial principle in the distribution of *phūlaí.* True, what Kleisthenes had changed was not only the naming and numbering of the *phūlaí* but also the actual constituency of the *phūlaí,* in that the subdivisions of old *trittúes* or *phrātríai* were replaced by subdivisions of new *trittúes,* further subdivided into territorial entities called *dêmoi.* Aristotle says explicitly, it is also true, that Kleisthenes did not reform the *phrātríai* or their constituencies, the *génē* 'lineages' (*Constitution of the Athenians* 21.6), so that the *phrātríai* could survive and in limited ways even cooperate with the *dêmoi.*[61] Still, the fact that the new *trittúes* were territorial units does not necessarily mean that the *phrātríai,* ousted from functioning as subdivisions of the *phūlaí,* had been devoid of any territorial principle. The subdivisions of the polis need not be conceived as marking differentiations exclusively in terms of territory or exclusively in terms of kinship (in the broader, political sense of the word). After all, the Athenian *dêmoi,* by virtue of being subdivisions of the new *phūlaí,* became functional determinants of actual ancestry.[62] Moreover, the concept of *trittús,* equated with *phrātríā* by Aristotle in the fragment that we have been considering, suggests some kind of territorially distributive mechanism: we may recall that the concept of the new *trittús,* as established after Kleisthenes, served to distribute each of the ten new *phūlaí* into three distinct territorial variations.

There still remain major problems, however, with the numbers recorded in Aristotle's report (*Constitution of the Athenians,* F 385 Rose) of the old subdivision of Athens into four *phūlaí,* each further subdivided into three *trittúes* or *phrātríai,* each further subdivided into thirty *génē.* The purported number of old *trittúes,* twelve, seems far too low in comparison with the number of new *trittúes* after Kleisthenes, that is, thirty. Perhaps a solution can be found if we do not assume that Aristotle's report applies to all of Athenian territory. The report begins by stating that the population was subdivided into *geōrgoí* and *dēmiourgoí,* and what then follows in the text may be interpreted to mean that each of these two subdivisions was further subdivided into four *phūlaí,* each further subdivided into three old *trittúes* or *phrātríai.* With this reckoning we would have a total of twenty-four *phrātríai* as a territorial grid for the even distribution of *phūlaí.*[63] There may be a parallel situation in

[61] Cf. Roussel 1976.139–151.

[62] Cf. Roussel p. 5.

[63] The emphasis on a numbering system in terms of four *phūlaí* rather than in terms of eight *phūlaí* could possibly be motivated by a desire for parallelism with the scheme of twelve months consisting of thirty days each, corresponding to twelve *phrātríai* consisting of thirty *génē* each. This parallelism is in fact the point of Aristotle's discussion. Moreover, we may still expect only four names for only four *phūlaí,* each further qualified as either *geōrgoí* or *dēmiourgoí.* In any case, we would still be left with a territorial grid of twenty-four rather than twelve *phrātríai.* All this is not to say that a scheme of twelve subdivisions, as emphasized by Aristotle, could not have preceded a scheme of twenty-four. We may recall

Corinth, where eight *phūlaí* seem to be further subdivided into three units each, yielding a territorial grid of, again, twenty-four units.[64] The eight-*phūlaí* system of Corinth apparently reflects the politics of the dynasty of tyrants known as the Kypselidai,[65] who promoted a clear delineation between countryside and city proper (Ephorus FGH 70 F 179; Aristotle *Constitution of the Corinthians,* F 516 Rose [cf. F 611.20]), and it may be argued that the Corinthian eight-*phūlaí* system reflects a countryside / city split of a modified Dorian four-*phūlaí* system.[66] There is a remote possibility that the system described by Aristotle as prevailing in Athens before Kleisthenes can be attributed to the tyranny of the Peisistratidai: in this case, if my interpretation of the Aristotle fragment has any merit, the basic Ionian four-*phūlaí* system was split along the lines of *geōrgoí* in the countryside, *dēmiourgoí* in the city proper.[67]

In any case, the principle of a twelve-part territorial division on the basis of four *phūlaí* subdivided into three *phrātríai* each should be compared with what Herodotus has to say about the sacred confederation of twelve Ionian cities in Asia Minor, modeled on an ancient twelve-part territorial division of the Ionians at a time when they were still supposedly settled in the Peloponnesus (1.145: *oíkeon*). Among the cities of the Ionian *dōdekápolis,* a notable exception to the pattern of retaining the

---

the myth that tells how Kekrops, primaeval king of Athens, divided all the territory into twelve "*póleis*" (Philochorus FGH 328 F 94). Aristotle's emphasis on the symbolic correlation of a twelve-part subdivision with the twelve months of the year should not be dismissed as an idiosyncratic exercise in numerology: the twelve months are a conventional mythopoeic device for expressing the totality of society and the equitable distribution of functions among its members. Consider the adoption of such a device by Solomon in I *Kings* 4.7ff, where the number 12 is surely correlated with the pre-existing ideology of the twelve *phūlaí* of Israel (e.g. *Joshua* 7.16–18; cf. Wolf 1946a).

64 See Stroud 1968, esp. p. 241; Jones 1980b.164–165 disagrees on the details of subdivision.

65 Jones pp. 187–193.

66 For the presence of the three basic Dorian *phūlaí* in the Corinthian daughter-cities of Syracuse and Corcyra, see the bibliography cited by Jones 1980b.187. Note, too, that Aletes, the founding hero of Corinth, who as we have seen was credited with dividing the city into eight *phūlaí* (*Suda* π 225 Adler s.v. *pánta oktṓ*), has two ancestors called *Phū̃lās*: see Robertson 1980.7. The younger ancestor is the paternal grandfather of Aletes, whereas the older *Phū̃lās* is not only the great-grandfather of the younger but also the grandfather of Tlepolemos, the founding hero of Rhodes (on whom see p. 285n53). As a possible parallel for the proposed split of a four-*phūlaí* system at Corinth into an eight-*phūlaí* system, we may compare the early split of the three Roman *tribūs* into six, where the old and the new three members of the ensemble are distinguished simply by the titles for "first" and "second," that is, *primi* and *secundi* Titienses, Ramnes, Luceres (Festus 468.3 Lindsay); on this split from three to six *tribūs* in Rome, see Alföldi 1974.63.

67 The tradition that insists on a three-way split among the *eupatrídai / geōrgoí / dēmiourgoí* (Plutarch *Theseus* 24–25) reflects political considerations that are different from those of the Peisistratidai: cf. the discussion of Figueira 1984, who detects tendencies of political polarization, fostered by the aristocracy, between *geōrgoí* and *dēmiourgoí.*

four basic Ionian *phūlaí* was Ephesus: this city was subdivided into five *phūlaí*, one of which was the *Epheseîs*, which was further subdivided into an unknown number of *khiliastúes*; among the six attested *khiliastúes* are the *Geléontes* and *Argadeîs*, names of the old Ionian *phūlaí*.[68] Significantly, Herodotus (1.147.2) reports that Ephesus (along with Kolophon) was exceptional among Ionian cities in that it did not celebrate the festival of the *Apatoúria*.

Now the Ionian *Apatoúria*, as we know from independent evidence, was the occasion for the seasonal reunion of the *phrātríai*.[69] Thus the absence of the *Apatoúria* at Ephesus seems to be correlated with the absence there of subdivision into *phrātríai*. Conversely, when we consider the *Apélla*, a Dorian institution analogous to the Ionian *Apatoúria*, we find that it, too, serves as the occasion for the seasonal reunion of the *phrātríai*.[70] In archaic Sparta there were three groups of nine *phrātríai* (Demetrius of Skepsis, in Athenaeus 142e–f)—presumably corresponding to the tripartition into three *phūlaí*.[71] I would surmise, on the analogy of the Athenian patterns, that the territorial distribution of the Spartan *phūlaí* and *phrātríai* would be in groupings of D1/H1/P1, D2/H2/P2, D3/H3/P3, . . ., not of D1/D2/D3 . . ., H1/H2/H3 . . ., P1/P2/P3 . . . (where D = *Dumânes*, H = *Hulleîs*, P = *Pámphūloi*; and where 1 2 3 . . . = the territorial order of the *phrātríai*).

To sum up the discussion of the *phrātríai* as they existed both before and after the reform of Kleisthenes: I conclude that this social subdivision is a matter of both kinship (in the broader, political sense of the word) and territoriality. The Athenian elimination of *phrātríai* as functional subdivisions of the polis reflects a movement away from a social structure that would have tended to exclude newer inhabitants by placing a stress on inherited kinship. The retention of the concept of *phūlḗ* as the largest political subdivision of Athens is thus but a camouflage for the fact that the kinship-related grouping of the *phrātríā* has been replaced by the territorial grouping of the *trittús* as the functional subdivision of the *phūlḗ*. If we follow this interpretation of Aristotle, then it may be that twenty-four old *phrātríai* are replaced by thirty new *trittúes* and four old *phūlaí* (times two) are replaced by ten new ones. As Aristotle observes elsewhere (*Politics* 1319b23–27), the successful formula for

[68] See Roussel 1976.211–212.

[69] See Burkert 1975.10.

[70] Burkert pp. 9–10.

[71] Cf. Plutarch *Lycurgus* 6: in the text of the *Great Rhetra*, the injunction about safeguarding the *phūlaí* is articulated in the context of prescribing the seasonal holding of *apéllai*. See also Robertson 1980.17: at Cos as well, there were three *phūlaí* apparently subdivided into nine *phrātríai* each.

achieving democracy in a polis is to increase the number of *phūlaí* and *phrātríai*, "so that all people may be mixed with each other as much as possible."

Aristotle's remark about "mixing" implies that social structuring along the lines of *phūlaí* and *phrātríai* is equivalent to the regulating of marriage along the lines of kinship. So also in the *Constitution of the Athenians,* Aristotle says that Kleisthenes distributed the entire population of the Athenians into ten new *phūlaí* in place of the old four *because he wanted to "mix" the population* (21.2): the "mixing" led to greater participation in the polity, which Aristotle (*ibid.*) connects with the expression *mḗ phūlokrīneîn* (μὴ φυλοκρινεῖν) 'not to make distinctions according to *phūlḗ*' as it applies to those who wish to verify the pedigrees (*génē*) of their fellow citizens. The injunction 'not to make distinctions according to *phūlḗ*' applies not to the new *phūlḗ* of the social reform but to the old *phūlḗ* that still reflects more faithfully the institutions of the tribe.[72] In fact, the notion 'to make distinctions according to *phūlḗ*' reveals something basic about the inherited semantics of both *phūlḗ* and *phûlon.* As Nicole Loraux points out,[73] the noun *phûlon* 'race, kind' conveys the *distinctiveness* of one entity as opposed to another: thus, for example, the *phûlon* of gods is distinct from the *phûlon* of men (*Iliad* V 441–442); the emphasis is on *closure of categories,* on *separation*—which is also why the plural *phūla* conveys the *diversity* of subcategories within a category.[74] Both notions, *distinctiveness* and *diversity,* are evident in the Homeric usage of *phûlon* as a synonym (or better, as a diachronic equivalent) of *phūlḗ*: in *Iliad* II 362, Agamemnon is advised to set up battle formations by arranging the warriors *katà phûla* 'according to *phūlaí*' and *katà phrḗtrās* 'according to *phrātríai*'.[75] Moreover, the verb for 'arrange' in this passage is *krīnein,* the same element that we find in the expression *phūlokrīneîn*; in other words, the act of arranging *katà phûla* and *katà phrḗtrās* is itself an act of selection, setting apart, distinguishing.[76] But there is another side of distinctiveness here, and that is complementarity: again in the same context, we see that each distinct military unit can then help the other (*Iliad* II 363)—while all along they fight in their own categories, *katà sphéas* (II 366). Thus group solidarity is not at odds with

[72] Cf. Day and Chambers 1962.112–114 and Bourriot 1976.496.

[73] Loraux 1978.77n78.

[74] See Loraux p. 54 on e.g. *phūla gunaikōn* at Semonides F 7.94 W.

[75] For testimonia on military formations arranged according to *phūlaí,* see e.g. Jones 1980a.197–198 on Herodotus 6.111.1; for details on military formations arranged according to *phūlaí* and *phrātríai,* see e.g. Robertson 1980.17 on Athenaeus 141e-f). Note, too, the reference in Tyrtaeus F 19.8 W to the three Dorian *phūlaí* of Sparta as they are deployed in battle.

[76] Note the nuances of *phūlokrīneîn* in the context of Thucydides 6.18.2.

the distinctiveness of subgroups. The semantics of categorization by *phûlon* are reminiscent of the opposition "marked/unmarked" in language: the *phûlon* is the marked member in an opposition with any other member of a totality. So also with the kinship term *phūlḗ*: 'to make distinctions about *phūlḗ*' is an exercise in maintaining categories of markedness. If we turn for just a moment to consider an analogue in a society that is otherwise very different from that of the Greeks, I am reminded of how the Tonga reportedly describe to outsiders the function of the main kinship subdivisions of their society: for them such a subdivision is their "flag."[77] It is something given to them by divinity "so that we could marry properly."[78]

In the case of the Tonga, proper patterns of marriage are achieved by the rule of exogamy among the kinship groups, which serves as "a primary mechanism for spinning the network of alliances between groups."[79] It seems fair to generalize, in fact, that the structure of any tribal society is shaped by its patterns of kinship grouping through exogamy, endogamy, or some combination of the two. In the case of the Greek polis, the evidence about patterns of marriage is insufficient, but one thing seems obvious: the *phrātríā* is by its very nature exogamous.[80] As for the *phūlḗ*, there is reason to think that there were constraints against certain patterns of intermarriage among *phūlaí*,[81] and we may compare the detailed rules against certain patterns of intermarriage among the *varṇa*-s of India.[82]

[77] Gluckman 1965.97.

[78] Gluckman p. 97.

[79] Gluckman p. 97. Cf. also p. 165 on the concept of *multiple and therefore divided loyalties.*

[80] In some cities, there is further differentiation, with the *phrātríā* further subdivided into *patríai* (cf. Roussel 1976.156 and 217n9 on the situation in Miletus); in other cities, however, the *patríā* seems to be the equivalent of what is called *phrātríā* elsewhere (cf. Roussel p. 154 on the situation in Thasos). As P.-Y. Jacopin points out to me, a narrower category of lineage (as in any existing opposition between a narrower category of *patríā* and a broader category of *phrātríā*) would most probably exclude junior branches.

[81] Cf. Gernet 1955.140n4; cf. also the semantics of *phūlokrīneîn*, as noted above. For a particularly valuable discussion of this word, see Bourriot 1976.501–508. For a report on a traditional interdiction of intermarriage between two particular Attic *dêmoi*, see Plutarch *Theseus* 13.2–3 and the helpful remarks of Gernet 1968.44–45 about the possible patterns of exogamy for males within a given *dêmos* and of endogamy for males within given groupings of *dêmoi*.

[82] Essentially, women of a higher *varṇa-* may not be given in marriage to men of a lower *varṇa-*, whereas women of a lower *varṇa-* may indeed be given to men of the next highest *varṇa-*: see Kane 1941.19–104 and Tambiah 1973, following Dumont 1980; also Yalman 1960. Ironically, the traditional constraints against intermarriage between the *varṇa*-s provided the ideological mechanism for integrating the emerging strata of society into the hierarchy of the *varṇa*-s: see Dumézil 1958.718–719 on *Manu* 10.46–50. They also provided the ideological mechanism for keeping a wide variety of differentiated strata at the bottom of the social pyramid: see Tambiah 1973. For example, the *sūta-* class, who tend horses and drive chariots, are the sons of a union between a female of the *brāhmaṇa-* class and a male of the *kṣatriya-* class. Here the ideological point of view motivates and perpetuates the

In this connection, it is interesting to note that Herodotus refers to the Aigeidai, a politically important lineage at Sparta, as a *phūlḗ* (4.149.1),[83] whereas Aristotle refers to them simply as a *phrātríā* (*Constitution of the Laconians,* F 532 Rose).[84] Aristotle concerns himself mostly with the lineage's claim to Theban origins,[85] whereas Herodotus is preoccupied with the lineage's political role in the history of Sparta:[86] significantly, tradition has it that the Aigeidai were connected by marriage to the royal line of the Herakleidai, in that Theras, an ancestor of the Aigeidai, whose father had fled in exile from Thebes to Sparta, was the maternal uncle of Eurysthenes and Prokles, the two Herakleidai who became the ancestors of the two royal houses of Sparta (Herodotus 6.52.2).[87] Now it so happens that lineages with royal connections or ambitions tend to practice endogamy,[88] as is clearly the case with the Bakkhiadai of Corinth (Herodotus 5.92).[89] Thus the reference by Herodotus to the Aigeidai as a *phūlḗ* at Sparta (again, 4.149.1) may perhaps reflect the endogamous tendencies of this lineage.[90]

Many uncertainties remain, and much further work is required on the problem of kinship patterns in ancient Greek society.[91] But at least this much seems to me certain: the Greek polis grew out of tribal institutions

genealogical point of view. In other words, it is not that the emergence of a type of "half-breed" led to the conceptualization of a new social class: rather, the emergence of new social functions led to the conceptualization of various categories of "half-breeds" as permutations of the old social functions. On the *sūta-* as a court poet, see Dillon 1975.54–55.

[83] Cf. the scholia to Pindar *Isthmian* 7.18a Drachmann.

[84] The Aristotle reference is in the scholia to Pindar *Isthmian* 7.18c.

[85] The Aigeidai of Sparta traced themselves, by way of their ancestor Aigeus (Herodotus 4.149.1), all the way back to Polyneikes, son of Oedipus (4.147.1–2). That the Aigeidai of Sparta originate from Thebes is proudly proclaimed in the words of Pindar *Isthmian* 7.14–15. There is an argument to be made that Pindar himself was a descendant of the original Theban branch of the Aigeidai: see Farnell 1932.178–179 and Hubbard 1985.129n83.

[86] On the restructuring of the family tree of the Aigeidai in the context of Spartan political history, see Vian 1963.219. According to Timagoras FGH 381 F 3, the Spartoi who fled from Thebes to Sparta (and these Spartoi were the Aigeidai: Vian p. 223) actually gave their name to Sparta. Aside from the Herodotean mention of the Aigeidai as a *phūlḗ* at Sparta, this polis is known for its three standard Dorian *phūlaí* of Dymanes, Hylleis, and Pamphyloi (e.g. Tyrtaeus F 19.8 W). In the account of a famous battle in the series of campaigns known as the Messenian Wars, Pausanias 4.7.8, there is a description of the battle line of the Spartans, where the left and the right wings are each commanded by one of the two Spartan kings, while the center is reserved for a descendant of the Aigeidai (4.7.8).

[87] See further Vian p. 218n4. Note, too, Vian's discussion of the Theban connections of Dorieus (p. 225).

[88] Cf. Gernet 1968 [1953].349–350.

[89] For Herodotus, endogamy on the level of lineage is a variation on the theme of incest, which in turn is correlated with the theme of the *húbris* of tyrants: see Vernant 1982.

[90] The early political power of the Aigeidai is formalized in the elliptic naming of Sparta after them, as reported by Timagoras (see n86 above).

[91] Facts and theories useful for comparison may be found e.g. in Brough 1953 on the

that reflect, albeit from a distance, an Indo-European heritage. The passage from tribe to polis, as is the case with any structure viewed through time, is a process where some aspects of the older phases of the structure fit in with those of the newer phases while other aspects are out of joint. We may not assume that difficulties of transition prove the lack of a historical connection between older and newer phases, any more than we may assume that instances of smooth transition prove the sameness of older and newer phases.

---

gotra- as an exogamous grouping of the *brāhmaṇa*-s and on the *pravara-*, a pattern of listing sequences of remote ancestors that serves as a test for maintaining exogamy. Note that a *kṣatriya-* is allowed to assume the *gotra-* of his *purohita-:* hence the application of the brahmanical *gotra*-title *Gautama* to the Buddha, who was actually from a *kṣatriya-* family (Brough p. 5n3). On the semantics of *gotra-,* see Lincoln 1975. Note, too, the interesting comments of Held 1935.96–97 on a five-generation framework (including the generation of the ego) for *sapiṇḍa*-relationships; cf. the symbolism of the number 5 in the Hesiodic myth of the five generations of mankind (on which see N 1979a.168–172).

CHAPTER 13

Unattainable Wishes: The Restricted Range of an Idiom in Epic Diction

εἰ γὰρ ἐγὼν ὣς
εἴην ἀθάνατος καὶ ἀγήρως ἤματα πάντα
τιοίμην δ' ὡς τίετ' Ἀθηναίη καὶ Ἀπόλλων,
ὡς νῦν ἡμέρη ἥδε κακὸν φέρει Ἀργείοισι

Iliad VIII 538–541

If only I were
immortal and unaging for all days to come,
and if only I were honored just as Athena and Apollo are honored,
—as surely as this day brings misfortune to the Argives

There have been problems with understanding the meaning of this passage, which features an extraordinary wish on the part of the speaker, the hero Hektor. At the root of these problems, I suspect, is an uneasiness on the part of many readers about the values underlying this wish, values that seem to disturb our own received notions of the Hellenic ideal as conveyed by epic.

The same problems recur in *Iliad* XIII 825–828, where Hektor expresses the same wish; verses 827–828 are identical with VIII 540–541, but the first two verses are slightly different:

εἰ γὰρ ἐγὼν οὕτω γε Διὸς πάις αἰγιόχοιο
εἴην ἤματα πάντα, τέκοι δέ με πότνια Ἥρη

Iliad XIII 825–826

If only I were the child of aegis-bearing Zeus
for all days to come, and the Lady Hera were my mother

The translations I offer here, based roughly on the rendition of Homer by Richmond Lattimore,[1] have been taken from a chapter I have written on the death of Hektor, where I adduce these two passages in arguing that the hero's hybristic wish to be a god draws him into a force field of antagonism with the gods, notably Athena.[2] In the view of F. M. Combellack, however, I and many others have misunderstood these passages.[3] He claims that "though what Hector says in these passages is grammatically a wish he does not express here any desire to be immortal or to be the child of Zeus."[4]

In making this claim, Combellack attempts to define an idiom that is at work here, citing a formulation found in Walter Leaf's comments on these passages: "a form of wish, where a thing is vividly depicted as certain by opposing it to an imaginary event which is obviously impossible."[5] What Hektor is really saying, Combellack insists, is "I wish I were as sure of immortality (or of being the son of Zeus) as I am that this day brings evil to the Greeks."[6] The author continues:[7]

> If I say, "I wish I were as certain of being elected President as I am that my taxes will go up this year," my sentence is grammatically a wish, but no one would imagine for a moment that I am expressing a desire to become President. I am using an idiom to emphasize my certainty that my taxes will go up. And Hector is merely emphasizing his certainty that evil is in store for the Greeks.

There is a serious flaw, however, in Combellack's reasoning here. He is assuming that the perspective of Hektor is the same as the perspective of the reader of Homer. What is an absurdity for the reader—or, to put it more rigorously, for the intended audience of Homeric poetry—is assumed to be an absurdity for the character who is speaking. This is to overlook a central feature in the composition of Homeric speeches, where a given character's perception of reality is frequently at odds with the reality that emerges from the overall narrative—that is, with the perception of reality by the intended audience of Homeric poetry. We shall explore some examples below, but it will suffice for the moment to cite a book on Homeric speeches that is well worth reading in this regard.[8]

[1] Lattimore 1951, 1965.
[2] N 1979a.42–50. See also p. 204n10 above.
[3] Combellack 1981.
[4] Combellack p. 116.
[5] Leaf 1900 1:368.
[6] Combellack p. 116.
[7] Combellack p. 116.
[8] Lohmann 1970.

A more serious flaw in Combellack's reasoning is that he has not examined exhaustively the Homeric parallels to the idiom that he has isolated in the two speeches of Hektor. Taking his examples from Leaf's incomplete list of Homeric passages where the same idiom occurs, he cites the following as formally the closest parallel:

αἲ γάρ μιν θανάτοιο δυσηχέος ὧδε δυναίμην
νόσφιν ἀποκρύψαι, ὅτε μιν μόρος αἰνὸς ἱκάνοι,
ὥς οἱ τεύχεα καλὰ παρέσσεται

Iliad XVIII 464–66

If only I could have the power to hide him from sorrowful death,
when his dreadful fate comes upon him
—as surely as there will be fine armor for him!

Hephaistos is here wishing for something that seems at the moment impossible, and the wish is linked by the adverb ὧδε 'so' with the conjunction ὡς 'as' introducing an absolute certainty,[9] that Achilles will have fine armor. In other words, the impossibility of the wish (that Achilles be saved from death) is supposedly correlated with the certainty of the premise (that Achilles will have fine armor). The αἲ γάρ (+ optative) of the wish and the ὧδε . . . ὡς that links it with the premise are parallel to the εἰ γάρ (+ optative) of Hektor's wish to be an immortal (VIII 538 and XIII 825) and the ὣς/οὕτω . . . ὡς that links his wish with his premise that disaster will surely befall the Achaeans (VIII 538–541 and XIII 825–828).

What has eluded Combellack, however, is that this same idiom can occur in situations where the wish introduced by εἰ γάρ or the variants αἲ γάρ and εἴθε is clearly not perceived as impossible by the speaker. For example, the disguised Odysseus has this to say to Eumaios:

αἴθ' οὕτως, Εὔμαιε, φίλος Διὶ πατρὶ γένοιο
ὡς ἐμοί, ὅττι με τοῖον ἐόντ' ἀγαθοῖσι γεραίρεις

Odyssey xiv 440–441

If only, Eumaios, you would be dear to Zeus the Father
as surely as you are dear to me, since you grace me, such as I am, with good things.

[9] In this presentation I will for the sake of convenience render Greek 'so . . . as' constructions consistently in the mode of '. . . so as . . .' (*pace* Combellack 1981.119).

αἴθ' οὕτως, Εὔμαιε, φίλος Διὶ πατρὶ γένοιο
ὡς ἐμοί, ὅττι μ' ἔπαυσας ἄλης καὶ ὀιζύος αἰνῆς

Odyssey xv 341–342

If only, Eumaios, you would be dear to Zeus the Father
as surely as you are dear to me, since you stopped my wandering and my dreadful sorrow.

Clearly, it is not impossible that Eumaios should be dear to Zeus. The implication seems to be that he probably is, and this probability is reinforced by the certainty of Odysseus' premise: that Eumaios is dear to Odysseus. In this connection, we may observe what Priam says ironically about Achilles: αἴθε θεοῖσι φίλος τοσσόνδε γένοιτο ὅσσον ἐμοί 'If only he would be dear to the gods as much as he is to me!' (*Iliad* XXII 41–42).

The idiom under consideration is frequently found in prayers, as when Telemachus exclaims:

αἲ γάρ, Ζεῦ τε πάτερ καὶ Ἀθηναίη καὶ Ἄπολλον,
οὕτω νῦν μνηστῆρες ἐν ἡμετέροισι δόμοισι
νεύοιεν κεφαλὰς δεδμημένοι, οἱ μὲν ἐν αὐλῇ,
οἱ δ' ἔντοσθε δόμοιο, λελῦτο δὲ γυῖα ἑκάστου,
ὡς νῦν Ἶρος κεῖνος ἐπ' αὐλείῃσι θύρῃσιν
ἧσται νευστάζων κεφαλῇ

Odyssey xviii 235–240

O Father Zeus, Athena, and Apollo, if only
in our house the suitors could be defeated
and bow their heads, some in the courtyard
and some inside the house, and the limbs be unstrung in each of them
—as surely as that Iros there is sitting at the courtyard gates,
bowing his head

Clearly, someone who prays is not contrasting the impossibility of his wish with the certainty of a situation (as Combellack's concept of the idiom would require); rather, he is appealing to this certainty as grounds for hope that the wish be fulfilled.

At times the premise for the wish is the immediate context itself, to which the speaker can refer with but one word, such as οὕτως 'so' = 'just as surely as what has happened in this context'. Thus when the suitor Antinoos strikes the disguised Odysseus, Penelope responds to this outrage by saying: αἴθ' οὕτως αὐτόν σε βάλοι κλυτότοξος Ἀπόλλων 'If only Apollo, famed for his bow, would strike you just as surely [as you struck Odysseus]!' (*Odyssey* xvii 494). Penelope's prayer is then seconded by Eurynome: εἰ γὰρ ἐπ' ἀρῇσιν τέλος ἡμετέρῃσι γένοιτο 'If only our prayers would be accomplished!' (xvii 496). The expression 'our prayers' here refers to those of Penelope and Eurynome combined, as formalized in these two one-line versions of the idiom under study. Again, the idiom is being used to express a wish that is intended as possible, not impossible.

In one instance, a speaker uses a curtailed form of the idiom and then overtly says that his wish is impossible—only to be corrected by another speaker who uses a full form. Telemachus wishes that the gods could give him the *dúnamis* 'power' to kill the suitors (αἲ γὰρ ἐμοὶ τοσσήνδε θεοὶ δύναμιν περιθεῖεν *Odyssey* iii 205); then, instead of giving a premise as grounds of hope, he gives up hope by claiming that the gods have granted such a power neither to him nor to his father (208–209). At this point Nestor responds by resorting to a full form of the idiom:

εἰ γάρ σ' ὣς ἐθέλοι φιλέειν γλαυκῶπις Ἀθήνη
ὡς τότ' Ὀδυσσῆος περικήδετο κυδαλίμοιο
δήμῳ ἔνι Τρώων

Odyssey iii 218–220

If only *glaukôpis* Athena would deign to love you
as surely as in those days she cared for glorious Odysseus
in the Trojan country

This time there is indeed a premise, there is reason to hope: if Athena does love you this much, Nestor is telling Telemachus, then the suitors will indeed be killed (223–224).

By building on something that is perceived as certain in order to wish for something that is less certain, it is also possible to extend a specific observation into a general one. One of the suitors, for example, makes the following ironic remark about the disguised Odysseus as the hero prepares to string the bow:

αἲ γὰρ δὴ τοσσοῦτον ὀνήσιος ἀντιάσειεν
ὡς οὗτός ποτε τοῦτο δυνήσεται ἐντανύσασθαι

Odyssey xxi 402–403

If only this person would find much profit
—as surely as he will have the power to string this.

The words are meant ironically, but the real irony is at the expense of the speaker. He wishes general failure for the stranger on the basis of what he expects to be the stranger's specific failure in not being able to string the bow. Instead, Odysseus will achieve a specific success with the bow and general success against the suitors. For another example, I cite what Agamemnon imagines a Trojan would say ironically, if Menelaos were killed:

> αἴθ' οὕτως ἐπὶ πᾶσι χόλον τελέσει' Ἀγαμέμνων,
> ὡς καὶ νῦν ἅλιον στρατὸν ἤγαγεν ἐνθάδ' Ἀχαιῶν
>
> *Iliad* IV 178–79
>
> If only Agamemnon could bring his anger to bear against all his enemies
> —as surely as he has led here in vain a host of Achaeans.

In this imaginary situation the Trojan is entertaining the possibility of general failure for Agamemnon on the basis of one specific failure.

There are times when the hyperbole achieved with this idiom reaches the point of hybris. Such seems to be the case with the words spoken by Odysseus to the Cyclops after the hero has blinded the monster. If only I could kill you, says Odysseus to Cyclops, as surely as your father Poseidon will not restore your eyesight (*Odyssey* ix 523–525)! The hybristic reality of blinding the son of a god who is antagonistic to the hero is the basis for the even more hybristic wish of actually killing him. Similarly, in the first two passages that we have considered, Hektor can actually entertain the possibility of becoming a god himself on the basis of his certainty that he is about to destroy the Achaean expedition. The first time that Hektor uses the idiom under study, he is expressing his certainty that, come next morning, he will defeat the Achaeans, most notably Diomedes (*Iliad* VIII 526–538); the second time, he is expressing the same certainty, although the focus of his attention has now shifted from Diomedes to Ajax (XIII 829–832). Of course, the perceived reality of Hektor's premise is at odds with the reality of the narrative: Hektor will not succeed in killing Diomedes or Ajax, nor for that matter will he succeed in repelling the Achaeans from Troy. Therefore, his hybristic wish to be a god is built on a premise of self-delusion, and its wording becomes an extended exercise in self-delusion. Since Hektor is speaking, we have no right to impose the reality of the narrative on Hektor's perception of reality: for him the wish to be a god is not contrary to fact, and it would be better for us to abandon the decidedly contrary-to-fact translations "If only I were immortal . . ." and "If only I were the child of aegis-bearing Zeus . . ." for VIII 538 and XIII 825, substituting something more neutral: "If only I could be immortal . . ." and "If only I could be the child of aegis-bearing Zeus. . . ."

There is a similar though far less grandiose exercise in self-delusion on the part of the evil goatherd Melanthios: if only Apollo or one of the suitors could kill Telemachus, says he, as surely as Odysseus has perished at sea (*Odyssey* xvii 251–253)! The interpretation of Combellack loses sight of the hybristic amplification evident in the wish of the goatherd: "I wish I were as certain that Apollo or the suitors would kill Telemachus today as I am that Odysseus' day of return has been lost afar."[10] I see no evidence to suggest that Melanthios is supposed to perceive the killing of Telemachus as an impossibility.

At times the premise of our idiom is deliberately falsified by the narrative. For example, when the god Apollo assumes the human identity of Hektor's maternal uncle, he goads the hero into valor with these words: αἴθ' ὅσον ἥσσων εἰμί, τόσον σέο φέρτερος εἴην 'If only I could be superior to you—as surely as I am that much inferior to you!' (*Iliad* XVI 722). Apollo goes on to say, in the guise of the uncle: if you were that much inferior, then you would retreat in battle (723). But, since Hektor is supposedly that much superior, he is of course expected not to retreat. What is hidden in these comparisons, however, is the relative stature of the god himself: the uncle is to Hektor as Hektor is to Apollo.[11] From the standpoint of Hektor, the premise in Apollo's use of the idiom is reality: the uncle is inferior to Hektor. From the standpoint of Apollo and the narrative, however, the premise is false: Apollo is superior, not inferior, to Hektor. Therefore the wish that is based on the premise is augmented: the "that much" of "let me be that much superior to you" is immeasurably more than Hektor might think.

By now I have discussed, besides those Homeric examples I have found myself, every example adduced by Combellack—except one. As Hektor lies mortally wounded, Achilles expresses a ghastly wish, though in attenuated terms: if only, says he, my *ménos* 'power' and *thūmós* 'spirit'[12] could impel me to eat your flesh raw (*Iliad* XXII 346–348)! The premise upon which this wish is founded is almost as hybristic as the wish itself: as surely as it is impossible for your corpse to be rescued from the dogs and to be ransomed by Priam himself (348–354). Yet this "impossibility" is precisely what comes to pass in the course of *Iliad* XXIV.[13] The eventual relinquishing of Achilles' premise is a function of the hero's eventual rehumanization as the narrative moves from *Iliad* XXII to XXIV: it is up to Achilles to release the corpse. But at the moment that he utters the premise, expressing his determination to leave Hektor's

[10] Combellack p. 118.

[11] For this and other uses of such a proportional equation in archaic Greek poetry, see Lohmann 1970.189n6.

[12] On the association of these words as they apply to Achilles, see N 1979a.136–137.

[13] On this correspondence between *Iliad* XXII and XXIV, see Lohmann 1970.161n6, 279, 280n18.

body exposed to the dogs and to refuse any ransom offered by Priam, the ghastly wish about cannibalism is as real as the almost as ghastly premise upon which it is founded. Achilles means what he wishes. It makes no sense to claim that "he mentions the cannibalism as the most impossible thing he can think of in order to emphasize the certainty of the dogs tearing Hektor's body."[14] This is no time for Achilles to be reassuring Hektor of a sort of modified bestiality, that he will go only so far as to expose Hektor's corpse to dogs but not so far as to eat it himself. Rather, the beastly wish is an amplification of an already beastly premise.

I come to the last example in my survey, a passage where Agamemnon has these words to say to Nestor:

> ὦ γέρον, εἴθ', ὡς θυμὸς ἐνὶ στήθεσσι φίλοισιν,
> ὥς τοι γούνατ' ἕποιτο, βίη δέ τοι ἔμπεδος εἴη
>
> *Iliad* IV 313–314

> Aged sir, if only your knees could keep up with the pace
> and your strength could remain steadfast—as surely as the spirit within you
> is steadfast!

The speaker is not telling the old man that it is impossible for him to keep up. Rather, he is paying tribute to an extraordinary man's extraordinary spirit by amplifying his admiration with a wish.[15]

For me this idiom, especially in the last example, serves as a metaphor for the Hellenization of Indo-European social ideology. If we may equate Hellenism with the ideal, the wish-fulfillment of human progress, then the Indo-European heritage of the Greek language, as an incomplete reflection of the past and the here-and-now, is a premise for that fulfillment.

[14]Combellack 1981.117.

[15]In the original version, I had added: "The same tribute is due to Sterling Dow, an extraordinary man of our own time."

Bibliography

Alexiou, M. 1974. *The Ritual Lament in Greek Tradition.* Cambridge.

Alföldi, A. 1974. *Die Struktur des voretruskischen Römerstaates.* Heidelberg.

Allen, T. W., ed. 1912. *Homeri Opera* 5 (Hymns, Cycle, fragments, etc.). Oxford.

——. 1924. *Homer: The Origins and the Transmission.* Oxford.

Allen, W. S. 1973. *Accent and Rhythm. Prosodic Features of Latin and Greek: A Study in Theory and Reconstruction.* Cambridge.

——. 1987. *Vox Graeca: The Pronunciation of Classical Greek.* 3rd ed. Cambridge.

Alty, J. 1982. "Dorians and Ionians." *Journal of Hellenic Studies* 102:1–14.

Andronikos, M. 1968. *Totenkult. Archaeologia Homerica* 3W, edited by F. Matz and H. G. Buchholz. Göttingen.

Arbman, E. 1926 / 1927. "Untersuchungen zur primitiven Seelenvorstellung mit besonderer Rücksicht auf Indien. I: Einleitendes. II: Altindischer Seelenglaube, sein Ursprung and seine Entwicklung." *Le Monde oriental* 20:85–226 / 21:1–185.

Austin, J. L. 1962. *How to Do Things with Words.* Oxford.

Bachelard, G. 1949. *La psychanalyse du feu.* Paris.

Balys, J. 1937. "Perkūnas lietuvių liaudies tikėjimuose." *Tautosakos darbai* 3. Kaunas.

Bartholomae, C. 1904. *Altiranisches Wörterbuch.* Strassburg.

Baumann, H. 1936. *Schöpfung und Urzeit des Menschen im Mythus der afrikanischen Völker.* Berlin.

Bausinger, H. 1980. *Formen der "Volkspoesie."* 2nd ed. Berlin.

Beekes, R. S. P. 1969. *The Development of the Proto-Indo-European Laryngeals in Greek.* The Hague.

Ben-Amos, D. 1976. "Analytical Categories and Ethnic Genres." *Folklore Genres,* edited by D. Ben-Amos, 215–242. Austin.

Benveniste, E. 1935. *Origines de la formation des noms en indo-européen.* Paris.

——. 1937. "Expression indo-européenne de l'éternité." *Bulletin de la Société de Linguistique de Paris* 38:103–112.

——. 1948. "Notes de vocabulaire latin." *Revue de Philologie* 22:122–124.

——. 1962. *Hittite et Indo-Européen.* Paris.

——. 1966. *Problèmes de linguistique générale.* Paris.

——. 1968. "Phraséologie poétique de l'indo-iranien." *Mélanges d'indianisme à la mémoire de Louis Renou* 73–79. Paris.

——. 1969. *Le vocabulaire des institutions indo-européennes.* 1. *Economie, parenté, société.* 2. *Pouvoir, droit, religion.* Paris. = *Indo-European Language and Society,* translated 1973 by E. Palmer. London and Coral Gables, Fl.

Benveniste, E., and Renou, E. 1934. *Vr̥tra et Vr̥θragna. Etude de mythologie indo-iranienne.* Paris.

Bérard, C. 1970. *L'hérôon à la porte de l'ouest.* Bern.

——. 1982. "Récupérer la mort du prince: Héroïsation et formation de la cité." *La mort, les morts dans les sociétés anciennes,* edited by G. Gnoli and J.-P. Vernant, 89–105. Cambridge and Paris.

Bergaigne, A. 1878–1883. *La religion védique* 1–3. Paris.

Bergren, A. L. T. 1975. *The Etymology and Usage of* ΠΕΙΡΑΡ *in Early Greek Poetry.* American Classical Studies 2, American Philological Association. New York.

Biezais, H. H. 1955. *Die Hauptgöttinnen der alten Letten.* Uppsala.

Bloom, H., ed. 1986. *Modern Critical Views: Homer.* New York.

Boas, F. 1898. *The Mythology of the Bella Coola Indians.* Memoirs of the American Museum of Natural History 2: The Jesup North Pacific Expedition. New York.

——. 1910. *Kwakiutl Tales.* Columbia University Contributions to Anthropology 2. New York and Leiden.

Boedeker, D. D. 1974. *Aphrodite's Entry into Greek Epic.* Leiden.

——. 1984. *Descent from Heaven: Images of Dew in Greek Poetry and Religion.* American Classical Studies 13, American Philological Association. Chico, Cal.

Böhme, J. 1929. *Die Seele und das Ich im homerischen Epos.* Leipzig.

Borgeaud, W. A. 1982. *Fasti Umbrici: Etudes sur le vocabulaire et le rituel des Tables eugubines.* Ottawa.

Borthwick, E. K. 1969. "The Verb ΑΥΩ and Its Compounds." *Classical Quarterly* 19:306–313.

Bourriot, F. 1976. *Recherches sur la nature du Genos: Etude d'histoire sociale athénienne, périodes archaïques et classiques.* 2 vols. Lille and Geneva.

Bowie, A. M. 1981. *The Poetic Dialect of Sappho and Alcaeus.* New York.

Bowra, C. M. 1961. *Greek Lyric Poetry.* 2nd ed. Oxford.

Brelich, A. 1949. *Vesta.* Zurich.

——. 1958. *Gli eroi greci.* Rome.

——. 1961. *Guerre, agoni e culti nella Grecia arcaica.* Bonn.

——. 1969. *Paides e Parthenoi.* Incunabula Graeca 36. Rome.

Bremmer, J. 1983. *The Early Greek Concept of the Soul.* Princeton.

Bremmer, J. N., and Horsfall, N. M. 1987. *Roman Myth and Mythography.* University of London Institute of Classical Studies Bulletin Supplement 52. London.

Brough, J. 1953. *The Early Brahmanical System of Gotra and Pravara.* Cambridge.

Brückner, A. 1926. "Mythologische Themen." *Archiv für Slavische Philologie* 40:1–26.

Brugmann, K. 1904/1905. "Griech. υἱύς υἱός υἱωνός und ai. *sūnús* got. *sunus.*" *Indogermanische Forschungen* 17:483–491.

Būga, K. 1921. "Priesagos *-ūnas* ir dvibalsio *uo* kilmė." *Lietuvos mokykla* 10/11:420–457. Reprinted 1959 in Būga's *Rinktiniai raštai* 2:331–376. Vilnius.

Bundy, E. L. 1962 [1986]. "Studia Pindarica I: The Eleventh Olympian Ode; II: The First Isthmian Ode." *University of California Publications in Classical Philology* 18, nos. 1–2:1–92. Both articles reissued 1986 as *Studia Pindarica.* Berkeley and Los Angeles.

——. 1972. "The 'Quarrel' between Kallimachos and Apollonios, Part I: The Epilogue of Kallimachos' *Hymn to Apollo.*" *California Studies in Classical Antiquity* 5:39–94.

Burkert, W. 1961. "Elysion." *Glotta* 39:208–213.

——. 1966. "Greek Tragedy and Sacrificial Ritual." *Greek Roman and Byzantine Studies* 7:87–121.

——. 1965. "Demaratos, Astrabakos und Herakles." *Museum Helveticum* 22:166–177.

——. 1970. "Jason, Hypsipyle, and the New Fire of Lemnos." *Classical Quarterly* 20:1–16.

——. 1972. "Die Leistung eines Kreophylos: Kreophyleer, Homeriden und die archaische Heraklesepik." *Museum Helveticum* 29:74–85.

——. 1975. "Apellai und Apollon." *Rheinisches Museum* 118.1–21.

——. 1979a. *Structure and History in Greek Mythology and Ritual.* Berkeley and Los Angeles.

——. 1979b. "Mythisches Denken." *Philosophie und Mythos,* edited by H. Poser, 16–39. Berlin and New York.

——. 1983. *Homo Necans: The Anthropology of Ancient Greek Sacrificial Ritual and Myth,* translated by P. Bing. Berkeley and Los Angeles. Originally published 1972 in German under the title *Homo Necans.* Berlin.

——. 1984. *Die Orientalisierende Epoche in der griechischen Religion und Literatur.* Heidelberg.

——. 1985. *Greek Religion,* translated by J. Raffan. Cambridge, Mass. Originally published 1977 in German under the title *Griechische Religion der archaischen und klassischen Epoche.* Stuttgart.

Burnett, A. P. 1983. *Three Archaic Poets: Archilochus, Alcaeus, Sappho.* Cambridge, Mass.

Byrne, J. 1971. "Tribes and Tribalism in Early Ireland." *Ériu* 22.128–166.

Calame, C. 1977. *Les choeurs de jeunes filles en Grèce archaïque.* 1: *Morphologie, fonction religieuse et sociale.* 2: *Alcman.* Rome.

——, ed., with commentary. 1983. *Alcman.* Rome.

——. 1986. *Le récit en Grèce ancienne.* Paris.

——. 1987. "Spartan Genealogies: The Mythological Representation of a Spatial Organisation." *Interpretations of Greek Mythology,* edited by J. Bremmer, 153–186. London.

Caland, W. 1893. *Altindischer Ahnenkult.* Leiden.

——. 1896. *Die altindischen Todten- und Bestattungsgebräuche.* Amsterdam.

Campbell, D. A., ed. 1976. *Greek Lyric Poetry: A Selection of Early Greek Lyric, Elegiac and Iambic Poetry.* Reprint, with addenda, of the 1967 ed. London.

——, ed., with translation. 1982. *Greek Lyric.* 1: *Sappho and Alcaeus.* Cambridge, Mass.

Caswell, C. P. 1986. "A Study of *Thumos* in Early Greek Epic." Doctoral dissertation, Boston University.

Cerri, G. 1969. "*Isos dasmos* come equivalente di *isonomia* nella silloge teognidea." *Quaderni Urbinati di Cultura Classica* 8:97–104.

Chantraine, P. 1968, 1970, 1975, 1977, 1980. *Dictionnaire étymologique de la langue grecque* I, II, III, IV-1, IV-2. Paris.

Christensen, A. 1916. "Reste von Manu-Legenden in der iranischen Sagenwelt." *Festschrift Friedrich Carl Andreas* 63–69. Leipzig.

——. 1918 / 1934. *Le premier homme et le premier roi dans l'histoire légendaire des Iraniens* 1/2. Uppsala / Leiden.

Christmann-Franck, L. 1971. "Le rituel des funérailles royales hittites." *Revue Hittite et Asianique* 29:61–111.

Clader, L. L. 1976. *Helen: The Evolution from Divine to Heroic in Greek Epic Tradition.* Leiden.

Clark, M. E., and Coulsen, D. E. 1978. "Memnon and Sarpedon." *Museum Helveticum* 35:65–73.

Claus, D. B. 1981. *Toward the Soul: An Inquiry into the Meaning of Soul before Plato.* New Haven.

Clay, J. S. 1984. *The Wrath of Athena. Gods and Men in the Odyssey.* Princeton.

Coldstream, J. N. 1976. "Hero-Cults in the Age of Homer." *Journal of Hellenic Studies* 96.8–17.

Combellack, F. M. 1981. "The Wish without Desire." *American Journal of Philology* 102:115–19.

Connor, W. R. 1987. "Tribes, Festivals and Processions: Civic Ceremonial and Political Manipulation in Archaic Greece." *Journal of Hellenic Studies* 107:40–50.

Cook, R. M. 1937. "The Date of the Hesiodic Shield." *Classical Quarterly* 31:204–214.

Crane, G. 1988. *Backgrounds and Conventions of the Odyssey.* Beiträge zur Klassischen Philologie 191. Frankfurt am Main.

Culler, J. 1975. *The Pursuit of Signs: Semiotics, Literature, Deconstruction.* Ithaca, N.Y., and London.

Darcus, S. M. 1979a. "A Person's Relation to ΨΥΧΗ in Homer, Hesiod, and the Greek Lyric Poets." *Glotta* 57:30–39.

——. 1979b. "A Person's Relation to ΦΡΗΝ in Homer, Hesiod, and the Greek Lyric Poets." *Glotta* 57:159–173.

——. 1980. "How a Person Relates to ΝΟΟΣ in Homer, Hesiod, and the Greek Lyric Poets." *Glotta* 58:33–44.

Darkevič, V. P. 1961. "Topor kak simvol peruna v drevnerusskom jazyčestve." *Sovetskaja Arxeologija* 4:91–102.

Davidson, H. R. E. 1965. "Thor's Hammer." *Folklore* 76:1–15.

Davidson, O. M. 1979. "Dolon and Rhesus in the *Iliad.*" *Quaderni Urbinati di Cultura Classica* 30:61–66.

——. 1980. "Indo-European Dimensions of Herakles in *Iliad* 19.95–133." *Arethusa* 13:197–202.

——. 1985. "The Crown-Bestower in the Iranian Book of Kings." *Acta Iranica, Hommages et Opera Minora* 10: *Papers in Honour of Professor Mary Boyce,* 61–148. Leiden.

——. 1987. "Aspects of Dioscurism in Iranian Kingship: The Case of Lohrasp and Goshtasp in the *Shāhnāme* of Ferdowsi." *Edebiyāt* 1:103–115.

Day, J., and Chambers, M. 1962. *Aristotle's History of Athenian Democracy.* Berkeley and Los Angeles.

Delcourt, M. 1965. *Pyrrhos et Pyrrha: Recherches sur les valeurs du feu dans les légendes helléniques.* Paris.

DELG. *See* Chantraine 1968–1980.

DELL. *See* Ernout and Meillet 1959.

Detienne, M. 1972. *Les jardins d'Adonis: La mythologie des aromates en Grèce.* Paris = *The Gardens of Adonis,* translated 1977 by J. Lloyd. Sussex.

——. 1973. *Les maîtres de vérité dans la Grèce archaïque.* 2nd ed. Paris.

——. 1977. *Dionysos mis à mort.* Paris = *Dionysos Slain,* translated 1979 by L. Muellner and M. Muellner. Baltimore.

——. 1981. *L'invention de la mythologie.* Paris.

Detienne, M., and Svenbro, J. 1979. "Les loups au festin ou la Cité impossible." In Detienne and Vernant 1979:215–237.

Detienne, M., and Vernant, J.-P. 1974. *Les ruses de l'intelligence: La* ΜΗΤΙΣ *des Grecs.* Paris. = *Cunning Intelligence in Greek Culture and Society,* translated 1978 by J. Lloyd. Sussex.

Detienne, M., and Vernant, J.-P., eds. 1979. *La cuisine du sacrifice en pays grec.* Paris.

Devoto, G., ed. 1937. *Tabulae Iguvinae.* Rome.

DGE. *See* Schwyzer 1923.

Diels, H., and Kranz, W., eds. 1951–1952. *Die Fragmente der Vorsokratiker.* 6th ed. Berlin.

Dieterich, A. 1913. *Nekyia.* Leipzig and Berlin.

Diggle, J., ed., with commentary. 1970. *Euripides, Phaethon.* Cambridge.

Dihle, A. 1970. *Homer-Probleme.* Opladen.

Dillon, M. 1975. *Celts and Aryans: Survivals of Indo-European Speech and Society.* Simla.

Dirlmeier, F. 1955. "Homerisches Epos und Orient." *Rheinisches Museum* 98:18–37.

Dittenberger, W., ed. 1915–1924. *Sylloge Inscriptionum Graecarum.* 3rd ed. Leipzig.

DK. *See* Diels and Kranz 1951–1952.

Dodds, E. R. 1951. *The Greeks and the Irrational.* Berkeley and Los Angeles.

——, ed. 1960. *Bacchae,* by Euripides. 2nd ed. Oxford.

Donini, G. 1967. "Osservazioni sui rapporti tra alcuni passi dell' *Iliade* riguardanti Enea." *Rivista di Filologia e di Istruzione Classica* 95:389–396.

Donlan, W. 1970. "Changes and Shifts in the Meaning of Demos." *La Parola del Passato* 135:381–395.

Drachmann, A. B., ed. 1903–1927. *Scholia Vetera in Pindari Carmina.* 3 vols. Leipzig.

Drekmeier, C. 1962. *Kingship and Community in Early India.* Stanford.

Duban, J. 1980. "Poets and Kings in the *Theogony* Invocation." *Quaderni Urbinati di Cultura Classica* 33:7–21.

Dubois, J. A. 1924. *Moeurs, institutions et cérémonies des peuples de l'Inde,* translated by H. K. Beauchamp, *Hindu Manners, Customs and Ceremonies.* 3rd ed. Oxford.

Dubuisson, D. 1978a. "Le roi indo-européen et la synthèse des trois fonctions." *Annales Economies Sociétés Civilisations* 33.21–34.

——. 1978b. "L'équipement de l'inauguration royale dans l'Inde védique et en Irlande." *Revue de l'Histoire des Religions* 193:153–164.

Duchesne-Guillemin, J. 1962. *La religion de l'Iran ancien.* Paris.

——. 1979. "La royauté iranienne et le *x^v arənah.*" *Iranica,* edited by G. Gnoli and A. Rossi, 375–386. Naples.

Ducrot, O., and Todorov, T. 1972. *Dictionnaire encyclopédique des sciences du langage.* Paris. = *Encyclopedic Dictionary of the Sciences of Language,* translated 1979 by C. Porter. Baltimore.

Duggan, J., ed. 1975. *Oral Literature: Seven Essays.* Edinburgh and New York.

Dumézil, G. 1941. *Jupiter Mars Quirinus* 1. Paris.

——. 1943. *Les mythes romains.* 2: *Servius et la Fortune, essai sur la fonction sociale de louange et de blâme et sur les éléments indo-européens du* cens *romain.* Paris.

——. 1953. "Les trois fonctions dans quelques traditions grecques." *Hommage à Lucien Febvre,* 25–32. Paris.

——. 1954. *Rituels indo-européens à Rome.* Paris.

——. 1958. *L'idéologie tripartie des Indo-Européens.* Paris.

——. 1959a. "Trois règles de l'Aedes Vestae." *Revue des Etudes Latines* 37:94–104.

——. 1959b. *Les dieux des Germains.* Paris.

——. 1961. "Vesta extrema." *Revue des Etudes Latines* 39:250–257.

——. 1966. *La religion romaine archaïque.* Paris.

——. 1968. *Mythe et épopée.* 1: *L'idéologie des trois fonctions dans les épopées des peuples indo-européens.* Paris.

——. 1969. *Idées romaines.* Paris.

——. 1971. *Mythe et épopée.* 2: *Un héros, un sorcier, un roi.* Paris.

——. 1973. *Mythe et épopée.* 3: *Histoires romaines.* Paris.

——. 1977. *Les dieux souverains des Indo-Européens.* Paris.

——. 1982. *Apollon sonore. Et autres essais. Vingt-cinq esquisses de mythologie* (1–25). Paris.

——. 1983. *La courtisane et les seigneurs colorés. Et autres essais. Vingt-cinq esquisses de mythologie* (26–50). Paris.

——. 1985. *L'oubli de l'homme et l'honneur des dieux. Et autres essais. Vingt-cinq esquisses de mythologie* (51–75). Paris.

Dumont, L. 1980. *Homo Hierarchicus: The Caste System and Its Implications,* complete revised English edition, translated by M. Sainsbury, L. Dumont, and B. Gulaiti. Chicago.

Dunkel, G. 1979. "Fighting Words: Alcman *Partheneion* 63: μάχονται." *Journal of Indo-European Studies* 7:249–272.

Durante, M. 1976. *Sulla preistoria della tradizione poetica greca.* 2: *Risultanze della comparazione indoeuropea.* Incunabula Graeca 64. Rome.

Dworak, P. 1938. *Gott und König: Eine religionsgeschichtliche Untersuchung ihrer wechselseitigen Beziehungen.* Bonn.

Edmunds, L. 1985. "The Genre of Theognidean Poetry." In Figueira and Nagy 1985:96–111.

Edwards, A. T. 1988. "ΚΛΕΟΣ ΑΦΘΙΤΟΝ and Oral Theory." *Classical Quarterly* 38:25–30.

Edwards, G. P. 1971. *The Language of Hesiod in Its Traditional Context.* Oxford.

Edwards, M. W. 1986. "Homer and Oral Tradition, Part 1." *Oral Tradition* 1:171–230.

——. 1988. "Homer and Oral Tradition, Part 2." *Oral Tradition* 3:11–60.

EG. *See* Page 1975.

Eliade, M. 1962. *The Forge and the Crucible*, translated by S. Corrin. New York and London.

——. 1963. *Patterns in Comparative Religion*, translated by R. Sheed. Cleveland and New York.

Else, G. F., ed., with commentary. 1957. *Aristotle's Poetics: The Argument.* Cambridge, Mass.

——. 1967. *Homer and the Homeric Problem.* Lectures in Memory of Louise Taft Semple, University of Cincinnati Classical Studies 1: 315–365. Princeton.

Endzelin, J. 1923. *Lettische Grammatik.* Heidelberg.

Ernout, A. 1954. *Aspects du vocabulaire latin.* Paris.

——. 1961. *Le dialecte ombrien.* Paris.

Ernout, A., and Meillet, A. 1959. *Dictionnaire étymologique de la langue latine.* 4th ed. Paris.

EWA. *See* Mayrhofer 1986–.

Farnell, L. R. 1921. *Greek Hero Cults and Ideas of Immortality.* Oxford.

——. 1932. *The Works of Pindar.* 2: *Critical Commentary.* London.

Feist, S. 1939. *Vergleichendes Wörterbuch der gotischen Sprache.* 3rd ed. Leiden.

FGH. *See* Jacoby 1923–.

Figueira, T. J. 1981. *Aegina.* New York.

——. 1984. "The Ten Arkhontes of 579/8 at Athens." *Hesperia* 53:447–473.

——. 1985. "The Theognidea and Megarian Society." In Figueira and Nagy 1985:112–158.

Figueira, T. J., and Nagy, G., eds. 1985. *Theognis of Megara: Poetry and the Polis.* Baltimore.

Finkelberg, M. 1986. "Is ΚΛΕΟΣ ΑΦΘΙΤΟΝ a Homeric Formula?" *Classical Quarterly* 36:1–5.

Finnegan, R. 1970. *Oral Literature in Africa.* Oxford.

——. 1977. *Oral Poetry: Its Nature, Significance, and Social Context.* Cambridge.

Floyd, E. D. 1980. "ΚΛΕΟΣ ΑΦΘΙΤΟΝ: An Indo-European Perspective on Early Greek Poetry." *Glotta* 58:133–157.

Fontenrose, J. 1978. *The Delphic Oracle: Its Responses and Operations, with a Catalogue of Responses.* Berkeley and Los Angeles.

Ford, A. L. 1985. "The Seal of Theognis: The Politics of Authorship in Archaic Greece." In Figueira and Nagy 1985:82–95.

Fraenkel, E. 1962 / 1965. *Litauisches etymologisches Wörterbuch* 1/2. Heidelberg.

Frame, D. 1978. *The Myth of Return in Early Greek Epic.* New Haven.

Fränkel, H. 1960. "Der kallimachische und der homerische Hexameter." *Wege und Formen frühgriechischen Denkens*, 100–156. 2nd ed. Munich.

——. 1975. *Early Greek Poetry and Philosophy*, translated by M. Hadas and J. Willis. New York.

Fraser, P. M. 1953. "The Tribal Cycles of Eponymous Priests at Lindos and Kamiros." *Eranos* 51:23–47.

Frazer, J. G. 1921. *Apollodorus* 1/2. London and New York.

——. 1930. *Myths of the Origin of Fire.* London.

Friedrich, J. 1952–. *Hethitisches Wörterbuch.* Heidelberg.

Friedrich, P. 1970. *Proto-Indo-European Trees.* Chicago and London.

Frisk, H. 1960–1970. *Griechisches etymologisches Wörterbuch.* Heidelberg.

Fritz, K. von. 1943. "ΝΟΟΣ and ΝΟΕΙΝ in the Homeric Poems." *Classical Quarterly* 38:79–93.

Gamkrelidze, T. V., and Ivanov, V. V. 1984. *Indoevropejskij jazyk i Indoevropejcy. Rekonstrukcija i istoriko-tipologičeskij analyz prajazyka i protokul'tury.* 2 vols. Tbilisi.

Garland, R. 1981. "The Causation of Death in the *Iliad*: A Theological and Biological Investigation." *Bulletin of the Institute of Classical Studies* 28:43–60.

Geldner, K. F. 1951–1957. *Der Rig-Veda, aus dem Sanskrit ins Deutsche übersetzt* 1–4. Cambridge, Mass., and Leipzig.

Gentili, B., and Prato, C., eds. 1979 / 1985. *Poetae Elegiaci* 1/2. Leipzig.

Gerber, D.E., ed. 1970. *Euterpe: An Anthology of Early Greek Lyric, Elegiac and Iambic Poetry.* Amsterdam.

——. 1982. *Pindar's Olympian One: A Commentary.* Toronto.

Gernet, L. 1953. "Mariages de Tyrans." *Hommage à Lucien Febvre,* 41–53. Paris. Reprinted in Gernet 1968:344–359.

——. 1955. *Droit et société dans la Grèce ancienne.* Paris.

——. 1968. *Anthropologie de la Grèce antique.* Paris. = *The Anthropology of Ancient Greece,* translated 1981 by J. Hamilton and B. Nagy. Baltimore.

GEW. *See* Frisk 1960–1970.

Gill, D. 1974. "Trapezomata: A Neglected Aspect of Greek Sacrifice." *Harvard Theological Review* 67:117–137.

Gimbutas, M. 1967. "Ancient Slavic Religion." *To Honor Roman Jakobson,* 738–759. The Hague and Paris.

Gluckman, M. 1965. *Politics, Law and Ritual in Tribal Society.* Oxford.

Gnoli, G. 1980. *Zoroaster's Time and Homeland: A Study on the Origins of Mazdeism and Related Problems.* Naples.

Goetze, A. 1954. "Some Groups of Ancient Anatolian Proper Names." *Language* 30:349–359.

Golden, L., and Hardison, O. B. 1981. *Aristotle's Poetics: A Translation and Commentary for Students of Literature.* Gainesville, Fl.

Gonda, J. 1954. *Aspects of Early Viṣṇuism.* Utrecht.

——. 1960. *Die Religionen Indiens* 1. Stuttgart.

——. 1976. *Triads in the Veda.* Verhandelingen der koninklijke nederlandse Akademie van Wetenschappen, afd. Letterkunde, Nieuwe Reeks, Deel 91. Amsterdam.

GP. *See* Gentili and Prato 1979 / 1985.

Grassmann, H. 1873. *Wörterbuch zum Rig-Veda.* Leipzig.

Griffith, M. 1983. "Personality in Hesiod." *Classical Antiquity* 2:37–65.

Grimm, J. 1875–1878. *Deutsche Mythologie* 1–3. 4th ed. Berlin.

Grottanelli, C. 1981. "Relazione." *Dialoghi di Archeologia* 2:55–67.

Grottanelli, C., and Parise, N. F., eds. 1988. *Sacrificio e società nel mondo antico.* Rome and Bari.

Gruppe, O. 1906. *Griechische Mythologie und Religionsgeschichte* 1. Munich.

——. 1912. "Die eherne Schwelle und der Thorikische Stein." *Archiv für Religionswissenschaft* 15.359–379.

Güntert, H. 1909. *Kalypso. Bedeutungsgeschichtliche Untersuchungen auf dem Gebiet der indogermanischen Sprachen.* Halle am Saale.

——. 1914. *Über Reimwortbildungen im Arischen und Altgriechischen. Eine sprachwissenschaftliche Untersuchung.* Heidelberg.

——. 1923. *Der arische Weltkönig und Heiland: Bedeutungsgeschichtliche Untersuchungen zur indo-iranischen Religionsgeschichte und Altertumskunde.* Halle am Saale.

Güterbock, H. G. 1952. *The Song of Ullikummi: Revised Text of the Hittite Version of a Hurrian Myth.* New Haven.

Haas, M. R. 1969. *The Prehistory of Languages.* The Hague.

Hack, R. K. 1929. "Homer and the Cult of Heroes." *Transactions of the American Philological Association* 60:57–74.

Hadzisteliou Price, T. 1973. "Hero-Cult and Homer." *Historia* 22:129–144.

Hainsworth, J. B. 1964. "Structure and Content in Epic Formulae: The Question of the Unique Expression." *Classical Quarterly* 14:155–164.

——. 1968. *The Flexibility of the Homeric Formula.* Oxford.

Hamm, E.-M. 1957. *Grammatik zu Sappho und Alkaios.* Berlin.

Hanell, K. 1934. *Megarische Studien.* Lund.

Hansen, P. A., ed. 1983. *Carmina Epigraphica Graeca saeculorum viii-v a.Chr.n.* Berlin and New York.

Hansen, W. F. 1977. "Odysseus' Last Journey." *Quaderni Urbinati di Cultura Classica* 24:27–48.

Harrison, J. E. 1927. *Themis: A Study of the Social Origins of Greek Relgion.* 2nd ed. Cambridge.

Haymes, E. R. 1973. *A Bibliography of Studies Related to Parry's and Lord's Oral Theory.* Cambridge, Mass.

Held, G. J. 1935. *The Mahābhārata: An Ethnological Study.* London and Amsterdam.

Henzen, W., ed. 1874. *Acta fratrum Arvalium quae supersunt.* Berlin.

Heubeck, A. 1959. *Lydiaka: Untersuchungen zu Schrift, Sprache und Götternamen der Lyder.* Erlangen.

Hillebrandt, A. 1927. *Vedische Mythologie* 1–2. 2nd ed. Breslau.

Hocart, A. M. 1936. *Kings and Councillors: An Essay in the Comparative Anatomy of Human Society.* Cairo.

Hoekstra, A. 1965. *Homeric Modifications of Formulaic Prototypes: Studies in the Development of Greek Epic Diction.* Amsterdam.

Hoffmann, K. 1965. "Av. *daxma-*." *Zeitschrift für Vergleichende Sprachforschung* 79:300. Reprinted in Hoffmann 1975:338.

——. 1974. "Ved. *dhánuṣ-* und *páruṣ-*." *Die Sprache* 22:15–25. Reprinted in Hoffmann 1975:327–337.

——. 1975 / 1976. *Aufsätze zur Indoiranistik* 1/2, edited by J. Narten. Wiesbaden.

Holoka, J. P. 1973. "Homeric Originality: A Survey." *Classical World* 66:257–293.

Householder, F. W., and Nagy, G. 1972. "Greek." *Current Trends in Linguistics* IX, edited by T. A. Sebeok, 735–816. The Hague.

Hubbard, T. K. 1985. *The Pindaric Mind: A Study of Logical Structure in Early Greek Poetry.* Leiden.

Humbach, H. 1961. "Bestattungsformen im Vidēvdāt." *Zeitschrift für Vergleichende Sprachforschung* 77:99–105.

Hunt, R. 1981. "Satyric Elements in Hesiod's *Works and Days*." *Helios* 8:29–40.

IG = *Inscriptiones Graecae*. Berlin. 1873–.

Ingalls, W. B. 1972. "Another Dimension of the Homeric Formula." *Phoenix* 24:1–12.

Ireland, S., and Steel, F. L. D. 1975. "*Phrenes* as an Anatomical Organ in the Works of Homer." *Glotta* 53:183–195.

Ivanov, V. V. 1958. "K ėtimologii baltijskogo i slavjanskogo nazvanii boga groma." *Voprosy slavjanskogo jazykoznanija* 3:101–111.

——. 1960. "L'organisation sociale des tribus indo-européens d'après les données linguistiques." *Cahiers d'Histoire Mondiale* 5:796–799.

Ivanov, V. V., and Toporov, V. N. 1968. "K semiotičeskomu analizu mifa i rituala (na belorusskom materiale)." Presented at the conference 'Semiotika', Warsaw. Reprinted 1970 in *Sign, Language, Culture*, 321–389. The Hague and Paris.

——, and Toporov, V. N. 1970. "Le mythe indo-européen du dieu de l'orage poursuivant le serpent: Reconstruction du schéma." *Mélanges C. Lévi-Strauss*, 1180–1206. The Hague and Paris.

——, and Toporov, V. N. 1974. *Issledovanija v oblasti slavjanskix drevnostej: Leksičeskie i frazeologičeskie voprosy rekonstrukcii tekstov*. Moscow.

Jacoby, F. 1918. "Studien zu den älteren griechischen Elegiekern." *Hermes* 53:1–44.

——, ed. 1923–. *Die Fragmente der griechischen Historiker*. Leiden.

——. 1933. "Homerisches I." *Hermes* 68:1–50. Reprinted 1961 in his *Kleine Schriften* 1:1–53. Berlin.

Jakobson, R. 1931. "Über die phonologischen Sprachbünde." *Travaux du Cercle Linguistique de Prague* 4:234–240. Reprinted in Jakobson 1962:137–143.

——. 1939. "Signe zéro." *Mélanges de linguistique, offerts à Charles Bally*, 143–152. Geneva. Reprinted in Jakobson 1971:211–219.

——. 1950. "Slavic Mythology." *Funk and Wagnell's Standard Dictionary of Folklore, Mythology, and Legend*, edited by M. Leach, 1025–1028. New York. Reprinted in Jakobson 1985:3–11.

——. 1952. "Studies in Comparative Slavic Metrics." *Oxford Slavonic Papers* 3:21–66. Reprinted in Jakobson1966:414–463. The Hague.

——. 1955. "While Reading Vasmer's Dictionary." *Word* 11:615–616. Reprinted in Jakobson 1971:636–637.

——. 1957. *Shifters, Verbal Categories, and the Russian Verb*. Cambridge, Mass. Reprinted in Jakobson 1971:130–147.

——. 1960. "Linguistics and Poetics." *Style in Language*, edited by T. Sebeok, 350–377. Cambridge, Mass.

——. 1962. *Selected Writings* 1. The Hague.

——. 1966. *Selected Writings* 4. The Hague.

——. 1971. *Selected Writings* 2. The Hague.

——. 1985. *Selected Writings* 7. Berlin, New York, and Amsterdam.

Janko, R. 1982. *Homer, Hesiod and the Hymns: Diachronic Development in Epic Diction*. Cambridge.

Jaskiewicz, W. C. 1952. "Jan Łasicki's Samogitian Gods." *Studi Baltici* 1:65–106.

Jeanmaire, H. 1939. *Couroï et Courètes: Essai sur l'éducation spartiate et sur les rites d'adolescence dans l'antiquité hellénique*. Lille.

Jerejian, A. V. 1953. "The *h*-zero Alternation in Classical Armenian." *Word* 9:146–151.

Johnson, B. 1980. *The Critical Difference: Essays in the Contemporary Rhetoric of Reading.* Baltimore. See esp. ch. 4, pp. 52–66: "Poetry and Performative Language: Mallarmé and Austin."

Jones, J. 1962. *On Aristotle and Greek Tragedy.* London.

Jones, N. F. 1980a. "The Order of the Dorian *Phylai.*" *Classical Philology* 75.197–215.

——. 1980b. "The Civic Organization of Corinth." *Transactions of the American Philological Association* 110:161–193.

——. 1987. *Public Organization in Ancient Greece: A Documentary Study.* Philadelphia.

Joseph, B. 1983. "Old English Hengest as an Indo-European Twin Hero." *The Mankind Quarterly* 24:105–115.

Kane, P. V. 1941. *History of Dharmaśāstra* 2, part 1. Poona.

Kelly, S. T. 1974. "Homeric Correption and the Metrical Distinctions between Speeches and Narrative." Doctoral dissertation, Harvard University.

KEWA. *See* Mayrhofer 1953–1980.

Kiparsky, P. 1976. "Oral Poetry: Some Linguistic and Typological Considerations." *Oral Literature and the Formula,* edited by B. A. Stolz and R. S. Shannon, 73–106. Ann Arbor, Mich.

Kirk, G. S., Raven, J.E., and Schofield, M. 1983. *The Presocratic Philosophers.* 2nd ed. Cambridge.

Koch, H. J. 1976. "ΑΙΠΥΣ ΟΛΕΘΡΟΣ and the Etymology of ΟΛΛΥΜΙ." *Glotta* 54:216–222.

Kock, T., ed. 1880–1888. *Comicorum Atticorum Fragmenta.* Leipzig.

Koller, H. 1954. *Die Mimesis in der Antike.* Bern.

——. 1956. "Das kitharodische Prooimion: Eine formgeschichtliche Untersuchung." *Philologus* 100:159–206.

——. 1968. "ΠΟΛΙΣ ΜΕΡΟΠΩΝ ΑΝΘΡΩΠΩΝ." *Glotta* 46:18–26.

——. 1972. "Epos." *Glotta* 50:16–24.

Kretschmer, P. 1894. *Die griechischen Vaseninschriften, ihrer Sprache nach untersucht.* Gütersloh.

——. 1940. "Die Stellung der lykischen Sprache." *Glotta* 28:103–104.

Krollmann, C. 1927. "Das Religionswesen der alten Preussen." *Altpreussische Forschungen* 4/2:5–19.

Kuhn, A. 1886. *Mythologische Studien* 1: *Die Herabkunft des Feuers und des Göttertranks.* 2nd ed. by E. Kuhn. Gütersloh.

Kuiper, F. B. J. 1964. "The Bliss of Aša." *Indo-Iranian Journal* 8:96–129.

Kuryłowicz, J. 1927. "Indoeuropéen et ḫ hittite." *Symbolae grammaticae in honorem Ioannis Rozwadowski* 1:25–104. Kraków.

——. 1945–1949 [1966]. "La nature des procès dits 'analogiques'," *Acta Linguistica* 5:15–37 (1945–1949); reprinted 1960 in Kuryłowicz's *Esquisses linguistiques,* 66–86. Wrocław / Kraków. Also reprinted 1966 in *Readings in Linguistics,* edited by E. P. Hamp, F. W. Householder, R. Austerlitz, 2:158–174. Chicago.

——. 1956. *L'apophonie en indo-européen.* Wrocław.

——. 1958. "Le hittite." *Proceedings of the Eighth International Congress of Linguists* 216–243. Oslo.

——. 1968. *Indogermanische Grammatik* 2: *Akzent / Ablaut.* Heidelberg.

Lamberton, R. 1988. *Hesiod.* New Haven and London.

Laroche, E. 1958. "Etudes de vocabulaire VII." *Revue Hittite et Asianique* 63:85–114 (esp. pp. 88–99).

Latacz, J. 1968. "ἄπτερος μῦθος—ἄπτερος φάτις." *Glotta* 46:27–47.

Latte, K. 1941. Article s.v. Phyle. Pauly-Wissowa, *Realencyclopädie der classischen Altertumswissenschaft* 21.1.994–1011.

Lattimore, R. 1951. *The Iliad of Homer.* Chicago.

——. 1965. *The Odyssey of Homer.* New York.

LDW. *See* Mühlenbach and Endzelin 1923–1925.

Leach, E. R. 1982. Critical Introduction to Steblin-Kamenskij, M. I., *Myth,* 1–20. Ann Arbor.

Leaf, W., ed. 1900. *The Iliad.* 2 vols. 2nd ed. London.

Lesher, J. H. 1981. "Perceiving and Knowing in the *Iliad* and *Odyssey.*" *Phronesis* 26:2–24.

Leumann, M. 1977. *Lateinische Laut- und Formenlehre.* 2nd ed. Munich.

Lévêque, P., and Vidal-Naquet, P. 1964. *Clisthène l'Athénien: Essai sur la représentation de l'espace et du temps dans la pensée politique grecque de la fin du VIe siècle à la mort de Platon.* Paris.

Lévi, S. 1898. *La doctrine du sacrifice dans les Brāhmaṇas.* Paris. Reprinted 1966.

Lévi-Strauss, C. 1967. "The Structural Study of Myth." *Structural Anthropology,* 202–228. New York

LEW. *See* Fraenkel 1962/1965.

Liddell, H. G., Scott, R., and Stuart Jones, H., eds. 1940. *Greek-English Lexicon.* 9th ed. Oxford.

Lidén, E. 1906. *Armenische Studien.* Göteborg.

Liebert, G. 1962. "Indoiranica I: Ap. *vazraka-*, aw. *vazra-*, ai. *vájra-*." *Orientalia Suecana* 11:126–154.

Lincoln, B. 1975. "Indo-Iranian **gautra-*." *Journal of Indo-European Studies* 3:161–171.

——. 1986. *Myth, Cosmos, and Society: Indo-European Themes of Creation and Destruction.* Cambridge, Mass.

Lindsay, W. M., ed. 1914. *Sexti Pompei Festi de uerborum significatu quae supersunt cum Pauli epitome.* Leipzig.

Lobel, E., and Page, D., eds. 1955. *Poetarum Lesbiorum Fragmenta.* Oxford.

Lohmann, D. 1970. *Die Komposition der Reden in der Ilias.* Berlin.

Lommel, H. 1939. *Der arische Kriegsgott. Religion und Kultur der alten Arier* 2. Frankfurt am Main.

Loraux, N. 1978. "Sur la race des femmes et quelques-unes de ses tribus." *Arethusa* 11.43–87.

——. 1981. "La cité comme cuisine et comme partage." *Annales Economies Sociétés Civilisations* 36:614–622.

Lord, A. B. 1938. "Homer and Huso II: Narrative Inconsistencies in Homer and Oral Poetry." *Transactions of the American Philological Association* 69:439–445.

——. 1951. "Composition by Theme in Homer and Southslavic Epos." *Transactions of the American Philological Association* 82:71–80.

——. 1960. *The Singer of Tales.* Cambridge, Mass.

——. 1968. "Homer as an Oral Poet." *Harvard Studies in Classical Philology* 72:1–46.

——. 1975. "Perspectives on Recent Work on Oral Literature." In Duggan 1975:1–24.

Loth, J. 1920. "Le gallo-latin *Brigantes.*" *Revue des Etudes Anciennes* 22:121–122.

Lowenstam, S. 1981. *The Death of Patroklos: A Study in Typology.* Beiträge zur Klassischen Philologie 133. Königstein/Ts.

LSJ. *See* Liddell, Scott, and Stuart Jones 1940.

LSS. *See* Sokolowski 1962.

Lucas, D. W., ed., with commentary. 1968. *Aristotle Poetics.* Oxford.

Macdonell, A. A. 1897. "Vedic Mythology." *Grundriss der Indo-Arischen Philologie und Altertumskunde* 3.1.A. Strassburg.

Mannhardt, W. 1936. *Letto-Preussische Götterlehre.* Riga.

Mansikka, V. J. 1922. *Die Religion der Ostslaven.* Folklore Fellows Communications 43. Helsinki.

Martin, R. P. 1983. *Healing, Sacrifice and Battle: Amēchania and Related Concepts in Early Greek Poetry.* Innsbrucker Beiträge zur Sprachwissenschaft 41. Innsbruck.

——. 1984a. "Hesiod, Odysseus, and the Instruction of Princes." *Transactions of the American Philological Association* 114:29–48.

——. 1984b. "The Oral Tradition." *Critical Survey of Poetry* (Foreign Language Series), edited by F. Magill, 1746–1768. LaCanada, Cal.

——. 1989. *The Language of Heroes: Speech and Performance in the* Iliad. Ithaca, N.Y., and London. = Vol. 1 in the present series.

Mayrhofer, M. 1953–1980. *Kurzgefasstes etymologisches Wörterbuch des Altindischen.* Heidelberg.

——. 1986. *Indogermanische Grammatik* 1(2): *Lautlehre.* Heidelberg.

——. 1986–. *Etymologisches Wörterbuch des Altindoarischen.* Heidelberg.

Meid, W. 1956. "Zur Dehnung praesuffixaler Vokale in sekundären Nominalableitungen" 1. *Indogermanische Forschungen* 62:260–295.

——. 1957. "Das Suffix *-no-* in Götternamen." *Beiträge zur Namenforschung* 8:72–108, 113–126.

Meillet, A. 1920. "Sur le rhythme quantitatif de la langue védique." *Mémoires de la Société de Linguistique de Paris* 21:193–207.

——. 1923. *Les origines indo-européennes des mètres grecs.* Paris.

——. 1925. *La méthode comparative en linguistique historique.* Paris.

——. 1926. "Le vocabulaire slave et le vocabulaire indo-iranien." *Revue des Etudes Slaves* 6:164–174.

Merkelbach, R., and West, M. L., eds. 1967. *Fragmenta Hesiodea.* Oxford.

Meulen, R. van der. 1907. *Die Naturvergleiche in den Liedern und Totenklagen der Litauer.* Leiden.

Michelini, A. 1978. "ΥΒΡΙΣ and Plants." *Harvard Studies in Classical Philology* 82:35–44.

Miller, A. M. 1979. "The 'Address to the Delian Maidens' in the *Homeric Hymn to Apollo*: Epilogue or Transition?" *Transactions of the American Philological Association* 109:173–186.

——. 1986. *From Delos to Delphi: A Literary Study of the Homeric Hymn to Apollo.* Leiden.

Minard, A. 1949/1956. *Trois énigmes sur les Cent Chemins* 1/2. Lyon and Paris.

Minkowski, C. Z. 1986. "The Maitrāvaruṇa Priest." Doctoral dissertation, Harvard University.

Mitchell, S. A. 1985. "The Whetstone as Symbol of Authority in Old English and Old Norse." *Scandinavian Studies* 57:1–31.

Momigliano, A. 1936. "Note sulla storia di Rodi." *Rivista di Filologia* 14:49–63.

——. 1962. Intervento in: *Accademia Nazionale dei Lincei* 359, *Quaderno* n. 54, *Problemi Attuali di Scienza e di Cultura, Atti del Convegno Internazionale sul Tema: Dalla Tribù allo Stato,* 189–191.

Mondi, R. J. 1978. "The Function and Social Position of the ΚΗΡΥΞ in Early Greece." Doctoral dissertation, Harvard University.

——. 1980. "ΣΚΗΠΤΟΥΧΟΙ ΒΑΣΙΛΕΙΣ: An Argument for Divine Kingship in Early Greece." *Arethusa* 13:203–216.

Monroe, J. T. 1972. "Oral Composition in Pre-Islamic Poetry." *Journal of Arabic Literature* 3:1–53.

Moore, S. F. 1964. "Descent and Symbolic Filiation." *The American Anthropologist* 66:1308–1320. Reprinted 1967 in *Myth and Cosmos: Readings in Mythology and Symbolism,* edited by J. Middleton, 63–75. Austin.

Morris, I. 1988. "Tomb Cult and the 'Greek Renaissance': The Past and the Present in the 8th Century B.C." *Antiquity* 62:750–761.

Muellner, L. 1976. *The Meaning of Homeric* ΕΥΧΟΜΑΙ *through its Formulas.* Innsbrucker Beiträge zur Sprachwissenschaft 13. Innsbruck.

Mühlenbach, K., and Endzelin, J. 1923–1925. *Lettisch-Deutsches Wörterbuch* 1–4. Riga.

Murr, J. 1890. *Die Pflanzenwelt in der griechischen Mythologie.* Innsbruck.

MW. *See* Merkelbach and West 1967.

N. *See* Nagy, G.

Nagler, M. N. 1967. "Towards a Generative View of the Oral Formula." *Transactions of the American Philological Association* 98:269–311.

——. 1974. *Spontaneity and Tradition: A Study in the Oral Art of Homer.* Berkeley and Los Angeles.

——. 1977. "Dread Goddess Endowed with Speech." *Archeological News* 6:77–85.

Nagy, G. 1968. "On Dialectal Anomalies in Pylian Texts." *Atti e Memorie del 1° Congresso Internazionale di Micenologia* (Incunabula Graeca 25:2), 663–679. Rome.

——. 1970. *Greek Dialects and the Transformation of an Indo-European Process.* Cambridge, Mass.

——. 1973. "Phaethon, Sappho's Phaon, and the White Rock of Leukas." *Harvard Studies in Classical Philology* 77:137–177. Rewritten as Chapter 9 in this book.

——. 1974a. *Comparative Studies in Greek and Indic Meter.* Cambridge, Mass.

——. 1974b. "Six Studies of Sacral Vocabulary relating to the Fireplace." *Harvard Studies in Classical Philology* 78:71–106. Rewritten as Chapter 6 in this book.

——. 1974c. "Perkūnas and Perunŭ." *Antiquitates Indogermanicae: Gedenkschrift*

für Hermann Güntert, edited by M. Mayrhofer, W. Meid, B. Schlerath, R. Schmitt, 113–131. Innsbruck. Rewritten as Chapter 7 in this book.
——. 1976a. Review of Edwards 1971. *Canadian Journal of Linguistics* 21:219–224.
——. 1976b. "Formula and Meter." *Oral Literature and the Formula*, edited by B. A. Stolz and R. S. Shannon, 239–260. Ann Arbor, Mich. Rewritten as Chapter 2 in this book.
——. 1979a. *The Best of the Achaeans: Concepts of the Hero in Archaic Greek Poetry*. Baltimore.
——. 1979b. "On the Origins of the Greek Hexameter." *Festschrift Oswald Szemerényi*, edited by B. Brogyanyi, 611–631. Amsterdam.
——. 1980. "Patroklos, Concepts of Afterlife, and the Indic Triple Fire." *Arethusa* 13: *Indo-European Roots of Classical Culture*, 161–195. Rewritten as Chapter 4 in this book.
——. 1981a. "Another Look at KLEOS APHTHITON." *Würzburger Jahrbücher für Die Altertumswissenschaft* 7:113–116. Rewritten as part of Chapter 5 in this book.
——. 1981b. "Essai sur Georges Dumézil et l'étude de l'épopée grecque." *Cahiers "Pour un temps": Georges Dumézil*, edited by J. Bonnet et al., 137–145. Aix-en-Provence. Rewritten as part of Chapter 1 in this book.
——. 1982a. "Hesiod." *Ancient Writers*, edited by T. J. Luce, 43–72. New York. Rewritten as part of Chapter 3 in this book, by permission of Charles Scribner's Sons, an imprint of Macmillan Publishing Company. Copyright © 1982 Charles Scribner's Sons.
——. 1982b. Review of Detienne 1981. *Annales Economies Sociétés Civilisations* 37:778–780.
——. 1982c. Review of Burkert 1977 (German version of Burkert 1985). *Classical Philology* 77:70–73.
——. 1982d. Review of Burkert 1980. *Classical Philology* 77:159–161.
——. 1983a. "*Sēma* and *Noēsis:* Some Illustrations." *Arethusa* 16:35–55. Rewritten as Chapter 8 in this book.
——. 1983b. "On the Death of Sarpedon." *Approaches to Homer*, edited by C.A. Rubino and C. W. Shelmerdine, 189–217. Austin. Rewritten as part of Chapter 5 in this book.
——. 1983c. Review of Bowie 1981. *Phoenix* 37:273–275.
——. 1984. "On the Range of an Idiom in Homeric Dialogue." *Studies Presented to Sterling Dow: Greek Roman and Byzantine Studies* 25:233–238. Rewritten as Chapter 13 in this book.
——. 1985a. "Theognis and Megara: A Poet's Vision of His City." In Figueira and Nagy 1985:22–81.
——. 1985b. "On the Symbolism of Apportioning Meat in Archaic Greek Elegiac Poetry." *L'Uomo* 9:45–52. Rewritten as Chapter 11 in this book.
——. 1986a. "Pindar's *Olympian* 1 and the Aetiology of the Olympic Games." *Transactions of the American Philological Association* 116:71–88.
——. 1986b. "Ancient Greek Praise and Epic Poetry." *Oral Tradition in Literature: Interpretation in Context*, edited by J. Foley, 89–102. Columbia, Mo.
——. 1986c. "Sovereignty, Boiling Cauldrons, and Chariot-Racing in Pindar's *Olympian* 1." *Cosmos* 2: 143–147.

——. 1986d. "Poetic Visions of Immortality for the Hero." In Bloom 1986:205–212.

——. 1986e. "The Worst of the Achaeans." In Bloom 1986:213–215.

——. 1987a. "The Indo-European Heritage of Tribal Organization: Evidence from the Greek *Polis.*" *Proto-Indo-European: The Archaeology of a Linguistic Problem. Studies in Honor of Marija Gimbutas,* edited by S. N. Skomal and E. Polomé, 245–266. Washington, D. C. Rewritten as Chapter 12 in this book.

——. 1987b. "Herodotus the *Logios.*" *Arethusa* 20:175–184, 209–210.

——. 1987c. "The Sign of Protesilaos." ΜΗΤΙΣ: *Revue d'anthropologie du Monde Grec Ancien* 2:207–213.

——. 1988a. "Sul simbolismo della ripartizione nella poesia elegiaca." In Grottanelli and Parise 1988:203–209.

——. 1988b. "Mythe et prose en Grèce archaïque: *l'aînos.*" *Métamorphoses du mythe en Grèce ancienne,* edited by C. Calame, 229–242. Geneva.

——. 1988c. "Homerische Epik und Pindars Preislieder: Mündlichkeit und Aktualitätsbezug." In Raible 1988:51–64.

——. 1988d. "Teaching the Ordeal of Reading." *Harvard English Studies* 15:163–167.

——. 1989. "Early Greek Views of Poets and Poetry." *Cambridge History of Literary Criticism,* edited by G. Kennedy, 1:1–77. Cambridge.

——. 1990. *Pindar's Homer: The Lyric Possession of an Epic Past.* Baltimore.

Nagy, J. F. 1985. *The Wisdom of the Outlaw: The Boyhood Deeds of Finn in Gaelic Narrative Tradition.* Berkeley and Los Angeles.

Nauck, A., ed. 1889. *Tragicorum Graecorum Fragmenta.* Leipzig. Revised by B. Snell et al., 1971–. Göttingen.

Newton, R. M. 1984. "The Rebirth of Odysseus." *Greek Roman and Byzantine Studies* 25:5–20.

Nilsson, M. P. 1906. *Griechische Feste.* Leipzig.

——. 1951. "The Ionian Phylae." Appendix 1 in *Cults, Myths, Oracles and Politics in Ancient Greece.* Skrifter utg. av Svenska Institutet i Athen 1:143–149.

——. 1967, 1961. *Geschichte der griechischen Religion* 1/2, 3rd ed./2nd ed. Munich.

Nussbaum, M. C. 1972. "ΨΥΧΗ in Heraclitus." *Phronesis* 17:1–16 / 153–170.

Nyberg, H. S. 1938. *Die Religionen des alten Iran.* Leipzig.

Oldenberg, H. 1917. *Die Religion des Veda.* 2nd ed. Stuttgart and Berlin.

O'Neill, E. G. 1942. "The Localization of Metrical Word-Types in the Greek Hexameter." *Yale Classical Studies* 8:102–176.

Otrębski, J. 1965. *Gramatyka języka litewskiego* 2. Warsaw.

Otten, H. 1951. "Pirva—Der Gott auf dem Pferde." *Jahrbuch für Kleinasiatische Forschung* 2:62–73.

——. 1958. *Hethitische Totenrituale.* Deutsche Akademie der Wissenschaften zu Berlin, Institut für Orientforschung, Publication 37. Berlin.

Page, D. L. 1951. *Alcman: The Partheneion.* Oxford.

——. 1953. "Corinna." The Society for the Promotion of Hellenic Studies *Supplementary Paper* 6. London.

——. 1955. *The Homeric Odyssey.* Oxford.

——. 1959. *History and the Homeric Iliad.* Berkeley and Los Angeles.

——, ed. 1962. *Poetae Melici Graeci.* Oxford.

——, ed. 1974. *Supplementum Lyricis Graecis.* Oxford.

——, ed. 1975. *Epigrammata Graeca.* Oxford.

Palmer, L. R. 1979. "A Mycenaean 'Akhilleid'?" *Serta Philologica Aenipontana* 3, edited by R. Muth and G. Pfohl, 255–261. Innsbrucker Beiträge zur Kulturwissenschaft 20.

——. 1980. *The Greek Language.* Atlantic Highlands, N. J.

Parke, H. W., and Wormell, D. E. W. 1956. *The Delphic Oracle.* 2 vols. Oxford.

Parry, M. 1928a. *L'épithète traditionnelle dans Homère.* Paris.

——. 1928b. *Les formules et la métrique d'Homère.* Paris.

——. 1930. "Studies in the Epic Technique of Oral Verse-Making. I. Homer and Homeric Style." *Harvard Studies in Classical Philology* 41:73–147.

——. 1971. *The Making of Homeric Verse: The Collected Papers of Milman Parry,* edited by A. Parry. Oxford.

Pedersen, H. 1931. *The Discovery of Language: Linguistic Science in the Nineteenth Century,* translated by J. W. Spargo. Reissued 1962. Bloomington, Ind.

Perpillou, J.-L. 1973. *Les substantifs grecs en* -ΕΥΣ. Paris.

Perry, B. E., ed. 1952. *Aesopica.* Urbana, Ill.

Peters, M. 1980. *Untersuchungen zur Vertretung der indogermanischen Laryngale im Griechischen.* Vienna.

Pfeiffer, R., ed. 1949/1953. *Callimachus.* 1/2. Oxford.

——. 1968. *History of Classical Scholarship: From the Beginnings to the End of the Hellenistic Age.* Oxford.

Pfister, F. 1909/1912. *Der Reliquienkult im Altertum.* 1/2. Giessen.

PMG. *See* Page 1962.

Porter, H. N. 1951. "The Early Greek Hexameter." *Yale Classical Studies* 12:3–63.

Pötscher, W. 1961. "Hera und Heros." *Rheinisches Museum* 104:302–355.

Poultney, J., ed. 1959. *The Bronze Tables of Iguvium.* American Philological Association Monographs 18. Baltimore.

Pucci, P. 1987. *Odysseus Polytropos: Intertextual Readings in the Odyssey and the Iliad.* Ithaca, N.Y., and London.

Puhvel, J. 1974. "Indo-European Structure of the Baltic Pantheon." *Myth in Indo-European Antiquity,* edited by G. J. Larson et al., 75–85. Berkeley and Los Angeles. Reprinted in Puhvel 1981:225–235.

——. 1975. "Remus et Frater." *History of Religions* 15:146–157. Reprinted in Puhvel 1981:300–311.

——. 1981. *Analecta Indoeuropaea.* Innsbrucker Beiträge zur Sprachwissenschaft 35. Innsbruck.

PW. *See* Parke and Wormell 1956.

Radin, P. 1956. With commentaries by Kerényi, K., and Jung, C. G. *The Trickster: A Study in American Indian Mythology.* London. Reissued 1972, with introductory essay by S. Diamond.

Radloff, W. 1885. *Proben der Volksliteratur der nördlichen türkischen Stämme.* 5: *Der Dialekt der Kara-Kirgisen.* St. Petersburg.

Raible, W., ed. 1988. *Zwischen Festtag und Alltag: Zehn Beiträge zum Thema Mündlichkeit und Schriftlichkeit.* Tübingen.

Rau, W. 1957. *Staat und Gesellschaft im alten Indien.* Wiesbaden.

Redfield, J. M. 1975. *Nature and Culture in the Iliad: The Tragedy of Hector.* Chicago.

Reichelt, H. 1913. "Der steinerne Himmel." *Indogermanische Forschungen* 32:23–57.

——. 1914. "Studien zur lateinischen Laut- und Wortgeschichte." *Zeitschrift für Vergleichende Sprachforschung* 46:313–316.

Renner, T. 1978. "A Papyrus Dictionary of Metamorphoses." *Harvard Studies in Classical Philology* 82:277–293.

Renou, L. 1937. "Infinitifs et dérivés nominaux dans le R̥gveda." *Bulletin de la Société de Linguistique de Paris* 39:69–87.

——. 1952. *Grammaire de la langue védique.* Lyon.

REW. *See* Vasmer 1953–1958.

Rhodes, P. J. 1981. *A Commentary of the Aristotelian* ΑΘΗΝΑΙΩΝ ΠΟΛΙΤΕΙΑ. Oxford.

Richardson, N. J., ed., with commentary. 1974. *The Homeric Hymn to Demeter.* Oxford.

Richter, G. 1950. *The Sculpture and Sculptors of the Greeks.* New Haven.

Risch, E. 1954. "Die Sprache Alkmans." *Museum Helveticum* 11:20–37. Reprinted in Risch 1981:314–331.

——. 1966. "Les différences dialectales dans le mycénien." *Proceedings of the Cambridge Colloquium on Mycenaean Studies,* edited by L. R. Palmer and J. Chadwick, 150–157. Cambridge. Reprinted in Risch 1981:451–458.

——. 1974. *Wortbildung der homerischen Sprache.* 2nd ed. Berlin.

——. 1976. "Il miceneo nella storia della lingua greca." *Quaderni Urbinati di Cultura Classica* 23:7–28. Reprinted in Risch 1981:527–548.

——. 1979. "Die griechischen Dialekte im 2. vorchristlichen Jahrtausend." *Studi Micenei ed Egeo-Anatolici* 20:91–111. Reprinted in Risch 1981:269–289.

——. 1981. *Kleine Schriften,* edited by A. Etter and M. Looser. Berlin.

——. 1987. "Die ältesten Zeugnisse für κλέος ἄφθιτον." *Zeitschrift für Vergleichende Sprachforschung* 100:3–11.

Robert, C. 1883. "Die Phaethonsage bei Hesiod." *Hermes* 18:434–441.

——. 1885. "Athena Skiras und die Skirophorien." *Hermes* 20:349–379.

Robertson, N. 1980. "The Dorian Migration and Corinthian Ritual." *Classical Philology* 75:1–22.

Rohde, E. 1898. *Psyche: Seelencult und Unsterblichkeitsglaube der Griechen.* 2 vols. Freiburg im Breisgau. Translated 1925 by W. B. Hillis. New York.

Rönnow, K. A. 1927. *Trita Āptya: Eine vedische Gottheit.* 1. Uppsala.

Rose, H. J. 1931. "De Actaeone Stesichoreo." *Mnemosyne* 59:431–432.

Rose, V., ed. 1886. *Aristoteles: Fragmenta.* Leipzig.

Roth, C. P. 1976. "The Kings and the Muses in Hesiod's Theogony." *Transactions of the American Philological Association* 106:331–338.

Roussel, D. 1976. *Tribu et cité.* Annales Littéraires de l'Université de Besançon 193. Paris.

Rudhardt, J. 1970. "Les mythes grecs relatifs à l'instauration du sacrifice." *Museum Helveticum* 27:1–15.

Russo, J. A. 1966. "The Structural Formula in Homeric Verse." *Yale Classical Studies* 20:217–240.

Rusten, J. 1982. *Dionysius Scytobrachion.* Papyrologica Coloniensia 10. Opladen.

Sacconi, A. 1960. "Il mito nel mondo miceneo." *La Parola del Passato* 15:161–187.

Sacks, R. 1974. "Studies in Indo-European and Common Germanic Poetic Diction: On the Origins of Old English Verse." A.B. dissertation, Harvard University.

Saïd, E. W. 1978. *Orientalism.* New York.

Saïd, S. 1979. "Les crimes des prétendants, la maison d'Ulysse et les festins de l'Odyssée." *Etudes de Littérature Ancienne* (Presses de l'Ecole Normale Supérieure), 9–49. Paris.

Sapir, E. 1929. "The Status of Linguistics as a Science." *Language* 5:207–214.

Saussure, F. de. 1916. *Cours de linguistique générale.* New critical ed. 1972, by T. de Mauro. Paris.

Schadewaldt, W. 1965. *Von Homers Welt und Werk.* 4th ed. Stuttgart.

Schein, S. L. 1984. *The Mortal Hero: An Introduction to Homer's Iliad.* Berkeley and Los Angeles.

Scheinberg, S. 1979. "The Bee Maidens of the Homeric Hymn to Hermes." *Harvard Studies in Classical Philology* 83:1–28.

Scherer, A. 1953. *Gestirnnamen bei den indogermanischen Völkern.* Heidelberg.

Schlerath, B. 1968. "Altindisch asu-, Awestisch ahu- und ähnlich klingende Wörter." *Pratidānam: Indian, Iranian and Indo- European Studies presented to F. B. J. Kuiper,* edited by J. C. Heesterman, G. H. Schokker, V. I. Subramoniam, 142–153. The Hague and Paris.

Schmeja, H. 1963. "Die Verwandtschaftsnamen auf -ως und die Nomina auf -ωνός, -ώνη im Griechischen." *Indogermanische Forschungen* 68:22–41.

Schmid, B. 1947. *Studien zu griechischen Ktisissagen.* Freiburg.

Schmitt, R. 1967. *Dichtung und Dichtersprache in indogermanischer Zeit.* Wiesbaden.

——, ed. 1968. *Indogermanische Dichtersprache.* Darmstadt.

——. 1974. "Nektar und Keine Ende." *Antiquitates Indogermanicae: Gedenkschrift für Hermann Güntert,* edited by M. Mayrhofer, W. Meid, B. Schlerath, R. Schmitt, 155–163. Innsbruck.

Schnaufer, A. 1970. *Frühgriechische Totenglaube: Untersuchungen zum Totenglauben der mykenischen und homerischen Zeit. Spudasmata* 20. Hildesheim.

Schulze, W. 1918. "Beiträge zur Wort- und Sittengeschichte." *Sitzungsberichte der Preussischen Akademie der Wissenschaften,* 320–332, 481–511, 769–791. Reprinted in Schulze 1966:148–210.

——. 1927. "Zufall?" *Zeitschrift für Vergleichende Sprachforschung* 54:306. Reprinted in Schulze 1966:215–216.

——. 1929. Note in *Zeitschrift für Vergleichende Sprachforschung* 56:287. Reprinted in Schulze 1966:361.

——. 1966. *Kleine Schriften.* Göttingen.

Schwartz, M. 1982. "The Indo-European Vocabulary of Exchange, Hospitality, and Intimacy." *Proceedings of the Berkeley Linguistics Society* 8:188–204.

Schwenck, K. 1859. "ἀπὸ δρυός, ἀπὸ πέτρης." *Philologus* 14:391–395.

Schwyzer, E., ed. 1923. *Dialectorum Graecarum exempla epigraphica potiora.* Leipzig. Reprinted, Hildesheim 1960.

——. 1939. *Griechische Grammatik* 1. Munich.

Scodel, R. 1980. "Hesiod Redivivus." *Greek Roman and Byzantine Studies* 21:301–320.

Searle, J. R. 1979. *Speech-Acts: An Essay in the Philosophy of Language.* Cambridge.

Sedov, V. V. 1953. "Drevnerusskoje svjatilišče v Peryni." *Kratkie soobščenija Instituta istorii material'noj kul'tury* 50:92–103.

——. 1954. "Novye dannye o jazyčeskom svjatilišče Peruna." *Kratkie soobščenija Instituta istorii material'noj kul'tury* 53:195–208.

Segal, C. P. 1962. "The Phaeacians and the Symbolism of Odysseus' Return." *Arion* 1:17–64.

——. 1983. "*Kleos* and Its Ironies in the *Odyssey*." *L'Antiquité Classique* 52:22–47.

Sergent, B. 1976. "La représentation spartiate de la royauté." *Revue de l'Histoire des Religions* 189:3–52.

——. 1977/1978. "Le partage du Péloponnèse entre les Héraclides." *Revue de l'Histoire des Religions* 190/191:121–136/3–25.

——. 1979. "Les trois fonctions des Indo-Européens dans la Grèce ancienne: Bilan critique." *Annales Economies Sociétés Civilisations* 34:1155–1186.

Seržputovski, A. K. 1930. "Prymxi i zababony belarusav- paljašukov." *Belaruskaja etnografija v dosledax i matar'jalax* 7. Mensk.

Shannon, R. S. 1975. *The Arms of Achilles and Homeric Compositional Technique.* Leiden.

SIG. *See* Dittenberger 1915–1924.

Sinclair, T. A., ed. 1932. *Hesiod, Works and Days.* London.

Sinos, D. S. 1980. *Achilles, Patroklos, and the Meaning of Philos.* Innsbrucker Beiträge zur Sprachwissenschaft 29. Innsbruck.

Slatkin, L. M. 1986. "The Wrath of Thetis." *Transactions of the American Philological Association* 116:1–24.

SLG. *See* Page 1974.

SM. *See* Snell and Maehler 1971, 1975.

Šmits, P. 1940. *Latviešu tautas ticējumi, sakrājis un sakārtojis Prof. P. Šmits.* Riga.

Snell, B., and Maehler, H., eds. 1971. *Bacchylides.* Leipzig.

——, eds. 1975. *Pindarus: Fragmenta.* Leipzig.

Snodgrass, A. M. 1971. *The Dark Age of Greece: An Archaeological Survey of the Eleventh to the Eighth Centuries.* Edinburgh.

——. 1980. *Archaic Greece: The Age of Experiment.* Berkeley and Los Angeles.

——. 1982. "Les origines du culte des héros dans la Grèce antique." *La mort, les morts dans les sociétés anciennes,* edited by G. Gnoli and J.-P. Vernant, 107–119. Cambridge and Paris.

——. 1987. *An Archaeology of Greece: The Present State and Future Scope of a Discipline.* Berkeley and Los Angeles.

Sokolowski, F., ed. 1962. *Lois sacrés des cités grecques. Supplément.* Paris.

Solmsen, F. 1901. *Untersuchungen zur griechischen Laut- und Verslehre.* Strassburg.

Sommer, F. 1914. *Kritische Erläuterungen zur lateinischen Laut- und Formenlehre.* Heidelberg.

Sommerstein, A. H., ed., with translation. 1980. *Aristophanes, Acharnians.* Warminster, Wiltshire.

Specht, F. 1932. "Die Flexion der *n*-Stämme im Baltisch-Slavischen und Verwandtes." *Zeitschrift für Vergleichende Sprachforschung* 59:213–304.

——. 1944. "Zur idg. Sprache und Kultur. II." *Zeitschrift für Vergleichende Sprachforschung* 68:191–200.

Stähler, K. P. 1967. *Grab und Psyche des Patroklos: Ein schwarzfiguriges Vasenbild.* Münster.

Stang, C. S. 1966. *Vergleichende Grammatik der baltischen Sprachen.* Oslo.

Stolz, B. A., and R. S. Shannon, eds. 1976. *Oral Literature and the Formula.* Ann Arbor, Mich.

Stroud, R. S. 1968. "Tribal Boundary Markers from Corinth." *California Studies in Classical Antiquity* 1:233–242.

Sulzberger, M. 1926. "ΟΝΟΜΑ ΕΠΩΝΥΜΟΝ. Les noms propres chez Homère." *Revue des Etudes Grecques* 39:381–447.

Svenbro, J. 1976. *La parole et le marbre: Aux origines de la poétique grecque.* Lund. 1984 Italian version, with changes and corrections, Torino.

——. 1982. "A Mégara Hyblaea: le corps géomètre." *Annales Economies Sociétés Civilisations* 37:953–964.

——. 1984. "La découpe du poème: Notes sur les origines sacrificielles de la poétique grecque." *Poétique* 58.215–232.

——. 1987. "The 'Voice' of Letters in Ancient Greece. On silent reading and the representation of speech." *Culture and History,* edited by M. Harbsmeier and M. T. Larsen, 2:31–47. Copenhagen. Recast as Ch.9 in Svenbro 1988.

——. 1988a. *Phrasikleia: anthropologie de la lecture en Grèce ancienne.* Paris.

——. 1988b. "Il taglio della poesia. Note sulle origini sacrificali della poetica greca." Grottanelli and Parise 1988: 231–252.

Szanto, E. 1901. "Die griechischen Phylen." *Sitzungsberichte der kais. Akademie der Wissenschaften in Wien, phil.-hist. Klasse* 145 (nr. 5) 1–74, reprinted 1906 in *Ausgewählte Abhandlungen,* 216–288. Tübingen.

Szegedy-Maszak, A. 1978. "Legends of the Greek Lawgivers." *Greek Roman and Byzantine Studies* 19:199–209.

Szemerényi, O. 1978. "Studies in the Kinship Terminology of the Indo-European Languages, with special reference to Indian, Iranian, Greek, and Latin." *Acta Iranica* 16:1–240.

Tambiah, S. J. 1973. "From Varṇa to Caste through Mixed Unions." *The Character of Kinship,* edited by J. Goody, 191–229. Cambridge.

Tarditi, G., ed. 1968. *Archilochus.* Rome.

Täubler, E. 1930. *Die umbrisch-sabellischen und die römischen Tribus.* Sitzungsberichte der Heidelberger Akademie der Wissenschaften, Philosophisch-historische Klasse, 1929/30. Heidelberg.

TGF. *See* Nauck 1889.

Thiel, H. van, ed. 1974. *Leben und Taten Alexanders von Makedonien: Der griechische Alexanderroman nach der Handschrift L.* Darmstadt.

Thieme, P. 1952. *Nektar / Ambrosia / Hades: Studien zur indogermanischen Wortkunde und Religionsgeschichte.* Berichte über die Verhandlungen der Sächsischen Akademie der Wissenschaften zu Leipzig, Philologisch-historische Klasse. Berlin. Reprinted in Schmitt 1968:102–153.

Thurneysen, R. 1907. Review of A. Walde, *Lateinisches etymologisches Wörterbuch* (Heidelberg 1906). *Göttingische Gelehrte Anzeigen,* 800.

——. 1912–1913. "Zur Wortschöpfung im Lateinischen." *Indogermanische Forschungen* 31:276–281.

Tischler, J. 1983. *Hethitisches etymologisches Glossar* 1. Innsbrucker Beiträge zur Sprachwissenschaft 20. Innsbruck.

Trautmann, R. 1906. "Etymologische Miscellen." *Beiträge zur Geschichte der deutschen Sprache und Literatur* 32:150–152.

V. *See* Voigt 1971.

Vadé, Y. 1977. "Sur la maternité du chêne et de la pierre." *Revue de l' Histoire des Religions* 191:3–41.

Vaillant, A. 1948. "Le suffixe *-ynji*." *Revue des Etudes Slaves* 24:181–184.

Van Brock, N. 1959. "Substitution rituelle." *Revue Hittite et Asianique* 65:117–146.

Vasmer, M. 1953–1958. *Russisches etymologisches Wörterbuch* 1–3. Heidelberg.

Vendryes, J. 1927. "Sur un nom ancien de l''arbre'." *Revue Celtique* 44:313–319.

Vermeule, E. D. T. 1965. "The Vengeance of Achilles: The Dragging of Hektor at Troy." *Bulletin of the Museum of Fine Arts. Boston* 63:34–52.

——. 1979. *Aspects of Death in Early Greek Art and Poetry*. Berkeley and Los Angeles.

Vernant, J.-P. 1960. "Le mythe hésiodique des races: Essai d'analyse structurale." *Revue de l'Histoire des Religions* 157:21–54. Rewritten in Vernant 1985:19–47.

——. 1962. "La catégorie psychologique du double. Figuration de l'invisible et catégorie psychologique du double: le colossos." Presented at the colloquium "Le signe et les systèmes de signes" (Royaumont). Rewritten in Vernant 1985:325–338.

——. 1963. "Hestia-Hermès: Sur l'expression religieuse de l'espace et du mouvement chez les Grecs." *L'Homme* 3:12–50. Rewritten in Vernant 1985:155–201.

——. 1966. "Le mythe hésiodique des races: Sur un essai de mise au point." *Revue de Philologie* 40:247–276. Rewritten in Vernant 1985:48–85.

——. 1969. *Les origines de la pensée grecque*. Paris.

——. 1974. *Mythe et société en Grèce ancienne*. Paris.

——. 1982. "From Oedipus to Periander: Lameness, Tyranny, Incest in Legend and History." *Arethusa* 15:19–38.

——. 1982–1983. "Étude comparée des religions antiques." *Annuaires du Collège de France, Résumé des cours et travaux,* 83:443–456.

——. 1985. *Mythe et pensée chez les Grecs*. 2nd ed., recast and repaginated. Paris.

Vetter, E. 1953. *Handbuch der italischen Dialekte* 1. Heidelberg.

Vian, F. 1960. "La triade des rois d'Orchomène: Eteoclès, Phlégyas, Minyas." *Hommage à Georges Dumézil* (Collection Latomus 45), 215–224. Brussels.

——. 1963. *Les origines de Thèbes: Cadmos et les Spartes*. Paris.

——. 1970. Review of Dumézil 1968. *Gnomon* 42:53–58.

Vidal-Naquet, P. 1981. *Le chasseur noir*. Paris.

——. 1986. "The Black Hunter Revisited." *Proceedings of the Cambridge Philological Society* 212:126–144.

Vieyra, M. 1965. "Ciel et enfer hittites." *Revue d'Assyriologie* 59:127–130.

Vine, B. 1977. "On the Heptasyllabic Verses of the Rig-Veda." *Zeitschrift für Vergleichende Sprachforschung* 91:246–255.

——. 1978. "On the Metrics and Origin of Rig-Vedic *ná* 'like, as'." *Indo-Iranian Journal* 20:171–193.

——. 1982. "Indo-European Verbal Formations in *-d-." Doctoral dissertation, Harvard University.

——. 1986. "An Umbrian-Latin Correspondence." *Harvard Studies in Classical Philology* 90:111–127.

Voigt, E.-M., ed. 1971. *Sappho et Alcaeus: Fragmenta.* Amsterdam.
W. *See* West 1971 / 1972.
Wackernagel, J. 1953. *Kleine Schriften.* 2 vols. Göttingen. 1953.
Wackernagel, J., and Debrunner, A. 1930. *Altindische Grammatik.* 3: *Nominalflexion—Zahlwort—Pronomen.* Göttingen.
——. 1954. *Altindische Grammatik* 2(2): *Die Nominalsuffixe.* Göttingen.
Wagler, P. 1891. *Die Eiche in alter und neuer Zeit. Eine mythologisch- kulturhistorische Studie* 1/2. Wurzen/Berlin.
Walcot, P. 1966. *Hesiod and the Near East.* Cardiff.
Wallace, P. W. 1974. "Hesiod and the Valley of the Muses." *Greek Roman and Byzantine Studies* 15:5–24.
Ward, D. 1968. *The Divine Twins: An Indo-European Myth in Germanic Tradition.* University of California Publications, Folklore Studies 19. Berkeley and Los Angeles.
Warden, J. 1971. "ΨΥΧΗ in Homeric Death-Descriptions." *Phoenix* 25:95–103.
Watkins, C. 1963. "Indo-European Metrics and Archaic Greek Verse." *Celtica* 6:194–249.
——. 1966. "Italo-Celtic Revisited." *Ancient Indo-European Dialects,* edited by H. Birnbaum and J. Puhvel, 29–50. Berkeley and Los Angeles.
——. 1969. "The Indo-European Origin of English." *The American Heritage Dictionary of the English Language,* xix-xx. New York.
——. 1970. "Studies in Indo-European Legal Language, Institutions, and Mythology." *Indo-European and Indo-Europeans,* edited by G. Cardona, H. M. Hoenigswald, and A. Senn, 321–354. Philadelphia.
——. 1971. "Hittite and Indo-European Studies: The Denominative Statives in *-ē-*." *Transactions of the Philological Society* 1971:51–93.
——. 1972. "An Indo-European Word for 'Dream'." *Studies for Einar Haugen,* edited by E. S. Firchow, K. Grimstad, N. Hasselmo, W. O'Neil, 554–561. The Hague.
——. 1973a. "Etyma Enniana: (1: *uegeō*; 2: *ceu*)." *Harvard Studies in Classical Philology* 55:195–206.
——. 1973b. "Language and its History." *Daedalus* 102.3:99–114.
——. 1974. "God." *Antiquitates Indogermanicae: Gedenkschrift für Hermann Güntert,* edited by M. Mayrhofer, W. Meid, B. Schlerath, R. Schmitt, 101–110. Innsbruck.
——. 1976. "Observations on the 'Nestor's Cup' Inscription." *Harvard Studies in Classical Philology* 80:25–40.
——. 1976b. "Syntax and Metrics in the Dipylon Vase Inscription." *Studies in Greek, Italic, and Indo-European Linguistics offered to Leonard R. Palmer,* edited by A. Morpurgo Davies and W. Meid, 431–441. Innsbruck.
——. 1976c. "The Etymology of Irish *dúan.*" *Celtica* 11:270–277.
——. 1978a. "ΑΝΟΣΤΕΟΣ ΟΝ ΠΟΔΑ ΤΕΝΔΕΙ." *Etrennes de septantaine: Mélanges Michel Lejeune,* 231–235. Paris.
——. 1978b. "Remarques sur la méthode de Ferdinand de Saussure comparatiste." *Cahiers Ferdinand de Saussure* 32:59–69.
——. 1979. "Is tre fír flathemon: Marginalia to *Audacht Morainn.*" *Ériu* 30:181–198.

——. 1982a. "Aspects of Indo-European Poetics." *The Indo-Europeans in the Fourth and Third Millenniums*, edited by E. Polomé, 104–120. *Linguistica Extranea*, Studia 14. Ann Arbor, Mich.

——. 1982b. "Notes on the Plural Formations of the Hittite Neuters." *Investigationes Philologicae Comparativae: Festschrift H. Kronasser*, edited by E. Neu, 250–262. Wiesbaden.

——, ed. 1985a. *The American Heritage Dictionary of Indo-European Roots.* Boston.

——. 1985b. "Greek *menoinâai*: A Dead Metaphor?" *International Journal of American Linguistics* 51:614–618.

——. 1986. "The Name of Meleager." *o-o-pe-ro-si: Festschrift für Ernst Risch zum 75. Geburtstag*, edited by A. Etter, 320–328. Berlin.

——. 1987. "How to Kill a Dragon in Indo-European." *Studies in Memory of Warren Cowgill (1929–1985)*, edited by C. Watkins, 270–299. Berlin.

——. 1989. "The Comparison of Formulaic Sequences." *Proceedings of the IREX Conference on Historical Linguistics, Austin, October 1986*, edited by E. Polomé, forthcoming. Amsterdam.

——. 1990. "Latin *tarentum*, the *ludi saeculares*, and Indo-European Eschatology." In *Proceedings of the IREX Conference on Indo-European Linguistics, USSR Academy of Sciences, June 1988*, edited by E. Polomé, forthcoming. Amsterdam.

Watt, W. M. 1962. "The Tribal Basis of the Islamic State." *Accademia Nazionale dei Lincei* 359, *Quaderno* n. 54, *Problemi Attuali di Scienza e di Cultura, Atti del Convegno Internazionale sul Tema: Dalla Tribù allo Stato*, 153–160.

Waugh, L. R. 1982. "Marked and Unmarked: A Choice between Unequals in Semiotic Structure." *Semiotica* 38:299–318.

Weber, M. [1956]. *Wirtschaft und Gesellschaft: Grundriss der verstehenden Soziologie.* 4th ed. by J. Winckelmann. Tübingen.

Wehrli, F., ed. 1944–. *Die Schule des Aristoteles.* Basel.

West, M. L. 1961. "Hesiodea III." *Classical Quarterly* 11:142–145.

——, ed., with commentary. 1966. *Hesiod: Theogony.* Oxford.

——, ed. 1971 / 1972. *Iambi et Elegi Graeci.* Oxford.

——. 1973a. "Greek Poetry 2000–700 B.C." *Classical Quarterly* 23:179–192.

——. 1973b. "Indo-European Metre." *Glotta* 51:161–187.

——. 1974. *Studies in Greek Elegy and Iambus.* Berlin.

——, ed., with commentary. 1978. *Hesiod: Works and Days.* Oxford.

——. 1982a. *Greek Metre.* Oxford.

——. 1982b. "Three Topics in Greek Metre." *Classical Quarterly* 32:281–297.

——. 1985. *The Hesiodic Catalogue of Women: Its Nature, Structure, and Origins.* Oxford.

Westermann, A., ed. 1843. ΜΥΘΟΓΡΑΦΟΙ: *Scriptores Poeticae Historiae Graeci.* Braunschweig.

Whallon, W. 1961. "The Homeric Epithets." *Yale Classical Studies* 17:97–142.

Whitley, J. 1988. "Early States and Hero-Cults: A Re-Appraisal." *Journal of Hellenic Studies* 108:173–182.

Whitman, C. H. 1958. *Homer and the Heroic Tradition.* Cambridge, Mass.

——. 1970. "Hera's Anvils." *Harvard Studies in Classical Philology* 74:37–42.

Whitney, W. D. 1896. *A Sanskrit Grammar.* 3rd ed. Leipzig.

Wickersham, J. M. 1986. "The Corpse Who Calls Theognis." *Transactions of the American Philological Association* 116:65–70.

Wikander, S. 1938. *Der arische Männerbund: Studien zur indo-iranischen Sprach- und Religionsgeschichte.* Lund.

——. 1950. "Sur le fonds commun indo-iranien des épopées de la Perse et de l'Inde." *La Nouvelle Clio* 1/2:310–329.

——. 1957. "Nakula et Sahadeva." *Orientalia Suecana* 6:66–96.

Wilamowitz-Moellendorff, U. von. 1897. "Der Chor der Hagesichora." *Hermes* 32:251–263. Reprinted 1935 in his *Kleine Schriften* 1:209–220. Berlin.

——. 1900. *Textgeschichte der griechischen Lyriker.* Berlin.

——. 1913. *Sappho und Simonides, Untersuchungen über griechische Lyriker.* Berlin.

——, ed. 1916. *Vitae Homeri et Hesiodi.* Berlin.

——. 1921. *Griechische Verskunst.* Berlin.

Wissowa, G. 1912. *Religion und Kultus der Römer.* 2nd ed. Munich.

Witzel, M. 1984. "Sur le chemin du ciel." *Bulletin d'Etudes Indiennes* 2:213–279.

Wolf, C. U. 1946a. "Terminology of Israel's Tribal Organization." *Journal of Biblical Literature* 65:45–49.

——. 1946b. "Some Remarks on the Tribes and Clans of Israel." *Jewish Quarterly Review* 36:287–295.

Wörrle, M. 1964. *Untersuchungen zur Verfassungsgeschichte von Argos im 5. Jahrhundert.* Erlangen.

Yalman, N. 1960. "The Flexibility of Caste Principles in a Kandyan Community." *Aspects of Caste in South India, Ceylon and North-West Pakistan,* edited by E. R. Leach, 78–112. Cambridge.

Zuntz, G. 1971. *Persephone: Three Essays on Religion and Thought in Magna Graecia.* Oxford.

General Index

Achilles, 12, 13, 14, 22, 24, 27, 28, 53, 70, 71, 89, 116, 123, 124, 125, 126, 127, 130, 136, 139, 176, 199, 200, 206, 215, 216, 218, 220, 221, 230, 238, 244, 245, 256, 296, 297, 300, 301; antagonism with Apollo, 12; as Doppelgänger of Apollo, 12; as homunculus, 88
Actaeon, 263, 264
Acts of the Arval Brethren, 156, 159, 161
Acusilaus FGH 2 F 2: 51
Adam of Bremen, 184
Adfertor, 167, 168, 169
Adonis, 4, 229, 234, 235, 255, 257, 261, 262
Aegina, 245
Aelian, *De natura animalium* 254: 273; *Varia Historia* 273: 274
Aeneas, 24, 27, 28, 133, 251; Aeneadae, 28
Aeschylus *Agamemnon* 1023: 259; 1147: 264; *Eumenides* 660: 231; *Persians* 514–515: 250; TGF 17: 140; 73: 237
Aesop, 50; *Fable* 348: 272; master of *aînos* 'fable', 275
African myths, 193
afterlife, concepts of, 86, 87, 89, 92, 93, 102, 116, 120, 121, 126, 170, 175, 225
Agamemnon, 28, 53, 77, 133, 143, 290, 299, 301
Agni, 99, 100, 101, 102, 103, 104, 105, 108, 109, 110, 111, 112, 113, 114, 117, 118, 119, 146, 147, 150, 156, 173
Ahiqar and Nadan, 71
Ahura, 94, 100, 119, 178
Aiaie, 237
Aigeidai, 292
Aigeus, 231, 292
Aigimios, 283, 284
Aigospotamoi, 258
Aitareya-Brāhmaṇa, 99, 102, 151
Aithiopes, 237, 242; Aithiopia, 235

Aithiopis, Epic Cycle, 130
Aithon, 274
Ajax, 299
Akkadian, 170, 171
Alcaeus F 69.5: 261
Alcman PMG 1: 223; 7: 4; 13a: 273; 39: 54; 45–49: 223; 49: 227, 234; 87: 256; passim: 273
Aletes, 288
Alexander, 251
Alexandrian scholars, accentual notation of, 40
Alkinoos, 44, 45, 205
alphabet, 37, 38; native Umbrian, 164, 166, 167
alter ego, 129, 193, 256
ambrosia, 141
amor uersus, theme of, 259
Amphidamas, 77
Amphidromia, 144
Anacreon PMG 376: 228, 233; 378: 233; passim: 230
analogy, fourth law of: *see* Kuryłowicz
ancestors: as heroes, 216; worship of, 11, 94, 116, 129
Anchises, 243, 248
Anecdota Graeca, 144
Aṅgiras-, 96, 151
antagonism between hero and god, 12, 49, 135, 204, 214, 215, 295
Antenoridai, 133
anthropogony: *see* first human
Antilokhos, 209, 210, 215, 217, 220
Antinoos, 271, 297
Apąm Napå, 100
Apām Napāt, 99, 100, 101, 102, 118
Aphrodite, 3, 4, 17, 46, 228, 229, 235, 242, 243, 246, 248, 249, 250, 251, 252, 253, 254, 255, 257, 258, 259, 260, 261, 262; *Melainís* 'the black one', 242, 254; Sappho's self-identification with, 4, 259, 260, 261, 262;
Apollo, 12, 37, 47, 51, 52, 56, 57, 58, 59, 60, 68, 75, 76, 130, 131, 141, 204, 206, 222, 234, 280, 294, 297, 300 ; Erithios, 229, 255; Leukatas, 227
Apollodorus 2.4.7: 232, 257; 2.5.4: 271; 2.8.3: 283; 2.8.4–5: 284; 3.14.3: 261; 3.15.5: 231; *Epitome* 1.24: 234
Apollonius of Rhodes 1.211 and scholia: 142; 3.1244 and scholia: 233
Arcadia, 214
Archilochus, 38, 49, 50, 51, 52
Arctinus, 79
Argonauts, 237
Argos, 233, 280, 284
Aristarchus, 230
Aristophanes *Acharnians* 34: 151; 180: 151; 321: 151; 325–341: 152; 332: 151; 333: 152; 349: 152; 350: 151; 609: 151; 612: 151; 668: 152; *Clouds* 599–600: 273; *Lysistrata* 758, scholia to: 144; *Ploutos* 627: 230, 231

Aristotle *Constitution of the Athenians* 3.5: 144; 21.2: 290; 21.2–6: 286; 21.6: 287; F 385: 286, 287; *Constitution of the Corinthians* F 516: 288; *Constitution of the Laconians* F 532: 292; *Constitution of the Orkhomenians* F 565: 49; *Poetics* 1452a30–32: 203; *Politics* 1264a8: 277; 1294a4–7: 271; 1306b40: 271; 1319b23–27: 289; 1322b: 144; *Problemata* 870a27: 264
Arjuna, 14
Arktos, 207, 253
Armenian: *harkanem* 'strike', 186; *orot* 'thunder', 186
Arnold, Matthew, 34
ars gratia artis, 54
Artemis, 57, 75, 77, 243, 250, 251, 252, 253, 263, 264, 265, 273; Artemis-of-the-Crossroads, 77; Orthia, 273;
Artemisia I, 229
ascending scale of affection, concept of, 203
Asclepiades FGH 12 F 71: 82
Asclepius, 38
ash spear, 23, 200
Askra, 49, 52, 53, 72, 73, 74
Asura, 94, 95, 98, 100
Aśvin-s, 12, 14, 93, 112, 255, 256, 258, 259, 281
Atē, 250
Atharva-Veda 1.13.2: 118; 1.21.1: 278; 3.21.1, 7: 102; 4.22.1: 284; 4.22.3: 278; 4.35.1d-6d: 139; 6.28.3: 97; 8.1.11: 102; 12.1.37: 102; 13.2.14: 99; 18.2.24: 120; 18.3.13: 96; 18.4.7: 97; 19.6.6: 284; passim: 87
Athena, 12, 17, 57, 113, 204, 250, 251, 254, 284, 285, 294, 295, 297, 298; *Sṓteira* 'Savior', 214
Athenaeus 69d-e: 229; 141e-f: 290; 142e-f: 289; 526a: 73; 620c: 51; 630f: 269; 687b: 260
Athens, 38, 63, 67, 144, 232, 273, 277, 282, 284, 285, 286, 287, 288, 289, 290
Atiedian Brethren, 144, 164, 165, 166, 167, 168
Atlantic, 238
Attica, 232, 286
Aulis, 77, 78
author, concept of, 17, 41, 42, 52, 53, 58, 59, 60, 61, 63, 64, 65, 66, 67, 70, 74, 76, 79, 80, 111, 143, 144, 170, 174, 194
Autocrates F 1: 273
Avesta *Vendidad* 1.8: 175; 1.12: 175; 1.16: 175, 177; 1.20: 176; 5.14: 177; 7.55: 178; 8.2: 177; 8.8: 174; 8.73: 175; 8.81–96: 178; 8.83: 174, 179; 8.84: 179; 8.87: 179; 8.91: 179; 8.96: 179; *Yasna* 2.5: 100; 9.3–4: 104, 146; 9.19: 120; 28.2: 120; 30.4: 120; 31.20: 120; 43.5: 119; 46.19: 119; 48.6: 119; 57.25: 120; 71.8: 177; *Yašt* 1.25: 119; 5.17–18: 176; 5.104: 176; 10.90: 100; 15.2: 176; 19.51: 100
Avestan: *acišta- ahu-* 'worst essence', 120; *ahu-* 'essence', 95, 119, 120, 121; *ahu-astuuant-* 'essence of bones', 120; *ahu- manahiia-* 'essence of *manah-*', 120; *Ahura-*, 94; *asan-/asman-* 'rock, stone, sky', 193; *auruuat̰.aspa-* 'having swift horses', 100; *daēuua-* 'demon', 94, 178; *daxma* (place of funeral), 177, 178, 179; *huuar-* 'sun', 100; *manah-*, 120; *parāhu-* 'higher existence', 119; *parō.asti-* 'higher existence', 119; *sairiia-* 'manure', 179; *sairiie.hiia-*, 174,

Avestan *(continued)*
178, 180; θ*uuaxš*- 'fashion', 149; *vahišta- ahu*- 'best essence', 120; *vīs* (unit of society), 281; *vīsō puθra*, 281; *vispa*- 'all', 281; *vohu*- 'good', 149; *x*^{v}*arənah*- 'brilliance of glory', 100; *yauuaētāt*- 'eternity', 125; *zantu* (unit of society), 281

Bakkhiadai, 292
Balios, 244
Bee Maidens, 59, 60
Bella Coola, 235, 240
Bellerophon, 207
Bhīma, 14
Black Figure iconography, 88, 217, 220
blame, 16, 17, 164; *see also* praise
Boeotia, 51, 53, 80
Boreas, 63, 81, 92, 142
Buddha, 293

Caeculus, 173
Caesar *Bellum Gallicum* 6.24.2: 25, 187
caesura, 31
Callimachus *Epigram* 6: 51; F 478: 229; *Hymn to Apollo* [2]: 58; *Hymn to Delos* [4]: 76
Callisthenes FGH 124 F 24: 273
cannibalism, 301
Capitolium, 161
Carmina Popularia PMG 869: 221
Catalogue of Ships, 78, 285
catalogue poetry, 54, 56, 238
Cato *De re rustica* 11.4: 162, 163; 16.3: 162; 75: 160; 76.2: 160; 113.1: 180; 143.2: 160
Cattle of the Sun, 225, 252
Catullus 62: 258; 85: 259
Centaur, 70, 271, 275
Chalkis, 77, 78
Charax FGH 103 F 14: 140
Charinos, 229
chariot, 88, 95, 100, 101, 113, 209, 210, 215, 216, 217, 218, 219, 220, 235, 241, 249, 261, 292
Charon of Lampsakos FGH 262 F 7: 230
Cheiron, 70, 71
Choerilus, 236, 239
Cicero *Against Catiline* 4.24: 166; *De domo sua* 106: 166; 123: 162; 124: 162; 143: 166; *De natura deorum* 3.37: 155; *De republica* 2.14: 278; *In Pisonem* 91: 166; *Philippics* 11.10: 106; *Pro Sestio* 90: 166; *Pro Sulla* 23: 164
Circe, 34, 237
city-state: *see* polis
Claudia Quinta, 162

Clearchus F 92: 38, 51
Clement *Stromateis*, 79
Clytemnestra, 143, 144, 174
Codex Vaticanus 909: 239
coincidentia oppositorum, 214, 237
colon, 31, 32
comparative philology, 7, 8
Compitalia, 172
compression (vs. expansion), principles of, 12, 15, 16, 55, 57, 203
constants (vs. tendencies), Jakobson's concept of, 24
Contest of Homer and Hesiod, 50, 51, 78
Corcyra, 288
Corinth, 292
Cos, 279, 280, 281
crane, 212, 213, 242
Crates of Pergamon, 54
Cratinus F 330: 229
cremation, practice of, 85, 86, 87, 89, 97, 112, 116, 117, 129, 170, 174, 175, 177, 178, 179, 180
Crete, 272
crystallization, hermeneutic model of, 42, 47, 51, 52, 61, 78, 79
cuckoo, 212
cult, working definition of, 10
cult hero, 1, 14, 48, 49, 50, 51, 68, 128, 134, 135, 136, 137, 138, 220
Cycle (Epic), 15, 16, 71, 79, 257; *see also Aithiopis* and *Cypria*
Cyclops (plural Cyclopes), 228, 299
Cypria F 1: 15, 16; Proclus summary, 16, 77
Cyprus, 46
Cythera, 46
Czech: *pelyn/pelun* 'wormwood', 188; *peru/prati* 'strike', 185; *perun* 'thunderbolt', 183; *prkno* 'board', 186

dactylic hexameter, 26, 27, 31, 32, 33, 51, 55, 58, 62, 63, 247, 248
Dahāka, 100
Dakṣiṇa, 108, 109, 110
dance, 56, 57, 58, 150, 191, 204, 223, 234, 260; Dance of the Lydian Maidens, 273
Dardanos, 229
Deioneus, 230, 257
DELG, 47, 76, 132, 139, 148, 190, 195, 202, 231
Deliades (Delian Maidens), 56, 58
DELL, 153, 155, 160, 163, 180, 185
Delos, 56, 58, 76; *see also* Deliades
Delphi, 37, 56, 59, 60, 68, 125; chief cult hero of, 12; dedication at, 258; ritual at, 275; *see also* Delphic Oracle
Delphic Oracle, 10, 222, 272; utterance no. 4 PW, 49
Demeter, 3, 136, 220, 283
Demetrius of Skepsis, 289
democracy, 67, 270, 280, 290

Demophon, 136
Deva, 94, 95, 97, 98, 110, 115, 118
DGE no. 62: 230; no. 96: 280; no. 200: 285; no. 251: 280; no. 251C: 283; no. 253: 280; no. 281: 285; no. 316: 125
Dharma, 12, 14
diachronic, working definition of, 20; *see also* synchronic
diaeresis, 31
Diagoras, 285
dialects: Attic, 148, 149; Boeotian, 61, 62, 63; Doric group, 51, 62; Ionic group, 51, 52, 61, 62, 63, 148, 149; Laconian, 224; "standard" Mycenaean, 148
Dichtersprache, 29
didactic poetry, 36
Diodorus Siculus, 12, 140, 239, 242
Diomedes, 299
Dione, 258
Dionysius of Halicarnassus 4.2.1–4: 173; 7.73: 220
Dionysius Scytobrachion, 239, 242
Dionysus, 43, 63, 75, 141, 231
Dios, father of Hesiod and Perses, 77
Dioskouroi, 93, 256, 258; *see also* Divine Twins
District of Dreams, 224, 225, 226, 234
Divine Twins, 4, 93, 218, 255, 256, 258
dog, 117, 175, 263, 264, 300, 301; Dog Star, 207
Dolopion, 133
Dorieus, 292
Doros, 283, 284
Drakanos, 43
dual kingship, 4
Dyaus, 94, 100, 112, 248
Dyman, 283
Dymanes: *see* Greek: *Dumânes*

economy, principle of: *see* thrift
elegiac, 51, 52, 270, 271, 272, 273, 274, 275
Eleusis, 136, 144
Elias, Saint, 214
Elpenor, 214, 215
Elysium, 127, 140, 190
Emathion, 242
endogamy, practice of, 291, 292
English: *ashes*, 151, 170; *by*, 203; *horse*, 256; *kindle*, 172; *king*, 145; *man*, 70; *willfire*, 196
Ennius *Annals*, 145
Eos, 130, 150, 237, 242, 243, 244, 246, 247, 248, 249, 250, 251, 252, 253, 254, 255, 257, 258, 261; *see also* Greek: *ēṓs*
Epeians, 225
Ephesus, 38, 82, 273, 286, 289
Ephialtes, 74

Ephorus of Kyme FGH 70 F 1: 75; F 15: 283; F 175: 274; F 179: 288
epic, 14, 19, 23, 24, 25, 27, 32, 34, 42, 46, 54, 61, 78, 80, 93, 133, 136, 138, 216; allusions to nonepic themes, 198; concept of justice in, 272; fame conferred by, 123, 127; and hero cult, 11, 12, 13; ideals conveyed by, 175, 294; incompatibility with local religious features, 128; Indic, 8, 9, 12, 14, 16; internal testimony about its genesis, 17; Kirghiz, 43; local, 47; metaphor as plotline in, 225; monumental, 55; and myth, 12, 13; as myth, 7, 8, 9, 37; pan-Hellenism in, 11; Persian, 100, 177; resistance to change, 29; Slavic, 8, 20, 26; specialization of, 15; specialization of heroes, 15, 16; subgenres of, 224; traces of a ritual dimension, 130; variant traditions, 28, 139
Epidauros, 38, 280
epithet, 13, 14, 22, 49, 55, 76, 93, 94, 99, 100, 101, 103, 104, 105, 109, 111, 113, 116, 117, 120, 124, 125, 126, 127, 140, 143, 147, 150, 155, 156, 164, 191, 194, 195, 198, 200, 204, 212, 226, 229, 235, 238, 246, 247, 249, 250, 251, 253, 254, 255, 256, 257, 259, 261, 274, 284, 285; distinctive, 22, 23; fixed, 22, 246, 247, 248; generic, 22, 23, 34
Erechtheus, 254
Eretria, 86, 87, 137
Eridanos, 236, 238, 239, 246, 256, 257, 262
Eris, 76
Eros, 233
Erysikhthon, 274
eschatology, 86, 87, 94
eternal return, 126
Etruscans, 278, 279
Etymologicum Magnum, 224, 245
Euboea, 77
Eubulus F 14: 229
euhemerism, 254
Eumaios, 44, 203, 205, 208, 243, 296, 297
Euripides *Cyclops* 163–168: 228, 234; 169–172: 234; *Hecuba* 70: 224; *Helen* 1465–1466: 256; *Herakles* 687–690: 58; *Hippolytus* 455: 242, 248; 735–741: 236; 736–737: 238; *Ion* 281: 254; 1579–1588: 277; *Iphigeneia in Tauris* 1150: 264; *Medea* 804–805: 250; *Phaethon* 48: 241; 51: 241; 61–62: 241; 227–235: 250; passim: 235; *Suppliants* 935: 140; TGF 821: 250; passim: 230, 254
Eurykleia, 203
Eurymakhos, 71
Eurynome, 298
Eurysthenes, 292
Eurystheus, 13
Eurytion, 271
EWA, 119, 151, 156, 157
exogamy, practice of, 143, 144, 174, 291, 293
expansion, principle of: *see* compression
exposition, practice of, 87, 174, 175, 176, 177, 179, 301
eye, symbol of: *see* Zeus: Eye of

fable, 50, 275; of the hawk and the nightingale, 65, 66; of the wolf as lawgiver and the ass, 272
Ferdowsi, 100, 177, 256
ferrymen, 255
festival, 38, 40, 41, 43, 50, 136, 214, 233, 273, 289
Festus, 157, 180, 288; *see also* Paulus ex Festo
fieldwork, 8, 9, 19, 20, 21, 24, 39, 40, 130
Finnish: *ahjo* 'fireplace', 151; *arina* 'hearthstone', 151
first human: king, 174; sacrificer/priest, 74, 104, 105, 110, 111, 146, 148, 151, 198; seer, 151, 198
five generations of mankind, Hesiodic myth of, 293
fixed text, concept of, 20, 23, 31, 38, 40, 41, 78
formula, 21, 22, 23, 25, 26, 29, 31, 32, 33, 34; modified working definition of, 29; Parry's definition of, 18
French: *feu* 'fire', 163
Freud, S., 241

Gades/Cadiz, 237
Ganymedes, 243, 245
Gārhapatya, 105, 106, 107, 108, 109, 110, 111, 169, 173
Gates of the Sun, 224, 225, 226
Gautama, 293
Gellius 12.1.6: 156
gēns Caecilia, 173
German: *Deutsch*, 278; *Donnerwetter*, 194; *Esse* 'smith's fireplace' = 'forge', 151, 170; *Hengst* 'stallion', 256; *jōk*, 164; *König* 'king', 145; *Notfeuer* 'willfire', 196
Germanic: *kuningaz 'king', 145; *Mannus*, 111; *Tuisto*, 111
Glaukos, 133, 137, 138
goat, 100, 101, 117, 197, 300
Gothic: *fairguni* 'mountain, mountain-range', 186; *kuni* 'race, family', 145
Great Rhetra, 289
Greek: *áella* 'gust of wind', 243, 245; *Aellṓ*, 245; *áesa* 'spend the night', 149; *agorā́* 'assembly', 52, 53; *aieí* 'forever', 125, 126; *Aigikoreîs*, 286; *ainéō* 'praise', 16, 17; *aínigma* 'riddle', 82; *aînos*, 221, 274, 275; *aiṓn* 'age', 123, 125, 126, 127; *Aíthōn*, 274; *aíthōn* 'burning [with hunger]', 274; *aíthops* 'with looks of fire, fiery-looking', 174; *aítion* 'cause', 275; *Akhaiós*, 284; *ákmōn* 'anvil', 192; *Akmōn*, 192; *alēthéa* 'true things', 45; *alēthéa gērū́sasthai / mūthḗsasthai* 'tell true things', 44, 45; *alētheíē* 'truth', 60; *álgea* 'pains', 12; *Alkínoos*, 205; *amboládēn* 'playing a prelude', 54; *ambrosíē* 'ambrosia', 141; *ámbroto-* 'immortalizing', 141; *amḗkhanos* 'irremediable', 204; *anagignṓskō* 'recognize', 203–205; *anagnṓrisis* 'recognition', 203; *anágō* (mystical meaning of), 258; *anak(t)-* 'king', 283; *ánaltos* 'insatiable', 157; *anapsū́khein* 'reanimate', 92; *anarpáxāsa* 'snatching up', 251; *Anaxílea*, 283; *androtēs* 'manhood', 111; *anélonto* 'seized', 244, 251; *ánemoi* 'spirits of the ancestors', 116; *ánemos* 'wind', 116; *anḗr* 'man', 174; *anereipsaménē* 'snatching up', 242–244, 253; *anēreípsanto* 'snatched up', 243, 244, 252; *anḗrpase* 'snatched up', 242, 243, 245; *anósteos* 'boneless one', 81, 82; *ánthrax* 'coal, charcoal', 151, 152; *ánthrōpos* 'human', 151, 173, 198; *Antínoos*, 206; *Aoidḗ* 'song' (name of Heli-

Greek *(continued)*
konian Muse), 60; *aoidós* 'singer, poet', 3, 26, 42, 43, 59, 60, 65, 76; *Aōtis*, 256; *Apatoúria*, 289; *Apélla, apéllai*, 289; *aphradées* 'without faculties', 92; *Aphrodī́tē*, 248; *áphthito-* 'imperishable', 123, 124, 125, 126, 127, 136, 138, 143; *apobátēs* (chariot athlete), 220; *arepuîa*, 245; *Argádai*, 286; *Argadeîs*, 286, 289; *Argeíā*, 285; *argikéraunos* 'he whose thunderbolt shines', 195, 200; *árgŭphos*, 187; *árgŭros* 'silver', 187; *áristos* 'best', 13; *áristos Akhaiôn* 'best of the Achaeans', 13; *arkhaiologikṓteroi* 'those more versed in the ancient lore', 230; *Arkhilókheion*, 51; *artokópos* 'baker', 195; *ásbolos / asbólē* 'soot', 152, 170; *Askrā* 'sterile oak', 74; *Asteríā*, 76; *ástu* 'city', 75; *atásthalos* 'reckless', 14; *athánatoi* 'immortals', 241; *átrikhos* 'hairless one', 82; *audḗ* 'voice', 47, 59; *aúō* 'take [fire]', 194; *aúōs* (Lesbian) 'dawn', 149, 261; *autós* 'self', 88; *basileús, basileîs* 'kings', 53, 67; *bathudī́nēs* 'deep-swirling', 238; *bíotos* 'life', 126; *boulàs bouleúei* 'plans his plans', 220; *boulḗ* 'planning', 204, 220; *daímōn* 'supernatural being, spirit', 68, 253; *daíō / daíomai* 'divide, distribute, apportion', 195, 271; *daís* 'feast', 271, 272; *daízō* 'distribute', 195; *dasmós* 'distribution', 270; *démas* 'body', 264; *dēmiourgós* 'artisan in the community', 3, 282, 287, 288; *Dēmophóōn*, 136; *dêmos* 'district, population, deme', 3, 132, 133, 135, 136, 137, 138, 152, 225, 226, 234, 270, 282, 285, 286, 287, 291; *dēmótai* 'fellow district-members', 152; *dérma* 'skin, hide', 263–264; *deúteron* 'next', 57; *diakrī́nō* 'separate, sort out', 64, 65, 88; *diī́philos* 'dear to Zeus', 34; *dikaiosúnē* 'justice', 71; *díkē* 'judgment' (short term) or 'justice' (long term), 53, 63, 64, 65, 66, 67, 68, 69, 73, 74, 75, 76, 211, 270, 272, 275; *dîon génos* 'descendant of Zeus', 75; *Diṓnē*, 258; *Dîos*, 75, 76, 77; *Diòs koûroi* 'sons of Zeus, Dioscuri', 250, 256; *Diòs thugátēr* 'daughter of the Sky', 247ff.; *dōdekápolis* (federation of 12 cities), 288; *dokeúei*, 253; *Dōriees* 'Dorians', 284; *Dōrieús*, 284; *dōrophágoi* 'gift-devouring', 64; *Dôros*, 283, 284; *dóru* 'wood, shaft', 143; *drûs ákrē* 'top of the oak', 74; *Dumā́n*, 283; *Dumânes*, 279, 280, 281, 283, 285, 289, 292; *dúnamis* 'power', 298; *ekhéphrones* 'aware', 66; *ekhthrós* 'enemy', 72; *ēlúsion* 'a place or field that has been struck by the thunderbolt', 140, 141, 190; *see also* Elysium; *enēlúsion, enēlúsios*, 140; *énthen apornúmenos* 'starting from there', 58; *ēṓs* 'dawn', 149, 150, 171, 246, 247, 248, 249, 261; *epesbólos* 'thrower of words', 164; *Epheseîs*, 289; *epikhthónios* 'earth-bound', 13; *epikraínousa* 'authorizing', 59; *épos, épea* 'utterance, epic utterances', 27, 28, 51, 221; *érgon, érga, érgmata* 'deed(s)', 54, 71; *êri* 'early', 246; *Ēridanós*, 239, 246; *see also* Eridanos; *ērigéneia* 'early-generated' or 'early-generating', 246; *éris* 'conflict, strife', 15, 16, 71, 76; *es méson, es tò méson* 'directed at the center', 270, 272; *eskhárā* 'fireplace', 148; *esthlós* 'good', 121, 204; *etḗtuma* 'genuine things', 64; *éthnos*, 277; *eú-* 'good', 94, 116, 120, 121; *Eunomíā*, 67, 271, 272; *eupatrídai*, 288; *euphrosúnē* 'merriment', 271; *ex halós* 'out of the sea', 214; *gastḗr* 'belly', 44, 45, 274, 275; *Geléontes*, 286, 289; *génē* 'lineages', 286, 287, 290; *génos andrôn hēmithéōn*, 56; *geōrgoí*, 'cultivators', 282, 287, 288; *géras basilḗion* 'honorific portion of kings', 134; *gérontes* 'elders', 53; *gignṓskō* 'recognize', 206, 208, 213; *(h)ábros* (Lesbian) 'luxuriant', 261; *(h)abrosúnā* 'luxuriance', 261; *habrótēs* 'luxuriance', 260; *Harmoníā*, 275; *harp-* 'snatch', 141; *Hárpagos* 'snatcher', 256; *harpázō* 'snatch', 141; *hárpuia* 'snatching wind, Harpy', 141, 243, 244, 245, 251; *hēgemónes* 'leaders', 282; *Hekátē*, 76; *Hékatos*, 76; *héleto* 'seized', 242,

Greek *(continued)*
244, 251; *hḗlios* 'sun', 235, 247; *hēmítheos* 'demigod', 15, 16, 54; *Heṓsphoros*, 258; *hḗrōs* 'hero', 10, 15, 94; *hḗrpase* 'snatched', 242, 245, 251, 252, 253; *Hēsíodos*, 47, 48, 58; *Hésperos*, 258; *hestíā* 'hearth', 143, 144, 146, 149, 171; *hetaîros* 'comrade', 69, 71, 72; *heúō* 'singe', 150; *hieropoioí* 'sacrificers, priests', 280, *hierós/hierón* 'sacred'/'sacred place', 140, 234; 282; *histíā* (*see also hestíā*), 148; *Homērídai* 'sons of Homer', 51; *Hómēros*, 48; *homóphūlos*, 286; *Hóplētes*, 286; *húbris* 'outrage', 65, 66, 68, 73, 74, 75, 76, 77, 271, 272, 292; *Hulleîs*, 279, 280, 281, 283, 284, 285, 289; *Húllos*, 283, 284; *húmnos*, 54; *hupémnēsen* 'reminded', 113; *Huperíōn*, *huperíōn* 'the one who goes above', 235; *Húpnos* 'Sleep', 131, 134, 138, 142; *Hurnáthioi*, 280; *iaúō* 'sleep', 149; *iētḗr* 'physician', 3; *īsonomíā*, 271, 272; *ísos* 'equal, equitable', 270; *ísos dasmós* 'equitable distribution', 270; *kaíō* 'burn', 195; *Kalupsṓ*, 254; *Kamirís*, 285; *katà phûla* 'according to *phūlaí*', 290; *katà phrḗtrās* 'according to *phrātríai*', 290; *katà sphéas*, 291; *kataphūladón*, 285; *keraízō* 'destroy, ravage', 194, 195; *kerameús* 'potter', 3; *keraunós* 'thunderbolt', 194, 195, 200; *kêrux* 'herald', 3, 52, 59, 60; *khiliastúes* (social division), 289; *khorós* 'place or occasion for dancing and singing', 58, 150; *khrḗmata* 'possessions', 68; *Khthoníā* 'the chthonic one', 254; *Kíssēs*, *Kisseús*, 74; *kléos* 'fame, glory', 26, 28, 46, 47, 54, 58, 94, 123, 125, 126, 127, 136, 137, 138, 215, 216, 217; *kléos áphthiton* 'fame . . . imperishable', 122, 123, 124, 125, 126, 127, 136; *Kluménē*, 254; *Klúmenos*, 254; *koéō* 'perceive', 76; *Koîos*, 76; *kôma* 'mystical sleep', 4; *kósmos*, 270, 271; *koûros* 'uninitiated male', 12; *kraínō* 'authorize', 59, 60; *Kreōphuleîoi* 'sons of Kreophylos', 51; *krī́nō* 'sort out, discriminate, arrange', 65, 290; *ktísis* ('foundation') poetry, 37, 43, 73, 74; *ktoínā*, 285; *ktoinétai* (Linear B *ko-to-ne-ta*), 285; *lā́iton* = *lḗiton*, 283; *Lampetíē*, 93, 249; *Lámpos*, 249; *lāoì . . . ólbioi*, 127; *lāós* 'people, host', 283; *Leimônes* 'Meadows', 49; *lênai* 'devotees of Dionysus', 63; *Lēnaiṓn*, 63; *lêstis* 'forgetting', 234; *Lēthaîos*, 234; *lḗthē* 'forgetting, forgetfulness', 211, 218, 234; *lḗthō* 'escape the mind of, forget', 44, 209, 210; *Leukàs pétrā* 'White Rock', 224, 227, 228, 230; *Leukippídes* 'bright horses', 256; *Leukopetrās*, 229; *leukópōloi* 'bright horses', 256; *loigós* 'devastation', 12; *Lukomḗdēs*, 231; *Lukoûrgos* 'he who wards off the wolf', 231, 272; *lúō* 'set loose', 88; *Maîra*, 198; *Makárōn nêsoi* 'Islands of the Blessed', 141; *mántis* 'seer', 3, 59, 60, 69, 76, 151, 198, 204, 205, 206; *Marīládēs* 'son of embers', 151; *marī́lē* 'embers of charcoal', 151, 198; *marmaírō* 'glow, flash', 198; *mḗ phūlokrīneîn* 'not to make distinctions according to *phūlḗ*', 290; *Meletḗ* 'practice' (name of Helikonian Muse), 60; *memnēménos* 'being mindful', 70, 213; *mênis* 'anger', 12, 28; *ménos*, 87, 88, 89, 90, 91, 92, 93, 94, 111, 113, 114, 115, 116, 120, 219, 226, 300; *ménos ēú*, 93, 94, 111, 115, 116, 120, 121; *Méntēs*, 113; *Merópē*, 198; *méropes*, 198; *Mérops*, 198, 250; *mêtis* 'artifice, strategem', 204, 205, 208, 209, 217; *mnē-* 'remember, have in mind', 44, 210, 213; *mnêma* 'reminder', 218; *mnḗmata* 'monuments', 220; *Mnḗmē* 'memory' (name of Helikonian Muse), 60; *Mnēmosúnē* 'Memory', 44, 45, 58, 59; *Mnēsiépēs*, 51; *mounogenḗs* 'only-born', 76, 77; *moûnon . . . génos* 'single birth', 76; *Mukhíā*, 254; *neikéō* 'blame', 16, 17; *múkhios* 'secreted', 254, 255; *mukhós* 'secret place', 254; *neîkos* 'quarrel, quarreling', 16, 53, 64, 65, 72, 76; *néktar* 'nectar', 139, 141, 190; *nékūs* / *nekrós* 'corpse', 139; *némō* 'distribute, apportion', 271; *néomai*, 92, 218, 219;

Greek *(continued)*

néphos 'cloud', 193; *Néstōr*, 218, 219, 225; *Noḗmōn*, 218; *noéō* 'perceive, take note, think, think through', 203, 205, 206, 208, 209, 210, 211, 212, 217, 218, 221; *nóēsis*, 203, 206, 209, 222; *nóos*, 92, 93, 126, 203, 204, 205, 207, 208, 211, 212, 213, 217, 218, 219, 220, 221, 225, 260; *nṓrops*, 174; *nóstos* 'return, homecoming', 92, 93, 123, 124, 125, 126, 127, 218, 219; *nússa* 'turning post', 230; *óar* 'wife', 253; *óaros* 'companionship, keeping company', 253; *Oidípous* 'he whose feet are swollen', 82; *oikéō* 'I have an abode', 274; *Oioklos* 'he who is famous for his sheep', 74; *Ōkeanós*, 99, 239; *Ōkupétē*, 245; *ólbioi*, 'blessed', 126, 127, 141; *ólbos* 'wealth', 126; *Ōríōn*, 253; *ornithomanteíā* 'divination by birds', 66; *oudé me/se/he lḗthei* 'and it does not escape my/your/his mind', 213; *Ouranós* 'Sky', 192; *palaíphatos* 'spoken of a long time ago', 198; *Pamphūliakón*, 285; *Pámphūloi*, 279, 280, 281, 282, 283, 285, 289; *Pámphūlos*, 283; *panéllēnes* 'pan-Hellenes, all Greeks', 37; *parà tà Anaxílea* 'at the precinct [called] Anaxílea', 281, 283; *parà tò Dāmā́trion* 'at the precinct of Demeter', 283; *parà tò Hērakleîon* 'at the precinct of Herakles', 283; *patéres* 'ancestors', 94; *patríā*, 291; *Patrokléēs* 'whose glory is that of the ancestors', 94, 115, 216, 218; *peírō* 'pierce, cross over', 190; *peníā* 'poverty', 72, 73; *peribállō* 'fling around [someone]', 263, 264, 265; *períblēma* 'garment', 264; *Perkṓsios* 'from *Perkṓtē*', 198; *Perkṓtē*, 198; *Pérsēs*, 74, 75, 76, 77; *Perseús*, 74; *pérthō* 'destroy', 75; *pétrā* 'rock', 223; *Pétrē Haimoníē*, 233; *Phaéthōn* 'bright, shining', 153, 235, 249, 255; *phaéthōn* 'the one who shines', 235, 249; *Phaéthousa*, 249; *Pháōn* 'bright, shining', 153, 235, 255; *phḗmē* 'prophetic utterance', 221; *pheréoikos* 'he who carries his house', 82; *phi* 'by', 203; *philíā* 'nearness and dearness', 203; *phílos* 'near and dear', 72, 203; *phlégō/phleg-éth-ō* 'be on fire, burn', 153, 235; *Phoíbē*, 76; *Phoîbos*, 76; *phrā́trā / phrātríā*, 277–292; *phrázomai*, 205, 208; *phrénes*, 89, 92; *phronéontes* 'aware', 65, 66; *phthi-* 'perish', 126; *phúlakes* 'guardians', 68, 282; *Phū́lās*, 285, 288; *phūlḗ*, 277 et passim; *phūlokrīneîn*, 290, 291; *phûlon* 'race, kind', 290, 291; *Pitúeia*, 198; *pítus* 'pine', 198; *plōtḗr*, 198; *Podárgē* 'bright/swift of foot', 238, 244, 245, 256; *pólis* 'city, city-state', 10, 75, 276, 277; *see also* polis; *pôlos* 'horse', 249, 250; *polútropos* 'of many turns', 13, 34; *póros*, 190; *porthmeús* 'ferryman', 228; *potamós* 'river', 238; *poús* 'foot', 82; *Prīnídēs* 'son of holm oak', 151; *prī́ninoi* 'made of holm oak', 151, 152; *prooímion* 'prelude', 53, 54; *prutaneîon* 'presidential building', 144, 283; *pseúdea* 'falsehoods', 44, 45, 47; *pseudómenoi* 'lying', 43; *pseúdontai* 'are liars', 44; *psūkhḗ*, 88, 89, 90, 91, 92, 93, 115, 116, 126, 142, 212, 219, 220, 226; *psū́khō* 'blow', 90, 116; *ptolíethron* 'city', 75; *púlai* 'gates', 225; *pulártēs* 'gate-closer', 226; *pulēdókos* 'he who receives [the *psūkhaí*] at the Gates', 226; *Púlos*, 225, 226; *pûr* 'fire', 155; *púraunos*, 194; *rhábdos* 'staff', 59, 60; *Rhákios* 'the man in rags', 73; *rhapsōidós* 'rhapsode', 38, 42; *sákos* 'cowhide-shield', 264; *Sarpēdṓn*, 141, 142; *Sarpēdónios*, 133; *sêma* 'sign, signal, symbol', 202, 203, 204, 205, 206, 207, 208, 209, 210, 211, 212, 213, 214, 215, 216, 217, 218, 219, 220, 221, 222, 230, 274; *skêptron* 'staff, scepter', 49, 52, 53, 60, 64, 143; *skhḗmata* 'configurations', 71; *Skī́rōn*, 231; *Skīrōnídes pétrai*, 231; *skîros/skírros*, 230, 231; *Skûros*, 230, 231; *Skúphios*, 232; *Skū́rios*, 231; *Skīrōnítēs*, 232, 239; *stiptoí* 'tough', 151; *súmmakhos* 'battle-ally', 259; *sunoikismós* 'urban consolidation', 278, 285; *Taráxippos* 'he who disturbs the

Greek *(continued)*
horses', 215; *tárīkhos* 'smoked fish, mummy', 139; *tarkhúō*, 131, 132, 133, 134, 136, 138, 139, 140, 141; *téktōn* 'carpenter', 3; *teléō* 'accomplish', 259, 260; *tēlephanḗs* 'shining from afar', 220; *témenos* 'sector of land, sacred precinct', 137, 138; *téndō* 'gnaw', 81; *térma* 'turning point', 209, 210, 215; *terpikéraunos*, 195, 200; *Thánatos* 'Death', 131, 134, 138, 142; *thêka* 'placed', 163; *thémis* 'divine law', 53, 63, 64, 65, 67; *themoí* 'ordinances', 59; *theoí* 'gods', 241, 243; *theôn génos* 'genesis of gods', 56; *therapeúō* 'be a *therápōn*', 135; *therápōn* 'attendant', 48, 129, 130, 135; *therápōn* of Ares, 48; *therápōn* of the Muses, 47, 48, 49; *théraps*, 129; *thesmoí* 'laws', 67; *thésphata* 'words of a *mántis* [seer] or of one who functions as a *mántis*', 198; *Thoríkios pétros* 'Leap Rock', 231, 239; *Thórikos*, 232, 257; *thorós* 'semen', 231; *thrṓiskō* 'leap, mount, fecundate', 231; *thúella* 'gust of wind', 243, 244, 245, 251; *thugátēr Diós*, 'daughter of the Sky', 247ff.; *thūmálōps* 'piece of burning wood, charcoal', 151; *thūmós*, 87, 88, 89, 90, 91, 92, 93, 99, 113, 115, 116, 199, 219, 237, 243, 246, 259, 260, 300; *tīmḗ* 'honor', 132, 133, 134, 135, 136, 137, 138, 204; *tíō/ tīmáō* 'honor', 132, 137; *tò kalón* 'what is beautiful', 260; *trapezṓmata*, 137; *trikhā́ïkes*, 284; *trikhthá* 'in three parts', 285; *trikhthà . . . oíkēthen kataphūladón* 'were settled in three parts, *phūlḗ* by *phūlḗ*', 285; *Triphūlíā*, 278; *trípous* 'three-footed', 82; **tris hērōei* (Linear B *ti-ri-se-ro-e*), 116; *trìs mákar*, 116; *tritopátores*, 116; *trittúes*, 286, 287; *trittús*, 287, 289; *Zeús*, 94, 248, 251; *see also* Zeus.
Grimm, J., 196
Grunau, Simon, 184
guslar, in South Slavic traditions, 39
Gyaros, 254

Hades, 86, 88, 89, 90, 91, 92, 212, 218, 219, 225, 226, 254
Hagesikhora, 223, 233
Hammerfest, 192
Haoma, 104, 146
Harpocration, 51 (s.v. Homeridai), 144 (s.v. παῖς ἀφ' ἑστίας), 220 (s.v. *apobátēs*)
Harpy, Harpies, 141, 238, 243, 244, 245, 251, 252, 256, 262; Harpy Tomb, 141; *see also* Greek: *hárpuia*
Hekate, 75, 76, 77
Hektor, 90, 139, 199, 204, 220, 294, 295, 296, 299, 300, 301; antagonism with Athena, 204, 295
Helen, 250, 256
Helikon, 53, 57, 58, 60, 74
Helios, 100, 235, 236, 237, 239, 240, 241, 242, 248, 254, 255; *see also* Greek: *hḗlios*
Hellanicus FGH 4 F 20: 51
Hellenism, 1, 2, 10, 301
Hellespont, 220
Hengest and Horsa, 256
Heosphoros, 258
Hephaestion, scholia to, 227
Hephaistos, 296
Hera, 17, 138, 221, 229, 234, 294

Heraclides, 230, 231

Heraclitus B 57: 36; B 93: 222
Herakleidai, 292
Herakles, 12, 13, 14, 140, 142, 225, 239, 254, 271, 280, 281, 283, 284
Hercynia silva, 187
Hermes, 34, 47, 53, 55, 57, 58, 59, 60, 156, 206, 226
Hermione, 254, 280
hero cult, 1, 10, 11, 12, 13, 14, 37, 48, 49, 50, 51, 68, 94, 116, 128, 132, 133, 134, 135, 136, 137, 138, 140, 141, 214, 220, 254, 274, 281
Herodotus: 1.65–66: 272; 1.65.3: 68; 1.65.4: 274; 1.118.2: 132; 1.144.3: 285; 1.145: 288; 1.147.2: 289; 1.152.1: 264; 1.168: 132; 2.53.2: 36; 2.93.1: 231; 3.39.2: 284; 3.115: 238; 3.142–143: 272; 3.142.3: 272; 4.8.2: 237; 4.36.2: 237; 4.149.1: 292; 5.66.2: 277, 286; 5.67.1: 38; 5.69.1: 286; 5.69.1–2: 286; 5.70.3: 284; 5.83: 49; 5.92: 292; 6.52.2: 292; 6.111.1: 290; 7.197.2: 283; 7.204: 284; 8.131.2: 284; 9.26.2–5: 283; 9.120: 139
Hesiod *Precepts of Cheiron*: 70, 71; *Shield of Herakles*: 79, 238; F 1: 56; F 23a.15–26: 77; F 23b: 77; F 25.25–28: 92; F 43: 274; F 70.7: 126; F 169.3: 198; F 193.9: 238; F 204.95–96: 15; 96: 16; 96–123: 15; 100: 15; 129: 82; F 233: 285; F 283: 70; *Theogony* 1: 55, 199; 1–2: 57; 1–21: 57; 1–7: 53; 1–963: 56; 3– 4: 57; 9: 58; 10: 47, 52; 11: 57; 11–20: 57; 14: 76; 16–19: 57; 20: 57; 22: 47; 22–34: 44, 45; 26: 74; 26–28: 45; 30: 49, 52, 58, 64; 31: 47, 59; 31–34: 198; 32: 59; 33–34: 59; 35: 182, 199; 36: 199; 36–103: 56, 57; 36–52: 57; 43: 47; 44: 56; 45: 57; 47: 57; 54: 44; 65: 47; 67: 47; 70: 57; 80–84: 64; 80–93: 53; 81–84: 53; 85: 53, 64; 85–86: 64; 86: 53, 64; 87: 64; 88: 66; 89: 53; 92: 53; 94–97: 55; 94–103: 59; 96: 53; 99–101: 47; 100: 48; 100–101: 61, 62; 104: 56; 105: 56; 105–962: 57; 115: 56; 119: 254; 133: 238; 135: 44; 192–193: 46; 225: 76; 229: 76; 242: 238; 267: 245; 267–269: 245; 337–338: 238, 239; 337–345: 238; 338: 238; 338–345: 238; 371–374: 235, 248, 255; 392–396: 134; 404–452: 75; 405–410: 76; 409: 76; 411–415: 75; 416–420: 75; 421– 422: 75; 423–425: 75; 426: 76; 435–438: 77; 448: 76; 626: 259; 901: 67; 901–1020: 80; 902: 67; 915: 44; 937: 275; 942: 140; 962: 56; 963: 55, 56; 965–1020: 56; 975: 275; 986–991: 242, 248, 252; 987: 235; 988–991: 246; 989–991: 253; 990: 242, 243, 248, 253; 991: 253, 254, 255; scholia to 990: 258; *Works and Days* 1–10: 63; 7: 67; 9: 63, 65, 67; 10: 64, 65; 11: 76; 11–12: 76; 11–26: 71, 76; 12–24: 76; 20: 71; 25–26: 3; 26: 71; 35: 64, 65, 72, 76; 36: 64; 37: 64, 68; 38: 64; 38–39: 64; 39: 64, 66; 40–41: 66; 42–105: 65; 106–201: 65; 109–110: 200; 109–126: 253; 109–142: 133; 116: 134; 121: 134; 122: 126; 122–126: 68; 123: 13; 124: 74; 126: 134; 127–128: 200; 132: 74; 134: 74; 134–137: 135; 137: 126; 138–139: 135; 141: 126; 142: 134; 143–145: 200; 161: 126; 162: 126; 166: 126; 167: 141; 171: 141, 238; 172: 126, 127, 141; 190–194: 65; 202, 65, 66; 202–212: 65; 206: 65; 207: 65; 208: 65; 209: 65; 210: 65; 213: 65; 217–218: 65, 66; 220–223: 65; 220– 224: 66; 221: 64; 224: 65, 66; 225–235: 73; 225–237: 65, 67; 232–233: 74; 234: 74; 236–237: 73; 238–247: 65, 67, 73, 75; 239: 75; 242: 75; 242–244: 74; 246: 73; 247: 74; 249: 64, 66; 249–255: 68; 250: 64; 256–262: 68; 256–269: 66; 263: 66; 264: 64; 267: 211; 267–269: 211; 268: 64; 269: 64, 66; 275: 66; 275–278: 66; 280–281: 66; 286: 67; 298: 70; 320: 68; 320–324: 66; 325–326: 66; 333–335: 69; 336–337: 71; 336–341: 70; 376–377: 76; 396: 66; 396–397: 67; 422: 70; 448–449: 212; 450: 212; 450–451: 212, 213; 483– 484: 212; 485–492: 212; 491–492: 212; 496–497: 82; 504: 63; 504–563: 81;

Hesiod *(continued)*
507–518: 81; 518: 82; 519–525: 81; 521: 81, 82; 524: 82; 524–525: 81; 525: 81, 82; 528: 37; 533: 82; 533–535: 82; 571: 82; 588–589: 224; 589: 233; 598–599: 253; 615–616: 253; 616: 70, 213; 618–623: 213; 622: 213; 623: 70, 213; 633–634: 72; 636: 72; 637: 73; 637–638: 73, 74; 638: 73; 639–640: 72; 640: 53; 641: 70; 650–651: 77; 651–653: 77; 654–656: 77; 656–657: 77; 657: 78; 657–658: 77; 660: 77; 687–688: 71; 707: 71; 708: 72; 708–722: 72; 710–711: 72; 711: 70; 717–718: 72; 720: 72; 727: 70; 728: 70; 729: 70; 742–743: 70; 757–758: 70; 828: 66; *see also* Greek: *Hēsíodos*

Hesperos, 258

Hestia, 143, 144, 146; *see also* Greek: *hestíā*

Hesychius: s.v. Ἄσκρη· δρῦς ἄκαρπος, 74; s.v. Ἠλύσιον, 140; s.v. Δρομιάμφιον ἦμαρ, 144; s.v. κτύναι ἢ κτοῖναι· χωρήσεις προγονικῶν ἱερειῶν ἢ δῆμος μεμερισμένος, 285; s.v. νῶροψ, 174; s.v. θεμούς· διαθέσεις, παραινέσεις, 59

hexameter: *see* dactylic hexameter

Hierapytna, 285

Hittite: *arš-* 'flow', 149; *aššu-* 'good', 145, 149; *ḫarki-* 'bright', 195; *ḫaš-* 'beget', 145, 148, 149, 170, 281; *ḫašša-* 'hearth, sacrificial fireplace', 145, 148, 149, 151, 152, 154, 170, 172; *ḫaššatar* 'begetting, gēns', 145; *ḫaššu-* 'king', 145, 170, 172, 281; *ḫekur* 'summit, mountain', 194; *ḫé-kur pí-ir-wa*, 194; *ḫuiš-* 'live', 149, 189; *ḫuišu-* 'alive', 189; *ḫuišwant-* 'alive', 149; *išḫuzzi-* 'belt', 191; *kunkunuzzi-*, epithet of megalithic monster, 191; *kwenzi* 'strike, kill', 191; *nepiš* 'sky', 193; *parḫ–* 'chase, drive, make (a horse) gallop', 191; *parku-* 'elevated', 189; *peru-* 'rock', 189, 190, 191, 193, 201; *peruna-* 'rock', 189, 190, 191; *tarḫ-* 'conquer, overpower, overcome', 132, 139, 189, 190, 191; *Tarḫu-*, 132, 189, 190; *tarḫu-* 'conquering, victorious', 132, 139; *tarḫuili-* 'heroic', 189; *Tarḫuna-*, 189, 190; *Tarḫunt-*, 189; *tarḫuzzi*, 189; *tarpan(alli)-* 'ritual substitute', 48, 129; *tarpašša-* 'ritual substitute', 129; *tweka-* 'body, person, self, one's own self', 264; [d]UTU*ši* 'my sun', 170; *warša-* 'dew', 149; *wašš-* 'be agreeable', 145; ZI = *ištanza-* 'animus', 171

Homer *Iliad* I 1: 12, 28; I 2: 12; I 3–4: 88; I 4–5: 175; I 5: 15, 222; I 15: 52; I 28: 52; I 52: 126; I 75: 12; I 96: 12; I 97: 12; I 103: 89; I 233–237: 143; I 238–239: 53; I 279: 52; I 341: 12; I 423–424: 237; I 477: 248; I 524–527: 221; I 543: 221; I 549: 221; II 46: 125, 143; II 86: 52; II 110: 48; II 186: 125, 143; II 275: 164; II 303–304: 77; II 308: 203; II 308–319: 204; II 320–332: 204; II 325: 122; II 353: 204; II 362: 285, 290; II 363: 290; II 366: 290; II 381: 258; II 386–387: 115; II 387: 88; II 485–496: 26; II 536: 114; II 547– 551: 254; II 548: 254; II 653–657: 285; II 655: 285; II 668: 285; II 819–823: 133; II 829: 198; II 831–832: 198; II 835: 198; II 877: 141; III 8: 114; III 100: 16; III 218: 52; III 374: 248, 251; IV 128: 250, 251; IV 178–79: 299; IV 313–314: 301; V 77–78: 133; V 78: 132, 133; V 269: 62; V 296: 88; V 312: 251; V 369: 88; V 370: 258; V 395–404: 225; V 397: 226; V 441–442: 290; V 470: 87; V 479: 141; V 646: 226; V 677: 92; V 696: 142; V 697: 142; VI 67: 48; VI 72: 87; VI 130–141: 231; VI 136: 231; VI 168: 207; VI 172: 141; VI 176: 207; VI 178: 207; VI 182: 114; VI 209: 94; VI 346: 243; VII 47: 204; VII 50: 139; VII 67–91: 139; VII 85: 139; VII 131: 90; VII 277: 52; VII 358: 221; VII 421–423: 99, 237, 238, 246; VII 458: 122; VIII 2: 195; VIII 123: 88; VIII 315: 88; VIII 367: 226; VIII 378: 62; VIII 485: 99, 237, 238, 239, 246, 257; VIII 526–538: 299; VIII 538: 296, 299;

Homer *(continued)*
VIII 538–541: 204, 294, 296; IX 97– 99: 53; IX 236: 204; IX 400: 125; IX 401–405: 125; IX 406–407: 125; IX 406– 409: 125; IX 408: 126; IX 412–416: 123; IX 413: 122, 123, 124, 125, 126, 136, 138; IX 414: 125; IX 415: 125, 126; IX 462: 89; IX 538: 75; X 32–33: 133; X 33: 132, 133; X 232: 89; X 249–250: 16; X 415: 220; X 482: 114; X 498: 88; XI 58: 132, 133; XI 58–60: 133; XI 200: 204; XI 223: 74; XI 291: 87; XI 508: 114; XI 671–761, 225; XI 735, 235, 249; XII 18: 114; XII 23: 15; XII 26– 32: 15; XII 232: 221; XII 252: 195; XII 310–321: 137; XII 319: 137; XII 322– 325: 138; XII 326–328: 138; XIII 216–218: 133; XIII 218: 132, 133; XIII 244: 204, 211; XIII 460–461: 28; XIII 487: 89; XIII 545: 253; XIII 726–735: 204; XIII 825: 296, 299; XIII 825–826: 294; XIII 825–828: 204, 294, 296; XIII 829–832: 299; XIV 238: 125; XIV 301–302: 237; XV 59–60: 114; XV 60: 90; XV 189: 285; XV 262: 90, 114; XVI 80–82: 78; XVI 149–151: 244, 245; XVI 150–151: 238, 256; XVI 151: 245; XVI 244: 130; XVI 313: 253; XVI 384–392: 68; XVI 384–393: 211; XVI 387–388: 65; XVI 388: 211; XVI 419–683: 127; XVI 440–457: 138; XVI 445: 138; XVI 446–447: 138; XVI 450–455: 138; XVI 453: 142; XVI 454: 142; XVI 454–455: 131; XVI 455: 132; XVI 456: 132, 133, 139, 141; XVI 456–457: 131, 134; XVI 456–674: 133; XVI 457: 133; XVI 604– 605: 133; XVI 605: 132, 133; XVI 669: 141; XVI 670: 141; XVI 671–673: 131; XVI 672: 134, 142; XVI 673: 132; XVI 674: 132, 133, 139, 141; XVI 674–675: 131, 134; XVI 675: 133; XVI 679: 141; XVI 680: 141; XVI 682: 142; XVI 683: 132; XVI 722: 300; XVI 723: 300; XVI 856: 88, 89; XVII 456: 114, 116; XVII 565: 114; XVIII 251–252: 204; XVIII 311: 204; XVIII 312: 204; XVIII 419: 92; XVIII 464–466: 296; XVIII 487–489: 253; XVIII 488: 253; XVIII 489: 141, 253; XVIII 497: 53, 64; XVIII 502: 53; XVIII 505–506: 53; XVIII 505–508: 64; XVIII 607: 238; XVIII 607–608: 238; XIX 1–2: 252; XIX 91: 250; XIX 95–133: 12; XIX 374–380: 220; XX 16: 195; XX 40: 90; XX 66–69: 252; XX 73: 238; XX 80: 120; XX 80: 93; XX 110: 114; XX 171: 88; XX 174: 87; XX 178–183: 28; XX 200–201: 27; XX 203–205: 27; XX 234: 243; XX 235: 243; XX 248–250: 27; XX 249: 24, 43; XX 302–308: 28; XX 340: 253; XX 440: 116; XXI 145: 89; XXI 195– 197: 238; XXI 569: 90; XXII 30: 207; XXII 30–31: 207; XXII 41–42: 297; XXII 116: 16; XXII 122: 199; XXII 123–125: 199; XXII 126–127: 200; XXII 127–128: 200; XXII 178: 195; XXII 346–348: 300; XXII 348–354: 300; XXII 418: 14; XXII 475: 90; XXIII 45: 215; XXIII 65–92: 89; XXIII 66: 89; XXIII 71: 89, 226; XXIII 72–74: 89; XXIII 75–76: 89; XXIII 76: 89; XXIII 103–104: 89; XXIII 167–169: 85; XXIII 190: 114, 116; XXIII 205–207: 237; XXIII 238: 116; XXIII 305: 217, 219; XXIII 313: 209; XXIII 314: 209; XXIII 315–318: 209; XXIII 319–321: 209; XXIII 320–321: 217; XXIII 322–325: 209; XXIII 323: 209, 220; XXIII 323–325: 210; XXIII 326: 209, 210, 215, 216; XXIII 326–328: 230; XXIII 327–345: 209, 210, 215; XXIII 329: 230; XXIII 331: 216, 218; XXIII 331–332: 216; XXIII 331– 333: 215, 230; XXIII 332: 216, 218; XXIII 332–333: 230; XXIII 333: 220; XXIII 341–345: 215; XXIII 414–415: 209, 210; XXIII 415: 209, 217; XXIII 417–441: 209; XXIII 418–441: 217; XXIII 426: 217; XXIII 568: 52; XXIII 586–611: 217; XXIII 590: 217; XXIII 604: 217; XXIII 612: 218; XXIII 619: 218; XXIII 648–649: 221; XXIII 650: 221; XXIII 652: 221; XXIII 880: 88; XXIV 6: 93, 111, 115, 120, 121; XXIV 29–30: 17; XXIV 294: 206,

Homer *(continued)*
207; XXIV 312: 206, 207; XXIV 364: 114; XXIV 792: 116; *Odyssey* i 1: 14, 33, 34; i 1–4: 13; i 2: 14; i 3: 14, 213; i 4: 14; i 8: 235; i 10: 250; i 23–24: 237; i 89: 89; i 105ff.: 113; i 241: 243; i 320: 113; i 320–322: 113; i 326–327: 47; i 338: 46; ii 1: 246; iii 130ff.: 215; iii 205: 298; iii 208–209: 298; iii 218–220: 298; iii 223–224: 298; iv 227: 250; iv 250: 203; iv 561–569: 92, 140; iv 568: 92; iv 727: 243; iv 809: 226; v 1–2: 252; v 121: 242, 244, 248, 251; v 121–124: 207, 242, 251, 252, 253; v 124: 251; v 160: 126; v 231: 264; v 271–277: 207; v 273–275: 253; v 274: 253; v 275: 141, 253; v 458: 90; vii 215–221: 44, 274; vii 216: 274; vii 221: 44; viii 94: 205; viii 390: 59; viii 429: 54; viii 533: 205; viii 536–638: 205; ix 3–11: 43; ix 116–141: 74; ix 215: 271; ix 507: 198; ix 523–525: 299; x 135: 237; x 190–193: 246; x 330: 33, 34; x 330–331: 34; x 492: 92; x 492–494: 219; x 493: 92, 212; x 494: 92, 212; x 508–512: 239; x 521: 88, 226; x 536: 88, 226; xi 21–22: 237; xi 29: 88, 226; xi 49: 88, 226; xi 75: 215; xi 75–78: 214; xi 90: 52; xi 91: 92; xi 121–137: 213; xi 126: 211, 212, 213, 215; xi 134: 214; xi 136–137: 127; xi 147–149: 92; xi 151: 198; xi 217: 250, 251; xi 222: 226; xi 305–320: 74; xi 317: 74; xi 368: 44; xi 476: 92; xi 601– 604: 92; xi 639: 238; xii 1–4: 237; xii 4: 150; xii 13–15: 214; xii 132: 249; xii 176: 235; xiii 79–95: 219; xiii 172: 198; xiii 221ff.: 215; xiii 369: 251; xiv 124–125: 44, 45, 274; xiv 371: 243; xiv 440–441: 296; xiv 508: 274; xv 235–236: 252; xv 242: 252; xv 249: 252; xv 250: 242, 248; xv 250–251: 242, 251; xv 251: 243, 252; xv 251–252: 252, 253; xv 341–342: 297; xvii 228: 157; xvii 232: 62; xvii 251–253: 300; xvii 279: 208; xvii 281: 208; xvii 381– 385: 3; xvii 494: 297; xvii 496: 298; xvii 514: 44; xvii 518–521: 44; xviii 204: 126; xviii 235–240: 297; xviii 366: 71; xviii 366–375: 71; xviii 369: 71; xviii 518: 44; xix 109–114: 275; xix 135: 3; xix 163: 182, 198; xix 177: 284; xix 183: 274; xix 203: 44, 274; xix 232: 205; xix 250: 205; xix 255– 257: 203; xix 320: 246; xix 433: 246; xix 433–434: 237, 238; xix 440: 114, 115; xix 562: 226; xx 61: 250, 251; xx 61–65: 99, 244, 251; xx 63: 245, 251; xx 63–65: 237, 245; xx 65: 246; xx 66: 244, 251; xx 66–81: 252; xx 67–72: 251; xx 73–74: 251; xx 77: 244, 252; xx 79: 245; xx 80–81: 246; xx 98–101: 221; xx 103–104: 221; xx 105: 221; xx 105–119: 221; xx 111: 221; xx 204–205: 211; xx 346: 206; xx 354: 206; xx 367–368: 206; xxi 205: 205; xxi 217: 203, 205; xxi 295–304: 271; xxi 402–403: 298; xxii 8–30: 206; xxii 32: 206; xxii 148: 264; xxii 203: 114; xxiii 73: 203; xxiii 206: 203; xxiii 246: 249, 250; xxiii 265–284: 213; xxiii 267–268: 214; xxiv 1: 226; xxiv 1–14: 224; xxiv 11: 224, 226, 230, 234; xxiv 11–12: 224; xxiv 12: 226, 234; xxiv 14: 234; xxiv 80–84: 215, 220; xxiv 85–92: 216; xxiv 93–94: 216; xxiv 329: 203; xxiv 349: 90; xxiv 520: 114; *see also* Greek *Hómēros*

Homer and Hesiod: as systematizers of civilization, 36

Homeric Hymn [1] *to Dionysus* 1–5: 43; 6: 43; 6–9: 43; 8–9: 75; 9: 46; [2] *to Demeter* 234: 136; 260–264: 136; 263: 138; 265–267: 136; 311–312: 132; 353: 132; 366–369: 132; [3] *to Apollo* 1: 76; 1–165: 57; 29: 58; 156: 58; 157: 58; 165–166: 56; 166–176: 54; 174–175: 58; 177–178: 56, 58; 179–544: 56, 57; 189–190: 58; 545: 56; 546: 56; [4] *to Hermes* 13: 34; 14: 226; 15: 226; 106: 62; 213–214: 206; 425–433: 47, 53, 57, 58; 426: 54; 427: 59; 434–512: 59; 439: 34; 511–512: 60; 531–532: 59; 533–549: 59; 550–566: 59; 559: 59; 560–561: 59; 562–563: 59; 578: 55; [5] *to Aphrodite* 21–32: 143; 81: 248; 107: 248; 191: 248; 196–197: 28; 202–203: 245; 202–217: 243; 208: 243, 245; 210–211: 245;

Homeric Hymn (continued)
217: 245; 218: 242, 248; 218–238: 243, 248; 227: 252; 236: 252; 293: 54; [15] *to Herakles* 1: 13; 2: 13; 5: 14; 5–6: 13; 6: 14; 9: 13; [18] *to Hermes* 5–9: 55; 10: 55; (*to other gods*) 25.1: 55; 25.2–3: 59; 25.2–5: 55; 25.6: 55; 26.5: 43; 29.3: 143; 31.18–19: 54, 56; 32.18–19: 54; as a *prooímion*, 54
Homeridai, 51
homunculus, 87, 88, 220
honey, fermented, 59, 60
horse, 88, 100, 101, 112, 114, 116, 191, 209, 215, 217, 220, 223, 224, 232, 233, 238, 239, 244, 245, 249, 250, 256, 291
Hylleis, 292
Hyllos, 283, 284
Hymen, 250; hymenaeus 'wedding-song', 62, 250, 258
Hyperion, 235, 248
hypostasis, 235, 241, 242, 248, 254, 259

Ialysos, 285; Ialysia, 285
Ibycus PMG 331: 258
IG XII v 651: 254
Iguvium, 278; Iguvine Tables, 155, 159, 164, 165, 166, 169, 170, 180, 278
Ikaria, 43
Ilos, 220
inauguration, of kings, 281
Indic: *abhyavadānyà-* 'apportioning', 186; *agní-* 'fire', 99; *see also* Agni; *ákṣita-* 'imperishable, unfailing', 123, 124; *ákṣiti śrávas* 'imperishable fame', 124; *alāta-* 'firebrand, coal', 157; *anala-*, 'the insatiable one', 157; *anasthá-* 'the boneless one', 81; *aṅgā́ra-* 'coal', 151; *áṅgiras-* 'fire-priest', 151; *ániti* 'blows', 116; *antárikṣa-* 'intermediate space', 102, 108, 109; *apā́m gárbha-* 'embryo of the waters', 102; *apā́ṃ nápāt* 'progeny of the waters', 99, 100, 118; *aptúr-* 'crossing over the water', 139, 190; *aráṇi-* 'fire-stick', 103, 105, 106, 156, 186; *árjuna-* 'bright', 187; *arṣ-* 'flow', 149; *ā́sa-* 'ashes', 151, 152, 170; *aśáni-* 'thunderbolt', 186; *áśman-* 'boulder', 192, 193, 194; *ásu-* , 87, 89, 93, 94, 95, 111, 112, 116, 117, 118, 119, 120, 121; *āśuhéman-* 'driving swift horses', 100; *ásuṃ páram* 'higher *ásu-*', 119; *ásunīti-* 'path leading to *ásu-*', 117, 120; *ásura-*, 94, 95; *see also* Asura; *asutṛ́pā* '*ásu*-robbers', 117; *áśva-* 'horse', 256; *avṛ̥kā́s* 'unharmed by the wolf', 117; *bhadrá-* 'good', 116, 117, 120; *brahma*, 282; *brāhmaṇa-*, 291, 293; *cákṣas-* 'eye', 147; *dā́nu-* 'fluid, dew', 246; *dā́ru-* 'wood', 187; *dārú-ṇa-* 'sturdy', 187; *devá-* 'god', 94, 95, 97; *see also* Deva; *devāsaḥ sarvayā viśā* 'gods, with the *viś-* complete', 281; *dhī-* 'think', 202, 221; *dhīyas* 'thoughts, consciousness', 114, 115, 220, 221; *dhrájīmat-* 'rushing', 113; *dhūmá-* 'smoke', 87, 89, 116; *dhyā-* 'think', 202, 221; *dhyāma* 'thought', 202, 220; *divá(s) duhitár-* and *duhitár- divás* 'daughter of the sky', 247ff.; *duróṣa-* 'hard to kindle', 150; *dūtá-* 'messenger', 150; *dyáus* 'sky', 94, 107, 248, 251, 255, 256; *see also* Dyaus; *dyotaní-* 'brightness', 186; *gárbha-* 'embryo', 102; *gautama*, 293; *girí-* 'mountain', 193; *gómad* 'rich in cattle', 126; *gotra-*, 293; *gṛhápati-* 'lord of the household', 105; *hánti* 'strike, kill', 191, 193; *hatámātṛ̥-* 'whose mother is killed', 155; *iddhā́gni-* 'whose fire is kindled', 155; *janáya-* 'beget, create', 147; *jīvá-* 'alive, living', 119; *kā́ma-*

Indic *(continued)*
'desire', 152; *kaví-* 'poet/seer', 76; *kṣatram* 'dominion, power', 282, 284; *kṣatriya-*, 284, 291, 293; *kṣipaní-* 'stroke of the whip', 186; *mánas-*, 87, 89, 93, 94, 111, 112, 113, 114, 115, 117, 120; *manth-* 'friction', 105; *mánu-*, 111; *see also* Manu; *manuṣvát-* 'like Manu', 110; *márya-*, 198, 250; *mātaríśvan-* 'swelling inside the mother', 103, 110, 156; *see also* Mātariśvan; *mr̥tyú-* 'death', 139; *nabhanyà-* 'bursting forth', 186; *nábhas* 'cloud', 193; *Nā́satyau*, 93, 112, 218, 249, 256, 259; *nr̥t-* 'dance', 150; *ójas-* 'power', 109; *óṣa-dhī-* 'plant', 102, 103, 112, 150; *óṣati* 'burn', 150; *parjánya-*, 186, 192; *parkatī*, 186; *párvan* 'joint [e.g. of sacrificial animal], knot [in plant]', 190, 193; *párvata-* 'boulder', 193, 194; *pitŕ̥-* 'ancestor', 87, 93, 94, 96, 97, 112, 115, 117, 118; *prajā́pati-*, 100; *pravara*, 293; *pravát-* 'downstream' = 'forward', 95, 96, 97, 118; *praváto nápāt* 'progeny of the *pravát-* stream', 118; *purohita-*, 293; *rājan-* 'king', 277, 278, 284; *rājanya-*, 284; *sádane vivásvataḥ* 'at the place of the Vivasvat', 104, 146; *sadhástha-* 'abode', 98, 99, 102; *śā́ka-* 'power', 152; *sapiṇḍa*, 293; *śará-* 'reed', 197; *śarā́ṇi-* 'malice', 186; *śā́ras-* 'ashes', 197; *śárīra-* 'body', 197; *śā́ru-* 'missile, arrow', 194, 197; *savitŕ̥-*, 93; *see also* Savitr̥; *śmaśrū-ṇá-* 'bearded', 187; *śraddhā*, 110; *śrávas* 'fame', 123, 124, 125; *śrávas . . . ákṣitam* 'fame . . . imperishable', 124, 125, 126; *śr̥ṇā́ti* 'shatter', 195, 197; *sū-* 'vivify', 93; *śū́dra-*, 281; *súmakha-*, 255; *sunīthá-* 'heading in the good direction', 95, 97; *sūnr̥tāvarī*, 150; *sū́rya-* 'sun', 247, 249; *see also* Sūrya; *sūryā́*, 249; *sūta-*, 291, 292; *takṣ-* 'fashion', 149; *tar(i)-* 'overcome, cross over', 139; *tarā́ṇi-* 'ship', 156, 190; *tárute, tū́rvati*, 189; *trisadhasthá-* 'having three *sadhástha*-s', 99; *tvác-* 'hide', 264; *tvakṣ-* 'fashion', 149; *udvát-* 'upstream', 95, 96; *uṣás-* 'dawn', 104, 149, 247; *vaiśya-* , 281, 282; *vā́ja-* 'generative power residing in vegetation, cattle, etc.', 197; *vā́javat* 'rich in booty', 125; *vájra-* , 109, 192, 193, 197; *vájrabāhu-* 'he who holds the *vájra-* in his arms', 109; *varṇa-*, 281, 282, 284, 291; *varṣ-* 'rain', 149; *vas-* 'spend the night', 149; *vas-/uṣ-* 'shine', 104, 146, 147, 149; *vásu-* 'good', 149; *vā́ta-* 'wind', 113; *vidyút* 'lightning', 100; *vípra-* 'priest', 114; *viś-* 'to settle', 282, 284, 285; *viś-* 'tribe, people', 277, 281; *viśaḥ pati-* 'lord of the *viś-* [singular]', 278; *viśām pati-* 'lord of the *viśaḥ* [plural]', 278; *viśpáti-* 'lord of the *viś-*', 105, 278; *viśpátnī* 'mistress of the *viś-*', 105; *viśva-* 'all', 277, 281; *viśvā́yur*, 124, 125; *vivásvat-* 'shining', 104, 146, 147; *see also* Vivasvat; *yamá-*, 111; *see also* Yama; *yóni-* 'uterus, female genitalia', 105, 106, 110, 169
Indo-European linguistics, 1, 7, 19
Indra, 12, 14, 95, 109, 124, 190, 192, 193, 194, 195, 196, 197
inhumation, practice of, 85, 86, 87, 129, 174, 175
Ino, 126
Ion of Chios, 236, 239
Iphigeneia, 77
Iphiklos, 257
Iphimede, 77
Irish: *Macc Cairthin* 'son of rowan-tree', 200; *Macc Daro* 'son of oak', 200; *Macc Ibair* 'son of yew', 200; *rí* 'king', 277; *rí tuaithe* 'king of the *tuath* [singular]', 278; *rí tuath* 'king of the *tuatha* [plural]', 278; *richis* 'glowing coals, live ember', 197; *teinm (laído)* 'gnawing [of marrow]', 81; *tuath* 'tribe, people', 277, 278, 281

Islands of the Blessed, 127, 141; *see also* Greek: *Makárōn nêsoi*
Isocrates 12.177f., 280; *Helen,* 51
Ištar, 3, 258
Isthmian Games, 50
Italian: *fuoco* 'fire', 163; *fuoco prendere,* 106
Ithaca, 219

Jaiminīya-Brāhmaṇa, 87
Joshua, Book of, 7.16–18: 288
Judgment of Paris, 15, 16, 17
Juno, 161
Jupiter, 161, 265

Kadmos, 275; Kadmeion, 141
Kalkhas, 204
Kalypso, 242
Kameiros, 285; Kameiris, 285
Kapaneus, 140
Kekrops, 288
Kephallenia, 227
Kephalos, 231, 232, 242, 245, 248, 254, 257
KEWA, 156, 186, 195, 197, 202
Khaironeia, 143
Kharites, 261
king, 4, 52, 53, 58, 59, 61, 63, 64, 65, 66, 67, 71, 129, 132, 133, 134, 137, 143, 144, 145, 170, 172, 173, 174, 275, 277, 281, 284, 288, 292
Kings, I *Book of,* 4.7ff.: 288
Kirghiz: *akyn* 'poet', 43
Kleisthenes, 286, 287, 288, 289, 290
Kleitos, 242, 243, 245, 251, 252
Kleomenes, 284
Klymene, 235, 240, 257
Kodridai, 230
Kolonos, 231, 232
Kolophon, 73, 74, 289
Kreophyleioi, 51
Kronos, sons of, 285
Kwakiutl, 235, 240
Kyme, 72, 73, 74, 75
Kypselidai, 288
Kyrnos, 69, 71, 72; *see also* Theognis

Laertes, 203
lamentation, practice of, 176, 274
Lampos, 249, 250; Lampetie, 249
Lampsakos, 230
Lapiths, 271

Latin: *aboleō* 'cause to atrophy, check the growth of, abolish', 159; *ācer* 'sharp', 151; *ăcuō* 'sharpen', 151; *adolēfaciō* 'cause to be nurtured', 159; *adoleō* 'burn, [nurture]', 157, 159; *adolēscēns* 'adolescent, young man', 160, 172; *adolēscō* 'become nurtured, grow', 159, 160; *adulēscēns* 'adolescent, young man', 160, 172; *aedēs*, 107, 108; *aetas* 'age', 126; *agnoscere* 'recognize', 208; *aeternus* 'eternal', 125, 126; *agō*, 164, 180; *alma māter*, 156; *alō* 'nurture', 155, 156, 159; *altāria* 'sacrificial fireplace, altar', 155, 170; *altilāneus* 'whose wool is nurtured', 155; *anculus*, 157; *animus* 'spirit', 116; *āra* 'sacrificial fireplace, altar', 145, 154; 145, 151, 154, 155, 160, 161, 170, 172; *ārae&focī*, 165, 166; *ardeō, ardēre* 'be on fire', 153; *ardor* 'burning', 153; *ārea* 'ground, space free of buildings or trees', 154; *āreō, ārēre* 'be dry', 153, 174; *āridus* 'dry', 153; *assus* 'roasted, broiled', 153; *aurōra* 'dawn', 149; *caueō* 'beware, take precautions, provide guarantees', 76; *corpus* 'body', 197; *crāpula*, 157; *cribrum*, 106, 168, 169; *ēlixus* 'boiled', 153; *exfir*, 180; *faciō* 'do, make, sacrifice', 163, 164; *Falernus*, 153; *fēcī*, 163; *fēlix*, 106; *fēlix māteria*, 169; *fimus* 'manure', 180; *fōculum*, 163; *fōculus*, 161, 163; *focus* 'domestic fireplace, hearth', 160, 161, 163, 164, 168, 172; *foueō* 'foster', 163; *fūmigō* 'fumigate', 180; *fūmus* 'smoke', 116, 180; *fundō* 'pour', 108; *futtile*, 108; *genitor*, 281; *gēns*, 145; *genus*, 145; *gignō* 'beget', 145; *iaciō* 'throw, hurl', 164; *ignem accipere*, 106; *ignem alere* 'nurture fire' = 'keep the fire going', 155, 156, 157, 159, 169; *ignis* 'fire', 99; *indicāre*, 64; *indolēs* 'inherent nature', 157; *Iuppiter Lapis*, 192; *Lār familiāris*, 172; *lepidus*, 261; *lepos*, 261; *libum*, 160; *māter* 'mother', 106; *māteria*, 106, 169; *nex* 'death', 139; *olēscō* 'increase, be nurtured', 157; *ornus* 'mountain-ash tree', 153; *pōnō*, 153; *pontifex*, 169; *porcae piāculāres*, 161; *Portūnus*, 185, 186, 187; *pergula* 'projection from an edifice', 186; *pūniceus* 'dyed with purple', 167; *pūrgāmentum*, 180; *pūrgō* 'purify', 180; *pūrigō* 'purify', 180; *quercus* 'oak', 185, 186, 190, 201; *Quirīnus*, 282; *Quirītes*, 282; *rēmigō* 'row', 180; *sacerdōs* 'priest', 156; *sacrificō*, 163; *signa sequī*, 207, 208; *signifer* 'standard-bearer', 207, 208; *signum* 'sign', 207, 208; *stercus* 'manure', 180; *subolēs* 'offshoot', 157; *suffiō* 'fumigate', 180; *suffitiō*, 180; *tabula* 'board', 106, 169; *templum*, 107; *tribūnus*, 185, 187; *tribuō*, 279; *tribus*, 165, 185, 187, 278, 279, 288; *uacca honorāria*, 161; *uectis* 'bolt, lever', 164; *uegeō* 'quicken, arouse', 197; *uersipellis* 'werewolf', 155, 265; *uigeō* 'thrive', 197; *ūrō* 'burn', 150; *Vesta*, 104, 146, 148, 149; *see also* Vesta
Latins, 278
Latvian: *pęlns* 'domestic fireplace, hearth' (singular) vs. *pęlni* 'ashes' (plural), 152; *Pērkōna ōzōls* 'oak of Pērkōns', 184; *pèrkuons* 'thunderbolt', 183ff.; *vìrsūne* and *vìrsuone* 'summit', 188; *vìrsus* 'summit', 188
Lavinia, 158
law, 10, 37, 67, 70, 82, 111; law code, 67, 69; Law Code of Manu, 10.46–50: 291; 4.45–48: 70; lawgiver, 67, 68, 69, 111, 272, 274
legend, term not used in this book, 8
Leonidas, 284
Leotychides, 284
Lesbos, 259, 261
Lesches, 79
Lethe, 274
Leukas, 227, 230, 232, 234, 257; *see also* White Rock

Leukippides, 256
Leukothea, 231; *see also* White Goddess
LEW, 164, 185, 186, 191, 197, 278
Liber, 162
Life of Aesop, 50; *of Archilochus*, 49; *of Hesiod*, 50, 79; *of Homer*, 79
Lindos, 285; Lindia, 285
Linear B: *ko-to-ne-ta* = *ktoinétai*, 285; *ti-ri-se-ro-e* = *tris hērōei, 116
Lithuanian: *akmuõ* 'rock, stone', 192; *dègti* 'burn', 154; *giñti* 'chase, drive (cattle) to pasture', 191; *ìš-dagas* 'arable land', 154; *juõkas*, 164; *karaliū́nas* 'prince', 185; *naktì-gonis* 'night-herder of horses', 191; *pẽlenas* 'domestic fireplace, hearth' (singular) vs. *pelenaĩ* 'ashes' (plural), 152; *pérgas* 'Einbaum, Fischerkahn', 186; *perkū́nas* 'thunderbolt', 182ff.; *perkū́nija* 'thunderstorm', 184; *Perkūnkalnis* 'summit of Perkūnas', 183; *Perkūno ąžuolas* 'oak of Perkūnas, 184; *per̃ti* 'strike', 185; *pir̃kšnys* 'glowing ashes', 197; *ùgnį im̃ti* 'take fire', 106; *viẽškelis* 'Landstrasse, öffentlicher Weg', 278; *viešpats* '[sovereign] lord', 278; *viršū́nė* 'summit', 188; *viršùs* 'summit', 188
Livy 3.28.3: 207; 5.30.1: 165; 10.6.7: 278; 21.1.4: 155; 22.2.6: 207; 23.35.7: 207, 208; 24.48.11: 207; 30.35.6: 207; 31.2.6: 278; 33.37.1: 278; 42.65.12: 207
Lokris, Ozolian, 50
lotus, 107; Lotus-Eaters, 218
Louvre Papyrus, 223
LSJ, 132, 230, 277
Luceres, 288
Lucretius 4.1232: 157; 4.1237: 158
Luvian: *Tarḫunt-*, 131, 139; *wašu-* 'good', 145, 149
Lycian: *trqqas*, 131
Lycophron, 141, 232
Lycurgus *Against Leocrates* 106–107: 272
Lycurgus, lawgiver of Sparta, 68, 272, 274
Lydia, 273
Lykomedes, 230, 231
Lykourgos, antagonist of Dionysus, 231
lyre, 49, 50, 52, 53, 59, 60, 204
lyric, 58, 228; choral, 51, 54
Lysander, 258

Magnesia, 234
Mahābhārata, 8, 9, 12, 14, 16, 87, 157, 173
Maiandrios, 272
Maitrāyaṇī-Saṃhitā, 104
Makēs, 229
Mantineia, 194
Mantios, 252
Manu, 70, 110, 111, 150
Marut, 281
Mātariśvan, 103, 104, 105, 110, 111, 156, 169
Megara, 51, 68, 73, 273, 274, 279
Melampous, 225, 252

Melanthios, 300
Melikertes, 50, 231
Memnon, 130, 242
Menander F 258: 227, 259
Menelaos, 209, 217, 251, 299
Mentes, 113
Merops, 235, 241
Messenia, 269, 284
Messenian Wars, 292
metaphor, 88, 172, 181, 193, 195, 199, 225, 240, 249, 250, 264, 265, 301; ritual use of, 265
Metis, 67
microcosm, 53, 99, 112, 149, 150, 171, 238
Miletus, 79, 286, 291
Minerva, 161
Mirror of Princes, 36
Mitra, 281
Mnesiepes, meaning of name, 51
Mnesiepes Inscription, 49, 50
Molouris, 231
Mongols, 177
Morning Star and Evening Star, 2, 258, 259
mourning: for Adonis, 262; as demonstrative self-humiliation and self-aggression, 4
multiform, concept of, 35, 111, 130, 131
Münster Hydria, 88, 94, 116, 217, 220
Muršiliš II, 171
Muses, 13, 26, 27, 33, 44, 45, 47, 48, 49, 52, 53, 55, 56, 57, 58, 59, 60, 64, 68, 74, 75, 76, 77, 198, 199, 250; Helikonian, 57, 58, 59, 60, 77; Olympian, 57, 58, 59, 60, 75
Mycenae, 143, 144, 174
myth, working definition of, 8
myth and ritual, relationship between, 3, 4, 10, 13, 101, 140, 141, 173, 230, 231, 239, 265, 275

Nakula, 14
Naxos, 43
Near East, 2, 3, 71, 81, 258
nectar, 139, 190, 141, 261
neoterics, 261
Nereids, 260
Nestor, 209, 210, 215, 216, 217, 218, 219, 220, 225, 230, 298, 301
New Persian: *daxma*, 177
Noemon, 218
Nonnus *Dionysiaka* 5.30–32: 275
Nostoi F 4: 257
Nyse, 43, 46, 75

ocean, 94, 98, 99, 100, 102, 107, 108, 237, 238; *see also* Okeanos
Ocresia, 172, 173
octopus, kenning for, 82
Odysseus, 12, 13, 14, 22, 23, 33, 34, 44, 45, 71, 92, 93, 127, 182, 198, 203, 205, 206, 207, 208, 212, 213, 214, 215, 217, 218, 219, 221, 224, 225, 237, 242, 243, 251, 253, 274, 275, 296, 297, 298, 299, 300; antagonism with Athena, 12, 214; antagonism with Poseidon, 12
Oedipus, 82, 241, 292
Oineon, 50
Okeanos, 57, 99, 141, 224, 230, 236, 237, 238, 239, 241, 244, 245, 246, 251, 252, 253, 256, 257, 258, 262
Old English: *feorh* 'life, soul', 200; *fercal* 'bolt', 186; *fíras* 'men', 200; *Hengest*, 256; *Horsa*, 256
Old Norse: *arinn* 'sacrificial fireplace', 151, 170; *esja*, 151; *fjǫr* 'life', 200; *Fjǫrgyn*, 183, 186; *hamarr*, 191; *kveikja* 'beget, kindle', 172; *mjǫllnir*, 183, 187
Old Persian: *vazraka-* 'endowed with generative power', 197; *viθ* 'royal house, court', 277
Old Prussian: *percunis*, 183
Old Russian: *na perunĕ, na peryni, na peruni*, 188; *peregynja* 'wooded hill', 187
Old Slavonic: *jasenĭ* 'ash tree', 153; *pelynŭ* 'wormwood', 188; *perǫ/pĭrati* 'strike', 185; *polěti* 'be on fire', 152; *pregynja* 'wooded hill', 187
oligarchy, 67, 280
Olympic Games, 10, 37, 46
Olympus, 46, 47, 55, 57, 58, 71, 135, 140, 233; Olympian model of gods, 10, 15, 28, 37, 46, 55, 56, 139, 251
Onetor, 133
ontogeny, 25
oral poetry, 8, 9, 18, 19, 20, 21, 24, 25, 28, 29, 30, 35, 39, 40, 41, 42, 43, 44, 45, 46, 47, 48, 51, 52, 55, 60, 79, 80, 130, 131; *see also* performance and composition; recomposition
Oreithuia, 142
Orientalism, 2
Orion, 207, 242, 244, 245, 248, 251, 252, 253
Orkhomenos, 49
Oscan: *aasa-* 'sacrificial fireplace, altar', 151, 154, 155, 170; *pūr-* 'fire', 155
Otos, 74
Ovid *Amores* 2.16.1: 279; *Fasti* 2.542: 161; 4.334: 162; 5.707: 154; 6.625–634: 173; *Metamorphoses* 1.755: 240; 3.13: 263; 10:173, 155; *Remedia Amoris* 808: 155
Oxyrhynchus Papyri 1787: 261; 1800: 275

Paeligni, 279
Pamphyloi, 292
Pamphylos, 283
Panathenaia, 38, 220
Pandareos, 244, 251, 252
Pāṇḍava-s, 12, 14, 16
Pandora, 65, 81

pan-Hellenism, 10, 11, 37, 38, 40, 41, 42, 45, 46, 47, 48, 49, 51, 52, 55, 56, 57, 58, 60, 61, 63, 67, 75, 76, 79, 128
Parjanya, 192
Parmenides, 141
Parnassos, 59
Paros, 49, 50, 51
Parsees, 176, 178
Partheneion, 223, 227
Parvata, 193
Patroklos, 85, 86, 88, 89, 92, 93, 94, 111, 115, 116, 121, 128, 129, 130, 131, 138, 209, 215, 216, 218, 219, 220; as homunculus, 88, 220
Paulus ex Festo, 106, 155, 156, 158, 169, 180; *see also* Festus
Pausanias 1.17.6: 230, 231; 1.33.8: 231; 1.43.1: 77; 1.44.7: 231; 1.44.8: 231; 2.2.4: 254; 2.6.7: 280; 2.12.5: 220; 2.13.1–2: 280; 2.26.1–2: 280; 2.30.10: 280; 2.34.5: 280; 2.35.10: 254; 2.35.9: 254; 3.16.1: 256; 3.20.4: 100; 3.22.1: 192; 4.7.8: 292; 4.36.2–3: 225; 6.20.15–19: 215; 8.6.5: 254; 8.7.2: 233; 9.2.3: 263; 9.27.5: 254; 9.29.1: 74; 9.29.2–3: 60; 9.40.11–12: 143; 9.44.4: 214; 10.29.9: 234; 10.32.6: 234; passim: 46
Peirithoos, 234
Peisistratidai, 288
Peloponnesus, 288
Pelops, 138
Penelope, 44, 99, 182, 198, 203, 205, 224, 243, 245, 246, 251, 297, 298
performance and composition, in oral poetry, 8, 20, 21, 24, 26, 29, 38, 39, 40, 41, 42, 43, 44, 47, 54, 55, 58, 60, 79, 270, 272, 273
Perkūnas, 183, 184, 185, 186, 187, 192, 196; Pērkōns, 183
Persephone, 92, 212, 250, 251
Perses: brother of Hesiod, 64, 65, 66, 67, 68, 71, 72, 74, 75, 76, 77; the god, 76
Persian: *Goshtāsp*, 256; *Lohrāsp*, 256
Perun, 183, 184, 185, 188, 192, 196
Petra Genitrix, 200
Petronius, 62, 155, 265
Phaenias F 33: 79
Phaethon, 223, 235, 236, 239, 240, 241, 242, 243, 245, 246, 248, 249, 250, 252, 253, 254, 255, 257, 261; Phaethousa, 249
Phaon, 223, 228, 229, 234, 235, 255, 257, 259, 261, 262
Phemios, 46, 47
Pherecydes FGH 3 F 16–17: 74, 239; F 80: 285; F 145: 142
Philochorus FGH 328 F 94: 288; F 215: 272, 273; F 216: 269, 272; passim: 272, 275
Philoitios, 203, 205
Philomele, 263, 264
Philostratus, 198
Phleious, 280
Phobos, 230
Phokaia, 230
Pholos, 271
Photius, 116 (s.v. *tritopátores*), 141 (s.v. Μακάρων νῆσος), 229, 234, 257, 262
Phylas, 288

phylogeny, 25
Pindar *Isthmian* 1:49: 275; 7.14–15: 292; 7.18a and 18c, scholia to: 292; 9.2–3: 283; *Nemean* 2.1: 51; 7.19–20: 219; 7.44–47: 12; *Olympian* 2.25: 140; 2.29: 126; 7.1, scholia to: 285; *Paean* 5.42: 76; 6.117–120: 12; F 33c 6: 76; *Pythian* 1.66: 256; 4.246, scholia to: 232, 233; 4.251: 237; 6.22, scholia to: 70; as descendant of the Aigeidai, 292; use of the word *aînos*, 275
Pirwa-, 194
Plato *Apology* 34d: 198; *Ion* 530a-b: 38; 530c: 51; 531a: 38, 51; 531a-d: 38; 532a: 38, 51; *Laws* 629b: 273; 843a: 286; *Phaedrus* 252b: 51; *Republic* 521c: 259; 544d: 198; 599d: 51; 600d: 38; *Theaetetus* 160e: 144
Plato Comicus, 50
Plautus *Amphitruo* 123: 155, 265; *Captivi* 847: 163; *Miles* 177: 180; *Poenulus* 320: 163
Pliny *Natural History* 8.34: 155, 265; 22.11: 162; 24.140: 156; 28.42: 180; 35.47: 156; 36.204: 172; 37.31–32: 237, 239
ploughing, as activity, 212, 213, 253
Plutarch *Aristeides* 17.10: 273; *Banquet of the Seven Sages* 162c: 49; *Consolation to his Wife* 608c: 198; *De mulierum uirtutibus* 255a-e: 230; *Lycurgus* 4.1: 274; 6: 289; 29.8: 31, 274; *Lysander* 12, 18: 258; *Romulus* 2.4–8: 173; *Solon* 23.4: 286; *Theseus* 10: 231; 13.2–3: 291; 24–25: 288; by way of Proclus, 49
Podarge, 238, 244, 245
poet and poetry, 21, 37, 40, 41, 42, 43, 44, 45, 46, 47, 48, 49, 50, 51, 52, 53, 54, 56, 58, 59, 60, 61, 63, 64, 66, 67, 68, 71, 73, 77, 131, 198, 199, 213, 222, 270, 272, 273, 274, 275, 278, 292
polemarch, 269
Polemon F 5: 140
polis, 10, 11, 37, 65, 67, 75, 116, 144, 269, 270, 271, 272, 273, 274, 275, 277, 278, 285, 286, 287, 289, 290, 291, 292, 293; of *díkē* and of *húbris*, 65, 67
Polish: *piołyn/piołun* 'wormwood', 188; *piorun* 'thunderbolt', 183
Pollux, 194
Polycrates, 272
Polydamas, 204
Polyneikes, 292
Poseidon, 28, 57, 74, 214, 232, 234, 299; *Petraîos*, 232, 233
Praeneste, 173
Praetorius, M., 183, 184, 197
praise, 16, 17, 221, 275; *see also* blame
Prajāpati, 100
prayer, 13
prelude, 53, 54, 55, 56, 57, 63
Priam, 28, 206, 207, 297, 300, 301
Procession of the Lydians, 273
Proitos, 207
Prokles, 292
Prometheus, 65, 80
Provençal: *trobador* (composer) and *joglar* (performer), 41
Proverbs of Solomon, 71
psychopomp, 97, 98, 101, 112, 117, 118, 226, 255

Pterelas, 230
Ptolemaios Chennos, 229, 234, 257, 262
Pūṣan, 97, 98, 99, 100, 101, 112, 113, 117, 255
Pylos, 225; *see also* Greek: *Púlos*
Pyrrhos, 12, 138

Rakṣas-, 94
Ramnes, 288
rebirth, concepts of, 86, 87, 93, 101, 112, 116, 127, 231, 241, 242, 246, 252
recomposition, 40, 42, 79, 273
Remus, 173
revenant, 68
REW, 183, 185
rhapsode, 38, 40, 41, 42, 47, 51, 52, 79
Rhodes, 278, 285, 288
Rig-Veda 1.9.7: 122, 124, 125, 126; 1.22.6: 99, 101; 1.32.1: 193; 1.32.2: 98; 1.32.2: 12, 102; 1.32.6: 193; 1.32.15: 109; 1.34.10: 113; 1.35: 95; 1.35.10: 94, 95, 98; 1.35.3: 95, 101; 1.35.5: 101; 1.35.6: 96; 1.35.7: 95, 96, 97; 1.37.7: 193; 1.38.5: 96; 1.40.4: 124; 1.42.2: 117; 1.44.1: 104, 146; 1.44.11: 110; 1.52.2: 193; 1.53.1: 104, 146; 1.57.6: 193; 1.58.1: 103; 1.61.12: 190; 1.68.4: 111; 1.71.4: 103; 1.79.1: 113; 1.83.4: 155; 1.92.11: 251; 1.93.6: 103; 1.96.2: 104, 146, 147; 1.96.4: 103, 156; 1.100.13: 192; 1.109.7: 109; 1.113.8–12: 150; 1.113.16: 118; 1.115.1: 112, 246; 1.115.2: 250, 255; 1.116.3: 255; 1.116.17: 249; 1.117.2: 113; 1.122.1: 94; 1.124.1: 11, 150; 1.125.6: 96, 118; 1.128.2: 111; 1.130.3: 192; 1.130.5: 98; 1.131.1: 94; 1.138.4: 100; 1.140.7: 119; 1.140.8: 119; 1.141.3: 103; 1.141.4: 102; 1.143.2: 100, 102, 103; 1.148.1: 103; 1.157.1: 113; 1.162.2–3: 100; 1.163.11: 113; 1.172.2: 197; 1.181.2: 112; 1.181.3: 95; 1.181.4: 255; 1.182.1: 256; 1.183.1: 112; 1.186.5: 100; 2.11.10: 192; 2.12.3: 192, 196; 2.13.7: 192; 2.19.3: 98; 2.23.2: 248; 2.30.5: 192, 194; 2.31.6: 100; 2.35: 100; 2.35.1: 100; 2.35.13: 101; 2.35.2: 100; 2.35.6: 101, 116; 2.35.15: 101; 2.40.4–5: 97; 3.1.12–13: 100; 3.2.13: 100, 102, 103; 3.5.9: 103, 156; 3.20.2: 99; 3.26.2: 103, 156; 3.29.1–2: 103, 105; 3.29.2: 156; 3.29.11: 156; 3.30.13: 104, 146; 3.30.17: 195, 197; 3.35.16–18: 282; 3.39.3: 256; 3.62.10: 115; 3.62.9–10: 98; 3.9.1: 100; 3.9.5: 103; 4.2.5: 100; 4.5.13: 247; 4.22.1: 192, 194; 4.26.2: 192; 4.3.11: 99; 4.4.3: 278; 4.42.33: 99; 4.43.6: 113, 256; 4.52.1: 251; 4.52.4: 150; 4.53.1: 94; 4.53.2: 100; 4.53.3: 114; 5.4.8: 99; 5.9.3–4: 156; 5.15.1: 100; 5.6.4: 99, 147; 5.31.1: 95; 5.31.3: 95; 5.31.11: 95; 5.51.11: 98; 5.73.4: 255; 5.75.9: 150; 5.76.1: 150; 5.79.8: 150; 5.81.1: 114, 115; 5.81.2: 114; 5.81.4: 98; 5.81.5: 98; 6.34.5: 124; 6.44.12: 192; 6.55.3–4, 6: 100; 6.55.4, 5: 255; 6.55.5: 255; 6.56.3: 97; 6.57.3: 100; 6.58.2: 97, 100; 6.6.2: 100, 102; 6.7.6: 147; 6.8.2: 102, 103, 104, 108; 6.62.3, 4: 112; 6.71.2: 114; 7.1.1: 156; 7.2.3: 100; 7.5.7: 147; 7.9.3: 102, 104, 146; 7.41.6: 150; 7.45.1: 101, 114; 7.47.2: 100; 7.50.3: 95; 7.63.3: 246; 7.72.4: 113; 7.75.5: 246, 255; 7.76.3: 250; 7.77.3: 249; 7.78.3: 246, 255; 7.78.4: 249; 7.80.1: 150; 7.88.2: 193; 7.104.19: 192, 194; 8.3.19: 193; 8.6.1: 192; 8.8.2: 113; 8.20.17: 94; 8.27.7: 155; 8.35.13: 281; 8.35.18: 282; 8.39.3: 103; 8.43.9: 102; 8.44.16: 99; 8.63.3: 255; 8.103.5: 124; 9.10.5: 104, 146; 9.26.4: 104, 146; 9.33.6: 99; 9.66.7: 124; 9.113.7–9: 96; 9.113.9: 96, 118; 10.2.7: 99; 10.7.9: 156; 10.12.1: 118; 10.12.4: 117; 10.14.1:

Rig-Veda (continued)
97, 111; 10.14.11: 117; 10.14.12: 117, 120; 10.14.3, 5: 96; 10.14.5: 104, 111, 146; 10.14.8: 96, 118; 10.15.1: 117; 10.15.14: 96, 117; 10.16: 175, 177; 10.16.2: 117; 10.16.3: 112; 10.16.4: 85, 117; 10.16.7: 85; 10.17.1: 104, 146; 10.17.3–6: 97; 10.17.4: 97, 118; 10.17.6: 98, 99; 10.20.1: 114; 10.21.5: 103; 10.30.3–4: 100; 10.45.1: 99, 109; 10.45.1–3: 102; 10.46.9: 99, 111; 10.52.5: 109; 10.59.5–6: 117; 10.65.2: 102, 109; 10.70.6: 251; 10.85.14: 113, 255; 10.90.11–12: 281, 282; 10.90.12: 284; 10.98.5, 12: 99; 10.107.2: 96, 118; 10.122.7: 150; 10.122.8: 150; 10.124.8: 277; 10.135.1: 96; 10.136.5: 99; 10.139.1: 95, 98; 10.142.2: 118; 10.149.2: 99; 10.152.2: 278; 10.154.5: 96, 118; 10.156.4: 99, 147; passim: 30, 32
ritual: working definition of, 10; ritual substitute, 48, 129, 135
Rome, 278, 288
Romulus, 173, 278
rotation, political principle of, 279, 280, 285
Russian: *begún* 'runner', 185; *peru/prat'* 'strike', 185; *perun* 'thunderbolt', 183; *Perunov dub* 'oak of Perun', 184

Sabines, 278
sacrifice, practice of, 4, 69, 70, 71, 74, 75, 77, 85, 99, 100, 101, 102, 103, 104, 105, 108, 110, 111, 112, 113, 114, 116, 118, 135, 137, 145, 146, 147, 148, 149, 150, 151, 152, 154, 155, 156, 158, 160, 161, 162, 163, 165, 166, 167, 168, 170, 171, 172, 173, 176, 180, 190, 191, 198, 220, 233, 250, 269, 270, 272, 280, 281, 282, 283
Sahadeva, 14
sailing, as activity, 72, 73, 77, 78, 213, 214, 220
Sallust *Catiline* 59.5: 165
Samos, 272, 286
Samudra, 98
Sappho F 1.15,16,18: 233; 1.21: 259; 1.26–27: 259; 1.28: 259; 2.13–16: 261; 5.1–4: 260; 44.4: 122; 58.13–15: 261; 58.19: 261; 58.25–26: 260, 261; 96.2– 5, 21–23: 260; 104: 258; 140: 261; 168: 262; 211: 228, 255, 262; passim: 227, 228, 234, 257, 258, 259, 262
Sarpedon, 92, 123, 127, 128, 130, 131, 133, 134, 136, 137, 138, 140, 141, 142
Savitr̥, 93, 94, 95, 96, 97, 98, 99, 100, 101, 112, 113, 114, 115, 117, 118
Savitr̥ Hymn, 96
Sāvitrī, 87
Sāyana, 256
Second Nekyia, 224
self-humiliation and self-aggression, 4
Selinus, 264
Semele, 140, 141, 263
Semonides F 7.61–62: 152; 7.94: 290
Servius, on *Aeneid* 1.704: 158; 6.603: 239; 7.678: 173; 11.339: 108; 12.118: 163
Servius Auctus, on *Aeneid* 3.134: 160
Servius Tullius, 172
Shāhnāma, 100, 177, 256

sheep, 74, 137, 156, 280, 283
shepherd's pipe, 60
Shield: of Achilles, 53, 64, 238; of Herakles, 79
Sikyon, 280
simile, 223, 224
Skiron, 231
Skironites, 232, 233
Skyphios, 232, 233
Skyros, 230, 232; Skyrios, 231
Slavic: *nebo* 'sky', 193; *perunŭ* 'thunderbolt', 182; *slava* 'glory' and *slovo* 'word, epic tale', 26
snail, kenning for, 82
snake, kenning for, 82
Socrates, 38
Socrates of Argos FGH 310 F 6: 285
Solomon, 288
Solon F 4.1–2: 271; 4.7–10: 270; 4.8, 13, 14, 16: 66; 4.14–16: 68; 4.32: 271; 4.33: 67; 4.35: 67; 4.36: 67; 5.5–6: 69; 6.1: 270; 13.1–4: 68; 13.5–6, 7–8, 16– 25: 68; 13.54: 206; 31: 67; 36.18–20: 67, 69; passim: 275
Soma, 104, 105, 146
Somali: traditions of performance, 41
Sophocles *Electra* 417–423: 143, 174; *Oedipus at Colonus* 27, 28, 92, 627, 637: 274; 670: 231; 1595: 231; *Oedipus Tyrannus* 393, 1525: 82
soul, 86, 200
South Slavic: *perperuna*, name for a virgin chosen to dance for rain, 191; oral poetry, 8, 19, 20, 21, 24, 39, 40
Spanish: *fuego* 'fire', 163
Sparta, 4, 51, 68, 100, 224, 256, 258, 269, 271, 272, 273, 274, 275, 284, 289, 290, 292
Spartoi, 292
Sphinx, riddle of, 82
Sprachbund, concept of, 3
Starkaðr, 12
Stesichorus PMG 178.1: 256; 236: 263–265
Strabo 4.6.9 C207: 187; 5.1.9 C215: 238; 7.1.3, 5 C290, 292: 187; 8.4.10 C362: 271, 273; 8.7.1 C383: 282; 9.1.4 C391: 231; 9.4.10 C427: 283;10.2.8–9 C452: 227, 229, 230, 232, 257; 14.1.18 C638: 51; 14.1.33–35 C 645: 51
subgenre, 224
Suda, 141, 277 (s.v. *pánta oktṓ*), 288 (s.v. same)
Sūrya, 246, 247, 248, 249, 255
Swedish: *ala* 'be on fire', 160
swooning, conceptualization of, 49, 90, 91, 92, 115, 142, 228
symbol, 64, 93, 100, 101, 106, 107, 108, 109, 116, 143, 144, 147, 174, 175, 176, 194, 214, 225, 233, 234, 235, 236, 253, 255, 256, 258, 265, 272, 274, 276, 281, 288, 293
synchronic, 21, 23, 24, 25, 29, 30, 31, 32, 35, 195, 207; working definition of, 20
Syracuse, 288

Tabulae Heracleenses, 230
Tacitus *Annals* 14.30: 158; 15.38: 155; *Germania* 2: 111; 45: 155; *Histories* 2.3: 158; 3.71: 155
Taittirīya-Āraṇyaka, 97, 99; *Taittirīya-Brāhmaṇa*, 100, 110, 112; *Taittirīya-Saṃhitā*, 95, 104, 111, 112
Tanaquil, 172, 173
Tantalos, 239
Taraxippos, 215
Tarquinius Priscus, 172
Taygetos, 100
Teiresias, 52, 92, 212, 213, 214, 215, 217, 219
Telemachus, 113, 243, 297, 298, 300
Telepinu-, 3
tendencies, Jakobson's concept of, 24
Teos, 286
Terpander, 273
Thaletas, 273
Thebes, 13, 15, 43, 141, 273, 274, 275, 292
theme: as regulator of formula, 23, 25; working definition of, 9
Theocritus 18.27: 212; 7.155–156: 214
Theognis 15–18: 273; 22: 54; 22–23: 52; 54: 271; 89 = 1082e: 72; 89–90: 72; 97–100: 72; 99–100: 71; 155–158: 72; 179–180: 73; 219–220: 69; 237–254: 52; 331–332: 69; 337–338: 68; 339–340: 68; 345: 68; 346–347: 68; 349: 68; 349–350: 68; 541–542: 271; 543–546: 69; 544: 69; 667–682: 270; 808: 222; 833–836: 73; 945, 72; 1089–1090: 72; 1103–1104: 73, 75; 1123–1125: 219; 1145: 71; 1147–1148: 71; 1164a-d: 72; 1197–1198: 213; 1197–1202: 213; 1198–1199: 213; 1202: 213; 1209–1210: 222, 274; 1210: 274; 1211–1213: 274; 1213–1214: 274; 1215–1216: 274; passim: 51, 52, 69, 274, 275; and Kyrnos, 71, 72; as revenant, 68
theogony, varieties of, 46, 47, 53, 56, 57, 58, 59, 60, 61
Theophrastus *On fire* 37: 151
Theras, 292
Thersites, 164
Theseus, 230, 231, 232, 234
Thespiai, 49, 52
Thetis, 231
Thoas, 133
Thor, 183, 186, 187, 196, 197
Thorikos, 232, 257
thrift, principle of, 21, 22, 23, 24, 25, 39
Thucydides 3.96: 50; 3.104.4: 54; 3.104.5: 58; 6.18.2: 290
thunder, 109, 139, 140, 141, 159, 181, 235, 254; thunderbolt, 182ff.
Thurian gold leaves, 140
Timagoras FGH 381 F 3: 292
Titanomachy F 6 p. 111 Allen: 71
Tithonos, 242, 243, 245, 248, 252, 261
Titienses, 288
Tlepolemos, 285, 288

Tocharian: *as-* 'dry', 153, 174
Tonga, 291
Tower of Silence, 176
tree animism, 200
trends, Jakobson's concept of, 24
tribe, not to be equated with Greek *phūlḗ*, 277; politics of, 277; working definition of, 276
trifunctionalism, 17, 278, 282, 283, 284
Triphylia, 278
Triple Fire, 86, 104, 105, 108, 109, 110
Trita Āptya, 109
Troy, 7, 14, 15, 23, 28, 77, 125, 138, 203, 204, 214, 218, 219, 299; Trojan War, 15, 16, 17, 23, 77, 78, 141, 205
Trozen, 280
Typhoeus, 67
tyrant, tyranny, 67, 272, 288, 292
Tyrtaeus F 4.1–2: 272; 19.8: 290, 292; passim: 51, 269, 270, 271, 272, 273, 274, 275
Tzetzes, 141

Ullikummi, 191
Umbrian: *ahti-* 'movable fireplace', 164, 166, 168, 169; *asa* 'sacrificial fireplace, altar', 145, 151, 154, 155, 170; *aso-*, 164, 169, 170; *cringatro/krenkatrum*, 168; *iuka* 'sacred words, formula', 164; *kařetu* 'let him call', 159; *pir* 'fire', 180; *tafla*, 169; *trifu-* 'tribe', 165, 278; *tuta* 'city, people', 278; *uřetu* 'let him burn', 157
Ur-form, concept of, 130
Uṣas, 117, 118, 146, 150, 246, 247, 248, 249, 250, 255, 256

Valerius Maximus, 161
Varro *De lingua latina* 6.14: 162; 6.32: 180; *De re rustica* 2.4.13: 156; *Rerum diuinarum*: 161
Varuṇa, 281
Vasiṣṭha, 150
Vāyu, 12, 14, 112
Vedas, 41
Velleius Paterculus 1.18.2: 273
Venus, planet, 3, 258
Vesta, 104, 105, 106, 107, 108, 146, 148, 149, 168, 169, 171, 180
Vestini, 279
Virgil *Aeneid* 1.704: 158; 6.659: 239; 7.71: 158; 8.189: 163; 12.169–170: 156; 12.285: 162; *Eclogues* 4.49: 157; 8.65: 159; *Georgics* 4.379: 154, 159
Virgins, Vestal, 106, 168, 169
Vita Homeri Romana, 54
Vitruvius, 107
Vīvahvant, 104, 146
Vivasvat, 103, 104, 105, 111, 146
Vǫluspá 56.10: 186
Vr̥tra, 109, 190, 193, 194

Vr̥trahan, 194
Vulcan, 173

werewolf, 155, 265
whetstone, 194
White Goddess, 126, 231
White Rock, 224, 225, 226, 227, 230, 233, 234, 239, 257, 258, 259, 262
wolf, 117, 231, 272; *see also* werewolf

Xanthos: horse, 116, 244; of Lycia, 133, 137, 141; = Skamandros, 238
Xenophanes of Kolophon, 36, 73

Yama, 87, 94, 96, 97, 104, 111, 117, 118, 146
Yāska (*Nirukta* 12.1), 255
Yima, 104, 146
Yudhiṣṭhira, 14

Zaraθuštra = Zoroaster, 176
Zephyros, 238, 244
Zeus, 13, 15, 16, 53, 56, 57, 58, 59, 61, 63, 64, 65, 66, 67, 68, 73, 74, 75, 77, 80, 94, 114, 116, 131, 135, 138, 139, 140, 141, 195, 200, 203, 204, 206, 211, 212, 221, 222, 229, 231, 234, 235, 243, 245, 247, 248, 250, 251, 254, 258, 294, 295, 296, 297, 299; Aphesios, 231; Eye of, 211; *homóphūlos*, 286; Idaios, 133; *Kappṓtās*, 192; Keraunos, 194; Nemeios, 50; Polieus, 280; Will of, 15, 221, 222
Zoroaster and Zoroastrianism, 146, 175, 176, 177, 178, 179, 180

Index of Scholars

Alexiou, M., 4, 11
Alföldi, A., 173, 278, 288
Allen, T. W., 51
Alty, J., 284
Andronikos, M., 85, 129, 133
Arbman, E., 87, 88, 90
Bachelard, G., 181
Balys, J., 183, 184, 185
Bartholomae, C., 174, 177, 178, 193, 197
Baumann, H., 193, 200
Beekes, R. S. P., 47, 148, 174
Benveniste, E., 1, 2, 8, 59, 109, 125, 126, 134, 145, 149, 186, 193, 194, 202, 207, 276, 277, 278, 279, 281, 282, 283, 284, 286
Bérard, C., 86, 87
Bergaigne, A., 102
Bergren, A. L. T., 190
Boas, F., 235
Boedeker, D. D., 150, 246, 250
Böhme, J., 87, 88, 90, 92
Borgeaud, W., 164, 167
Borthwick, E. K., 194
Bourriot, F., 286, 290, 291
Bowra, C. M., 264
Brelich, A., 11, 50, 51, 173, 273
Bremmer, J., 86, 87, 88, 173
Brough, J., 292, 293
Brugmann, K., 152
Būga, K., 188
Burkert, W., 3, 4, 8, 10, 12, 14, 51, 137, 138, 140, 141, 144, 265, 272, 289
Byrne, J., 277, 278
Calame, C., 256, 273, 276
Caland, W., 175, 177
Campbell, D. A., 224, 233, 261
Caswell, C. P., 86, 88
Cerri, G., 270, 271
Chambers, M., 290
Chantraine, P., 132, 133 (*see also* DELG)
Christensen, A., 111, 174
Christmann-Franck, L., 85
Clader, L. L., 250
Clark, M. E., 130
Claus, D. B., 86
Clay, J. S., 12
Coldstream, J. N., 11
Combellack, F. M., 295, 296, 297, 300, 301
Connor, W. R., 220
Coulsen, D. E., 130
Darcus, S. M., 86
Darkevič, V. P., 183
Davidson, H. R. E., 197
Davidson, O. M., 12, 93, 100, 111, 176, 256, 272
Day, M., 290
Debrunner, A., 124, 156, 157, 186, 187
Detienne, M., 8, 16, 25, 26, 45, 60, 205, 217, 269, 270, 272, 275
Devoto, G., 164, 169
Dieterich, A., 228, 239
Diggle, J., 235, 237, 239, 240, 250, 254, 258
Dillon, M., 277, 292
Dirlmeier, F., 200
Donini, G., 28
Donlan, W., 270, 282
Dow, S., 301
Drekmeier, C., 277, 284
Dubois, J. A., 180
Dubuisson, D., 281

Duchesne-Guillemin, J., 176, 178
Ducrot, O., 20
Dumézil, G., 7, 8, 9, 12, 13, 14, 16, 17, 100, 104, 106, 107, 108, 146, 148, 172, 173, 180, 278, 281, 282, 284, 291
Dumont, L., 291
Dunkel, G., 79
Durante, M., 42, 79
Dworak, P., 181
Edmunds, L., 274
Edwards, A. T., 122
Edwards, G. P., 23, 24, 39, 61
Edwards, M. W., 22, 31
Eliade, M., 200, 237
Else, G. F., 34
Endzelin, J., 188
Ernout, A., 156, 167, 169
Farnell, L. R., 254, 292
Feist, S., 186
Figueira, T. J., 5, 288
Finkelberg, M., 122, 127
Finnegan, R., 41
Floyd, E. D., 122, 124, 125
Fontenrose, J., 273
Frame, D., 92, 93, 126, 203, 211, 217, 218, 219, 225, 236, 237, 249, 252, 256, 259
Fränkel, H., 31, 33
Fraser, P. M., 285
Frazer, J. G., 181, 235
Friedrich, P., 185
Fritz, K. von, 92
Gamkrelidze, T. V., 4
Garland, R., 86
Geldner, K. F., 193
Gernet, L., 143, 291, 292
Gill, D., 137
Gimbutas, M., 183, 188
Gluckman, M., 277, 291
Gnoli, G., 176
Goetze, A., 194
Gonda, J., 180, 197, 278, 282, 284
Grassmann, H., 191
Griffith, M., 48
Grottanelli, C., 272
Gruppe, O., 230, 232
Güntert, H., 93, 111, 185, 186, 194, 242, 246, 254, 255, 256, 258
Güterbock, H. G., 191
Haas, M. R., 1, 20
Hack, R. K., 128
Hadzisteliou Price, T., 137
Hainsworth, J. B., 31, 32
Hamm, E.-M., 261
Hanell, K., 73, 274
Hansen, W. F., 12, 214
Hauschild, R., 156
Held, G. J., 293
Henzen, W., 156, 161
Heubeck, A., 131
Hillebrandt, A., 112
Hocart, A. M., 193
Hoffmann, K., 177, 190
Holoka, J. P., 22
Householder, F. W., 29, 130, 139, 148, 149, 224
Hubbard, T. K., 292
Humbach, H., 176, 177
Ingalls, W. B., 31, 32, 33
Ireland, S., 86
Ivanov, V. V., 4, 182, 183, 184, 185, 186, 187, 188, 191, 192, 193, 194, 196
Jacoby, F., 28, 230, 272
Jakobson, R., 3, 24, 29, 182, 186, 187, 188, 191
Janko, R., 61, 63, 79
Jaskiewicz, W. C., 184
Jeanmaire, H., 230, 231
Jones, J., 203
Jones, N. F., 279, 280, 288, 290
Joseph, B., 93, 256
Kane, P. V., 291
Kelly, S. T., 27
Kiparsky, P., 41
Koller, H., 27, 54, 198, 221
Kretschmer, P., 132, 133, 232, 245
Krollmann, C., 184
Kuhn, A., 196
Kuiper, F. B. J., 193
Kuryłowicz, J., 149, 150, 152, 154, 189
Kuryłowicz's Fourth Law of Analogy, 154
Lamberton, R., 78, 79
Laroche, E., 131, 132, 139, 189, 191
Latte, K., 277, 285
Lattimore, R., 295
Leach, E. R., 8
Leaf, W., 295, 296
Lesher, J. H., 217
Leumann, M., 153, 157, 180
Lévêque, P., 286
Lévi, S., 70, 110, 111
Lévi- Strauss, C., 240, 241
Lidén, E., 186
Liebert, G., 197
Lincoln, B., 86, 200, 293
Lobel, E., 261
Lohmann, D., 295, 300
Lommel, H., 192, 193
Loraux, N., 270, 290
Lord, A. B., 8, 9, 18, 19, 21, 22, 24, 25, 26, 35, 39, 40, 41, 55, 130, 131
Loth, J., 200
Lowenstam, S., 85, 130
Macdonell, A. A., 103
Mannhardt, W., 184, 185, 192, 197
Mansikka, V. J., 187, 188

Martin, R. P., 8, 9, 36, 43, 204
Mayrhofer, M., 47, 148, 156 (*see also* EWA and KEWA)
Meid, W., 186, 187, 188, 189
Meillet, A., 29, 30, 123, 185, 186
Meulen, R. van der, 200
Minard, A., 103, 150
Minkowski, C. Z., 52
Mitchell, S. A., 194
Momigliano, A., 285
Moore, S. F., 276
Muellner, L., 53
Murr, J., 239
Nagler, M. N., 25
Newton, R. M., 93, 127, 231
Nilsson, M. P., 3, 233, 282
Nyberg, H. S., 176, 177
O'Neill, E. G., 32
Oldenberg, H., 87, 102, 104, 105, 192
Otrębski, J., 185
Otten, H., 85, 128, 132, 170, 171, 194
Page, D. L., 7, 9, 21, 22, 29, 224, 226, 261
Parry, M., 8, 9, 18, 19, 20, 21, 22, 23, 24, 31, 34, 39, 40, 41, 130
Pedersen, H., 19
Perpillou, J.-L., 74, 75
Peters, M., 47, 149
Pfister, F., 50, 273
Porter, H. N., 32
Pötscher, W., 94
Poultney, J., 164, 278
Propp, V., 4
Puhvel, J., 111, 184
Radloff, W., 43
Rau, W., 282
Redfield, J. M., 88
Reichelt, H., 154, 192, 193, 194
Renner, T., 265
Renou, L., 31, 186, 193, 194
Richardson, N. J., 133, 136
Richter, G., 264
Risch, E., 124, 141, 148
Robert, C., 230, 236, 239
Robertson, N., 285, 288, 289, 290
Rohde, E., 10, 11, 37, 94, 116, 128, 133, 134, 140, 215
Rönnow, K. A., 109
Rose, H. J., 263
Roussel, D., 277, 279, 284, 285, 286, 287, 289, 291
Rudhardt, J., 133
Russo, J. A., 31, 32
Rusten, J., 239, 242
Sacconi, A., 116
Sacks, R., 30
Saïd, E., 2
Saïd, S., 272
Sapir, E., 19
Saussure, F. de, 20
Schadewaldt, W., 130
Scheinberg, S., 59
Scherer, A., 258
Schlerath, B., 94, 95, 119, 120
Schliemann, H., 7
Schmeja, H., 188, 195
Schmid, B., 73
Schmitt, R., 114, 122, 124, 139, 141, 247, 248
Schnaufer, A., 88, 89, 90, 91, 92
Schulze, W., 106, 157, 185
Schwartz, M., 203
Schwenck, K., 192
Schwyzer, E., 152, 153
Scodel, R., 50
Segal, C. P., 219, 225
Sergent, B., 284
Seržputovski, A. K., 183, 184
Shannon, R. S., 23, 200
Sinclair, T. A., 81
Sinos, D. S., 130, 135, 215, 216
Snodgrass, A. M., 9, 10, 11, 37, 48, 277
Solmsen, F., 149
Sommer, F., 153
Sommerstein, A. H., 151, 152
Specht, F., 185, 188, 189, 200
Stähler, K., 88, 94, 116, 217, 220
Stang, C. S., 188
Steel, F. L. D., 86
Stroud, R. S., 288
Svenbro, J., 44, 45, 71, 203, 222, 270, 271, 272, 274
Szanto, E., 286
Szegedy-Maszak, A., 274
Szemerényi, O., 276
Tambiah, S. J., 291
Täubler, E., 279
Thieme, P., 139, 141
Thurneysen, R., 157, 180
Tischler, J., 145, 149
Todorov, T., 20
Toporov, V. N., 182, 183, 184, 185, 186, 191, 192, 193, 194, 196
Trautmann, R., 186
Vadé, Y., 200
Vaillant, A., 187
Van Brock, N., 48, 129
Vendryes, J., 185, 197, 200
Vermeule, E. D. T., 77, 141, 142
Vernant, J.-P., 11, 13, 15, 65, 68, 80, 88, 126, 143, 144, 148, 205, 217, 269, 292
Vetter, E., 155
Vian, F., 16, 292
Vidal-Naquet, P., 286

Vieyra, M., 85
Vine, B., 29, 47, 165, 198
Wackernagel, J., 40, 124, 156, 157, 186, 187
Wagler, P., 196
Walcot, P., 81
Wallace, P. W., 72
Ward, D., 93, 256
Warden, J., 88, 91
Watkins, C., 1, 20, 29, 36, 70, 81, 113, 121, 122, 124, 131, 132, 182, 187, 189, 195, 197, 204, 211, 278
Watt, W. M., 276
Weber, M., 277
Welcker, F. G., 71
West, M. L., 15, 29, 59, 63, 65, 66, 70, 71, 74, 75, 77, 80, 81, 82, 126, 199, 211, 212, 235, 238, 270
Whallon, W., 23
Whitley, J., 11
Whitman, C. H., 192, 226
Whitney, W. D., 155
Wikander, S., 250, 256
Wilamowitz-Moellendorff, U. von, 50, 54, 224, 227, 228, 229, 230, 258
Wissowa, G., 161
Witzel, M., 4, 94, 96
Wolf, C. U., 288
Wörrle, M., 280, 286
Yalman, N., 291
Zuntz, G., 140

Nagy, Gregory.
Greek mythology and poetics / Gregory Nagy.
p. cm. — (Myth and poetics)
Includes bibliographical references.
ISBN 0-8014-1985-9 (alk. paper)
1. Greek poetry — History and criticism. 2. Mythology, Greek, in literature. 3. Mythology in literature. I. Title. II. Series.
PA3015.R4N34 1990 89-17447
881′.0109—dc20